2013

Lewison's Drafting Business Leases

2013

Lewison's Drafting Business Leases

Eighth Edition

Janet Bignell
MA (Cantab), BCL (Oxon)
Barrister

Consultant editor

Lord Justice Lewison
Lord Justice of Appeal

SWEET & MAXWELL

THOMSON REUTERS

First Edition	1980
Second Edition	1986
Third Edition	1989
Fourth Edition	1993
Fifth Edition	1996
Sixth Edition	2000
Seventh Edition	2007
Eighth Edition	2013

Published in 2013 by Sweet & Maxwell, 100 Avenue Road, London NW3 3PF part of Thomson Reuters (Professional) UK Limited (Registered in England & Wales, Company No 1679046.
Registered Office and address for service: Aldgate House, 33 Aldgate High Street, London EC3N 1DL)

For further information on our products and services, visit *www.sweetandmaxwell.co.uk*

Typeset by Letterpart Ltd, Reigate, Surrey

Printed and bound in Great Britain by CPI Group (UK) Ltd, Croydon, CR0 4YY.

No natural forests were destroyed to make this product; only farmed timber was used and re-planted.

A CIP catalogue record of this book is available for the British Library.

ISBN: 978-0414-02498-4

Preface

The last edition of this book was published in 2007 before the recession. In the intervening years, case law has focussed on tenants' break clauses, the pursuit of sureties, assignment and service charge issues. As in the previous editions, I have tried to incorporate new material which is relevant for the purposes of understanding the general legal background to the drafting, negotiating and interpretation of business leases, concentrating on those developments which give rise to drafting points.

Looking to the future, it remains to be seen how the recent application of the Competition Act 1998 to land agreements, the increasing importance of sustainability issues and the development of new retail models will affect lease drafting, but I have made some suggestions.

I am grateful to Sir Kim Lewison for his invaluable assistance as Consultant Editor in reading and commenting on the typescript. I alone bear responsibility for any errors which remain.

I also owe a debt of thanks to Joanna Lampert and to Damian Fleming and Elizabeth Thompson of Berwin Leighton Paisner LLP for their time and thoughts about green leases.

The law is, in general, stated as at September 2012.

Janet Bignell
Falcon Chambers
London, EC4Y 1AA

TABLE OF CONTENTS

8. SERVICE CHARGES

List of Examples

TABLE OF CASES

TABLE OF STATUTES

TABLE OF STATUTORY INSTRUMENTS

TABLE OF EUROPEAN LEGISLATION

CHAPTER 1

THE INTERPRETATION OF LEASES

A lease of business property is a commercial contract. It must, therefore, be drafted and perused against the background of the principles developed by the courts for construing commercial contracts. The most important of these principles are briefly set out below. A fuller treatment of the principles applicable to the interpretation of contracts may be found in *The Interpretation of Contracts*, 5th edn (London: Sweet and Maxwell, 2011) by the Consultant Editor. **1–01**

1. GENERAL PRINCIPLES OF INTERPRETATION

The object sought to be achieved in construing any commercial contract is to ascertain what the mutual intentions of the parties were as to the legal obligations each assumed by the contractual words in which they chose to express them (*Pioneer Shipping Ltd v BTP Tioxide Ltd* [1982] A.C. 724). When one speaks of the intention of the parties to the contract one is speaking objectively: the parties cannot themselves give direct evidence of what their intention was. What must be ascertained is the intention that a reasonable person would have had if placed in the situation of the parties. What the court must do is place itself in thought in the same factual matrix as that of the parties (*Reardon Smith Line Ltd v Hansen-Tangen* [1976] 1 W.L.R. 989). The principles have been summarised as follows: **1–02**

(1) Interpretation is the ascertainment of the meaning which the document would convey to a reasonable person having all the background knowledge which would reasonably have been available to the parties in the situation in which they were at the time of the contract.
(2) The background was famously referred to by Lord Wilberforce as the matrix of fact, but this phrase is, if anything, an

understated description of what the background may include. Subject to the requirement that it should have been reasonably available to the parties and to the exception to be mentioned next, it includes absolutely anything which would have affected the way in which the language of the document would have been understood by a reasonable man.

(3) The law excludes from the admissible background the previous negotiations of the parties and their declarations of subjective intent. They are admissible only in an action for rectification. The law makes this distinction for reasons of practical policy and, in this respect only, legal interpretation differs from the way we would interpret utterances in ordinary life. The boundaries of this exception are in some respects unclear.

(4) The meaning which a document (or any other utterance) would convey to a reasonable man is not the same thing as the meaning of its words. The meaning of words is a matter of dictionaries and grammars; the meaning of the document is what the parties using those words against the relevant background would reasonably have been understood to mean. The background may not merely enable the reasonable man to choose between the possible meanings of words which are ambiguous but even (as occasionally happens in ordinary life) to conclude that the parties must, for whatever reason, have used the wrong words or syntax.

(5) The rule that words should be given their natural and ordinary meaning reflects the commonsense proposition that we do not easily accept that people have made linguistic mistakes, particularly in formal documents. On the other hand, if one would nevertheless conclude from the background that something must have gone wrong with the language, the law does not require judges to attribute to the parties an intention which they plainly could not have had. Thus if detailed semantic and syntactical analysis of words in a commercial contract is going to lead to a conclusion that flouts business common sense, it must be made to yield to business common sense (*Investors Compensation Scheme v West Bromwich Building Society* [1998] 1 All E.R. 98, and see *BCCI v Ali* [2001] 1 A.C. 251; *Rainy Sky SA v Kookmin Bank* [2011] 1 W.L.R. 2900).

2. BACKGROUND

The principles summarised above have not been universally welcomed, but are the established starting point in the interpretation of a contract. The point has been made, with particular reference to leases, that an assignee of a lease may have no knowledge of the background at the time of the original grant (*National Bank of Sharjah v Dellborg* Unreported July 9, 1997, and see the speech of Lord Collins in a different context in *Re Sigma Finance Corp* [2010] 1 All E.R. 571). However, the influence of background on questions of interpretation is unquestionable (see *Chartbrook Ltd v Persimmon Homes Ltd* [2009] A.C. 1101, per Lord Hoffmann at [40]). The court will always consider the factual background even if the wording of that contract might be regarded as unambiguous or sensible (*Persimmon Homes (South Coast) Ltd v Hall Aggregates (South Coast) Ltd* [2008] EWHC 2379 (TCC)). The question is what a reasonable person would understand the parties to mean by the words of the contract to be construed. The reasonable person must be taken to have all the background knowledge which would reasonably have been available to the parties in the situation in which they were at the time of the contract (*Rainy Sky SA v Kookmin Bank* [2011] 1 W.L.R. 2900). However, where the instrument in question is a public document (as some registered conveyancing documents are) then background has a more limited role to play. But even in such a case, the court will take account of objective background facts. **1–03**

For example, the standard of repair required by a covenant to keep property in repair will be determined by reference to the age, character and locality of the demised property at the time of the demise (*Proudfoot v Hart* (1890) 25 Q.B.D. 42). So also the size of the property may be relevant to the interpretation of the use covenant (*Basildon Development Corp v Mactro Ltd* [1986] 1 E.G.L.R. 137 per O'Connor L.J.), as may its physical layout (*Levermore v Jobey* [1956] 1 W.L.R. 697). Equally, in construing a rent review clause, the court has been aided by a consideration of valuation methods which the parties must have envisaged would be applied at the review date (*Pivot Properties v Secretary of State for the Environment* (1980) 41 P. & C.R. 248), and by the terms of a supplemental agreement to the lease (*Scottish Widows Fund and Life Assurance Society v BGC International* [2012] 142 Con. L.R. 27). In construing a restriction on use, an apparently unrelated series of specific prohibitions was explained by reference to leases already in existence at the date of grant (*Ashworth Frazer v Gloucester City Council* [2000] 1 E.G.L.R. 44).

Where the extent of the demise is ambiguous or lacks definition, oral evidence will be admitted to identify it (*Bisney v Swanston* (1972) 225 E.G. 229). An ambiguity in an executed lease may be resolved by a consideration of an agreement for lease, and a draft annexed to it, pursuant to which the lease was granted (*Ladbroke Group Plc v Bristol City Council* [1988] 1 E.G.L.R. 126, and *KPMG LLP v Network Rail Infrastructure Ltd* [2007] EWCA Civ 363).

In general, however, the intention of the parties is to be ascertained from the words of the lease itself and oral evidence will not be admitted to vary or contradict the written document. The courts do not easily accept that people have made linguistic mistakes, particularly in formal documents (see *BCCI v Ali*, as cited above, and *Chartbrook Ltd v Persimmon Homes Ltd* [2009] A.C. 1101). Thus, where a covenant in a lease provided for the payment of rent in advance, the tenant was not entitled to prove an antecedent oral agreement under which he was to pay by way of bill of exchange maturing some time after tender (*Henderson v Arthur* [1907] 1 K.B. 10). There are some exceptions to the rigours of this rule: an oral agreement was allowed to be proved where it formed one comprehensive contract with the written lease (*Walker Property Investments (Brighton) Ltd v Walker* (1947) 177 L.T. 204); and a tenant in breach of the user covenant in his written lease was allowed to prove an antecedent oral collateral contract permitting the breach complained of (*City and Westminster Properties (1934) Ltd v Mudd* [1959] Ch. 129).

Nevertheless, the aim of the draftsman must always be to ensure that the lease as executed represents the full intention of the parties. The parties cannot, however, by an express statement of intention alter the legal consequences of their bargain. Thus an express term that a transaction is not intended to be a lease but is intended to be a licence will not be given effect (*Street v Mountford* [1985] A.C. 809). Similarly, where a clause in a written agreement states that exclusive possession is not granted to the occupier, the clause will not be taken into account in deciding whether a licence or a tenancy is created (*Family Housing Association v Jones* [1990] 1 W.L.R. 779).

3. ORDINARY AND TECHNICAL WORDS

Where there is nothing to show that the parties have used language in any other than its strict and ordinary sense, and where the words interpreted in that sense are sensible with reference to extrinsic circumstances, it is an inflexible rule of construction that the words shall be interpreted in that strict and primary sense even though they may be capable of some popular or secondary interpretation and even though the most conclusive evidence of the intention to use them in such popular sense is tendered (*Enlayde Ltd v Roberts* [1917] 1 Ch. 109: obligation to reinstate property destroyed by fire included an obligation to reinstate where the destruction was caused by incendiary bombs). If the parties wish to give an ordinary word some special meaning, an express definition clause should be included. Where a definition in a lease states that a defined term "includes" a particular meaning, the term may also be construed in its ordinary sense, even if that sense is not within the definition (*Adelphi (Estates) v Christie* [1984] 1 E.G.L.R. 19). **1–04**

Technical words will be construed in a technical sense. Many words and phrases commonly found in leases are terms of art for example, "the usual quarter days". These will be given the meaning they bear among lawyers. In some cases evidence may be admitted to show that a word is used in a technical or local meaning. An odd example of the rule is provided by an old case in which it was proved that 1,000 rabbits meant 1,200 rabbits (*Smith v Wilson* (1832) 3 B. & Ad 728). A more modern example is "prime position" as applied to a shop (*Ashburn Anstalt v Arnold* [1989] Ch. 1). Even the meaning of a word such as "supermarket" may be proved by oral evidence (*Calabar (Woolwich) Ltd v Tesco Stores Ltd* [1978] 1 E.G.L.R. 113). Where a word used in a lease has multiple meanings, one of which is its ordinary meaning and the other of which is some technical meaning, there must be some objective evidence that the parties intended the technical meaning to be adopted, otherwise the word will be construed in its ordinary sense (*Holt & Co v Collyer* (1881) 16 Ch. D. 719).

4. LEASE CONSTRUED AS A WHOLE

1–05 The court must take into consideration the whole of the lease and the purposes for which it was granted, and then see what is the proper construction of a particular covenant (*Bickmore v Dimmer* [1903] 1 Ch. 158). The draftsman must, therefore, express himself consistently throughout the lease, for a word used in one part of the lease will probably be construed as having the same meaning if used in another part of the same document. Thus, where the draftsman used the phrase "adjoining premises" in one part of the lease and the phrase "adjoining or neighbouring premises" in another part of it, it was held that the former phrase only applied to property that came into physical contact with the demised property because the words "or neighbouring" must have added something to the word "adjoining" (*White v Harrow* (1902) 86 L.T. 4). The danger of inconsistency is most pronounced where the draftsman takes parts of his draft from different precedents.

Where there is an apparent inconsistency, the court will do its best to resolve it. Thus where there was a covenant against alterations without the landlord's consent, and an absolute covenant against the making of waste, spoil or destruction, the covenant against waste was interpreted as not applying to anything covered by the qualified covenant against alterations (*FW Woolworth v Lambert* [1937] Ch. 37). Where a lease placed an obligation upon the landlord to keep the building in repair and to give the tenant quiet enjoyment, the court construed the obligations so as to coexist on a basis of parity not priority and held that the threshold for disturbance by repairs was the taking of all reasonable precautions rather than all possible precautions (*Goldmile Properties Ltd v Lechouritis* [2003] 1 E.G.L.R. 60). A tenant's covenants to yield up and to reinstate have also been construed such that apparent conflict was resolved (*Fairgate International Ltd v Citibank International Plc* [2005] 2 E.G.L.R. 48). Where the repairing obligations in a lease resulted in the landlord and tenant having overlapping obligations, it was held that the lease ought to be construed to avoid such an impractical result unless it was literally impossible to do so (*Toff v McDowell* (1995) 69 P. & C.R. 535; *Petersson v Pitt Place (Epsom) Ltd* [2001] L.&T.R. 21).

If there is an inconsistency between lease and counterpart prima facie the lease prevails. However, where there is an ambiguity on the face of the lease it is permissible to look at the counterpart to explain it. Thus, a proviso for re-entry on breach of the "covenant" contained in the lease was construed as extending to all covenants in the lease (*Matthews v Smallwood* [1910] 1 Ch. 777).

5. CLEAR WORDS

In some cases, the court applies a particularly exacting standard to the interpretation of a clause. Instead of simply interpreting the clause, it requires clear words to be used before it will interpret a clause as having a particular effect. Thus, where a lease required the tenant to pay rent "without deduction", it was held that clear words were necessary in order to exclude the tenant's remedy of equitable set-off, and that the words "without deduction" were not clear enough (*Connaught Restaurants Ltd v Indoor Leisure Ltd* [1994] 1 W.L.R. 501). Similarly, where landlords sought to argue that various forms of rent review clause entitled them to receive a "headline rent" on review it was held that only the most unambiguous of clauses would be interpreted as having that effect (*Co-operative Wholesale Society Ltd v National Westminster Bank Plc* [1995] 1 E.G.L.R. 97). It is by no means clear in what circumstances this principle will apply, but it seems to emerge whenever the court would otherwise be forced to an interpretation which it considers is unfair. **1–06**

6. CONSTRUCTION AGAINST GRANTOR

It is a well-known maxim of construction that in case of doubt or ambiguity a contract is construed *contra proferentem*. However, reliance on the maxim is generally very much as a last resort (*Landlord Protect Ltd v St Anselm Development Co Ltd* [2009] 2 P. & C.R. 9). **1–07**

In the case of a lease this will usually mean that the ambiguity will be construed against the landlord (*Killick v Second Covent Garden Property Co Ltd* [1973] 2 All E.R. 337, although in *Amax International Ltd v Custodian Holdings Ltd* [1986] 2 E.G.L.R. 111, Hoffmann J. suggested that, technically, the tenant might be the *proferens*). The landlord is usually the party who settles the form of the lease (albeit it may be amended many times before execution) and most of the covenants are inserted for his protection. He will, therefore, usually be the *proferens*. But this does not mean that a dispute about the interpretation of the lease must be decided against the landlord if it possibly can be. Thus, where the issue is the width of the use covenant, the application of the *contra proferentem* rule points towards greater freedom of use on the part of the tenant rather than narrower, even if the tenant is arguing for a narrower use so as to secure a benefit on rent review (*Skillion v Keltec Industrial Research* [1992] 1 E.G.L.R. 123). However, some parts of the lease will be construed against the tenant, since by a legal fiction he may be treated as a grantor. This is seen at its most capricious in the case of exceptions and reservations. It is a settled rule of construction that where there is a grant and an exception out of it the exception is taken as inserted for the benefit of the grantor and is to be construed in favour of the grantee (*Savill Brothers Ltd v Bethell* [1902] 2 Ch. 523). In the case of an exception the grantor will be the landlord and the grantee will be the tenant. However, where the lease contains a reservation in favour of the landlord it is construed as if the right reserved had been granted to the landlord by the tenant. Any ambiguity will be construed against the tenant (*St Edmundsbury & Ipswich Diocesan Board of Finance v Clark (No.2)* [1975] 1 All E.R. 772).

A covenant by a surety will be construed strictly against the principal creditor (*Eastern Counties Building Society v Russell* [1947] 2 All E.R. 734).

7. IMPLIED TERMS

1–08 Certain terms will be implied in a lease by operation of law, although many such terms may be excluded by agreement. Thus, the use of the word "demise" will give rise to two implied covenants on the part of the landlord, i.e. that he is entitled to grant some term in the demised property and that the tenant shall have quiet enjoyment of the demised property. However, there is no room for the implication of the covenant in a demise if the landlord enters into an express covenant for quiet enjoyment (and gives no covenant for title). The reason for this is that an express covenant as to one branch of the covenant implied by the word "demise" excludes the other branch on the principle that *expressio unius est exclusio alterius* (the expression of one thing is the exclusion of another) (*Miller v Emcer Products Ltd* [1956] Ch. 304). The court is, however, reluctant to find implied terms in commercial contracts especially where there is a formal document which, on the face of it, represents the apparently complete bargain between the parties (*Westminster (Duke) v Guild* [1985] Q.B. 688). An unexpressed term can be implied if, and only if, the court finds that the parties must have intended that term to form part of their contract: it is not enough for the court to find that such a term would have been adopted by the parties as reasonable men if it had been suggested to them. It must have been a term that went without saying, a term necessary to give business efficacy to the contract, a term that, although tacit, formed part of the contract the parties made for themselves (*Trollope & Colls Ltd v North West Metropolitan Regional Hospital Board* [1973] 1 W.L.R. 601).

The circumstances in which a term may be implied as part of the process of interpreting contracts is a matter of the construction of the contract as a whole in its commercial setting (*Transfield Shipping Inc v Mercator Shipping Inc* [2009] A.C. 61, per Lord Hoffmann). The starting point for deciding whether a term should be implied into a contract is now *Attorney-General of Belize v Belize Telecom Ltd* [2009] 1 W.L.R. 1988. The court has no power to improve upon the instrument it is called upon to construe or to introduce terms to make it fairer or more reasonable. The court is concerned only to discover what the instrument means. That is the meaning the instrument would convey to a reasonable person having all the background knowledge which would reasonably be available to the audience to whom the instrument is addressed (see *Investors Compensation Scheme Ltd*, as cited above). This is the only question, even though it may be formulated in different ways, including that the implied term must "go without saying" or must be "necessary to give business efficacy to the contract" (*Attorney General of Belize* per Lord Hoffmann). The most usual inference where an instrument includes no express provision for what is to happen when some event occurs is that nothing is to happen. A term will only be implied to spell out what the instrument means where the reasonable addressee would consider that the only meaning consistent with the other provisions of the instrument, read against the background, is that something is to happen.

Thus, the court has refused to imply a term that a landlord entitled to recover the cost of insurance from his tenant is obliged to choose the cheapest method of insuring (*Bandar Property Holdings Ltd v Darwen (JS) (Successors) Ltd* [1968] 2 All E.R. 305) or that the tenant is under an obligation not to use the demised property for an immoral purpose (*Burfort Financial Investments Ltd v Chotard* [1976] 2 E.G.L.R. 53) or that the landlord is entitled to interest on a retrospective increase in rent (*Trusthouse Forte Albany Hotels Ltd v Daejan Investments Ltd* [1980] 2 E.G.L.R. 123) or that a landlord would lose his right to review the rent under a lease by virtue of an unexpressed time limit (*Iceland Foods Plc v Dangoor* [2002] 2 E.G.L.R. 5).

However, the court will readily imply the grant of such easements as may be necessary to give effect to the common intention of the parties with reference to the manner and purposes for which the demised property is to be used. It is essential for this purpose that the parties intend that the demised property should be used in some definite and particular manner. It is not enough that the property should be intended to be used in a manner that may or may not involve this definite and particular manner (*Pwllbach Colliery Co Ltd v Woodman* [1915] A.C. 634). Thus, where a tenant covenanted to use a basement as a restaurant, not to cause any nuisance, to control and eliminate all smells and to comply with Food Hygiene Regulations, he was entitled to an easement to erect a ventilation duct on his landlord's wall (*Wong v Beaumont Property Trust Ltd* [1965] 1 Q.B. 173).

Business efficacy also dictated the implication of a term where a landlord alone had the power to apply to the President of the RICS for the appointment of a surveyor to determine the rent on review under an upwards downwards rent review clause, but no time limit was placed upon that step such that the tenant would have no effective means of knowing what the rent might be. The court implied a term that the landlord should make the application within a reasonable time, with the result that it was open to the tenant to serve notice to make time of the essence (*Northern & Midland Holdings v Magnet Ltd* [2004] EWHC 120).

Certain other terms are implied into leases by virtue of statute and these are dealt with in their respective contexts. In some cases a term implied by statute may not be excluded by agreement.

8. PRINCIPLES OF CONSTRUCTION

(a) *Expressio unius est exclusio alterius*

This principle of construction has already been touched on. Its basic principle is: where one specific thing is mentioned but another is not, that other thing is taken to have been deliberately not mentioned. Where, for example, a tenant covenants "to keep in repair the demised property and the windows, window frames, boilers and air-conditioning plant" it might be successfully argued on their behalf that they are not liable to repair the doors because the doors were not mentioned in the catalogue. Thus, the draftsman should be especially careful before embarking on a long list of matters that fall within a particular covenant. However, this principle is of little weight where it produces an unfair and unreasonable result (*Basingstoke and Deane BC v Host Group* [1988] 1 W.L.R. 348). **1–09**

Similarly, where an agreement specifies the time for doing three things (e.g. taking procedural steps towards a rent review) and two of the three are stated to have a time limit which is of the essence of the contract and the other one does not, then it follows that, in all probability, where it is not stated to be of the essence, it is not intended to be of the essence. If the parties, when they wish something to be made of the essence, say so in terms, then obviously it is of the essence if they do say so, and the probability is, that where they do not say so, it is not intended to be of the essence (*Amherst v Walker (James) Goldsmith & Silversmith Ltd* [1980] 1 E.G.L.R. 86).

(b) Express terms negative implied terms

An express term in a lease generally excludes the possibility of the implication of a term dealing with the same subject matter as the implied term. Thus, where a lease contained a covenant to build certain buildings by a specified date and an obligation to keep them in repair, it was held that once the tenant had failed to build the buildings on time, no further covenant to build could be implied from the covenant to repair (*Stephens v Junior Army and Navy Stores* [1914] 2 Ch. 516). Similarly where a transfer of land contained an express right to park it was said that the circumstances **1–10** would have to be quite exceptional for a further right of a similar character to be implied (*Waterman v Boyle* [2009] 2 E.G.L.R. 7).

An implied obligation not to derogate from grant was not excluded by the presence of an express restriction where the content of the implied obligation was held to be substantially different (*Oceanic Village Ltd v Shirayama Shokusan Co Ltd* [2001] L.&T.R. 35).

(c) *Ejusdem generis*

1–11 The *ejusdem generis* rule is an important principle of construction. If one can find that the things described by particular words have some common characteristic one ought to limit the general words that follow them to things of that genus (*Lambourn v McLellan* [1903] 2 Ch. 268). Thus, where there was a contract for the sale of land and "buildings material, etc." it was held that the word "etc" referred to "material" and did not embrace a right of way (*Re Walmsley and Shaw's Contract* [1917] 1 Ch. 93). Similarly, a power entitling a landlord to re-enter for "building sites or planting or other purposes" did not entitle him to re-enter in order to build a sports stadium (*Coates v Diment* [1951] 1 All E.R. 890).

The rule usually applies only where a genus can be found. For example, where a tenant covenanted to yield up certain articles together with "all doors, wainscots, shelves, presses, dressers, drawers, locks, keys, bolts, bars, staples, hinges, hearths, chimney pieces, mantelpieces, chimney-jambs, floor-pans, slabs, covings, window-shutters, partitions, sinks, water-closets, cisterns, pumps, and rails and water-tanks and other additions, improvements, fixtures and things" it was held that there was no discernible genus which restricted the general words (*Wilson v Whateley* (1860) 1 J. & H. 436). It is, therefore, possible by sheer verbosity to defeat the operation of the rule; but this is hardly a method to be recommended. However, the absence of a genus does not of itself preclude the operation of the rule: it is an indication that the parties did not intend the general words to be restricted (*Chandris v Isbrandtsen-Moller* [1951] 1 K.B. 240; *Skillion v Keltec Industrial Research* [1992] 1 E.G.L.R. 123). One method of avoiding the operation of the rule is to reverse the order of the two parts of the clause so that the general words are placed first and the list of specific items are prefaced by a phrase like "for example", or "without prejudice to the generality of the foregoing", or "such as".

(d) Party not to take advantage of his own wrong

A lease will be construed, so far as possible, so as not to permit a party to it to take advantage of his own wrong. Thus the tenant will not be permitted to rely on his own breach of his repairing obligations in order to depress the rent payable on review (*Harmsworth Pension Funds Trustees v Charringtons Industrial Holdings* (1985) 49 P. & C.R. 297), and a surety who had guaranteed the obligations of a tenant was not allowed to rely on the tenant's failure to register an assignment with the landlord in order to escape liability under his surety covenant (*Cerium Investments v Evans* (1991) 62 P. & C.R. 203). **1–12**

9. UNCERTAINTY

The court is always reluctant to find a provision void for uncertainty, particularly where the provision is contained in a commercial agreement. **1–13**

> "No doubt there may be cases in which the draftsman's ineptitude will succeed in defeating the court's efforts to find a meaning for the provision in question; but only if the court is driven to it will it find a provision is void for uncertainty." (*Brown v Gould* [1972] Ch. 53, per Megarry J.)

A provision will be void for uncertainty where there is real conceptual uncertainty, for example, an option to renew "at a rent to be agreed" where there was no indication of how the rent was to be agreed, nor on what basis, nor what was to happen if the parties failed to agree (*King's Motors (Oxford) v Lax* [1970] 1 W.L.R. 426). But even in such a case, the court may be able to give contractual effect to the stipulation by implying a term to the effect that the rent must be a reasonable rent (*Corson v Rhuddlan BC* [1990] 1 E.G.L.R. 255). The Court would not, however, imply or write in details of a specification for a permanent office building that the lessee was obliged to build in accordance with a specification agreed and signed by the parties on the date of execution of the lease ex post facto, where no letter had ever existed. It held that the manifest intention of the parties was to agree the content and detail of the specification and that the specification should not be left open for later agreement but should be set out in the lease. The covenant to build was, therefore, void for uncertainty (*UYCF Ltd v Forrester* [2001] 3 E.G.C.S. 131).

Where the difficulty is one of applying the provision rather than a conceptual uncertainty, the court will not hold it to be void (*Brown v Gould* [1972] Ch. 53); and a provision in a lease will not be uncertain if it can be made certain. Thus, a lease which contains a rent review clause will not be uncertain merely because the amount of the rent is not known at the date of the lease. To attract the remedy of distress, however, the rent must be certain at the time it falls due (*United Scientific Holdings Ltd v Burnley BC* [1978] A.C. 904).

The principle is different in relation to the term for which a lease is granted. A term created by a lease must be expressed either with certainty and specifically or by reference to something that can at the time the lease takes effect be looked to as a certain ascertainment of what the term is meant to be (*Lace v Chantler* [1944] K.B. 368: lease "for the duration of the war" was void for uncertainty). Thus a tenancy granted until the land was required for road widening was void for uncertainty (*Prudential Assurance Co v London Residuary Body* [1992] 2 A.C. 386). If the draftsman wishes to create a lease for a period that cannot be made certain at the time of the demise the only way is to express it as being granted for a fixed term subject to a power to break at the expiry of the period. In the case of a lease granted to an individual a term which is otherwise uncertain may take effect as a lease for 99 years terminable on the death of the tenant.

10. PRIMA FACIE ASSUMPTIONS

1–14 Sometimes the court lays down a prima facie assumption applicable to a certain kind of provision (e.g. the rule that time is not of the essence of a rent review timetable, see *United Scientific Holdings Ltd v Burnley BC* [1978] A.C. 904 and *British Gas Corp v Universities Superannuation Scheme Ltd* [1986] 1 W.L.R. 398). These rules are very important, because they bring consistency to the interpretation of leases and enable parties buying and selling leases and reversions to obtain more reliable advice on what their rights and liabilities are likely to be. Thus the court will not fritter away the prima facie assumption on small differences in drafting (*Laura Investments v Havering LBC* [1992] 1 E.G.L.R. 155).

11. STATUTORY RULES OF CONSTRUCTION

In a number of cases, statute has intervened. Thus, in all leases granted after 1925, unless the context otherwise requires: **1–15**

(1) "month" means calendar month;
(2) "person" includes a corporation;
(3) the singular includes the plural and vice versa;
(4) the masculine includes the feminine and vice versa (s.61 of the Law of Property Act 1925).

Many leases repeat these definitions, although it is unnecessary to do so. Where a definition is qualified by a phrase like "unless the context otherwise requires", the context may displace the defined term (for an example in an insurance policy, see *Deutsche Genossenschaftsbank v Burnhope* [1995] 4 All E.R. 717).

Similarly, an instrument that is expressed to be "supplemental" to a previous instrument is construed as if the supplemental instrument contained a full recital of the previous instrument (s.58 of the Law of Property Act 1925). In construing the supplemental instrument the whole of the previous instrument may be looked at (*Plumrose Ltd v Real and Leasehold Estates Investment Society Ltd* [1970] 1 W.L.R. 52).

Stipulations in a contract, as to time or otherwise, which according to rules of equity are not deemed to be of the essence of the contract, are construed at law in accordance with the same rules (s.41 of the Law of Property Act 1925). After a flurry of litigation it is now settled that stipulations as to time in a rent review clause are, prima facie not of the essence (*United Scientific Holdings Ltd v Burnley BC* [1978] A.C. 904); nor is an obligation to prepare service charge accounts (*West Central Investments Ltd v Borovik* [1977] 1 E.G.L.R. 29). However, it is not certain how far this rule of construction extends. Would it, for example, apply to a covenant to redecorate the demised property in the seventh year of the term? It is suggested that if the timetable is important (as for example, a development timetable in a building lease) the draftsman should provide expressly that time is to be of the essence.

Sometimes, a lease incorporates parts of a statute by reference (e.g. the "disregards" in s.34 of the Landlord and Tenant Act 1954). It is important for the draftsman to make clear whether amendments to the statute are also incorporated (cf. *Brett v Brett Essex Golf Club Ltd* [1986] 1 E.G.L.R. 154). Moreover, part of a statute incorporated by reference will be construed in accordance with the ordinary canons of construction as applied to the lease, not necessarily in accordance with the way the statute itself is construed.

Where a lease defines something by reference to a statute or statutory instruments (e.g. the Town and Country Planning (Use Classes) Order 1987), a change in the statute or statutory instrument will not alter the terms of the lease (*Brewers Co v Viewplan* [1989] 2 E.G.L.R. 133).

12. DATE FOR APPLYING RULES OF CONSTRUCTION

1–16 In the ordinary course, the rules of construction must be applied as at the date of execution of the lease: thus a word will be interpreted in the sense it bore at the time (*Texaco Antilles Ltd v Kernochan* [1973] A.C. 609: the phrase "public garage" was given the meaning it bore in 1933 and not the one it bore at the date of the litigation; *St Marylebone Property Co Ltd v Tesco Stores Ltd* [1988] 2 E.G.L.R. 40 construing the word "grocer"; *Joint London Holdings Ltd v Mount Cook Land Ltd* [2005] 3 E.G.L.R. 119 construing the words "victualler, vintner, tavern-keeper, vendor of malt liquor, restauranteur or coffee-house keeper" in a 1950 lease). The same principle probably applies where the lease refers to an Act of Parliament or statutory instruments by name. Thus, where the user covenant permits the tenant to use the demised property for any purpose falling within a class of the Town and Country Planning (Use Classes) Order 1972 (SI 1972/1385) the covenant will be construed as referring to the use class as it existed at the date of the demise. Thus a covenant in that form will not allow the tenant to take advantage of the much greater flexibility of use permitted by the Town and Country Planning (Use Classes) Order 1987 (SI 1987/764) (*Brewers Co v Viewplan* [1989] 2 E.G.L.R. 133), or the Town and Country Planning (Use Classes) Order 1987 as amended by the Town and Country Planning (Use Classes) (Amendment) (England) Order 2005 (SI 2005/84), which came into force on April 21, 2005. In order to avoid this result, the draftsman should define a reference to an Act of Parliament, etc. as including a reference to that Act, etc. as amended or re-enacted from time to time.

Equally, the standard of repair demanded by a covenant to keep the demised property in repair will be determined by reference to the age, character and locality of the property at the date of the demise. If the locality deteriorates during the term the standard of repair required will not (*Anstruther-Gough-Calthorpe v McOscar* [1924] 1 K.B. 716).

13. MAKING IT WORK

All the above rules of construction will yield to the overriding importance of making the lease work. Where a term of a contract is open to more than one interpretation, it is generally appropriate to adopt the interpretation which is most consistent with business common sense (*Rainy Sky SA v Kookmin Bank*, as cited above). If detailed semantic and syntactical analysis of words in a commercial contract is going to lead to a conclusion that flouts business common sense, it must be made to yield to business common sense (*The Antaios* [1985] A.C. 191). **1–17**

Thus the court has modified a use covenant in a lease for the purposes of a rent review (*The Law Land Company Ltd v Consumers Association Ltd* [1980] 2 E.G.L.R. 109, in which Brightman L.J. recognised that some modification had to be made to the strict wording of the rent review clause if it was to work. He justified that approach on the basis that "the lease is a commercial document and we have to find a commercial solution to the problem posed"). Similarly, the court has implied the grant of a right of way, solely for the purpose of a rent review, in order that the rent review clause should have a practical effect (*Jefferies v O'Neill* [1984] 1 E.G.L.R. 106) and has enlarged a definition of "lessor" in a lease in order to give effect to a general scheme for the maintenance of a building and the recovery of a service charge (*Adelphi (Estates) Ltd v Christie* [1984] 1 E.G.L.R. 19). In construing a 1965 lease to determine "the gross amount of total sales" for the purpose of calculating turnover rent in 2004, the court considered that whilst VAT did not exist in 1965 and could not have formed part of the thinking of the parties, purchase tax did exist at that date and was imposed on wholesalers of goods. In the real world, purchase tax affected ultimate prices just like VAT and, accordingly, the parties would have regarded VAT as included within the definition (*Debenhams Retail Plc v Sun Alliance & London Assurance Co Ltd* [2005] 3 E.G.L.R. 34).

The development of this approach to commercial documents is continuing, and may well lead to greater judicial activity in shaping the mutual obligations of the parties. At its most extreme, it may result in the court rewriting the terms of a lease in order to do what is fair and reasonable between the parties in circumstances which they did not foresee at the date of the lease (*Pole Properties Ltd v Feinberg* [1981] 2 E.G.L.R. 38).

14. PRACTICALITIES

1–18 "A lease is not intended to be either a mental exercise or an essay in literature; it is a practical document dealing with a practical situation" (*Levermore v Jobey* [1956] 2 All E.R. 362 at 370, per Dankwerts L.J).

For this reason, in drafting a lease the draftsman should constantly have in mind the nature of the demised property and the parties' own agreed heads of terms. A long lease of a large property acquired for investment may well require far different treatment from a lease of second rate property let to a small businessman at a rack rent. Many of the burdensome covenants inserted in the former kind of lease will be wholly inappropriate to the latter. Although the draftsman may never see the lease again once it has been executed, others will have to live with it and try to manage the property according to its terms. An over-sophisticated document may make that task far more difficult than it need be.

This approach is reflected in the basic forms in the Appendix. Although some of them have been drafted in an "institutional" style and are intended as a framework for the kinds of specific drafting found by way of example throughout the book, others have been deliberately kept simple. The simpler forms are designed for less prestigious or valuable property. The essential point is that the draftsman always has the choice.

Example 1.1 Definitions clause for business lease

(1) The following definitions apply:

"Act" means an Act of Parliament whenever passed and a reference to a specific Act includes any legislation amending or replacing it or made under it

"Approved" means approved in writing by the Landlord
"Authorised guarantee agreement" means an agreement authorised by section 16(2) of the Landlord and Tenant (Covenants) Act 1995
"Consent" means the Landlord's written consent
"Insured Risks" means the risks covered by the policy of insurance arranged by the Landlord to include (subject to cover being available on reasonable terms) loss or damage by fire storm tempest flood earthquake aircraft and articles dropped from them terrorism riot or civil commotion labour disturbances malicious damage impact bursting and overflowing of pipes tanks and other apparatus and any other risks insured against by the Landlord
"Landlord" includes all persons from time to time entitled to the immediate reversion to this Lease and where there is a superior landlord includes him as well
"Last Year" means the period of twelve months ending on the Termination of the Term
"Lease" includes any documents supplemental to this Lease
"Legislation" means any regulation or directive of the European Union, any Act and any subordinate legislation made under or by virtue of them
"Notice" means written notice
"President" means the President for the time being of the Royal Institution of Chartered Surveyors or a person acting on his behalf
"Tenant" includes the successors in title of the original tenant
"Term" includes both the term expressly granted by this Lease and also any statutory continuation of it
"Termination of the Term" includes termination by effluxion of time notice forfeiture surrender disclaimer or any other means

(2) Where a party consists of two or more persons the obligations of that party are joint and several
(3) Any covenant by a party to this Lease to do something includes an obligation to ensure that it is done
(4) Any covenant by the Tenant not to do something includes a covenant not to permit or allow that thing to be done by any person

(5) References to liability include (where the context allows) claims demands proceedings damages losses costs and expenses

(6) All payments to be made by the Tenant are exclusive of Value Added Tax.

CHAPTER 2

FORMAL REQUIREMENTS AND REGISTERED LEASES

Unless the lease takes effect in possession for a term not exceeding three years at the best rent that can reasonably be obtained without taking a fine (s.54(2) of the Law of Property Act 1925), the lease must be made by deed (s.52(1) of the LPA 1925). **2–01**

To be a deed the document:

(1) must be in writing;
(2) must make clear on its face that it is intended to be a deed by the person making it or the parties to it (either by the document describing itself as a deed or expressing itself to be executed as a deed "or otherwise"); and
(3) must be validly executed as a deed by the person making it or one or more of the parties to it (s.1 of the Law of Property (Miscellaneous Provisions) Act 1989).

Merely sealing a document will not make it a deed (s.1(2A) of the Law of Property (Miscellaneous) Provisions Act 1989), introduced by the Regulatory Reform (Execution of Deeds and Documents) Order 2005)).

Where the deed relates to land in England and Wales, it is the law of England and Wales that applies to the form and execution of the deed. There is no prescribed form for a lease of registered land, but the deed must be in such form as Land Registry may direct or allow (Land Registration Rules 2003 r.212). **2–02**

Subject to four exceptions, any lease granted on or after 19 June 2006 where the lease is a disposition of a registered estate in land (s.4(1)(c) of the Land Registration Act 2002), and is required to be completed by registration (s.27(2)(b) of the LRA 2002), must contain the standard prescribed clauses contained in cll.LR1 to LR14 of Sch.1A to the Land Registration Rules 2003 (The Land Registration (Amendment) (No.2) Rules 2005 (SI 2005/1982). **2–03**

The four exceptional cases when a lease does not have to contain the prescribed clauses are when the lease is granted in a form expressly required either by an agreement entered into before 19 June 2006; by an order of the court; by or under any enactment; or by a necessary consent or licence (for example of a superior landlord) for the grant of the lease given before 19 June 2006.

2–04 Accordingly, in the case of a grant out of a registered title, the leases that must contain the prescribed lease clauses are as follows:

(a) The grant of a term of years absolute for a term of more than seven years from the date of grant (s.27(2)(b)(i) of the LRA 2002).
(b) The grant of a term of years absolute as a reversionary lease giving the tenant a right to possession of the leased property more than three months from the date of grant of the lease (rather than immediately) (s.27(2)(b)(iii) of the LRA 2002).
(c) The grant of a term of years absolute under which the right to possession is discontinuous (s.27(2)(b)(iv) of the LRA 2002). For example, under a lease of an office or a market stall where possession is granted for a specified number of days a week or for a specified week or weeks or specified month or months.
(d) The grant of a term of years absolute where the registered estate is a franchise or manor (s.27(2)(c) of the LRA 2002).

2–05 In the case of a grant out of an unregistered freehold or leasehold legal estate in land which, at the time of the grant, has more than seven years to run (s.4(2) of the LRA 2002), the lease must contain the prescribed clauses if it is:

(a) The grant of a term of years absolute for more than seven years from the date of grant provided the lease is either for valuable or other consideration, by way of gift or in pursuance of an order of any court (s.4(1)(c) of the LRA 2002). This provision catches estates that have a negative value (s.4(6) of the LRA 2002).
The reference to a transfer or grant by way of gift will include transfers or grants for the purpose of setting up a trust under which the settlor does not retain the whole of the beneficial interest, or to unite the bare legal title and the beneficial interest in property held under a trust under which the settler

did not on constitution retain the whole of the beneficial interest when the trust was set up (s.4(7) of the LRA 2002).

(b) The grant of a term of years absolute as a reversionary lease giving the tenant a right to possession of the leased property more than three months from the date of grant of the lease (rather than immediately) (s.4(1)(f) of the LRA 2002).

(c) The grant of a discontinuous lease for a term of more than seven years (s.4(1)(c) of the LRA 2002).
The length of term is calculated by multiplying the number of complete weeks each year that the property is demised by the number of years granted. If the total is more than 364 complete weeks (seven years), the lease must be registered.

(d) The grant of a lease out of an unregistered estate in land where the owner of the reversionary estate was subject to a duty to apply for the estate to be registered under s.6 of the LRA 2002 when the lease was granted (r.38 of the LRR 2003).

The clauses may also be included in a lease that is to be the subject of voluntary first registration. If the clauses are used in non-compulsory circumstances, omissions and mistakes in the completion of the clauses will not result in the rejection of the application for registration of the lease. In contrast to the compulsory circumstances, separate applications will be required on Forms AP1, FR1, AN1, UN1 as appropriate, in any event. A lease is voluntarily registrable: **2–06**

(1) Where a tenant holds a lease in possession but is granted another lease of the same land to take effect in possession or within one month of the expiry of the first lease, the two terms can be treated as creating one continuous term (s.3(7) of the LRA 2002). If the two terms total more than seven years, Land Registry will register both leases together on the same title.

(2) Where a discontinuous lease of any length is granted out of unregistered land (s.3(4) of the LRA 2002).

(3) Where a public private partnership lease constitutes a public-private partnership agreement (s.90 of the LRA 2002).

Example 2.1 The prescribed clauses

LR1. Date of lease	
LR2. Title Number(s)	
	LR2.1 Landlord's Title Number(s) *Title Number(s) out of which this lease is granted. Leave blank if not registered.* **LR2.2 Other Title Numbers** *Existing Title Number(s) against which entries of matters referred to in LR9, LR10, LR11 and LR13 are to be made.*
LR3. Parties to this lease *Give full names and addresses of each of the parties. For UK incorporated companies and limited liability partnerships, also give the registered number including any prefix. For overseas companies, also give the territory of incorporation and, if appropriate, the registered number in the United Kingdom including any prefix.*	

	Landlord **Tenant** **Other parties** *Specify capacity of each party, for example "management company", "guarantor", etc.*
LR4. Property *Insert a full description of the land being leased or* *Refer to the clause, schedule or paragraph of a schedule in this lease in which the land being leased is more fully described.* *Where there is a letting of part of a registered Title, a plan must be attached to this lease and any floor levels must be specified.*	**In the case of a conflict between this clause and the remainder of this lease then, for the purposes of registration, this clause shall prevail.**

LR5. Prescribed statements, etc. *If this lease includes a statement falling within LR5.1, insert under that sub-clause the relevant statement or refer to the clause, schedule or paragraph of a schedule in this lease which contains the statement.* *In LR5.2, omit or delete those Acts which do not apply to this lease.*	
	LR5.1 Statements prescribed under rules 179 (dispositions in favour of a charity), 180 (dispositions by a charity) or 196 (leases under the Leasehold Reform, Housing and Urban Development Act 1993) of the Land Registration Rules 2003. **LR5.2 This lease is made under, or by reference to, provisions of:** *Leasehold Reform Act 1967* *Housing Act 1985* *Housing Act 1988* *Housing Act 1996*

LR6. Term for which the property is leased *Include only the appropriate statement (duly completed) from the three options.* **Note: The information you provide, or refer to, here will be used as part of the particulars to identify the lease under rule 6 of the Land Registration Rules 2003.*	*From and including* *To and including* *OR* *The term as specified in this lease at clause/schedule/paragraph* *OR* *The term is as follows:*
LR7. Premium *Specify the total premium, inclusive of any VAT where payable.*	

LR8. Prohibitions or restrictions on disposing of this lease *Include whichever of the two statements is appropriate.* *Do not set out here the wording of the provision.*	This lease does not contain a provision that prohibits or restricts dispositions. *OR* This lease contains a provision that prohibits or restricts dispositions.
LR9. Rights of acquisition, etc. *Insert the relevant provisions in the sub-clauses or refer to the clause, schedule or paragraph of a schedule in this lease which contains the provisions.*	

	LR9.1 Tenant's contractual rights to renew this lease, to acquire the reversion or another lease of the Property, or to acquire an interest in other land **LR9.2 Tenant's covenant to (or offer to) surrender this lease** **LR9.3 Landlord's contractual rights to acquire this lease**
LR10. Restrictive covenants given in this lease by the landlord in respect of land other than the property *Insert the relevant provisions or refer to the clause, schedule or paragraph of a schedule in this lease which contains the provisions.*	
LR11. Easements *Refer here only to the clause, schedule or paragraph of a schedule in this lease which sets out the easements.*	
	LR11.1 Easements granted by this lease for the benefit of the Property **LR11.2 Easements granted or reserved by this lease over the Property for the benefit of other property**

LR12. Estate rentcharge burdening the property *Refer here only to the clause, schedule or paragraph of a schedule in this lease which sets out the rentcharge.*	
LR13. Application for standard form of restriction *Set out the full text of the standard form of restriction and the Title against which it is to be entered. If you wish to apply for more than one standard form of restriction use this clause to apply for each of them, tell us who is applying against which Title and set out the full text of the restriction you are applying for.* *Standard forms of restriction are set out in Schedule 4 to the Land Registration Rules 2003.*	The Parties to this lease apply to enter the following standard form of restriction [against the Title of the Property] or [against Title Number]

LR14. Declaration of trust where there is more than one person comprising the tenant *If the Tenant is one person, omit or delete all the alternative statements.* *If the Tenant is more than one person, complete this clause by omitting or deleting all inapplicable alternative statements.*	The Tenant is more than one person. They are to hold the Property on trust for themselves as joint tenants. *OR* The Tenant is more than one person. They are to hold the Property on trust for themselves as tenants in common in equal shares. *OR* The Tenant is more than one person. They are to hold the Property on trust [*Complete as necessary*].

1. COMPLETION OF THE PRESCRIBED CLAUSES

The prescribed clauses are an integral part of a compulsorily registrable lease and must form part of the bound and executed lease and counterpart. They must appear at the front of the lease or, if the lease contains a front sheet (including a contents sheet and/or **2–07** index sheet if placed at the beginning of the lease), immediately after that front sheet (defined in r.58A(4) of the LRR 2003). They must come before the Particulars page, if the lease has one.

The clauses may be set out in tabular form, or the text of the clauses can be set out alone. The numbered headings and subheadings of the prescribed clauses must be replicated even where there is no relevant information to complete them, or different terms or definitions are used in the remainder of the lease. To avoid confusion, the sensible approach would be to attempt to use the definitions deployed in the prescribed clauses throughout the body of the lease.

It is important that the clauses are completed correctly as Land Registry will use the information to complete registration of the lease and, unless the property is the subject of a voluntary application for first registration, will complete that registration solely on the information provided in the clauses. Land Registry will reject applications for registration that are substantially defective. Accordingly, if the application is rejected the tenant runs the risk that it may lose priority to a subsequent interest during the period before the lease can be rectified. If the error is such that the application is accepted but ancillary rights such as easements, covenants and options to renew are not registered with the lease, the tenant will run the risk that such rights will not bind a subsequent purchaser from the landlord.

2–08 Reference should be made to Land Registry's Practice Guide 64 for full guidance on the formalities. As some of the prescribed clauses dictate the choice of an option from a list and others require the insertion of information from the lease by setting out the information in full or cross-referencing to the location of the relevant provision within the lease, great care must be taken to use the acceptable form of response in relation to each clause. Where there is an option to cross-refer, all relevant clauses must be listed. The draftsman should avoid reference to "all such matters in the lease", or any reference to the contents of a numbered page.

Where the terms of the lease refer to the terms of an incorporated document, for example where an underlease incorporates the terms of a head lease, the draftsman should ensure that it is clear to which document reference is made.

In addition to the directions for completion made as part and parcel of the prescribed lease clauses, the following general points may be made about the completion of certain of the clauses. 2–09

LR1. Date of lease

Land Registry uses the format "19 June 2006".

LR2.2 Other title numbers

The clause must be completed with any Title Numbers other than the landlord's, against which an application is made to make entries of the matters referred to in cll.LR9, LR10, LR11 and LR13 (easements, options, restrictive covenants, etc.). If the panel is not completed, a separate application may have to be made in respect of these matters as Land Registry is not obliged to make the entry.

The application will be rejected if this clause is not completed. Insert "None" if that is the appropriate response.

LR3. Parties to the lease

The full names must be set out. Cross-referencing to the description in the body of the lease is not permitted in the case of this clause.

LR4. Property

This clause is very important. In the case of a conflict between the clause and the details in the remainder of the lease, it is this clause that will prevail.

The registration of the lease will be completed solely on the basis of the content of cl.LR4.

Where the property description is being set out in this clause, the description should include:

(a) Postal number or name;
(b) Floor level;
(c) Road name;
(d) Locality;
(e) Town;
(f) Administrative area;

(g) Postcode.

An application should not contain any discrepancy between the parcels and the plan in a recently executed deed. Plans described as "for identification only" are not satisfactory for land registration purposes.

Any physical exceptions from the demised property must also be set out in this clause, for example mines and minerals and roads.

LR5. Prescribed statements, etc.

The precise wording of the required statements is set out in the rules mentioned in clause 5.1.

The statement must either be set out in full in this clause or reference must be made to the clause, schedule or paragraph of a schedule in the body of the lease that contains the statement in full.

Clause 5.2 can be omitted or deleted in the case of a business lease. If omitted or deleted the subsequent clauses must not be re-numbered.

LR6. Term for which the property is leased

The appropriate option must be selected and completed. The application will be rejected if the clause is not completed.

LR7. Premium

This clause must be completed if a premium is being paid. If no premium is being paid, insert "None" or leave blank. It is not permissible to make reference to the clause, schedule or paragraph in the body of the lease that contains this information.

Where the premium includes an element of VAT it must either be stated that the sum is "£x inclusive of VAT", or "£x plus VAT of £y". The draftsman should not simply state that the rent is "x plus VAT".

In the absence of evidence that VAT was payable, Land Registry will assume that the premium and rent quoted in a deed include any VAT element payable. The fees will be assessed on the VAT inclusive sum and the information in cl.LR7 will be used to make an entry in the register of the price paid.

LR8. Prohibitions or restrictions on disposing of this lease

Where the lease contains a provision or restriction, the information should be given in general form as the form of entry in the register is not dependent on the wording of the lease.

If the clause is not completed, a separate application must be made for an entry to be made on the register.

LR9. Rights of acquisition, etc.

The appropriate selection must be made and the relevant information set out in general terms only. The relevant clause/s of the lease are not to be recited in full. Land Registry will make an entry in the register where the clause is completed to show that the lease contains a provision which prohibits or restricts dispositions (r.6(2) of the LRR 2003).

Any such rights must be included in this clause either by setting out the full text of the relevant provision or referring to the clause, schedule or paragraph of a schedule in the body of the lease that contains the option or right.

If any of the tenant's rights affect Title Numbers other than the landlord's, the additional Title Numbers should be listed in cl.LR2.2 so that Land Registry will be obliged to make an entry of the interest.

LR9.2 Tenant's covenant to (or offer to) surrender this lease

The full text of the relevant provision may be set out, or reference can be made to the clause, schedule or paragraph of a schedule in the body of the lease that contains the covenant.

A provision of this kind may constitute an estate, contract, even though no payment may be made for the surrender and therefore an interest affecting the leasehold estate (*Greene v Church Commissioners* [1974] Ch. 457).

Land Registry will record the existence of the interest in a note to the particulars of the lease in the tenant's Title.

Land Registry will not, however, make any entry in respect of such a covenant if it forms part of a clause which includes a requirement as to service of a notice.

LR9.3 Landlord's contractual rights to acquire this lease

The clause must be completed with details of any contractual right on the part of the landlord to acquire the lease, such as a right of pre-emption.

The full text of the relevant provision may be set out, or reference made to the clause, schedule or paragraph of a schedule in the body of the lease that contains the option or right.

Land Registry will record the existence of the interest by making a note to the particulars of the lease in the tenant's Title.

LR10. Restrictive covenants given in this lease by the landlord in respect of the land other than the property

Details of any restrictive covenants that bind land owned by the landlord, other than the reversionary interest in the leasehold property, are to be completed in this clause.

The full text of the covenant may be set out, or reference can be made to the clause, schedule or paragraph of a schedule in the body of the lease that contains the covenants. If the land bound is not registered in the landlord's Title mentioned in LR2.1, the additional Titles must be listed in LR2.2 if Land Registry is to be obliged to make an entry of the interest.

No reference should be made to personal covenants, restrictive covenants entered into by the tenant, or restrictive covenants entered into by the landlord so far as relating only to the reversionary interest in the property.

LR11. Easements

This is an important clause. The clause must be completed to refer to all easements in the lease that benefit the property and to which the property is subject.

The easements are not to be set out in full. Reference should be made to the clause, schedule or paragraph of a schedule in the lease that contain the easements.

If the clause is not completed, a separate application will have to be made if the easements are to be completed by registration and appear in the register of affected Titles.

LR11.1 Easements granted by this lease for the benefit of the property

Easements contained in the lease for the benefit of the property are a registrable disposition (s.27(2)(d) of the LRA 2002) and will not take effect at law unless completed by registration. The burden must also be noted in the appropriate register, and if the burdened land is in Title Numbers other than the landlord's Title Number mentioned in cl.LR2.1 the additional Title Numbers must be listed in cl.LR2.2 so that Land Registry is obliged to enter notice in the burdened register.

LR11.2 Easements granted or reserved by this lease over the property for the benefit of other property

The clause must be completed with details of any easements granted or reserved over the land demised for the benefit of other land. This includes easements reserved to benefit land contained in the registered Title of the landlord out of which the lease was granted or to benefit land contained in other registered Titles of which the landlord is the registered proprietor. It also includes easements granted or reserved to benefit land in other registered Titles of which a third party, such as a management company is proprietor, or granted or reserved to benefit unregistered land.

Where the easements benefit registered Titles other than the landlord's Title mentioned in cl.LR2.1, those other Titles must be mentioned in cl.2.1 if Land Registry is to be obliged to complete the registration.

LR12. Estate rentcharge burdening the property

This is a reference to a rentcharge as defined in s.1(2)(b) of the LPA 1925. The provisions of the estate rent charge should not be set out in full. Reference should simply be made to the clause, schedule or paragraph of the schedule containing the charge.

No reference should be made in this clause to the rent reserved.

LR13. Application for standard form of restriction

This clause may be omitted or deleted. It is safer, however, simply to answer "None", if that is the appropriate response.

If the clause is not completed, a separate application must be made to enter a standard restriction. If the restriction is not a standard one no reference should be made to it in this clause, and a separate application should be made on Form RX1.

If the restriction affects Title Numbers other than that of the demised property or the landlord's Title, these must be listed. If the restriction affects only part of a Title, that must be made clear.

Land Registry Practice Guide 19 sets out the circumstances when additional evidence may be required to enter a restriction. This is likely to be rare in the case of prescribed form leases, but if such evidence is required a statement must be inserted following the wording of the appropriate panel on Form RX1 and either the necessary evidence or a certificate that the necessary evidence is held must be inserted.

LR14. Declaration of trust where there is more than one person comprising the tenant

This clause and/or the relevant wording may be omitted or deleted if inapplicable. It is sensible, however, to include the clause and to state that it does not apply.

The declaration of trust relates only to the original tenants named in cl.LR3.

An application should be made in cl.LR3 if the existence of a trust is to be reflected by the entry of a restriction in Form A against a sole proprietor.

2. PLANS

2–10 The Land Registry has detailed provisions with regard to plans. These are set out in para.3–04. Reference should be made to Land Registry Practice Guide 40 for a full account of Land Registry requirements.

3. THE REGISTER

Inspections of the register

The parties' draftsmen should keep well in mind that since 13 October 2003, all leases received at Land Registry are open to public inspection and copying under s.66(1) of the Land Registration Act 2002, see also Land Registry Practice Guide 57, "Exempting Documents from the General Right to Inspect and Copy". **2–11**

Subject to the exceptions listed below, any person can now apply to inspect or obtain official copies of:

(a) the Register or Caution Register of any Title;
(b) any Title Plan or Caution Plan of an individual Title;
(c) any document referred to in the Register; and
(d) any other document kept by the Registrar and not referred to in the Register which relates to an application made to him.

If any term of the proposed lease is highly sensitive, the parties may wish to consider whether they should agree that the term of the lease is to be of a duration that is not subject to the registration requirements of the LRA 2002 (see para.2–03 above).

The exceptions that relate to registered leases are: **2–12**

(1) Exempt Information Documents;
(2) an Edited Information Document which has been replaced by another Edited Information Document;
(3) Form EX1A;
(4) Form CIT and any form which has been attached to Form CIT together with any documents or copy documents prepared or sent by the Registrar in response to the application.

If the lease will contain favourable terms that are not found in other leases granted by the landlord, the landlord may wish to attempt to exclude that information. An application to designate a document as an "Exempt Information Document" ("EID", see r.136(1) of the LRR 2003) will, however, only succeed if the document contains "prejudicial information". That is, if the information: **2–13**

(a) is information that relates to an individual who has applied for the document to be an EID, which if disclosed to other persons (whether to the public generally or specific persons) would, or would be likely to, cause substantial unwarranted distress to the applicant or another; or

(b) information that if disclosed to other persons (whether to the public generally or specific persons) would, or would be likely to, prejudice the commercial interests of the person who has applied for the document to be an EID (r.131 of the LRR 2003).

Unless the Registrar is satisfied that the applicant's claim is not groundless he must designate the document as an EID (r.136(3) of the LRR 2003).

2–14 If a landlord wishes to make an application to have parts of the lease classified in this way, the landlord should contract with the tenant to ensure that the landlord's application to exclude any prejudicial information is made at the same time as the tenant's application to register the lease. If it does not do so and the tenant registers the lease (as it is required to), any information already extracted from the lease that appears in the register will not be removed by an application for an EID. Where an application for exemption accompanies another application for registration, the parties may specify that the application for registration is not to proceed in the event that the application for exemption is unsuccessful.

It should also be noted that, in the event that information is excluded, the document will appear in redacted form. It will be obvious, therefore, that an exemption has been made and where that exemption falls within the document.

2–15 Even if a document is designated an EID, the privacy of the confidential information cannot be absolutely guaranteed. Applications can be made under r.137 of the LRR 2003, or under the Freedom of Information Act 2000 for inspection or a copy of the document. The Registrar may also cancel the application if he considers that the designation could prejudice the keeping of the Register (r.136(4) of the LRR 2003).

Any EID is also personal to the applicant and cannot be assigned. In the event of an assignment, an application by the original applicant to remove the EID should be made simultaneously with the assignee's application for an EID and to register the assignment.

CHAPTER 3

DESCRIPTION OF PROPERTY

Careful thought must be given to the way in which the property to be let is to be described. The parties and their advisers should seek to place themselves in the position of third parties who will be required to read and interpret the chosen description many years after the date of grant. The more accurate and objectively precise the description used within the lease the more limited is the scope for later disagreement and dispute. **3–01**

The importance of accurate and unambiguous drafting is underlined by the fact that, the courts have consistently rejected the admission of extrinsic evidence which contradicts the clear terms of the contract (*Partridge v Lawrence* [2004] 1 P. & C.R. 176 at 187; and *Horn v Phillips* [2003] EWCA Civ 1877, where extrinsic evidence was not admissible to contradict a transfer with an annexed plan which clearly showed the boundary as a straight line and even contained a precise measurement of distance).

1. LAND OR BUILDINGS "KNOWN AS"

The interpretation of a description which speaks of the land or building as being "known by" a given number or name, or "known as" a given number or name, renders it permissible, indeed inevitable, that a court will have to resort to extrinsic evidence to identify the property that was intended to be described as at the date of the lease (*Freeguard v Rogers* [1999] 1 W.L.R. 375; *Targett v Ferguson* (1996) 72 P. & C.R. 106). It is clearly preferable to avoid any potential for later uncertainty as to the precise subject matter and extent of the letting by placing the identity of the land or building beyond doubt at the outset. The property should be described as accurately and fully as possible in writing in any given circumstances. The use of a plan is commonplace. Annotated photographs may also assist in certain cases, for example in **3–02** identifying specific elements of an unusual property, or plant or machinery that are affixed to the property at the date of the lease.

2. THE USE OF PLANS

3–03 It is important to ensure that the plan and description of the property are accurate and relate to the current state of the property. Where the demised property is clearly bounded there is no need for a plan to be included in the lease. In other cases a plan is desirable, provided that the plan is drawn on sufficiently large a scale not to be merely confusing.

(a) Land Registry's requirements

3–04 An application to register a lease at Land Registry must always be accompanied by a plan unless the demised property is clearly defined on the title plan to a lessor's existing registered title and can be described verbally. The lease plan should be prepared to fulfil the detailed plan requirements set out in the LRR 2003 and explained in Land Registry Practice Guide 40. Compliance is vital when the lease is registrable. If the plan is rejected the transaction will be delayed. Worse still, if the application for registration is cancelled because of inadequacies in the plan submitted, priority search protection will expire and the tenant and any lender will be exposed to the risk of a loss of priority.

The plan should:

(a) be drawn to scale and show its actual scale;
(b) show its orientation;
(c) use preferred scales of 1/1250 to 1/500 for urban properties;
(d) use preferred scales of 1/2500 for rural properties;
(e) be based on a metric scale;
(f) not be reduced in scale, unless the actual scale is stated in place of the original scale, the original scale has been deleted and it is endorsed with a statement that it is a reduced copy;
(g) not be marked or referred to as being for identification only;
(h) not show statements of disclaimer used under the Property Misdescriptions Act 1991;
(i) show sufficient detail to be identified on the Ordnance Survey map;

(j) show its general location by showing roads, road junctions or other landmarks;
(k) show the land included within the property including any garage or garden;
(l) show buildings in their correct or intended position;
(m) show access drives or pathways if they form part of the property boundaries;
(n) show the land properly and clearly, by edging, colouring or hatching;
(o) have edgings of a thickness that do not obscure any other detail;
(p) show separate parts by suitable plan markings: offices, car parking space, refuse store;
(q) identify different floor levels where appropriate;
(r) show intricate boundaries with a larger scale or inset plan;
(s) show measurements in metric units only, to two decimal places;
(t) show undefined boundaries accurately and where necessary, by reference to measurements;
(u) show measurements that correspond, so far as possible, to scaled measurements.

It is self evident that the guidance provides a useful good practice checklist even in circumstances where the lease is not registrable.

Where an approved estate plan exists, any plan used in the lease must be based on the current approved version. A verbal description referring only to plot numbers on an estate plan or to a postal address is not acceptable. Unless all the land above and below the surface is included in the application, a plan of the surface on, under, or over the land to be registered, together with sufficient information to define the vertical and horizontal extents, must be provided. Complex floor plans may be shown on a supplementary plan or on an enlargement to the title plan.

The lessor must sign the plan to the lease. Where the lessor is a company the plan should be signed by officers of the company with authority to sign on behalf of the company.

In preparing the Title plans, Land Registry follows the conventions published by the British Standards Institute in the British Standards for Construction Drawing Practice. It will avoid difficulties on registration if these conventions are adopted in preparing the lease plan. This is particularly important with regard to rights of way as the colours mentioned in the deed may not otherwise be replicated on the Title plan.

(b) The importance of the plan

3–05 In every case, the draftsman should consider whether the plan is to prevail over the verbal description or vice versa. On this decision will depend the phrase by which the plan is referred to in the parcels clause itself. If the plan is small scale or consists of an extract of the Ordnance Survey map, it is suggested that the verbal description should prevail. In the former case, the plan is unlikely to provide sufficient information to enable the boundaries to be accurately ascertained, while in the latter case the plan will reflect features on the ground rather than boundaries between different owners. It is absolutely essential that each parcel should be described with such particularity and precision that there is no room for doubt about the boundaries of each, and for such purposes if a plan is intended to control the description of part only of a building, an Ordnance map on a scale of 1:2500 is worse than useless (*Scarfe v Adams* [1981] 1 All E.R. 843; *Clarke v O'Keefe* (2000) 80 P. & C.R. 126). However, it must also be remembered that Land Registry will not accept a plan that is marked or referred to as being for identification only. Nevertheless since registration takes effect with general boundaries only, the verbal description may be of importance in ascertaining precise boundaries.

The following phrases will prevent the plan from prevailing over the verbal description:

- "for the purpose of identification only"
- "for the purpose of facilitating identification only"
- "only for the purposes of identification"

(*Hopgood v Brown* [1955] 1 W.L.R. 213; *Webb v Nightingale* (1957) 169 E.G. 330).

On the other hand, the following phrases will prevent the verbal description from prevailing over the plan:

- "more particularly delineated"
- "more particularly described"

- "more precisely delineated"

(*Eastwood v Ashton* [1915] A.C. 900; *Wallington v Townsend* [1939] Ch. 588).

A middle course may be achieved by the phrase "for the purpose of delineation only", which has been held to mean that the plan must not be taken to be drawn to scale but the lines are correct diagrammatically (*Re Freeman and Taylor's Contract* (1907) 97 L.T. 39).

Where the plan is subordinate to the verbal description, it may be referred to in order to elucidate boundaries, so long as it does not conflict with anything explicit in the verbal description (*Wiggington & Milner v Winster Engineering* [1978] 1 W.L.R. 1462, recently approved in *Taylor v Lambert* (2012) 156 S.J.L.B. 39).

3. FORMS OF PLAN

There is no implied warranty that a plan used in a lease is accurate **3–06**
(*Re Sparrow and James' Contract* [1910] 2 Ch. 60). Nevertheless, an inaccurate plan that prevails over the verbal description may have the same effect as a verbal misdescription. The landlord may also owe the tenant a duty of care as regards the preparation of accurate plans (see Tromans, *Commercial Leases*, 2nd edn (London: Sweet & Maxwell, 1996), p.40). Accordingly, the draftsman should so far as possible ensure that the plan is accurate.

The lease plan is often based on an extract from the Ordnance map. The Title plan to a registered Title is always based on the Ordnance map. Ordnance maps only show the general boundaries of land. It will not, therefore, be possible to identify the position of the legal boundary if the Ordnance map or the Title plan is used to identify the demised premises (unless in the latter case the boundaries have been fixed under s.60 of the LRA 2002 and r.120 of the LRR 2003). The Ordnance map may well show the boundary of the parcel as the centre line of any boundary feature, irrespective of its legal ownership (see *Fisher v Winch* [1939] 1 K.B. 666). Judicial notice is taken of this practice (*Davey v Harrow Corp* [1958] 1 Q.B. 60). Accordingly, where the parcels are described simply by references to the Ordnance map (either by specifying the numbers of the enclosures or by a plan that prevails over a verbal description) the parcels will be taken to be those shown on the

Ordnance map (*Fisher v Winch* [1939] 1 K.B. 666). The tenant may, therefore, find that his demise does not include the whole of a boundary feature, contrary to the intention of the parties. This problem can usually be resolved by the standard preliminary inquiries.

The Ordnance map is subject to specified accuracy tolerances which means that measurements scaled between features shown on the maps will not exactly match the actual distance measured between the same distances on the ground. Where the Ordnance map is used as the basis of the lease plan the draftsman should ensure that the edition he has used is clearly specified in the lease. A problem that arises from time to time is that a new edition of the Ordnance map is published with altered enclosure numbers and often altered enclosures. In using any Ordnance map or the Title plan prepared from that map, the draftsman should also ensure that there have been no significant physical alterations to the demised premises since the map was drawn. The Title plan is prepared using the version of the Ordnance map that is current at the time that the land is first registered and if there have been physical changes to the property or locality since the map was prepared they will not appear. The use of enclosure numbers taken from an old edition together with current measurements must be consistent. They may well be internally contradictory (*Drake v Fripp* [2012] 1 P. & C.R. 4).

A plan usually shows the boundaries of the property in question at ground level (or floor level). If the Ordnance map is used that only shows permanent physical features and normally at ground level. Where the demised property is an entire building with curtilage this will usually be sufficient. Where the property is part only of a building the draftsman should also consider whether some further visual description is necessary. Although the use of vertical elevations or sectional drawings is rare in leases there is no reason why they should not be used; and where the property overhangs or interlocks with another property they may be the only practical or readily comprehensible way of describing it. The same problem may also arise where the demised property is to include some projection. Developments in modern technology make it possible for three dimensional models of the property to be stored on computer.

When construing a plan, an objective approach must be assumed, namely that a plan is addressed to a lay reader and is to be construed by the ordinary reasonable observer. It must not be construed in isolation, but in context, including Replies to Inquiries Before Contract and the surrounding circumstances. The question is: what would the reasonable layman think he was buying? (*Toplis v Green* [1992] E.G.C.S. 20).

The problems that can result from drafting that fails to take account of each of the matters identified above is well illustrated by the facts of *Taylor v Lambert* (2012) 156 S.J.L.B. 39. In that case a conveyance dated 8 April 1974 defined the land conveyed as: **3–07**

> "All that messuage or dwellinghouse and saleshop with the outbuildings yard garden and conveniences thereto adjoining and belonging situate in High Street at Barnby Dun near Doncaster in the County of York known as Bridge Stores which said premises contain an area of 553.4 square yards or thereabouts and are for the purposes of identification only delineated on the plan annexed hereto and thereon coloured pink."

This wording, which might at first be thought to provide a full description, was held only to be capable of interpretation by reference to historic extrinsic evidence. On analysis, the descriptive wording was found to be rather general, and the various elements of the description internally inconsistent. It was not clear in 2012:

(a) quite what premises had been "known as Bridges Stores" on 8 April 1974; and
(b) what "outbuildings yard garden and conveniences" had existed as a matter of fact on 8 April 1974.

Furthermore, whilst the wording was rather precise as to the area measured, the measurement was stated to be "or thereabouts", and the plan:

(i) was for "identification only";
(ii) had not been produced by a surveyor;
(iii) was not of good quality; and
(iv) showed the general intention of a boundary in a position that produced a square footage that did not match the stated measurement, but did accord with a boundary wall on site.

Looked at as a whole, in the light of the remainder of the description, the plan, and contemporaneous evidence, it was the measurement that was disregarded.

4. BOUNDARIES

3–08 It must be ensured that the description of the property accords with the provisions set out in the remainder of the lease. The description of the property and its boundaries will not fall to be considered in isolation: the lease will be interpreted as a whole (see *Strachey v Ramage* [2008] 2 P. & C.R. 8 and *Drake v Fripp* [2012] 1 P. & C.R. 4).

(a) Hedges and ditches

3–09 Unless the relevant parcels of land were within common ownership and occupation at the date that the ditch was created, prima facie, the boundary runs along the edge of the ditch away from the hedge. The rationale behind this presumption is that the ditch-digger is assumed to have dug the ditch at the extremity of his own land and then to have thrown the spoil onto his own land to make a bank on which the hedge is planted (*Fisher v Winch* [1939] 1 K.B. 666). The utility of the rule has been reaffirmed by the House of Lords (*Alan Wibberley Building v Insley* [1999] 1 W.L.R. 894).

(b) Roads

3–10 Prima facie, a lease of land adjoining a road operates to pass one half in width of the road, even where the road is a private one (*Long v House* (1961) 178 E.G. 801). The presumption probably only operates where the conveyancing history of the land is unknown, and may not operate at all where the land in question is part of a building estate (*Giles v County Building Constructors (Hertford) Ltd* (1971) 22 P. & C.R. 978). In any event the presumption is rebuttable and will be fairly easily rebutted where a developer needs to retain ownership of the road in order to build it or to dedicate it as a public highway. There is no similar presumption in relation to land bounded by a railway (*Thompson v Hickman* [1907] 1 Ch. 550).

(c) External wall

In the case of a demise of one floor of a building, or of a room on any floor that is bounded or enclosed on one or more sides by an outside wall, unless the outside wall is excepted or reserved, or there is some context which leads to the contrary conclusion, prima facie, the premises demised comprise both sides of the outside wall (*Hope Brothers Ltd v Cowan* [1913] 2 Ch. 312, per Joyce J.; *Goldfoot v Welch* [1914] 1 Ch. 213; *Sturge v Hackett* [1962] 3 All E.R. 166; *Delgable Ltd v Perinpanathan* [2006] 1 E.G.L.R. 78). If such walls are not excepted, the landlord may, for example, be restrained from maintaining an advertisement on the walls enclosing the demise (*Re Webb's Lease* [1951] Ch. 808). **3–11**

(d) "Eggshell tenancies"

A demise of an enclosed space that excludes the main structure of the building, save for the internal skin of that part of the building occupied by the tenant, is known as an "eggshell tenancy". Many multi-let units comprise internal space surrounded by a decorative skin limited to plastered walls and floor and ceiling finishes. **3–12**

As an eggshell with no structural element can be demolished and reconstructed within the meaning of s.30(1)(f) of the LTA 1954 (*Pumperninks of Piccadilly Ltd v Land Securities Plc* [2002] 2 E.G.L.R. 147), a tenant taking such a tenancy should be warned that he is, effectively, giving up a considerable part of his security of tenure under the Act.

Before taking such a tenancy, particularly for a long term, a tenant should consider whether it, or an assignee, may potentially wish to carry out alterations which may involve works of a structural nature. If so, consideration should be given as to whether the proposed demise can be extended so that the tenancy is not an "eggshell". If an eggshell tenancy is granted, a tenant's covenant not to make structural alterations without the landlord's consent will be meaningless because the demise will not include any part of the structure. As such, the landlord has the right to refuse an application to carry out a structural alteration, even unreasonably, because any such alteration would necessarily trespass upon their retained land (*Iqbal v Thakrar* [2004] 3 E.G.L.R. 21 at 25E (CA), per Peter Gibson L.J., where the lease was granted for 999 years).

(e) Horizontal divisions

3–13 There are no clear presumptions relating to horizontal divisions between individually let parts of buildings. It is, however, established that the demise of one floor of a building extends at least as far as the underside of the joists supporting the floor above it (*Sturge v Hackett* [1962] 3 All E.R. 166). The ordinary expectation is that the tenant will be entitled to occupy all that space between the floor of his demise and the underside of the floor above, unless there are cogent reasons to assume otherwise (*Graystone Property Investments Ltd v Margulies* [1984] 1 E.G.L.R. 27). So the demise of a flat or a particular floor of a building will include a roof space accessible only from that flat where there is no reservation to the landlord of any rights relating to the roof space (*Hatfield v Moss* [1988] 2 E.G.L.R. 58). However, a demise of a "suite of rooms" on the top floor of a building will not include the common roof (*Cockburn v Smith* [1924] 2 K.B. 119), and a demise of the first, second and third floors of a three-storey building has been held not to include the roof (*Delgable Ltd v Perinpanathan* [2006] 1 E.G.L.R. 78). Equally, it has been said that half the ceiling structure and half the floor structure is included in a lease of the space between them (*Phelps v City of London Corp* [1916] 2 Ch. 255). The position is different where the demise is freestanding or is a building in a terrace. In such a case the roof and the airspace above it will normally be included in the demise (*Straudley Investments Ltd v Barpress Ltd* [1987] 1 E.G.L.R. 69; *Tennant Radiant Heat Ltd v Warrington Development Corp* [1988] 1 E.G.L.R. 41).

If the precise boundaries of the demised property are of importance, as where the tenant covenants to keep "the demised property" in repair, the draftsman should make express provision for horizontal divisions. Obligations to repair simply drafted in terms of the "structure" or the "main structures" of a building have proved particularly difficult to apply (see *Toff v McDowell* (1993) 69 P. & C.R. 535, with regard to the obligation to repair the floor between two flats; *Hallisey v Petmoor Developments Ltd* [2000] N.P.C. 114 and *Ibrahim v Dovecorn Reversions Ltd* [2001] 2 E.G.L.R. 46, with regard to balcony floors; and *Marlborough Park Services Ltd v Rowe* [2006] 23 E.G. 166, in relation to wooden floor joists between first and second floor flats which not only supported the floor but also provided lateral support to the partition walls between maisonettes).

Where a tenant is concerned about the possibility of liability to carry out remedial work to contaminated land, the tenant's adviser should stipulate that the demise is not to extend beneath the floor covering on the ground floor of the premises so that the tenant takes what is commonly termed a "pie crust lease". Such a lease may, however, be particularly vulnerable to the landlord's right to oppose the grant of a new business tenancy under s.30(1)(f) of the Landlord and Tenant Act 1954 (*Pumperninks of Piccadilly Ltd v Land Securities Plc* [2002] 2 E.G.L.R. 147, see para.3–12 above).

Where the property is air-conditioned, consideration should be given to the question whether the air-conditioning units should be included in or excluded from the demise. Many landlords prefer to retain air-handling units within their control, particularly in a multi-let building, so that the air-conditioning system may be dealt with as an integrated whole.

(f) Roofs

Roofs deserve special consideration because of their specific potential as a separate income producing asset for landlord or tenant. A landlord may wish to exclude the roof from the demise of the building so that it has the freedom to grant a licence to a third party for the installation of telecommunications apparatus or a Feed-in Tariffs Lease for the installation of roof top equipment to which the electricity generator has access. Pholtovoltaic or solar panels and wind turbines are included within the Feed-In Tariffs scheme. A long leaseholder may wish to include the roof within its demise for similar reasons. **3–14**

Even if the roof is to be demised to the tenant, the landlord may wish to consider the inclusion of a tenant's covenant expressly precluding the tenant from sub-letting the roof space to a telecoms operator. Regardless of the position under the Landlord and Tenant Act 1954 Part II, telecoms operators enjoy their own quasi-statutory security of tenure under the Electronic Communications Act 2000. Feed-in Tariffs Leases are often contracted out of protection.

Any decision whether to exclude or include the roof space within the demise for commercial reasons must also take into account the burden of responsibility for repair of the roof during the term of the lease. If the roof space is reserved to the landlord, the landlord's responsibility for the repair of the roof must be considered in terms of the practical inter-relationship between the landlord's obligations to the tenant in the lease of the whole or part of the remainder of the building and the repairing obligations that are likely to be set out in a separate lease or licence of the whole or part of the roof space.

Any lease of premises consisting solely of roof space and airspace, or of part of the roof surface and airspace, or of those elements together with certain structural parts of the roof, will require bespoke drafting. A standard lease precedent will not suffice because there is no surrounding structural envelope. The height and dimensions of the airspace will require to be defined and demised, together with the grant of identified rights to install and thereafter to access, and the grant of any ancillary rights to connect to the requisite services and to the National Grid in the case of a Feed-in Tariffs Lease. The parties will also have to consider how the equipment is to be fixed to the roof.

If the landlord assumes responsibility for repair of the roof, on the basis that repairs to the roof may well require to be carried out to the roof as a whole to be effective, and in order to safeguard its ability to perform its obligations to other tenants of the building, then the landlord will need to reserve rights to inspect the area and to ensure that the roof top equipment can be shut down or temporarily removed in the event that works are required.

The landlord's advisers and the draftsman acting for tenants of other parts of a multi-occupied building will wish to investigate the likely impact of any roof top lease on the insurance premium payable in respect of the building if roof top equipment is installed, and to make appropriate consequential provision. In any case, both the landlord granting a roof top lease, and a tenant of any floor within a building that is or may be subject to a roof top lease, will also wish to ensure that a tenant installing roof top equipment is obliged to operate that equipment in accordance with statutory requirements, and that the roof top tenant is obliged not to cause a nuisance or annoyance in the way it uses the installation.

(g) Airspace and underground

In the past it has often been stated that in the absence of indications to the contrary a conveyance of land includes not only everything on the surface but everything beneath it down to the centre of the earth and the space directly above (*Grigsby v Melville* [1974] 1 W.L.R. 80). However, the stopping point, so far as subterranean property is concerned, has more recently been described as the place where pressure and temperature make concepts of ownership absurd (*Bocardo v Star Energy* [2010] 3 W.L.R. 654), and, nowadays, different considerations affect airspace. **3–15**

In the absence of indications to the contrary, a conveyance of land may include a cellar below ground level that can only be reached from an adjoining shop (*Grigsby v Melville*, as cited above). Similarly, part of a room that projected above ground level into the property conveyed has been held to pass in the conveyance (*Laybourn v Gridley* [1892] 2 Ch. 53).

In terms of the rights of a freehold owner of land in the airspace above his land it appears that such rights extend only to such height as is necessary for the ordinary use and enjoyment of the land and any structure upon it (*Bernstein of Leigh (Baron) v Skyviews & General Ltd* [1978] Q.B. 479). Nevertheless, in the absence of a reservation the landlord may find that he is unable to display advertisements on his adjoining property or that he is unable to redevelop adjoining property economically if those activities would involve a trespass to his tenant's airspace (see, for example, *Kelsen v Imperial Tobacco Co Ltd* [1957] 2 Q.B. 334; *Woollerton & Wilson Ltd v Costain (Richard) Ltd* [1970] 1 W.L.R. 411).

A lease of the top floor of a building which includes the roof may well carry with it the airspace over the building, thereby entitling the tenant to enlarge the premises into the airspace (*Davies v Yadegar* [1990] 1 E.G.L.R. 71; *Haines v Florensa* [1990] 1 E.G.L.R. 73). However, whilst the tenant is entitled to the enjoyment of such airspace above the roof as is reasonably necessary for the enjoyment of the demise itself (*Dorrington Belgravia v McGlashan* [2009] 1 E.G.L.R. 27), there is no presumption that a lease of, or including, a roof extends upwards to the full height of the airspace available to the landlord (*Roseberry v Rocklee* [2011] L. & T.R. 21). The question will be one of interpretation of the individual lease.

As discussed by reference to roofs above, where the demise includes the whole of a building (or the top floor) the draftsman may wish to consider whether the airspace above the building should be excluded from the demise. The advantage of so doing, from the landlord's point of view, is that the tenant will not be entitled to raise the height of the building (e.g. by adding additional floors, plant, masts or aerials) without committing a trespass. Accordingly, if the question should later arise, the landlord will be free to demand a premium or an increased rent as the price of a demise of the airspace. But if the airspace is excluded from the demise, the tenant's adviser should ensure that the tenant obtains a right to enter the airspace for the purpose of performing his covenants.

(h) Projections

3–16 Prima facie, an external feature (whether ornamental or not) fixed to an external wall enclosing the demise will itself be part of the demised property (*Sturge v Hackett* [1962] 3 All E.R. 166). Likewise, where the footings or eaves of a building project beyond the edge of an external wall they will be included in the demised property, although the column of air between them will not (*Truckell v Stock* [1957] 1 All E.R. 74).

(i) Fences

3–17 In the case of wooden fences it is likely to be inferred that in the absence of freeboard the owner of land will use his land to the fullest extent; and the fence will be deemed to belong to the person on whose side the rails and posts are placed, the palings being placed on his neighbour's side (*Halsbury's Laws of England* (2006 reissue), Vol.27(1), para.167).

(j) Windows

3–18 The lease should make clear whether windows are included in or excluded from the demise, especially where the responsibility for repair is divided between landlord and tenant (*Reston v Hudson* [1990] 2 E.G.L.R. 51). Specific reference to windows should avoid the difficult questions of interpretation that frequently arise when the court has to determine whether or not references in any given lease to the "main structure", "the exterior", or the "main walls", were or were not intended to include responsibility for the repair and/or decoration of the windows. The draftsman should consider not only window glass, but also window frames, window sills, mastic joints, soffits. If the building is constructed with glazed curtain walling, care must be taken over the precise words used.

5. MEASUREMENT

If premises are to be defined by measurement, the draftsmen must ensure that they are expressly agreed as to exactly what is to be included and excluded from the measurements. It is not sufficient simply to make reference to the "RICS Code of Measuring Practice: A Guide for Surveyors and Valuers, 6th edn (2007)". The Code provides non-mandatory guidance on measuring different buildings for different purposes. The core definitions it uses are Gross External Area (GEA), Gross Internal Area (GIA) and Net Internal Area (NIA). In general terms, subject to specified inclusions and exclusions set out in the Code: **3–19**

- GEA is the area of a building measured externally at each floor level;
- GIA is the area of a building measured to the internal face of the perimeter walls at each floor level; and
- NIA is the usable area within a building measured to the internal face of the perimeter walls at each floor level.

Whilst the NIA is commonly used for rent reviews on retail shops and offices, the interpretation of NIA can often give rise to matters of pure judgment in determining whether a particular area falls within the definition or not (see *Kilmartin SCI (Hulton House) Ltd v Safeway Stores* [2006] 1 E.G.L.R 59, where reference was made to the RICS Code, 5th edn.

The draftsman should consider the inter-relationship between the description of the component elements of the demised premises, the definitions used in the Code, and alterations to the physical layout that a tenant might make as part of its fit out.

Example 3.1 Parcels clause of office suite

ALL THAT suite of rooms on the [ ] floor of the building known as [ ] (excluding the outer faces of the walls and the windows enclosing the said building its roof and roof structure but including the structure supporting the floor of the said rooms) and for the purpose of identification only edged in red on the attached plan.

Example 3.2 Parcels clause of open land

ALL THAT parcel of land in [ ] and numbered [ ] on the Ordnance Map ([ ] edition) a copy of which is attached hereto (including the entirety of the hedge and ditch on the western boundary of enclosure number [ ] but excluding the entirety of the hedges and ditches on the northern boundaries of those enclosures and the entirety of the road on their southern boundaries).

Example 3.3 Parcels clause of building excluding airspace

ALL THAT Building known as [ ] shown edged red on the attached plan but excluding the airspace lying above the existing roof of that building together with a right for the tenant with or without workmen to enter that airspace for the sole purpose of inspecting the building or carrying out any works for which the tenant is liable under this lease.

Example 3.4 Parcels clause with details of boundaries: multi-occupied building

ALL THAT the [ ] floor of the Building known as [ ] ("the Property") including:

(1) all non-loadbearing walls situated wholly within the red edging on the attached plan
(2) one half (severed vertically) of all non-loadbearing walls separating the property from any other part of the Building
(3) all plaster or other decorative finish applied to any wall bounding the property and not included in paragraph (1) or (2) above or applied to any column or loadbearing wall within the Property
(4) the whole of all doors door frames windows window frames (including mastic joints or seals) bounding the Property
(5) all ceilings bounding the Property and any void between any suspended ceiling and the structural slab above
(6) all floor finishes and floor screeds including raised floors and floor jacks supporting such floors

(7) all light fittings and air-conditioning units incorporated in any ceiling but not any other part of the air-conditioning system.

Example 3.5 Parcels clause with details of boundaries: unit

The Property as briefly described in [ ] and edged red on the Plan

(1) including:
  (a) non load bearing walls and columns completely within the Property
  (b) the internal plaster or other surfaces of any load bearing walls and columns within the Property and of walls which form boundaries of the Property
  (c) the doors door frames and any glass relating to the doors
  (d) the flooring
  (e) the plaster or other surfaces of the ceilings within the Property
  (f) the Conduits and any other equipment and apparatus which exclusively serve the Property
  (g) all landlord's fixtures and fittings in or forming part of the Property
  (h) machinery plant and equipment situated within and exclusively serving the Property and any improvements and additions made to the Property and to fixtures and fittings within the Property

(2) excluding
  (a) the structural parts load bearing frame roof foundations joists and external walls of the Property
  (b) the Conduits machinery plant and equipment within but not exclusively serving the Property
  (c) the Tenant's trade fixtures and fittings.

Example 3.6 Definition of Conduits

Includes drains sewers conduits flues gutters gullies channels ducts shafts watercourses pipes cables wires and mains.

6. PARTY STRUCTURES

Where the landlord retains no property adjoining the demised property, the question of party structures will rarely arise as between him and his tenant. In such cases, the best course is for the lease to remain silent, leaving problems to be resolved as and when they arise. **3–20**

Where the landlord retains adjoining property, or where he lets a building in separate parts, party structures must be considered.

The former distinction between party structures in Inner London and party structures elsewhere was abolished by the Party Wall, etc. Act 1996. The 1996 Act applies to the whole of England and Wales. It applies to cases where the line of junction is not built on, or is built on only to the extent of a boundary wall (s.1) and to cases where the line of junction is built on or a boundary wall, being either a party fence wall or the external wall of a building, has been erected (s.2). The Act contains a comprehensive code of rights for the building owner and the adjoining owner. The structures to which it applies are party structures, which can include floor partitions (s.20). There are rights of entry to carry our works authorised by the Act (s.8). A tenant will qualify as an owner for this purpose unless he is a tenant from year to year or has a lesser interest (s.20).

Example 3.7 Declaration as to party structures

It is hereby agreed that:

(1) one half in thickness of every internal wall floor and ceiling separating the demised property from any adjoining property is included in this demise

(2) each such structure is a party structure

(3) the tenant shall maintain each of them as such and shall be liable to pay a fair proportion of the cost of repairing or maintaining any such structure which shall have been incurred by any adjoining occupier or tenant or by the landlord such proportion to be determined (in default of agreement) by an arbitrator appointed by the President for the time being of the Royal Institution of Chartered Surveyors.

7. APPURTENANCES AND CURTILAGE

3–21 Property is often demised together with the "appurtenances" or the "curtilage" belonging to it. Each of these expressions deserves consideration.

Strictly, land cannot be appurtenant to other land. Thus, a lease of a shop "with appurtenances thereto" was held not to pass the forecourt immediately in front of the shop (*Owens v Thomas Scott & Sons (Bakers) Ltd* [1939] 3 All E.R. 663). However, appurtenances will include incorporeal hereditaments such as rights of way

(*Hansford v Jago* [1921] 1 Ch. 322) and in the case of a demise of a house they will also include an orchard, yard, garden or curtilage (*Trim v Sturminster RDC* [1938] 2 K.B. 508) but not a paddock (*Methuen-Campbell v Walters* [1979] Q.B. 525). What is included in the appurtenances of property is a question of fact. It is doubtful whether a right of way over other land belonging to the landlord can ever be an appurtenance, strictly so called (*Re Walmsley and Shaw's Contract* [1917] 1 Ch. 93).

A curtilage has been said to be a small and necessary area of land about a building (*Dyer v Dorset CC* [1989] Q.B. 346). However, it is not an essential ingredient of a curtilage that it is small. The curtilage of a building will include the ground that is used for the comfortable enjoyment of that building even though it has not been marked off or enclosed in any way (*Sinclair-Lockhart's Trustees v Central Land Board* (1950) 1 P. & C.R. 195). However, it is not sufficient to constitute two pieces of land parts of one and the same curtilage that they should have been conveyed or demised together, for a single conveyance or lease can comprise more than one parcel of land, neither of which need be in any sense an appurtenance of the other or within the curtilage of the other; nor is it sufficient that they have been occupied together; nor is the test whether the enjoyment of one is advantageous or convenient or necessary for the full enjoyment of the other. For one corporeal hereditament to fall within the curtilage of another the former must be so intimately associated with the latter as to lead to the conclusion that the former in truth forms part and parcel of the latter (*Methuen-Campbell v Walters* [1979] Q.B. 525).

General words will be implied in all leases (other than an agreement for lease for a term exceeding three years (*Borman v Griffith* [1930] 1 Ch. 493)) unless a contrary intention appears in the lease. By the Law of Property Act 1925 s.62, a lease of land with buildings thereon will include all outhouses, cellars, areas, courtyards, sewers, drains, ways, passages and other rights appertaining or reputed to appertain to the property or at the time of the conveyance occupied or enjoyed therewith.

Where a building is demised together with its curtilage, or where the draftsman chooses not to exclude the operation of s.62, consideration should be given to the taking of special covenants from the tenant. For example, it will be of importance to some tenants (particularly cafe operators, greengrocers and other shop-keepers) to know whether they are entitled to trade from a forecourt. This should be dealt with expressly in the lease. Equally, the landlord may wish to ensure that a yard adjoining a building does not become obstructed by trade empties or unrestricted car-parking. Failure to deal with these matters on the grant of the lease often leads to complaints from adjoining tenants and sometimes to an action against the landlord for derogation from his grant.

Easements may be acquired either by grant or by prescription. In the case of a grant the grant may be express or implied. An implied grant may arise by virtue of s.62 of the Law of Property Act 1925 or by the operation of the rule in *Wheeldon v Burrows* (1879) 12 Ch. D. 31. Whether the grant is express or implied, in the case of a lease it is made at the date of the lease. If the draftsman wishes to ensure that the tenant only acquires easements expressly granted to him, s.62 should be expressly excluded.

Example 3.8 Exclusion of s.62 of the Law of Property Act 1925
Provided always that nothing in this lease shall operate to grant by way of implication or otherwise any estate right or easement over any land owned by the landlord (whether now or in the future) unless it is expressly granted either by this lease or by subsequent deed executed by the landlord.

Example 3.9 Express exclusion of the right to light
Excepting and reserving all rights to the access of light or air from the adjoining property known as Cambridge House and Oxford House to any of the windows of the demised property.

8. ACCESS

(a) Roads

3–22 If access is gained by a road that serves only the demised property, the draftsman should include the road in the demise. The landlord will have no need to retain day-to-day control over it and any necessary restrictions can be imposed by covenant. In this way, the tenant will also be under an obligation to keep the road in repair if he covenants to keep "the demised property" in repair.

If other properties in the landlord's ownership are also served by the road it may be more convenient for him to retain it. Although no tenant will be directly responsible for the repair and maintenance of the road the landlord may recover his outlay by way of a suitably drawn service charge. In such a case the tenant's adviser should insist on an express covenant by the landlord to keep the road in repair and the grant of an express easement to the tenant to use the road.

Where the landlord retains a roadway he may be under a positive duty to the tenant to prevent obstruction of it (*Hilton v Smith (James) & Sons (Norwood) Ltd* [1979] 2 E.G.L.R. 44).

The mode of use of the road should be clearly defined, although some restriction on user may be implicit in the physical nature of the road itself (*St Edmundsbury & Ipswich Diocesan Board of Finance v Clark (No.2)* [1975] 1 W.L.R. 468). If the right of way is in terms a right to use it with vehicles it will be difficult, in the absence of express words, to show that it is restricted to a particular type or size of vehicle. In many cases, therefore, the draftsmen should take express instructions on the capacity of the road and as to whether the tenant has any specific operational requirements which will effect the way in which it wishes to use the road.

The grant of a right of way over a road will, depending on the words of the grant and the physical circumstances of the demised premises and their immediate surrounding area (*B&Q Plc v Liverpool and Lancashire Properties Ltd* [2001] 1 E.G.L.R 92), include the following ancillary rights:

(1) the right to stop for such time as is necessary to load and unload vehicles (*McIlraith v Grady* [1968] 1 Q.B. 468) but only where there is no other convenient place to stop (*London and Suburban Land v Carey* (1991) 62 P. & C.R. 480); and
(2) the right to a sufficiency of vertical space immediately above the road for the purpose of loading and unloading (*VT Engineering Ltd v Borland (Richard) & Co Ltd* (1968) 19 P. & C.R. 890).

It will not, however, include:

(a) any lateral space outside the limits of the road (*VT Engineering Ltd v Borland (Richard) & Co Ltd* (1968) 19 P. & C.R. 890); or

(b) a right to visibility splays beyond the edges of the road (*Hayns v Secretary of State* (1977) 36 P. & C.R. 317).

3–23 These implied ancillary rights may be excluded by agreement; but the tenant's adviser should not agree to their exclusion unless the tenant has access to delimited loading bays and an express right to load and unload. Special restrictions on loading and unloading may be imposed. It will usually be desirable for the landlord to have power to make regulations about traffic management. This is normally done by imposing upon the tenant a covenant to comply with regulations made from time by the landlord. The tenant's adviser should seek to restrict the power to the making of reasonable regulations. Even if there is no express power to do so, the dominant owner will usually be entitled to introduce a scheme of traffic management in the interests of safety (*Celsteel Ltd v Alton House Holdings Ltd* [1985] 1 W.L.R. 204).

If the draftsman wishes to restrict the identity of the persons whom the tenant may authorise to use the road (e.g. staff but not customers) this must be done expressly (see *Woodhouse & Co Ltd v Kirkland (Derby) Ltd* [1970] 2 All E.R. 587).

Example 3.10 Right of way: unlimited times and vehicles

The right in common with the landlord and all others having the like right to pass and repass (but not to park or except in emergency to stop) with or without vehicles at all times and for all purposes connected with the use of the demised property (but not otherwise) over the road coloured [ ] on the attached plan.

Example 3.11 Right of way: limited times and vehicles, right to load, etc.

The right in common with the landlord and all others having the like right to pass and repass on foot and with vehicles not exceeding [ ] feet in length or [ ] tonnes (unladen weight) at any time between 6 am on Monday and 8 pm on Friday in each week (except public holidays) for all purposes connected with the use of the demised property (but not otherwise) over the road coloured [ ] on the attached plan and to park any such vehicle for such period as may be reasonable for the purpose only of loading or unloading it.

Example 3.12 Right of way: right to load, etc. in loading bay
The right at all times with or without vehicles to pass and repass over the road leading from [ ] to the demised property (but not to halt or park any vehicle thereon except in case of emergency) for all purposes connected with the use of the demised property and the right for the same purposes to use the loading bay coloured [ ] on the attached plan for loading and unloading any such vehicle.

(b) Stairs and passages

In a lease of property on an upper floor of a building there will be **3–24**
implied an easement of necessity to use a staircase that is its sole means of access (*Altmann v Boatman* (1963) 186 E.G. 109). The tenant will also have implied rights to use any passages or corridors that are necessary means of access. Nevertheless, it is good practice to grant the tenant express rights of access over the common parts of the building. The landlord may seek to restrict access over common parts to specified parts of the day, or to "normal working hours". In the case of a self-contained building, this should not be accepted by the tenant. But in the case of a single floor of an office building or a unit in a covered shopping centre, the landlord may have a legitimate concern to avoid the necessity of providing services (e.g. heating, lighting, hot water, and security) for one tenant only. The tenant's adviser has two approaches. If the additional expenditure would be recoverable by the landlord through the service charge, he may reasonably point out that the landlord will not suffer any actual loss. Consequently, the landlord has no financial interest in preventing the tenant from using the building round the clock, and may have a financial interest in permitting him to do so, since the rent may be enhanced on review. If, however, the expenditure is not so recoverable, the tenant may have to agree either to forego such services out of hours or to pay the costs of them. In any case, however, the landlord should insist that the tenant either pays for the costs of security, or indemnifies the landlord against third party claims arising out of the use of the building out of hours. It should also be noted that a covenant limiting hours of access may not limit hours of use of the demised property, provided that the tenant arrives before permitted hours cease and leaves after they recommence.

The tenant's adviser should ensure that the landlord undertakes responsibility for the repair, maintenance and cleaning of the common parts. In the absence of express provision certain duties are imposed on the landlord at common law and by statute. At common law the landlord will be liable to take reasonable care to keep in repair any essential means of access retained in his possession. Similarly, if the access is useless without artificial lighting he will be liable to take reasonable care to maintain adequate lighting (*Liverpool City Council v Irwin* [1977] A.C. 239). In the case of buildings let in separate parts for use as factories, more onerous duties are imposed on the landlord. He will in such cases be under an absolute duty to keep floors, stairs, passages and gangways maintained in an efficient state and in good repair (Factories Act 1961 ss. 122 and 176(1); *Galashiels Gas Co Ltd v O'Donnell* [1949] A.C. 275). Similar duties are imposed on employers (Workplace (Health, Safety and Welfare) Regulations 1992 (SI 1992/3004) Regs 15, 17 and 18).

Example 3.13 Right of way: limited times
The right in common with the landlord and all others having the like right at all times between 8.30 am and 6.30 pm on weekdays and between 8.30 am and 1.30 pm on Saturdays (but not on public holidays) to pass and repass on foot only through the main entrance to the building of which the demised property forms part and over the stairs and corridors leading therefrom to the demised property.

(c) Lifts

3–25 A right to use a lift may be implied in the case of a letting on, say, the tenth floor of a block (*Liverpool City Council v Irwin* [1977] A.C. 239) or where it would be inconvenient and uneconomic for the tenant to use the stairs (*Dikstein v Kanevsky* [1947] V.L.R. 216). A right to use a lift is in the nature of an easement.

Where property is demised together with the use of the lift the landlord will be under a duty to provide a working lift (*De Meza v Ve-Ri-Best Manufacturing Co Ltd* (1952) 160 E.G. 364). Equally, where the lift is an essential means of access he will be under a duty to take reasonable care to keep it in working order (*Liverpool City Council v Irwin* [1977] A.C. 239). Such an obligation may be enforced against the landlord by way of specific performance

(*Francis v Cowcliffe Ltd* (1976) 33 P. & C.R. 368). In the case of a building let in separate parts for use as factories, the landlord will be under an absolute duty to keep lifts in an efficient state and in good repair (ss.122(1) and 176(1) of the Factories Act 1961). A corresponding duty is imposed on "employers" in relation to premises where the Health and Safety at Work Act 1974 applies, such as factories, agricultural premises, offices, shops, hospitals, hotels and places of entertainment. The definition of "employers", includes a person who has control to any extent (in connection with the carrying on by him of a trade, business, or other undertaking, Reg.3(5)): of lifting equipment; a person at work who uses or supervises or manages the use of lifting equipment; or the way in which lifting equipment is used, and to the extent of his control (Reg.3(3) of The Lifting Operations and Lifting Equipment Regulations 1998 (SI 1998/2307).

In addition, the landlord and "employer" (as defined in Reg.3(3) of The Lifting Operations and Lifting Equipment Regulations 1998) must ensure that every hoist or lift is thoroughly examined by a competent person at least once in every six months in the case of lifting equipment for lifting persons and in the case of other lifting equipment, at least every 12 months (s.122(2) of the Factories Act 1961); The Lifting Operations and Lifting Equipment Regulations 1998 Reg.9(3)(a)). This will usually be done by the landlord entering into a long-term maintenance contract with a specialist. In such cases the draftsman should provide for the costs of periodic maintenance and inspection to be recoverable from the tenants, for they may not always fall within a provision to pay the cost of repairs.

The Lifting Operations and Lifting Equipment Regulations 1998 do not apply if the equipment provided is to be used primarily by members of the public, for example lifts in shopping centres, but is regulated by the Health and Safety at Work Act 1974.

In most cases, the tenant should not be permitted to load the lift to an unlimited extent. This may be achieved either by way of limitation in the grant of the right itself or by way of separate covenant. It may also be necessary to specify in the lease the lifts that are passenger lifts and those that are goods lifts.

Example 3.14 Right to use passenger lift

The right at all times in connection with the use of the demised property (but not otherwise) to use the lifts in the building for the carriage of passengers only and their hand luggage provided that the landlord shall not be liable for any loss or damage caused by a temporary failure of the lifts.

Example 3.15 Right to use passenger and goods lift
The right in common with the landlord and all others having the like right during normal office hours to use:
(1) the lift marked [ ] on the attached plan for the carriage of passengers only and their hand luggage
(2) the lift marked [ ] on the attached plan for the carriage of goods provided that the lift shall not be loaded in excess of the permitted weight displayed therein.

9. CAR PARKING

3–26 Where there is car parking space attached to the building or development in question, the draftsman has two basic methods of dealing with it. On one hand, he may include individual parking spaces within each demise; on the other hand, he may grant each tenant a general right to park cars, either limited to a specified number of cars per tenant or on a daily "first come first served" basis. The grant of a right to park in a defined area takes effect as a legal easement (*Newman v Jones* unreported, 1982; *London and Blenheim Estates v Ladbroke Retail Parks* [1992] 1 W.L.R. 1278, *Hair v Gillman* (2000) 80 P. &C.R. 108). In addition, a tenant granted rights during normal business hours to use parking spaces to the exclusion of others may also acquire the protection of the Landlord and Tenant Act 1954 Part II (*Pointon York Group Plc v Poulton Land* [2007] 1 P. & C.R. 6)

The inclusion of specified car parking spaces within each demise has the advantage that each tenant knows precisely how many cars he (or his staff or visitors) may park, and where. However, it has the disadvantage that there is no flexibility in available space. Thus, if a tenant's business expands or becomes more labour-intensive, unauthorised encroachments may be made into the parking spaces of other tenants, or there may be parking on access and service roads. It is by no means unusual for an aggrieved tenant to sue the landlord for derogation from his grant.

The grant of a right, but not the exclusive right, to park cars has the advantage of flexibility. However, the very fact that the right to park is not exclusive means that one tenant may appropriate more than his fair share of parking spaces. If the landlord attempts to take counter measures (e.g. by erecting lockable posts in some spaces and issuing keys to some of the tenants and not others) he may face an action for interfering with the other tenants' easements. If the right is a right to park on such defined area of land as may from time to time be specified by the landlord, the landlord must specify an area, and will derogate from his grant if he withdraws a specification or does not specify at all (*Saeed v Plustrade Ltd* [2002] 2 E.G.L.R. 19).Accordingly, the draftsman should attempt to combine both methods. He should include in each demise a small number of spaces, the availability of which the tenant can be sure. In addition, the tenant should be granted a non-exclusive right to park in a delineated area, subject to the availability of space from time to time. It may also be desirable to set aside a small area for short-term parking and the shared use of that area may be restricted to the tenants' visitors. If this is done the tenants and their staff should be expressly prohibited from using the visitors' car park and time limits on parking there should be imposed.

The right to park is often limited to "private" motor vehicles. A "private" motor vehicle is one which is used for personal or domestic purposes, not for business purposes (*Bell v Franks (Alfred) & Bartlett Co Ltd* [1980] 1 All E.R. 356). It is suggested, therefore, that if the tenant wishes to park vehicles actively used for business purposes, the word "private" should be deleted from the draft lease.

Example 3.16 Composite rights of parking

Together with:

(1) the parking spaces numbered [ ] and marked on the attached plan

(2) the right in common with the landlord and all others having the like right to park private motor vehicles belonging to the tenant and the tenant's staff (subject to the availability of space from time to time) in the area designed "Staff Car Park" on the attached plan

(3) the right for the tenant's visitors in common with the visitors of other tenants in the building to park private motor vehicles for temporary periods not exceeding one hour in any period of

twenty four hours (subject to the availability of space from time to time) in the area designated "Visitors' Car Park" on the attached plan.

10. ADVERTISEMENTS, SIGNS AND NAMEPLATES

3–27 In the absence of agreement to the contrary the tenant will be entitled to exhibit advertisements, signs and nameplates in any part of the property included in the demise. The nature of the advertisements is not restricted to purposes connected with the tenant's business (*Clapman v Edwards* [1938] 2 All E.R. 507). Conversely, the landlord will not be entitled to maintain an advertisement on any part of the demised property, even if the advertisement was in position at the beginning of the tenancy (*Re Webb's Lease* [1952] Ch. 808).

These rights concern only the property actually demised; not the common parts. If a tenant takes only an upper floor of a building and has no more than a right to use the entrance hall for the purposes of approaching the property demised he must stipulate for the right to put a nameplate outside the property (other than that part demised to him) if he desires this convenience (*Berry (Frederick) Ltd v Royal Bank of Scotland* [1949] 1 K.B. 619 at 621, per Lord Goddard C.J.). If such a right is granted to the tenant it will take effect as a legal easement (*Moody v Steggles* (1879) 12 Ch. D. 261; *William Hill (Southern) Ltd v Cabras Ltd* [1987] 1 E.G.L.R. 37).

The draftsman should either designate in the lease the place where the advertisement may be maintained, or grant the tenant a right to maintain an advertisement in such place as may be designated from time to time by the landlord or his surveyor. The form of the advertisement may either be left to the discretion of the landlord (or his surveyors) or be dealt with in the lease. If the draftsman chooses the latter course it is suggested that the tenant be permitted to display any advertisement permitted by the Town and Country Planning (Control of Advertisements) Regulations 1992 (SI 1992/666).

If further restrictions on displaying advertisements are to be imposed, the tenant's adviser should ensure that the tenant still has sufficient ability to carry on his business efficiently (e.g. by exhibiting advertisements as part of a window display).

The landlord should specifically provide that the tenant is to remove its signage and advertisements and make good at the determination of the lease.

Example 3.17 Right to display advertisement permitted by regulations
The right to display in and on the demised property any advertisement permitted to be displayed without the express consent of the local planning authority by virtue of the Town and Country Planning (Control of Advertisements) Regulations 1992 or any modification or replacement thereof.

Example 3.18 Right to display advertisement in prescribed form
The right to display on the front door of the demised property a name plate not exceeding [ ] in area and advertising the business carried on in the demised property and to display the name or style of that business on the name board situated in the entrance hall of the building of which the demised property forms part with letters provided by the landlord.

11. SANITARY FACILITIES

Where the demised property consists of part only of a building the **3–28** draftsman may either include sanitary facilities in each demise or he may grant each tenant a right to use communal facilities. The right to use a lavatory will take effect as a legal easement (*Miller v Emcer Products Ltd* [1956] Ch. 304) as will a right to use a washroom (*Heywood v Mallalieu* (1883) 25 Ch. D. 357); but a right to a supply of hot water is a matter of personal contract rather than an easement (*Regis Property Co Ltd v Redman* [1956] 2 Q.B. 612).

Sanitary facilities may be included in a demise where the building is amply provided with them or where the position of the lavatories and washrooms is such that access cannot be directly obtained from the common parts. In all other cases it is advisable to grant tenants easements to use the facilities in common with the other tenants in the building. The principal reason for so doing is the effect of statutory duties imposed on the landlord in respect of the provision of sanitary facilities in a multi-occupied building.

Where part of a building is let off as a separate factory, the landlord will be responsible for providing and maintaining in efficient working order and good repair sufficient and suitable sanitary conveniences for the persons employed in the factory (s.122 of the Factories Act 1961). A corresponding duty is imposed on him in respect of lettings of offices and shops (ss.42(6) and 43(4) of the Offices, Shops and Railway Premises Act 1963).

The number of conveniences required to be provided varies according to the number of persons employed in the building (Workplace (Health, Safety and Welfare) Regulations 1992 (SI 1992/3004) Reg.20). The draftsman should, therefore, consider whether to impose on the tenant a limit to the number of persons who may be employed in the demised property in order to avoid overloading the available facilities.

In the absence of an express obligation, the landlord will have no duty to keep in repair any pipe or drain through which the tenant discharges soil or water, even if the pipe or drain is retained in the possession of the landlord (*Westminster (Duke) v Guild* [1984] 3 All E.R. 144). However, the tenant has the implied right to enter the landlord's land in order to carry out any necessary works of repair. This situation is unlikely to be satisfactory to either party especially if the pipe is shared or runs under a shared access. Accordingly, provision should be made for the expenses of cleaning and maintaining the sanitary facilities. This may be done by including such expenses among the items for which the landlord is entitled to recover a service charge.

Example 3.19 Easement to use sanitary facilities
The right in common with the other tenants of the building to use the ladies' lavatories and washrooms on the [ ] floor of the building and the gentlemen's lavatories and washrooms on the [ ] floor of the building.

12. Telecommunications

3–29 The tenant must consider whether the needs of his business require the grant of rights to maintain electronic communications apparatus on or in the building. This encompasses both fixed line and wireless facilities:

(a) any apparatus within the meaning of the Communications Act 2003 which is designed or adapted for use in connection with the provision of an electronic communications network;

(b) any apparatus within the meaning of the Act that is designed or adapted for a use which consists of the sending or receiving of communications or other signals that are transmitted by means of an electronic communications network;
(c) any line;
(d) any conduit, structure, pole or other thing in, on by or from which any electronic communications apparatus is or may be installed, supported, carried or suspended (s.106(1) of the Communications Act 2003, and para.1(1) of Sch.2 to the Telecommunications Act 1984, as amended by Sch.3 of the 2004 Act).

If so, this should be covered by the grant of an express right. Although provision is made for the acquisition of such rights under the Electronic Communications Code (Telecommunications Act 1984 Sch.2, as amended by Communications Act 2003 Sch.3), it is unwise merely to rely on the statutory machinery. A covenant prohibiting alterations has effect in relation to the installation and running of telecommunication systems as if it were a covenant not to alter without the landlord's consent such consent not to be unreasonably withheld (Communications Act 2003 s.134). Reasonableness is determined having regard to the principle that no person should unreasonably be denied access to an electronic communications network or to electronic communications services.

It is common for freeholders to impose restrictions as to the particular telecoms operators used by the tenants or to prohibit their tenants from entering into telecoms agreements. Even if the landlord is not directly bound by the agreement, once any electronic communications apparatus has been installed the apparatus will enjoy the benefit of statutory protection (Communications Act 2003 para.21). As a result, even if the lease is contracted out of the protection of the Landlord and Tenant Act 1954, Part II, the landlord will not be able to enforce the removal of such apparatus without complying with the Code procedure and serving a para.21 notice. If the operator serves a counternotice in response, a court order must then be sought to require removal. It is not possible to contract out of paras 20 or 21.

If a tenant wishes to take a lease containing a break clause and to enter a telecoms agreement, the tenant should consider the inter-relationship between the statutory protection provided to telecoms operators and its potential ability to exercise the break clause in its lease if its right to break is made conditional upon the delivery up of the premises with vacant possession at the break date. The tenant should either exclude all communications apparatus from the scope of its obligation to deliver up vacant possession, or, if it cannot, it must seek to ensure that it will be able to obtain vacant possession by the relevant date (although there is authority under the Rent Acts which suggests that a tenant may not be held in breach, see *Reynolds v Bannerman* [1922] 1 K.B. 719, *Watson v Saunders-Roe* [1947] K.B. 437 and the discussion in *Woodfall Landlord and Tenant* (looseleaf, para.19.006).

If the tenant is permitted to enter agreements with a telecoms operator, a landlord may wish to provide in the lease for notice of any agreement to be given to it well before the expiry of the lease so that it can commence the para.21 procedure if it so chooses.

13. EXCEPTIONS AND RESERVATIONS

3–30 Although used almost interchangeably the words "exception" and "reservation" are, strictly, different mechanisms. An exception is always of part of the thing granted, and only a thing that exists can be excepted. A reservation is of a thing not in existence, but newly created or reserved out of land (27(1) *Halsbury's Laws of England* (2006 reissue), para.167 et seq.). Thus, the retention of an exterior wall will be an exception, but the retention of a right to enter the demised property will be a reservation. The practical significance of this distinction is that in cases of ambiguity an exception will be construed against the landlord, while a reservation will be construed against the tenant (*St Edmundsbury & Ipswich Diocesan Board of Finance v Clark (No.2)* [1975] 1 All E.R. 772).

(a) Right to enter

3–31 Where the landlord has undertaken obligations to repair or decorate the demised property, he has an implied right to enter the demised property for that purpose (*Saner v Bilton* (1878) 7 Ch. D. 815). In the exercise of that right the landlord may exclude the tenant from occupation, but only for a reasonable time, and only if to do so is essential for the execution of the work (*McGreal v Wake* [1984] 1 E.G.L.R. 42). But where the landlord has no such obligations, then in the absence of an express right he is not entitled to enter the demised property in order to carry out repairs even where the tenant has failed to repair and is in breach of covenant (*Regional Properties Ltd v City of London Real Property Co Ltd* [1981] 1 E.G.L.R. 33). Accordingly, the draftsman should reserve to the landlord a right to enter the demised property for the purposes of inspecting the state of repair and making good defects if the tenant fails to do so. Where the demised property is part only of a building the right should extend to entering the demised property for the purpose of repairing other parts of the building not included in the demise. A right of entry to repair will not entitle the landlord to enter to carry out improvements (*Rothschild v Moser* [1986] N.P.C. 46).

The draftsman should therefore consider whether the landlord should have the right to enter the demise for other purposes also, for example the right to enter for the purpose of testing the property, taking samples from it, carrying our surveys to require compliance with environmental legislation from time to time, reading meters, or measuring the property for the purpose of rent review. Some specificity is required in the drafting of the reservation, however it must also be remembered that, without more, the draftsman's choice of wording will be construed as it would have been understood as at the date of the grant of the lease. In the Scottish case of *Possfund Custodian Trustee Ltd v Kwik-Fit Properties Ltd* [2009] 1 E.G.L.R. 39, it was held that the reservation of a right for the landlord to "enter upon the premises generally to inspect and examine the same, to view the state and condition thereof and to take a schedule of the landlord's fixtures and of any wants of compliance by the tenant with its obligations hereunder", did not permit the landlord to carry out intrusive works of investigation over several days to test for soil contamination where those works involved cordoning off an area and the drilling of six boreholes of a depth ranging from 6m to 30m deep. Equally, in *Heronslea (Mill Hill) Ltd v Kwik-Fit Properties Ltd* [2009] Env. L.R. 208, it was held that the reservation to the landlord of the "right to enter the premises (on reasonable notice) for the purpose of making surveys and drawings of the premises" did not permit the landlord to dig boreholes under the premises or to take samples, even if those steps were part of an environmental assessment survey.

However, the draftsman should not draw the right too widely. If, for example, the landlord is entitled to enter the demised property in order to carry out substantial improvements or to reconstruct it the tenant may be able to defeat a claim to determine his tenancy on the ground of demolition and reconstruction (*Heath v Drown* [1973] A.C. 498). Thus, where a landlord was entitled to enter the demised property to carry out such improvements, additions and alterations as he considered reasonable, he was held to be entitled to demolish and reconstruct all the existing buildings comprising the demised property without putting an end to the tenancy (*Price v Esso Petroleum Co Ltd* [1980] 2 E.G.L.R. 58). A power to carry out improvements will not usually entitle a landlord to replace existing buildings with buildings in which the tenant cannot carry on the business permitted under the lease (*Leathwoods Ltd v Total Oil (Great Britain) Ltd* [1985] 2 E.G.L.R. 237). The landlord will have to make good damage to decorations caused by carrying out of works by him (*Bradley v Chorley BC* [1985] 2 E.G.L.R. 49). But it is good practice for the tenant's adviser to ensure that a right of entry is expressly conditional on the landlord making good any damage caused by his entry. Consideration should be given to the question whether "damage" is to be restricted to physical damage or is to extend to loss of profits caused by disturbance of the tenant's business.

(b) Right to develop adjoining property

3–32 Where the landlord retains adjoining property, a right to develop it should be reserved. If it is not, the landlord will be unable to deal with the property if to do so would interfere materially with the demised property (*Aldin v Latimer Clark Muirhead & Co* [1894] 2 Ch. 437; *Platt v London Underground Ltd* [2001] 2 E.G.L.R. 121). Even the erection of temporary scaffolding may amount to a breach of covenant for quiet enjoyment (*Owen v Gadd* [1956] 2 Q.B. 99) These restrictions originate in the doctrine of non-derogation from grant. It has been held that such restrictions will apply equally to land acquired by the landlord after the date of the lease (*Johnston & Sons Ltd v Holland* [1988] 1 E.G.L.R. 264), although a provision in an underlease that disabled the undertenant from objecting to the development of land belonging to the landlord or "of any land not comprised in the underlease" was held only to apply to land of the landlord at the date of the underlease (see *Paragon Finance Plc v City of London Real Property Co Ltd* [2002] 1 E.G.L.R. 97). Where such a right is reserved, it will give the landlord power to interfere with easements granted to the tenant, provided that the interference stops short of total extinguishment (*Overcom Properties v Stockleigh Hall Residents Management* (1989) 58 P. & C.R. 1). The tenant's adviser should, therefore, ensure that such a power is kept as narrow as possible.

(c) Right to alter common parts

Leases often contain fixed definitions of common parts. Yet **3–33** sometimes landlords wish to alter them. For example, it is not unusual for the landlord of a retail park to wish to construct a new unit on land originally designated for car parking. If this is a live possibility, it is desirable for the lease not only to provide that the landlord may build on adjoining land, but also to give him the express right to alter common parts. This should include power to remove areas of land from any definition of common parts and to substitute new areas. But the tenant will wish to ensure that the landlord's power cannot be exercised so as to leave him with substantially less convenient common parts than he had before.

In the case of a multi-occupied building or shopping centre or leisure development, the landlord will also wish to ensure that it retains the express right to regulate and control the use of the common parts, and also to use the common parts for displays or promotions from time to time. The tenant's adviser will wish to ensure that the landlord is obliged to act reasonably.

(d) Right to use services

In general terms, a reservation of a right to the free passage of **3–34** water, gas and electricity through the demised property will be constructed as a right to use the existing system and will not entitle the landlord to introduce any new wires or pipes (*Taylor v British Legal Life Assurance Co* [1925] Ch. 395). If the landlord wishes to have the right to introduce new wires and pipes it must be expressly reserved. It should be made clear that the right is to extend to wires such as computer cables (*Trailfinders Ltd v Razuki* [1988] 2 E.G.L.R. 46).

The landlord may also wish to reserve the right to divert services along different routes. But in such a case, the tenant's adviser should seek to ensure that a supply is maintained to the demised property at all times, and that any new route will not involve the tenant in extra expense.

(e) Light

3–35 Whether the grant of a right to light is express or implied, it is made at the date of the lease.

However, it is also the case that under s.3 of the Prescription Act 1832 a right to light may arise by the enjoyment of light that takes place *subsequent* to the grant of the lease. As a result, the landlord may wish to guard against the possibility of the tenant acquiring such a right during the term in addition to excluding s.62 of the Law of Property Act 1925. Section 3 provides: "When the access and use of light to and for any dwelling house, workshop, or other building shall have been actually enjoyed therewith for the full period of 20 years without interruption, the right thereto shall be deemed absolute and indefeasible, any local usage or custom to the contrary notwithstanding, unless it shall appear that the same was enjoyed by some consent or agreement expressly made or given for that purpose by deed or writing." The acquisition of the right to light is not therefore dependent on the terms of the lease; it is dependent on the established facts and the absence of a consent or agreement that satisfies the concluding part of s.3. The enjoyment of light does not need to be "as of right" as that expression is generally used in the law of easements.

A prescriptive right under s.3 is not confined to a freehold right. As such, it is possible for a tenant to acquire a prescriptive right to light against his landlord. In order to guard against this possibility the landlord and tenant must enter an agreement so as to prevent the enjoyment of light from being deemed to be "absolute and indefeasible". If an agreement provides for the enjoyment of light not to be absolute and indefeasible it will be sufficient to prevent the deeming provision from taking effect (*RHJ Ltd v (1) FT Patten (Holdings) Ltd (2) FT Patten Properties (Liverpool) Ltd* [2008] Ch. 341 (CA)). Whilst such an agreement is often found in substance in the reservation of the landlord's rights to develop, it is sensible to make express reference to rights to light.

(f) Other rights

Where the tenant has been granted rights (e.g. a right of support) the landlord will be entitled to rights that are in their nature reciprocal to the rights he has granted, or is taken to have granted, to the tenant (*Re Webb's Lease* [1952] Ch. 808). Nevertheless, it is good practice to reserve such rights expressly. **3–36**

Example 3.20 Exceptions and Reservations

Excepting and reserving to the landlord:

(1) easement rights and privileges over the demised property corresponding to those expressly granted to the tenant over the other parts of the building

(2) the right to build on develop deal with use any adjoining or neighbouring property retained by the landlord in such manner as he thinks fit even though the amenity of the demised property or the access of light or air to it may be lessened and without making any compensation to the tenant

(3) the right at reasonable times and on reasonable notice (except in emergency) to enter the demised property for the purposes of:
   - (a) inspecting its condition and state of repair
   - (b) carrying out any works (whether of repair or otherwise) for which the landlord or the tenant is liable under this lease
   - (c) carrying out any works (whether of repair or otherwise) to any property adjoining the demised property or to any party structure sewer drain or other thing used by the tenant in common with others
   - (d) measuring testing or valuing the demised property (including the right to take samples of materials and to open up parts of the demised property which would otherwise be inaccessible) but making good any damage caused by such an entry

(4) the right for the landlord and the other tenants of the building to pass through the demised property in case of fire or other emergency.

Example 3.21 Reservation of right to develop

Except and reserving to the landlord the full and free right to erect build rebuild and/or alter as it may think fit at any time and from time to time any buildings or bays or projections to buildings on any land adjoining the demised property and/or on the opposite sides of the adjoining streets and access ways.

Example 3.22 Sample rights reserved in respect of the common parts of a shopping centre

Notwithstanding any other provisions or covenants contained in this Lease the right to regulate and control the use of the Common Parts and in particular the right:

1. to exclude the general public from the Centre outside the trading hours of the Tenant;
2. to make reasonable regulation for the control and regulation of all vehicular and pedestrian traffic;
3. in the case of emergency only to vary change the use of or control access temporarily to the whole or any part of the Common Parts subject to the provision of suitable alternative access;
4. to erect signage and information boards and to install information desks;
5. to erect advertising displays and hoardings;
6. to install kiosks booths carts stalls vending machines public internet access terminals seating areas and other similar structures or facilities;
7. to use the Common Parts for temporary displays exhibitions themed events or promotional activity;

PROVIDED THAT the Landlord shall act reasonably and have regard to the benefit to the Centre as a whole and to the interests of the tenants as a whole.

Example 3.23 Express consent or agreement for the purposes of s.3 of the Prescription Act 1832

It is agreed that for the purposes of s.3 of the Prescription Act 1832 and otherwise the access of light to the demised property and the use of light within the demised property is enjoyed by consent.

Example 3.24 Definition of service pipes

"Service pipe" means any pipe drain sewer flue duct gutter wire cable optic fibre conduit channel or other means of passage or transmission of water soil gas air smoke electricity light information or other matter and all ancillary equipment or structures.

Example 3.25 Right to redesignate Common Parts
The right to remove from any area defined or designated as Common Parts such part of that area (up to and including the whole) as the landlord thinks fit provided that the landlord substitutes for the area removed an equivalent area to be used for similar purposes as the area removed.

14. FIXTURES

The general maxim of the law is that what is annexed to the land becomes part of the land. Whether annexation is sufficient depends on the circumstances of each case, and mainly on two circumstances, as indicating intention, namely the degree of annexation and the object of the annexation (*Holland v Hodgson* (1872) L.R. 7 CP 328, per Blackburn J.). If an object is annexed to land in order to enjoy it as a chattel (e.g. a carpet held by carpet grippers, or removable carpet tiles) it will not become a fixture but will remain a chattel. It will not therefore form part of the demised property and obligations relating to the demised property will not apply to it. **3–37**

Where an article has become a fixture it is treated as part of the demise during the term. Accordingly, the landlord may not distrain upon it (*Crossley v Lee* [1908] 1 K.B. 86). But at the expiry of the term the tenant has the right to remove those fixtures which are tenant's fixtures. Tenant's fixtures are those fixtures which the tenant fixes into the property for the purposes of his trade, but which do not become part of the structure itself (*New Zealand Government Property Corp v HM&S Ltd* [1982] 1 All E.R. 624). The essential qualities of a tenant's fixture are that it may be removed without causing irreparable damage to the building and that it may be set up and used again in another building or place (*Webb v Bevis (Frank) Ltd* [1940] 1 All E.R. 247; *Young v Dalgety Plc* [1987] 1 E.G.L.R. 116). Accordingly, fixtures such as office partitioning which cannot be removed without destroying the partitions will be a landlord's fixture rather than a tenant's fixture.

The tenant may exercise his right to remove tenant's fixtures so long as he is in possession as a tenant, whether under the original contract of tenancy or a new tenancy or by holding over (*New Zealand Government Property Corp v HM&S Ltd* [1982] 1 All E.R. 624). Where the right is exercised, the tenant must make good damage caused by the removal of the fixtures (*Mancetter*

Developments Ltd v Garmanson [1986] Q.B. 1212). However, it is important to remember that the tenant has a right and not a duty to remove tenant's fixtures, unless the fixtures were affixed in breach of covenant (*Never-Stop Railway (Wembley) Ltd v British Empire Exhibition (1924) Inc* [1926] 1 Ch. 877). But if the tenant chooses to leave fixtures, they must be left in repair. Accordingly, when damages for dilapidations at the end of the term come to be assessed, the tenant is entitled to have the damages assessed according to the cheaper option of stripping out the fixtures or leaving them in repair. This position may be altered by agreement. Thus, a tenant may contract to yield up the demised property including tenant's fixtures (*Leschallas v Woolf* [1908] 1 Ch. 641). Conversely, the tenant may be placed under an express obligation to remove all tenant's fixtures at the end of the term (see *Wessex Reserve Forces & Cadets Association v White* [2006] 1 E.G.L.R. 55, where the tenant's fixtures included a portakabin, a garden shed and sectional concrete buildings), or may contract to remove fixtures either unconditionally, or conditionally, upon being requested to do so by the landlord.

In a case where substantial fitting out work is in contemplation, it is suggested that the draftsman should give the landlord the right to require the removal of fixtures and, in particular, its partitions and associated lighting and wiring. Thought should also be given as to the consequential impact that the removal of partitions may have upon the state and condition of carpeting and ceiling tiles. Where the landlord has such a right to require the removal of fixtures, it is often overlooked in practice, and the landlord does not make a requirement until it is too late. Accordingly, the draftsman should consider imposing on the tenant an obligation to ask the landlord, say six months before the expiry of the term which (if any) fixtures the landlord requires him to remove.

The draftsman should ensure that the yielding up obligations placed upon the tenant are self-explanatory and, if a range of separate obligations is placed upon the tenant, that those obligations are consistent. *Fairgate International Ltd v Citibank International Plc* [2006] 1 P. & C.R. 2, provides an example of the difficulties that a tenant may face in complying with its obligations if those obligations are not drafted clearly. In that case, the tenant was obliged to yield up the premises in repair and, if required by the landlord so to do, both to remove all furnishings, fixtures and fittings installed by the tenant, restoring the premises to their original condition (cl.2(8)(B)(i)), and to fit out and equip the premises in accordance with a detailed specification set out in a schedule to the lease (cl.2(8)(B)(ii)). The landlord served notice upon the tenant requiring it to reinstate in accordance with both clauses. At face value, the notice required performance of mutually inconsistent requirements. The Court of Appeal construed the provisions as entitling the landlord to require the tenant to carry out work under the first provision except to the extent that it was inconsistent with the second provision.

The tenant should consider the need for bespoke drafting if it is to lease equipment from an equipment-leasing company, such as lighting and air conditioning, and that equipment, once installed, will be fixed to, and become part of, the premises. One approach is for the landlord to become the owner of the equipment, subject to a "landlord's waiver" entered into with the equipment-leasing company. Under the waiver, the landlord is obliged not to deprive the equipment-leasing company of its interest in the equipment, and the equipment-leasing company has a contractual right to enter the premises and detach the equipment so as to resume ownership of it. The waiver provides that in the event that the landlord determines the lease, it will give the equipment-leasing company notice of the termination and thereafter 28 days in which to remove the equipment (see *Michael Gerson (Leasing) Ltd v Greatsunny Ltd* [2010] Ch. 558).

In the case of Feed-in Tariff Leases, the tenant may wish to include declarations within the lease confirming that the equipment belongs to the tenant and is not intended to be a permanent improvement.

Example 3.26 Covenant to yield up tenant's fixtures
At the expiry or sooner determination of the tenancy to yield up the demised property including all tenant's fixtures in good repair and clean and tidy.

Example 3.27 Covenant to remove tenant's fixtures if required
If so required by the landlord by written notice given not later than three months before the term date to remove (or pay for the removal of) all fixtures affixed to the demised property by the tenant or such of them as may be specified in the notice.

Example 3.28 Covenant by tenant to inquire about removal of fixtures
Not later than six months before the expiry of the term to inquire in writing of the landlord which (if any) tenant's fixtures the landlord requires the tenant to remove on the termination of the term.

Example 3.29 Authorisation for landlord to remove and sell tenant's fixtures
The tenant authorises the landlord at the expiry or sooner determination of the tenancy to remove any tenant's fixtures and/or other items left in the demised property and dispose of them on such terms as the landlord considers fit.

15. RENEWAL LEASES

(a) Extent of the demise

3–38 Although the tenant is entitled to the protection of Part II of the Landlord and Tenant Act 1954 in respect of the whole of the property comprised in his tenancy, he is only entitled to be granted a new tenancy of his holding. The tenant's holding is that part of the property occupied by him (whether or not for business purposes) or by an employee of his employed in the business giving rise to protection (s.23(3)). If there is no agreement as to the extent of the holding, it is designated by the court by reference to the circumstances existing at the date of the order (s.32(2)).

The court cannot normally order the grant of a new tenancy of part only of the holding (*Fernandez v Walding* [1968] 2 Q.B. 606). However, where the landlord opposes the grant of a new tenancy on redevelopment grounds, the tenant may be entitled to a new tenancy of an economically separable part of the holding if the landlord's redevelopment would not be impeded (ss.31A and 32(1A)).

Equally, the court cannot normally order the grant of a new tenancy of more than the holding. But the landlord has an absolute right to require the tenant to take a new tenancy of the whole of the property comprised in the current tenancy even though the tenant does not occupy the whole of it (s.32(2)).

(b) Ancillary rights

Where the current tenancy includes rights enjoyed by the tenant in connection with the holding, those rights are included in the new tenancy unless the landlord and tenant agree or the court determines otherwise (s.32(3); *Pointon York Group Plc v Poulton Land* [2007] 1 P. & C.R. 6). However, the court cannot create new rights over the landlord's land and cannot elevate informal personal privileges into property rights (*Orlik (G) (Meat Products) Ltd v Hastings and Thanet BS* (1974) 29 P. & C.R. 126; *Picture Warehouse Ltd v Cornhill Investments Ltd* [2008] 1 E.G.L.R. 29). In addition the rights must still be subsisting at the date of the court's order (*Kirkwood v Johnson* (1979) 38 P. & C.R. 392). **3–39**

(c) Section 62 of the Law of Property Act 1925

By s.62 of the Law of Property Act 1925, a lease of land will include all liberties, privileges, easements, rights, and advantages whatsoever appertaining or reputed to appertain to the land or any part thereof at the date of the lease, demised, occupied, or enjoyed with or reputed or known as part or parcel of or appurtenant to the land or any part thereof. Where the tenant is already in occupation at the date of execution of the lease, s.62 may convert mere personal licences into legal rights, provided that they are rights known to the law (*Wright v Macadam* [1949] 2 K.B. 744; *Goldberg v Edwards* [1950] Ch. 247). Section 62 may be excluded by the terms of the lease (s.62(4)). The draftsman should give consideration to doing so in all renewal leases (see Form 15, below) but if this is done, the tenant's adviser must ensure that all necessary ancillary rights are expressly granted by the lease. **3–40**

(d) Alterations carried out under previous lease

In many cases, the tenant renewing his lease will have carried out alterations to the property during the term of the expired lease. He may have undertaken obligations to reinstate. The draftsman should ensure that those reinstatement obligations are carried forward into the new lease, so that the tenant remains under an obligation to reinstate when the new lease comes to an end. **3–41**

The tenant's adviser should ensure that the rental value of any alterations carried out under the expired lease is ignored in assessing the rent payable on any rent review under the new lease.

CHAPTER 4

PARTIES AND COVENANTS

1. LANDLORD AND TENANT (COVENANTS) ACT 1995

The Landlord and Tenant (Covenants) Act 1995 applies to new tenancies and also changed the law in certain respects in relation to old tenancies A new tenancy is one which is granted on or after January 1, 1996. However, a tenancy granted on or after that date will not be a new tenancy if it is granted pursuant to: **4–01**

(1) an agreement for lease made before that date;
(2) an option granted before that date (irrespective of the date when the option is exercised); or
(3) a court order (e.g. for the grant of a new tenancy) made before that date.

The rules which apply only to new tenancies are:

(a) the new rules introduced for the running of covenants;
(b) the abolition of privity of contract, and associated changes;
(c) the amendment of s.19 of the Landlord and Tenant Act 1927;
(d) the ability of the landlord to seek a release from privity of contract on assignment of the reversion.

Since the rights and liabilities of the parties differ according to whether the lease is a new lease or not, the lease should state whether it is a new lease or not.

Example 4.1 Statement whether lease is a new lease
This lease [is][is not] a new lease of the purposes of the Landlord and Tenant (Covenants) Act 1995.

2. THE RUNNING OF COVENANTS

4–02 The Act abolished the traditional distinction between covenants which run with the land and covenants which do not (s.2 of the Landlord and Tenant (Covenants) Act 1995). All covenants now run with the land. The exceptions to this principle are:

(1) a covenant does not bind an assignee if it did not bind the assignor immediately before the assignment (personal waivers and releases being disregarded for this purpose); and
(2) a covenant will not bind an assignee if it is expressed to be personal to the assignor (s.3 of the Landlord and Tenant (Covenants) Act 1995).

Thus where, for example, the tenant is a government department, and the lease contains a covenant by the tenant to insure, but it is subject to a proviso that for as long as the tenant is a government department it may carry its own insurance, the proviso would be a personal waiver or release, so that an assignee would be bound by the covenant to insure. And where, for example, the original tenant is given the personal right to use the property for some special purpose, that right will not pass to an assignee on assignment. It seems highly unlikely that these changes will affect traditional drafting practices.

It is specifically provided that, where a covenant is expressed (in whatever terms) to be personal to any person, the Act does not make that covenant enforceable against any other person. The formula "in whatever terms" requires that the language of the tenancy, read in its context, expresses or otherwise implicitly conveys that the covenant is not to be annexed to the tenancy or the reversion (*First Penthouse Ltd v Channel Hotels & Properties (UK) Ltd* [2004] E.G.L.R. 16. This point was not considered on appeal). An obligation that is expressed to be personal to the original landlord will continue to bind the original landlord after he has assigned the reversion to the lease. It is not a "landlord's" covenant, as it is not a covenant to be performed by the person who may from time to time be entitled to the reversion on the tenancy (s.28(1) of the Act). It will not, therefore, be capable of release using the notice procedure in the Act (*BHP Petroleum Great Britain Ltd v Chesterfield Properties Ltd* [2002] Ch. 194).

A covenant may be drafted so that it ceases to bind a person after he has parted with his interest in the property by specifically limiting his liability to the period whilst he holds the reversion, or term (*Avonridge Property Co Ltd v Mashru* [2006] 1 E.G.L.R. 15). In the event of a lawful assignment, such a covenant will effect an automatic release without the need to follow the release procedure in the Act. The provision will not fall foul of the anti-avoidance provisions contained in the Act. This form of drafting is normally found in the case of landlord's covenants and landlords would be well advised to limit their liability to the period when they are landlords of the premises.

The draftsman may also limit the landlord or tenant's liability to the extent of the assets of a particular fund. This may be done, for example, where the tenant is the trustee of a trust fund and does not wish to accept liability in excess of the assets of the trust fund (*Warborough Investments Ltd v Berry* [2005] L. & T.R. 17), or where the landlord or tenant is a partnership and the liability under the lease is to be limited to partnership assets and is not to extend to the personal assets of individual partners. In such circumstances, care must be taken to ensure that the limitation is by way of personal concession and is not intended to alter the relationship between any other potentially interested parties and that the provisions of the Contract (Rights of Third Parties) Act 1999 are excluded (*Prudential Assurance Co Ltd v Ayres and Grew* [2008] 1 All E.R. 1266).

The Act applies not only to covenants contained in the lease itself, but also to covenants contained in collateral agreements (see, for example, *First Penthouse Ltd v Channel Hotels and Properties (UK) Ltd; Channel Hotels & Properties (UK) Ltd v Tamimi* [2004] E.G.L.R. 16). A collateral agreement may be an agreement which is made before the grant of the lease (s.28(1)). This raises the question whether obligations undertaken in an agreement for lease, for example by a developer, will bind a subsequent purchaser, for example a pension fund. In order to avoid this potential problem, it is good practice to provide expressly in the agreement for lease that development obligations are personal to the developer.

Example 4.2 Limitation on landlord's liability

The Landlord covenants with the Tenant (but not so as to impose any liability on the Landlord after it has parted with its reversion) as follows:

OR
The Landlord covenants with the Tenant but not, in the case of [X Company only], so as to be liable after the Landlord has disposed of its interest in the Premises:

[N.B. in the case of registered leases, this is subject to the impact of the "registration gap." Following an assignment the landlord will remain liable until its successor is registered as proprietor at Land Registry (*Brown & Root Technology v Sun Alliance & London Assurance* [1997] 1 E.G.L.R. 39).]

3. Enforcement of covenants

(a) Benefit

4–03 The benefit of tenant covenants of the tenancy will pass to the landlord for the time being. It is also possible for covenants to be made for the benefit of a person who is not a party to a lease. For example, a covenant to keep the property in repair, or a covenant not to use it except for some specified purpose, may be given not only to the landlord but also to other tenants in a scheme of development. This is more common in residential leases than in business leases. Since the Contracts (Rights of Third Parties) Act 1999, a third party may enforce a term in a contract to which he is not a party if either the contract says he can or the term purports to confer a benefit on him (s.1). Whether a term purports to confer a benefit on a third party is a question of construction of the contract. The third party may be identified by name, as a member of a class, or as answering a particular description, but he need not be in existence when the contract is made. Where the alienation provisions of the lease require the tenant to impose particular obligations on a subtenant, the draftsman should consider making those obligations directly enforceable by the landlord. In addition, the Act may do away with the need for collateral warranties given by the professional and construction team responsible for the building of a new building. It will now be possible for the contract with the developer to provide that the benefit of the contract may also be claimed by any tenant of the completed building.

Where a third party has a right to enforce a term of a contract, the parties to the contract may not generally vary it so as to alter his entitlement without his consent (s.2). However, this may be modified by the terms of the contract (s.2(3)). If express provision is made for the possibility of varying the lease, careful consideration should be given to the potential impact of a variation on the liability of a guarantor or former tenant.

Example 4.3 Declaration that covenants may not be enforced by third parties
It is agreed that, save in accordance with the provisions of the Landlord and Tenant (Covenants) Act 1995, no term of this lease is intended to be enforceable by any person who is not a party to it.

Example 4.4 Declaration that some covenants may be enforced by third parties
It is agreed that the provisions of clauses [ ] and [ ] may be enforced by any person who is for the time being a tenant of any other part of the Estate in addition to any person who is entitled to enforce those provisions by virtue of the Landlord and Tenant (Covenants) Act 1995.

Example 4.5 Provisions for modification
The landlord and the tenant for the time being may vary the terms of this lease without the consent of any other person entitled to the benefit of any covenants contained in it.

(b) Burden

The Contracts (Rights of Third Parties) Act 1999 does not alter the **4–04**
general rule that the burden of a contract cannot be assigned or imposed on a third party. However, under the Landlord and Tenant (Covenants) Act 1995, the burden of landlord covenants and tenant covenants will pass to an assignee.

4. RELEASE OF COVENANTS ON ASSIGNMENT

If the tenant assigns the premises demised to him, he is released **4–05**
from the tenant covenants of the tenancy, and ceases to be entitled to the benefits of the landlord covenants (s.5 of the Landlord and Tenant (Covenants) Act 1995). The tenant covenants of the tenancy will include not only covenants contained in the lease, but also any covenant contained in a collateral agreement (e.g. a side letter or

licence granted during the tenancy) (s.28(1)). Where the assignment is of part only, the release extends only to the extent that the covenants fall to be complied with in relation to the part assigned.

The automatic release does not apply on an excluded assignment. An excluded assignment is one which is in breach of a covenant of the tenancy, or an assignment which takes place by operation of law (s.11). However, the automatic release will apply to the next assignment which is not itself an excluded assignment.

If the landlord assigns his reversion, he is not automatically released. However, he has the right to apply to be released, either by agreement with the tenant or if the county court declares that it reasonable for him to be released (ss.6–8). Where a landlord negotiates an automatic release a tenant should consider inserting an automatic release of their own obligations. The express provisions for the statutory release of tenants only apply where the landlord applies to be released, and not where the lease contains an automatic release (ss.6(2)(b), 6(3)(b), 7(4)).

Unless each lease within a multi-let building contains a provision for automatic release or all the tenants agree to release the landlord, there is potential for future difficulty where a building is subject to multiple tenancies. If some tenants automatically release the landlord or agree to do so, and some do not, and the assignee later defaults, the former landlord will not be liable to those tenants who released it (and who have themselves been released), but will remain liable to others. In circumstances where, for example, the discharge of the former landlord's liability requires it to pay a sum of money in order to remedy the current landlord's breach, say a failure to pay the insurance premium for the building, and that sum could have been recouped by the current landlord from all the tenants under their leases of part, the former landlord's recovery will be limited to recovery from those tenants who did not release it and who were not themselves released. It will therefore suffer a shortfall proportionate to the numbers of tenants released.

Example 4.6 Provision for both landlord and tenants to be released in the event of automatic release of the landlord

Each Landlord is liable under the landlord covenants (and has the benefit of the tenant covenants) only for the period that it is the Landlord and each Tenant is liable under the tenant covenants (and has the benefit of the landlord covenants) only for the period that it is the Tenant.

5. Authorised guarantee agreements

Although the tenant is automatically released from liability under his covenants on assignment, he may be required to guarantee the obligations of the immediate assignee. This is done by an authorised guarantee agreement. The agreement must comply with the formal requirements of s.16 of the Act. In addition, the tenant may only be required to enter into such an agreement where he is required to do so as a condition (lawfully imposed) of consent to the assignment (s.16(3)(b)). The circumstances in which such a condition may be imposed are discussed in Chapter 12. **4–06**

6. Joint and several liability

Where two or more persons are bound by the same covenant in consequence of the Act, they are jointly and severally liable (s.13(1)). Moreover, where two or more persons are jointly and severally liable by virtue of the Act, a release of one of them will not release the others (s.13(2)). This reverses the general law under which the release of one contracting party releases the others unless the creditor expressly reserves its rights against co-debtors in the agreement or a term to that effect is necessarily to be implied from the circumstances which existed at the time of the agreement (*Deanplan v Mahmoud* [1992] 3 W.L.R. 467, *Chelsea Building Society v Nash* [2011] B.P.I.R. 381 (CA), although see *Sun Life Assurance Society Plc v Tantofex (Engineers) Ltd* [1999] 2 E.G.L.R. 135). However, the statutory provision applies only to persons bound by virtue of the Act, and so will not apply to persons who are bound independently of the Act (e.g. two original tenants who are bound jointly and severally solely by contract). **4–07**

7. Overriding leases

Where a former tenant or guarantor makes full payment of any sum which he has been required to pay under s.17 of the Act, i.e. a payment of a fixed charge which was the primary liability of the tenant in possession he is entitled to claim an overriding lease of the property (s.19 of the Landlord and Tenant (Covenants) Act 1995). The overriding lease will be granted for a term of three days longer than the unexpired residue of the lease, and (subject to any agreed **4–08** modifications) will be on the same terms as the underlying lease, barring personal obligations and spent obligations. An overriding lease must state:

(1) that it is a lease granted under s.19; and
(2) whether or not it is a new tenancy for the purposes of s.1 (s.20). An overriding lease will be a new tenancy if (and only if) the underlying lease is a new tenancy.

Example 4.7 Statement contained in overriding lease
This lease:
(1) is a lease granted under s.19 of the Landlord and Tenant (Covenants) Act 1995; and
(2) is [not] a new tenancy for the purposes of s.1 of that Act.

8. VARIATIONS

4–09 A subsequent variation of a lease will not bind a former tenant or guarantor if at the time when the variation was made the landlord had the absolute right to refuse to allow it, or would have had that right but for a previous variation (Landlord and Tenant (Covenants) Act 1995 s.18). At common law, an original tenant is not bound by a variation of the lease (*Friends Provident Life Office v British Railways Board* [1995] 2 E.G.L.R. 55) and unless the contract otherwise provides, a guarantor would be wholly discharged by such a variation (*Holme v Brunskill* (1877) 3 Q.B.D. 495). At common law, the parties may agree what they please, but the parties cannot contract out of the Act (s.25). It appears therefore that even if the former tenant or guarantor expressly consents to the variation, he will not be bound by it. However, the Act does not appear to prevent a person from entering into a fresh guarantee of the lease as varied, although it is arguable that a fresh guarantee would be struck down by the extremely wide anti-avoidance provisions contained in s.25 (see para.4–11 below).

9. FIXED CHARGES

4–10 The Act limits the liability of former tenants and guarantors in respect of fixed charges. This limitation applies to all leases, not merely new tenancies. A fixed charge is:

(1) rent;
(2) any service charge;
(3) any amount payable under a tenant covenant of the tenancy providing for the payment of a liquidated sum in the event of a failure to comply with any such covenant (Landlord and Tenant (Covenants) Act 1995 s.17(6)).

Where the landlord wishes to recover a fixed charge from a former tenant or a guarantor, he must serve a notice within the period of six months from the date when the charge became due. The notice must be in the prescribed form, and must inform the recipient:

(1) that the charge is now due; and
(2) that the landlord intends to recover from the recipient such amount as is specified in the notice and (where payable) interest calculated on the basis specified in the notice (s.17(2), (3)).

If no such notice is served in time, the former tenant or guarantor is not liable for the fixed charge. Where the amount of the fixed charge has not been finally determined (e.g. there is a pending rent review, or service charge accounts have not been finalised) the notice need not inform the recipient of the possibility that liability may be determined subsequently as every former tenant is taken to know the contents of the lease (*Scottish & Newcastle Plc v Raguz* [2008] 1 W.L.R. 2494). In such a case, the landlord may recover the amount finally determined, if he serves a further notice within three months of the final determination (s.17(4)).

These provisions apply only to fixed charges (as defined). They will not apply to claims for unliquidated damages (e.g. damages for dilapidations). The tenant may seek to extend protection against liability under all covenants. It is unlikely that, except in a strong tenants' market, the landlord will agree to forego all claims against the tenant. A possible compromise is that the landlord must first have attempted to pursue others who may be jointly and severally liable with the tenant.

Example 4.8 Restriction on landlord's ability to sue original tenant

(1) At any time after the lawful assignment of this lease by [name of original tenant] the landlord shall not be entitled to enforce

against him (either as former tenant or as guarantor under an authorised guarantee agreement) the tenant's obligations under this lease unless the landlord has first

(a) recovered judgment against all other persons against whom the landlord is or has become entitled to enforce those obligations either as principal or surety and
(b) attempted to levy execution upon such judgment

(2) upon payment by [name of original tenant] of any sum due under such judgment the landlord shall assign to him the benefit of it
(3) "authorised guarantee agreement" has the same meaning as in the Landlord and Tenant (Covenants) Act 1995.

10. ANTI-AVOIDANCE

4–11 Section 25 of the Act contains stringent anti-avoidance provisions. Any agreement relating to a tenancy is void to the extent that:

(1) it would otherwise have effect to exclude, modify or otherwise frustrate the operation of any provision of the Act;
(2) it provides for:
    (a) the termination or surrender of the tenancy; or
    (b) the imposition on the tenant of any penalty, disability or liability, in the event of the operation of any of the provisions of the Act; or
(3) it provides for any of the matters referred to in (2)(a) or (b) and does so (whether expressly or otherwise) in connection with, or in consequence of, the operation of any provision of the Act.

However, a covenant against assignment does not fall foul of these provisions merely because it prohibits assignment, and an authorised guarantee agreement similarly does not fall foul of them. The limitation of a party's liability to the period whilst he holds the reversion or term will not fall foul of the anti-avoidance provisions (*Avonridge Property Co Ltd v Mashru* [2006] 1 E.G.L.R. 15, see para.4–02).

CHAPTER 5

THE TERM OF THE LEASE

1. PRACTICAL PROBLEMS

The length of the term that the landlord is prepared to grant, and the tenant to take, is usually outside the draftsman's province. It is almost always determined by commercial considerations. The draftsman should, nevertheless, be aware of some of the practical problems that arise in connection with the choice of tenancy to be granted and in appropriate cases should draw them to the attention of his client. The Code for Leasing Business Premises in England and Wales 2007 (the successor to the Commercial Leases Codes of Practice published in 2002 and 2005) simply recommends that the length of term should be clear. **5–01**

For many years, investment considerations dictated that the norm for the duration of commercial leases was 25 years. The landlord required security of income for a long period, and this was specially desirable where the landlord was an investing institution which pays out pensions or insurance policies, because a period of 25 years' secure income facilitates the actuarial calculations necessary in order to determine the level of payments which the landlord can make. Since such institutions are the heaviest investors in commercial property, their requirements drove the market, so that even landlords who were not institutions required an "institutionally acceptable" investment. In addition, income security for a long period decreases the risks associated with the investment. This in turn diminishes the yield (or rate of return) required by an investor. Since the capital value of an investment is determined by a multiple of the rent, and the multiplier (or years' purchase) is the reciprocal of the yield, the lower the yield, the higher the capital value of the investment.

However, in the recession of the early 1990s, landlords became less able to impose these requirements on tenants who were unwilling to enter into such a long-term contractual commitment.

Although the basic pattern of a 25-year lease remained largely intact, tenants were able to secure the right to terminate the lease before its expiry. In addition, the pace of development in technology meant that office buildings had a shorter economic life, so that landlords recognised the need to refurbish at intervals more frequent than 25 years. Changes in accounting practice, which require tenants to carry contingent liabilities on their balance sheets, also militated against the acceptance of long terms. The implementation of the Landlord and Tenant (Covenants) Act 1995 and the abolition of privity of contract of the original tenant after assignment appear, however, to have had little impact on the attraction of the 25-year term for landlords and tenants.

5–02 Since the late 1990s a variety of economic, legislative and procedural factors have combined to cause a reduction in the length of leases granted. Whilst some premises are still let for 25-year terms, for example major corporation's headquarters buildings and premises let for a use that involves substantial works of fitting out (e.g. cinemas, other leisure facilities and major supermarkets), there has been an influx of overseas investors into the market who are not necessarily looking for the same pattern of lease as traditional investors. There has also been a reduction in the proportion of property to equities held by the pension funds who favoured long leases.

The introduction of Stamp Duty Land Tax ("SDLT") has also caused lease terms to be reduced as all leases are now capitalised at a standard 3.5 per cent discount rate for the term of the lease and duty is charged to the occupier at 1 per cent of the amount by which the capitalised value exceeds £150,000. Previously, higher duty was only payable on leases for over 100 years' and leases of seven years or less in length where the rent was less than £5,000 per annum did not attract duty at all. A 15-year lease will now attract a greater tax payment on execution than a shorter lease, but a tenant on a short lease who wished to remain in occupation will have to renew its lease several times over that same 15-year period and will have to pay the appropriate tax by reference to the new rental on each occasion.

Since 13 October 2003, all new leases granted for a term in excess of 7 years and all reversionary leases that will not take effect in possession within 3 months must be registered at Land Registry. Previously, only leases granted for a term in excess of 21 years were required to be registered. The lease and any side agreements intended to bind the tenant's successors in title must be lodged at Land Registry and will then be open to public inspection. Although there is a procedure for redacting commercially sensitive information (see para.2–13), if confidentiality is a serious issue the simplest method to achieve this will be to ensure that the lease is granted for a term of less than 7 years.

The Office of the Deputy Prime Minister's March 2005 Report, "Monitoring the 2002 Code of Practice for Commercial Leases", confirmed then market sentiment that there had been a continuing fall in average lease length since the late 1990s. Its research demonstrated that better quality and new properties tended to be let for longer terms than lower value and second hand property. The fall in lease length had also been more marked in office and industrial property than in the retail sector. The Report concluded that around a third of retail leases by value were granted for terms of 15 years, whilst 10 years was the then average lease length for larger tenants, 8 years was the average lease length for medium size tenants and 6 years was the average lease length term for small tenants.

The British Property IPD Annual Lease Review 2010 evidences a continuation of this pattern and that lease lengths have shortened again. There has also been an increase in the proportion of leases with tenant's break clauses. This is apparent across all sectors and on leases of all lengths, but mostly on longer leases.

Where the landlord has redevelopment plans for the property in **5–03**
question, the term of the lease should be short enough for him to be able to recover possession in time to redevelop. This is of great importance in practice because planning permissions are invariably granted subject to a condition that the permitted development is begun within a stipulated time. It is often forgotten that the service of a notice determining the tenant's tenancy under s.25 of the Landlord and Tenant Act 1954 is only the first step in the process of recovering possession. After the service of the notice, the tenant is entitled to apply to the court for a new tenancy. The application will take several months (or longer) to come on for hearing. Even if the application is dismissed, the tenant's tenancy will continue for a further 3 months plus time for appeal, which is currently 21 days. Moreover, except by consent, the court cannot make an order for possession against the tenant in the application; so that if the tenant

refuses to leave at the expiry date of his tenancy, the landlord will be compelled to take fresh proceedings against him. It is, therefore, quite possible that the tenant is still in occupation of the demised property 2 or more years after his tenancy was expressed to expire.

Where the landlord is the owner of other property adjoining the demised property, or where the demised property is part only of a building, the date on which the tenancy is expressed to expire may be of importance. On the one hand, if the landlord has redevelopment plans or if a higher rent could be achieved on a reletting of a greater part of the building, it will be in the landlord's interest to ensure that all tenancies are expressed to expire on the same date. On the other hand, if the landlord is likely to relet the demised property at the end of the tenancy without incorporating it into any greater unit it may be prudent to spread the termination dates so as to prevent a cash flow crisis, which might be occasioned by too many voids at the same time.

Where the landlord is himself a leaseholder, the draftsman should have in mind the length of the landlord's own lease. If he grants a sublease for a term longer than the term of his own lease, the grant may take effect as an assignment of that lease (contrast *Milmo v Carreras* [1946] K.B. 306 and *Parc Battersea Ltd v Hutchison* [1999] 2 E.G.L.R. 33 with *Skelton (William) & Son v Harrison & Pinder Ltd* [1975] Q.B. 361). If he retains a short but more than nominal reversion he may find that at the expiry of the sub-lease he is unable to relet the property. Or, if his reversion is less than 14 months longer than the sub-lease, on the expiry of the sub-lease he will not be the competent landlord for the purposes of Part II of the Landlord and Tenant Act 1954 if his own landlord is prompt in serving a s.25 notice. In that case, he will not be able to increase the rent payable under the sub-tenancy or to oppose the grant of a new tenancy to the subtenant should he wish to do so.

5–04 The tenant's adviser should have in mind and advise the tenant about the obligations assumed by an original tenant, discussed in Chapter 4. The tenant should be advised that he will assume liability for performance of covenants during the period of his own tenure, and that he may be required to guarantee performance of covenants by his assignee. In addition to the statutory mechanism for the protection of tenants, the tenant's adviser should also consider:

(1) regular tenant's break clauses throughout the term; and
(2) the reservation of a right of re-entry on assignment.

In view of the fact that a tenant may be required to guarantee the payment of rent by his immediate assignee, who may hold over under the Landlord and Tenant Act 1954, it is considered that it is still in the landlord's interest to define the term so that it includes statutory continuation, and to include an express contractual liability to pay any interim rent which may become payable under s.24A of that Act. But it has, surprisingly, been held that a definition of the term as including any continuation period prevented the term from being a "term of years certain" with the result that a purported contracting out of security of tenure under Part II of the Landlord and Tenant Act 1954 was ineffective (*Newham LBC v Thomas-Van Staden* [2009] 1 E.G.L.R. 21). In the absence of express provisions to this effect, liability under an authorised guarantee agreement will not extend to these payments (*City of London Corp v Fell* [1994] 1 A.C. 458). If, however, there is an express contractual liability to pay rent during a continuation period and to pay interim rent, it is considered that liability under an Authorised Guarantee Agreement will extend to these amounts (*Herbert Duncan v Cluttons* [1992] 1 E.G.L.R. 101).

Example 5.1 Definition clause making tenant liable for rent during holding over period
"The term" includes not only the term expressed to be granted by this lease but also any period after the date on which the term is expressed to expire during which the tenancy continues under the Landlord and Tenant Act 1954.

Example 5.2 Clause making the tenant liable to pay rent and interim rent
Promptly to pay the rent reserved by this lease without any deduction or set-off and any rent substituted for it either as a result of a rent review under this lease or the agreement or determination of a rent payable by virtue of section 24A of the Landlord and Tenant Act 1954.

2. TENANCY AT WILL

5–05 Part II of the Landlord and Tenant Act 1954 does not apply to tenancies at will (*Hagee (London) Ltd v Erikson (AB)* [1976] Q.B. 209). The essence of such a tenancy is that either party may determine it at will. Accordingly, it may at first sight seem advantageous to a landlord to grant such a tenancy. However, the court will look very carefully at any agreement that is alleged to be a tenancy at will, particularly if the circumstances are not the classic circumstances of holding over or holding pending negotiation. Only a genuine tenancy at will, will escape the provisions of the 1954 Act. A tenancy that is something else, that is to say, either periodic or for a term certain but described as a tenancy at will, will inevitably be caught (*Hagee v Erikson* [1976] Q.B. 209 at 217, per Scarman L.J.). Features that will tend towards a tenancy at will are:

(1) the absence of a right of re-entry;
(2) the absence of onerous repairing covenants;
(3) the absence of a prohibition against assignment;
(4) the absence of any specified period of notice;
(5) a rent payable on demand.

Since machinery now exists that permits a term certain to be contracted out of the 1954 Act's security of tenure, it is unwise, except in special circumstances, for a landlord to take the risk of granting a tenancy at will. It is safer to grant a tenancy for a term certain, subject to a break clause, that is contracted out of the 1954 Act (*Scholl Mfg Co Ltd v Clifton (Slim-Line) Ltd* [1967] Ch. 41 at 51; *Receiver for the Metropolitan Police District v Palacegate Properties* [2000] 3 W.L.R. 519). Equally, from the tenant's point of view the interest granted him under a tenancy at will is so precarious that he would almost always be better off with a fixed term to which the 1954 Act did not apply.

Example 5.3 Informal tenancy at will
Dear Sirs,
Our clients [name] are prepared to permit you to occupy [parcels] from [date] on the following terms:
(1) You will have exclusive possession of the premises as tenant at will only.

(2) Throughout your occupation you will pay rent calculated at the rate of £[ ] per annum payable on demand in advance (but periodic demands shall not convert this tenancy into a periodic tenancy).
(3) A proportionate part of any advance payment will be refunded to you if this tenancy is determined before the expiry of the period which such payment is intended to cover.
(4) You may use the premises for the sole purpose of [ ].
(5) You will keep the premises clean and tidy and will leave them in no worse condition than that in which they are at the date of this letter and free from rubbish.
(6) You may not do or permit to be done in the premises anything which may invalidate or increase the premium payable for any policy of insurance maintained by our clients and you will comply with all requirements and recommendations of our clients' insurers.
(7) You may not allow any other person to occupy the whole or any part of the premises. If you agree to the above terms, please sign the enclosed copy of this letter and return it to us.

Yours etc

3. TERM CERTAIN

The term certain, or fixed term tenancy, is the most common form of business letting. It is only one species of the term of years absolute (defined in s.205(1)(xxvii) of the Law of Property Act 1925). Its main characteristic is that it can be predicated with certainty before the commencement of the term that it will come to an end (subject to any right of re-entry or option to determine) on a known date. Thus, a tenancy for a term of "seven years and thereafter from year to year" is not a term certain because the tenancy will not come to an end until notice is served. **5–06**

From the landlord's point of view, one principal advantage of the term of years certain is that it can be contracted out of the security of tenure that would otherwise be provided by the Landlord and Tenant Act 1954. This may be done by agreement with the tenant and serving the appropriate statutory notice (s.38(A) of the Landlord and Tenant Act 1954). A term certain of less than one year may also be contracted out (*Re Land and Premises at Liss, Hants*

[1971] Ch. 986). The existence of a break clause in the lease does not prevent it from being a term certain (*Metropolitan Police District v Palacegate Properties* [2000] 3 W.L.R. 519). But, as mentioned above, it has been held that a definition of the term as including any continuation period prevented the term from being a "term of years certain" with the result that a purported contracting out of security of tenure was ineffective (*Newham LBC v Thomas-Van Staden* [2009] 1 E.G.L.R. 21). From the tenant's point of view, he has assured security for the term of the lease, subject to compliance with his obligations and continuing solvency.

The legal requirement that a term must be certain means that it is not possible to create a tenancy which will last until the occurrence of an uncertain future event (e.g. until land is required for road widening). The correct way of dealing with this situation is to create a term certain for a long period and then to insert a break clause exercisable on the happening of the event in question (*Prudential Assurance Co v London Residuary Body* [1985] 2 A.C. 386).

A miscellaneous series of incidents attach to various lengths of term. For convenience, the most important of them are set out below:

Term	**Characteristic**
Indefinite	For the calculation of Stamp Duty Land Tax, a periodic tenancy or other interest or right terminable by a period of notice, a tenancy at will, and any other interest or right terminable by notice at any time, is classified as a lease for an indefinite term (Sch.17A, para.4(5) of the Finance Act 2003) and is treated in the first instance as if it were a lease for a fixed term of one year. If the lease continues after the end of that year it is treated as if it were a lease for a fixed term of two years, and so on (Sch.17A para.4(5) of the Finance Act 2003).

6 months Part II of the Landlord and Tenant Act 1954 does not apply to a tenancy for a term of years certain not exceeding 6 months unless:

(1) it contains provision for renewing the term or extending it beyond 6 months from its beginning; or

(2) the tenant has been in occupation for a period which, together with any period during which any predecessor in his business was in occupation, exceeds 12 months (s.43(3) of the Landlord and Tenant Act 1954).

1 year A tenant may only serve a request for a new tenancy under s.26 of the Landlord and Tenant Act 1954, if his tenancy was granted for a term of years certain exceeding 1 year or for a term of years certain and thereafter from year to year (s.26(1) of the Landlord and Tenant Act 1954).

3 years A lease taking effect in possession for a term not exceeding 3 years at a rack rent need not be made by deed and may be made orally (s.54 of the Law of Property Act 1925; s.2 of the Law of Property (Miscellaneous Provisions) Act 1989).

A tenancy granted for a term of years certain of which not less than 3 years remain unexpired is an owner's interest for the purpose of serving blight notices (s.168 of the Town and Country Planning Act 1990).

5 years

The tenant's right to compensation under s.37 of the Landlord and Tenant Act 1954, may be excluded or modified by agreement unless:

(1) during the whole of the 5 years immediately preceding the date on which the tenant under a tenancy to which the Act applies is to quit the holding, premises being or comprised in the holding have been occupied for the purposes of a business carried on by the occupier or for those and other purposes; and

(2) if, during those 5 years, there was a change in the occupier of the premises, the new occupier was a successor to the business carried on by the old occupier (s.38(2) and (3) of the Landlord and Tenant Act 1954).

Note that the crucial date is the date on which the occupier quits, not the date on which the lease is expressed to expire.

7 years A lease for a term of more than 7 years from the date of the grant, whether continuous or discontinuous, must be registered at Land Registry if that grant is made for valuable or other consideration, is by way of gift, or results from a court order (s.4(1)(c) of the Land Registration Act 2002).

If a lease is granted for a term of less than 7 years and the chargeable consideration does not exceed the zero rate threshold it is not notifiable for the purposes of SDLT: (s.77(1)(a) and s.77(A)(5)) of the Finance Act 2003, as amended by the Finance Act 2008 s.94).

The grant of a lease for chargeable consideration for a contractual term of 7 years or more where any chargeable consideration other than rent is less than £40,000 and the relevant rent is less than £1,000 is not notifiable for SDLT (s.77(1)(a) and s.77(A)(4) of the Finance Act 2003, as amended by the Finance Act 2008 s.94).

The Leasehold Property (Repairs) Act 1938 does not apply to a tenancy granted for a term of years certain of less than 7 years (s.7 of the Leasehold Property (Repairs) Act 1938).

14 years The tenant will be entitled (in certain circumstances) to compensation under s.37 of the Landlord and Tenant Act 1954, equal to the production of the appropriate multiplier and twice the rateable value of the holding if:

(1) during the whole of the 14 years immediately preceding the termination of his tenancy, premises being or comprised in the holding have been occupied for the purposes of a business carried on by the occupier or for those and other purposes; and

(2) if during those 14 years, there was a change in the occupier of the premises, the new occupier was the successor to the business carried on by the old occupier (s.37(2) and (3) of the Landlord and Tenant Act 1954). In all other cases, the amount of the compensation will be equal to the product of the appropriate multiplier and the rateable value of the holding.

21 years A lease for a term certain exceeding 21 years is a major interest for the purposes of VAT (s.96(1) of the Value Added Tax Act 1994).

40 years Where a term of more than 40 years is created the tenant may, after the expiry of 25 years of the term, apply to the court for the discharge of any restriction affecting the user of the demised property (s.84(12) of the Law of Property Act 1925).

A building lease for a term of more than 40 years, where the lessor is not a public body, is freely assignable even if it contains a qualified covenant against alienation (s.19(1)(b) of the Landlord and Tenant Act 1927).

50 years	A lease for a term of more than 50 years is a long lease for the purposes of Income and Corporation Taxes. There is a series of complex rules for determining the true length of a lease (s.38 of the Income and Corporation Taxes Act 1988; s.303 of the Income Tax (Trading and Other Income) Act 2005). A lease will usually be a wasting asset for the purposes of capital gains tax when its duration does not exceed 50 years (Sch.8 para.1 of the Taxation of Chargeable Gains Act 1992).
60 years	A lease for a term not exceeding 60 years is a depreciating asset for the purposes of rollover relief (s.154(7) of the Taxation of Chargeable Gains Act 1992).
Any	All leases granted out of unregistered land must be registered at Land Registry if they are to take effect in possession more than 3 months after the date of the grant (s.4(1)(d) of the Land Registration Act 2002).

4. COMMENCEMENT OF THE TERM

The date on which the term is to begin should always be clearly expressed in the lease. It is normal for a fixed term tenancy to begin on one of the usual quarter days (25 March, 24 June, 29 September and 25 December). This practice is convenient both for the purposes of managing the property (since most managing agents, or their computers, send out rent demands by reference to quarter days) and for the purpose of calculating the rent (since broken periods can often be avoided). If the rent is payable monthly it is usually best that the tenancy should begin on the first of the month. 5–07

If possible, the term should be expressed as a whole number of years. This will ease the calculation of important dates during the term (for example, rent review dates or years in which the tenant is liable to paint). If the tenant is let into possession or the lease is completed at a time that makes this inconvenient, the commencement date should be back-dated to a convenient date. For the purposes of calculation the term will then run from the date on which it is expressed to begin, although the tenant's interest will not vest until the date on which the lease is actually executed (*Cadogan (Earl) v Guinness* [1936] Ch. 515).

Where a lease creates a term of years which is expressed to run from some date earlier than that of the execution of the lease, the term created will be a term which begins on the date the lease is executed, and not the earlier date. No act or omission before the date on which the lease is executed will normally constitute a breach of the obligations of the lease. These principles do not prevent the parties from defining the expiration of the term by reference to a date before that of execution of the lease, or from making contractual provisions which take effect by reference to such a date, as by defining the period for the operation of a break-clause or an increase of rent. There is nothing in these principles to prevent the lease from creating obligations in respect of any period before the execution of the lease. Whether in fact any such obligations have been created depends on the construction of the lease; and there is nothing which requires the lease to be constructed in such a way as to avoid, if possible, the creation of such obligations (*Bradshaw v Pawley* [1980] 1 W.L.R. 10, where liability for rent was held to be retrospective). Normally, rent review dates and dates for the exercise of options will be calculated from the date on which the term is expressed to begin, rather than the date of execution of the lease (*Beaumont Property Trust v Tai* [1983] 1 E.G.L.R. 122; *Page v Mallow Investments Ltd* (1974) 29 P. & C.R. 168, but see *Bisichi Mining Ltd v Bass Holdings Ltd* [2002] 2 E.G.L.R. 4 where the lease was interpreted to contrary effect).

The term of a lease is often expressed to run from a particular date. Prima facie, the term will be treated as beginning at midnight between the named date and the day following it (*Meggeson v Groves* [1917] 1 Ch. 158). Thus, a lease for 5 years "from 25 March 2012" will begin at midnight between 25 March 2012 and 26 March 2012; and it will end at the stroke of midnight at the end of 25 March 2017. However, this presumption may be easily rebutted.

The court will, for example, try to construe a lease so that all payments of rent fall due during the term and in respect of periods that fall wholly within it (*Ladyman v Wirral Estates Ltd* [1968] 2 All E.R. 197; *Whelton Sinclair v Hyland* [1992] 2 E.G.L.R. 158). Thus, where rent is payable quarterly in advance on the usual quarter days a term of "5 years from 25 March" will be construed as beginning at the first moment of 25 March, so that the first payment of rent will fall due on the first day of the term and the last payment of rent would be made in respect of a complete quarter, which ends at the last moment of the term. Conversely, if the rent is payable quarterly in arrears the term will be taken to begin at the first moment of 26 March, so that the last payment of rent will fall due on the last day of the term rather than the day after its expiry by effluxion of time.

The safest course for the draftsman to adopt is to express the term as "beginning on" a particular date. If the rent is payable in advance, the date chosen should be a rent day. If the term is expressed to begin or start "on 25 March 2012" for 5 years, that term will usually be considered to start at midnight on 25 March 2012 and will end at the stroke of midnight on 24 March 2017. If the rent is payable in arrear, the date chosen should be the day after a rent day. If the term is expressed to begin in the middle of a rental period, this may distort other parts of the lease; for example, a rent review timetable (*East v Pantiles (Plant Hire) Ltd* [1982] 2 E.G.L.R. 111).

5. BREAK CLAUSES

In recent years there have been many cases before the courts **5–08** involving the interpretation of break clauses. For tenants the commercial imperative has been to exercise their right to terminate successfully in order to divest themselves of surplus or over-rented premises. For landlords the imperative has been to seek to retain their tenants and to maintain their income stream. The downturn in the economy has highlighted that issues regarding the drafting of break clauses can provide a key battleground in times when the interests of landlords and tenants are directly opposed.

In drafting a break clause the draftsman should consider:

(1) who may exercise the break clause;
(2) the time at which the break clause may be exercised;
(3) the manner in which it may be exercised;
(4) whether the circumstances in which the break clause may be exercised should be limited in any way;
(5) the effect on other parts of the lease of the inclusion of a break-clause.

(a) The benefit of the break clause

5–09 In theory, either the landlord or the tenant may be entitled to determine a term certain at a date earlier than that on which it would otherwise expire by effluxion of time. If the landlord is to have such a power it must be expressly conferred on him; if the lease is silent as to the person by whom it is exercisable it will be exercisable by the tenant alone (*Wingfield (LR) v Clapton Construction Co Ltd* (1967) 201 E.G. 769).

A break clause is sometimes expressed to be personal to the first tenant or to a specific assignee. Once the lease has been assigned, the benefit of such a break clause will be lost, even if the lease is subsequently reassigned to the first tenant or to the relevant assignee (*Max Factor v Wesleyan Assurance Society* [1992] 2 E.G.L.R. 210; *Equinox Industrial (GP2) Ltd v Sketchley Ltd* [2003] EWHC 2 (Ch), and *Norwich Union Life & Pensions Ltd v Linpac Mouldings Ltd* [2009] EWHC 1602, (Ch)). A tenant who wishes to retain the benefit of a personal right to break should seek to agree terms for an assignment that will terminate its own personal liability to the landlord on what would have been the break date, or should consider the benefits of sub-letting rather than assignment.

If the tenant company is a group company it may wish to provide that a personal break clause will be capable of assignment to another company within that group (*Harbour Estates Ltd v HSBC Bank Plc* [2005] 1 E.G.L.R. 107). If it does not do so, the benefit of the break clause will be lost if the lease is assigned within the group as part of any corporate restructuring exercise (*3M United Kingdom Plc v Linklaters & Paines (a firm)* [2006] 2 E.G.L.R. 53 (CA)).

The benefit of a personal break clause will not be taken into account on rent review, unless the lease specifically provides for it (*St Martins Property Investments Ltd v CIB Properties Ltd* [1999] L. & T.R. 1).

(b) Time of exercise

5–10 A break clause is a species of option properly so called. Accordingly, any prescribed time-limits must be strictly complied with unless there is express provision to the contrary. The long established principle is that the time for serving a break notice is of the essence (*United Scientific Holdings Ltd v Burnley BC* [1978] A.C. 904).

A break clause may be exercisable on a specified date; for example "at the expiry of the seventh year of the term". This form is not to be recommended to a landlord, because if his power is restricted to a power to determine for certain specified purposes, he may lose the power altogether if he cannot establish the purpose at the crucial date. A better form is "at any time after the expiry of the seventh year of the term." However, from the tenant's point of view this is undesirable. Even if he is able to negotiate a minimum fixed term before the landlord's power to break can be exercised, once that period has expired a notice can come at any time. This greatly impairs proper business planning and may well paralyse investment by the tenant in the property. The tenant is better served if the landlord's power to break arises only at fixed intervals. One matter for the landlord to consider is the impact of the break clause on rent review (*R & A Millett (Shops) Ltd v Legal and General Assurance Society Ltd* [1985] 1 E.G.L.R. 103; *St Martins Property Investments Ltd v CIB Properties Ltd* [1999] L.&T.R. 1). It must also be remembered that if the tenant's ability to exercise a right to break is tied to the dates for rent review under the lease and the landlord alone has the power to trigger a rent review, the right to break will not become exercisable unless and until the landlord triggers the rent review (*Johnsons of London Ltd v Protec Trust Management* (2000) E.G.C.S. 114).

Alternatively, a break clause may be exercisable on the happening of an uncertain event; for example, if a dangerous structure notice is served or if planning permission for a particular use is refused. If the break clause is of this kind, the party entitled to break may equally need flexibility in his choice of time at which to exercise the power. For example, if the tenant has the right to break if the local planning authority refuses to renew a temporary planning permission he may wish to appeal against that refusal. In those circumstances he would be wise to insist that provision be made for a late exercise of the break clause following an unsuccessful appeal. Any draftsman should take care when making a matter conditional upon planning permission that it is clear whether outline planning permission, a permission in relation to reserved matters, or a permission in relation to part only of a proposed development, will be sufficient.

The draftsman should also be aware of the incidence of compensation under s.37 of the Landlord and Tenant Act 1954. If, for example, the landlord has the right to break at the expiry of the twelfth year of the term, rather than at the expiry of the fourteenth year of the term, the tenant's right to compensation on quitting may be halved.

(c) Manner of exercise

5–11 A break clause is usually exercisable by notice in writing. The server must give such notice as satisfies the terms of the lease. If the notice is to be served by recorded delivery at the landlord's registered office then that is how and where the notice should be sent (see, for example, *Orchard (Developments) Holdings Ltd v Reuters Ltd* [2009] 1 E.G.L.R. 13). In some cases it has been held that a method of service described in a contract is not the only possible method of service (*Ener-G Holdings Plc v Hormell* [2012] EWCA Civ 1059). The draftsman should make it clear whether prescribed methods of service are intended to be exclusive.

Thus if the break clause provides that the notice will not be treated as validly served unless it is served on the landlord at its registered office and copied to the landlord's property manager at its own office as well, then the notice must be so served and copied prior to the last date for service if it is to be effective (*Hotgroup Plc v Royal Bank of Scotland Plc (as trustee of Schroder Exempt Property Unit Trust* [2010] 2 P. & C.R. DG23). An effective provision to ensure that the property manager with day-to-day responsibility of a landlord's property portfolio is aware of the tenant's intention in good time, but a provision that is all too likely to be forgotten by the tenant by the date of service unless it reviews its lease carefully.

The draftsman should keep well in mind that, without more, an option to determine may only be exercised by the person in whom the relevant interest is vested at law. Beneficial entitlement is generally insufficient (*Brown & Root Technology Ltd v Sun Alliance & London Assurance Co Ltd* [2001] Ch. 733). As a result, if the drafting states that the notice is to be given by the "landlord" or the "tenant", it must be given by that party, or by an authorised agent on their behalf. If the lease is granted to two companies as tenant, both must serve the notice (*Prudential Assurance Co Ltd v Exel Ltd* [2010] 1 P. & C.R. 7). Some tenants have also fallen foul of the law where the lease is vested in them but a group company physically occupies the premises and actually pays the rent (*Lemmerbell Ltd v Britannia LAS Direct Ltd* [1998] 3 E.G.L.R. 67; *Havant International Holdings Ltd v Lionsgate (H) Investment Ltd* [2000] L. & T.R. 297).

The length of notice is a matter of negotiation between the parties. Where the tenancy in question is one to which Part II of the Landlord and Tenant Act 1954 applies, it is often convenient if the minimum period of notice is 6 months and the form of the notice is capable of being that prescribed for the purposes of s.25 of that Act. In that way, the landlord need serve only one notice (the s.25 notice), which will be effective to bring the tenancy to an end, even if the landlord is not going to oppose any application for a new tenancy (*Scholl Mfg Co Ltd v Clifton (Slim-Line) Ltd* [1967] Ch. 41; *Rene Claro (Haute Coiffure) Ltd v Halle Concerts Society* [1969] 2 All E.R. 842; *Keith Bayley Rogers & Co v Cubes Ltd* (1975) 31 P. & C.R. 412). If notice is given that is sufficient to satisfy the terms of the lease but not the provisions of the 1954 Act, the effect of the notice will be to convert the tenancy from a fixed term tenancy into a tenancy continuing by virtue of s.24 of the 1954 Act (*Weinbergs Weatherproofs Ltd v Radcliffe Paper Mill Co Ltd* [1958] Ch. 437). In those circumstances, the landlord will have to serve a further notice under s.25 of the Landlord and Tenant Act 1954. The s.25 notice may expire any time after the expiry of the break notice. This method of operating the break clause may be advantageous to the landlord in that he may delay the service of a s.25 notice until he is in a position to establish a ground of opposition to an application for a new tenancy.

Where a lease contains a tenant's break clause, and the tenancy is protected by the Landlord and Tenant Act 1954, the tenant cannot serve a s.26 request to take effect on the break date (*Garston v Scottish Widows Fund and Life Assurance Society* [1998] 1 W.L.R. 1583). This means that former drafting practices (such as requiring the tenant to give more than twelve months notice to exercise a break) need no longer be adopted. And once the tenant has served a break notice, he loses the right to make a request for a new tenancy (s.26(4) of the Landlord and Tenant Act 1954).

If a landlord's notice expires in the middle of a rental period, rent paid in advance may need to be apportioned and part repaid. The tenant's adviser would do well to include an express provision to that effect.

In the case of a tenant's notice a requirement that rent be apportioned may work to the prejudice of the landlord since he will need time to arrange a reletting. The landlord should therefore resist such a provision. The general principle, subject to specific drafting, is that if the break date is a quarter day a quarter's rent will fall to be paid by the tenant on that date in any event (see, for example, *Quirkco Investments Ltd v Aspray Transport Ltd* [2012] L. & T.R. 19). The Apportionment Act 1870 does not apply where rent is payable in advance (*Ellis v Rowbotham* [1900] 1 Q.B. 740). From a landlord's point of view, the correspondence between a break date and a quarter day is justifiable both when the break clause is unconditional, and hence it is likely to be unclear up to the actual break date whether the premises will or will not be vacated by the tenant in an appropriate state for an early re-letting, and when the break clause is conditional, such that it will be again be unclear whether the tenant will or will not have performed the requisite conditions precedent in order for the lease to determine. Equally, if the rent is payable in advance on the usual quarter days and the break is exercisable between quarter days, there will be no scope for apportionment unless the lease contains an express apportionment provision. In the absence of such a provision the tenant must pay the entire quarter's rent (see, again by way of example, *PCE Investors Ltd v Cancer Research UK* [2012] 2 P. & C.R. 5).

The tenant's adviser will however wish to consider whether the break date can be identified as the day before the next rental instalment will fall due, so 24 March if a quarter's rent is payable on 25 March, or whether the landlord will agree to the inclusion of an express apportionment provision.

(d) Circumstances of exercise

Landlord's rights to break

5–12 It is rare nowadays for the landlord to have an unrestricted power to determine a lease. The usual way in which his power is circumscribed is by limiting it to a right to break for certain specified purposes. The commonest of these purposes are those of redevelopment and of occupation for the purposes of a business carried on by the landlord. It will be a condition precedent to the exercise of the break clause that the landlord has the necessary bona fide intention (*IRC v Southend-on-Sea Estates Co Ltd* [1915] A.C. 428). However, some latitude is allowed if the landlord has only one opportunity to determine the lease on a specified date. Thus, where landlords were entitled to determine a 21 year lease "at the expiration of 14 years if they shall require the premises for the purposes of a business carried on by them" it was held to be sufficient for them to show that they would need at least part of the premises before the date on which the lease would otherwise have expired by effluxion of time (*Parkinson v Barclays Bank Ltd* [1951] 1 K.B. 368). On the other hand, where a landlord was entitled to determine a lease for "building sites or planting or other purposes", he was held not to be entitled to determine it for the purpose of constructing a sports stadium (*Coates v Diment* [1951] 1 All E.R. 890).

The most satisfactory solution for the landlord (and probably for the tenant) is for the power to break to be modelled closely on the provisions of s.30(1)(f) or (g) of the Landlord and Tenant Act 1954 and for the power to be exercisable on or after a specified date. In that way, the determination of the lease and of the tenant's rights under the 1954 Act can proceed in tandem. Moreover, the weight of authority on the construction of those two subsections will enable both the landlord and the tenant to be more certain of the legal scope of the power. However, it is not advisable to incorporate the section itself. First, the section deals only with "the holding" which may not be the whole of the demise; and secondly the impact of s.31A of the Act may need to be considered. Both these features give unnecessary complexity to the termination of the contractual relationship.

The draftsman must also consider the interrelationship between the date that the landlord needs to demonstrate that the condition precedent is made out for the purposes of the break notice and the date that the landlord needs to prove its intention for the purposes of s.30(1) of the Landlord and Tenant Act 1954. For the purposes of the Landlord and Tenant Act 1954, Part II the relevant date at which the landlord must prove its intention (including, potentially, with a board resolution, planning evidence and evidence of finance) is the date of hearing (*Betty's Cafes Ltd v Phillips Furnishing Stores Ltd* [1957] 1 Ch. 67). As such, if the break clause is to be modelled on the statutory ground, it is suggested that the break clause contains express provision to the effect that the landlord's intention is an intention to occupy or to redevelop at the date of expiry of the notice, and that the landlord need not demonstrate such an intention at the date that the notice is served as well.

If the break clause merely requires the landlord to have a desire (as opposed to an intention) to redevelop, there is no need for the landlord to have worked up a scheme before exercising the break (*Aberdeen Steak Houses Group v Crown Estate Commissioners* [1997] 2 E.G.L.R. 107).

Where the tenancy is protected by the Landlord and Tenant Act 1954, a break clause which relates to only part of the property is wholly ineffective (*Southport Old Links Ltd v Naylor* [1985] 1 E.G.L.R. 66). If it is desired to resume possession of part of the property to be let to a tenant, that part should be demised by a separate lease. The two tenancies may be contained in a single document (*Moss v Mobil Oil Co Ltd* [1988] 1 E.G.L.R. 71). Alternatively, the break clause should relate to the whole property, leaving the landlord free to oppose the grant of a new tenancy.

Tenant's rights to break

5–13 Conditions may also be attached to the exercise of a tenant's break clause. The tenant's adviser should resist the exercise of the break clause being conditional on compliance with the tenant's covenants, for strict compliance will be necessary (*West Country Cleaners (Falmouth) Ltd v Saly* [1966] 3 All E.R. 210); see further at para.5–20. Alternatives which the tenant's adviser should seek are:

(1) that the tenant should have committed no "substantial" or "material" breach of covenant which is subsisting on the termination date;
(2) that the tenant should have "reasonably" performed his covenants; or
(3) that the tenant should have undertaken to pay the cost of remedying any breach found to exist on the termination date.

Depending on the context, the words "material" and "substantial" are interchangeable (*Fitzroy House Epworth Street (No.1) Ltd,*

Fitzroy House Epworth Street (No.2) Ltd v The Financial Times Ltd [2006] 1 W.L.R. 2207). The issue of material compliance is assessed on an objective basis by reference to the ability of the landlord to relet or sell the property without delay or additional expenditure. Where a break-clause is conditional on reasonable performance by the tenant of his obligations, the requirement of reasonableness may be stricter in the case of a break clause than in the case of an option to renew (*Reed Personnel Services v American Express* [1997] 1 E.G.L.R. 229).

Whilst the landlord will wish to ensure that the premises are delivered back to it in a state and condition that will allow it to re-let at the earliest opportunity, the tenant's advisers should resist the exercise of the break clause being conditional on compliance with all the tenant's covenants in the lease in any event. Such compliance can be an impossible task to achieve, particularly if there is scope for a legitimate difference of opinion as to what does or does not amount to performance, or where there is potential for a third party's actions to foil the tenant's attempts at compliance shortly prior to the break date, for example in terms of the tenant's compliance with its covenants to repair or to deliver up vacant possession. The Code for Leasing Business Premises in England and Wales 2007 recommends that the only pre-conditions to tenants exercising any break clauses should be that they are up to date with the main rent, give up occupation and leave behind no continuing sub-leases. The recommendation is that disputes about the state of the premises, or what has been left behind or removed, should be settled later (as if the lease had expired at the end of the term).

At one time it was common for the exercise of the break clause to be conditional on payment by the tenant of a multiple of the annual rent in order to compensate the landlord for the void which will ensue. If there is a time by which such a payment must be made, the time limit must be strictly complied with (*Dun & Bradstreet Software Services (England) v Provident Mutual Life Assurance Association* [1998] 2 E.G.L.R. 175).

If the covenant to pay rent is a condition precedent, the draftsman should consider whether the intention is that the basic rent alone is to be paid, or whether the intention is that all sums reserved as rent are to be paid. If the latter, the tenant's adviser should investigate the interrelationship between the service charge provisions and the break date to ensure that the tenant will not be placed at a practical disadvantage. In such circumstances, the tenant's adviser should also seek to include a provision that the tenant is to be provided with a complete statement of account for the purposes of break clause compliance no later than 14 days prior to the break date if payment of such sums is to be a condition precedent of its right to break. The tenant's adviser should also consider an express exclusion of any interest required to be paid as rent (see, *Avocet Industrial Estate LLP v Merol Ltd* [2012] 1 E.G.L.R. 65).

A break clause that is conditional upon the tenant yielding up the entirety of the demised premises, without more, may cause uncertainty. In the absence of any specific provisions in the break clause, the issue at the break date will be whether the tenant's acts clearly manifest the intention to determine the lease and whether the landlord can occupy the premises without difficulty or objection. So, the question is whether the property is empty of people such that the landlord is able to assume and enjoy immediate and exclusive possession, occupation and control of it, and whether the property is empty of chattels, although this obligation is likely only to be breached if any chattels left in the premises substantially prevent or interfere with the landlord's enjoyment of the right of possession of a substantial part of the property (see *NYK Logistics (UK) Ltd v Ibrend Estates BV* [2011] 4 All E.R. 539, and the discussion in *Legal & General Assurance Society Ltd v Expeditors International (UK) Ltd* [2007] 2 P. & C.R. 10). From a tenant's point of view, it would appear sensible to make the landlord's requirements express, and to provide that the tenant must not leave any chattels in the premises that substantially prevent or interfere with the enjoyment of a substantial part of the premises.

(e) Effect of break clause

5–14 The draftsman should be aware of two important consequences of the insertion of a break-clause.

Firstly, whether the power is exercisable by the landlord or the tenant, the effect of its exercise will be to determine the tenancy prior to the expiry of the term. Thus, any covenant that takes effect at a date calculated by reference to the expiry of the term, will be unenforceable if the power is exercised. For example, where a tenant covenanted to paint in the "last quarter of the said term" it was held that the exercise of a break clause relieved him from his obligation (*Dickinson v St Aubyn* [1944] K.B. 454). It would have been otherwise if he had covenanted to paint in the quarter "preceding the expiry or sooner determination of the said term".

Secondly, if the tenant is entitled to break at a specified date linked to a rent review, the effect of the break clause may be to make time of the essence as far as the review is concerned (*United Scientific Holdings Ltd v Burnley BC* [1977] 2 All E.R. 62 at 77 and 98). This is so even where there is only one date for breaking the lease under the break clause but many reviews. The effect of the linked break clause is to make time of the essence in respect of each review (*Central Estates v Secretary of State for the Environment* [1997] 1 E.G.L.R. 239). If the parties wish to link a tenant's break to a rent review, one solution would be to link it not to the review date itself, but to the date on which the new rent is agreed or otherwise determined. However, if this is done, in the tenant's interest there must be a limit on the landlord's power to operate the review retrospectively. In the normal course of events, the exercise by the tenant of a break clause will prevent him from applying to the court for the grant of a new tenancy (ss.26(4) and 69(1) of the Landlord and Tenant Act 1954; defining "notice to quit" in s.24(2)).

On a commercial note, it may well be that the insertion of a landlord's break will reduce the market rent obtainable for the **5–15**
property, a fact which will doubtless manifest itself at the time of the first rent review after the landlord's power to break has become exercisable. Conversely, the existence of a tenant's right to break may increase the market rent.

On a practical note, it has been held that a landlord and a head tenant cannot effectively agree that, notwithstanding the head tenancy's determination by a break notice, a subtenant will none the less be entitled to retain possession against the landlord for the contractual duration of the subtenancy (*PW & Co v Milton Gate Investments Ltd* [2004] 3 E.G.L.R. 103).

Example 5.4 Landlord's right to break

(1) The landlord shall be entitled to determine this tenancy by not less than six months' notice in writing expiring on or after [date] if he intends at the expiry of such notice either:

    (a) to demolish or reconstruct the demised property or a substantial part of it or to carry out substantial work of construction on the demised property or part of it or

(b) to occupy the demised property for the purposes or partly for the purposes of a business to be carried on by him

(2) The service of a notice under section 25 of the Landlord and Tenant Act 1954 shall be sufficient notice and good service for the purposes of the preceding sub-clause.

Example 5.5 Tenant's right to break on refusal of planning permission

The tenant shall be entitled to determine this tenancy by not less than three nor more than six months' notice in writing served not more than one month after the happening of any of the following events:

(1) the refusal or deemed refusal by the local planning authority to renew the planning permission dated [*date*] permitting the use of the demised property for [ ]

(2) the dismissal by the Secretary of State or an appointed person of any appeal against any such refusal

(3) the expiry of the said planning permission.

Example 5.6 Tenant's conditional right to break

The tenant shall be entitled to determine this tenancy on [ ] if:

(1) he gives twelve months' written notice to that effect and

(2) both at the date of the notice and at the date of its expiry there are neither any outstanding arrears of rent nor any subsisting breach of covenant by the tenant for which the landlord would be entitled to recover damages of more than a nominal amount.

Example 5.7 Tenant's conditional right to break (alternative form: vacant possession)

The tenant shall be entitled to determine this tenancy on [ ] if

(1) it gives not less than six months' written notice to the Landlord at its registered office to that effect and

(2) on the expiry of the notice there are no outstanding rent arrears and

(3) on the expiry of the notice the tenant delivers up the whole of the Premises with vacant possession.

The determination of the tenancy will not affect any liability of the Tenant arising from any other breach of covenant or condition which has occurred before then.

Example 5.8 Tenant's conditional right to break (alternative form: payment)

The tenant shall be entitled to determine this tenancy on [ ] if:

(1) he gives thirteen months' written notice to that effect and
(2) on or before the expiry of the notice he pays to the landlord a sum equivalent to one year's rent at the rate payable at the date when the notice was given and
(3) on the expiry of the notice there are no outstanding rent arrears and no substantial breach of any of the tenant's covenants.

6. OPTIONS TO RENEW

Since the introduction of Stamp Duty Land Tax, it is generally thought that it may be in a tenant's interest to structure its lease as a short lease with an option to renew, rather than as a longer lease with a break option. When a new lease is granted, SDLT is payable both on the premium and on the rent payable for the whole term of the lease; the SDLT on the rent being calculated as 1 per cent of the net present value of the right to receive the rent (inclusive of VAT). As a result, if a short lease is granted with a tenant's option to renew for a further term, the tenant will pay SDLT on the short lease without reference to the option (although, if the option is exercised SDLT will become payable at that stage on the new lease). By contrast, break clauses are inefficient for SDLT purposes. If the tenant takes a longer term lease with a break clause, SDLT will be calculated at the outset on the entire term of the lease. If the tenant exercises the break clause, the tenant will not receive any SDLT rebate in respect of the unexpired residue of the term originally granted. It is, therefore, a matter for the tenant to weigh the SDLT consequences of its favoured lease term against the psychological security of obtaining a lease for the entirety of that term, the risk that it may fail to exercise the option to renew successfully at the relevant date, and the fact that the SDLT payable on the grant of the further lease may be higher by the time that the option is exercised than it would have been originally. The two leases will very probably also be "linked" for SDLT purposes, such that relief will not be available for the new lease if it has been used up by the original lease. **5–16**

Prior to the introduction of SDLT, options to renew had become less frequent in commercial leases since the passing of the Landlord and Tenant Act 1954. There was little reason for the tenant to seek to incorporate an option to renew in his lease unless by reason of his bargaining strength he could secure that the rent payable under the new lease would be lower than that which would be fixed by the court on an application for a new tenancy under the 1954 Act. The only circumstances in which an option to renew would be of practical value to the tenant were where the landlord might be able successfully to oppose the grant of a new tenancy, in such circumstances, however, it was unlikely that the landlord would be prepared to grant an option to renew.

An option to renew might also be granted where the tenancy has been "contracted out" of the Landlord and Tenant Act 1954. The grant of a "contracted out" tenancy, followed by the grant of an option to renew for a term which will not be contracted out is a useful mechanism to achieve a position where the tenant's loss of security of tenure is only temporary. In such cases, the tenant's adviser should ensure that exercise of the option is not conditional on the performance by the tenant of his covenants. However, there may be cases where the landlord requires that the tenant should not acquire security of tenure. In such circumstances the draftsman should ensure that any new tenancy is also "contracted out." Once the tenant exercises the option, he is committed to take the new lease, and it is then too late for the landlord to serve the "health warning notice" that must be served before the tenant is contractually bound to take the new lease. The most reliable method to ensure that the new lease is contracted out is, therefore, to require the tenant to serve a "pre notice" stating that it is minded to exercise the option to renew. The landlord can then serve the "health warning" notice and obtain the tenant's declaration in response, before the tenant is entitled to serve the actual notice exercising the option. The drawback is that it is thought that the tenant will be confined to an action for breach of covenant in the event that the landlord frustrates the process by failing to serve the warning notice.

In any event, the grant of an option to renew may depress the value of the landlord's reversion and reduce the number of potential purchasers of it since the plans of a purchaser who wishes to redevelop or to occupy the property for the purposes of his own business may be frustrated by the exercise of the option.

The following matters must be dealt with in drafting an option to renew:

(1) who may exercise the option;
(2) the time at which it may be exercised;
(3) the manner in which it may be exercised;
(4) the conditions (if any) which the tenant is required to fulfil;
(5) the terms of the new lease;
(6) registration of the option.

(a) Who may exercise the option

If the option is to be personal to the original tenant this must be stated. If the tenant is a group company and the premises are to be occupied by a different group company, an express provision should be included permitting that group company to serve notice (see, for example, *William Page & Co Ltd v BNP Paribas Securities Services Custody Bank Ltd* [2009] L. & T.R. 8). **5–17**

Example 5.9 Personal option to renew

The benefit of this clause is personal to the original tenant who may not dispose of it in any way.

This clause shall become void on the first assignment of this lease and shall remain void even if this lease is later re-assigned to the original tenant.

N.B. Reference should be made to the original tenant rather than the tenant, throughout the clause.

(b) Time of exercise

It is usual to provide that the tenant must exercise the option within a few months before the expiry of the lease. Such time limits must be strictly observed unless there is express provision to the contrary. However, the draftsman should choose his words with care. For example, an option exercisable six months before the "expiry of the tenancy" might permit the tenant to exercise the option during any continuation tenancy (under s.24 of the Landlord and Tenant Act **5–18**

1954); conversely, an option exercisable six months before "the date on which the term hereby granted is expressed to expire" would not. The clause should also state the earliest date upon which the option may be exercised. If no date is specified the court would probably conclude that it was to be exercised within a reasonable period ending on the last day for exercise (*Multon v Cordell* [1986] 1 E.G.L.R. 44).

(c) Manner of exercise

5–19 An option to renew is usually exercisable by notice in writing. There is rarely any need to specify a form of notice, although it is sensible to provide for service of the notice. This is usually done by incorporating the provisions of s.196 of the Law of Property Act 1925, or those of s.23 of the Landlord and Tenant Act 1927. Which of the two is incorporated is largely a matter of taste. It is suggested that one or other method of service be expressly incorporated. Although s.196(5) of the Law of Property Act 1925 (which incorporates the method of service therein prescribed) applies to all leases unless a contrary intention appears, it applies only in respect of notices "required" to be served by the lease in question. It does not apply to notices "permitted" to be served by the lease. It is probable that notices exercising options do not fall within s.196(5) (*Wandsworth LBC v Attwell* [1996] 1 E.G.L.R 57). In some cases it has been held that a method of service described in a contract is not the only possible method of service (*Ener-G Holdings Plc v Hormell* [2012] C.P. Rep. 47; [2012] 45 E.G. 96). The draftsman should make it clear whether prescribed methods of service are intended to be exclusive.

There is no need to take any special measures in order to comply with s.2 of the Law of Property (Miscellaneous) Provisions Act 1989. The service of a traditional form of notice exercising an option is sufficient to bring a binding contract into existence, provided that the original grant of the option (i.e. the lease) was in writing and contained all the terms of the option (*Spiro v Glencrown Properties* [1991] 2 W.L.R. 931).

(d) Conditions precedent

If conditions precedent are prescribed the tenant must fulfil them strictly. In some cases, however, the court may be able to imply a term that even if a condition precedent is not fulfilled, it will not prevent exercise of the option (*Little v Courage* (1994) 70 P. & C.R. 469). It is common for an option to provide that the tenant must have paid all the rent and performed all the covenants. If this form is chosen even a trivial breach of covenant will defeat the tenant's option (*West Country Cleaners (Falmouth) Ltd v Saly* [1966] 3 All E.R. 210; *Bairstow Eves (Securities) Ltd v Ripley* (1992) 65 P. & C.R. 220). However, a breach for this purpose means a subsisting breach, not a "spent" breach in respect of which the landlord no longer has a cause of action (*Bass Holdings Ltd v Morton Music Ltd* [1987] 2 All E.R. 1001). The strict approach was questioned but nevertheless applied in *Kitney v Greater London Properties Ltd* [1984] 2 E.G.L.R. 83. In almost all cases an obstructive landlord will be able to find some subsisting breach of covenant on the tenant's part and thereby defeat the option. This form may, therefore, work hardship to tenants, particularly where there is a genuine dispute as to liability. **5–20**

The tenant's adviser should, therefore, insist that the requirement be that the tenant shall have "reasonably" performed his covenants. In such a case, the exercise of the option will be good if the tenant has performed his covenants to the extent that a reasonably-minded tenant would have done (*Gardner v Blaxill* [1960] 2 All E.R. 457). The inclusion of the word "reasonably" gives the court a discretion which will be exercised in the tenant's favour where for example he has made one or two late payments of rent, but not where he has been persistently in arrear throughout the term (*Bassett v Whiteley* (1982) 54 P. & C.R. 87). Alternatively, the tenant's adviser should insist that the requirement be that the tenant has "materially complied" with all his covenants. The issue of material compliance is assessed on an objective basis by reference to the ability of the landlord to relet or sell the property without delay or additional expenditure. The words "material" and "substantial", depending on the context, are interchangeable (*Fitzroy House Epworth Street (No.1) Ltd, Fitzroy House Epworth Street (No.2) Ltd v The Financial Times Ltd* [2006] 1 E.G.L.R. 19).

This does not, however, mean that the tenant can ignore his obligations. A total failure to comply with an important obligation in a lease (such as a covenant to keep in good decorative condition) is not reasonable compliance with covenants (*Reed Personnel Services v American Express* [1997] 1 E.G.L.R. 229).

The draftsman should next consider whether the conditions are to be fulfilled at the time of the service of the notice or at the end of the term. If they are to be fulfilled at the time of the service of the notice then, for example, the landlord may not be able to rely on a breach of covenant to decorate "in the last year of the term" since no breach of that covenant can be positively asserted until the expiry of the complete year. On the other hand, if the conditions are to be fulfilled at the expiry of the term, the tenant will have the opportunity to remedy any breach of covenant between the service of the notice and its expiry (*Simons v Associated Furnishers Ltd* [1931] 1 Ch. 379). This latter form is fairer to both parties.

(e) Terms of the new lease

5–21 The terms of the new lease should be clearly specified in the grant of the option. Usually, the terms of the new lease will be the same as the terms of the old, but there is no reason why the parties should not provide for variations in those terms. The draftsman should take care in dealing with the option to renew itself. If the option to renew is included in the terms of the new lease, the lease may be treated as a perpetually renewable lease taking effect as a term of 2,000 years (*Parkus v Greenwood* [1950] Ch. 644; *Caerphilly Concrete Products Ltd v Owen* [1972] 1 W.L.R. 372; s.145 and Sch.15 of the Law of Property Act 1922). However, where an option clause enabled the tenant to renew for a term of seven years, and provided that the new lease was to "contain a like covenant for renewal for a further term of seven years on the expiration of the term thereby granted", it was held that the tenant was entitled to renew twice only (*Burnett (Marjorie) Ltd v Barclay* [1981] 1 E.G.L.R. 41). It is difficult to see any significant differences between that case and those in which a perpetually renewable lease has been found to have been created. Accordingly, where the draftsman wishes to create more than one right to renew, it is suggested that a perpetually renewable lease should be expressly negatived.

5–22 As far as the new rent is concerned, options fall into four categories:

(1) options to renew "at a rent to be agreed": such options are void for uncertainty unless some provision is made for determination of the rent in default of agreement (*King's Motors (Oxford) Ltd v Lax* [1969] 3 All E.R. 665) or some provision is made for a minimum or a maximum rent (*Corson v Rhuddlan BC* [1990] 1 E.G.L.R. 255);
(2) options to renew at a rent to be determined in accordance with some stated formula, without any effective machinery for working it out: if necessary the court will supply the machinery in such cases (*Brown v Gould* [1972] Ch. 53);
(3) options with machinery but no detailed formula: in such cases the court is likely to imply a term that the rent is to be fair and reasonable between the landlord and the tenant and will supply machinery for its determination (*Sudbrook Trading Estate Ltd v Eggleton* [1983] A.C. 444);
(4) options which provide both a formula and the machinery for working it out: the draftsman should attempt to make his draft fall into this category.

If the term of the new lease is to exceed, say, five years, the **5–23** draftsman should make provision for the inclusion in the new lease of machinery for reviewing the rent. In the absence of express provision to this effect, the person responsible for determining the new rent will not be able to include rent reviews, nor will he be able to fix a stepped rent (*National Westminster Bank Ltd v BSC Footwear Ltd* [1981] 1 E.G.L.R. 89; *Bracknell Development Corp v Greenlees Lennards Ltd* [1981] 2 E.G.L.R. 105). In Example 5.10 below, the arbitrator is given the powers exercisable by the court on a renewal under the 1954 Act. Those powers contain the power to include in the new lease provision for varying the rent (s.34(3) of the Landlord and Tenant Act 1954).

The drafting of a suitable formula is considered in more detail in the context of rent review.

The parties should consider whether alterations carried out under the original lease are to be rentalised or disregarded under the new lease. The parties will also need to provide for the re-execution of any surety covenants, side letters or rent deposit arrangements. The tenant's advisers should ensure that any superior landlord's or mortgagee's consent to the further lease are obtained before the first lease is executed.

(f) Registration

5–24 An option for renewal is registrable as a Class C(iv) land charge (*Beesly v Hallwood Estates Ltd* [1961] Ch. 105). If it is not registered it will be void against a purchaser of the reversion where the land in question is unregistered land. Where the land is registered land at the time of the demise, if the tenant is in actual occupation of the property the option to renew will be an overriding interest under Sch.1 to the Land Registration Act 2002, and will be enforceable against such a purchaser. Nevertheless, the option should be protected by notice on the register, not least because the protection is confined to the land actually occupied, and because the protection that was given by s.70(1)(g) of the Land Registration Act 1925 to persons who were not in actual occupation of registered land but were in receipt of rent and profits is not replicated by the LRA 2002. A notice cannot be entered in respect of a lease granted for a term of 3 years or less and which is not otherwise required to be registered: s.33(b) of the LRA 2002.

If the option is defeated against a purchaser of the reversion for want of registration, it appears that the tenant may still maintain an action against the original landlord for breach of covenant (*Wright v Dean* [1948] Ch. 686), unless in the meantime the original landlord has been released from liability under the procedure laid down by the Landlord and Tenant (Covenants) Act 1995. It will, therefore, be in the landlord's interest as well as the tenant's to ensure that the option is protected by registration in the appropriate register. This may be done by including in the grant of the option a proviso that it is to be void if it is not registered as an estate contract within, say, 3 months from the date of the lease, or is not protected by the registration of a notice in accordance with the Land Registration Act 2002 if the length of the term is sufficient to enable a notice to be registered.

Example 5.10 Option to renew

(1) The tenant may by notice in writing served not less than six months before the date on which the term hereby granted is expressed to expire call upon the landlord for a further lease of the demised property ("the further lease") provided that up to that date he has paid the rent and reasonably performed and observed his covenants

(2) The further lease shall be for a term of five years from the said date upon the same terms and conditions as this lease (save as to rent and as to this option for renewal) and at a rent to be agreed between the parties or in default of agreement to be determined by a single Arbitrator to be appointed by the President for the time being of the Royal Institution of Chartered Surveyors

(3) In determining the rent payable under the further lease the Arbitrator shall have the same powers as would be enjoyed by the court determining a rent for the demised property under section 34 of the Landlord and Tenant Act 1954 and shall disregard the same matters as are specified in that section

(4) This option shall be of no effect if the tenant fails to register it as an estate contract within three months from the date of this lease or properly registers a notice of the option at the Land Registry against the landlord's title within one month from the date of this lease.

Example 5.11 Option to renew contracted out tenancy

If:

(1) the tenant wishes to take a further tenancy of the demised property for a term of five years from the expiry date of the term hereby created and

(2) the tenant gives written notice of his desire to the landlord not more than six nor less than three months before the expiry of the term and

(3) up to the date of the notice the tenant has paid the rent and substantially performed his covenants and

(4) the landlord gives the tenant a Landlord's Security of Tenure Exclusion Notice in a form complying with the requirements of Schedule 1 to the Regulatory Reform (Business Tenancies) (England and Wales) Order 2003 and

(5) the tenant gives to the landlord a Tenant's Security of Tenure Exclusion Declaration in a form complying with the requirements of Sch.2 to the Regulatory Reform (Business Tenancies) (England and Wales) Order 2003 and

(6) [there has been no assignment of the term of the Lease after the landlord has given the Landlord's Security of Tenure Exclusion Notice]

then the option may be exercised by the tenant giving notice to the landlord to that effect, and the landlord shall let the demised property to the tenant for a term of five years from the expiry of the term hereby created at a rent to be agreed between the parties or in default of agreement to be determined by arbitration and otherwise upon the terms of this lease (except this option for renewal).

Example 5.12 Clause negativing perpetual renewal
Nothing in this clause shall entitle the tenant to renew the tenancy for any term expiring more than twenty years after the beginning of the term of this lease.

7. RENEWAL LEASES

(a) Duration of tenancy

5–25 The duration of a new tenancy granted under the Landlord and Tenant Act 1954 is to be such term as is reasonable in all the circumstances (s.33 of the Landlord and Tenant Act 1954). However, unless the landlord and the tenant agree, the court cannot order the grant of a term exceeding 15 years.

The following factors are among those which are taken into account:

(1) the length of the previous tenancy or tenancies (*Betty's Cafes Ltd v Phillips Furnishing Stores Ltd* [1957] 1 Ch. 67 at 88);
(2) any period during which the tenant has held over pending resolution of his application (*London and Provincial Millinery Stores Ltd v Barclays Bank Ltd* [1962] 1 W.L.R. 510);
(3) the landlord's intentions as regards his own occupation of the property (*Wig Creations Ltd v Colour Film Services Ltd* (1969) 113 S.J. 688, where it was held that the new tenancy should expire shortly after the landlord would become entitled to rely upon s.30(1)(g) of the Landlord and Tenant Act 1954);
(4) the prospects of redevelopment of the property (*Reohorn v Barry Corp* [1956] 2 All E.R. 742; *London and Provincial Millinery Stores Ltd v Barclays Bank Ltd* [1962] 1 W.L.R. 510);

(5) the balance of hardship, and the relative bargaining positions of the parties (*Upsons Ltd v Robins (E) Ltd* [1956] 1 Q.B. 131; *Amika Motors Ltd v Colebrook Holdings Ltd* [1981] 2 E.G.L.R. 62);
(6) the tenant's business needs (*CBS United Kingdom Ltd v London Scottish Properties Ltd* [1985] 2 E.G.L.R. 125);
(7) the tenant's personal circumstances (e.g. his wish to retire from business) (*Becker v Hill Street Properties* [1990] 2 E.G.L.R. 78);
(8) the desirability of maintaining stability in the letting market and the effect of a short lease on the landlord's reversion (*Ganton House Investments v Crossman International* [1995] 1 E.G.L.R. 239).

(b) Break clauses

Where the landlord asserts that there are redevelopment prospects, the court will usually order the new tenancy to contain a break clause enabling the landlord to terminate the lease for redevelopment. It is no part of the policy of the Landlord and Tenant Act 1954 to give security of tenure to a business tenant at the expense of preventing redevelopment (*Adams v Green* [1978] 2 E.G.L.R. 46). The duty of the court to strike a reasonable balance between the conflicting interests of the landlord and the tenant entitles the court to order the grant of a tenancy which will delay the development, but not for so long as to frustrate it (*Davy's of London (Wine Merchants) v City of London Corp* [2004] 3 E.G.L.R. 39). **5–26**

Accordingly, where the landlord proves an intention to redevelop not immediately capable of implementation, the court will order the inclusion of a break clause exercisable when the landlord is ready. It does not matter that the redevelopment is likely to be carried out by a purchaser from the landlord rather than the landlord himself (*Adams v Green* (1978) 247 E.G. 49; *Davy's of London (Wine Merchants) Ltd v City of London Corp* [2004] 3 E.G.L.R. 39)); nor that the redevelopment proposals are very tentative (*JH Edwards & Sons Ltd v Central London Commercial Estates Ltd* [1984] 2 E.G.L.R. 103). The function of the court in such circumstances is to strike a reasonable balance between the conflicting considerations of not preventing redevelopment on the one hand, and giving the tenant a reasonable degree of security of tenure on the other. The court has two objects in mind: first, to give the tenant security for as long as the holding is not required for development; secondly, to ensure that when the landlord is ready to proceed with the development, the development is not held up by rights possessed by the tenant (*National Car Parks v Paternoster Consortium* [1990] 1 E.G.L.R. 99). But the court may take into account hardship to the tenant. Thus, where the tenant had been innocently misled into believing that he would obtain a long term, and had invested heavily in the property next door, whereas the landlord in fact had plans for immediate redevelopment, the Court of Appeal upheld an order for a break clause exercisable after the first 3 years of the term (*Amika Motors Ltd v Colebrook Holdings Ltd* [1981] 2 E.G.L.R. 62).

The court will take into account the fact that the landlord must prove a statutory ground of opposition in order effectively to operate the break clause (*Adams v Green* [1978] 2 E.G.L.R. 46) and accordingly will not attach much weight to objections which could be raised by the tenant when the landlord seeks to operate the break-clause (*Amika Motors Ltd v Colebrook Holdings Ltd* [1981] 2 E.G.L.R. 62).

In the present state of the law, the landlord is in a strong position if he wishes to include a break clause in a new lease.

Where the landlord seeks a break clause on renewal, the tenant should press for any right to break to be mutual. If the tenant accepts that the property may be redeveloped he will probably wish to be looking for alternative accommodation sooner rather than later, and he will wish to move in and terminate his liability under his existing lease as soon as he finds it.

(c) Options

5–27 The court has no jurisdiction to order a new tenancy to contain an option entitling the tenant to purchase the landlord's reversion (*Kirkwood v Johnson* (1979) 38 P. & C.R. 392).

It is suggested that the court would not order a new lease to contain a contractual option to renew, since the Landlord and Tenant Act 1954 itself contains the code for enabling tenants to renew their leases.

CHAPTER 6

RENT AND RENT REVIEW

1. THE INITIAL RENT AND RENT FREE PERIODS

The fixing of the initial rent is obviously beyond the province of the draftsman. However, there are some drafting points which should be considered.

(a) Stamp Duty Land Tax

The first concerns Stamp Duty Land Tax ("SDLT"). Whilst a full treatment of SDLT is outside the scope of this work and reference should be made to a specialist text, the following general points should be taken into consideration. SDLT is chargeable on land transactions (ss.42(1), 43(1) and 48(1) of the Finance Act 2003, other than those exempt from charge, as to which, for example, see Sch.3 of the Finance Act 2003), and not instruments. The charge applies to leases other than tenancies at will (s.48(2)(c)(i) of the Finance Act 2003). It also applies when an agreement for lease is "substantially performed" (s.44(4)–(7) and (8) of the Finance Act 2003, as amended by the Stamp Duty and Stamp Duty Land Tax (Variation of the Finance Act 2003) Regulations 2003 and the Finance Act 2004); when the lease is formally "granted" (s.77 and 77A of the Finance Act 2003, as substituted by s.94(1) and (2) of the Finance Act 2008); on any variation; on any assignment; on a surrender; and on the exercise of any option to renew. It also applies by whatever means the transaction is effected, whether by act of the parties, by operation of law or by order of the court (s.43(2) of the Finance Act 2003). Liability to pay SDLT is the liability of the acquiring party (s.85 of the Finance Act 2003). **6–01**

The chargeable consideration for the transaction is, subject to certain exceptions, any consideration in money or money's worth given for the subject matter of the transaction, directly or indirectly, by the purchaser or a person connected with him (Sch.4 para.1 of the Finance Act 2003). It is charged by reference to both premium and rent (Sch.5 para.9 of the Finance Act 2003, as amended by the Finance Acts 2008 and 2011). The consideration will include VAT, other than VAT payable by virtue of waiver or exemption from VAT made subsequent to the effective date of the transaction (Sch.4 para.2 of the Finance Act 2003, as amended by the Value Added Tax (Buildings and Land) Order 2008). No discount will be made if payment of part of the consideration is postponed (Sch.4 para.3 of the Finance Act 2003). Market value is taken as the consideration in certain cases, such as where the transaction is between connected companies (Sch.4 paras 4, 5, 6 and 7 of the Finance Act 2003), and in the case of connected companies (ss.53 and 54, as amended by the Finance Act 2004).

6–02 The following do not count as chargeable consideration on the grant of a lease (Sch.17A para.10 of the Finance Act 2003, as amended by the Finance Act 2004 and the SDLT (Amendment to the Finance Act 2003) Regulations (SI 2006/875):

- any undertaking by the tenant to repair, maintain or insure the demised premises;
- any undertaking by the tenant to pay any amount in respect of services, repairs, maintenance or insurance or the landlord's costs of management;
- any other obligation undertaken by the tenant that is not such as to affect the rent that a tenant would be prepared to pay in the open market;
- any guarantee of the payment of rent or the performance of any other obligation of the tenant under the lease;
- any penal rent, or increased rent in the nature of a penal rent, payable in respect of the breach of any obligation of the tenant under the lease;
- any other obligation of the tenant to bear the landlord's reasonable costs or expenses of or incidental to the grant of a lease.

In the case of the grant, assignment or surrender of a lease a reverse premium does not count as chargeable consideration. A "reverse premium" means, in relation to the grant of a lease, a premium moving from the landlord to the tenant (Sch.17A para.18 of the Finance Act 2003, inserted by the Finance Act 2004).

A lease premium will, however, include (Sch.4 of the Finance Act 2003, as amended):

- consideration or money's worth, including surrenders of existing leases or sale and leaseback arrangements;
- VAT on any lump sum payable;
- leases granted in satisfaction of indebtedness;
- leases granted where there are related obligations to carry out works, whether upon the leased land or other land. "Works" is defined to include works of construction, improvements, repairs or other works to enhance the value of the land (Sch.4 para.10(1) of the Finance Act 2003). The SDLT is payable upon the open market cost of the works. The exclusion from charge for the tenant's own works is only available where these take place after "the effective date" of the grant of the lease (Sch.4 para.10(1)(a) and para.2);
- the provision of services; and
- sums payable periodically.

Where the whole or part of the chargeable consideration is contingent, the amount or value of the consideration will be determined on the assumption that the outcome of the contingency will be such that the consideration is payable or does not cease to be payable (s.51(1) of the Finance Act 2003, as amended by the Finance Act 2004). A refund will be made if the contingency does not happen (s.80 of the Finance Act 2003, as amended by the Finance Act 2004). This would apply if the lease was granted at a basic premium and contained provision for an additional sum to be paid if a planning permission was obtained.

Where the whole or part of the premium is uncertain or unascertained, its amount or value will be determined on the basis of a reasonable estimate of what will eventually be payable with an obligation to report and pay tax or claim a refund (ss.51(2) and 80 of the Finance Act 2003, as amended by the Finance Act 2004). Separate rules relating to rent apply where the amount of rent varies in accordance with provisions in the lease, or is contingent, uncertain or unascertained (Sch.17A para.7 of the Finance Act 2003, amended by the Finance Act 2004).

The amount of tax payable is a percentage of the chargeable consideration. The percentage payable is dependent upon the premium, the rent payable under the lease and whether the property is or is not residential (as defined in s.116 of the Finance Act 2003), or includes land that is not residential property (s.55 of the Finance Act 2003, as amended by the Finance Acts 2006, 2009 and 2010).

The following percentages are applicable to non-residential or mixed property (s.55 Table B of the Finance Act 2003, as amended):

Table 1: Non-residential land or property rates and thresholds

Relevant consideration	**SDLT Rate (%)**
Up to £150,000	0
More than £150,000 but not more than £250,000	1
More than £250,000 but not more than £500,000	3
More than £500,000 but not more than £1,000,000	4
More than £1,000,000	5

For these purposes the annual rent is the highest annual rent known to be payable in any year of the lease, not the net present value used to determine any tax payable on the rent as described below.

6–03 Where there is chargeable consideration other than rent, in other words a premium, the nil rate band does not apply if the rent exceeds £1,000 per annum. The annual rent is taken as the average annual rent payable under the lease and, in such a case, the rent that would have fallen into the nil rate band is taken to fall within the one per cent band (Sch.5 para.9 of the Finance Act 2003, as amended by the Finance Acts 2008 and 2011). Chargeable consideration for the grant of a lease which is in respect of a period before the lease is granted is not rent for SDLT purposes, even if described as such, but may be taxed as a premium (see the Guidance provided by HM Customs & Revenue, SDLTM17110).

Where a new non-residential or mixed use lease has a substantial annual rent, SDLT is payable on both (a) the lease premium or purchase price (as set out in Table 2 below) and (b) the net present value of the rent payable (Sch.5 para.2 Table B of the Finance Act 2003).

Table 2: SDLT on rent for new leasehold properties (non-residential or mixed use)

Net Present Value of Rent: Non-Residential	SDLT Rate
£0–£150,000	0
Over £150,000	1% of the value that exceeds £150,000

The SDLT chargeable in respect of so much of the chargeable consideration as consists of rent is a percentage of the net present value of the rent payable over the term of the lease (Sch.5 para.2 of the Finance Act 2003). The percentage again depends upon whether the property is or is not residential (as defined in s.116 of the Finance Act 2003), or includes land that is not residential property (Sch.5 para.2) of the Finance Act 2003, and see the Guidance provided by HM Customs & Revenue, SDLTM18410).

If property is mixed use in a disadvantaged area, the residential part may qualify for Disadvantaged Areas Relief (check Sch.6 of the Finance Act 2003, subject to the provisions for repeal in the Finance Act 2012 for transactions with an effective date on or after April 6, 2013 and the time limit for all residential relief claims of April 5, 2014, and transitional provisions).

The formula for determining the amount of the rent upon which the SDLT is to be charged is:

$$v = \sum_{i=1}^{n} \frac{r_i}{(1 + T)^i}$$

Where "v" is the net present value of the rent;
"r" is the rent payable in year "i";
"i" is the first, second, third etc years of the term;
"n" is the term of the lease; and
T is the temporal discount rate, currently 3.5 per cent but subject to change by statutory instrument.

Basically, the formula is an attempt to capitalise the rent by aggregating the rent payable over the term of the lease, subject to suitable discounts.

6–04 Leases where the rent is constant throughout the term, or where the rent is expressed to increase to agreed stepped levels or where the rent is linked to the Retail Prices Index are treated as certain rents such that the tax is calculated on actual figures (subject to RPI adjustments). Separate rules apply where the amount of rent varies in accordance with provisions in the lease, or is contingent, uncertain or unascertained (Sch.17A para.7 of the Finance Act 2003, as amended by the Finance Act 2004). Turnover rents, profit sharing rents and leases containing rent review clauses to market rent are all variable and uncertain. The normal rules relating to contingent consideration apply as regards rent payable up to the end of the fifth year of the term. After the end of the fifth year, the annual rent is assumed to be the highest amount payable in respect of any consecutive twelve-month period in the first five years of the term (Sch.17A para.7(3) of the Finance Act 2003). This assumed rent is applied for all years of the term after the fifth year. Broadly speaking, if the rent has doubled or more than doubled since the fifth year it will be classified as an "abnormal" increase in rent under the Act, even if made in accordance with a provision in the lease, a further SDLT return must be made and tax is chargeable on the excess (Sch.17A paras 14 and 15 of the Finance Act 2003, as amended by the Finance Acts 2004 and 2006; and see the discussion "SDLT and Abnormal Rent Increases: Seven Anomalies", Paul Clark, *Landlord & Tenant Review* (2008) p.206).

6–05 There are issues surrounding the reservation of matters such as service charge as rent. Sums are to be treated as rent where a single sum is expressed to be payable either in respect of rent or in respect of rent and other matters but not apportioned (Sch.17A para.6 of the Finance Act 2003, inserted by the Finance Act 2004). So, where a single sum is payable in respect of rent and service charge and/or the service charge is not separately provided for in the terms of the lease, then the sum is to be treated entirely as rent for SDLT purposes.

However, the fact that a service charge is reserved in the lease as rent does not make it rent for SDLT purposes. Service charges payable from tenant to landlord are not chargeable consideration for stamp duty purposes and are excluded from the calculation of tax so long as payment of the service charge has either been (1) provided for in the lease as a separate figure or (2) expressed in the lease as part of an inclusive rent payment and apportioned on a just and reasonable basis. Where apportionment of an inclusive figure is needed this must be made on a just and reasonable basis for SDLT purposes and will not necessarily be the same as any apportionment set out in the lease itself. If the service charge element is included in the rent, and is likely to vary, this will make the rent "uncertain" for SDLT purposes. This treatment applies equally to other non-chargeable consideration.

It will be essential for advisers to carry out the relevant calculations prior to the grant of the lease in order to identify the length of term that is most suitable to meet the clients' overall requirements. The potential impact of SDLT may suggest that it will be in a tenant's interest to take a short-term lease, perhaps with an option to renew. The option will be ignored in determining the term of the lease (Sch.17A para.2 of the Finance Act 2003, as amended by Finance Act 2004), but it has yet to be resolved whether a lease which comes into being as a consequence of an option to renew is a linked transaction.

(b) VAT

Secondly, the draftsman must now consider the potential impact of **6–06**
VAT. The following matters are of importance, however an in-depth treatment of this subject is beyond the scope of this work, and the reader should refer to a specialist text. Where there is a direct causal link between the grant of a rent free period and the carrying out by the tenant of work to the property, and the tenant is obliged to carry out such work (e.g. shopfitting), for the landlord's benefit the tenant will be treated as making a supply to the landlord of an amount equivalent to the rent foregone. The tenant will be liable for the VAT (*Ridgeons Bulk v Commissioners of Customs & Excise* [1994] S.T.C. 427, discussed in [1994] E.G.C.S. 68, and the Tribunal case of *Port Erin Hotels* (MAN/89/722). However, rent free periods will not be treated as consideration for supplies by the tenant where the rent free periods are offered in order for the tenant business to fit out the premises to its own specifications (thereby not being able to use the premises fully during that time), or in order to reduce the

actual rent to a market level while the lease still shows the higher level (see HM Customs & Excise Guidance, VATSC47000).

In addition, where the landlord pays an inducement to the tenant in order to persuade the tenant to take up the lease, for example payments by the landlord to the tenant to carry out building works to improve the property by undertaking necessary repairs or upgrading or re-equipping of the property, that is a payment on which the tenant must account for VAT (*Gleneagles Hotel* [1986] V.A.T.T.R. 196 and *Nevile Russell v Commissioners of Customs & Excise* [1987] V.A.T.T.R. 194. It is not considered that the decisions in these cases were affected by the European Court of Justice's findings in para.26 of the ECJ's *Mirror Group Plc* (C-409/98) decision, and *Trinity Mirror Plc v C&E Commrs* [2003] S.T.C. 518; HM Revenue & Customs VATSC47000]).

If there is clear evidence that a tenant is acting as an "anchor tenant" in a (normally retail) development, and is paid an inducement for this, affording the landlord the right to use that tenancy generally to market the development or enabling the landlord to obtain finance for the project, the tenant will be regarded as an "anchor" for VAT purposes, and treated as supplying a taxable benefit (HM Revenue & Customs VATSC46800). Taxable benefits for which reverse premiums constitute consideration also include cases where a tenant undertakes to move a business to the new property and, in so doing, dispose of old property under conditions set by the new landlord (HM Revenue & Customs VATSC46800).

Lease obligations to which a tenant is normally bound do not constitute supplies for which inducement payments on entering into leases are consideration (see *Trinity Mirror Plc v C&E Commrs* [2003] S.T.C. 518).

6–07 The general principle for VAT is that consideration for a supply is inclusive of VAT unless otherwise stated. Thus, if the landlord has elected to waive the exemption from VAT in respect of a particular building, he will not be able to add VAT to the rent if it is expressed as a single figure. If the rate of VAT changes, he will be able to pass on any increase. However, if the landlord has not elected to waive the exemption from VAT, VAT will not be chargeable on the rent. If he subsequently decides to waive the exemption, he will be able to add VAT unless that is forbidden by the terms of the lease (s.89 of the VAT Act 1994, as amended by the Value Added Tax (Buildings and Land) Order 2008). A term in a lease does not negative this rule unless it refers specifically to VAT or to s.89 of the Act (s.89 of the VAT Act 1994). The tenant should ensure that in the event that the landlord waives the exemption from VAT the tenant will not be liable for any additional sums of VAT in respect of rent until such time as the correct documentation has been supplied to the tenant. By so doing, the tenant can ensure that payments of VAT cannot accrue due without the tenant's knowledge (*Foreign Properties APS v Secretary of State for Health* [2004] 2 P. & C.R. 5).

The exemption can only be waived on a building-by-building basis. However, it seems that if the exemption is waived for a building as a whole, but if a lease of part of the building prohibits the addition of VAT, the landlord will have to account to HMRC for VAT out of the net rent. Some tenants prefer, however, to seek to obtain from the landlord a covenant not to waive the exemption. If this route is taken it will be necessary, from the tenant's point of view, for the landlord to covenant to procure a similar covenant from successors in title.

Special provisions for the taxation of reverse premiums are now to be found in the Income Tax (Trading and Other) Income Act 2005 and the Corporation Tax Act 2009.

Example 6.1 Clause preventing landlord from charging VAT

In the event that the landlord elects to waive any exemption from value added tax in relation to the demised property or the building of which it forms part, no value added tax shall be added to the rent reserved by this lease.

Example 6.2 Clause preventing landlord from waiving exemption from VAT

(1) not to elect to waive any exemption from value added tax in relation to the demised property or the building of which it forms part

(2) on any assignment of the whole or part of the reversion expectant on this lease, or the grant of any concurrent lease of the whole or part of the property, to procure that the assignee or lessee gives a covenant in the terms of this clause.

2. DEDUCTIONS FROM RENT

6–08 There are a number of circumstances in which a tenant is entitled to withhold some or all of the rent which is otherwise payable. Some of these are laid down by statute. For example, where rent is paid to a non-resident landlord, the Revenue can require the tenant to deduct income tax from the amount of the rent (s.944 of the Income Tax Act 2007). Other statutes enable a tenant to make deductions where he has paid the cost of certain works (s.212 of the Highways Act 1980, s.10 of the Coast Protection Act 1949 and s.33 of the Local Government (Miscellaneous Provisions) Act 1976, as amended). In other cases, the tenant has a right at common law to make deductions; for example, where he pays for repairs which are the landlord's responsibility (*Lee-Parker v Izzet* [1971] 1 W.L.R. 1688), or ground rent (*Jones v Morris* (1849) 3 Exch. 742) or mortgage interest (*Johnson v Jones* (1839) 9 Ad. & El. 809) which is the landlord's liability. In addition, the tenant is entitled to set off against his liability to pay rent any cross-claim (whether liquidated or unliquidated) which arises out of the lease itself or the relationship of landlord and tenant (*British Anzani (Felixstowe) v International Marine Management* [1980] Q.B. 137). In certain circumstances, the landlord may set off a claim for damages resulting from the tenant's failure to pay service charges against the tenant's claim for damages for disrepair (*Bluestorm v Portvale Holdings* [2004] 2 E.G.L.R. 38).

The tenant's right to deduct may be excluded by the express terms of the covenant to pay rent (except in certain cases where statute prohibits contracting out). But where the draftsman wishes to exclude the tenant's right to set off, clear words must be used (*Connaught Restaurants Ltd v Indoor Leisure Ltd* [1994] 1 W.L.R. 501). The phrase "without deduction" is not clear enough to exclude the right to set off. It is considered that only the use of the words "set off" themselves will be clear enough (see *Altonwood Ltd v Crystal Palace FC (2000) Ltd* [2005] EWHC 292 (Ch), where the words "without set off" were held to include equitable as well as legal set off). An anti set-off clause is not invalidated by the Unfair Contract Terms Act 1977 (*Unchained Growth III v Granby Village (Manchester) Management Co* [2000] 1 W.L.R. 739). However, an anti set-off clause will only apply to a claim for misrepresentation if it is reasonable (s.3 of the Misrepresentation Act 1967, *WRM Group v Woods* [1998] C.L.C. 189).

Example 6.3 Covenant to pay rent
To pay the rent promptly and without deduction or legal or equitable set-off.

(a) Generally

6–09 A payment of rent before it is due is not a fulfilment of an obligation to make that payment. If a payment is made in advance of the due date it will not count towards payment of the rent unless there is an express or implied agreement to that effect (*De Nicholls v Saunders* (1870) 5 L.R.C.P. 589; *Lord Ashburton v Nocton* [1915] 1 Ch. 274). An erroneous payment in respect of turnover rent was not treated as a prepayment of or discharge of the future obligation to pay rent, in particular the basic rent: (*Altonwood Ltd v Crystal Palace FC (2000) Ltd* [2005] EWHC 292 (Ch)).

(b) Interest

6–10 Provision should be made for the payment of interest in the event of the late payment of rent. If the rent payable is a set amount payable on a set day, it is reasonable for interest to be charged from the day that payment is due. In the case of irregular payments, tenants should be given a period of grace, for example 10 business days, before interest is charged. If no payment is made during that period of grace, interest should be charged from the date of default. The contractual interest rate has traditionally been set at three per cent over the base rate in recent years.

A landlord may wish to include provision for interest to be paid in the event that a tenant is in breach of covenant and the landlord rejects a tendered payment in order to avoid waiving the breach. If the landlord is found to have been wrong, or the tenant's breach is held to be trivial, no interest should be payable. However, if the tenant is found to be in material breach of covenant, the landlord should be entitled to interest on the outstanding rent from the date that it fell due. The tenant's adviser should press for interest to be payable at the base rate in such circumstances.

3. RENT REVIEW

6–11 In recent years, it has become the practice in leases granted for more than five years or so to contain some machinery for enabling the rent to be reviewed, either continuously or at periodic intervals. The rent review clause, or the indexation of rent, is the product of the conflict between the tenant who wishes to have the maximum length of term and the landlord who wishes to have the maximum return on his investment. It is nowadays quite unrealistic for a tenant even to attempt to secure a long letting of commercial property at a fixed rack rent; and no well-advised landlord would grant such a lease. Since the value of a property investment is primarily the receipt of a secure rent, the rent review clause is the most important provision in the whole lease.

The revision of rents can be achieved in a number of ways. The most common is for the rent to be periodically revised to a figure agreed between the parties, with procedure for determination by a third party if the landlord and tenant fail to agree. This is the best method because it is most closely related to the value of the property itself. It is not, however, the only method and others are considered below.

The Code for Leasing Business Premises in England and Wales 2007 presently recommends that headline rent review clauses should not be used, and that in negotiation landlords should on request offer alternatives to their proposed option for rent review priced on a risk-adjusted basis. An example given as an alternative to an upwards only review is an upwards or downwards review to market rent with a minimum of the initial rent, or reference to another measure such as annual indexation. The Code also recommends that leases should allow both landlords and tenants to start the review process.

4. INDEX-LINKED RENTS

6–12 Draftsmen have sometimes attempted to link the rent payable under a lease to movements in an official index, such as the Index of Retail Prices (as happened in *Blumenthal v Gallery Five Ltd* (1971) 220 E.G. 33). It is understood that such clauses are more common on the Continent. Commercially, such a rent review clause may work to the disadvantage of either party. On the one hand, if the chosen index rises faster than rents, or if rents fall, the tenant may find himself paying a rent in excess of the market rent; on the other hand, if rents rise faster than the chosen index, the landlord may find himself receiving an uneconomic return from his property. In addition, a rent which is index-linked will not reflect any change in the property itself. Thus, if an out of town retail park or superstore is developed during the term of the lease the trading potential of a high street shop may be severely affected, but an index-linked rent will not be capable of reflecting that change.

Sometimes, the parties may choose an informal index. Where, for example the rent of a petrol filling station was to be increased by reference to the rise in rents of other comparable filling stations, the Court of Appeal held that, in effect, the parties had chosen to index link the rent to rental values of filling stations generally (*British Railways Board v Mobil Oil* [1994] 1 E.G.L.R. 46).

The drafting of an indexation clause presents various problems. Firstly, the parties must agree on their chosen index. Various indices now exist and it may be that the choice of index should to some extent be determined by the nature of the property. Thus, the rent of a shop might be determined by reference to the Index of Retail Prices, the rent of a warehouse by reference to the Index of Wholesale Prices, and the rent of a builder's merchant's yard by reference to an index of construction costs. The index most often used for this purpose is the General Index of Retail Prices published by the Office for National Statistics, although the government's preferred measure is now the Consumer Price Index. Some of the larger firms of surveyors produce property indices, but the statistical sample is probably too small to enable them to be reliable.

Secondly, the parties should be aware that the items taken into account in compiling the index may vary from time to time. **6–13**
Accordingly, the basis on which the rent is calculated may itself be changed through a change in the composition of the index. This was the problem that arose in *Blumenthal v Gallery Five Ltd* (1971) 220 E.G. 33 and *Cumshaw v Bowen* [1987] 1 E.G.L.R. 30. It is unusual to provide expressly for this contingency and the lease is probably best left silent on this point. A major change in the composition of the index is one of the gambles inherent in this form of rent review.

Thirdly, the base figure upon which the index is calculated may be updated. Thus, if the index starts with a base figure of 100 in, say, January 2013 and rises to 300 by September 2033, the index may be recalculated from October 2033 onwards by reference to the figure shown in the index for September 2033, which becomes the new base figure of 100. The draftsman must provide expressly for this contingency, otherwise the landlord will face a sudden drop in the rent if the base figure used for the index is recalculated. There are two principal methods of dealing with this. One is to provide that the rent shall be calculated as if the index had not been adjusted. This method works fairly well provided that the publishers of the index provide a conversion table enabling the current figures to be related to earlier figures, and usually they do so. However, it may give rise to the necessity for a fairly sophisticated mathematical calculation if a conversion table is not published. If the clause provides for the substitution of figures, it is important to ensure that all necessary mathematical information is given to enable the rent to be calculated (see *Wyndham Investments v Motorway Tyres and Accessories* [1991] 2 E.G.L.R. 114 for a case where this was not done, and the index-linked rent failed completely).

The alternative method is to provide that upon any adjustment of the base figure, the rent payable immediately before the adjustment becomes a fixed amount payable under the terms of the lease (or is substituted for a fixed amount previously reserved). The indexation process then begins again, using the new figures. The advantage of this method is that there is no need for any conversion from one set of figures to another. However, the disadvantage from the tenant's point of view is that the minimum rent payable under the lease will be increased. Accordingly, he will be unable to take the benefit of any fall in the index.

6–14 The fourth point that the draftsman must cover is the possible abandonment of the index. It may become impossible to calculate the index-linked rent. Again, there are two principal methods of dealing with this contingency. First, the draftsman may provide for the substitution of a different index to be agreed between the parties or determined by a third party in default of agreement. Alternatively, he may provide for a change in the method of rent review, and if this is done it is usual to revert to the more traditional method of periodic reviews to market rent. Another choice is to leave the new method of rent review open for agreement at the time indexation proves to be impossible. In this way, either party will be able to take advantage of any significant change in market practice during the currency of the lease.

Fifthly, the clause must be mathematically correct. Since it is often difficult to translate mathematical concepts into words (see *London Regional Transport v Wimpey Group Construction* [1986] 2 E.G.L.R. 41 for judicial commendation of algebra), the formula must be checked mathematically either with a calculator or a computer. One unfortunate error which is made from time to time is that the indexation relates back to the beginning of the lease, so that inflation is double counted. Although this may not be noticeable in the early years of a lease, its compound effect over time may be disastrous.

Allied to the indexation of rent is the reservation of rent calculated by reference to the price of some specified commodity, such as gold, or by reference to the value of the pound in relation to a foreign currency. In *Treseder-Griffin v Co-operative Insurance Society Ltd* [1956] 2 Q.B. 127, the rent reserved was 1,900 "either in gold sterling or Bank of England notes to the equivalent value in gold sterling". The Court of Appeal held that the rent payable was 1,900 rather than the realisable value of 1,900 gold sovereigns. The decision was based on two grounds. First, it was held by Denning L.J. that a "gold clause" in a domestic contract was void as being contrary to public policy. Secondly, it was held that on the proper construction of the lease the provisions relating to gold regulated the manner of payment rather than the amount of payment. It is suggested that the first of these reasons would no longer be valid if litigated again (see *Multiservice Bookbinding Ltd v Marden* [1979] Ch. 84, where Browne-Wilkinson J. upheld a mortgage under which the interest payments were linked to the value of the Swiss franc, cited with apparent approval by Lord Denning M.R. in *Staffordshire Area Health Authority v South Staffordshire Waterworks Co* [1978] 3 All E.R. 769). The second of these reasons can be overcome by careful drafting. **6–15**

Example 6.4 Index-linked rent: upwards only from initial rent

YIELDING AND PAYING the annual sum of £[ ] ("the Basic Rent") payable quarterly in advance on the 25th of March the 24th of June the 29th of September and the 25th of December in each year and in addition such sum payable on each of the above dates in advance ("the Index-Linked Rent") as bears the same proportion to one quarter of the Basic Rent as is borne by the figure shown in the General Index of Retail Prices ("the Index") for the month immediately preceding the month in which payment of any particular instalment of rent is due to the figure [ ] (which is the figure shown in that Index for the month of [ ]) minus one quarter of the Basic Rent PROVIDED THAT

(1) if after the date of this Lease the Index is calculated by reference to a different base date or base figure then the Index-Linked Rent shall be calculated as if that change had not taken place

(2) if the Index ceases to be published or if for any reason it becomes impossible or impracticable to calculate the Index-Linked Rent then either the Landlord or the Tenant may by notice require the rent to be thenceforth reviewed at such times and in such manner as may be agreed between them or in default of agreement be determined by a single arbitrator to be appointed by the President for the time being of the Royal Institution of Chartered Surveyors who shall have regard to market practice prevailing at the time of such notice in relation to new lettings of property of the same type as the demised property

(3) in no circumstances shall the total rent payable under this Lease be less than the Basic Rent.

5. TURNOVER RENTS

6–16 Rents linked to the tenant's turnover have been common for many years, particularly in mining leases. Recently, they have been applied to other commercial lettings, notably to lettings of shops, hotels and restaurants and they have become increasingly popular. In times of recession, turnover rents are more favourable to tenants because the tenant's liability to pay rent is related to its ability to pay.

However, it has been judicially observed that the objection to a rent representing a percentage of the tenant's turnover is that, if the price of a commodity rises at a faster rate than the cost of living, pressure is likely to develop on dealers in that commodity to reduce their margin of profit or rate of commission (*Naylor v Uttoxeter UDC* (1974) 231 E.G. 619, per Brightman J.). Accordingly, the tenant may find that the proportion of rent to profit increases. The same result may occur even if the tenant does not consciously reduce his profit margin. For example, if the government were to increase the rate of VAT gross turnover may increase (and with it the rent) while the tenant's net profit remains static. This problem arose in a rather more specialised form in *Tucker v Granada Motorway Services Ltd* [1977] 3 All E.R. 865. In that case, the Minister of Transport granted the tenant a lease of a motorway service area at a fixed rent and an additional variable rent. The variable rent payable each year was a percentage of the gross takings for the previous year from the petrol filling station and catering services provided and from any other business activities on the service area. The gross takings included the amount of tobacco duty concealed in the selling price of tobacco. Thus, when the Chancellor of the Exchequer increased tobacco duty, the tenant's rent increased, although its ratio of profit to turnover decreased and its actual profit on each packet of cigarettes was generally speaking not favourably affected. The tenant's business was rendered uneconomic and eventually the terms of the lease were renegotiated at a cost of £122,220 to the tenant.

Today, a tenant would expect to see VAT expressly excluded from the definition of "turnover". In *Debenhams Retail Plc v Sun Alliance & London Insurance Co Ltd* [2005] 3 E.G.L.R. 34, the tenant held department store premises under a lease granted in 1971 for a term of 99 years from 1965. The lease reserved a basic rent together with an additional rent calculated by reference to the store's turnover, defined as "the gross amount of the total sales". The Court of Appeal held that whilst the lease had to be construed in its 1965 context, its purposes and values were applicable in the changed factual circumstances. Accordingly, VAT had to be regarded as a substitute for the purchase tax payable before VAT was introduced, and the words "gross amount of total sales" meant everything that was taken at the till, including VAT, without deduction.

The tenant's advisers should study carefully the definition of turnover upon which the rent is to be calculated. It should as far as possible be related to the actual profit made by the tenant. However, from the landlord's point of view too close a relationship between rent and profit means that his income will depend to a large extent on the efficiency with which the tenant carries on business rather than on the value of the demised property.

Further matters must be taken into account when drafting a turnover rent. Should a basic rent be reserved? This is usually done, and is often between 70 per cent and 90 per cent of the open market rental. Sometimes, there is a guaranteed minimum reviewed at periodic intervals. Next, the tenant's adviser should ensure that there is a minimum turnover figure, which is not to be taken into account in assessing the rent, and possibly a maximum figure above which turnover is ignored.

Where the tenant's business includes a substantial number of transactions in which he gives credit to his customers the draftsman will have to consider whether the amount of the transaction should be brought into account at the time of the transaction or at the time of payment, whether interest payments are to be included in the calculation of turnover and whether the tenant is to have an allowance for bad debts. Conversely, where the tenant is likely to give discounts to certain customers (e.g. those who pay by cash, or employees), or where he is likely to have sales or special offers, his advisers should attempt to ensure that it is the amount he receives rather than the full retail price which is to be included in the calculation of turnover.

The landlord's adviser should also consider the impact of sales of store vouchers and gift cards and also of new shopping models, such as the way in which the retailer accounts for profits resulting from shoppers' and tenant's use of the internet. Orders made via the internet on in-store computers should be attributed to that store's turnover rather than (perhaps) being notionally allocated to a different shop in the tenant group as a matter of the tenant's accounting practice. Orders placed remotely on the internet but collected from the store should also be attributed to the store where the collection is made. If the lease is to include rent review provisions it is common for the base rent to be reviewed to the open market rental level disregarding the turnover provisions. The parties should also consider whether the provisions as to payment of a turnover rent are to continue if the lease is assigned or a sub-letting takes place, or are to be made personal to the original tenant. If the provisions are to terminate the full market rent should become payable.

A landlord's adviser will wish to couple a turnover rent clause with a tenant's covenant to keep open to attempt to ensure that the demised property is kept open and trading. Although an injunction to compel the tenant to trade is unobtainable (*Co-Operative Insurance Society v Argyll Stores (Holdings)* [1998] 1 A.C. 1), a positive obligation will give the landlord a remedy in damages (*Costain Property Development Ltd v Finlay & Co Ltd* [1989] 1 E.G.L.R. 237; *Transworld Land Co v J Sainsbury* [1990] 2 E.G.L.R. 255). The tenant's adviser should ensure that the clause excludes circumstances where the store is, for example, closed for repairs, refitting, stocktaking, works required to comply with statutory obligations or as a result of damage caused by insured risks. The landlord may wish to include a term for the rent to revert to the open market rental level if the closure is in excess of a certain period.

If a base rent is payable, then the lease will provide that the base rent is to be paid in conventional instalments in advance. However, because the turnover for each year can only be established following the end of the relevant year, most landlords will also normally wish to provide for a provisional sum to be paid in advance on account of the turnover rent on the same dates as the basic rent is payable. Terms should also be included setting out the appropriate machinery. For example, (a) the provision by the tenant to the landlord of a turnover certificate signed by a qualified accountant at the end of the turnover period within an agreed time period; (b) potentially, for the production of audited accounts, and (c) for the tenant to make available to the landlord its accounts and all relevant supporting documentation for inspection. The tenant's adviser will wish to ensure that confidentiality provisions are included to ensure that the landlord does not disclose the tenant's private business information, and that it uses that information solely to calculate the turnover rent. The machinery should also provide for the payment of the turnover rent once determined. It is common to see provisions for the payment by the tenant on demand of any additional sums due from the tenant to the landlord and for the repayment by the landlord of any overpaid sums by way of credit to the tenant.

The demised property may be part only of the premises on which the tenant carries on business and in such cases the turnover may need to be apportioned. For example, a tenant who uses the demised **6–17** property for the business of a dry cleaner, may receive goods for cleaning on the property but process them elsewhere. The place at which the cleaning is actually carried out may be entirely dependent on reception centres, yet the tenant may be paying rent for it. In such circumstances if the turnover of the reception centres is not apportioned in some way, the tenant will in effect pay double rent for the place at which the cleaning is carried out.

The draftsman must provide for the landlord to have sufficient power of inspection of the tenant's books to satisfy himself that any information supplied by the tenant is correct. There should probably be a provision for independent determination (by an accountant rather than a surveyor) in case of dispute. However, the tenant should not be subjected to oppressive powers of inspection and he should resist an attempt to make him pay the costs of an inspection, although it would be fair that he should pay the costs if there is a material discrepancy between the information supplied by him and the results of an inspection. Reliance on the tenant's audited accounts for the purpose of calculating turnover may be unwise for the landlord, not because those accounts may be inaccurate but because they may not be settled until well after the end of the rental period in question. Accordingly, the tenant should be required to supply regular certificates of his turnover, and there might also be a provision for the payment of interest on rent in case of delay in supplying them.

Clearly, if the demised property ceases to be used for trading, the landlord's income will drop or possibly cease. The draftsman should, therefore, insert in the lease a positive covenant to keep the demised property open for trading during normal hours (rather than relying on a negative user covenant "not to use the property otherwise than as . . ."', which would permit the tenant not to use the property at all). In this way any loss of rent may be claimed as damages for breach of covenant (see *Transworld Land Co v J Sainsbury* [1990] 2 E.G.L.R. 255 for the scope of such a claim). Nevertheless, it may be prudent to provide expressly for the payment of rent where, for example, the property remains empty while the tenant is seeking to assign his lease. This may be done by deeming a certain level of turnover during any such period or by reverting to the open market rent. If the former method is chosen, the draftsman should beware lest the deemed turnover relates to the period immediately preceding the void, since the tenant may have been running down his business in preparation for a move. If the tenant is to be obliged to use its best endeavours to obtain maximum revenue, a specific covenant to that effect should be included (see *Burford UK Properties Ltd v Forte Hotels (UK) Ltd* [2003] EWCA Civ 1800; [2003] NPC 159, where a landlord's claim for damages on the basis that a proviso to use best endeavours fell to be interpreted as a covenant, failed).

A similar problem may arise when the tenant allows someone else into occupation of part of the demised property, either as a subtenant or by way of licence or franchise agreement. The draftsman should ensure that any licence fee or sub-rent is taken into account in the calculation of the tenant's turnover; indeed, he may think it appropriate to cover the contingency that the tenant grants a licence of part of the demised property at less than the market rate. This may be done, for example, by providing that the turnover of the subtenant or licensee is to be taken into account in calculating the tenant's turnover. In addition to Example 6.5, Forms 12 and 13 contain examples of rents based on turnover. **6–18**

Example 6.5 Turnover rent

YIELDING AND PAYING THEREFOR by equal quarterly payments in advance on the usual quarter days:

(1) the annual sum of £[ ] ("the basic rent") and
(2) such sum as is calculated in accordance with the Schedule hereto ("the turnover rent")

SCHEDULE

(1) In this Schedule the following expressions have the following meanings:
    (a) "gross turnover" means the aggregate of all sums:
        (i) received by the tenant in return for goods supplied or services rendered in the course of any trade or business carried on by him in the demised property or partly in the demised property and partly elsewhere; and
        (ii) payable to the tenant by any person in consideration of the use or occupation of the whole or any part of the demised property
    (b) "a rental year" means a period of twelve calendar months beginning on [ ]

(c) "net turnover" means the gross turnover less:
  (i) any sum actually paid by the tenant to HM Revenue and Customs by way of valued added tax or other tax chargeable on the supply of goods or services
  (ii) any sum refunded by the tenant to his customers in respect of defective or unsatisfactory goods or services
  (iii) [ ] per cent of any sums received by the tenant in return for services for which orders are received at the demised property but are performed wholly elsewhere
(d) "qualified accountant" means a member of the Institute of Chartered Accountants in England and Wales

(2) The turnover rent for a rental year shall be:
  (a) [ ] percent of the net turnover for the year immediately preceding that rental year exceeding [ ] but less than [ ] and
  (b) [ ] percent of the net turnover for the year immediately preceding that rental year exceeding [ ] but less than [ ]

(3) Within one month after the beginning of each rental year (time being of the essence) the tenant shall deliver to the landlord a certificate signed by a qualified accountant of the tenant's gross turnover and net turnover for the year immediately preceding that rental year

(4) The tenant shall upon reasonable notice permit the landlord or his agent to inspect and take copies of the tenant's books of accounts or any other document or record which in the opinion of the landlord or such agent is relevant to the determination of the turnover rent and shall bear the costs of such inspection if there shall be any material discrepancy between the information supplied by the tenant under paragraph (3) above and the results of such inspection

(5) The turnover rent shall be determined by a qualified accountant (acting as an expert) and whose decision shall be final (except so far as concerns matters of law) to be appointed by the President for the time being of the Institute of Chartered Accountants in England and Wales:

(a) if the tenant fails to supply a certificate in accordance with paragraph (3) above (in which case the landlord's costs of the determination and the expert's fee shall be borne by the tenant) or

(b) if there shall be any dispute between the parties as to the calculation of the turnover rent (in which case the costs of the determination and the expert's fee shall be borne as the expert directs)

(6) Until the determination of the turnover rent for any rental year the tenant shall continue to pay rent at the rate payable immediately before the beginning of the rental year in question and upon such determination there shall be due as arrears of rent or as the case may be refunded to the tenant the difference (if any) between the rent paid by the tenant for that year and the rent which ought to have been paid by him for that year plus (if the turnover rent is determined by an expert) such amount of interest as may be directed by the expert

(7) If the turnover rent for any rental year falls below [ ] the landlord may by notice in writing served on the tenant not more than one month after the determination of the turnover rent for that year (time not being of the essence) require that there be substituted for the basic rent and the turnover rent for that year the amount for which the demised property might reasonably be expected to be let on the open market at the beginning of the year in question for a term equal to the residue of this lease then unexpired and on the same terms as this lease (save as to rent but on the assumption that the rent may be revised every five years) there being disregarded the matters set out in section 34 of the Landlord and Tenant Act 1954 (as amended) and in default of agreement the said amount shall be determined by an independent surveyor (acting as an expert not as an arbitrator) to be appointed by the President for the time being of the Royal Institute of Chartered Surveyors whose decision shall be final and whose fee shall be borne as he directs.

Example 6.6 Turnover rent for theatre or cinema based on box office receipts

(1) In this Schedule:

(a) "box office receipts" means the gross amount of all moneys payable to the tenant or any group company on the sale of tickets for theatrical cinematic or other performances in the demised property or the right to stage productions or hold conferences or other events (whether public or private) in the demised property and any moneys payable on the sale of programmes souvenirs or similar items:

(i) treating any sale by credit card as having been a sale in consideration of the net amount recoverable by the tenant from the credit card company

(ii) treating any amount which the tenant is entitled to receive by way of grant gift or sponsorship as part of the box office receipts and

(iii) deducting any value added tax payable by the tenant to HM Revenue & Customs

(b) "bar receipts" means the gross amount of all moneys payable to the tenant or any group company for the supply of food and drink in the demised property:

(i) treating any sale by credit card as having been a sale in consideration of the net amount recoverable by the tenant from the credit card company

(ii) allowing the tenant a reduction of 2 per cent for wastage

(2) The rent payable by the tenant shall be the aggregate of:

(a) [ ] per annum

(b) 5 per cent of the first 60 per cent of the box office receipts for any year

(c) 10 per cent of the remainder of the box office receipts

(d) 7.5 per cent of the bar receipts payable annually in arrear on 31 December in each year

(3) The tenant shall pay on account of the rent on 1 January, 1 April, 1 July and 1 October:

(a) in the first year of the term [ ] by four equal instalments

(b) in the second and every subsequent year of the term payments at the rate of the rent payable for the last preceding year of the term by four equal instalments and as soon as possible after the end of the second and each subsequent year the amounts payable for that year under paragraph (2) above shall be agreed or otherwise determined and all necessary adjustments (whether by way of further payment by the tenant or credit given by the landlord) shall be made

(4) The tenant shall:
   (a) keep full and accurate books or records of account
   (b) permit the landlord (or a person nominated by the landlord) to inspect the books or records of account (but not more often than once every three months) and if so required to provide the books or records in a readily legible form

(5)
   (a) at the end of each year of the term either the landlord or the tenant may require an audit of the tenant's books and records by an independent auditor (acting as an expert) to be appointed (in default of agreement) by the President of the Institute of Chartered Accountants in England and Wales
   (b) the auditor shall certify the amount of the box office receipts and the bar receipts for the year in question and his certificate shall be binding on the parties (except in so far as concerns matters of law)
   (c) the auditor has power to determine how his costs and the costs of any representations to him shall be borne.

6. RENT GEARED TO SUB-RENTS

Where the landlord lets property that the tenant will sublet, it is not uncommon for the rent due under the headlease to be geared to the rents due under subleases granted by the tenant. The rent due under the headlease will usually be a basic rent plus a percentage of the sub-rents. This concept is mainly found in development leases, where the parties are in economic (though not legal) partnership. The landlord puts in the land, the tenant puts in the construction costs and his development skills, and the result is an investment in which both landlord and tenant participate. The landlord will require a return on the land value; the tenant will require a return on the costs and risk of development; and both parties may wish to participate in any super profit. This kind of scheme is often known as a side by side scheme. In these cases, the rental income is often divided between the landlord and the tenant in slices, each slice **6–19** representing a particular return on investment by landlord and tenant respectively. If this is done, care must be taken to ensure that each slice receives its proper priority in order of payment, otherwise one party may take the lion's share of the income at the expense of the other. As with index-linked rents, any mathematical formula should be carefully checked by calculator or computer.

Where the head rent is a fraction of market rental value rather than rents receivable, slightly different problems may arise.

(a) Receipts

6–20 The principal receipt will be the rents payable under the subleases. But there may also be:

(1) receipts of mesne profits in the case of subtenants holding over;
(2) premiums paid for surrenders or lease variations;
(3) money payable under insurance policies for damage to the scheme or for loss of rent and commissions paid by the insurers to the tenant;
(4) damages for breach of covenant (e.g. dilapidations);
(5) interest on late rent, on reviewed rent, and on damages;
(6) grants or other public money paid for works to the scheme;
(7) compensation for compulsory acquisition.

All these ought to be considered. The court will not readily interpret a clause as entitling the landlord to participate in compensation awarded to the tenant for loss to his own interest (*Standard Life Co Ltd v Greycoat Devonshire Square Ltd* [2001] L. & T.R. 25). Where "gross rents" are defined as "the aggregate of all rents fees and other moneys from whatever source payable to the tenant in respect of the rental year directly or indirectly by virtue of its estate or interest in the demised premises", a one-off payment in the nature of a premium will form part of the gross rents, but a compensatory payment for accrued dilapidations will not (*Standard Life Co Ltd*, as cited above). The court differentiates between enabling the landlord to participate in the monetary advantages to be gained from the exploitation of the demised estate and compensation for damage inflicted on that interest.

(b) Deductions

If the head tenant is liable to pay the rates under the terms of some or all of the subleases, and is also liable to pay the rates under the terms of the headlease, the rates should be deducted from the gross amount of the sub-rents for the purposes of the rent review under the headlease. Similarly, if the head tenant collects VAT from the subtenants in respect of any services which he provides for them, the amount of such VAT should also be deducted. Where VAT is payable on the sub-rents, that should also be deducted, whether or not VAT is charged on the head-rent. **6–21**

Problems may also arise where the head tenant provides services to his subtenants, particularly where the subtenants' service charge is reserved as rent. It will clearly be in the interest of the head tenant if the service charge is left out of account for the purposes of the rent review under the headlease. On the other hand, if the head tenant charges a profit element or management fee to the subtenants, the landlord may argue that profit ought to be taken into account. Such a profit element may include not only a straightforward management fee but also a hidden profit, such as a discount, which may be given to the head tenant under a block policy of insurance.

The tenant may also find that in order to attract subtenants he must pay inducements, often in the form of a contribution to the subtenant's fitting-out costs. This must be deducted from the income received. There is considerable debate among valuers about the correct method of amortising such payments. Preferably the parties' surveyors should agree on an appropriate method of amortising such payments, which can then be written into the lease.

In addition, the tenant may have to pay compensation to occupying subtenants for non-renewal of tenancies under the Landlord and Tenant Act 1954 and may himself have to pay damages for breach of obligation (e.g. an unreasonable refusal of consent to assign). He will seek to ensure that these are permitted deductions.

(c) Premiums

6–22 It may be that the head tenant will grant subleases in consideration of a premium and a low rent. The premium may be a payment in cash or a payment in kind (such as the carrying out of substantial repairs or improvements). The draftsman should cover this possibility and there are at least four methods of doing so.

Firstly, the draftsman may provide that a specified proportion of the premium be paid by the head tenant to the landlord. If this is expressly provided for in the lease the parties will not fall foul of s.144 of the Law of Property Act 1925. A payment of this kind may be capital or income (for tax purposes) in the hands of the landlord, depending on the circumstances. The draftsman should consider this question as well as whether the landlord's cash flow position would be appreciably helped by the payment of a proportion of premiums exacted by the head tenant.

Secondly, he may provide for the premium to be decapitalised, either at a fixed number of years' purchase or at the rate prevailing at the time of the subletting, with the amount thus calculated being added to the rent reserved by the sublease for the purposes of the rent review under the headlease. The tenant may well benefit from this arrangement since he will have in his hands a lump sum before he is called upon to make any payment to his own landlord.

Thirdly, he may provide that for the purposes of the rent review under the headlease, the sublet property shall be deemed to be let at a rack rent. This is probably the most satisfactory method for the landlord since the regularity of his cash flow will be maintained. However, the tenant's advisers must study closely the terms of the deemed subletting. First, is the deemed subletting to be at a fixed rent or at a rent subject to review? It is probably in the tenant's interest for a fixed rent to be assumed. However, if a review is to be assumed the tenant should ensure that the notional review coincides with the actual review under the headlease, otherwise there may be periods when the head tenant's profit rent is eroded. If there is to be a review, the rent review clause should specify whether the review is to be upwards only or simply a review to market rent.

Fourthly, the terms of the lease may prohibit letting except at a rack rent. This is the most common method of dealing with the problem. From the point of view of the landlord, the income payable by the head tenant remains secured by the income payable by the subtenants. The calculation of the head-rent is also easier if there are subleases in existence. From the point of view of the tenant, he has the security of the rents payable by the subtenants, and is not called on to find income from other resources.

(d) Voids

The tenant's advisers should attempt to secure some allowance for the tenant in case of voids. This may well be resisted by the landlord on the basis that the risk of unlet property should fall on the tenant. In addition the risk of voids may already be reflected in the percentage of rent which the landlord is entitled to receive. If the landlord proves the stronger, the draftsman should make provision for the assessment of rent for empty property. This is best done by assuming a letting at a rack rent for a reasonable length of term, say, 10 years. Nevertheless, the tenant should insist that he be given a reasonable rent free period in which to find a new subtenant. If there is to be a rent review of the rent obtainable under the notional letting, the tenant should resist any suggestion that such a review should be upwards only. The purpose of a notional letting is to compensate the landlord for the share of income which he is not receiving due to the void, and if the tenant were to secure a subtenant, that subtenant would only be prepared to pay the market rent (whatever it happened to be) at the date of the letting. If the landlord is entitled to an upwards only rent review during a void period, he is over-insulated against fluctuations in the market. **6–23**

Another variant is for the rent to be assessed on the assumption that the tenant continues to receive rent at the rate last payable when the void property was let. In a falling market this may mean that the tenant is required to pay rent to the landlord based on an historic rent which he could not obtain in the real world. This form of notional receipt should therefore be resisted by the tenant.

Where the head rent is based on rents received, so that the scheme is a side by side scheme, the landlord should be satisfied by a covenant by the tenant to do his best to keep the scheme fully let. Thus, the risk of voids will fall on both parties, and both will suffer the loss in the proportions in which they are entitled to participate in income.

(e) Occupation by the head tenant

6–24 The draftsman should provide expressly for the occupation of the whole or part of the demised property by the head tenant. This was forgotten by the draftsman in *British Railways Board v Elgar House Ltd* (1969) 209 E.G. 1313, where it was nevertheless held that for the purposes of the rent calculation parts of the demised property occupied by the head tenant should be deemed to be let at a rack rent. The court will try to prevent the tenant from cheating the landlord out of his share of the rental income (*Freehold & Leasehold Shop Properties Ltd v Friends Provident Life Office* [1984] 2 E.G.L.R. 133, per Griffiths L.J.). Thus where the rent was to be the highest of (a) a fixed sum; (b) the rent payable during the previous rent period; and (c) eight per cent of the rents receivable by the tenant, it was held that where the tenant was in occupation, the rents receivable by him were the rents he would have received if he had sublet the premises (*Ashworth Frazer v Gloucester City Council* [1997] 1 E.G.L.R. 104). As with the case of voids the terms of any deemed subletting should be carefully considered by the tenant's advisers.

If the draftsman provides for a notional lease to be valued while the tenant is in occupation, it should be made clear whether any revaluation is to be on an upwards only basis or is simply to be a revaluation to market rent. In the case of a side by side sharing, it is suggested that the review should not be upwards only because if, instead of occupying the property himself, the tenant were at any given time to sublet he would only receive the then going rate.

(f) Improvements

6–25 A rent geared to sub-rents is most commonly found in building leases. Accordingly, the tenant will have carried out substantial improvements, the cost of which will form a large part of the consideration given by him for the grant of the lease. His sublettings, on the other hand, will be sublettings of the improved property. It is, therefore, important that the value of those improvements be taken into account in assessing the rent of any part of the property deemed to be sublet. Accordingly, the draftsman should not provide for the usual disregard of tenant's improvements in the valuation formula. However, it should be borne in mind that the subtenants may themselves carry out improvements which, as against the tenant, are to be disregarded on rent review. Normally, it is unnecessary to make special provision for this since the rent the tenant pays is linked to the rent he receives. In a special case, however, it may be appropriate to deal expressly with improvements made by subtenants.

(g) Other obligations

Since the landlord's income will usually depend on rents generated by actual lettings of the property, the landlord will require the tenant to enter into a series of obligations designed to ensure that the scheme is kept fully let at rack rents. Those obligations will include: **6–26**

(1) a covenant to try his best to keep the scheme fully let;
(2) a covenant not to let at less than the market rent obtainable at the date of the letting;
(3) a covenant not to grant rent free periods or concessionary rent periods without the landlord's consent;
(4) a covenant not to sublet except in defined subletting units;
(5) a covenant not to waive or commute any rental payments under subleases;
(6) a covenant not to accept any surrender of any sublease without the landlord's consent;
(7) a covenant to enforce subtenants' covenants in subleases;
(8) a covenant not to permit any sub-underletting of a sublet part.

All these obligations are designed to ensure that the tenant keeps up the real value of the scheme and that the landlord's income remains as high as possible.

In addition, the draftsman should prohibit the assignment of the lease to a person holding an interest inferior to the lease. The object of such a provision is to prevent circumstances arising in which a sublease could be merged in the headlease. If a merger were to take place, the landlord might find that the rental being paid under a sublease would cease to be payable to the tenant with a resulting loss in rental income to the landlord. In many cases, the lease will be one to which s.19(1)(b) of the Landlord and Tenant Act 1927 applies. The draftsman must be particularly careful to ensure that any restrictions on alienation are not avoided by that subsection.

Section 19(1)(b) will not, however, apply to an assignment of a tenancy which is a new tenancy for the purposes of the Landlord and Tenant (Covenants) Act 1995. See Chapter 14.

Example 6.7 Rent geared to sub-rents receivable

YIELDING AND PAYING THEREFOR by equal quarterly payments in advance on January, 1 April, 1 July and 1 October in each year [ ] per cent of the net rents which the tenant is entitled to receive for the whole or any part of the demised property and calculated in accordance with the Schedule hereto

SCHEDULE

(1) In this Schedule the following expressions have the following meanings:
   (a) "full rack rental value" means the best rent at which the demised property (or as the case may be the part of the demised property in question) might reasonably be expected to be let in the open market by a willing landlord to a willing tenant:
      (i) in the case of property falling within paragraph (2) below on the terms (other than as to rent or other pecuniary consideration) upon which it is actually occupied
      (ii) in the case of property falling within paragraph (3) below on the terms (other than as to rent or other pecuniary consideration) of this lease
      (iii) in the case of property falling within paragraph (4) below on the terms (other than as to rent or other pecuniary consideration) upon which it was last occupied and in any case disregarding the matters set out in paragraphs (a) and (b) of section 34(1) of the Landlord and Tenant Act 1954 (as amended) and on the assumption that the rent so determined will be revised every five years
   (b) "qualified accountant" means a member of the Institute of Chartered Accountants in England and Wales or the Association of Certified Accountants

(2) If the tenant lets or permits to be occupied the whole or any part of the demised property in return for any pecuniary consideration other than the full rack rental value thereof as at the date of such letting or permission or in return for no pecuniary consideration then he shall be deemed for the

purposes of this Schedule to be entitled to receive the full rack rental value thereof determined as at the date of such letting or permission and redetermined (upwards only) as at every fifth anniversary thereof

(3) If the tenant himself occupies the whole or any part of the demised property then he shall be deemed for the purposes of this Schedule to be entitled to receive the full rack rental value thereof determined as at the date on which he went into occupation and redetermined (upwards or downwards) as at every fifth anniversary thereof

(4) If the whole or any part of the demised property remains vacant for three months or more then at the expiry of such period of three months the tenant shall until the same is next occupied be deemed to be entitled to receive the full rack rental value thereof determined as at the date upon which the said period expired and redetermined (upwards or downwards) as at every fifth anniversary thereof

(5) The tenant shall one month before the beginning of each quarter (time being of the essence) deliver to the landlord a certificate signed by a qualified accountant showing a true summary of:

(a) the gross amount of all rents and licence fees which the tenant is entitled (or deemed to be entitled) to receive in respect of the demised property and each part thereof for that quarter and

(b) the amount of any sum included in (a) above which the tenant is entitled to recover from any subtenant or occupier of the whole or any part of the demised property either by way of value added tax or by way of service charge in respect of services or works performed or to be performed

(6) Subject to paragraph (7) below the net rents shall be the difference between the two amounts shown in the said certificate

(7) The net rents shall be determined by a single arbitrator to be appointed by the President for the time being of the Royal Institution of Chartered Surveyors if:

(a) the tenant fails to deliver a certificate in accordance with paragraph (5) above (in which case the tenant shall pay interest on the net rents at the rate of [ ] percent from the quarter day in question until payment) or

(b) any dispute or difference arises between the parties in connection with the calculation of the net rents (in which case the arbitrator shall determine the amount of interest if any to be paid by the tenant)

(8) The tenant shall permit the landlord or his agent to inspect and take copies of the tenant's books or accounts or any other document or record (and if necessary the tenant shall procure any computer printout) which in the opinion of the landlord or such agent is relevant to the calculation of the net rents and shall bear the costs of such inspection if there shall be any material discrepancy between the certificate delivered by the tenant under paragraph (5) above and the results of such inspection.

Example 6.8 Side by side rent sharing

SCHEDULE

(1) In this Schedule:

(a) "rental income" means the aggregate of:

(i) any yearly or other periodical sums payable under an occupational lease including sums payable by virtue of any enactment

(ii) any sums payable by way of interest under an occupational lease

(iii) any sums payable by way of damages or compensation for any breach of a tenant's obligation under an occupational lease

(iv) any sum payable by a guarantor of a tenant's obligation under an occupational lease pursuant to his guarantee

(v) any premium paid or other capital payment made by a tenant under an occupational lease in connection with the grant assignment variation or surrender of an occupational lease

(vi) any sum payable under a policy of insurance in respect of loss of rent or other income

(b) "permitted deductions" means the aggregate of:

(i) expenses reasonably incurred by the tenant in order to comply with its obligations as landlord under an occupational lease

(ii) legal costs incurred by the tenant in enforcing obligations under occupational leases except to the extent that the tenant recovers those costs from a party to an occupational lease

(iii) the amount of any compensation or damages which the tenant is liable by statute or ordered to pay to any party to an occupational lease whether for non-renewal of a tenancy breach of covenant breach of obligation compensation for improvements or otherwise

(iv) the cost of management and rent collection not exceeding [ ] per cent of rental income

(c) "notional rental income" means the rack rental value of any lettable unit which is either unlet or vacant or occupied by the tenant or by a group company the value to be determined as at the date on which the unit in question ceased to be let or occupied or as the case may be become occupied by the tenant or a group company and redetermined every year

(d) "lettable unit" means a part of the property which is designed constructed or adapted for letting to an occupying retail trader

(e) "occupational lease" means a lease under which physical possession of a lettable unit was granted by the tenant

(f) "rack rental value" of any lettable unit at any time means the rent at which that unit might reasonably be expected to be let in the open market for a term of not less than 10 years with an upwards only rent review on every fifth anniversary of the beginning of the term and on such other terms as would be expected to be negotiated in the open market (including such financial inducements and concessions as are usual in the market at that time)

(g) "group company" means a company which would be treated as a member of the same group of companies as the tenant for the purposes of the Landlord and Tenant Act 1954 (as amended)

(h) "divisible income" means the difference between:

(i) rental income plus notional rental income and

(ii) permitted deductions but divisible income shall never be less than nil

(i) "the first slice" means such part of divisible income as does not exceed [ ]
(j) "the second slice" means such part of divisible income as exceeds [ ] but does not exceed [ ]
(k) "the top slice" means such part of divisible income as exceeds [ ]

(2) The rent payable by the tenant is the aggregate of:
(a) [ ] per cent of the first slice
(b) [ ] per cent of the second slice and
(c) [ ] per cent of the top slice
to be paid by equal quarterly payments on the usual quarter days.

7. RENT GEARED TO HEAD RENT

6–27 Some subleases reserve a rent which is linked to the rent payable under the headlease. The reasons which prompt such a bargain are a desire on the part of the landlord to ensure that he suffers no rental shortfall, and in some cases a desire to have a guaranteed profit rental.

If faced with such a clause, the tenant's adviser should ensure that the tenant ascertains the amount of the head rent and receives advice from a valuer as to whether it is a fair rent (*County Personnel Ltd v Alan R Pulver & Co* [1987] 1 All E.R. 289). If the rent under the sublease is made to increase at the same rate as the rent under the headlease, and the rent under the headlease is less than a market rent at the date of grant of the sublease, the rent under the sublease may well exceed the true market rent after the first rent review.

The draftsman of a clause linking the sub-rent to the head rent must make it clear what is to happen if the head landlord does not exercise his right to a rent under the headlease, or if the headlease is surrendered. In *Lorien Textiles v SI Pension Trustees Ltd* [1981] 2 E.G.L.R. 100, the rent under the sublease was to be assessed "on the basis set out" in the headlease. It was held that this merely incorporated the words of the headlease, and that the continuing existence of the headlease was not a condition precedent to the right to review the rent under the sublease. So also where a sublease provided for the rent to be a proportion of the rent "payable" by the landlord "in the manner fixed" under the headlease, it was held that the rent review clause in the sublease was capable of operation despite the surrender of the headlease (*R&A Millett (Shops) Ltd v Leon Allan International Fashions Ltd* [1989] 1 E.G.L.R. 138).

If the sublease merely incorporates the valuation formula and machinery contained in the headlease, the rent review clause in the sublease will be capable of operation whether or not the rent review clause is exercised in the headlease. However, the corollary is that the rent review under the headlease and the rent review under the sublease will in effect be independent valuations and consequently there is a risk that the rent payable under each will be different.

Example 6.9 Definition of rent linked to head rent

"the reviewed rent" means the highest of

(1) the rent contractually payable immediately before the relevant review date

(2) the market rent and

(3) [   ] per cent of the rent payable under the headlease (assuming if it is not the fact that the headlease is in existence on the relevant review date).

Example 6.10 Alternative definition

If at any time the rent payable under the headlease is increased the rent payable under this lease shall be increased with effect from the date as from which the rent payable under the headlease is increased so as to equal [   ] per cent of that rent.

8. PERIODIC REVIEW TO MARKET RENT

The periodic review to market rent is the most common form of rent review clause found in occupational business leases. Its principal advantage is that it most accurately reflects changes in the value of the demised property rather than the business efficiency of a particular tenant or inflation generally. In most cases, the clause will operate by postulating a hypothetical letting of the demised property in the open market. Under normal circumstances, this is as fair a valuation method to both parties as can be achieved. However, there are cases (such as property specially built or adapted for a particular occupier) where modifications are needed. **6–28**

Judicial statements abound that the purpose of a rent review clause is to ensure that the rent payable reflects changes in the value of money and the value of the property let (e.g. *Basingstoke and*

Deane BC v Host Group [1988] 1 W.L.R. 348; *British Airways v Heathrow Airport* [1992] 1 E.G.L.R. 141). However, there are two different perspectives from which this general purpose can be viewed. The first perspective is that the purpose of the rent review is to revalue the original bargain between the parties in the light of changes in the value of money and of the property. This perspective leads to the conclusion that, in the absence of clear words to the contrary, the hypothetical letting will be on the same terms as the actual letting. But the second perspective is that the rent review clause is the landlord's price for the grant of a long term, in the absence of which he would have granted a shorter term. Thus, the purpose of a rent review clause is not to revalue the original bargain between the parties, but to give the landlord the income which he would have got, on the terms on which he would have let, if he had had the property in hand on the rent review date. This would mean that in the absence of clear words, the terms of the hypothetical letting would be dictated by the market at the review date, and not by the terms of the lease. So far, the courts have approached rent review clauses from the first perspective only. But the parties are not confined to the first perspective. Many of the failures of rent review clauses result from a failure to consider carefully the object which the clause is designed to achieve.

A well-drawn rent review clause must provide for each of the following:

(1) the review dates;
(2) the method of initiating the review;
(3) the procedure for resolving disputes;
(4) the timetable;
(5) the valuation formula.

6–29 It should also state whether time is or is not of the essence at any of the procedural stages. The choice of review dates is one of the basic terms of the lease which will have been agreed between the parties before the matter passes into the hands of solicitors. Some landlords attempt to introduce a review date on the last or penultimate day of the term. The purpose of doing so is to attempt to obtain for the landlord a higher rent than would be awarded by the court on an application by the landlord for an interim rent under s.24A of the Landlord and Tenant Act 1954 (although both landlord and tenant can now make such application, s.24(A)(1) of the Landlord and Tenant Act 1984). The tenant will always be better off without such a review, and consequently should resist its introduction. Moreover, in the normal course of events the interim rent will be the rent payable for the new tenancy, back-dated to the date when the old tenancy ended. The advantage to the landlord has therefore been largely eliminated. If, however, it is agreed that there should be a review at the end of the term, the draftsman should ensure that the term of the hypothetical lease is long enough to be realistic. Clearly, letting for the residue of the actual term will not produce a worthwhile rent.

There are two methods of defining the review dates. One is to specify the actual dates of review in the lease. This produces certainty, but the tenant's adviser should be careful to ensure that the hypothetical lease has proper provision for rent review. The problem does not arise where the review takes place on the assumption of a hypothetical letting for the residue of the actual term. However, where the assumption is a letting for a term expiring after the actual term on the terms of the actual lease, the hypothetical lease may have a long period without review. For example, a lease provides for rent reviews at fixed dates in the years 2015, 2020 and 2025. The term of the lease is limited to expire in 2030. The review clause provides for a hypothetical lease for a term of 15 years from the rent review date but otherwise on the terms of the actual lease. A literal interpretation of these terms would mean that on the second rent review date what was to be assumed was a lease expiring in 2035 with a rent review in 2025 only, leaving 10 years without review at the end of the hypothetical lease. The effect on the final rent review would be even more drastic. The second method is to define review dates by reference to the anniversaries of the commencement of the lease. The draftsman must, however, make it clear whether the periods are to be measured from the date from which the term of the lease is computed or from the date of the lease itself. Prima facie a clause which specifies review date by reference to the commencement of the term requires the measurement to be taken from the date from which the term is computed, and not the date of the lease (*Beaumont Property Trust v Tai* [1983] 1 E.G.L.R. 122).

The valuation date will usually be the rent review date, and the court will lean in favour of a construction which produces the result **6–30** that the rent is valued by reference to values prevailing at the start of the period for which it is payable (*Glofield Properties v Morley (No.2)* [1989] 2 E.G.L.R. 118). But if the clause clearly specifies another valuation date, the court will give effect to the clause (*Prudential Assurance Co v Gray* [1987] 2 E.G.L.R. 134; *Parkside Investments v German Food Centre* [1990] 2 E.G.L.R. 265).

If provision is made for service of a late notice, the parties should expressly state the date from which the revised rent is to be payable as well as the date at which the revised rent is to be determined (see *H Turner & Son Ltd v Confederation Life Insurance Co (UK) Ltd* [2003] 2 E.G.L.R. 11, where it was held that the rent was to be reviewed as at the defined rent review date, but was only to be payable from the expiry of the subsequent "late notice").

9. TIME LIMITS IN RENT REVIEW PROCEDURE

(a) The presumption

6–31 Much of the early litigation about rent review clauses concentrated on the question whether limits were of the essence. That question was thought to have been partially settled by the House of Lords in *United Scientific Holdings Ltd v Burnley BC* [1978] A.C. 904, where it was held that prima facie time limits are not of the essence, with the result that if a time limit is missed the review can still take place.

However, it was said that the prima facie rule could be displaced:

(1) by express words;
(2) by contra-indications in the rent review clause;
(3) by the inter-relationship of the rent review clause and other clauses in the lease.

(b) The presumption rebutted

(i) By express words

6–32 The parties may always provide expressly that time limits are to be of the essence. If they do so, the court will give effect to their expressed intention, even if this means overriding words in the reddendum (*Weller v Akehurst* [1981] 3 All E.R. 411). However, if the draftsman wishes to make time of the essence of some but not all of the procedural steps he should be particularly careful to make it clear which steps carry strict time limits and which do not (as the draftsman made clear in *Lancecrest Ltd v Dr Ganiyu Asiwaju* [2005] 1 E.G.L.R. 40, where time was not of the essence of the time limit relating to service of the landlord's trigger notice but was of the essence for service of the tenant's counternotice, and as the draftsman failed to do in *Bradley (C) & Sons Ltd v Telefusion Ltd* [1981] 2 E.G.L.R. 94 and *Art & Sound v West End Litho* [1992] 1 E.G.L.R. 138). If it is not clear that time is of the essence of a particular procedural provision, the presumption that time is not of the essence will apply (*Panavia Air Cargo Ltd v Southend-on-Sea BC* [1988] 1 E.G.L.R. 124).

Should the parties agree that time is to be of the essence? From the tenant's point of view such an agreement has much to commend it. If the review is upwards only he is highly unlikely to want to initiate the review himself, but the uncertainty of not knowing what his rent is may hamper him in conducting or investing in his business, or in disposing of his lease. If time is of the essence, the business tenant knows where he stands.

On the other hand, as Lord Salmon observed in *United Scientific Holdings Ltd v Burnley BC* [1978] A.C. 904:

> "I would add that a well-advised landlord is hardly likely to agree to a rent revision clause which laid down that its provisions as to time were of the essence of the contract. Were he to do so, it would mean that should he take any step later than the time specified in the clause then however slight the delay and however little it affected the tenant, he would lose the benefit of the clause for the next five, seven or 10 years or whatever the intervals for revision might be."

By contrast, where time is not of the essence for the service of a landlord's notice calling for a rent review, mere delay by the landlord, however lengthy and even if coupled with hardship to the tenant, does not of itself destroy the contractual right which the landlord has to serve a notice. In order to show that a landlord is precluded from exercising his right to call for a rent review, the tenant must show that the lease or the rent review clause has been abrogated by mutual consent or that the landlord's conduct has been such that he is estopped from exercising his right to a rent review (*Amherst v Walker (James) Goldsmith & Silversmith Ltd* [1983] 2 All E.R. 1067; and *Bello v Ideal View* [2010] 1 E.G.L.R. 39, where a 13 year delay was held not to prevent the landlord reviewing the rent). The practical consequences of time limits which are not of the essence of the contract are such that they are virtually meaningless. If, therefore, the parties agree that the rent review is to be initiated and conducted according to a timetable laid down in the lease, it is suggested that time should be of the essence of the timetable. If the parties do not wish to be bound by time limits there should be none in the lease.

6–33 One possible solution is for the last step in the procedure to be the subject of a strict time limit. Normally, that step is the reference of a dispute to an independent third party. If the chosen third party is an expert, the court cannot interfere with the contractual time limit. However, if the chosen third party is an arbitrator, the court can extend time, even if only one party has the right to refer the matter to arbitration (*Pittalis v Sherefettin* [1986] Q.B. 868). But the circumstances in which the court can extend time are extremely limited (s.12 of the Arbitration Act 1996).

The tenant's adviser should press for the tenant to have the right to serve notice on the landlord in the event of delay, calling upon the landlord either to exercise the rent review or abandon it. Such a notice may also contain a proposal by the tenant as to the amount of the rent. It should be made clear that any time limit within which the landlord is to act is to be of the essence. But even if there is no such express provision, it is likely that the court would hold that time was of the essence anyway (*Banks v Kokkinos* [1999] 3 E.G.L.R. 133, following the Scottish case of *Visionhire v Britel Fund Trustees* [1992] 1 E.G.L.R. 128. This is consistent with the decision in *Fifield v WR Jack* [2001] L. & T.R. 4 and *Starmark Enterprises v CPL Distribution* [2002] 2 W.L.R. 1009).

(ii) By contra-indications in the rent review clause

6–34 It is extremely difficult to extract any coherent principles from the decisions of the court in relation to contra-indications in the rent review clause. This only serves to emphasise the desirability of stating expressly whether time is or is not to be of the essence.

In *Drebbond Ltd v Horsham DC* [1978] 1 E.G.L.R. 96, the landlord was entitled to require arbitration by notice in writing given to the tenant within three months after the review date "but not otherwise". The words "but not otherwise" were held to be a sufficient contra-indication to make time of the essence. In *First Property Growth Partnership LP v Royal & Sun Alliance Property Services Ltd* [2003] 1 E.G.L.R. 39, it was held that the words "not at any other time" made time of the essence where the landlord was entitled to serve notice requiring the rent be reviewed and "such notice may be given at any time not more than twelve months before the expiration of the following years of the said term that is to say every fifth year thereof but not at any other time." In *Touche Ross & Co v Secretary of State for the Environment* [1983] 1 E.G.L.R. 123, the lease provided that the question of what was a fair market rent was to be referred to an expert "as soon as practicable and in any event not later than" three months after service of a rent review notice. It was held that time was not of the essence. Dillon L.J. pointed out that small differences in language will lead in some cases to opposite conclusions. In other cases, the fact that the rent was to be "conclusively fixed" by the landlord's trigger notice if the tenant failed to give counternotice in time was held to be a sufficient indication that time was of the essence (*Mammoth Greeting Cards v Agra* [1990] 2 E.G.L.R. 124; *Barrett Estate Services v David Greig (Retail)* [1991] 2 E.G.L.R. 123). All those cases turned on the effect of particular words in the rent review clause. In other cases, however, the court has relied more on the procedure for review laid down in the lease.

In *Lewis v Barnet* [1982] 2 E.G.L.R. 127, the lease provided that in default of agreement the rent was to be determined by a surveyor appointed by the President of the RICS on the application of the landlord made not less than three months before the review date. It was further provided that if the parties had not agreed the rent six months before the review date, and the landlord had not made the application to the President, then any notice given by the landlord to trigger the review should be void and of no effect. It was held that that provision was sufficient to make time of the essence of the time limit for the landlord's application. By contrast, where the lease provided for the landlord to serve a notice, for the tenant to serve a counternotice and said that if the tenant did not serve a counternotice, the figure in the landlord's notice would stand as the rent payable, it was held that this was insufficient to rebut the presumption that time was not of the essence (*Bickenhall Engineering Co v Grandmet Restaurants* [1995] 1 E.G.L.R. 110). In *Iceland Foods Plc v Dangoor* [2002] 2 E.G.L.R. 5, it was provided that the landlord should serve a trigger notice not more than 12 months and not less than three months before the review date (para.2), and that if the parties had not agreed the rent not less than two months prior to the review date or within three months of the trigger notice, the rent was to be determined by a surveyor to be agreed not less than one month before the review date, and, in default, by the President (para.3). It was further provided that, if the parties had not agreed the rent at least two months before the review date and the landlord had neglected to make an application to the President, the trigger notice already given would be void (para.6). The landlord served a trigger notice after the rent review date. It was held that time was not of the essence of paras 2 or 3, and the landlord was entitled to review the rent. However, the terms of para.6 and the word "neglect" in relation to the failure of the landlord to apply for an appointment indicated that notwithstanding the absence of a specific time limit, the landlords were under a duty to get on with the review and the landlord had a reasonable time only under para.6 to apply for the appointment.

In *Smith's (Henry) Charity Trustees v AWADA Trading and Promotion Services Ltd* [1984] 1 E.G.L.R. 116, the rent review clause prescribed an elaborate procedure of notices and counternotices. At each stage, the clause set out the consequence of failure to serve the requisite notice or counternotice. The court held that time was of the essence of the timetable. That decision was approved in *Starmark Enterprises Ltd v CPL Distribution Ltd* [2002] Ch. 306 (overruling *Mecca Leisure Ltd v Renown Investments (Holdings) Ltd* (1985) 49 P. & C.R. 12), where the rent review clause entitled the landlord to serve a rent notice during the last six months of the current period specifying the amount of rent payable in respect of the next period, and provided that if the tenant failed to serve a counternotice within one month of receipt of the rent notice, the tenant would be "deemed to have agreed to pay the increased rent specified in that notice". Similarly, in *Greenhaven Securities Ltd v Compton* [1985] 2 E.G.L.R. 117, the review clause prescribed three alternative ways in which the rent was to be determined, two of them introduced by "if" clauses. It was held that time was of the essence.

In *Secretary of State for Communities and Local Government v Standard Securities Ltd* [2008] 1 P. & C.R. 23, time was also held to be of the essence where the amount of the current market rental value of the premises at each review date was to be agreed in writing between the landlord and tenant not later than two calendar months before such review date and failing agreement to be determined by an independent surveyor to be appointed by the President of the RICS on the written request of the landlord "provided always that if no such agreement or written request is made by the review date applicable the yearly rent payable for the year ending on such review date shall continue to be the rent reserved by this Lease for the next seven years of the term."

Where the parties have not only required a step to be taken within a specified time but have expressly provided for the consequences in case of default, this provides an indication, of greater or less strength, that time is to be of the essence, but it is not necessarily decisive. Whether it is so or not depends on all the circumstances of the case including the context and wording of the provisions, the degree of emphasis, the purpose and effect of the default clause and any other relevant consideration. In the end, the matter is one of impression. As a result of these cases, it is clear that relatively small differences in the drafting of a rent review clause may have great practical consequences. In all cases it is suggested that the parties must consider whether or not to have strict time limits and ensure that their intention is clearly expressed. **6–35**

(iii) By the inter-relationship of the rent review clause and other clauses in the lease

The classic case of the inter-relationship of the rent review clause and other clauses in the lease making time of the essence is a case where the tenant has an option to determine the term by the service of a break-notice. Whether the right to review the rent and the right to determine are contained in the same sub-clause of the lease (*Al Saloom v Shirley James Travel Service Ltd* (1981) 42 P. & C.R. 181) or in different sub-clauses (*Legal & General Assurance (Pension Management) Ltd v Cheshire CC* [1984] 1 E.G.L.R. 102) makes no difference. Nor does it matter whether the tenant may give notice after the last date for service of a rent review notice (*Coventry CC v J Hepworth & Son Ltd* [1983] 1 E.G.L.R. 119) or at a time which coincides with time during which a landlord may serve such a notice (*Legal & General Assurance (Pension Management) Ltd v Cheshire CC* [1984] 1 E.G.L.R. 102). Where **6–36** there is only one break but multiple rent reviews, the existence of the break clause will make time of the essence for all reviews, including those which are not linked with the break (*Central Estates v Secretary of State for the Environment* [1997] 1 E.G.L.R. 239). Where, however, the tenant also had the right to initiate the rent review and the date for the tenant's notice terminating the lease was linked to a date over which the landlord had no control (the decision of the arbitrator), the link between the rent review and the break clause was held not to make time of the essence (*Metrolands Investments Ltd v JH Dewhurst Ltd* [1986] 3 All E.R. 659). The essential feature to displace the presumption is a link between a rent review timetable and the timetable for the exercise of the tenant's right to determine the lease. Where there is no such interrelation, as where the landlord does not have to serve a notice in order to exercise his right to review the rent, the mere existence of a tenant's break clause will not lead the court to impose time limits on the landlord (*Woodhouse (Edwin) Trustee Co Ltd v Sheffield Brick Co Plc* [1984] 1 E.G.L.R. 130). The same conclusion would probably be reached if the tenant's break notice had to be served before the last date for service of the landlord's notice calling for a rent review.

However, if the tenant has the right to determine the lease, the draftsman must be careful lest that right should have the effect of making time limits in the rent review procedure of the essence. This danger may be met in two ways. Firstly, the draftsman may insert in the rent review clause an express provision that time is not to be of the essence. If he chooses this method, the landlord may serve a late notice, but the tenant will not be able to serve a late break notice. Accordingly, his break notice must be given in ignorance of what the new rent would be. Secondly, the draftsman may ensure that the two timetables are not interrelated. This may be done by conferring on the tenant a right to serve a late notice in the event that the rent has not been determined in accordance with the timetable specified in the lease. Alternatively, the draftsman may dispense with a timetable for the rent review, and dispense with the requirement for the landlord to serve a rent review notice in order to exercise the right to review the rent.

In an appropriate case, a time limit may be implied. Where a rent review clause requires or entitled a landlord or tenant to take a step within a specified time, in respect of which time is not of the essence, the other party can make time of the essence by serving an appropriate warning notice (*United Scientific Holdings v Burnley BC* [1978] A.C. 904; *Barclays Bank Plc v Savile Estates Ltd* [2002] 2 E.G.L.R. 16).

Example 6.11 Tenant's power to make time of the essence

(1) If the landlord fails to take any step in the procedure for rent review within a period of time prescribed by this lease (whether or not that step could also have been taken by the tenant) the tenant may give the landlord written notice:
  (a) referring to the step which the landlord has failed to take
  (b) requiring the landlord to take that step within such period of not less than twenty-one days as may be specified in the notice and
  (c) informing the landlord that if he fails to take that step within the period specified in the notice he will be precluded thereafter from taking it and that time is of the essence of the period so specified

(2) If the landlord fails to take the step specified in a notice under paragraph (1) within the time specified in that notice (time being of the essence) he shall thereafter be precluded from taking it.

Example 6.12 Express provision that time is not of the essence and to ensure that inter-relation with break clause does not make time of the essence

1. Time is not of the essence in agreeing or determining the reviewed rent
2. The Tenant's right to determine the tenancy under clause [ ] does not make time of the essence in agreeing or determining the reviewed rent under Schedule [ ].

10. REVIEW PROCEDURE

(a) Initiating the review

Many rent review clauses provide for the procedure to be initiated by the service of a notice. The principal advantage of such a requirement is that it signals, in a formal way, that the procedure is under way. If the lease requires the service of a notice, informal discussions between the parties are unlikely to be held to amount to a review of the rent (*Esso Petroleum Co Ltd v Anthony Gibbs* 6–37

Financial Services Ltd [1983] 2 E.G.L.R. 112). However, unless the rent review is to be conducted in accordance with a prescribed timetable, there is much to be said for dispensing with notices, and removing a fertile source of potential dispute.

Some review clauses require a review notice to be in a particular form (for example, proposing a new rent); others do not. Unless one of the steps in the review machinery is the service of a counter notice by the person upon whom the review notice is served, it is better not to stipulate for a particular form of notice because the fewer the requirements that have to be complied with the less scope there is for litigation. It is, however, a fundamental requirement of a review notice that it leaves the recipient in no doubt that it is intended to be the formal document invoking the landlord's right to review the rent (*Shirlcar Properties Ltd v Heinitz* [1983] 2 E.G.L.R. 120).

If a particular form of notice is prescribed, failure to serve notice in the prescribed form will not generally invalidate the notice (*Dean and Chapter of Chichester Cathedral v Lennards Ltd* (1977) 35 P. & C.R. 309); although where the timetable is tight and the landlord's notice is required to state a rental figure it may be of the essence that the notice should do so (*Commission for New Towns v R Levy & Co* [1990] 2 E.G.L.R. 121). If the general presumption does not apply in the particular case, a defective notice may usually be followed by a late notice in proper form. The general presumption might not apply where a notice initiating the review is to be followed by a counternotice objecting to the rent proposed in the initial notice. In such a case, unless the initial notice specifies the proposed rent, a counternotice cannot be served.

Where the rent may go up or down on review, the courts have sometimes found that the landlord is under an obligation to serve a trigger notice. If he has such an obligation, but fails to serve a notice, the court may substitute its own machinery for determining the rent (*Royal Bank of Scotland v Jennings* [1997] 1 E.G.L.R. 101; *Addin v Secretary of State* [1997] 1 E.G.L.R. 99). Whether the landlord has an obligation to serve a notice or merely an option to do so is a question of construction of the lease. In *Hemingway Realty Ltd v Master Wardens & Commonalty of Freemen of the Art or Mystery of Clothworkers' of the City of London* [2005] 2 E.G.L.R. 36, it was held that there was no presumption that a rent review clause, even an upwards or downwards clause, ought to be capable of exercise by both parties to the lease, and if the right to initiate the review was, on the true interpretation of the lease, exclusive to the landlord, the landlord would be able to refuse to implement the review machinery and avoid a downwards review. In the case of an upwards or downwards review, the tenant's adviser should ensure that the tenant has an opportunity either to initiate the review or to compel the landlord to do so.

(b) Counternotices

Where the initiator of the review is required to specify the proposed new rent, it is sometimes provided that the figure so specified shall be the new rent unless the other party serves a counternotice within a given period. Usually, it is the landlord who initiates the review and the tenant who is obliged to serve the counternotice. Generally, the period for serving the counternotice will not be of the essence, however the existence of a deeming provision expressly setting out that in the absence of a counternotice the tenant is deemed to have agreed the rent specified in the landlord's notice is a virtually decisive contra indication that time is of the essence (*Starmark Enterprises v CPL Distribution* [2002] W.L.R. 1009). **6–38**

It is often the case that the service of a counternotice is the only step in the review procedure of which time is expressly made of the essence (*Lancecrest Ltd v Dr Ganiyu Asiwaju* [2005] 1 E.G.L.R. 40). The tenant's adviser should be on his guard against such a provision since it is little more than a trap for the tenant, particularly since the figure specified by the landlord need not be a bona fide and genuine pre-estimate of the market rent (*Amalgamated Estates Ltd v Joystretch Manufacturing Ltd* [1981] 1 E.G.L.R. 96). The tenant's adviser should, therefore, delete from the draft any provision making time of the essence in relation to the service of a counternotice; or he should delete the entire requirement to serve a counternotice. He may derive some support from the statement of Templeman L.J. in *Amalgamated Estates Ltd v Joystretch Manufacturing Ltd*:

> "I think it is a great pity that any landlord should require, or that any tenant should accept, a provision making time of the essence when the consequences are so onerous."

If the landlord will not accept the amendment, then the tenant's adviser should seek to ensure that any dispute about the rent is determined by arbitration rather than by an expert. A unilateral right to require a dispute about the rent to be referred to arbitration is "an agreement to refer future disputes to arbitration" (s.5 of the Arbitration Act 1996; *Pittalis v Sherefettin* [1986] Q.B. 868) and the court has limited power to extend the time for service of a counternotice (s.12 of the Arbitration Act 1996). However, the previous liberal attitude towards extensions of time for commencing arbitration (*Patel v Peel Investments (South)* [1992] 2 E.G.L.R. 116) no longer applies (*Fox & Widley v Gurham* [1998] 1 E.G.L.R. 91).

In addition, the tenant's adviser should seek to ensure that the form of trigger notice to be served by the landlord is required to contain a clear reminder to the tenant of his right to serve a counternotice and the consequences of a failure to do so.

(c) Agreeing the new rent

6–39 There should be a period in which the parties are able to agree the amount of the new rent before the necessity for independent determination. In the normal case three months should suffice and the period should be made to run from the service of a review notice. If the landlord is not required to serve a notice in order to initiate the review, then no fixed timetable will be necessary.

The right to have an independent determination arises when negotiations between the parties have broken down; but what if the parties have never tried to agree? A phrase such as "in default of agreement" does not imply that the parties must have tried to agree (*Re Essoldo (Bingo) Ltd's Underlease* (1971) 23 P. & C.R. 1), and neither does the phrase "in the event of the parties failing to reach agreement" (*Wrenbridge Ltd v Harries (Southern Properties) Ltd* [1981] 2 E.G.L.R. 5). It is suggested that whichever phrase is used, the court would be reluctant to construe it as imposing on the parties a positive obligation to negotiate.

(d) Independent determination

6–40 Three questions arise in drafting a provision for determination of the new rent by an independent person. Firstly, who is to have the power to require such determination? Secondly, should the determination be made by an expert or by an arbitrator? Thirdly, should the lease lay down any particular procedure to be followed?

Both parties should have the right to apply for the appointment of the expert or arbitrator, even if the landlord alone has the right to initiate the rent review. If the lease is silent on the point, either party may apply (*United Scientific Holdings v Burnley BC* [1978] A.C. 904 at 960). Where either party may apply the tenant is not entitled to serve notice making time of the essence of the landlord's right to apply: if he is prejudiced by delay his remedy is to make the application himself (*Factory Holdings Group Ltd v Leboff International Ltd* [1987] 1 E.G.L.R. 135). Where only the landlord can apply, the time when the entitlement to do so arises will be a matter of construction, and time cannot be made of the essence until the obligation to apply arises and the landlord has then had a reasonable time to apply (*Northern and Midland Holdings Ltd v Magnet Ltd* [2004] EWHC 120 (Ch); [2004] NPC 7). This minor disadvantage to the tenant does not outweigh the advantage to the tenant in being able to initiate the determination of the rent. Where the rent review clause is not upwards only, it is of particular importance that the tenant should be able to initiate the machinery for determining the rent. The draftsman should specify the person who is to nominate the expert or arbitrator. That person is frequently the President of the RICS who has set up an efficient administrative machinery for such appointments. If the clause specifies the President as the appointor of the expert or arbitrator, it is thought that he must do so personally. Some clauses therefore provide that an appointment may be made by a duly authorised deputy, or a person acting on behalf of the President. If, for some reason, the nominated appointor cannot or will not make an appointment, the court is likely to provide alternative machinery for determining the rent (*Sudbrook Trading Estate Ltd v Eggleton* [1982] 3 All E.R. 1; s.18 of the Arbitration Act 1996). Similarly, where one of the parties has an obligation to apply for the appointment of an arbitrator, and refuses to do so, the court may regard this as a case of the machinery having broken down, unless the rent review clause itself provides for the consequence of a failure to apply (contrast *Harben Style v Rhodes Trust* [1995] 1 E.G.L.R. 118 and *Royal Bank of Scotland v Jennings* [1997] 1 E.G.L.R. 101). Where a clause requires the making of an application to the President of the RICS it is sufficient for the applicant merely to send a letter making the application, even though the application will not be processed (and hence will not come to the attention of the other party) until the requisite fee is paid (*Staines Warehousing Co Ltd v Montagu Executor & Trustee Co Ltd* [1987] 2 E.G.L.R. 130). The tenant's adviser should therefore press for an obligation on the landlord to notify the tenant of any application made by him to the President. Alternatively the tenant's adviser could amend the timetable by requiring the landlord to apply to the President and pay any requisite fee within the prescribed period.

6–41 The appointor is usually required to appoint "an independent surveyor." This formula may be unnecessarily restrictive where the new rent is to be determined by an arbitrator (rather than an expert). For example, if the only issue between the parties is a point of construction of the lease it may be better to have a solicitor or barrister as arbitrator. This would be possible if the lease provided for the appointment of "an independent person". If a surveyor is specified as the arbitrator, he may well in practice appoint a legal assessor to advise him on any contested point of law.

Before deciding whether to provide for determination by expert rather than by arbitration, it is essential to appreciate the differences between them. An arbitrator is a person who is appointed to resolve a formulated dispute between the parties. He will hear evidence and submissions from each party (although these may be written rather than oral) and is bound to make his decision solely on the evidence presented to him. If the strict rules of evidence apply, the evidence in question must be admissible evidence, and it will not include previous awards of other arbitrators relating to comparable properties (*Land Securities v Westminster CC* [1993] 1 W.L.R. 286). Despite the abolition of the rule against hearsay in civil proceedings (Civil Evidence Act 1995) it is probable that previous awards remain inadmissible. But the arbitrator may disapply the strict rules of evidence if he chooses to (s.34 of the Arbitration Act 1996). He has a wide range of powers under the Arbitration Act 1996, including the power to order discovery of documents and attendance of witnesses. His award may be enforced as if it were a judgment of the court, and there is a limited right of appeal from his award to the High Court on a point of law. He also has power to make an order as to the costs of the arbitration, and any clause in the lease which provides that a particular party is to pay his own costs (or the costs of the other party) is void (s.60 of the Arbitration

Act 1996; *Windvale Ltd v Darlington Insulation Co Ltd*, *The Times*, 22 December 1983). In addition, as has been noted, the court has power to extend the time within which an arbitration must be commenced (s.12 of the Arbitration Act 1996).

If the arbitrator dies or is unwilling or incapable of acting a new arbitrator may be appointed under the Arbitration Act 1996, and as long as he acts in good faith an arbitrator is immune from liability for negligence (s.29 of the Arbitration Act 1996).

On the other hand, an expert is a person appointed to fix the new rent. He is not bound to afford the parties an opportunity to tender evidence or submissions; and, even if a right to do so is conferred upon them by the terms of the lease, it is doubtful whether the expert need pay any attention to them. He is not bound by the strict rules of evidence. He acts on his own skill and judgment in reaching his decision, and that decision will be binding on the parties even if it is wrong (*Campbell v Edwards* [1976] 1 All E.R. 785; *Morgan Sindall v Sawston Farms (Cambs)* [1999] 1 E.G.L.R. 90). At one time it was thought that an expert's award was binding even though it contained an error of law on its face. But it has now been held by the House of Lords that, where parties agree to have a contractual dispute resolved by an expert, they intend him to resolve that dispute on the basis of a correct interpretation of the contract. Thus the expert's legal rulings can be reviewed by the court (*Mercury Communications v Director-General of Telecommunications* [1996] 1 W.L.R. 48, qualified in *British Shipbuilders Ltd v VSEL Consortium* [1997] 1 Lloyd's Rep. 106, where Lightman J. analysed the various decisions in which the court's jurisdiction to intervene had been considered). Since there is no statutory prohibition on challenging the legal rulings of an expert, unlike the restrictions on appealing against an arbitrator's award, it may be that the parties will have greater access to the courts when the rent is to be determined by an expert than they do when it is to be determined by an arbitrator. **6–42**

If the expert is negligent he may be sued by either party (*Arenson v Casson Beckman Rutley & Co* [1977] A.C. 405). He has no power to order disclosure of documents or the attendance of witnesses or to make any order as to costs (unless such power is expressly conferred on him by the lease); and if he dies or becomes incapable or unwilling to continue, it is doubtful whether another expert could be appointed under the lease. However, the death or incapacity of experts does not seem to have presented any problem in practice, and in any event the court would not allow a rent review to be frustrated by a breakdown in the machinery.

Which method should the draftsman choose? In general terms, it is suggested that determination by expert is quicker and cheaper than determination by arbitrator. On the other hand, the expert will not have had the benefit of hearing the arguments, and some observers have suggested that expert valuers rarely assess rents from the tenant's point of view.

Where the demised property is of a common type both in character and size, determination by expert is likely to be the better method. Comparables will be fairly easy to find and the determination will be able to proceed quickly. In addition, the costs of the determination will remain a reasonable proportion of the rental value of the property. In a time of rapidly changing markets, or where the true market is obscured by confidentiality clauses attached to the terms of transactions, some tenants fear that a concentration on comparable evidence which is capable of proper proof is in itself a distortion of the market. There is therefore a growing feeling among tenants that, since an expert is not tied to the rules of evidence, his judgment may be a more accurate reflector of the real market. Of course, while this point may work in the tenant's favour in a falling market, it is just as likely to work in the landlord's favour in a rising market.

6–43 Where the demised property is unusual either in size or in character, or where it is so valuable that small points have large financial consequences, determination by arbitration may be the better method since there will be an opportunity for full argument. The draftsman should, however, consider whether the categories of admissible evidence should be extended by agreement, e.g. to allow the parties to rely on awards of experts and arbitrators relating to comparable properties. Arbitration is also the better method where points of law may arise or where extensive disclosure might be needed. If no particular difficulties arise at the time of the rent review the costs of the arbitration need not be great since evidence and submissions can be presented informally. In some cases, it may be desirable for the choice of method of determination of the rent to remain flexible. If so the draftsman should consider giving one of the parties (usually the landlord) the right to choose whether the person to be appointed to determine the new rent should act as expert or arbitrator. Such a right should be made exercisable by notice given before the earliest date upon which an appointment may be made.

The procedure to be adopted should be left to the discretion of the person conducting the reference. In the case of an arbitrator, the court has a supervisory jurisdiction over his conduct of the reference. No such jurisdiction exists in the case of an expert. However, it is nevertheless suggested that the draftsman is unlikely to be able to provide a satisfactory procedure for future disputes without losing most of the advantages of determination by expert. For example, some leases require the expert to receive submissions or evidence from the parties. Almost invariably they are written. It is suggested that it is unsatisfactory to allow the rent to be fixed in reliance on assertions made by the parties which cannot be challenged by cross-examination, and where the expert is not to be given an opportunity of seeing and evaluating the quality of the witnesses. If the parties wish to adduce evidence in support of their cases, the appropriate way of determining the rent is by arbitration. A formal hearing may be dispensed with if the parties do not wish to avail themselves of their right to have one.

In the absence of consent of all parties, or an express term in the **6–44**
lease, an arbitrator cannot order a dispute referred to arbitration to be heard or determined together with another dispute involving a stranger, even though the two disputes are closely related, and a consolidated hearing would be convenient (*Oxford Shipping Co Ltd v Nippon Yusen Kaisha* [1984] 3 All E.R. 835; s.35 of the Arbitration Act 1996). Where the draftsman can anticipate this problem arising (e.g. where the lease in question is a sub-lease or is one of a parade of identical shops) he should consider enlarging the powers of the arbitrator.

Example 6.13 Rent review machinery; Notice, Counternotice reference to arbitration

(1) the landlord may serve upon the tenant not earlier than one year before the review date in question a notice ("a Review Notice") calling for a review of the rent;
(2) if the landlord serves a Review Notice then the rent payable with effect from the review date to which it relates shall be:
    (a) such sum as may be specified in the Review Notice or

   (b) the higher of the rent payable immediately before that review date and the Market Rent if (but only if) the tenant so elects by Counternotice in writing served on the landlord not later than two months (time being of essence) after the service of a Review Notice
(3) if the tenant serves a Counternotice the Market Rent shall be determined in default of agreement within two months after the service of the Counternotice by arbitration.

Example 6.14 Rent review machinery; no notice; determination by expert

(1) if the landlord and the tenant have not agreed the Market Rent three months before the relevant review date it shall be determined by an independent surveyor acting as an expert
(2) the independent surveyor shall:
   (a) be appointed in default of agreement by the President
   (b) give the landlord and the tenant an opportunity to make representations to him and to reply to each other's representations (but shall not be bound by them)
   (c) have power to determine how the costs of the reference shall be borne
   (d) publish his decision within two months of his appointment
(3) if the independent surveyor dies delays or becomes unwilling or incapable of acting or if for any reason the President thinks fit he may discharge the independent surveyor and appoint another in his place and may repeat this procedure as often as necessary.

Example 6.15 Landlord's option to select method of resolving disputes

If the landlord and the tenant have not agreed the Market Rent three months before the relevant review date it shall be determined by arbitration or (if the landlord so elects by notice in writing given not later than one month before the relevant review date time being of the essence) by an independent surveyor acting as an expert.

Example 6.16 Disputes procedure for inclusion in an underlease

If the landlord and the tenant have not agreed the Market Rent three months before the relevant review date it shall be determined by:

(1) an independent surveyor acting as an expert appointed in default of agreement by the President of the Royal Institution of Chartered Surveyors or
(2) at the election of either party (made not later than the making of an application to the President for an appointment time being of the essence) by the person (if any) appointed to determine the rent payable under the headlease acting in the capacity in which he is appointed under it.

Example 6.17 Either party to initiate the procedure
(1) either the landlord or the tenant may serve on the other of them a written notice ("a Review Notice") calling for a review of the rent
(2) a Review Notice may be served not earlier than six months before the review date to which it relates or at any time after that review date
(3) if the landlord and the tenant have not agreed the amount of the rent to be paid with effect from the review date in question by the review date itself, the question shall be determined by an independent expert
(4) in default of agreement the expert shall be appointed by the President of the Royal Institution of Chartered Surveyors (or a person acting on his behalf) on the application of either the landlord or the tenant.

Example 6.18 Clause permitting reliance on other awards
In the case of any arbitration either party shall be entitled to rely on the award of an expert or arbitrator relating to a transaction alleged to be comparable as evidence of the truth of the matters stated in the award, and the arbitrator shall give the award such weight as he thinks fit.

11. VALUATION FORMULA

The most important part of the rent review clause is the valuation formula since this will define the method of calculating the new rent. In recent years, this part of the rent review clause has become more sophisticated; perhaps over-sophisticated. If the rent review clause proposed in any particular case is unusual then the draftsman or the tenant's adviser should seek to ensure that it is studied by the landlord's (or the tenant's) surveyor before it is finally agreed. **6–45**

It is expected that green leasing provisions will gradually fall to be considered on rent review. Their relevance in any given case will depend upon the exact nature of the statutory provisions and regulations in force from time to time, whether the terms agreed between any given landlord and tenant are contained in the lease or in a time limited non legally binding Memorandum of Understanding for example, and the individual nature of such terms and obligations. Green provisions may impact upon the assumed energy efficiency of the hypothetical premises, the treatment of tenant's improvements, and the drafting of assumptions and disregards. The draftsman should also consider whether the inclusion of bespoke green lease provisions is likely to make it difficult to value the premises by reference to comparables on review and, if so, the best review machinery to adopt. Green leasing, including the potential interrelationship between rent review and green leasing provisions, is discussed in Chapter 11.

(a) The basic definition

6–46 Minor variations in language in the basic definition can have surprisingly different results. For example, if the new rent is to be "a reasonable rent for the demised premises" that rent must be assessed without regard to the fact that the tenant may have spent a large amount of money in improving the property: in effect he will have to pay for his improvements twice: once when he carries them out and again on the rent review (*Ponsford v HMS Aerosols Ltd* [1979] A.C. 63). On the other hand, if the new rent is to be "such rent as is reasonable in all the circumstances" or "such rent as would be reasonable for the landlord and the tenant to agree" the tenant's expenditure would not give rise to an increase in the rent (*Thomas Bates & Son Ltd v Wyndham's (Lingerie) Ltd* [1981] 1 All E.R. 1077; *Lear v Blizzard* [1983] 3 All E.R. 662). Moreover, there have been widely divergent expressions of judicial opinion as to whether the expression "a reasonable rent" permits or precludes the valuer from taking into account freak bids or rents obtainable in the open market by special circumstances (*Cuff v Stone (J&F) Property Co Ltd* [1979] A.C. 87 at 90, per Megarry J.; *Ponsford v HMS Aerosols Ltd* [1979] A.C. 73 at 74E, per Lord Wilberforce; at 77D, per Viscount Dilhorne; at 81F, per Lord Salmon; at 83H, per Lord

Fraser and, at 85G, per Lord Keith). In view of the uncertainty surrounding the meaning of these phrases, it is better to avoid them.

Even the expression "rack rent" may mean different things in different circumstances. In a lease granted at a time when there is in force some long-standing statutory control or inhibition on the right to recover rent it will mean the maximum amount recoverable under that control (*Newman v Dorrington Developments Ltd* [1975] 3 All E.R. 928); but in a lease granted at a time when such control was not in the contemplation of the parties it will mean the rent unrestricted by such control (*Compton Group Ltd v Estates Gazette Ltd* (1978) 36 P. & C.R. 148). Notwithstanding the temporary control of business rents between 1972 and 1975 it is suggested that the re-imposition of such control is so unlikely that it is unnecessary any longer to make express provision for it.

The time-honoured formula is the rent at which the demised property might reasonably be expected to be let in the open market on the review date by a willing landlord to a willing tenant.

This formula operates by reference to a hypothetical letting of the demised property in the open market. It therefore requires an objective approach. Some clauses in use require the surveyor to assess the amount which in his opinion ought to be the rent for the demised property "having regard to rental values" current at the review date. The term "having regard" is almost of necessity bound to create difficulties. How much regard is to be had, and what weight is to be attached to the regard when it has been had? (*English Exporters (London) Ltd v Eldonwall Ltd* [1973] 1 All E.R. 726 at 737, per Megarry J.). It may also be objected that a direction to the surveyor to have regard to rental values of other property may cause difficulties if there are no real comparables, or if some other method of valuation (e.g. a rent based on barrelage or through-put of petrol or profits) would be appropriate. Unless there are special reasons for adopting a subjective approach it is suggested that the objective approach does better justice between the parties.

However, the courts have said that there is little difference between **6–47** a variety of phrases in common use. Thus "full" adds nothing to "rack rent"; "market" does not add anything to "rack rent"; "open" does not add anything to "market" and the word "highest" only adds emphasis to what would be implicit anyway (*Royal Exchange Assurance v Bryant Samuel Properties (Coventry)* [1985] 1 E.G.L.R. 84; *Sterling Land Office Developments v Lloyds Bank*

[1984] 2 E.G.L.R. 135; *Daejan Investments v Cornwall Coast Country Club* (1985) 50 P. & C.R. 157).

Nevertheless, tenants are rightly suspicious of clauses which require the ascertainment of the "best" rent, since that will undoubtedly entitle the landlord to the advantage of any special purchaser. If the actual tenant is the occupier of adjacent property he may find himself in the position of a special purchaser, since there is no rule of law which excludes him from the market (*First Leisure Trading v Dorita Properties* [1991] 1 E.G.L.R. 133). The evidence may establish that in his capacity as adjoining occupier the tenant would outbid the rest of the market. If so, his overbid may be taken into account (*Secretary of State for the Environment v Reed International* [1994] 1 E.G.L.R. 22). The remedy against this is to extend the scope of the disregard of the tenant's occupation to include property (other than the demised property) which is occupied by the tenant.

The reference in the basic definition to the open market predicates the existence of an open market in which the hypothetical tenant will compete, and requires that the successful competitor will be able to use the property on offer (*Law Land Company Ltd v Consumers Association Ltd* [1980] 2 E.G.L.R. 109). If there are parts of the lease which are inconsistent with that basic assumption the court will modify the lease accordingly.

It is advisable to provide expressly for the assumption of a willing landlord and a willing tenant, since this removes the scope for arguing that the property would fail to be let at any particular review date. The general principles to be applied to the construction of such a clause were considered in *Evans (FR) (Leeds) Ltd v English Electric Co Ltd* (1978) 36 P. & C.R. 185. The assumption of a willing landlord or a willing tenant must not, however, be used to distort the reality of the market (*Dennis & Robinson Ltd v Kiossos Establishment* [1987] 1 E.G.L.R. 133). In some cases there may, in reality, be only one tenant who would take the property if it were to be offered in the market. In such a case the willing tenant will have the attributes of the actual tenant (*Hoare v National Trust* [1999] 1 E.G.L.R. 155).

A rent review clause in the conventional form does not permit the agreement or determination of a stepped rent, that is, a rent rising in stages over the review period (*Beegas Nominees v BHP Petroleum*

[1998] 2 E.G.L.R. 57). If the parties wish to leave this possibility open, the lease should provide for it expressly.

(b) The property to be valued

Normally, the property to be valued for the purposes of the rent review will be the demised property and this will also be the court's default position in the absence of clear and specific drafting to the contrary (see, for example, *Airways Aero Associations Ltd v Wycombe District Council* [2010] EWHC 1654 (Ch)). In the case of a large property consideration should be given to the question whether account should be taken of the potential of the property for letting in parts. Where the rent is to be reviewed to a fraction of the market rental value, and the fraction is intended to take account of the tenant's position as mesne landlord, this is particularly important (*Royal Exchange Assurance v Bryant Samuel Properties (Coventry) Ltd* [1985] 1 E.G.L.R. 84). **6–48**

The draftsman should also ensure that the property to be valued is capable of being successfully let as a separate entity with all necessary rights of access and other easements. If it is not, he should provide for the assumption of those rights in the hypothetical letting (*Jefferies v O'Neill* [1984] 1 E.G.L.R. 106, where the demised property in fact had no independent access but it was held that that fact ought to be disregarded for the purposes of the rent review. In *J Murphy v Railtrack* [2002] 2 E.G.L.R. 48, the Court of Appeal refused to imply such a disregard into s.34 of the Landlord and Tenant Act 1954).

In some cases it may be necessary to provide for the valuation of property other than the demised property. For example, the demised property may be of an unusual character making the finding of comparables difficult (see *St Martins Property Investments Ltd v Cable & Wireless UK Plc* [2007] EWHC 582 (Ch), where the premises comprised a computer data centre and the reviewed rent was originally to be set on the assumption that "the demised premises comprise high class professional or commercial offices with a new internal area of 124,019 sq ft"). If a rent review clause requires the valuation of a notional building the court will construe the clause so as to produce a valuation method which can reasonably have been intended to apply to the actual premises (*Dukeminster (Ebbgate House One) Ltd v Somerfield Properties Co*

Ltd [1997] 2 E.G.L.R. 125). In construing a counter factual assumption, the court will adopt a minimalist approach in the absence of express direction (see *McDonalds Real Estate LLP v Arundel Corp* [2008] 2 E.G.L.R. 53, where the rent review clause provided that the rent payable after review should be the open market value of either the actual restaurant building on the site or a notional modern single storey warehouse, whichever was the greater). The draftsman should consider not simply the nature of the notional building, but also the inclusion of appropriate drafting to reflect the assumed specification of, and facilities to be enjoyed by, the notional premises as at the review date/s (see, for example, *HMV UK v Propinvest Friar Ltd Partnership* [2012] 1 Lloyd's Rep. 416, where the issue was whether the notional premises enjoyed the benefit of a secondary fire escape).

The draftsman should also consider the question of planning permission if a notional use is to be assumed. Is the relevant permission to be assumed to exist, or is the valuer to take into account the prospect of a successful application being made to obtain the requisite planning permission? In *McDonalds Real Estate LLP* (as cited above), the issue was whether the valuer was to assume the notional warehouse on the site was a retail or non retail warehouse. It was held there was no basis for assuming that planning permission for retail use existed in relation to the notional warehouse. However, in the absence of any provision limiting the use of the notional warehouse to use for distribution and storage, there was nothing to prevent the valuer taking into account the prospect of obtaining planning permission for such use.

If a lease of a unit on a business park is granted when that business park is largely undeveloped such that there may be no comparables available on review, an assumption may be included that the evidence of rental value of premises with specified characteristics within other specified areas is evidence of market rental value as if those other premises were situated on the business park. However, unless it is expressly provided that an allowance or discount is made from the rent in respect of premises in a better, more highly-rented location, or better established location, no discount will be made from higher values simply because the premises in question are situated in the specified areas and not in the business park (*Beegas Nominees Ltd v Decco Ltd* [2003] 3 E.G.L.R. 25).

If the property is to be valued as a cleared site on terms which include a covenant to erect a building, the draftsman should specify whether the building is to be constructed in accordance with plans that were approved by the landlord at the date the lease was granted (*Margram Plc v Dorant Ltd* [2006] 47 E.G. 180 (CS)), or whether it is to be constructed in accordance with the plans that would be drawn up for such a building at the review date (*Bellow Properties Ltd v The Master Fellows & Scholars of the College of the Holy and Undivided Trinity, Cambridge* [2002] 1 P. & C.R. DG6).

If the property to be valued is to be assumed to have a lawful use different from that of the actual property, it is essential that the clause makes it clear that the notional property is physically suitable for that use. In *Trusthouse Forte Albany Hotels Ltd v Daejan Investments Ltd* [1980] 2 E.G.L.R. 123, the property consisted of an hotel, but the reviewed rent was to be assessed on the basis of a hypothetical letting of parts of the ground floor only on the assumption that those areas were "actually let or available for letting for shopping or retail purposes". It was held that the clause required the assumption that the property could be used for the specified purpose without illegality or breach of covenant, but did not require the further assumption that the property was physically adapted or fit for the specified use. Similarly, where a rent review clause provided for a hypothetical letting "for office purposes" it was held that the clause required the assumption that the property could lawfully be used for that purpose (*Bovis Group Pension Fund Ltd v GC Flooring & Furnishing Ltd* [1984] 1 E.G.L.R. 123).

Where the lease contained an acknowledgment by the tenant that the premises were fit for use as offices, the acknowledgment did not require the assumption that the property was in a physical condition which differed from its actual condition; it merely precluded the tenant from arguing that in its actual condition the property could not be used as offices (*Orchid Lodge v Extel Computing* [1991] 2 E.G.L.R. 116). If the draftsman wants to provide for a review of the property in an improved physical condition, clear words are needed.

The property may be suitable for letting either as a whole or in parts. If the review clause expressly says that the letting is to be a letting as a whole, then there is no scope for aggregating the sums of the constituent parts. But if the clause says that the letting may be a letting either as a whole or in parts, then the valuer may value the property in natural lots, provided that those lots can be created without breach of covenant (*Westside Nominees v Bolton MBC* (2000) 81 P. & C.R. 130).

(c) Fit for use

6–49 Although the general rule is that the property is to be valued in its actual condition at the relevant date, it is nevertheless to be assumed that the tenant has removed from the property those fixtures which he is entitled to remove (*New Zealand Government Property Corp v HM & S Ltd* [1982] Q.B. 1145; *Young v Dalgety Plc* [1987] 1 E.G.L.R. 116). In order to avoid the potentially depreciatory effect on the rent which such an assumption might have, and in order to counter the additional argument that the hypothetical tenant would be granted a rent free period, it is now usual to include in the rent review clause an assumption that the property is fit for immediate use and occupation. This form does not entirely overcome the difficulty, because it leads to the question: use as what? It is suggested therefore that the draftsman states expressly that the property is to be assumed to be fit for use for the purposes permitted by the lease. Some more extreme forms of lease go on to provide that the property is to be assumed to be fitted out. The phrase "fitted out" goes beyond merely "fit". The latter may simply mean free from defects and ready for fitting out; the former means that all partitions, shop fittings, office furniture, etc. have been installed (*Pontsarn Investments v Kansallis-Osake Pankki* [1992] 1 E.G.L.R. 148). Where a lease provided for the assumption that all tenant's works required by the hypothetical tenant had been completed, it was held that this meant that the hypothetical tenant did not want further or different work from that carried out by the actual tenant, whose improvements were in any event to be disregarded (*London & Leeds Estates v Paribas* (1993) 66 P. & C.R. 218). One difficulty is that the draftsman has not had in his mind's eye a mental picture of the building to be valued. In addition, provisions dealing with the physical condition of the building are often scattered through the rent review clause, sometimes as assumptions and sometimes as disregards. There is much to be said for collecting these provisions together, which will help avoid the risk that one provision may be effectively cancelled out by another.

If the parties agree that the property is to be treated as having been fitted out, it is important to specify at whose expense the fitting out is assumed to have been done. In some cases, the landlord will in fact have paid for the fitting out through a contribution to the tenant's initial costs. In those cases, it may be fair to assume that the hypothetical fitting out is also carried out at the expense of the landlord, at least during the life of the original actual fitting out. But where the tenant has fitted out at its own expense, it is unfair for the rent to be assessed on the basis of a fitted-out building unless that expense to the tenant is also taken into account.

In buildings finished by the developer to "shell and core" it is customary for the tenant to specify the fitting-out works but for the landlord to contribute towards them. In such cases one solution which is frequently adopted is for the parties' surveyors to prepare a "rent review specification" which is annexed to the lease. For the purposes of rent review, the building is assumed to be in the condition specified in the rent review specification. The rent review specification must be sufficiently detailed to enable the valuer to form a clear picture of the imaginary physical condition of the building. An alternative would be to build in an assumption that the hypothetical tenant receives a similar contribution towards fitting out from the hypothetical landlord. Provision would need to be made for index-linking the amount of the contribution. This method has the advantage that the landlord is not tied to a rent review specification formulated at the beginning of the lease, but can respond to changes in the requirements of a modern building. **6–50**

Example 6.19 Rent review clause requiring valuation of a notional building

(1) The expression "the Market Rent" means the product of:
   (a) the net lettable area of the demised property (measured in accordance with any codes of practice promulgated from time to time by the Royal Institution of Chartered Surveyors) expressed in square metres and
   (b) the rate per square metre at which the notional building could reasonably be expected to be let in the open market on the review date by a willing landlord to a willing tenant

(2) The notional building referred to in clause (1) above is:

(a) located in the business centre of [ ]
(b) constructed to a standard similar to the demised property
(c) [ ] square metres in area
(d) available for letting with vacant possession on the terms of this lease (subject to any necessary modifications) together with all necessary ancillary accommodation
(e) fit for immediate occupation and use for the purposes permitted by the terms of this lease.

Example 6.20 Assumptions about the physical condition of the property

The Market Rent shall be assessed on the assumption that the demised property:

(1) is in a condition consistent with performance by the tenant of his obligations under this lease
(2) has not been altered by the tenant in such a way as to affect its rental value (unless the alterations were carried out by the tenant under an obligation to the landlord)
(3) has had removed from it all tenant's fixtures and partitioning and that all consequential damage has been made good
(4) has not been destroyed or damaged by any insured risk
(5) is free from physical defects
(6) is to be fitted out by and at the expense of the hypothetical tenant during a rent free period of such length as is reasonably necessary for that purpose.

(d) Duration of the tenancy

6–51 The next matter to be considered is the duration of the hypothetical letting. If the clause is silent, a letting for the residue of the term will be presumed (*Norwich Union Life Insurance Society v Trustee Savings Bank Central Board* [1986] 1 E.G.L.R. 136). It used to be the general rule that the longer the letting the higher the rent was likely to be. However, recent economic conditions, and a growing awareness of the onerous liabilities of an original tenant have combined to alter tenants' desires, and it does not appear that these have changed in the light of the abolition of privity of contract by the Landlord and Tenant (Covenants) Act 1995. The optimum length of term varies according to the nature of the property and its location. There are three basic possibilities in specifying the duration of the hypothetical letting. Firstly, the clause may provide for the length of the hypothetical tenancy to be equal to the unexpired residue of the actual term on the review date. This formula may produce different results according to which review is being operated. For example, on the fourth quinquennial review under a 25 year lease the rent will be assessed as if a 5 year term was being granted. A 5 year term, particularly of a large building, may not be attractive to potential tenants and the rent obtainable on that review may be depressed on that account. This effect may be countered by specifying a minimum length of term. For example, the hypothetical tenancy may be expressed to be for "a term equal to the unexpired residue of the term of this lease or for a term of 10 years from the review date whichever is the longer."

Secondly, the clause may provide for the term of the hypothetical tenancy to be equal to the original term of the lease. It has been suggested that such a formula is unfair to the tenant. However, since the tenant has actually had a longer lease than the unexpired residue of the term, there is no compelling reason why he should not be charged rent on that basis, especially if the fact that the tenant is in occupation is to be disregarded in so far as it would otherwise affect the rent (*Lynnthorpe Enterprises v Sidney Smith (Chelsea)* [1990] 2 E.G.L.R. 131, per Staughton L.J.). Before adopting this formula, the draftsman should consider the likely effect of the assumption in relation to the last review. Even in the case of a new building let for, say, 25 years, the landlord might have difficulty in finding a tenant to accept a full repairing lease for a further 25 years, if the building is 20 years old at the date when the question arises.

In *Canary Wharf Investments (Three) v Telegraph Group Ltd* [2003] 3 E.G.L.R. 31, the lease had been made on 4 March 1994 for a term of 25 years commencing on April 1993. The "open market rent" was defined as the rent at which the premises, subject to certain assumptions:

> "could be expected to be let as a whole at the Relevant Rent Review Date by a willing landlord to a willing tenant with vacant possession and without payment or receipt by any person of any premium or any consideration, under the rent, for the grant thereof, the term of 25 years and otherwise on the terms and conditions and subject to the covenants and provisions contained in the hypothetical lease…".

The court held that the natural reading of the draftsman's wording was that the hypothetical 25 year term ran from the relevant review date and not from the date from which the term of the actual lease ran. Whilst welcomed by property professionals, the decision in the *Canary Wharf* case is regarded as exceptional. If the draftsman wishes to adopt this formula, the words of the clause must be clear.

The court generally leans in favour of a construction which, wherever possible, accords with reality. Accordingly, a clause which provided for the length of the hypothetical term to be "equivalent to the term hereby granted" was held to require the assumption of a letting for a period equal to the residue of the actual term (*The Ritz Hotel (London) Ltd v Ritz Casino Ltd* [1989] 2 E.G.L.R. 135; *Lynnthorpe Enterprises v Sidney Smith (Chelsea)* [1990] 2 E.G.L.R. 131). A similar conclusion was reached in relation to an assumption of a term equal in duration to the original term (*St Martins Property Investments Ltd v CIB Properties Ltd* [1999] L. & T. 1), and in relation to hypothetical letting "for a term equal to the term originally granted under this lease" (*Chancebutton Ltd v Compass Services UK & Ireland Ltd* [2004] 2 E.G.L.R. 47). If the draftsman wishes to avoid this result, it is best to quantify the length of the hypothetical term to avoid ambiguity (e.g. "for a term of 15 years beginning on the relevant review date").

6–52 Thirdly, the draftsman may adopt a flexible formula. For example, the hypothetical tenancy may be assumed to be granted "for such a term as will command the best rent". This formula has obvious attractions for the landlord. However, since it will always result in the tenant having to pay the highest rent for the property, irrespective of the actual duration of the residue of the term, it is suggested that the tenant's adviser should resist this formula. A variant of this approach is to provide for a term "not exceeding" a particular duration. The court has held that a flexible term should be assumed where the terms of the hypothetical lease excluded the possibility of rent review. Thus, the assumed term was that which a willing landlord would have been prepared to grant under a lease with no rent review (*Prudential Assurance v Salisbury's Handbags* [1992] 1 E.G.L.R. 153). A flexible term may also be assumed where the actual term is very long and the rent is a geared rent (*Brown v Gloucester City Council* [1998] 1 E.G.L.R. 95; *Westside Nominees v Bolton MBC* (2000) 81 P. & C.R. 130).

From the tenant's point of view, a formula based on the unexpired residue of the term, perhaps with a minimum period, is the best solution. If any other formula is chosen the tenant's adviser must make sure that the hypothetical term contains rent reviews at the same frequency as those in the actual term.

In assessing the rent for the hypothetical tenancy, the valuer may take into account the hypothetical tenant's prospects of renewing the tenancy under Part II of the Landlord and Tenant Act 1954 even where the lease specified a term "not exceeding" a stated number of years (*Pivot Properties Ltd v Secretary of State* (1981) 41 P. & C.R. 248). Occasionally clauses provide for statutory controls on rent and security of tenure to be disregarded (e.g. *Toyota (GB) Ltd v Legal & General (Pensions Management) Ltd* [1989] 2 E.G.L.R. 123). Such clauses would almost certainly reduce the rent which would otherwise be payable, and should be avoided.

Where the transaction takes the form of the grant of a lease and a reversionary lease, the draftsman must ensure that the existence of the reversionary lease is taken into account in assessing the rent under the lease in possession. If this is not done, the tenant may receive a windfall benefit by an assumption of a short hypothetical term whereas in reality he has the benefit of the reversionary lease as well. The court will avoid this result if possible, and may be able to imply a term to the effect that the existence of the reversionary term is to be taken into account (*Toyota (GB) Ltd v Legal & General (Pensions Management)* [1989] 2 E.G.L.R. 123). But it is not safe to rely on an implication.

(e) Terms of letting

The terms of letting should be clearly stated in the clause. The court will lean against construing a rent review clause so as to make the tenant pay for something which he has not got and cannot compel the landlord to give him (*Pearl Assurance Plc v Shaw* [1985] 1 E.G.L.R. 92). Accordingly, if no terms are stated, the presumption is that the terms are to be those of the actual lease (*Basingstoke and Deane BC v Host Group Ltd* [1988] 1 All E.R. 824). **6–53**

This is known as the presumption in favour of reality (*Lynnthorpe Enterprises v Sidney Smith (Chelsea)* [1990] 2 E.G.L.R. 131). However, this inference may be displaced if some of the terms of the actual lease are inconsistent with the fundamental concept of review to market rent (*Sterling Land Office Developments Ltd v Lloyds Bank Plc* [1984] 2 E.G.L.R. 135). Further modifications may be made where the terms of the actual lease are inconsistent with some assumption which must be made for the purposes of the hypothetical lease.

Thus, in *Sheerness Steel Co v Medway Ports Authority* [1992] 1 E.G.L.R. 133, property was let as a steel rolling mill. The rent review clause required the assumption that the property was let for industrial purposes and that the tenant had an obligation to build buildings corresponding to those on site at the rent review date. It was held that the use restrictions which limited use to a particular form of industrial activity (i.e. steel rolling) and the restrictions on alterations could not be part of the hypothetical lease because they were inconsistent with the assumption that the property would be let for industrial purposes generally, and that the incoming tenant would have to adapt the property to make it suitable for the industrial use of his choice. Similarly, where a rent review clause provided for a hypothetical letting for retail purposes it was held that restrictions in the lease on the type of retail use permitted were not to be included in the hypothetical lease (*Postel Properties v Greenwell* (1992) 65 P. & C.R. 244).

As a general rule, the tenant's adviser should seek to ensure that the terms of the hypothetical tenancy correspond with those of the actual tenancy.

(i) Alienation

6–54 The terms of the covenant against alienation may have a significant effect on the rent obtainable on the review. If the tenant is absolutely prohibited from subletting a large building, the available market will be restricted to those tenants capable of occupying the whole, which may have the effect of reducing rental levels. Similarly, if the tenant is prohibited from sharing occupation (as well as prohibited from assigning or subletting part of the property) the restriction may well be reflected in the reviewed rent. The effect of such a restriction may be particularly marked where the demised property is a department store (where the tenant would be unable to enter into franchise agreements or licences) or a large office where the tenant would be unable to share the accommodation with a subsidiary company. Many clauses prohibit subletting at a rent less than the rent passing under the lease itself. In a falling market, such a clause may mean that the property is effectively incapable of being sublet. This in turn may have a depressing effect on rental value. The draftsman should, therefore, be careful not to impose greater restrictions on the tenant than those necessary for the protection of the landlord. Moreover, the restrictions on alienation should always be read together with the restrictions on use.

(ii) Use

The greater the restrictions on the permitted use of the demised property, the less the market rent is likely to be, until the point comes at which the permitted use of the property is so restrictive that the court is able to reject it as being inconsistent with the concept of review in the open market. Use clauses may be divided into a number of categories for this purpose. **6–55**

Firstly, there are clauses which restrict the use of the property to a particular category of use, unless the landlord's consent is obtained, such consent not to be unreasonably withheld (see, for example, *Kalford Ltd v Peterborough CC* [2001] E.G.C.S. 42). Such clauses are known as "open" clauses, and form the norm for valuation purposes. Any material deviation from this type of clause is likely to have an effect on the rent.

Secondly, there are clauses which restrict the use of the property to a particular category of use unless the landlord's consent is obtained, but do not provide that the landlord's consent is not to be unreasonably withheld. In such a case the valuer may have regard to the possibility that the landlord will consent to a change of use, since the change of use will not involve a variation of the terms of the lease, but is expressly contemplated by them (*Forte & Co Ltd v General Accident Life Assurance Ltd* [1986] 2 E.G.L.R. 115).

Thirdly, there are clauses which restrict the use of the property to a particular category of use, but make no provision for any change of use. In such a case the valuer may not take into account the possibility that the covenant will be varied by agreement between the parties, or waived by the landlord (*Plinth Property Investments Ltd v Mott, Hay & Anderson* (1978) 38 P. & C.R. 361). Even if the landlord does purport unilaterally to waive or vary the clause otherwise than at the request of the tenant, the waiver or variation is to be ignored (*C&A Pensions Trustees Ltd v British Vita Investments Ltd* [1984] 2 E.G.L.R. 75).

Fourthly, there are clauses which restrict the use of the property to use by a named tenant. Where that use is the only permitted use under the lease then for the purpose of the rent review the name of the hypothetical tenant will be substituted for that of the actual tenant. In *Law Land Co Ltd v Consumers Association* [1980] 2 E.G.L.R. 109, the use covenant provided that the property was not without the prior written consent of the landlord to be used other than as offices of the Consumers' Association and its associated organisations. The Court of Appeal held that for the purposes of the rent review clause it was to be assumed that the property could lawfully be used as offices of the hypothetical original tenant. The court held that to conclude otherwise would frustrate the purpose of the rent review, since there would then only be one possible tenant in the market. Similarly, in *Sterling Land Office Developments Ltd v Lloyds Bank Plc* [1984] 2 E.G.L.R. 135, the use was defined as "not. . .for any purpose other than as a branch of Lloyds Bank Ltd." The rent review clause was silent as to the terms of the hypothetical letting. Harman J. held that for the purposes of the rent review the use covenant should be read as prohibiting use for any purpose other than as premises of the hypothetical willing tenant.

A similar conclusion was reached where the use was restricted to the lessees' business of mortgage finance and insurance consultants (*SI Pension Trustees v Ministerio de la Marina Peruana* [1988] 1 E.G.L.R. 119). On the other hand, where there is both a restriction on use to use by a named tenant and an alternative use provided for in the lease, the reasoning of those two cases does not apply. The existence of the alternative use means that there will be hypothetical tenants in the market for that use and consequently there is no need to modify the restriction on use to the named tenant (*James v British Crafts Centre* [1987] 1 E.G.L.R. 139; *Orchid Lodge (United Kingdom) v Extel Computing* [1991] 2 E.G.L.R. 116).

The lesson for the draftsman is not to impose on the tenant any restrictions greater than those necessary for the protection of the landlord. Some rent review clauses meet the problem by providing for the restrictions on use to be disregarded in assessing the rent. Although this approach protects the landlord, it is clearly unfair to the tenant who is compelled to pay for something which he does not have. The tenant's adviser should therefore delete the provision. Paradoxically, however, if the draftsman tightens the use clause so that use is restricted to the named original tenant only, the use clause in the hypothetical lease will be opened up on review. But the process of opening the lease will only make the property usable by the hypothetical original tenant. For practical purposes, therefore, the hypothetical lease will be unassignable.

Once the parties have agreed upon a use covenant the court will not modify it in a new lease granted under Part II of the Landlord and Tenant Act 1954 merely to give one party a rental advantage. This applies equally to a landlord seeking to widen the use covenant (*Clements (Charles) (London) Ltd v Rank City Wall Ltd* [1978] 1 E.G.L.R. 47) and to a tenant seeking to narrow it (*Aldwych Club Ltd v Copthall Property Co Ltd* (1962) 185 E.G. 219).

As the Competition Act 1998 now applies to land agreements (see Chapter 10), there is theoretically potential for the value to be attributed to an exclusivity clause to be an issue on a rent review on the grounds that it may be open to challenge.

(iii) Assumed compliance with terms

Many rent review clauses contain an express assumption that the **6–56** tenant has complied with his covenants. It seems that such an assumption would be implied by the court even if the review clause was silent on the point (*Harmsworth Pension Funds Trustees Ltd v Charringtons Industrial Holdings Ltd* [1985] 1 E.G.L.R. 97). This is consistent with the general principle of law that a person is not entitled to rely upon his own wrong. How this principle applies to the landlord's covenants is less clear. In *Plinth Property Investments Ltd v Mott, Hay & Andersen* (1978) 38 P. & C.R. 361, Brandon L.J. said that an arbitrator directed to have regard to the provisions of the lease had to consider the rights and obligations imposed by the lease and "to assume that the rights will be enforced and that the obligations will be performed."

This dictum would suggest that it should be assumed that the landlord has performed his covenants also. But in *Fawke v Chelsea (Viscount)* [1979] 3 All E.R. 568, the Court of Appeal held that in fixing an interim rent on the landlord's application under s.24A of the Landlord and Tenant Act 1954, the court should have regard to the actual state of repair of the property. In that case the landlord was under an obligation to repair. Thus, the application of the principle that a person cannot take advantage of his own wrong produced the converse result in the case of a landlord. It may however be questioned whether the same result would follow in a rent review case. The rent fixed by the Court of Appeal was a differential rent, in the sense that it was to increase once the property was put into repair. By contrast, a rent fixed upon review is a constant rent (*Clarke v Findon Developments Ltd* [1984] 1 E.G.L.R. 129). Accordingly, if the tenant was to enforce the landlord's repairing obligation against him by specific performance, he might achieve occupation of a repaired building at a rent reflecting the disrepair. The likely resolution of this conflict is that the rent should be assessed having regard both to the actual state of the building but taking into account the existence and enforceability of the landlord's covenants.

(iv) Geared rents

6–57 Leases sometimes provide for the tenant to pay a rent fixed as a percentage of market value. The percentage may be less than 100 where the tenant has carried out substantial building works as part of the consideration for the grant. Conversely, it may be greater than 100 where the landlord has carried out special works of adaptation to the building which are of benefit to the particular tenant but which would be unlikely to affect the rental value of the building in the market. In such circumstances the draftsman should provide for the hypothetical lease to contain a rent review clause to 100 per cent of rack rental value. This is best done by specifying that the terms of the hypothetical lease are to exclude the terms of the actual lease as regards the gearing. If the draftsman fails to do this, the court will usually reach the conclusion that the gearing provisions should be omitted from the hypothetical lease anyway (*Guys 'n' Dolls v Sade Brothers Catering* [1984] 1 E.G.L.R. 103; *Buffalo Enterprises v Golden Wonder* [1991] 1 E.G.L.R. 141; *Prudential Assurance v 99 Bishopsgate* [1999] 1 E.G.L.R. 119; *Nissim v Ablethird Ltd* [2009] EWHC 585 (Ch)). There can be exceptions to this (*Norwich Union Life Insurance Society v British Telecommunications* [1995] E.G.C.S. 148).

Example 6.21 Example of geared rent
The rent payable by the tenant shall be 125 per cent of the open market rent (as agreed or determined in accordance with this clause). But in agreeing or determining the open market rent it shall be assumed that the tenant is liable to pay no more than the open market rent itself.

(v) Personal rights

Some leases grant personal rights to the original tenant (e.g. the right to use the property for a particular purpose or the right to sublet or assign to a company within the same group). The approach adopted by the court is that since such rights would not be enjoyed by an assignee, they would not be enjoyed by a hypothetical tenant, and consequently rights personal to the tenant should be excluded from the hypothetical lease (*James v British Crafts Centre* [1987] 1 E.G.L.R. 139; *Orchid Lodge (United Kingdom) v Extel Computing* [1991] 2 E.G.L.R. 116). The same is true of a personal break clause (*St Martins Property Investments Ltd v CIB Properties Ltd* [1999] L. & T.R. 1). However, since the tenant enjoys these rights, the landlord may consider that he ought to pay for them. This result can be achieved by an assumption in the rent review clause that any rights or privileges personal to the person who is the actual tenant at the date of the rent review are to be assumed to be granted to the hypothetical tenant. The tenant should ensure that personal rights are not to be assumed to be granted to the hypothetical tenant after they have lapsed in reality. **6–58**

(f) Disregards

(i) Tenant's occupation

The tenant's adviser should ensure that as far as any effect on rent is concerned, the fact that the tenant has been in occupation of the demised property is disregarded. If this is not expressly provided, the new rent may be fixed taking into account that the tenant might pay more for the property simply in order to avoid having to move. The disregard does not of itself require vacant possession to be assumed (*Scottish & Newcastle Breweries Plc v Sir Richard Sutton's Settled Estates* [1985] 2 E.G.L.R. 130 at 136E), nor does it exclude from consideration all evidence derived from the tenant's occupation. Such evidence is excluded only to the extent that it affects rent (*Cornwall Coast Country Club Ltd v Cardgrange Ltd* [1987] 1 E.G.L.R. 146 at 151E). Thus far, the disregard of the tenant's occupation is a standard term in rent review clauses. However, the tenant's adviser should consider whether it goes far enough to protect the tenant. In particular, it may be advisable to disregard the occupation of the tenant's subtenants and licensees, **6–59** and it may also be desirable to disregard the tenant's occupation of other property (e.g. an adjoining building, or another unit in the same shopping centre, or a piece of land used as a car park). If this is not done then the fact that the tenant occupies adjoining property may be taken into account in fixing the rent (*First Leisure Trading v Dorita Properties* [1991] 1 E.G.L.R. 133).

(ii) Goodwill

6–60 Equally, the tenant's adviser should ensure that goodwill is disregarded in assessing the new rent, otherwise a tenant who is efficient in running his business will be charged extra on account of his efficiency. It is well known, however, that some property is valued by the profits method; that is, by ascertaining what average annual profit is likely to be made by a competent trader before deduction of rent, and then by apportioning that profit between the landlord and the tenant. If a profits method is likely, consideration should be given to deleting or modifying this disregard. For example, in the case of a letting of a public house, it may be appropriate to disregard the effect on rent of goodwill to the extent that it exceeds the goodwill likely to have been generated by a tenant of average competence. Further drafting problems raised by this valuation method are discussed below. Where the lease requires the disregard of the effect on rent of the tenant's occupation it will usually follow as a matter of necessary implication that his goodwill must also be disregarded (*Prudential Assurance Co v Grand Metropolitan Estates* [1993] 2 E.G.L.R. 153).

(iii) Part of the property

6–61 Clear words must be used if the court is to conclude that the parties intended the valuation to be a valuation of part only of the property comprised in the lease. In *Safeway Stores v Legal & General Assurance Society* [2005] 1 P. & C.R. 9, the demised premises comprised a retail supermarket and a petrol filling station but the rent review clause made clear that the valuation was to be of the supermarket, disregarding the potential of the filling station.

(iv) Improvements

Unless the lease provides to the contrary, the new rent will be determined for the demised property as it stands on the review date irrespective of the identity of the person who paid for improvements (*Ponsford v HMS Aerosols* [1978] 2 All E.R. 837) except where the formula describing the rent allows the personal circumstances of the parties to be taken into account (as in *Thomas Bates & Son Ltd v Wyndham's (Lingerie) Ltd* [1981] 1 All E.R. 1077). This has been said to be an important prima facie assumption, which is not to be frittered away on minor differences in drafting (*Laura Investments v Havering LBC* [1992] 1 E.G.L.R. 155). Sometimes, however, it has been possible to discern a clear distinction between part of the demised property (e.g. the site on which it was constructed) and structures erected on the site, such that only the site is to be valued for the purposes of the rent review (*Ipswich Town Football Club v Ipswich BC* [1988] 1 E.G.L.R. 146; *Braid v Wallsall MBC* (1998) 78 P. & C.R. 94; *Coors Holdings Ltd v Dow Properties Ltd* [2007] 2 P. & C.R. 22; *Sahota v RR Leisureways (UK) Ltd* [2010] EWHC 3114). But such cases are rare (see *Goh Eng Wah v Yap Phooi Yin* [1988] 2 E.G.L.R. 148; *Ravenseft Properties v Park* [1988] 2 E.G.L.R. 164; *Laura Investments v Havering LBC* [1992] 1 E.G.L.R. 155 and *Sheerness Steel v Medway Ports Authority* [1992] 1 E.G.L.R. 133, in all of which tenants' improvements were included in the valuation). In the normal case of property taken at a rack rent, the tenant's adviser should ensure that the tenant is not required to pay rent for his own improvements. Where, however, part of the consideration for the grant of the lease is the carrying out of improvements, it is fair that the landlord should receive the benefit of those works on review. So also where the tenant is recompensed for the carrying out of works by paying a proportion of the rack rental value of the property, or a proportion of rents received or receivable for the property, it is fair for the property to be valued as it stands on the rent review date. But there is one important qualification. The tenant's adviser should ensure that improvements carried out by any subtenants should be disregarded on the review. If this is not done, then the tenant may find himself in a position of rental shortfall, since he may have to pay rent for the improvements carried out by his subtenants, while being unable to recover that rent from the subtenants themselves. **6–62**

If improvements are to be disregarded, the first question is to determine what improvements are. An improvement, for this purpose, is generally considered to be something which alters the structure of the demised property or which amounts to a landlord's fixture (*New Zealand Government Property Corp v HM&S Ltd* [1982] Q.B. 1145). There is no connotation of objective amelioration of the property in the word "improvement". What is an improvement is to be judged from the point of view of the tenant, and therefore it is quite possible that an "improvement" may diminish the market rental value of the property (see *Shalson v John Lyon's Free Grammar School* [2003] 3 W.L.R. 1, a decision under the Leasehold Reform Act 1967).

The second question to ask is: improvements to what? Most clauses are either silent on the point, or require the disregard of improvements to the demised property. If the clause is silent on the point, it is likely that the word will be construed as meaning improvements to the demised property (cf. *Brett v Brett Essex Golf Club* [1986] 1 E.G.L.R. 154 at 158H). It follows that the starting point is the property in the condition in which it was when demised. This means that work carried out by a tenant under a previous tenancy will not fall within the scope of the disregard, because it will ordinarily have become part of the property itself and therefore would form part of the demise (*Panther Shop Investments Ltd v Keith Pople Ltd* [1987] 1 E.G.L.R. 131). This is a particularly important point for the tenant's adviser in the case of a renewal lease. In the case of a new letting where the tenant has been let in to carry out fitting-out work a short time before the grant of the lease itself, the court may by a purposive construction conclude that work carried out in anticipation of the grant of the lease falls within the scope of the disregard (*Hambros Bank Executor & Trustee Co Ltd v Superdrug Stores Ltd* [1985] 1 E.G.L.R. 99). But in the case of a renewal lease, there is far less scope for such a robust conclusion, and the tenant's adviser must ensure that the lease makes it clear that improvements carried out during a previous tenancy are to be disregarded. Even in the case of a new letting the point may be of significance, for it has been held that a modification to the original design of a building at the request and expense of the tenant, which resulted in the building of a structure different from that contemplated by the landlord was not an improvement for this purpose (*Scottish & Newcastle Breweries Plc v Sir Richard Sutton's Settled Estates* [1985] 2 E.G.L.R. 130 at 137).

The tenant's adviser should also consider the inter-relationship between works that the tenant wishes to undertake outside the demised property in order to use the demised property for a specific purpose and rent review. If the rent review clause contains a disregard of improvements to the demised property then the impact of any improvements outside the demise is likely to be rentalised in the absence of express agreement to the contrary (see the facts of *Cordoba Holdings Ltd v Ballymore Properties Ltd* [2011] Arb. L.R. 19, where the tenant converted its premises into a data centre and upgraded the power supply to the entire building in order to accommodate that change of use, the majority of the requisite works being outside the demised property).

The third question is how to identify the improver. If the lease **6–63** names the original tenant and then defines him as the tenant it may be possible to conclude that all work carried out by that named person, whenever carried out, potentially falls within the disregard (*Hambros Bank Executor & Trustee Co Ltd v Superdrug Stores Ltd* [1985] 1 E.G.L.R. 99). But if the lease identifies the improver as being tenant at the time the work was carried out (as does s.34 of the Landlord and Tenant Act 1954), then unless the person carrying out the work had either a legal tenancy at the date the work was carried out (*Euston Centre Properties Ltd v Wilson (H&J) Ltd* [1982] 1 E.G.L.R. 57) or had an enforceable agreement for a lease (*Scottish & Newcastle Breweries Plc v Sir Richard Sutton's Settled Estates* [1985] 2 E.G.L.R. 130), the improvements will fall outside the scope of the disregard. In addition the tenant's adviser should ensure that improvements carried out by persons deriving title under the tenant (e.g. subtenants and licensees) are within the scope of the disregard. However, where the tenant arranges for an improvement to be carried out by a third party and is involved in the identification, supervision or financing of the works, it may be possible to conclude that the works were carried out by the tenant (*Durley House v Cadogan* [2000] 1 W.L.R. 246).

The tenant's adviser should not lose sight of the possibility that improvements may be carried out by the landlord at the expense of the tenant, for example by recovery through the service charge. Such improvements ought to be treated in the same way as improvements carried out by the tenant himself. In addition, where the landlord carries out improvements under an obligation to the tenant, many tenants feel that such an improvement should be disregarded. However, an improvement which the landlord has actually funded stands on a different footing to an improvement which, although carried out by the landlord, has been funded by the tenant. The landlord should therefore not accept a disregard of improvements which he himself has funded. It is uncommon for the tenant to be entitled to the benefit of a disregard of all improvements. The usual provision extends to improvements carried out otherwise than in pursuance of an obligation to the landlord. The tenant's adviser should ensure that if this form of disregard is adopted, the exclusion from the disregard is limited to improvements carried out in pursuance of obligations contained in the lease. Although the court will be slow to construe a licence to make alterations as being an obligation for this purpose, nevertheless it has recognised that the obligation may be contained in some contractual document other than the lease (*Godbold v Martin the Newsagents Ltd* [1983] 2 E.G.L.R. 128). The tenant's adviser should also be on his guard against hidden obligations to carry out improvements. Landlords sometimes limit the disregard to tenants' improvements carried out with the consent of the landlord. The reasoning behind this limitation is that the landlord (particularly if he is a successor in title) wishes to avoid disputes over what improvements have actually been carried out. The requirement that the consent of the landlord be obtained before the improvements can be disregarded is a strong incentive to the tenant to comply with the obligations in the lease as regards alterations, and will normally ensure that the improvements are properly documented. If they are not, then they will not be disregarded, even if the lease contains an express assumption that the tenant is to be assumed to have complied with his obligations (*Hamish Cathie Travel England Ltd v Insight International Tours Ltd* [1986] 1 E.G.L.R. 244). If such a clause is put forward the tenant's adviser should at least ensure that improvements may be disregarded if consent was not required under the terms of the lease, or, if required, was unreasonably withheld.

6–64 There is a feeling on the part of many landlords that the giving to the tenant of a rent free period is in effect a contribution by the landlord to the tenant's initial fitting-out costs. If the draftsman's client is of this school of thought, the disregard of improvements could be limited to those carried out after the expiry of any rent free period contained in the lease.

In addition where the parties have agreed that the property is to be valued on the basis that it has been fitted out or is fit for immediate use and occupation, a disregard of tenant's improvements may conflict with the assumption. Thus, careful consideration must be given to the question what types of improvement should fall within the disregard.

From 1 October 2004, the Disability Discrimination Act 1995 placed service providers under a statutory duty in relation to the physical features of their premises to make them accessible to disabled people. The DDA was largely replaced by the Equality Act 2010 in October 2010. Service providers who own or occupy land where they provide a service may be under an obligation to make reasonable changes to the physical features of the premises to ensure that a person with a disability is not substantially disadvantaged in accessing those services. It is not yet established whether works that a tenant may carry out will be works that the tenant would be required to carry out in order to perform its covenant to comply with statutory requirements. As rent review clauses often disregard improvements unless they were carried out pursuant to an obligation to the landlord, for example under the tenant's covenant to comply with statutory requirements, the tenant's adviser should insist upon specific wording excluding the value of any works carried out by the tenant to comply with its duties under the Equality Act.

The final series of questions relates to the instruction to be given to the valuer as to the method of carrying out the disregard. In essence there are three possibilities.

(1) To disregard the improvements themselves. This requires the valuer to assume that the improvements have never been carried out. If the improvements in question are such that any incoming tenant would carry them out, then the disregard of the improvements themselves may give the tenant a greater credit than the value of the actual (secondhand) improvements at the review date. This possibility was recognised in *GREA Real Property Investments Ltd v Williams* [1979] 1 E.G.L.R. 121.

(2) To disregard the effect on rent of improvements. This is the formula which is most usually adopted, and which was considered in *GREA Real Property Investments Ltd v Williams* [1979] 1 E.G.L.R. 121 and *Estates Projects Ltd v Greenwich LBC* [1979] 2 E.G.L.R. 85. The main disadvantage of this formula is that nobody knows what it means, and nobody knows how to disregard the effect on rent of improvements without disregarding the improvements themselves.

(3) To make a fair allowance to the tenant on account of improvements. This method avoids the conceptual difficulties inherent in the other two methods, while at the same time preventing the tenant from arguing that he should receive the equivalent of a rent free period on each rent review. It must of course be recognised that this method entails a subjective approach leaving much to the discretion of the valuer, but it is better to leave arguments about value to valuers than to lawyers. This approach was adopted in a standard form of rent review clause published by the Incorporated Society of Valuers and Auctioneers.

Example 6.22 Disregard of improvements

Disregarding any effect on rent of any improvement carried out:

(1) to the demised property or any part of it

(2) by the tenant or any person deriving title under the tenant or by the landlord at the expense of the tenant

(3) with the consent of the landlord where required under this lease (unless consent was unreasonably withheld)

(4) otherwise than in pursuance of an obligation to the landlord (apart from an obligation to comply with statutes)

(5) either during the term or in anticipation of its grant.

Example 6.23 Extension of disregard to improvements under previous lease

Disregarding any improvements carried out to the property demised by this lease but in the state in which it was on [ ] and either carried out at any time by the tenant named as party to this lease or a person deriving title under him or carried out by the tenant under any previous lease of the property granted on or after [ ].

(v) *Unusual terms of the lease*

Where the lease contains unusual terms the draftsman should consider whether they should be disregarded for the purposes of the rent review. In some cases, the court is able to imply a disregard; for example where the unusual term requires the tenant to pay a rent additional to the market rent of the property (*Lister Locks Ltd v TEI Pension Trust Ltd* [1982] 2 E.G.L.R. 124; *Guys 'n' Dolls Ltd v Sade Brothers Catering Ltd* [1984] 1 E.G.L.R. 103; *Buffalo Enterprises v Golden Wonder* [1991] 1 E.G.L.R. 141) or a rent which is a proportion of market rental value (*Prudential Assurance v 99 Bishopsgate* [1992] 1 E.G.L.R. 119). However, in a case where the unusual term is not inconsistent with the rent review, the court would have to give it effect. The effect to be given to a term in a lease is its real effect, and not the artificial effect which it would have if repeated verbatim in the hypothetical lease. Thus, where a lease contained a break clause operable after the twelfth year of the term on six months' notice, it was held that the rent to be paid on the rent review at the expiry of the twelfth year of the term should be assessed on the footing of a hypothetical lease terminable on six months' notice (*Millett (R&A) Shops Ltd v Legal & General Assurance Society Ltd* [1985] 1 E.G.L.R. 103). **6–65**

One of the terms of the lease which should always be excluded is the amount of rent payable. However, the tenant's adviser should ensure that the rent review clause itself is not excluded. A considerable amount of litigation has taken place to determine whether on its true construction a lease was or was not intended to exclude the rent review clause from the hypothetical lease. Most of this litigation was unrealistic, since it can scarcely be supposed that parties who inserted rent review clauses into their leases precisely because they could not accurately assess a proper rent for the whole term of the lease intended the rent to be assessed on review on precisely the basis that they had rejected when fixing the initial rent. Nevertheless, judges managed to arrive at the conclusion that the parties had so intended. Ultimately, the court has reached the conclusion that in the absence of clear words directing the rent review clause to be disregarded, the court will give effect to the underlying purpose of a rent review clause and hold that the hypothetical lease is to contain provisions for rent review on the same terms as the actual lease (*British Gas Corp v Universities Superannuation Scheme Ltd* [1986] 1 W.L.R. 398). This approach has been welcomed and approved by the Court of Appeal (*Equity and Law Life Assurance Society Plc v Bodfield Ltd* [1987] 1 E.G.L.R. 124), although it was stressed that no guidelines as to construction can entitle the court to construe not the clause which the parties have entered into but the different clause which they would have entered into if they or their advisers had thought more deeply about how the clause would work in practice. The tide of authority is now firmly against the conclusion that the hypothetical lease contains no rent review clause (*Electricity Supply Nominees v FM Insurance Co Ltd* [1986] 1 E.G.L.R. 143; *Amax International Ltd v Custodian Holdings Ltd* [1986] 2 E.G.L.R. 111; *British Home Stores Ltd v Ranbrook Properties Ltd* [1988] 1 E.G.L.R. 121; *Arnold v National Westminster Bank Plc* [1991] 2 W.L.R. 1177).

6–66 However, there has been the occasional aberration (*General Accident Fire & Life Assurance Corp Plc v Electronic Data Processing Co Plc* [1987] 1 E.G.L.R. 112), and the unusual case of *Equity & Law Life Assurance Society Plc v Bodfield Ltd* [1987] 1 E.G.L.R. 124. The particular feature in that case which complicated matters was the fact that the rent review clause was to a fraction only of market rent, and the construction advanced by the tenant would have required a partial disregard of the rent review clause anyway. Where the rent review clause is to a fraction of market rent the review clause should provide specifically for the disregard of the fraction as one of the terms of the hypothetical lease. In the case of a lease containing a normal review to a rack rent, it is sufficient if the rent review clause provides for a hypothetical letting "on the terms of this lease other than the amount of the rent."

The tenant's adviser should nevertheless beware of words which do require the disregard of the rent review clause itself. Words which have this effect are words such as "disregarding the provisions of this clause" (*Pugh v Smiths Industries Ltd* [1982] 2 E.G.L.R. 120) or "on the terms of this lease save for this proviso" (*Safeway Food Stores Ltd v Banderway Ltd* [1983] 2 E.G.L.R. 116) or "there being disregarded this clause" (*Securicor Ltd v Postel Properties Ltd* [1985] 1 E.G.L.R. 102). The particular problem usually arises where a rent review clause appropriate to a short term with only one review date has been inserted into a lease containing numerous rent reviews.

(vi) Incorporation of the statutory disregards

Many leases incorporate the disregards contained in s.34 of the Landlord and Tenant Act 1954. In a simple case this is convenient shorthand, but the draftsman should be aware of some of its limitations. Firstly, the disregards apply only to the "holding" (i.e. that part of the demised property occupied by the tenant) so that if sub-letting is envisaged the tenant may not reap the full benefit of the disregards. Secondly, the parties should specify whether the disregards are to be incorporated in the form in which they were originally enacted or as amended by the Law of Property Act 1969 (cf. *Brett v Brett Essex Golf Club Ltd* [1986] 1 E.G.L.R. 154). Thirdly, if the disregard is incorporated in its amended form, it will extend only to improvements carried out by a person who was tenant at the time when the improvement was carried out; whereas if the disregard is incorporated in its unamended form it may extend to improvements carried out by the named tenant even before he became tenant (*Hambros Bank Executor & Trustee Co Ltd v Superdrug Stores Ltd* [1985] 1 E.G.L.R. 99), unless the works were carried out long before the grant of the lease (*Brett v Brett Essex Golf Club Ltd* [1986] 1 E.G.L.R. 154). Fourthly, the references in s.34(2) to improvements having been carried out not less than 21 years before the making of the "application for the new tenancy" is inappropriate in the context of a rent review, although the court may be able to construe them as meaning the rent review. **6–67**

(g) Planning

The disregard of the effect on rent of an improvement does not require the disregard of planning permission pursuant to which it was carried out (*Railstore Ltd v Playdale Ltd* [1988] 2 E.G.L.R. 133, see also *Fattal v Keepers and Governors, etc. of the Free Grammar School of John Lyon* [2005] 1 W.L.R. 803, a case under the Leasehold Reform Act 1967), for the potential for improvement is part of the property itself. Where the use permitted under the terms of the lease is not permitted under the Town and Country Planning Act 1990, or is permitted under a planning permission personal to the tenant, special provision should be made in the rent review clause. For an example, see *Bovis Group Pension Fund Ltd v GC Flooring & Furnishing Ltd* [1984] 1 E.G.L.R. 123, where an **6–68** assumption that property was to be assumed to be let "as offices" carried with it an assumption that office use was lawful. The valuer is not entitled to take into account the possibility that the tenant may commit a breach of planning control (*Compton Group Ltd v Estates Gazette Ltd* (1978) 36 P. & C.R. 148) but the hope of obtaining planning permission may be taken into account (*Rushmoor EC v Goacher* [1985] 2 E.G.L.R. 140; *6th Centre v Guildville* [1989] 1 E.G.L.R. 260). Where there is a difficulty over planning the draftsman should provide for an assumption that the property may be lawfully used by any person for the purposes permitted by the terms of the lease.

But the fact that a use is to be treated as lawful does not mean that the property is to be treated as having been notionally adapted physically for that use (*Orchid Lodge (United Kingdom) v Extel Computing* [1991] 2 E.G.L.R. 116). If the draftsman intends that the property should be physically suitable for an alternative use, this must be specified clearly in the rent review clause.

(h) Vacant possession

6–69 Many review clauses require the valuer to assume vacant possession at the review date. In most cases this is not unfair to either party. However, where the property was originally let subject to existing tenancies, the tenant's adviser should seek to ensure that such tenancies are taken into account. As a general rule the valuer should take incumbrances, including tenancies, into account (*Oscroft v Benabo* [1967] 2 All E.R. 548). This applies especially to leases which were in existence when the lease was granted (*Forte & Co v General Accident Life Assurance* [1986] 1 E.G.L.R. 115). But subleases granted after the date of the lease may be taken into account where rent review dates in the subleases coincide with rent review dates in the headlease (*Scottish & Newcastle Breweries v Sir Richard Sutton's Settled Estates* [1985] 2 E.G.L.R. 130) or where improvements carried out by subtenants are to be disregarded in fixing the rent under the subleases but are taken into account in fixing the rent under the headlease (*Laura Investments v Havering LBC (No.2)* [1993] 1 E.G.L.R. 124). However, there may be indications in the lease which produce a contrary result (*Avon CC v Alliance Property Co Ltd* [1981] 1 E.G.L.R. 110, where the indications were first, use of the phrase "rack rent", secondly, the assumption that the letting was to be of the demised property as a whole and, thirdly, the lack of an express requirement to take the subtenancies into account).

There may also be cases where it is to the landlord's advantage for the property to be valued subject to such tenancies as subsist on the rent review date. Where the tenant does not intend to occupy the property, but rather to sublet it and hold it as an investment, an assumption of vacant possession may seriously reduce the rental value of the property on the rent review because the incoming tenant would face an immediate void, instead of obtaining an immediate income (*Bishopsgate (99) Ltd v Prudential Assurance Co Ltd* [1985] 1 E.G.L.R. 72).

If subtenancies are to be taken into account the draftsman should ensure that the alienation provisions require the subtenancies to contain rent reviews coincident with the rent review dates in the lease. This in itself may lead to the inference that the property is to be valued subject to subsisting subtenancies (*Scottish & Newcastle Breweries Plc v Sir Richard Sutton's Settled Estates* [1985] 2 E.G.L.R. 130).

(i) Statutory control of rents

Between 1972 and 1975, there was statutory control of rents **6–70** payable under business tenancies. The form of control affected only the amount of rent which the landlord was entitled to receive, and did not affect the landlord's ability to call for a rent review. Some clauses provide that if at a future date there is any statutory restriction on the landlord's right to recover rent the review is to be postponed until the lifting of that restriction. That method of dealing with the problem is satisfactory only if the statutory control is temporary; if it is permanently imposed then it may be that the review can never take place. Other clauses direct the valuer to ignore the effect of any statutory control of rents. There is no legal objection to this method (*Langham House Developments Ltd v Brompton Securities Ltd* [1980] 2 E.G.L.R. 117), although if business rents were to be subjected to control it might be difficult to assess a new rent based on a hypothesis so far removed from reality. Of course, if the valuer is directed to disregard such control the rent actually recoverable after the review will still be subject to control (i.e. the recoverable rent will be less than the reserved rent).

Example 6.24 Valuation formula for occupational lease

"Market Rent" means the rent at which the demised property might reasonably be expected to be let as a whole in the open market with vacant possession by a willing landlord to a willing tenant without a premium for a term equal to the unexpired residue of the term at the relevant review date (or 10 years if longer) upon the terms of this lease (other than the amount of the rent) and upon the assumptions that:

(a) the tenant has complied with his covenants
(b) the demised property is fit for immediate use for the purposes permitted by this lease and will be fitted out by and at the expense of the incoming tenant during a period when no rent is payable

and disregarding:

(1) the fact that the tenant has been in occupation of the whole or part of the demised property
(2) any goodwill attached to the demised property by reason of the carrying on there of the tenant's business
(3) any improvement carried out at the expense of the tenant or a person deriving title under him otherwise than in pursuance of an obligation imposed on him by this lease (but in case of conflict between this paragraph and assumption (b) above assumption (b) shall prevail)
(4) any restraint or restriction on the right to recover rent imposed by or by virtue of any Act of Parliament.

Example 6.25 Alternative valuation formula

"Market Rent" means the rent at which the demised property might reasonably be expected to be let in the open market either as a whole or in parts without payment of a premium by a willing landlord to a willing tenant or tenants for such a term (not exceeding the length of the term originally granted) as would command the best rent with vacant possession at the beginning of the term and upon the same terms (other than the amount of the rent) as this lease and on the assumptions that:

(a) the tenant has observed and performed all his covenants
(b) the demised property is fit for immediate use and occupation for the use permitted by this lease
(c) the demised property may be lawfully used by any person for that use

(d) in case the demised property has been damaged or destroyed it has been fully reinstated

but disregarding:

(1) the fact that the tenant or his subtenants have been in occupation of the demised property
(2) any goodwill attached to the demised property by reason of the carrying on there of the business of the tenant or his subtenants or their predecessors in their respective businesses
(3) any works carried out by the tenant or his subtenants which would diminish the rental value of the demised property
(4) the effect on rent of any improvement carried out at the expense of the tenant or his subtenants (other than improvements carried out either during a rent free period or in pursuance of an obligation imposed by this lease or an agreement to grant it) and completed not more than twenty-one years before the rent review date in question.

Example 6.26 Valuation formula: "Market Rent", short form

"Market Rent" means the rent at which having regard to the terms of the tenancy (other than the amount of the rent) the demised property might reasonably be expected to be let in the open market with vacant possession for a term equal to the term of this lease by a willing landlord to a willing tenant assuming that the tenant has complied with his covenants and disregarding those matters set out in paragraphs (a), (b) and (c) of section 34(1) of the Landlord and Tenant Act 1954 (as amended) which would be disregarded if the tenant were applying for a new tenancy of the demised property and were in occupation of the whole of it for the purposes of a business carried on by him.

Example 6.27 Valuation formula: disregard of review clause and no disregard of tenant's improvements (for use in a building lease)

"Reviewed Rent" means [   ] percent of the best rent at which the demised property might reasonably be expected to be let either as a whole or in parts in the open market by a willing landlord to a willing tenant or tenants:

(1) for such a term as would command the best rent
(2) with vacant possession at the beginning of the term

(3) upon the same terms as this lease (subject to any necessary modifications) but excluding this rent review clause and any obligation to erect buildings
(4) on the assumption that the hypothetical lease or leases contain provisions enabling the rent to be revised upon such terms as may be reasonable having regard to market practice current at the time
(5) on the assumptions that the tenant has performed all its covenants that the demised property is fit for immediate use and occupation for the purposes permitted by this lease that no work has been carried out to the demised property which would diminish its rental value and that in case the demised property has been damaged or destroyed it has been fully reinstated but disregarding:
   (a) the fact that the tenant or its subtenants have been in occupation of the demised property
   (b) any goodwill attached to the demised property by reason of the carrying on there of the business of the tenant its subtenants or their predecessors in their respective business
   (c) any improvement carried out by a person deriving title under the tenant and holding a leasehold interest at a rack rent other than an assignee of this lease or part of it
   (d) any restraint or restriction on the right to recover rent imposed by or by virtue of any Act of Parliament.

Example 6.28 Review to modern ground rent

(1) With effect from each review date the rent payable shall be the higher of:
   (a) the rent payable immediately before that review date and
   (b) the modern ground rent.
(2) The modern ground rent is the rent for which the demised property might reasonably be expected to be let in the open market on the relevant review date by a willing landlord to a willing tenant on the following assumptions:
   (a) the letting is with vacant possession
   (b) all buildings landlord's fixtures and fixed plant have been demolished or removed and the site has been cleared for development
   (c) obligations relating to the removal or treatment of pollution waste or noxious or hazardous substances have

been complied with and no such obligations will be imposed on the willing tenant as a result of anything done or omitted to be done before the rent review date

(d) there is in force planning permission (not subject to onerous conditions) authorising the use of the demised property for any purpose within Class B1 or B2 or B8 of the Town and Country Planning (Use Classes) Order 1987 (or any amended class which includes that use) and authorising the erection of buildings suitable for those uses and having an area no less than the area of buildings then comprised in the demised property

(e) no planning permission would be granted for any other use of the demised property

(f) mains services for water gas electricity telecommunications and other usual or necessary services are laid to appropriate points on the perimeter of the demised property and the demised property has adequate provision for surface water and foul drainage

(g) the letting is for a term of 125 years from the relevant review date

(h) the terms of the letting are those of this lease except that:
 (i) there is no obligation to build
 (ii) there is no restraint on alienation except that during the last seven years of the term the tenant may not without the landlord's consent assign or sublet the whole or any part of the demised property
 (iii) the demised property may be used for any purpose falling within the use classes specified in paragraph (d) above.

(j) Rent free period

In the cases of new lettings in the open market, it is conventional for **6–71**
the tenant to be given a period of occupation under the lease during which he pays no rent or a concessionary rent. There is no satisfactory explanation for why this happens. Sometimes it is said to be in order to allow the tenant to fit out the property, but the length of the rent free period rarely bears any discernible relationship to the time or cost of fitting out. It may be little more than a reflection of the bargaining strength of the respective parties.

It is common in a disputed rent review for the tenant to seek the equivalent of a rent free period, on the ground that had the hypothetical letting really taken place in the market, the hypothetical tenant would have been given such an inducement to take the lease. Since the reviewed rent must be a constant figure in the absence of express agreement to the contrary (*Clarke v Findon Developments Ltd* [1984] 1 E.G.L.R. 129; *Beegas Nominees v BHP Petroleum* [1998] 2 E.G.L.R. 57) the only way to give effect to the notional rent free period is to spread it over some period. When the problem first arose valuers spread the notional rent free period either to the next rent review or to the end of the hypothetical term. The tenant's valuer would usually favour the former and the landlord's valuer the latter. Now, however, many valuers favour a middle ground and will spread the notional rent free period over an intermediate period (such as ten years). An alternative way in which the tenant can put the case is to adjust his analysis of comparable lettings in order to reflect the rent free period actually granted. If the rent review clause provides for the disregard of rent free periods, either in relation to the subject property or in relation to comparables, the result will be to distort the market and to lead to a difficult valuation. In addition, it may work against the landlord, since if rent free periods are to be disregarded, the effective rent of comparable properties (where rent free periods were in fact agreed) will be diminished. This in turn will lower the rent to be paid for the demised property.

In *Cooperative Wholesale Society v National Westminster Bank* [1995] 1 E.G.L.R. 97, the Court of Appeal considered four different drafting responses to this problem. It was held that only the most unambiguous of clauses would succeed in achieving for the landlord a headline rent, although the court was more sympathetic to a clause which merely sought to neutralise the tenant's argument that the hypothetical tenant would have to incur expenses associated with moving in. One of the drafts provided for an assumption that any rent free period had expired immediately before the review date. The court held that if the rent free period had expired, it could have no part to play in the negotiations which took place on the review date itself. Another provided for the rent to be payable at the rate payable following the expiry of a rent free period which might be granted on "a new letting" of the property. The court held that this referred to a rent free period attributable to the fact of the letting being new and was therefore to be confined to a rent free period given for fitting out purposes. A third provided for an assumption that no reduction or allowance was to be made on account of any rent free period. The court held that this meant that no reduction was to be made from the rent which would have been fixed without the assumption, and that the assumption did not entitle the landlord to increase the rent to the headline rate. The fourth, and only successful clause, provided for the rent to be that which would become payable after the expiry of a rent free period of such length as would be negotiated in the open market. The court held that since the notional rent free period was still to come, it could play a part in the hypothetical negotiations, and since its length was governed by the open market, it could not be restricted to a rent free period for fitting out. This form of clause was suggested in the third edition of this book. But it is vital not to combine this method with a disregard of rent free periods otherwise the two methods will cancel each other out (*City Offices v Allianz Cornhill International Insurance Co* [1993] 1 E.G.L.R. 126. It is extremely difficult to persuade a court that a rent review clause produces a headline rent (*St Martins Property Investments Ltd v CIB Properties Ltd* [1999] L. & T.R. 1)).

The unprecedented recession of the early 1990s failed to compel landlords to lower "headline" rents enough to reflect fully the decline in the market. Instead, they bought off tenants with extended rent free periods. This has meant that some clauses agreed in the boom of the late 1980s have been found to work unfairly against tenants. The problem is that where a clause requires the assumption of a rent free period which would be granted in the market, there is no easy way of separating out a rent free period granted to recognise the need to fit out the property, and a rent free period granted as a pure inducement to keep up the level of "headline rent" (*Broadgate Square v Lehman Bros* [1995] 1 E.G.L.R. 97). The tenant's adviser should not accept such a clause unless the rent free period which is to be assumed (or the absence of which is to be disregarded) is limited to a reasonable fitting out period. **6–72**

An alternative way of coping with the problem is not to refer to rent free periods at all but to build in an assumption that the tenant has had access to the property for fitting out purposes. Where the rent review clause provides for the assessment of a headline rent, and the hypothetical lease is to contain a rent review clause in similar terms, the tenant may argue that the rent review clause itself is an onerous clause which justifies a discount from what would otherwise be the headline rent. Some draftsmen sidestep this argument by providing for a hypothetical lease containing a different form of rent review clause.

Example 6.29 Valuation formula with built in rent free period
"Market Rent" means the highest rent which would become payable immediately after the expiry of a rent free period of such length as would reasonably be required for fitting out the demised property on a letting of the demised property between a willing landlord and a willing tenant in the open market on the review date with vacant possession for a term equal to the original duration of this lease and on the same terms (save for the amount of the rent but including this rent review clause) on the assumptions that:
(a) the tenant has complied with all his covenants
(b) the demised property is fit for immediate occupation but disregarding
    (1) the fact that the tenant has been in occupation of the demised property
    (2) any improvement carried out by the tenant during the term otherwise than pursuant to an obligation imposed by this lease.

Example 6.30 Assumption that tenant has had access for fitting out
Assuming that the hypothetical tenant has had sufficient access to the demised property before the relevant review date during a period in which he did not pay rent for the purpose of enabling him to fit out to his requirements.

(k) VAT

6–73 VAT is charged on sales of new commercial buildings. Thus, an investor will have to pay more for the same building than would have been the case if VAT had not been imposed. In order to mitigate this, a landlord has the option to charge VAT on the rent payable. The option may be exercised on a building-by-building basis. If the option is exercised, the VAT payable on the rent may be retained by the landlord until he has offset the VAT payable on the construction or acquisition of the building. The option may be exercised in relation to a building whether it is a new building or not. If the tenant is a trading company with considerable output VAT, this will not matter to the tenant, since the VAT payable on the rent will be absorbed as input tax and will merely result in a smaller net payment being made to HM Revenue & Customs. But if the tenant does not have sufficient output tax to absorb the VAT on rent, the result of the exercise of the option will be to add 20 per cent to the rent. This may in turn depress the rental bid of the hypothetical tenant, or at least produce a two tier market, as between those buildings where VAT is not payable (either because they are not new, or because the option has not been exercised) and those buildings where it is. The problem will arise only in the case of new buildings (i.e. those less than five years old) and those where the option has been exercised, and does not therefore require to be dealt with in every case. In addition in areas where there is a high concentration of occupiers who are exempt from VAT and who cannot therefore absorb VAT on rent (e.g. in the City of London) the exercise of the option to tax is extremely rare. Where the point does arise the problem for the draftsman is similar to that encountered over rent free periods, and it is suggested that the response should be the same. Thus, the rent review clause should contain an assumption that the tenant will be able to absorb any VAT payable on the rent. The market rent should also be defined as being exclusive of VAT, in order to avoid any argument by the tenant that the amount determined as the market rent is inclusive of VAT.

There is a school of thought, however, which argues that the inclusion of VAT assumptions is sufficiently complex as to distort the hypothetical market and that the safest course is to leave well alone. Until the courts have considered the effect of VAT assumptions, it is impossible to predict whether these fears are unfounded.

Example 6.31 Assumption about VAT

On the assumption that the hypothetical tenant is and tenants in the market generally are registered for the purposes of value added tax and will be able to set off in full by way of input tax any value added tax payable in respect of any payment of rent against the output tax payable by him or them.

Example 6.32 Alternative assumption about VAT
Assuming that the hypothetical tenant is a person who for the purposes of value added tax is a taxable person who makes only taxable supplies and no exempt supplies.

(l) Profits valuation

6–74 In many cases a lease of commercial property will contain a normal rent review clause requiring the ascertainment of the market rent for the property, but instead of valuing by reference to comparables, the valuers will carry out a profits valuation. A profits valuation proceeds by ascertaining what average annual profit is likely to be made by a competent trader before deduction of rent, and then apportions that profit (usually called the divisible balance) between the landlord and the tenant. A profits valuation is relatively common in the case of leisure properties (see *WJ Barton Ltd v Long Acre Securities Ltd* [1982] 1 All E.R. 465 for other examples). Where a profits valuation is a likely method to be employed at the rent review, several points should be considered.

Firstly, it will clearly be desirable to know what profits the actual tenant has made. This may work to the landlord's advantage if the tenant seeks to put forward too gloomy an estimate, or to the tenant's advantage if the landlord seeks to put forward too optimistic an estimate. But in the absence of a specific clause requiring the tenant to disclose his profits, they are inadmissible in evidence (*Cornwall Coast Country Club v Cardgrange Ltd* [1987] 1 E.G.L.R. 146 at 154; *Electricity Supply Nominees Ltd v London Clubs Ltd* [1988] 2 E.G.L.R. 152) although they may be obtainable on discovery (*Urban Small Space v Burford Investment Co* [1990] 2 E.G.L.R. 120). However, if the lease specifically so provides, then the tenant's accounts and other records may be made available and relied on by either party (*Electricity Supply Nominees v London Clubs* [1988] 2 E.G.L.R. 152).

Secondly, if a profits valuation is carried out, particularly if it is reliant upon the tenant's actual profits, the valuer may find it difficult to disentangle that part of the profit which is attributable to the tenant's goodwill. Accordingly, the draftsman should consider not including the customary disregard of tenant's goodwill. The tenant may well wish to resist this, as he will clearly be unwilling to pay rent for his own commercial success. But it is inherent in the concept of a profits valuation, that the gross profit (which necessarily comes partly from the trader's goodwill) is divided between landlord and tenant, so that the landlord does obtain a share of the tenant's goodwill. One possibility is for goodwill to be disregarded only to the extent that it exceeds the goodwill which would have been generated by a tenant of average competence. This is reflected in the practice in rent reviews of licensed premises of ascertaining the "fair maintainable trade". This is the trade which a trader of reasonable competence would achieve.

Thirdly, it may be desirable to make special provision for the treatment of improvements. The gross profit will be ascertained from the conduct of the business as it is, i.e. from improved premises. Some valuers deal with improvements in profits valuations by deducting from the gross profit an annual sum representing interest on capital employed in carrying out the improvement plus a writing down allowance. It may be desirable to provide for this (or some other method) specifically.

Example 6.33 Clause admitting accounts

For the purpose of ascertaining the open market rent either party shall be at liberty to rely upon the actual trading history of the demised property and the tenant shall if so required by the landlord make available to the landlord such accounts and other trading records as the landlord shall reasonably require.

Example 6.34 Alternative clause admitting accounts

On the assumption that the hypothetical tenant has had access to such accounts and information as would be made available by a reasonable tenant to a purchaser of the tenant's business (in so far as conducted in the demised property) as a going concern.

12. REVIEW OF REVIEWS

Where the term of the lease is exceptionally long, the draftsman **6–75** should consider providing for machinery whereby the intervals between review dates may be reconsidered so as to bring those intervals into line with market practice. To a limited extent such a provision is also in the tenant's interest because an unusually long period between reviews is likely to increase the rent which would otherwise be payable.

Example 6.35 Review of review periods

(1) Subject to paragraph (2) below the landlord may from time to time serve on the tenant a notice (a "Review Frequency Notice") requiring the substitution for the review dates of more frequent review dates

(2) A Review Frequency Notice shall not be served before the expiry of the twenty fifth year of the term nor less than twenty five years after the service of an earlier Review Frequency Notice nor during a year ending on a review date

(3) A Review Frequency Notice shall contain the landlord's proposals as to the dates to be substituted

(4) In default of agreement within two months after the service of a Review Frequency Notice the question at what dates it would be reasonable for the rent to be reviewed shall be determined by an independent surveyor acting as an expert to be appointed in default of agreement by the President of the Royal Institution of Chartered Surveyors

(5) The independent surveyor shall have regard to market practice current at the date of the Review Frequency Notice in relation to new lettings with vacant possession of property comparable to the demised property

(6) If the independent surveyor shall determine that it would be reasonable for the rent to be reviewed at dates more frequent than the review dates then the dates so determined shall become the review dates.

13. INTERIM PROVISIONS AND INTEREST

6–76 The draftsman should provide for the making of payments on account pending the determination of the reviewed rent. This is particularly important where the review is automatic otherwise there is a danger that no rent will be payable after the review date and before the new rent is settled (*Kenilworth Industrial Sites Ltd v Little (EC) & Co Ltd* [1975] 1 All E.R. 53; *Accuba Ltd v Allied Shoe Repair Ltd* [1975] 3 All E.R. 782) although in some cases the court will be able to interpret the lease as making provision for a minimum rent (*London and Manchester Assurance Co Ltd v Dunn & Co (GA)* [1983] 1 E.G.L.R. 111 at 117, per Slade L.J.). The rent payable pending the determination of the new rent is usually the unreviewed rent, although there is no reason why it should not be some higher figure (e.g. 115 per cent of the unreviewed rent). Indeed, in *Smith's (Henry) Charity Trustees v AWADA Trading and Promotion Services Ltd* [1984] 1 E.G.L.R. 116, the tenant was required to make payments on account at the rate demanded by the landlord in the review notice. This provision was described by Griffiths L.J. as being a "powerful pointer" to the conclusion that time was of the essence of the timetable.

Provision should be made for the payment of the difference between the payments on account and the amount of the new rent (or for refunding to the tenant any overpayment) once the new rent has been settled. The tenant should insist that any overpayment is repaid to him rather than simply credited towards payment of the next instalment of rent so that he is not required to make the landlord a free loan. If there is a requirement that interest be paid it should operate in the tenant's favour if there is any overpayment.

If the lease so provides, the reviewed rent will operate retrospectively (*Bailey (CH) Ltd v Memorial Enterprises Ltd* [1974] 1 All E.R. 1003). However, it is likely that it cannot be distrained for until it has been determined (*United Scientific Holdings Ltd v Burnley BC* [1977] 2 All E.R. 62) and it will not be in arrear until after the rent day next following the determination (*South Tottenham Land Securities Ltd v R&A Millett (Shops) Ltd* [1984] 1 All E.R. 614, where O'Connor L.J. remarked on the desirability of dealing specifically with what is to happen where there is a delay in arriving at a new rent beyond the review date). Where a lease permitted a trigger notice to be served in accordance with a timetable and then gave the landlord power to serve a late notice expiring on a date later than the review date, the reviewed rent was held to be payable from the expiry of the late notice and not from the review date (*H Turner & Son v Confederation Life Insurance Co (UK)* [2003] 2 E.G.L.R. 11). However, in most review clauses the reviewed rent is back-dated to the review date itself. Where the review may be operated long after the review date has passed the tenant may find that he has substantial arrears to pay. His advisers should, therefore, seek to limit the power to back-date any increase in the rent to, say, one year before the service of a review notice or, alternatively to insert a provision enabling such arrears to be paid in instalments rather than in one lump sum. At common law, the landlord is not entitled to recover damages for delay if the rent is not paid on time, and the court has no power to award interest if the rent is paid before the issue of proceedings (*President of India v La Pintada da Navegacion SA* [1984] 2 All E.R. 773). Nor will the court imply a term that interest should be paid (*Trusthouse Forte Albany Hotels Ltd v Daejan Investments Ltd* [1980] 2 E.G.L.R. 123) even where the interest sought is interest upon money actually expended by the landlord (*Frobisher (Second Investments) Ltd v Kiloran Trust Co Ltd* [1980] 1 All E.R. 488).

6–77 Accordingly, the draftsman should provide for the payment by the tenant of interest on all overdue payments. The rate of interest should be tied to a readily ascertainable yardstick (e.g. base lending rate of a clearing bank) and provision should be made for substituting a different rate should the selected yardstick cease to exist.

Since the reviewed rent will not become due until the rent day following its determination (*South Tottenham Land Securities Ltd v R&A Millett (Shops) Ltd* [1984] 1 All E.R. 614) special provision must be made to deal with interest following a rent review. The tenant's adviser should seek to limit the rate of interest charged. While it is reasonable for the landlord to seek interest at a high rate where the tenant has defaulted in paying money due under the lease, it is not reasonable for the same rate to be adopted where the tenant is not in default. The tenant's adviser should also ensure that interest is not payable for any greater period than would have been the case if the reviewed rent had been ascertained by the review date.

Example 6.36 Definition of rate of interest

"The Prescribed Rate" means three percent above the base lending rate from time to time of [ ] Bank plc or (if the landlord chooses) the rate of interest which the landlord has to pay from time to time for short-term unsecured borrowing.

Example 6.37 Alternative definition of rate of interest

"The Prescribed Rate" means three per cent above the base lending rate from time to time of:

(1) [ ] Bank plc or

(2) Such other UK Clearing Bank as the landlord may from time to time nominate or

If that rate cannot be ascertained such comparable rate of interest as may be agreed between the landlord and the tenant and in default of agreement determined by arbitration.

Example 6.38 Payment on account pending rent review
Pending the ascertainment of the rent the tenant shall continue to make payments at the rate payable immediately before the Review Date in question and upon the ascertainment of the rent the tenant shall pay to the landlord the shortfall if any together with interest at the Prescribed Rate calculated as if the rent had been ascertained at the Review Date.

Example 6.39 Review to market rent: upwards only
1. In this Schedule:
   1.1 "Review Date" means the [ ] of [ ] and every [ ] anniversary of that date.
   1.2 "Market Rent" means the best rent at which the Property might reasonably be expected to be let on the relevant Review Date in the open market without a premium by a willing landlord to a willing tenant for such a term as would then command the best rent and upon the terms of this lease (other than the amount of the rent) upon the assumptions that:
      (a) the tenant has complied with all his covenants and
      (b) the property is fit for immediate use and occupation (any damage having been repaired or reinstated) and disregarding:
         (i) the fact that the tenant has been in occupation of the property
         (ii) any restriction imposed by this lease upon the use of the property
         (iii) any goodwill attached to the property by reason of the carrying on there of the tenant's trade or business

   and making a fair allowance to the tenant on account of any improvement to the property carried out at his expense during the period of twenty one years immediately preceding the relevant Review Date other than an improvement carried out (1) during a rent free period or (2) in pursuance of any obligation to the landlord

2. From each Review Date the rent payable by the tenant shall be the rent contractually payable immediately before that Review Date or the Market Rent on that Review Date whichever is the higher
3. The Market Rent on any Review Date shall be determined in default of agreement between the landlord and tenant by arbitration (but no arbitrator shall be appointed before the relevant Review Date)
4. Pending the ascertainment of the Market Rent the Tenant shall continue to make payments on account at the rate of 115 per cent of the rent payable immediately before the Review Date in question and upon the ascertainment of the Market Rent the tenant shall pay to the landlord the shortfall (if any) together with interest at the rate of three per cent below the Prescribed Rate calculated as if the Market Rent had been ascertained on the Review Date
5. The Basic Rent payable from any Review Date shall be recorded in a written memorandum as soon as it has been ascertained
6. If at any Review Date the landlord's right to recover or increase the rent is restrained or restricted by or by virtue of any Act of Parliament the landlord may by notice in writing given to the tenant call for an additional review of the rent upon such date as may be specified in the notice and that date shall thereupon become a Review Date and this Schedule shall apply accordingly.

Example 6.40 Alternative form of review to market rent: upwards only

(1) In this clause:

"Review Date" means the [ ] of [ ] in the years [ ] and any date which becomes a Review Date under subclause (7)

"Market Rent" means the highest yearly rent which would become payable after the expiry of a rent free period of such length as is necessary to fit out the demised property on a letting of the demised property in the open market between a willing landlord and a willing tenant:

(a) for a term equal to the unexpired residue of the term or (if longer) 15 years
(b) with vacant possession

(c) for the use or uses permitted under this lease (taking into account all variations and licences)
(d) on the terms of this lease assuming:
    (i) that all the covenants in this lease have been performed
    (ii) that any rights personal to the actual tenant would be granted to the hypothetical tenant
    (iii) that the demised property may be lawfully occupied for the purposes permitted by this lease

but disregarding:

(a) goodwill attached to the demised property because the tenant has carried on business there
(b) any effect on rent of any improvement to the demised property made:
    (i) with the landlord's written consent
    (ii) either without obligation by the tenant or pursuant to an obligation to comply with statutes
    (iii) during the term or during the currency of an agreement to grant this lease
(c) any depreciating effect of anything done by the tenant in the demised property or installed or affixed to it by him
(d) the fact that the tenant has been in occupation of the demised property

"Surveyor" means a chartered surveyor agreed in writing by the landlord and the tenant or in default of agreement appointed by the President

"The President" means the President of the Royal Institution of Chartered Surveyors or a person acting on his behalf

(2) From each Review Date the rent shall be the higher of:
    (a) the Market Rent on that Review Date and
    (b) the rent contractually payable immediately before that date
(3) If the landlord and the tenant have not agreed the market rent four months before the Review Date in question it shall be determined by a surveyor who
    (a) shall be appointed in default of agreement by the President and
    (b) shall act as an arbitrator unless the landlord requires him to act as an expert.
(4) If the surveyor acts as an expert he shall

(a) give the landlord and the tenant an opportunity to submit written representations and cross representations to him
(b) disclose each party's representations and cross representations to the other before reaching his decision

(5) If the surveyor refuses to act or is incapable of acting then the President may appoint another in his place
(6) If the rent is not ascertained by a Review Date:
(a) the tenant shall continue to pay rent on account at the rate payable immediately before the Review Date and
(b) seven days after the ascertainment of the rent the tenant shall pay the difference (if any) for the period from the Review Date to the expiry of that seven day period between the amount paid on account and the Market Rent together with interest on the difference at the rate of two percent above the prescribed rate

(7) If on any review date legislation restricts the landlord's right to recover the rent then on the lifting of the restriction the landlord may give one month's notice requiring an additional rent review on a quarter day specified in the notice and that quarter day shall become a Review Date
(8) Time is not of the essence
(9) The rent shall be endorsed on the lease and counterpart whenever it is reviewed.

Example 6.41 Review to market rent upwards only

(1) The Landlords shall be entitled to require the rent to be reviewed with effect from each Review Date
(2) This right is exercisable by written notice given not earlier than six months before the Review Date
(3) The Landlords and the Tenant may agree the amount of the revised rent at any time after the service of such a notice
(4) If the Landlords and the Tenant have not agreed the revised rent within 56 days after the service of such a notice either the Landlords or the Tenant may require it to be determined by a single arbitrator under the Arbitration Act 1996
(5) The arbitrator shall be appointed by agreement or, in default of agreement, by the President of the Royal Institution of Chartered Surveyors
(6) The arbitrator shall determine the market rent of the Property

(7) The market rent is the rent at which the Property might reasonably be expected to be let on the Review Date in question
  (a) with vacant possession
  (b) on the then subsisting terms of this lease
  (c) assuming that any personal licence or concession (apart from a financial concession) enjoyed by the Tenant would (subject to the terms of the licence or concession in question) be enjoyed by the hypothetical tenant personally
  (d) for a term equal to the unexpired residue of the term of this lease
  (e) assuming that the Tenant has complied with all his obligations
  (f) disregarding any work carried out by the Tenant which has decreased the rental value of the Property (including any work carried out by any tenant under a previous lease of the property unless the Landlords have in the meantime recovered vacant possession of the property)
  (g) disregarding any effect on the rental value of the Property of any improvement carried out by the Tenant (including any work carried out by any tenant under a previous lease of the Property unless the Landlords have in the meantime recovered vacant possession of the Property)

(8) If the revised rent has not been agreed or determined before the Review Date in question the Tenant shall continue to make payments on account at the rate of the rent payable immediately before that Review Date

(9) Once the revised rent has been agreed or determined any shortfall (together with interest) shall be paid by the Tenant on the next usual quarter day after it has been agreed or determined

(10) Under no circumstances may the rent be reduced as a result of the operation of this clause.

14. SUBLEASES

Where the lease in question is a sublease, the draftsman will usually wish to make the terms of the sublease mirror the terms of the headlease. However, it is not always enough merely to repeat the **6–78** words verbatim. Each review clause will have to be applied to a particular set of facts, and the interaction between the facts and the clause will produce the rent. This may be illustrated by two cases concerning the same casino. Both *Daejan Investments Ltd v Cornwall Coast Country Club* [1985] 1 E.G.L.R. 77 and *Cornwall Coast Country Club v Cardgrange Ltd* [1987] 1 E.G.L.R. 146 concerned Crockford's Casino, the rent of which fell to be reviewed on the same date both under the headlease and under the sublease. Both leases provided for the disregard of the effect on rent of improvements carried out by the tenant and both leases provided for the disregard of any additional value attributable to the existence of a gaming licence if it belonged to the tenant or an associate of the tenant. The head tenant had carried out improvements, but the subtenant held a gaming licence. The consequence was that under the headlease, what was reviewed was an unimproved building, but taking into account the existence of the gaming licence in the hands of the subtenant, while under the sublease what fell to be reviewed was the improved building but disregarding the value attributable to the gaming licence. Thus the same form of words applied to different factual situations produced very different results. This is perhaps an extreme example, but it shows that care must be taken, and that it is not enough merely to repeat the words in the headlease without thinking through the consequences of doing so.

15. RENEWAL LEASES

6–79 On a renewal under Part II of the Landlord and Tenant Act 1954, the rent will be determined in accordance with s.34 of the Act. Under s.34(3), the court is expressly given power to determine that the terms of the new tenancy should include such provision for varying the rent as may be specified in the determination. The discretion given to the court is very wide. In the light of *O'May v City of London Real Property Co Ltd* [1983] 2 A.C. 726, it seems likely that where the current tenancy contains provisions for rent review the court would start with a preference for the form of clause contained in the current tenancy. In *Charles Follet Ltd v Cabtell Investment Co Ltd* [1986] 2 E.G.L.R. 76, the current tenancy contained an upwards only rent review clause in which time was of the essence of the timetable. That form of clause was carried into the new tenancy.

It does not appear that the tenant argued for an upwards or downwards review as a matter of principle, and the judge's decision on this point was not appealed. Initially, in the only cases where the point appears to have been argued, the court has refused to order the inclusion of an upwards only review clause (*Stylo Shoes Ltd v Manchester Royal Exchange Ltd* (1967) 204 E.G. 803; *Janes (Gowns) Ltd v Harlow Development Corp* [1980] 1 E.G.L.R. 52). However, in subsequent county court cases, judges have been divided on the point (*Boots the Chemist v Pinkland* [1992] 2 E.G.L.R. 98; *Amarjee v Barrowfen Properties* [1993] 2 E.G.L.R. 133; *Fourbouys v Newport BC* [1994] 1 E.G.L.R. 138 (upwards/downwards) and *Blythewood Plant Hire v Spiers* [1992] 2 E.G.L.R. 103 (upwards only)). It is suggested that it would be wrong in principle for the court to order the inclusion of an upwards only review clause, since it would only be of any practical effect if it resulted in the tenant having to pay more than the market rent. Since the court is required by s.34(1) to determine the market rent and no more, an upwards only review clause would be contrary to the spirit if not to the letter of the law. Accordingly, the tenant should insist on an upwards or downwards review.

The tenant's adviser should pay particular attention to the disregard of improvements, so as to ensure that any improvements carried out under the current tenancy will be disregarded on review under the new tenancy.

CHAPTER 7

INSURANCE

1. INSURANCE

It is usual to include in a lease a provision requiring one or other party to insure the demised property. This requirement should always be considered in conjunction with a requirement as to reinstatement of the demised property and a proviso for abatement of rent. Within the framework of the insurance covenant itself the draftsman should specify: **7–01**

(1) who is to insure;
(2) the risks against which the property is to be insured;
(3) the amount of the cover; and
(4) the application of insurance moneys.

(a) Who is to insure?

In many cases the draftsman will have no control over who is to insure, but if he has then the following matters should be considered. **7–02**

(i) Existing obligations

One of the parties may already be under an obligation to insure the property. Usually, it will be the landlord. For example, the landlord may himself be a leaseholder and under an obligation to his own landlord to insure, or he may be obliged to insure under the terms of his mortgage. The tenant is unlikely to be under an obligation to insure unless he has paid a premium for the lease, in which case he too may be so obliged by the terms of his own mortgage. If both parties are under similar obligations their respective liabilities under the lease can only be resolved by negotiation, but it is suggested that it is better for the landlord to insure in such a case. **7–03**

The Code for Leasing Business Premises in England and Wales 2007 recommends that where landlords are insuring the landlord's property, the insurance policy terms should be fair and reasonable and represent value for money, and be placed with reputable insurers.

(ii) The nature of the property

7–04 If the demised property is part only of a building that belongs to the landlord, or if it is part of a trading estate or town centre development that belongs to the landlord, it is usually better for the landlord to insure. The advantages are that only one insurance policy need be maintained for the whole property (and, therefore, any common parts will be covered) and if the landlord is his own agent there may be a discount that can be passed on to the tenants. If the landlord wishes to retain for his own benefit any discount or commission this should be expressly provided in the lease. In the absence of such provision the tenant may be entitled to require the landlord to account to him for moneys had and received. Further, the landlord will probably be in a better position to assess the amount of cover required and the tenants will not be subject to the risk that part of a building will be uninsured. The disadvantage to the tenant is that he will be unable to control either the company with which the property is insured or the amount of the cover. This may lead to difficulties with his mortgagee, particularly if the business carried on by him is such that insurance against special or unusual risks is required. In such a case, the tenant should stipulate for a measure of control over the risks against which the landlord insures.

If the demised property is a self-contained building it will often be more convenient for the tenant to insure. If this is the case, the landlord should retain some control over the insurance; the policy should be in joint names so that a payment by the insurers does not pass wholly into the hands of the tenant, and the landlord should also be entitled to prescribe the risks against which the property is insured and the amount of the cover. The disadvantage to the tenant of insuring is that the risk of under insurance will fall on him, in the sense that failure adequately to insure will be a breach of the covenant to insure. If the landlord is to insure in the case of a self-contained building, the tenant should be given the opportunity to influence the choice of insurer and the scope of the insured risks.

This may be appropriate for landlords who do not have block policy, but may not be appropriate if the landlord does have such a policy.

Fixtures

Whenever the landlord is to insure, the tenant should consider the need to provide for the insurance of its fixtures and its fit out to the property, as well as its chattels within the property. A tenant should not accept a provision that prohibits it from arranging its own insurance unless the landlord is obliged to extend the policy cover at the tenant's request. If such matters are to be included within the landlord's policy, then the landlord must be given appropriate details, and the tenant should be obliged to reimburse the landlord for the cost of arranging the additional insurance on its behalf. **7–05**

From a landlord's point of view, it is also important to consider whether an obligation to extend the cover at the request of one tenant might raise the premiums of other tenants through a block policy. If so, it might be preferable for the landlord to insure the building and landlord's fixtures and plant and equipment, and for the tenant to be permitted to maintain separate insurance for its trade fixtures and fit out.

(iii) Other provisions of the lease

If there is to be a service charge in the lease it may be convenient for the landlord to insure and to recover from the tenant the appropriate premium by way of service charge rather than by way of an insurance rent. Conversely, if the tenant's use of the property is a high insurance risk it may be better for him to insure, thereby preventing problems of apportioning a premium for a policy that covers property in addition to the demised property. **7–06**

Whichever party is to insure the other party should have the right to require production of the policy (and the last receipt for the premium) and also the right to require insurance against unusual risks (on payment of any increased premium thereby occasioned).

Some landlords resist this, especially where a block policy is concerned, since they regard the details of other properties as being confidential. But the tenant should persist, for he is entitled to be satisfied by proper evidence that insurance cover is in force, especially where he is paying for it. If the landlord will not produce the policy, it may be possible to authorise the tenant to correspond directly with the insurers in order to be satisfied that the policy is in force.

Where the landlord insures and the amount of the insurance premium is increased by reason of any improvement carried out by the tenant, the tenant must pay the landlord the amount of the increase, which is recoverable from him as rent (s.16 of the Landlord and Tenant Act 1927).

(iv) Policy terms

7–07 Where the landlord is responsible for property insurance, policy terms should be competitive. However, care should be taken that undue emphasis is not placed upon cost rather than value. In recognition of this possibility, the British Property Federation/ British Council of Offices Model Clauses for an FRI Lease of Whole require the landlord to insure with a reputable and substantial insurer and on terms and conditions which are usual. The Model Clauses also refer to obtaining insurance on the London insurance market to prevent the landlord from obtaining insurance other than from an established market.

Example 7.1 Landlord's covenant to insure
The Landlord shall insure the [demised property] [the building of which the demised property forms part] and keep it insured with a reputable insurer or underwriters subject to such exclusions excesses and limitations as are normal in the United Kingdom insurance market and as may be imposed by the insurers.

(b) Risks

7–08 It is clearly impracticable to specify every risk against which the property is to be insured, particularly in a long lease. However, the draftsman should avoid such expressions as "comprehensive risks" or "insurable risks" since they have no clear meaning.

If the tenant is required by the lease to insure in a named insurance office, but the lease is silent as to the risks, his obligation is to effect such a policy as is the usual policy from time to time of the named company (*Upjohn v Hitchens* [1918] 2 K.B. 48). In most cases this will be satisfactory, but where there is a possibility that the use of the property will require cover against additional risks a power to specify such risks should be reserved. Thus, if the tenant is to insure he should be required to insure against "loss or damage by fire and such other risks as the landlord may from time to time reasonably prescribe." If the landlord is to insure he should be required to insure against "loss or damage by fire and such other risks as he thinks fit and (upon payment by the tenant of any increased premium occasioned thereby) against such risks as the tenant may from time to time reasonably request."

Some draftsmen prefer to specify a long list of risks against which the insuring party must insure. If this is done, provision must be made for the possibility that cover against some listed risks is no longer available or is only available on unreasonable terms (e.g. insurance of commercial buildings against terrorist activities, which might otherwise be required to be obtained under an obligation to insure against explosion and/or malicious damage, or, increasingly, the prohibitive costs of obtaining insurance of buildings against flood damage). Thus the obligation to insure against listed risks should be qualified by a proviso that:

(1) the obligation is subject to such limitations, exclusions and excesses as may be imposed by insurers; and
(2) the obligation is subject to the availability of insurance in the market on reasonable terms and at a reasonable premium.

The tenant's adviser should note that if the tenant is required to insure in a named insurance office "or in some other responsible insurance office to be approved by the landlord" the landlord has an absolute right to withhold approval of any insurance company other than that named in the lease (*Tredegar v Harwood* [1929] A.C. 72). Accordingly, any such draft should be amended by inserting a proviso that the landlord's approval is not to be unreasonably withheld. It is, however, unusual to find an obligation to insure in a named office.

Example 7.2 Definition of insured risks
The risk of:
(a) fire lightning explosion aircraft (except damage caused by hostile aircraft as part of a terrorist incident as defined in the Terrorism Act 2000 or following the outbreak of war) and other aerial devices or articles dropped from aircraft riot civil unrest strikes or malicious persons storm or tidal wave flood

bursting or overflowing of natural or artificial water courses water tanks apparatus or pipes earthquake impact collapse resulting from subsidence ground heave or landslide and accidental damage to Conduits whether under or above ground fixed or plate glass

(b) such other risks and perils against which the Landlord acting reasonably may insure from time to time

but excluding at the reasonable discretion of the Landlord any risk for which cover is not available in the normal market in the United Kingdom on reasonable commercial terms and subject to such exclusions terms and conditions as the insurers may reasonably require.

(i) Terrorism

7–09 It is also necessary to consider the scope of a general term used to describe a particular insured risk, and to consider whether there is a shared understanding as to what is or is not intended to be covered, and what will or will not be capable of insurance within that description. This is particularly so in the case of a reference to "terrorism" (for a discussion of the insurance of risks such as terrorism after September 11, 2001, see "Landlords hunt for cover", *Estates Gazette*, January 8, 2005), but would also apply to the use of the term, "global warming", for example. There may well be a need to consider more specific terminology.

Whilst the Terrorism Act 2000 (as amended), defines "terrorism" for the purposes of the Act as follows, the traditional *Pool Re* definition, for example, is rather narrower. Section 1 of the Terrorism Act, covers both the actions of an organisation and of an individual. The definition is:

> "The use or threat of action where-
> (1) ...
> (a) the action falls within subsection (2),
> (b) the use or threat is designed to influence the government or an international governmental organisation or to intimidate the public or a section of the public, and
> (c) the use or threat is made for the purpose of advancing a political, religious racial or ideological cause.
> (2) Action falls within this subsection if it-
> (a) involves serious violence against a person,

(b) involves serious damage to property,
(c) endangers a person's life, other than that of the person committing the action,
(d) creates a serious risk to the health or safety of the public or a section of the public, or
(e) is designed seriously to interfere with or seriously to disrupt an electronic system.

(3) The use or threat of action falling within subsection (2) which involves the use of firearms or explosives is terrorism whether or not subsection (1)(b) is satisfied.

(4) In this section-
(a) 'action' includes action outside the United Kingdom,
(b) a reference to any person or to property is a reference to any person, or to property, wherever situated,
(c) a reference to the public includes a reference to the public of a country other than the United Kingdom, and
(d) "the government" means the government of the United Kingdom, of a part of the United Kingdom or of a country other than the United Kingdom.

(5) In this Act a reference to action taken for the purposes of terrorism includes a reference to action taken for the benefit of a proscribed organisation."

By contrast, the traditional *Pool Re* definition of "terrorism" has focused on activities "by or on behalf of or in connection with any 'organisation'", and would not therefore cover the actions of a lone individual.

Again, a plain reference to "terrorism" as an insured risk might result in insurance cover being obtained against physical loss and damage and associated business interruption costs, whereas it might also be sensible, in given circumstances, to provide for the consequences of any chemical or biological attack which renders property incapable of occupation.

(c) Amount of cover

Either the landlord or the tenant can be severely prejudiced if the property is underinsured. For that reason the obligation to insure should be drawn so as to specify how much cover is required. If the requirement is merely to insure "adequately" the obligation is fulfilled if the amount of cover is such an amount as the insurance company recommends, even if that amount in fact turns out to be too little (*Mumford Hotels Ltd v Wheeler* [1963] 2 All E.R. 250). Even a requirement that the property is to be insured to "its full **7–10** value" may not be sufficient because such an expression is capable of meaning the full market value of the property, which may be considerably less than its reinstatement cost. Accordingly, it is suggested that the obligation should be to insure the property "for the full cost of reinstatement". If the landlord is to insure, the choice of such an expression will permit him to insure for the full cost of reinstatement calculated on the basis that the destruction of the property may not occur until the end of the year for which the premium is current and that there may then be a substantial delay before the work of reinstatement begins. Thus, the landlord will be entitled to take inflation of building costs into account in fixing the amount of the cover (*Gleniffer Finance Corp Ltd v Bamar Wood & Products Ltd* [1978] 2 Lloyd's Rep. 49). In addition to basic building costs, the obligation to insure should be expressly extended to cover architects' and surveyors' fees and other professional fees. It is sometimes forgotten that the rebuilding of the property may require planning permission which will necessitate expense in legal fees. Similarly, the cover should be extended to include the cost of any work required by local or public authorities in order to secure compliance with up-to-date legislation, and it should be remembered that such works may have to extend to parts of the property that are not damaged.

Provision can also be included for cover against the costs of emergency temporary repair works, and the costs of protecting the site (for example, against vandalism, or looting), following the insured event and during the period whilst work is carried out.

It is now common for the insurance cover to include the loss of rent for a specified period (usually three years, sometimes five years in the case of large premises or those that would be difficult to reconstruct). The landlord should satisfy himself that the prescribed period is likely to be adequate, having regard to possible planning delays in addition to the basic contract period. The tenant for his part should not accept an obligation to pay for insurance against loss of rent unless the lease includes a proviso for the abatement of rent after damage or destruction of the demised property. No such proviso will be implied even if the tenant pays the cost of the insurance (*Cleveland Shoe Co Ltd v Murray's Book Sales (King's Cross) Ltd* (1973) 229 E.G. 1465). If there is no rent abatement clause, the landlord will suffer no loss of rent, and consequently insurers will not pay for loss of rent anyway.

The British Property Federation and British Council for Offices has recommended that the insurance rent for a full repairing and insuring lease of the whole of a building should include the cost of insurance valuations. It is believed reasonable for the tenant to pay this cost as long as valuations are not carried out more than once in every three years (for example, Model Clauses for an FRI Office Lease of Whole, 2003).

Example 7.3 Definition of insurance rent
Insurance Rent - a fair and reasonable proportion of a sum which is equal to the aggregate of:
(a) the gross insurance premiums chargeable to the Landlord from time to time for effecting and maintaining insurance in accordance with schedule [ ]; and
(b) the reasonable and proper cost of valuations and inspections for insurance purposes (but not more than once in every three years).

Example 7.4 Definition of reinstatement cost
The full costs of reinstatement including the cost of propping or shoring up demolition and site clearance architects' surveyors' planners' and other professionals' fees (and irrecoverable VAT (if any)) which would be incurred in reinstating the Building in accordance with the requirements of this Lease at the time when such reinstatement is likely to take place having regard to all relevant factors including any increases in building costs expected or anticipated to take place at any time up to the date on which the Building shall be fully reinstated.

(d) Amount of premium

In the absence of any provision to the contrary the landlord is under no obligation to choose the cheapest method of insuring, even where the tenant is obliged to reimburse the amount of the premium (*Bandar Property Holdings Ltd v JS Darwen (Successors) Ltd* [1968] 2 All E.R. 305). Where the lease required the tenant to reimburse the amount which the landlord should "properly" pay for insuring the premises, it was held that the landlord was entitled to recover the amount he actually paid, provided that it was no more than the "going rate" for insurance charged by the particular insurer with whom he chose to do business (*Havenridge Ltd v Boston* 7–11

Dyers Ltd [1993] 2 E.G.L.R. 73). If the tenant wishes to have some control over the premium, and in particular if the tenant wishes the landlord to have an obligation to shop around, this must be expressly provided for in the lease.

Sometimes the landlord is entitled to a rebate from insurers. This may be given because he has entered into a long-term contract of insurance, or because he maintains a block policy for a number of buildings. Tenants will often argue that they are entitled to the benefit of any such rebate. The problem can be avoided if the draftsman provides that the tenant is liable to contribute to the gross cost of the premium before any discount or commission. The alternative that was put forward by the British Property Federation/British Council of Offices by way of fair compromise is for landlords to keep commission, but for any discount to be passed on to tenants. They acknowledge that there may be difficulties in differentiating between the two (Model Clauses for an FRI Office Lease of Whole, 2003).

(e) Application of insurance moneys

7–12 The application of insurance moneys should be expressly dealt with in the lease, and the draftsman should provide for the possibility that reinstatement turns out to be impossible. If the tenant pays the cost of insurance, even if the policy is in the landlord's name, it appears that he can require the landlord to lay out the insurance moneys, as far as they will go, in the reinstatement of the property (*Mumford Hotels Ltd v Wheeler* [1963] 3 All E.R. 250); but there appears to be no such right in favour of the landlord if the tenant insures in his own name. Accordingly, if the tenant is to insure he should be expressly required to reinstate the demised property. It should be pointed out that both parties have a statutory right to require insurance moneys to be laid out in reinstatement, but the right is only effective if a request is made to the insurance company concerned before the insurance moneys are paid out and it only applies in cases of fire damage (s.83 of the Fires Prevention (Metropolis) Act 1774, which applies to the whole of England).

It may happen that reinstatement is impossible or that neither party wishes the building to be reinstated. The draftsman should provide for the division of the insurance moneys in such an event. In the absence of express provision the court must draw inferences from the terms of the lease and the relevant provisions of any insurance policy. In a case where the landlord covenanted to insure and reinstate, and the tenant reimbursed the insurance premium, the court was able to draw the inference that the basic right of the parties was to have the building rebuilt for their mutual benefit, and that where they treated the insurance moneys as standing in place of the building, the moneys were to be divided between them in shares proportionate to their respective interests in the building immediately before the fire (*Beacon Carpets Ltd v Kirby* [1984] 2 All E.R. 726). But where the tenant covenanted to keep the property in repair, to insure in the joint names of landlord and tenant, and to apply insurance moneys in reinstatement, the court drew the inference that the purpose of the insurance was to secure performance of the tenant's obligations so that the insurance moneys were held to belong to the tenant alone (*Re King* [1963] 1 All E.R. 781).

It is suggested that in all but the most unusual cases the fair solution is for the insurance moneys to be divided between the parties in proportion to the values of their respective interests immediately before the loss, after giving credit to the landlord for insurance in respect of loss of rent. Upon such division the lease should be brought to an end.

(f) Reinstatement

Some aspects of the covenant to reinstate have already been touched upon. Some further aspects require comment. **7–13**

Firstly, the covenant to reinstate is often limited to an obligation to lay out insurance moneys received in reinstatement. Several consequences flow from this form of obligation. There can be no breach of this obligation until insurance moneys have in fact been received (*Re King* [1962] 2 All E.R. 66 at 77). It is likely that the court would imply an obligation to pursue the insurance claim diligently (*Vural v Security Archives* (1989) 60 P. & C.R. 258), but if the insurers do not pay the covenant does not bite. Also, if the insurance moneys are insufficient to enable reinstatement to take place, neither party is liable to make up the shortfall. The insufficiency may arise because the property was underinsured (with the consequential application of average in the case of a partial loss) or because the insurers exercise the option commonly found in insurance policies to pay on the basis of market value rather than the cost of reinstatement. Additionally, the covenant should clearly provide for insurance moneys payable for loss of rent to be excluded from the obligation. It may be doubted, however, whether the parties can effectively ensure that the landlord retains the benefit of insurance moneys payable for loss of rent in view of the wide provisions of s.83 of the Fires Prevention (Metropolis) Act 1774 which gives the tenant the right to require "the insurance money" to be laid out in reinstatement. The solution to this problem may be solved by placing the insurance at Lloyd's, rather than in an insurance office, since the 1774 Act does not apply to Lloyd's (*Portavon Cinema Co Ltd v Price* [1939] 4 All E.R. 601). A covenant limited to an obligation to lay out moneys received has obvious attractions to the covenantor. It ensures that he can never be out of pocket. Usually this limitation is found in landlords' covenants and rarely in tenants'. It is suggested that the tenant should not accept this form of covenant. If the landlord is entitled to fix the amount of the cover he should in principle bear the risk of underinsurance; it should not be shifted onto the tenant. Equally, if the tenant is to insure, the risk of underinsurance should be his.

Secondly, where a landlord covenants to reinstate, his obligation is often qualified by an expression such as "unless the insurance is avoided by reason of any act or omission of the tenant." In a case where the landlord's obligation is merely to lay out moneys received, this qualification is unnecessary. However, it should be inserted in any other case for the protection of the landlord. If the insurance is thus avoided, the tenant only has himself to blame; but equally, he should insist on being supplied with a copy of the policy and copies of all recommendations made by the landlord's insurers so that he knows what acts and omissions will avoid the policy. The tenant should, however, resist the extension of such a qualification to acts and omissions of his subtenants and licensees, as there is no reason why he should be the landlord's insurers for their behaviour. Equally, in the case of a letting of part only of a building the tenant should not accept a proviso which releases the landlord from liability to reinstate if the policy is avoided by the acts or omissions of other tenants in the building.

7–14 Thirdly, where the landlord is to reinstate, the draftsman should ensure that the tenant's repairing covenants exclude liability for repairing damage by insured risks (except where the insurance is avoided by any act or omission of the tenant). If the tenant is not himself liable to repair, but is liable to pay the cost of repair by way of service charge, his liability should exclude liability to pay for the repair of damages caused by insured risks. If this is not done a landlord who had underinsured would effectively be able to charge the tenant with any shortfall. In addition, where the tenant is under an absolute obligation to repair, insurers of the landlord's interests under an indemnity policy might be entitled to refuse to pay on the ground that the landlord had suffered no loss.

Fourthly, consideration should be given to the question whether "reinstatement" is what the parties want. There is no satisfactory judicial definition of what is meant by reinstatement. However, it has been held at first instance that a covenant to reinstate obliges the covenantor to restore the building to the precise form in which it existed immediately before the loss, unless such restoration would be pointless (*Camden Theatre Ltd v London Scottish Properties Ltd*, unreported, 1984, per Nicholls J., where a landlord was liable for breach of covenant for painting in gold paint mouldings in a discotheque which had originally been covered in gold leaf). The test has also been said to be whether the restored building element produces as efficient a result as the element which was damaged or destroyed (*Vural v Security Archives* (1989) 60 P. & C.R. 258, where a landlord was in breach by replacing a wooden factory floor with high quality linoleum). In a case where the property is not brand new, a more appropriate obligation might be for the covenantor to undertake to provide a reasonable modern equivalent. At the least, the draftsman should consider the inclusion of an express provision entitling the covenantor to build something which is not identical to that which existed before the loss, and/or that reasonably complies with, and conforms to, current statutory standards and obligations. In addition, where the property is part only of a building or an estate, the draftsman should enable the landlord to carry out work in the order of his choice, and not according to the speed or tenacity with which the tenants pursue their claims.

Fifthly, consideration should be given to specifying a timetable. If none is specified, the court will imply a term to the effect that reinstatement must take place within a reasonable time (*Farimani v Gates* (1984) 271 E.G. 887). From the tenant's point of view, it would be desirable to have an option to terminate the lease if reinstatement has not been completed within a specified time.

Finally, where the demised property forms part of a larger building or complex, the tenant's adviser should ensure that the landlord's reinstatement obligation extends to common parts (especially means of access to the demised property).

(g) Subrogation

7–15 Where an insurer pays out on a policy of insurance he is generally entitled to be subrogated to any claim that the insured has in respect of the subject matter of the claim. However, in most cases, the right of subrogation will not extend to a claim in negligence against the tenant, since the intention of the parties to the lease will be taken to require the landlord's loss to be recouped from his insurers alone (*Mark Rowlands Ltd v Berni Inns Ltd* [1986] Ch. 211).

Nevertheless, it may be worthwhile for the tenant's adviser to attempt to remove the right of subrogation. It is thought that this may be done in one of two ways. Firstly, the landlord's right to sue the tenant may be removed by the insertion of a suitable exemption clause. If such a clause is inserted the insurers will have nothing to which they can be subrogated. Secondly, the landlord may covenant to procure that the tenant's interest be noted on the policy. It is thought that the noting of the tenant's interest on the policy effectively deprives the insurers of their right of subrogation. This method has been chosen in Example 7.6 below.

Example 7.5 Tenant's covenant to insure and reinstate

(1) To keep the demised property insured with reputable insurers approved by the landlord (such approval not to be unreasonably withheld) in the joint names of the landlord and the tenant against loss or damage by fire and such other risks as the landlord may from time to time reasonably prescribe for an amount equal to its full reinstatement cost (including all professional fees and the cost of any work which might be required by or by virtue of any Act of Parliament) and two years' loss of rent

(2) To produce to the landlord on demand the policy of insurance maintained by the tenant and the receipt for the premium payable for it

(3) If the demised property or part of it is destroyed or damaged by fire or by any other peril against the risk of which the tenant is liable to insure forthwith to reinstate the demised property or such part of it as may have been so damaged or destroyed

(4) If it is impossible or impracticable to reinstate in accordance with sub-clause (3) above any moneys received under the policy of insurance (except payments in respect of loss of rent which shall belong to the landlord absolutely) shall be divided between the landlord and the tenant according to the value at the date of the damage or destruction of their respective interests in the demised property (to be determined in default of agreement by a single arbitrator to be appointed by the President for the time being of the Royal Institution of Chartered Surveyors).

Example 7.6 Landlord's covenant to insure and reinstate

(1) To keep the demised property insured against loss or damage by fire and such other risks as he thinks fit and (upon payment by the tenant of any increased premium occasioned thereby) against such risks as the tenant may from time to time reasonably request for an amount equal to its full reinstatement cost (including all professional fees and the cost of any work which might be required by or by virtue of any Act of Parliament) and two years' loss of rent

(2) To produce to the tenant on demand the policy of insurance maintained by the landlord and the receipt for the last premium payable for it and to try his best to cause the tenant's interest to be noted on any such policy

(3) If the demised properly is destroyed or damaged by fire or any other peril against the risk of which the landlord has insured and the policy of insurance not being vitiated by some act or omission by the tenant or any subtenant or licensee of his forthwith to reinstate the demised property or such part of it as shall have been so destroyed or damaged

(4) If it is impossible or impracticable to reinstate in accordance with sub-clause (3) above any moneys received under the policy of insurance (except payments in respect of loss of rent which shall belong to the landlord absolutely) shall be divided between the landlord and the tenant according to the value at the date of the damage or destruction of their respective interests in the demised property (to be determined in default

of agreement by a single arbitrator to be appointed by the President for the time being of the Royal Institution of Chartered Surveyors).

Example 7.7 Proviso for protection of landlord

PROVIDED THAT:

(1) The landlord is under no obligation to reinstate the demised property in the form in which it existed immediately before the damage or destruction in question

(2) If the damage or destruction affects other property in which the landlord has an interest the landlord is under no obligation to reinstate the demised properly until that other property has been reinstated.

Example 7.8 Alternative covenant by landlord to insure and either reinstate or provide modern equivalent

(1) Subject to any exclusions excesses and conditions imposed or required by insurers to keep the demised property insured against loss or damage by the Insured Risks:
   (a) for such sum as the landlord considers appropriate to cover the cost of reinstatement (assuming total loss) together with site clearance debris removal professional fees value added tax and two years' loss of rent
   (b) in a reputable insurance office or at Lloyd's

(2) To use reasonable efforts to negotiate a policy under which insurers have no right of subrogation against the tenant

(3) If:
   (a) the property is destroyed or damaged by any of the Insured Risks and
   (b) the landlord (taking all reasonable steps) obtains all necessary licences and consents

   the landlord shall lay out the insurance money received by him (apart from moneys received for loss of rent) in either:
      (i) reinstating the demised property or the damaged part of it or
      (ii) at his option providing a reasonable modern equivalent

(4) "Insured Risks" means those of the following risks for which cover can be obtained on reasonable terms from reputable insurers: fire storm tempest flood earthquake aircraft and

articles dropped from them riot or civil commotion malicious damage impact damage explosion bursting or overflowing of pipes tanks and other apparatus subsidence or heave and such other risks as may be specified by the landlord or by the tenant.

Example 7.9 Landlord to insure in unspecified amount. Reinstatement or modern equivalent: demised property forming part of larger building

(1) If (and only if) the tenant pays the insurance rent to keep the building insured with reputable insurers against the Insured Risks in an amount decided by the landlord together with three years' loss of rent or such other period as the landlord reasonably requires

(2) To produce to the tenant on demand the policy of insurance maintained by the landlord (or in the case of a block policy extracts from it) and the receipt for the last premium payable for it

(3) If the demised property or any means of access to it is damaged or destroyed by an Insured Risk and the policy of insurance remains in force to lay out the insurance moneys (except loss of rent insurance) in either:
  (a) reinstating the demised property or the means of access or the damaged part of them or
  (b) at the landlord's option providing a reasonable modern equivalent

(4) If it is impracticable to reinstate or provide a modern equivalent in accordance with subclause (3) above within three years after the event giving rise to the loss then:
  (a) the landlord shall be entitled to retain the insurance moneys for his own use and benefit and
  (b) either party shall be entitled to terminate this lease by six months' written notice to that effect

(5) The Insured Risks are [see example 7.8].

(h) Proviso for abatement of rent

In the absence of provision to the contrary the tenant will be liable to pay the rent even if the demised property is wholly destroyed by fire; and a proviso for abatement will not be implied even if the tenant pays the cost of insuring (*Cleveland Shoe Co Ltd v Murray's* **7–16**

Book Sales (King's Cross) Ltd (1973) 229 E.G. 1465). Accordingly, the tenant should ensure that such a proviso is included in the lease, especially where the insurer is to cover the loss of rent. If loss of rent is covered by the insurance policy, but the rent does not abate, then unless the tenant is the insured or one of the insured, the insurers will not pay, because the landlord will have suffered no loss. If, however, the tenant takes out consequential loss insurance in respect of his business, then if the rent does abate, the extent of his claim on his own policy will, to that extent, be diminished.

Several points need to be considered in drafting a proviso for the abatement of rent. Firstly, the draftsman should ensure that the rent does not abate if the insurance is vitiated by any act or omission of the tenant, otherwise the landlord will be both deprived of his income and unable to recover under his policy.

Secondly, the draftsman should consider whether the rent is to abate even in the case of minor damage. For example, it might be provided that the rent shall not abate if the demised property is repaired or reinstated within, say, three months of the occurrence of the damage. Loss of access to the demised property should also be covered.

Thirdly, a proviso for the abatement of rent will reduce the rent payable for the demised property while it is in operation. This may be of significance if the proviso comes into operation shortly before a rent review where the reviewed rent is to be at least the rent payable for the demised property immediately before the review date. If market rents have fallen since the date of the lease (or the last review) an upwards only review will lose its force. Similarly, if there were to be a recurrence of statutory control of rents in the same form as that prevailing between 1972 and 1975 the rent might be incapable of an increase above the abated rent. It is possible to provide contractually that the abatement of rent shall not affect the operation of a rent review. However, it is difficult to see how the draftsman can provide against the imposition of statutory control on the rent payable on a given date. It may be that by providing that the rent shall be "suspended" rather than "shall cease to be payable" the draftsman will be able to protect the landlord. This suggestion is entirely speculative since if statutory control is reimposed its effect will of course depend on the construction of the particular statute.

7–17 Fourthly, where the demised property is part of a larger building or complex, the loss may not have caused damage to the demised property itself, but only to common parts (e.g. means of access). If damage to common parts has made the demised property unusable, even though physically undamaged, the rent should abate.

Fifthly, the parties should consider whether it is only the occupation rent which is to abate, or whether the tenant should also be entitled to an abatement of service charges. The tenant will argue that if he cannot occupy the building, then he should not have to pay any costs. The landlord will retort that many services (e.g. repairs) have to be provided anyway, whether or not the tenant can occupy. The court will not be inclined to construe a lease as allowing for the abatement of anything other than the occupation rent (*P&O Property Holdings v International Computers* [2000] 2 All E.R. 1015).

Sixthly, the parties must consider the date at which the rent abatement period is to end. The landlord will naturally want it to end as soon as the fabric of the building which he let is reinstated. But it is likely that at the beginning of the lease the landlord allowed the tenant a rent free period in which to fit out. The tenant will naturally wish that rent free period to be replicated until he has reinstated his own fit out.

Where the building has suffered a total loss, the tenant has little option but to find alternative accommodation. He will usually have to take the alternative accommodation on a lease for a normal commercial term. Once he has done so he is quite likely not to want to return to the destroyed property. In those circumstances a rent abatement clause is insufficient protection for him, because once the period of abatement comes to an end the tenant will resume liability to pay rent. The tenant's adviser should press for a tenant's break-clause in the event of a total loss. Equally, the landlord may wish to redevelop the building in the event of a total loss in which case he will wish to terminate existing leases. Even where the loss is not total, he may wish to realign services or the layout of the building, and the existence of leases may hamper that task. Accordingly, it will often be in both parties' interest that the lease should be capable of termination by either of them if there is a major loss. **7–18**

If this is impossible to agree, the tenant should press for safeguards. First, he should be given full information about the progress of reinstatement works. Second, he should require a period of notice **7–19** before he is obliged to recommence paying the rent. This will enable him to dispose of any temporary accommodation he has acquired in the meantime. Third, he should try to ensure that the obligation to recommence paying the rent does not arise until the whole of the property is fit for reoccupation.

Example 7.10 Proviso for abatement of rent

(1) If the demised property or any principal means of access to it is so damaged or destroyed by a peril against the risk of which the demised property is insured as to become unfit for occupation in whole or in part and the sum insured is not wholly or partly irrecoverable by reason of any act or omission of the Tenant or any subtenant or licensee of his then the rent or a fair proportion of it shall be suspended until the demised property is again fit for occupation

(2) Sub-clause (1) above shall not apply if the damage is repaired or reinstated within three months after the occurrence of the damage or destruction in question

(3) Any dispute as to the proportion shall be determined by a single arbitrator to be appointed by the President for the time being of the Royal Institution of Chartered Surveyors

(4) Any reviewed rent for the demised property shall be assessed as if subclause (1) above was not in operation at the review date and as if the damage or destruction had not occurred.

Example 7.11 Tenant's break clause on total loss

If the demised property or any principal means of access to it is so damaged or destroyed by any peril against the risk of which the demised property is insured as to become unfit for occupation and to remain unfit for occupation for more than six months the tenant shall be entitled to determine this tenancy by not less than three months' written notice given to the landlord at any time after the expiry of that period of six months.

Example 7.12 Mutual break clause on total loss

If the demised property or any principal means of access to it is so damaged or destroyed by any peril against the risk of which the demised property is insured as to become unfit for occupation and use and to remain unfit for occupation and use for more than three years either the landlord or the tenant shall be entitled to determine this tenancy by not less than three months' written notice given at any time after the expiry of that period of three years.

(i) Insurance and use

The tenant's use of the property may have repercussions on the amount of the premium payable for insurance. For that reason, it is good practice to include in the lease a covenant on the tenant's part not to do anything that would avoid the insurance policy or increase the premium payable. In practice the problem faced by landlords is that tenants fail to comply with recommendations made by the landlords' insurers. Often the landlord does not know whether non-compliance with those recommendations will cause the insurers to come off risk. Accordingly, it is suggested that the draftsman should extend the usual form of covenant to include a positive obligation on the tenant's part to comply with all recommendations of the landlord's insurers. Such a covenant not only has the advantage that the tenant may be restrained by injunction from using the property in such a way as to cause an increased premium to be payable (*Chapman v Mason* (1910) 103 L.T. 390) but also, it is submitted, the tenant may be ordered to execute works recommended by the insurers. **7–20**

The tenant's advisers should note that if the tenant covenants not to cause any increase in the premium the landlord will not be under a similar correlative obligation. Thus, he will be entitled to let adjoining property for a use that causes an increased premium to be payable for the demised property (*O'Cedar Ltd v Slough Trading Co Ltd* [1927] 2 K.B. 123).

Example 7.13 Tenant's covenant not to avoid insurance or to cause increase in premium

Not to do permit or suffer to be done in the demised property anything which may avoid any policy of insurance maintained by the landlord in respect of the demised property or increase the rate of any premium payable for it and to comply at his own expense with all recommendations of the insurers under it.

(j) Insurance other than fire insurance

(i) Plate glass

7–21 Plate glass is often insured under a separate policy from the building. In most shop lettings it is more convenient for the tenant to insure against damage to plate glass. However, the draftsman should ensure that any proviso for abatement of rent does not come into operation merely because the shop window is cracked. It will usually be sufficient if the proviso does not come into operation if the demised property is reinstated within, say, three months, because in practice any shop tenant will want to repair his shop window as soon as possible.

(ii) Lifts and boilers

7–22 The insurance of lifts, boilers and other expensive plant is usually included in a regular maintenance contract. Accordingly, the person responsible for such maintenance should be made liable for their insurance. If, as is often the case, the landlord maintains and insures and recovers the cost by way of service charge, the tenant should ensure that he is not required to contribute to a sinking fund for the replacement of such plant in addition to being liable to pay for such a contract.

(iii) Public liability

7–23 Landlords often require tenants to pay the cost of insuring the landlord against public liability by reason of any defect in the demised property or, more usually, the common parts. It is questionable whether tenants ought to accept such an obligation. If the landlord is responsible for the repair of common parts he should bear the risk of defects in them causing injury to people. Conversely, it might well be in the interest of landlords to require tenants to effect public liability insurance since a tenant faced with a substantial claim for personal injuries may find it impossible to continue to pay rent.

(k) Uninsured risks

As stated above, a covenant to insure should be qualified so that it applies only to the extent that the specified insured risks can be insured against in the UK market or at reasonable commercial rates. If one of the insured risks cannot be insured against, a landlord's covenant to reinstate will not apply and the tenant will not receive a rent abatement. Historically, the risk of damage to property by an uninsured risk has rested with tenants. If a tenant's repairing covenant has been drafted widely, it is also possible that the tenant might be required to make good the damage, whilst paying the rent. 7–24

Over recent years, there has been a move to change. The Code for Leasing Commercial Business Premises in England and Wales 2007 recommends that rent suspension should apply if the property is damaged by an uninsured risk (other than one caused by the deliberate act of the tenant), and that if the property is damaged so as to prevent occupation, tenants should be allowed to terminate their leases unless landlords agree to reinstate at their own cost.

The Code's first recommendation has not, however, found general favour in practice because the entirety of the risk and cost is placed upon the landlord. One alternative approach is for the risk to be shared as follows. The landlord is given a period within which to elect whether to reinstate the damage at its own cost, normally twelve months. During the period before the landlord serves notice, the tenant's covenants to repair relevant damage should be suspended. Once the notice has been served, the rent abatement provisions apply until the reinstatement is completed. If the landlord fails to serve notice within the set period then either landlord or tenant should be able to terminate the lease. Such an approach has the advantage of enabling the landlord to investigate whether relevant consents and funding can be obtained in order to decide whether reinstatement is indeed feasible. The draftsman must however consider the impact of the Landlord and Tenant Act 1954 Part II if the lease is not contracted out of the statutory security of tenure provisions. If the landlord serves notice to terminate, the tenant can, in theory apply for a new tenancy. The drafting should therefore provide that in such circumstances the tenant should reinstate the property at its own expense and pay the rent.

An alternative approach to rent abatement in the event of an uninsured risk is to oblige the tenant to pay a specific amount of rent in the event that the landlord elects to rebuild, for a stated maximum period. This is sometimes made payable during the construction process and sometimes payable as a lump sum once the construction is completed.

It is also suggested that these provisions should apply in the event that a substantial element of the property is rendered inaccessible.

CHAPTER 8

SERVICE CHARGES

1. SERVICE CHARGES

The purpose of a service charge is to ensure that the landlord recovers the rent payable under the lease free from the risk that he will have to spend part of it in maintaining or repairing the demised property or otherwise incurring running costs. In other words, the risk is transferred from the landlord to the tenant. The existence of a service charge can have significant effects on the capital value of the landlord's reversion. Indeed, many of the financial institutions will not buy reversions on leases that do not contain service charges. Since the norm in the market is for "institutionally acceptable" leases, the service charge is a vital component of the lease. Accordingly, in many cases the form of the service charge is not negotiable. However, from the tenant's point of view, the service charge represents a very large part of his cost of occupation. And an onerous service charge will almost always play a part in reducing rent on review. For those reasons the draftsman should try to ensure that a service charge not only protects the landlord's interest but is also fair to the tenant. **8–01**

The British Council of Shopping Centres, British Council for Offices, British Property Federation, British Retail Consortium and the Property Managers Association Shopping Centre Management Group support and endorse the Royal Institution of Chartered Surveyors' publication, "Service Charges in Commercial Property: RICS Code of Practice" (2nd edn, October 2011). The current RICS Code is based on the voluntary "Service Charges in Commercial Property: Guide to Good Practice" (2nd edn, August 2002) and the "Service Charges in Commercial Property: RICS Code of Practice" (1st edn, June 2006), and supersedes both. The RICS Code has the status of a RICS Guidance Note, and contains advice and recommendations. Its stated aims are to improve general standards and promote best practice, uniformity, fairness and transparency in the management and administration of service charges in commercial property. The City of London Law Society has drawn up a series of lease provisions specifically designed to comply with the principles and provisions of the Code. The Code is effective from 1 October 2011, and the RICS has recommended that its provisions are appropriately implemented in all new leases. Whilst the RICS Code has been designed for larger properties, the principles are intended to apply to smaller properties as well.

(a) Green lease provisions

8–02 It is to be expected that green lease provisions will play an increasing role in the way in which energy, water and waste costs are attributed to either landlord or tenant and/or are provided by landlords to their tenants in future. Green leasing is discussed in Chapter 11 below.

(b) Mixed use schemes

8–03 Over the last 10 years there has been a real increase in new mixed use developments with residential units being introduced into commercial developments. The Landlord and Tenant Act 1985 (amended by the Housing Act 1996 and the Commonhold and Leasehold Reform Act 2002), imposes statutory constraints on the recovery of service charges for residential properties. As a result, and regardless of any other provisions in the lease, the landlord of a lease including both residential and non-residential elements must follow the statutory procedures, including the consultation requirements, to ensure that non-recovery does not result (*Heron Maple House Ltd v Central Estates* [2002] 1 E.G.L.R. 35; *Oakfern Properties Ltd v Ruddy* [2006] EWCA Civ 1389). In *Daejan Investments Ltd v Benson* [2011] 1 W.L.R. 2330, the landlord's failure to comply fully with the statutory consultation procedures limited service charge recovery to £250 per leaseholder. In *Brent LBC v Shulem B Association Ltd* [2011] 4 All E.R. 778, a failure to give a section notice under s.20B of the Landlord and Tenant Act 1985 meant that the landlord could not recover all of the cost of major works.

It is suggested that reference is made to the RICS Information Papers "Managing Mixed Use Developments" and "Apportionment of Service Charges in Mixed Use Developments", for a full discussion of the specific service charge considerations involved in relation to mixed use properties.

(c) The key five aspects of standard commercial service charge

In practice, five aspects of service charges give rise to problems: 8–04

(1) the method of payment of service charges;
(2) the items that may be recovered as part of the charge;
(3) the apportionment of charges as between tenants;
(4) the provision of reserve or sinking funds; and
(5) the certification of charges.

(d) Method of payment

There are two schools of thought as to whether the service charge should be reserved as rent. In practice, it usually is. Those who believe it should, do so for the following reasons: 8–05

(1) the landlord will be able to forfeit the lease for non-payment of the charge without the need to serve a s.146 notice beforehand; and
(2) the landlord will be entitled to distrain for any unpaid charge, at least once it has been quantified (*Re Knight, Ex p. Voisey* (1882) 21 Ch. D. 442) and for any interim charge if that is also reserved as rent (*Walsh v Lonsdale* (1882) 21 Ch. D. 9).

Those who prefer a covenant to pay retort that:

(1) if a s.146 notice must be served, the period for remedying the breach of covenant may be short;
(2) the landlord cannot distrain while the service charge is in dispute (*Concorde Graphics Ltd v Andromeda Investments SA* ([1983] 1 E.G.L.R 53);
(3) there is a theoretical liability to pay a modest amount of additional stamp duty; and
(4) if the lease is forfeit for non-payment of service charge the tenant does not have the same automatic right to relief against

forfeiture as he does for non-payment of rent although in practice he is highly likely to obtain relief if he can pay the arrears.

8–06 Whether the service charge is reserved as rent or not, it is regarded by HM Revenue & Customs as part of the consideration for the grant of the lease for the assessment of VAT. Thus, the service charge will be treated in the same way as the rent. So if the rent carries VAT, so will the service charge; if the rent does not carry VAT nor will the service charge. But this does not apply to services to the demised property itself. Whether such services carry VAT depends on the nature of the service (see also HM Revenue & Customs Brief 67/09 confirming that the UK's treatment of service charges is unchanged following the European Court of Justice case of *RLRE Tellmer* (C-572/07)).

8–07 If service charge is reserved as a single sum with the rent, it will be taxed accordingly for SDLT (Sch.17A, para.6 of the Finance Act 2003, inserted by the Finance Act 2004). So, where a single sum is payable in respect of rent and service charge and/or the service charge is not separately provided for in the terms of the lease, then the sum is to be treated entirely as rent for SDLT purposes.

However, the fact that a service charge is reserved in the lease as rent does not make it rent for SDLT purposes. Service charges payable from tenant to landlord are not chargeable consideration for stamp duty purposes and are excluded from the calculation of tax so long as payment of the service charge has either been (1) provided for in the lease as a separate figure or (2) expressed in the lease as part of an inclusive rent payment and apportioned on a just and reasonable basis. Where apportionment of an inclusive figure is needed this must be made on a just and reasonable basis for SDLT purposes and will not necessarily be the same as any apportionment set out in the lease itself. If the service charge element is included in the rent, and is likely to vary, this will make the rent "uncertain" for SDLT purposes.

On balance, it is suggested that from the landlord's point of view the service charge is better reserved as rent, mainly because of the remedy of distress for undisputed or minimum charges. This is the most common practice.

The draftsman should make it clear that the service charge is not to abate if the demised property is destroyed or damaged or is inaccessible as a result of an insured risk except to the extent that services are not provided to the tenant. Moreover the service charge should not be caught by the provisions for rent review inevitably found in a lease containing a service charge. **8–08**

It is rare to find a service charge in a modern lease where sums are payable on demand. Although such a scheme is found in older leases, it is unsatisfactory, since it is impossible to budget for. It can only be appropriate where expenditure is likely to be extremely infrequent and to amount to no more than the cost of repairing party walls, etc. **8–09**

(i) Interim payments and balancing payments

Some provision should therefore be made for payments in advance. The landlord has to fund expenses out of his own pocket before he can recover them from the tenant (often up to a year later) and in the absence of a specific provision in the lease, he will not be entitled to charge the tenants with interest on moneys expended, even if the landlord has actually had to pay it (*Frobisher (Second Investments) Ltd v Kiloran Trust Co Ltd* [1980] 1 All E.R. 488). It will be unacceptable for the landlord to have to wait until the end of an accounting period to recover the capital cost. Accordingly, it is suggested that the tenant should accept a provision for payment in advance. **8–10**

What provision should be made for such payments? In essence there are two methods. The lease may provide for a payment on account which is fixed in the first year of the term, and thereafter is a specified percentage of the previous year's actual charge. The percentage may be less than or more than 100. This method can only work if the tenant is required to contribute towards a reserve fund to meet non-annual expenditure (for example, external redecorations). In other cases this method will not work fairly to either party. In a year in which substantial non-annual expenditure is incurred the landlord will not recover enough to enable him to meet that expenditure as it falls due, while in the following year the tenant's advance payment will be far too high. Alternatively, the lease may provide for the tenant to pay a sum fixed each year either by the landlord or his surveyor. The tenant should not accept an obligation to pay whatever the landlord asks for, since he may find himself being used as a source of free loans. He should stipulate for the advance payment to be based on a budget for the year in question, prepared by someone exercising an independent judgment. In addition a copy of the budget should be supplied to the tenant. If there is a tenants' association (as in a shopping centre) it may be appropriate to provide for major items of expenditure to be discussed with the association before inclusion in the budget. Advance payments should be payable at the same time as the rent.

There will be an implied obligation on the part of the landlord to provide estimates (*Gordon v Selico Co Ltd* [1986] 1 E.G.L.R. 71). Where there is an express obligation on the landlord to obtain estimates in advance of carrying out work, the court will probably interpret this as a condition precedent to the right to a service charge for that work. This has the result that if the landlord fails to obtain estimates in advance, he cannot recover any service charge for that item even if the cost was otherwise reasonable (*CIN Properties v Barclays Bank* [1986] 1 E.G.L.R. 59; *Northways Flats Management Co (Camden) v Wimpey Pension Trustees* [1992] 2 E.G.L.R. 42; and see *Leonora Investment Co Ltd v Mott McDonald Ltd* [2008] 2 P. & C.R. DG 15, where the court concluded, as a matter of interpretation, that a balancing payment had not fallen due at a time when the tenant had not been provided with a statement of expenditure in accordance with which the service charge was payable). It is therefore prudent for the draftsman to provide that failure to comply with the machinery is not to make the service charge irrecoverable.

From a tenant's point of view, it is sensible to place the landlord under an obligation to provide a statement of expenditure within a set period following the end of the service charge year such that any balancing payment or re-payment can be made promptly (see also *Redrow Homes (Midlands) Ltd v Hothi* [2012] L. & T.R. 8, where the Upper Tribunal implied a term into a residential lease that the landlord will compute the final service charge within a reasonable time of the end of the relevant service charge year). Again, a landlord's adviser will wish to ensure that time is not to be regarded as of the essence for this purpose.

(ii) Fixing costs

As stated above, all-inclusive rentals have traditionally proved unpopular in the investment market, and the discussion in this Chapter therefore focuses on the standard variable service charge provisions that will be included in the majority of business leases. There are, however, circumstances in which either a landlord or a tenant will seek to agree that a pre-determined service charge is payable throughout the term. In such cases, a tenant will take an internal lease or leases of a number of floors and the landlord will retain responsibility for the repair and maintenance of all other elements of the building, including the common parts, and will be obliged to provide services and utilities to the demised premises. **8–11**

A detailed all-inclusive service charge in a pre-determined amount will provide the tenant with certainty, and, to an extent, that may also provide the landlord with some assurance that the tenant will be likely to meet the agreed sums. The landlord will also have comfort that its building will be kept in repair during the term. However, the disincentive for the landlord is that its estimate may prove inaccurate, or that the tenant's use of the premises may result in the need for unanticipated works or bills. Accordingly, the consideration for the landlord's agreement to a fixed cost provision should include restrictive assignment provisions, agreed business hours within which the tenant may use the building, and careful structuring of the landlord's obligations to make any necessary improvement, and to provide services and utilities.

It is suggested that such arrangements are necessarily best suited to short term lettings. In the event that the letting is of any real duration, provision should be made for periodic review of the fixed charge. In the event that the lease is to be of a length that also justifies the inclusion of a rent review clause, careful thought must be given to the inter-relationship of a fixed charge provision with a rent review clause, and the impact of the fixed cost provision on future rental value.

(e) Landlord's obligation

The aim of the tenant's adviser should be to ensure that the landlord enters into an obligation to provide the services for which the service charge is to be levied. Landlords sometimes attempt to make **8–12** obligations to provide services conditional upon payment by the tenant of the service charge. The court will be reluctant to construe a lease as having the effect that the landlord is entitled to withhold essential services merely because the tenant is in arrear with payments (*Yorkbrook Investments Ltd v Batten* [1985] 2 E.G.L.R. 100), but careful drafting linking the tenants and their payments on the one hand and the landlord and its responsibilities on the other could produce a clause which stated clearly that such was the parties' intention. The tenant should not accept such a provision. The landlord should consider its position carefully if it depends entirely for its ability to run the building upon the contributions from the tenants (*Bluestorm Ltd v Portvale Holdings Ltd* [2004] 2 E.G.L.R. 38).

The desire of the tenant is to ensure that the landlord has an absolute obligation to provide the services. If the landlord is willing to enter into such an obligation then the services must be provided even if this would involve the landlord in substantial capital expenditure (*Yorkbrook Investments Ltd v Batten* [1985] 2 E.G.L.R. 100) and the landlord will be in breach of such an obligation even if he cannot afford the necessary expenditure (*Francis v Cowcliffe Ltd* (1976) 33 P. & C.R. 368). The draftsman should therefore consider whether the landlord's obligation should be limited to an obligation to use "best" or "reasonable" endeavours to provide the services. An obligation to use "best" endeavours may be acceptable to the tenant, although an obligation merely to use reasonable endeavours may not be. A halfway house would be an obligation to use "all reasonable" endeavours (*UBH (Mechanical Services) Ltd v Standard Life Assurance Co*, *The Times*, November 13, 1986). If the obligation to provide services is expressed in absolute terms, it is usual to qualify it by exempting the landlord from liability for temporary interruptions in services for reasons beyond his control.

The mere fact that the tenant pays a service charge does not necessarily mean that the landlord is under an obligation to provide the service (*Russell v Laimond Properties* [1984] 1 E.G.L.R. 37). Conversely, the court has recognised that what may nominally be a landlord's obligation to provide services is also his right, since the corollary of the provision of the services is the tenant's obligation to contribute to their cost (*Plough Investments v Manchester City Council* [1989] 1 E.G.L.R. 244).

In some cases, however, an obligation to provide services has been implied from the tenant's obligation to pay. This is easier where the tenant pays a rent quantified in advance and which is payable in any event (*Barnes v City of London Real Property Co* [1918] 2 Ch. 18), although such an obligation has been implied in other cases also (*Edmonton Corp v WM Knowles & Son* (1961) 60 L.G.R. 124). But such an obligation will not usually be implied (*Westminster (Duke of) v Guild* [1984] 3 All E.R. 144; *Tennant Radiant Heat Ltd v Warrington Development Corp* [1988] 1 E.G.L.R. 41).

The landlord will often seek to restrict his obligation to the provision of essential services (e.g. repair of the structure, exterior and common parts; provision of air-conditioning, etc.), while leaving himself a discretion to provide other services (e.g. floral arrangements or security) if he so chooses. In principle, this is not objectionable provided that the list of services which the landlord is obliged to provide is extensive enough to meet the tenant's foreseeable needs. If the landlord has a discretion whether to provide services or not, the tenant's adviser should ensure that the discretion must be exercised reasonably. In addition, it is desirable from the tenant's point of view to provide that the landlord must consult the tenants before instituting or discontinuing a service.

(f) Trust funds

In the hands of the landlords or their agents interim payments are **8–13**
part of their general funds to be applied in accordance with the contractual arrangements between them. They are not impressed by any trust, nor are they held by the landlords or their agents as stakeholders (*Frobisher (Second Investments) Ltd v Kiloran Trust Co Ltd* [1980] 1 All E.R. 488; *Secretary of State for the Environment v Possfund (North West) Ltd* [1997] 39 E.G. 179). If, however, the moneys are set aside in a separate bank account then a trust may be created (*Re Chelsea Cloisters Ltd (In Liquidation)* (1980) 41 P. & C.R. 98). In relation to dwellings, however, s.42 of the Landlord and Tenant Act 1987 (and the Commonhold and Leasehold Reform Act 2002 ss.156 and 157, and Sch.10, para.15) requires service charge contributions to be held in trust. Normally this need not concern the draftsman of a commercial lease, but in the case of a lease of a part of a mixed development or even of a

lock-up shop under separately let flats, the draftsman will need to consider whether the service charge should be held on trust so as to provide uniformity of management.

Some leases provide for the service charge to be paid to a maintenance company which holds the contribution upon trust to apply the funds towards certain specified purposes (e.g. repair, maintenance and insurance). Under this arrangement, the company is only obliged to apply the money actually received, so that if a tenant defaults, the maintenance company is not liable to make good the deficit or to carry out work for which it does not have the necessary funds (*Alton House Holdings Ltd v Calflane (Management) Ltd* [1987] 2 E.G.L.R. 52). Moreover, if the tenant has a complaint about the way that the money is spent, his remedy is not an action for damages for breach of covenant, but an action for the administration of the trust (*Gordon v Selico Co Ltd* [1986] 1 E.G.L.R. 71). Procedurally this is more cumbersome than an action for damages and/or specific performance of the covenant, and in any event the tenant is less well protected by a scheme which only requires expenditure of moneys received rather than one which places an absolute obligation on the landlord (or a maintenance company) to repair and carry out other works. The tenant should not be deceived by the illusion that a trust affords him protection, when in fact it operates to deprive him of common law remedies. Trusts of reserve and sinking funds are dealt with in (f) below.

Where service charge monies are to be held in a separate bank account, and based on the principle that property owners should not profit from the supply of services, all interest earned should be credited to the service charge account. Provision should be made for deductions for items such as bank charges and tax.

(g) Recoverable items

8–14 In each case, the draftsman should consider the nature and type of the property as the levels and standards of services provided should differ according to these factors. Whether a particular item is recoverable by way of service charge depends on the construction of the lease in question. Where parties entrust the determination to an expert, they usually intend the expert to apply his expertise to the contract properly interpreted, and his interpretation may be reviewed by the court (*Mercury Communications v Director-General of Telecommunications* [1996] 1 W.L.R. 48).

Where the charge is payable by reference to costs "incurred" by the landlord, no costs will be "incurred" until the landlord has either disbursed the costs or become immediately liable to do so (*Capital & County Freehold Equity Trust Ltd v BL Plc* [1987] 2 E.G.L.R. 49). The tenant should not accept anything more favourable to the landlord. The lease will usually provide that the amount of service charge is measured by reference to the cost incurred by "the landlord". That phrase will usually be defined by reference to the holder of the immediate reversion.

If the lease in question is a sub-lease, it will be important to ensure that the definition is wide enough to include costs incurred by the superior landlord. Similarly, if the lease is an overriding lease (e.g. granted under s.19 of the Landlord and Tenant (Covenants) Act 1995), it will be necessary to ensure that the service charge payable by the occupational tenant is calculated by reference to expenditure incurred by the superior landlord. In practice, the court is likely to take a robust view of technical arguments based on the details of the definition of "landlord" (*Adelphi (Estates) v Christie* [1984] 1 E.G.L.R. 19).

Some leases reserve to the landlord a power to alter the services provided during the term, but it is questionable how far the terms of the bargain may be altered in this way. Nevertheless, it is suggested that the draftsman would be correct in including such a power in a long lease since it may well be impossible to predict what services will be required in the later years of the term.

The draftsman's aim should be to provide the landlord with a complete indemnity against the cost of complying with his covenants. But it does not follow that where a service charge echoes the landlord's obligations the service charge will necessarily cover those obligations (*Rapid Results College Ltd v Angell* [1986] 1 E.G.L.R. 53).

Thus far, a service charge is likely to be acceptable to the majority of tenants. However, some service charges seek to go further. For example, it is not uncommon to find a provision entitling the landlord to recover from the tenant the cost of collecting the rent. Rent collection is a service of dubious value to the tenant and a well-advised tenant may not accept having to pay for it. The RICS Code also now recommends that rent collection costs (and asset management costs) should be excluded from the service charge management fee.

Equally, some landlords seek to include in the service charge the cost of renewing, rebuilding or even improving the demised property. Such a provision should not be accepted by the tenant. Any inducements and concessions to attract other tenants to the landlord's building or centre should also be borne by the owner and not spread amongst other tenants.

Some items will now be considered in more detail.

(i) Management charges

8–15 The management charge is defined in the RICS Code as the reasonable price for the total cost of managing the provision of the services at the location, and relates only to work carried out in managing and operating the services and administering the service charge. The management charge might comprise two elements:

(1) the management fee, being the fee charged by the manager for the management and supervision of the services to the site; and
(2) the site management costs, being the cost of site-specific management staff, whether based on site full-time or part-time.

Because no two buildings are identical in the way that they need to be run to meet the interest of all parties, the appropriate level of services needs to be considered in each case, and the management charges need to be set at a correspondingly appropriate level.

(1) Management fees

8–16 Save in exceptional circumstances, the landlord will not be entitled to recover the cost of management fees or charges unless the lease expressly so provides (*Embassy Court Residents Association v Lipman* [1984] 2 E.G.L.R. 60). But there can be no objection in principle to a landlord seeking to recover from the tenant the cost of employing a managing agent to organise and supervise the various services provided for the tenant under the lease, provided that the cost is reasonable. The RICS Code recommends that management fees charged should be reasonable costs and overheads in relation to the operation and management of the services. It recognises that whoever is providing the service is entitled to cover their costs and overheads including a reasonable profit element.

It used to be common practice for agents to be paid a percentage of the service charge. However tenants reasonably object that this encourages overspending, and is a disincentive to the delivery of value for money. The RICS Code requires that fees are set on a fixed price basis rather than being calculated as a percentage of expenditure. The recommendation is that the management fee should be a fixed fee subject to annual review or indexation.

Where the landlord is entitled to recover the cost of management, he may employ his own company as managing agent, unless this is merely a sham (*Skilleter v Charles* [1992] 1 E.G.L.R. 73). But if the lease simply provides that the landlord shall be entitled to recover the cost of employing agents he will not be entitled to an allowance for himself if he does not employ any. Nor will he be able to dress himself up as his own agent (*Finchbourne Ltd v Rodrigues* [1976] 3 All E.R. 581). Accordingly, the draftsman should expressly provide for the landlord to be entitled to a reasonable allowance in respect of the performance of any function that could reasonably be delegated to a managing agent. The RICS Code recommends that where the landlord manages the property they should be able to support the basis of their fees when benchmarked against other comparable service providers. Some leases provide that the landlord is to be entitled to recover a proportion of his general administrative overheads. It is suggested that the tenant should not accept such a provision but should instead accept that the landlord should have remuneration for services that he in fact performs or supervises.

(2) Site management costs, including staff and staff accommodation

The RICS Code defines site management costs to include the full employment costs for sufficient on-site or part-time staff who perform according to defined management standards. The fact that a landlord may employ staff has long been recognised. In the case of lettings of office suites, the desirability of providing staff was judicially noted in the last century as follows: 8–17

> "It is far better for the tenants that there should be some central authority who should appoint a housekeeper to look after the house generally than that each of them should be left to make provision of that kind for himself.

> It would not be possible for any one individual, having to make arrangements of that sort, to ensure that the occupants of the other rooms would be as careful as he might be himself in the selection of a housekeeper; and when once you had five or six different sets of cleaners coming in to perform the services of cleaning and dusting and so on, there would be very much inferior security to the tenants that there should not be all sorts of improper people getting in to the house and perhaps making arrangements for burglary and theft, or acquiring information which it was very desirable should not go outside the particular office." (per Sargant J. in *Barnes v City of London Real Property Co* [1918] 2 Ch. 18.)

The same considerations might be applied to lettings of consulting rooms to doctors or dentists where a receptionist is to be employed, for example.

These days, in any given circumstances, the staff employed by a landlord may range from a management team in a shopping centre, to a security guard at the gate of a business park, and to the cleaners responsible for the common parts of an office block. As an alternative, off-site emergency support might also be provided, full time or out of hours. Provision should be made for the reasonable costs of this service to be recoverable through the service charge if this course is or might be adopted during the term.

If it is contemplated that the landlord will provide staff, the draftsman should ensure that the landlord is entitled to recover more than merely the wages or salary of such staff. The total cost of the staff will include wages, national insurance, tax, compliance with statutory requirements, training, appropriate benefits and Christmas bonuses. If the landlord's entitlement is restricted to "wages and salaries" it is arguable that it would not extend to those items to which the employee is not strictly entitled under his service contract. Accordingly, it is suggested that the landlord should be entitled to recover "the full cost" or "total cost" of employing staff.

In some cases, the RICS Code states that site management costs might also make provision for an "administration charge", a fee representing the human resources and payroll costs associated with dealing with staff. Where reviews of staffing levels are undertaken, the RICS Code recommends that it is reasonable that costs associated with achieving beneficial change, such as the termination of employment contracts, should be recoverable under the service charge provided such costs can be justified following the analysis of reasonable options; the purpose being to achieve greater value for money and effectiveness.

In the interests of transparency, it is advisable that the landlord's costs of commissioning any specialist expert reports, and consultancy services, for example, fire risk assessments, Equality Act reports and assessments, asbestos surveys, health and safety reports and the costs of any procurement specialists employed, should be excluded from the management fees, and made specifically recoverable as a separate service charge item.

Where on-site staff oversee more than one property, their costs and any appropriate accommodation and any administrative support costs, should be adjusted proportionately, so that each property is only responsible for a fair share of their cost.

Although it has been held by the Court of Appeal that notional rent foregone by the landlord in respect of accommodation provided for staff is part of the "cost" of providing services (*Agavil Investments Ltd v Corner*, unreported, 3 October 1975; *Lloyds Bank v Bowker Orford* [1992] 2 E.G.L.R. 424; *Gilje v Charlegrove Securities* [2002] 1 E.G.L.R. 41) it is nevertheless suggested that the draftsman should provide expressly for the inclusion of notional rent in the service charge. If the lease is ambiguous, the notional rent will not be recoverable. From a tenant's point of view, a tenant's adviser should resist the inclusion of a notional rent if the particular premises would have been unlettable or incapable of beneficial occupation for any other purpose. In such cases, there is no rent "foregone".

(ii) The relationship with the landlord's obligations

Where a lease reserves additional rent in respect of office cleaning and other similar services there will be implied a correlative obligation on the landlord to provide the service for which the tenant has covenanted to pay (*Barnes v City of London Real Property Co* [1918] 2 Ch. 18). Such an obligation may be specifically enforceable (*Posner v Scott-Lewis* [1986] 3 All E.R. 513) and the tenant may be awarded damages if it is broken and the landlord may be restrained by injunction from selling or disposing of accommodation intended to be occupied by resident staff (*Hupfield v Bourne* (1974) 28 P. & C.R. 77). Since staff may prove difficult to obtain, the draftsman should expressly declare that the landlord is not to be liable to the tenant for failure to provide staff. **8–18**

(iii) *Heating, water and electricity*

8–19 The cost of heating the demised property has traditionally been an item commonly included in a service charge. The drafting of this item requires some care. Where the tenant pays a percentage of a global sum, the item should be the cost of heating the whole building (or development) rather than the cost of heating the demised property, otherwise the tenant will not pay the proper cost of heating his own accommodation (*Pole Properties Ltd v Feinberg* [1981] 2 E.G.L.R. 38). Similarly, where other services such as mains water and electricity are provided direct to a tenant, as common services, the parties must make clear whether the costs are to be included within the service charge account or as a separate charge. The fairest apportionment of cost to reflect actual consumption by an individual tenant may increasingly be based on separate metering or sub-metering of the leasehold premises together with a formula to reflect the costs incurred in relation to the common parts or the estate or development. This is also discussed in terms of green leasing in Chapter 11. The RICS Code recommends that an additional provision should be made for the recovery of a reasonable administrative charge in this regard; that best practice includes the reading of meters by third parties, and that this cost should also be expressed to be recoverable.

The draftsman should avoid a provision that refers to specific dates between which heating is to be maintained. If the landlord is only entitled to recover the cost of heating the premises between, say, 1 October and 1 May in each year the tenant may refuse to pay for heating the premises during a cold September. Conversely, he may complain if they are not heated during April. But if the landlord has the discretion to fix the heating season, he cannot nullify the covenant to supply heat by making an arbitrary choice of dates (*Regis Property Co v Redman* [1956] 2 Q.B. 612).

Equally, it is unwise to specify a temperature to which the property is to be heated. Moreover, the draftsman should ensure that the landlord is not liable to the tenants for a temporary breakdown in the heating system (cf. *UBH (Mechanical Services) Ltd v Standard Life Assurance Co*, *The Times*, 13 November 1986).

As it is becoming commonplace for utility companies to request that property owners pay large security deposits or higher energy rates, the draftsman should consider, in an appropriate case, making provision for the inclusion of a security deposit as a service charge cost. In such case, the tenant must ensure that the lease allows for the tenant's proportion of such deposit to be reimbursed:

(1) upon the expiry or sooner determination of the term;
(2) in the event of a change of landlord; or
(3) if the deposit is reimbursed by the utility company.

The RICS Code suggests that the payment of a deposit can be included in on account payments demanded for the relevant service charge year, then credited back to the tenant at the end of the year, and then re-budgeted for the following year. As a result, if the lease expires in any given period, the tenant will receive an appropriate credit in their final service charge balance without more.

Example 8.1 Obligation on tenant to pay for utility use attributed to their leasehold property
The Tenant covenants:
To pay for all gas electricity and water consumed on the Property all charges for meters and all standing charges.

(iv) Plant and machinery

The most important items to be considered under this head are lifts, boilers and air-conditioning equipment. The landlord will usually arrange for these to be maintained under comprehensive maintenance contracts. Such contracts often include payments on account of the eventual cost of replacing the plant or equipment in question. The draftsman should, therefore, ensure that the whole of the cost of such a contract is recoverable from the tenant. Accordingly, the service charge should not be limited to the "repair and maintenance" of the equipment but should extend to include all payments made under a contract for the repair and maintenance of the equipment, including any provision made thereunder for the periodic renewal of such equipment. The tenant's adviser should scrutinise a service charge provision of this nature in order to eliminate any separate requirement to contribute to a reserve fund for the renewal of the same equipment. **8–20**

All items of plant have a finite life, and all of them reach the point at which it is a question of judgment whether to continue to repair them or whether the time has come to replace them. The lease should make it clear whether the landlord has power to charge for the replacement of plant and machinery either at the end of their useful life or at a time when a prudent building owner would decide to replace them. If the position is not made clear and the item is not in disrepair, it has been held that the fact that an item of plant has reached the end of its recommended lifespan as suggested by industry guidelines does not mean that it would be reasonable for the landlord to replace it at the tenant's expense (*Fluor Daniel Properties Ltd v Shortlands Investments Ltd* [2001] 2 E.G.L.R. 103). The court will not, however, be astute to read into a service a charge a limitation which prevents the landlord from recovering capital, as opposed to revenue, costs (*Lloyds Bank v Bowker Orford* [1992] 2 E.G.L.R. 44).

In addition, the draftsman should provide for the landlord not merely to be able to replace items of plant, but to do so with a reasonable modern equivalent. The RICS Code suggests that, whilst service charge costs should not include improvement costs above the costs of normal maintenance, repair or replacement, service charge costs may extend to include improvements or enhancement of the fabric, plant or equipment where such expenditure can be justified following the analysis of reasonable options and alternatives, and having regard to a cost benefit analysis over the term of the tenant or tenants' leases. Relevant factors might include reduction in on-going maintenance costs, and increased energy efficiency.

Against this background, it is suggested that in any case where a long lease is to be granted, or a lease is to be granted at a time when the plant within the property is reaching the end of its economic life (such that it is more economic for a landlord to replace it than to retain and maintain it), it will be in the interests of both landlord and tenant to consider and address these issues at the outset. Express provision can then be made as to whether or not the cost of any potential improvements is to be included in the service charge and, if so, to what extent. The various ways of addressing these issues are considered further in Chapter 11.

(v) Air conditioning

8–21 From 1 January 2015, it will be illegal to top up air conditioning systems with the HCFC gas R22 (see Chapter 9, para.9–13). In the absence of any incentive, new or renewing tenants will not want to sign a lease that requires them to maintain, repair and, where necessary, renew plant and machinery that incorporates an air conditioning system using R22, and/or to comply with the relevant European Regulation 1005/2009 (or any modification or amendment). On the same basis, a new or renewing tenant will wish to ensure that the costs of replacement by the landlord of a system using R22 are not put through the service charge accounts. The parties may also wish to regulate the use of air conditioning as part of a green leasing agenda (see Chapter 11).

Example 8.2 Landlord's power to replace plant and express exception for air conditioning plant using R22

Where under this lease:

(1) the landlord is required or entitled to keep in repair or proper working order any plant or machinery; and

(2) in the reasonable opinion of the landlord the cost of so doing would be uneconomic or imprudent when compared with the anticipated lifespan of that item of plant or machinery the landlord may replace that item with a modern equivalent and the cost of the replacement shall be deemed to be a repair unless the reason for replacement is compliance with European Regulation 1005/2009 or any modification or amendment of that Regulation.

(vi) Repairs

The repair and redecoration of buildings give rise to most problems in practice. Unfortunately the problems cannot usually be solved by careful drafting. Three areas of dispute are common. **8–22**

Firstly, tenants often refuse to pay the whole of a demand resulting from repairs on the ground that the repairs were badly executed. If the landlord undertakes any form of repairing obligation it is probable that he will be held to be liable to repair to a reasonable standard. A term to this effect may now be implied by s.13 of the Supply of Goods and Services Act 1982.

Secondly, expenditure is challenged on the ground that it was incurred in improving the property rather than in repairing it (e.g. *Mullaney v Maybourne Grange (Croydon) Management Co Ltd* [1986] 1 E.G.L.R. 70, and *Tingdene Holiday Parks Ltd v Cox* [2011] UKUT 310 (LC); [2011] 3 E.G.L.R. 30, where it was held that the landlord could not recover the cost of carrying out improvements since these did not rank as either repairs or maintenance). This area of dispute can be cut down by providing expressly that the landlord is to be entitled to recover the cost of improvements. However, it is unlikely that a well-advised tenant would agree to the landlord being so entitled except in very limited circumstances (such as in the case of improvements required by statute). There is a common sense argument to justify inclusion of the cost of minor "improvements" within the service charge when replacing components of a building. It is proposed that the cost of minor replacement works that go beyond the minimum specification necessary to effect a repair may be justified if the tenants will benefit from the improvement through reduced bills and maintenance costs, and a reasonable payback period on the investment can be justified. An example would be of a new piece of equipment added to an existing boiler better to control fuel consumption.

Thirdly, a demand may be resisted on the ground that the work in respect of which it is made could have been carried out more cheaply, or that not all the work was strictly necessary. In general, neither of these grounds will defeat the landlord's claim. The landlord is under no obligation to his tenant to choose the cheapest method of performing work (*Bandar Property Holdings Ltd v JS Darwen (Successors) Ltd* [1968] 2 All E.R. 305); nor is he obliged to patch up the property rather than spending more money on a permanent job (*Manor House Drive Ltd v Shahbazian* (1965) 195 E.G. 283). Moreover, in many cases the question whether to carry out a patch repair rather than a more permanent job is a matter of professional judgment. Provided that the landlord acts reasonably, the court will normally uphold his decision (*Postel Properties v Boots the Chemist* [1992] 2 E.G.L.R. 60, but see *Princes House Ltd v Distinctive Clubs Ltd* [2007] 1 P. & C.R. DG20, where, contrary to its repairing covenant, it was held that the landlord had failed to use all reasonable endeavours to complete the works in the relevant time). However, the amount charged to the tenant must be fair and reasonable (*Finchbourne Ltd v Rodrigues* [1976] 3 All E.R. 581). A term to this effect may be implied by s.15 of the Supply of Goods and Services Act 1982. In addition, where the residue of the term is short, and expenditure is restricted to that which is "reasonably and properly" incurred, the landlord may be precluded from recovering the cost of a permanent job where a patch repair would have lasted until the expiry of the term (*Scottish Mutual Assurance v Jardine*

Public Relations [1999] E.G.C.S. 43; *Fluor Daniel Properties Ltd v Shortlands Investments Ltd* [2001] 2 E.G.L.R. 103).

The landlord may find difficulties arising out of an obligation to redecorate the property at fixed intervals. If, for example, he is obliged to redecorate in every fourth year but delays the work until the fifth year, he may be met with a claim for damages for breach of covenant on the basis that in a time of rapidly rising building costs the redecoration would have been cheaper had it been carried out a year earlier (see *Postel Properties v Boots the Chemist* [1992] 2 E.G.L.R. 60). The draftsman can meet this difficulty by providing that the landlord shall redecorate "as often as in his opinion is reasonably necessary", rather than by imposing a timetable on him.

The draftsman must also ensure that the landlord is entitled to recover the cost of repairing parts of the building. Extreme care must be taken if using phrases such as things "used in common" (*Rapid Results College Ltd v Angell* [1986] 1 E.G.L.R. 53) which may not require the tenant of the ground floor to contribute to, say, the repair of the roof. However, it has been held that where the tenant of a ground floor flat in a house was required to contribute to the cost of repair of "mutual structures" he was liable to contribute to the cost of repairing the roof (*Twyman v Charrington* [1994] 1 E.G.L.R. 243).

(vii) Annual contracts

Many of the services that the landlord is to provide will be provided by contractors. The RICS Code contains a number of recommendations, including that the landlord should keep costs under review and, where appropriate, regularly require contractors and suppliers either to submit competitive tenders or to provide competing quotations. It is suggested that tendering and benchmarking should be undertaken at least once every three years. The landlord should be entitled to use a procurement specialist to obtain these services so long as the purpose is to achieve greater value for money and cost effectiveness. Where contracts are reviewed it is not unreasonable for the landlord and the tenant to agree that costs associated with achieving beneficial change, such as termination of contracts, should be recovered under the service charge where such costs can be justified following the analysis of reasonable options and the proposal achieves greater value for money. **8–23**

(viii) Promotional expenses

8–24 Some landlords of shopping developments actively promote them by advertising, marketing and promotions. A promotion may, without more, take place both within and outside the development and either regularly or irregularly (see *Boots UK Ltd v Trafford Centre Ltd* [2008] EWHC 3372 (Ch)).

The expenditure involved may be modest, but in some cases it may be the most substantial item on the service charge account. If the landlord wishes to recover some or all of the expenditure from the tenants, the draftsman must provide for it expressly. There is justification for such recovery as the promotional expenditure is calculated to increase goodwill, and with it the tenant's trading profits. However, the tenant may reasonably object that the landlord also derives substantial benefits in the form of increased rental values and that he too should bear some proportion of the cost. The RICS Code recommends that the funding of promotional activities should be recognised as a shared cost to be borne by both the owner and occupiers. The Code also recommends that the joint funding should cover not just the actual marketing and promotions, but also the costs of providing specialist staff (and accommodation), whether directly or through an agency agreement.

It is particularly important for the tenants to have some form of control over the level of expenditure in this respect, which has no definite limits. The tenant's adviser may do this by limiting expenditure to, say, two per cent of the annual rent roll. In addition, expenditure on promotional activities is a prime example of an item where consultation between landlord and tenant would be of mutual benefit. Some leases therefore provide for promotional expenses not to exceed a specified limit without the consent of the tenants' or merchants' association. The service charge budget should state what the gross expenditure on promotions is and how much is contributed by the owner.

The marketing of vacant units within a scheme should not be included as a service charge item, and nor should re-branding. These are expenses that should be borne by the landlord.

Example 8.3 Services: shopping centre, promotional expenses
50% [fifty percent] of the costs of promoting the Centre including the costs of advertising sponsorship staging events promoting the Centre and of employing advertising agents and consultants.

(ix) Amenities and entertainment

The cost of a landlord arranging attractions, Christmas and seasonal decorations, entertainments and events within a shopping centre or development (including the erection of a big screen to show a sporting event, for example), is not usually considered to be a marketing and promotional cost, and should be regarded as amenities or facilities. Where such costs are included within the service charge they would not normally be jointly funded. **8–25**

In *Boots UK Ltd v Trafford Centre Ltd* [2008] EWHC 3372 (Ch), for example, the lease defined "Promotion" to mean "advertising and other forms of promotion of the Centre intended to bring additional custom to the Centre which shall be reasonable and proper". The landlord's regular engagement of entertainers, such as a jazz band, a string quartet, and an animated character called Barney Bear to walk the malls, and the provision of Christmas decorations and a Santa's Grotto, were all held to be properly classified as a facility, an amenity or an attraction of the Centre, but not a "Promotion".

The treatment, for service charge purposes, of the landlord's installation of a "Sky Wall" in *Boots UK Ltd v Trafford Centre Ltd* illustrates the need to consider how the costs of, and income generated by, a single item may fall to be categorised under a number of different heads in the service charge account. The Sky Wall was a large permanent television screen mounted in the food court to give diners information about the Centre generally. It was also used by retailers and restaurants to advertise their presence (in which case the net income received from the individual retailer went directly back into the service charge account), and by some external advertisers. For the remainder of the time the Wall was used for playing music videos. It was held that when the Sky Wall was used to provide information about the Centre the costs were properly classified as a "Promotion", but otherwise the Sky Wall was a facility, amenity or an attraction and not a form of "Promotion" of the Centre.

(x) Environmental sustainability

The emergence of green leases, and the introduction of the Energy Performance Certificate ("EPC"), illustrates the increasing importance of addressing environmental sustainability issues (see Chapter **8–26**

11). Failure to do so may have a negative impact on the value of the reversion and the term. It is therefore sensible for the parties to consider the potential need for environmental improvement measures, or for the levying of additional charges, during the term of the lease. Provision should be made for the recovery through the service charge of the reasonable costs of mandatory compliance and for the introduction of such new systems as objectively justify, given the unexpired term of the lease, improvement costs above the costs of normal maintenance, repair or replacement. The reduction of energy and water consumption and waste production should be in the interests of both landlords and tenants as increased charges are introduced.

The cost of obtaining an EPC would not normally be considered to be an appropriate service charge cost as it is only required when a building is sold or rented, but addressing the issues that are identified in such an EPC could be classified as an appropriate cost.

Example 8.4 Services: multi-occupied premises, Memorandum of Understanding relating to discretionary green issues
The costs of implementing matters recorded in the Memorandum of Understanding including the costs of employing consultants and of commissioning a recommendation report if reasonably required from time to time.

(xi) Legal costs

8–27 The landlord will not be able to recover through the service charge his legal costs of suing tenants for arrears of rent or breach of covenant unless the lease expressly so provides (*Sella House v Mears* [1989] 1 E.G.L.R. 65). A general power to employ agents and professionals will not suffice. The clause in the service charge must be specific.

(xii) Bank borrowing

8–28 The Code recommends that the landlord should be entitled to recover the cost of borrowing to fund major non-cyclical expenditure as a cost to the service charge,

(xiii) Sweeping up

No draftsman can accurately predict precisely what services will be required over the term of a long lease. Accordingly, the list of items for inclusion in the service charge should always include provision for variation in the services. Normally, such provision will be construed ejusdem generis with the preceding items, with the result that the landlord will not be entitled to recover the cost of providing a service of a wholly different kind (*Jacob Isbicki & Co Ltd v Goulding & Bird Ltd* [1989] 1 E.G.L.R. 236). Sometimes, however, such a clause will allow the landlord to recover the cost of introducing a new facility, e.g. a window cleaning cradle and track (*Sun Alliance & London Assurance Co Ltd v British Railways Board* [1989] 2 E.G.L.R. 237). Some draftsmen negative the effect of this principle of construction by drafting the sweeping up clause very widely. This should be resisted by the tenant. The clause should either be limited to additional services of the same general description as the other items, or the consent of a majority of the tenants should be required before the introduction of any service of a radically different kind. **8–29**

Generally, sweeper clauses tend to be construed narrowly by the courts. If plant is in proper working order and is capable of rendering the particular service the landlord has covenanted to provide, a sweeper clause is unlikely to be construed to enable the landlord to recover expense incurred in renewing or improving that plant (*Fluor Daniel Properties Ltd v Shortlands Investments Ltd* [2001] 2 E.G.L.R. 103).

If the term of the lease is long, the parties may wish to consider whether the cost of an improvement should be recoverable if the additional expenditure incurred in carrying out the improvement can be justified on the basis of a cost benefit analysis. An improvement that will reduce future maintenance bills, or insurance premiums would fall within this category.

Example 8.5 Services: sweeper clause

PROVIDED ALWAYS that the Landlord may at its reasonable discretion add to extend vary or make any alteration in the nature or delivery of the Services if the Landlord reasonably considers it desirable to do so for the more efficient conduct and management of the Building.

(h) Apportionment of charges

8–30 The recommendations contained within the RICS Code include:

(1) Apportionment of costs to each occupier should be on a fair and reasonable basis, in accordance with the principles of good estate management and applied fairly and consistently throughout the property having regard to the physical size, nature of use and the benefit to the occupier or occupiers.
(2) An apportionment schedule should be available showing the total apportionment for each unit within the building or complex.
(3) The occupiers should not be charged through the service charge or otherwise collectively towards the costs attributable to unlet premises.
(4) The landlord should meet the cost of any special concession given by an owner to any one occupier. A properly constituted weighting formula is not a special concession.
(5) The landlord should bear a fair proportion of costs attributable to his use of the property, for example where there is a management suite.
(6) Where there is a separate cost/profit centre within a complex that generates income for the landlord which is not credited to the service charge account, for example a car park, the costs associated with maintaining and running that cost centre should not be allocated to the service charge account. If they are, a procedure will be required to for the landlord to estimate and declare a contribution to the service charge to reflect the benefit and use of the common services enjoyed.
(7) Where services are provided for the benefit of specific occupiers only, these costs should be allocated to the specific occupiers that benefit from or need them.
(8) If the property is fully let the landlord should normally be able to recover all expenditure on services through the service charge.
(9) The estimated budget of service charge expenditure and certified accounts should set out the method and calculation used to determine each occupier's share of the costs and how costs are apportioned.

There are five basic methods of apportioning service charges between tenants: **8–31**

(1) according to rateable value of each letting;
(2) according to floor area of each letting, or weighted floor area;
(3) according to anticipated use of each tenant;
(4) by fixed proportion;
(5) by fixed amount.

None of these methods achieves perfect equity between the tenants.

(1) Rateable value

Where the apportionment is by rateable value, the apportionment will vary according to the rateable value from time to time of the property in question (*Moorcroft Estates Ltd v Doxford* [1980] 1 E.G.L.R. 37). As rateable values will change over a period of years, with the occupier having the right to appeal against any reassessment, many owners have adopted a policy of using those rateable values that exist in the rating list at the time of calculating the service charge. Appeals against rating assessments can take a considerable period to resolve and could otherwise result in the reimbursement of any overpayment of service charge to an individual tenant and the need to recalculate the apportionment payable by all the other occupiers and the recovery of further balancing payments a considerable time after the service charge year concerned has ended. If provision is made to use the rateable value in the list at the date of calculation, any reassessment will be used in future calculations. **8–32**

An apportionment by rateable value is particularly vulnerable in a development such as a town shopping centre where identical units may have different rateable values according to their trading positions. Equally, the rateable value of a particular unit may be increased if the tenant carries out substantial improvements. In either case, the tenant's use of the services may not be changed, although his contribution to their cost would be.

Where the development is to include residential accommodation, an apportionment based on rateable value may well be impossible, if the residential element was constructed or redeveloped after the abolition of domestic rating.

The RICS Code states that rateable values are no longer recommended as an appropriate method for calculating service charge apportionments (para.1.5.6).

(2) Floor area/weighting

8–33 Floor area is the most common, and often the simplest method of apportionment. The standard floor area apportionment is simply the ratio that the demise bears to the total lettable parts of the building. An apportionment by floor area can often work satisfactorily where the units are unlikely to be subdivided. However, if the units may be subdivided the apportionment is likely to be distorted by the creation of access corridors, fire lobbies and other areas that make little demand on the services. In addition, the measurement of property is a fertile area for dispute (see, for example, *Kilmartin SCI (Hulton House) Ltd v Safeway Stores Plc* [2006] 1 E.G.L.R 59. The main definitions of measurement used are Gross Internal Area (GIA), applied to industrial and warehouses (including ancillary offices), and Net Internal Area (NIA), applied to offices and shops (see the "RICS Code of Measuring Practice: A Guide for Surveyors and Valuers" (6th edn, 2007) and para.3–19 above)).

A variant on this method, particularly prevalent in shopping areas, is the use of a weighted floor area to discount the percentage the tenant will pay over a certain size to reflect the benefit of the services provided. This method is intended to avoid discrimination against large space users (who are often also the anchor tenants and who enjoy financial privileges). Under the weighted floor area apportionment method, the first, say, 500^2 of a unit will be counted in full, the next, say, $500m^2$ will be counted at 80 per cent of the actual area, the next $2000m^2$ at 70 per cent , the next $2000m^2$ at 60 per cent, and the excess over $5,000m^2$ at 50 per cent. Similarly, the floor area of ancillary basement and upper floors accommodation, or remote storage, might be discounted.

The RICS Code states that a reasonable and fairly administered weighting formula cannot usually be considered as a concession. However, if there is a risk that the weighting will be calculated to provide the anchor tenant with a concession, the cost of the concession being spread amongst the remaining occupiers, the tenant's adviser should ensure that the landlord should meet the cost of that special concession.

A further variant on the weighting method of apportionment may be appropriate to take account of the fact that different tenants may enjoy the benefit of the services provided to varying extents. Whilst a café may be open from breakfast to late at night, a nightclub may only open in the evening. One method is to use opening hours and to count visitor footfall.

Example 8.6 Apportionment by floor area, basic provision
"The Tenant's Proportion" means a fair and reasonable proportion of the Expenditure based on the gross internal area of the Premises relative to the gross internal area of the Other Premises (excluding any areas that are not rentalised) measured in accordance with the RICS Code of Measuring Practice: A Guide for Surveyors and Valuers (6th edn, 2007).

(3) Anticipated use

An apportionment according to anticipated use would be the fairest method of apportionment if practicable. However, the use of certain services may change dramatically on an assignment or subletting or simply by a change in the tenant's business practice. Moreover, in order to work properly, an apportionment of every item would have to be made; for example, should the ground floor tenant be required to pay for the lift, or a labour intensive business a greater proportion of the cost of cleaning the lavatories? It is suggested that the apportionment of the service charge should be by way of fixed proportions written into the lease at the beginning of the term. The principal merit of this method is that it produces certainty. However, its disadvantage is that it may result in unfairness if the use of the premises changes significantly during the term. For example, if a shop becomes a restaurant the tenant will inevitably make a greater demand on the hot water system. For that reason, the draftsman should include some machinery for reviewing the fixed proportions. This could be done either by providing for a review at stated intervals or, more satisfactorily, by providing for the proportion to be reassessed if there is a material change in circumstances. **8–34**

The tenant's adviser should insist on a stipulation that the aggregate of the proportions payable by the tenants collectively should not exceed 100 per cent. If the landlord wishes to make a profit on the provision of services this should be openly and expressly stated.

(i) Unlet parts

8–35 In apportioning a service charge between tenants some provision should be made for a contribution by the landlord in respect of unlet parts. If the tenants are required to make fixed contributions to the cost of services the landlord will not be provided with a complete indemnity if part of the building in question is unlet. Conversely, if the tenants are required to contribute to a reserve fund the fund may be depleted if no contributions are made in respect of an unlet part. It is suggested that the risk of voids is one that should fall on the landlord rather than on the tenants; accordingly, the draftsman should provide for the landlord to make contributions to the cost of services (especially any reserve fund) in respect of unlet parts. It should also be provided that the landlord should pay interest on any unpaid service charge in respect of any unlet parts in the same way and on the same basis as the tenant is required to pay interest if its service charge is not paid on the due date.

(ii) Landlord's own occupation

8–36 If the landlord occupies any part of the property for its own purposes, for example where on-site management premises are also used for other purposes unconnected with the day-to-day management of the building and services, the RICS Code recommends that the landlord should be responsible for bearing a fair proportion of the costs attributable to such use.

(iii) Depreciation funds

8–37 Depreciation funds are rare (see, for example, *Secretary of State for the Environment v Possfund (North West) Ltd* [1997] 2 E.G.L.R. 56), where the lease contained a provision requiring the tenant to pay a depreciation allowance in respect of the cost of maintaining and replacing certain fixtures and fittings, in particular the air conditioning plant). They are based upon the initial cost of an installation, rather than the future cost of repair or replacement. The charge enables the landlord to include an amount in the service charge to reflect the "cost" of the annual depreciation of plant and equipment. The landlord will normally treat the money as its own and when major plant and equipment requires replacement the landlord will be solely responsible for the costs. There is a risk for both landlords and tenants that the landlord will not have sufficient funds when major outlay is required.

(iv) Non-core income or "commercialisation" or "mall income"

There should be a clear statement of policy in leases of shopping centres, retail and leisure parks as to how costs and income generated from services and activities are to be treated. It is increasingly common for landlords to seek additional non-core income streams from their properties. **8–38**

Where the landlord retains income from common part areas and the use of space is of a permanent or semi-permanent nature, for example the traditional kiosks, barrows, and flower stalls in shopping centres, and, more recently, the erection of mobile phone masts, advertising walls, and free-standing pods in car parks, the landlord often includes the income as rent and the space should be included in the service charge apportionment. As an alternative, a sum should be credited to the service charge to reflect the contribution to the benefit of the services enjoyed, such as lighting and cleaning the common parts.

Income derived from the provision of a service or activity, the finance for which is included in the service charge, for example income from, the installation of ATMs, vending machines, photo booths, amusements and children's' rides, photocopiers, public access internet terminals, advertising on street furniture and bins, the provision of public telephones, the sale of recyclable waste, exhibitions, car park receipts, wheel clamping fees, and income from hand car wash services in car parks should be treated as a service charge credit.

Income derived from a promotional activity should also be credited to the promotional expenditure budget (see *Boots UK Ltd v Trafford Centre Ltd* [2008] EWHC 3372 (Ch), and the fees received from the Sky Wall, as discussed at para.8–25 above). Income should be credited to the service charge after calculation of the management fee.

In considering the potential for the landlord to receive non-core income, the tenant's adviser should also consider whether any future development of the common parts might impact upon the tenant's own business. It may be necessary for the tenant to seek a covenant from the landlord restricting the landlord's ability to use a defined area in front of a store if that might interfere with its visibility or otherwise obstruct trade, or to specify that any exclusivity that the tenant has obtained should extend not only to restrict the use of other units, but also the use of the common parts.

(4) Fixed proportion

8–39 Sometimes a lease will provide for the tenant to pay a "fair" or "proper" or "due" proportion of the relevant costs. Unless there is clear machinery for determining what is a fair, proper or due proportion of the costs, phrases such as these are likely to give rise to dispute and should be avoided (*Hackney LBC v Roy Thompson* [2001] L. & T.R. 7.

(5) Fixed amount

8–40 Payment of a fixed amount will be most suitable for short leases where costs are unlikely to vary or where a limited scope of services is to be provided.

(i) The need to provide for future apportionment

8–41 Where the service charge is based on a floor area or a specified percentage, it has long been suggested that the lease should provide for the landlord's surveyor to be able to vary the proportions, or to change the method of apportionment, in order to allow for: changes in the lettable areas of the development; and circumstances where a destination occupier ceases to trade, and for cessation of supply of services (see *Law Society Gazette*, 9 April 1986, p.1056; and "Floor exercises don't always pay off", Simon Hughes, *Estates Gazette*, 23 February 2008). Not all tenants will find it acceptable to leave the discretion in the hands of the landlord or the landlord's surveyor.

Example 8.7 Service charge apportionment
The Service Charge to be paid by the Tenant shall be a fair proportion of the actual or anticipated Service Costs for each Service Charge Year which shall be assessed by the Landlord or its Surveyor according to a reasonable and proper basis for apportionment applicable from time to time to the Premises.

(j) Reserve and sinking funds

The treatment of reserve and sinking funds in leases is often haphazardly dealt with. In addition to regular annual expenditure on services, landlords and tenants often need to make provision for infrequent expensive outlays on replacing major items, such as plant, and for regular major expenditure, such as external decoration. A sinking fund (or "replacement fund") is a replacement fund by which the landlord aims to build up over time, a fund to pay for repair and replacement of major items of plant and equipment. A reserve fund is a fund built up to equalize expenditure in respect of regularly recurring service items so as to avoid fluctuations in the amount of service charge payable each year. **8–42**

In the first place it is important to consider what the money is intended to cover. Is it to provide for the eventual replacement of expensive capital items (such as lifts) or is it to spread the load of non-annual expenditure (such as redecoration) over the period between the recurrence of such expenditure? In the case of the former, the tenant's adviser should seek to ensure that the fund is held on trust (so that it is protected from the landlord's creditors) and invested until the time comes for its expenditure. It has long been the law that a non-charitable purpose trust cannot validly be created but trusts for the improvement of a settled estate have been upheld (*Re Bowes* [1896] 1 Ch. 507) as has a trust to maintain land as a sports ground (*Re Denley's Trust Deed* [1969] 1 Ch. 373) and a trust for the construction and/or improvement of a building (*Re Lipinski's Will Trusts* [1977] 1 All E.R. 33). In each case the trust was upheld by treating it as a trust for the benefit of ascertainable beneficiaries. It is suggested that a trust of a sinking fund would be upheld if it could also be treated as being for the benefit of ascertainable beneficiaries, i.e. the tenants.

Where a trust for beneficiaries is created it must conform to the rule against perpetuities. It is possible to specify a perpetuity period of 125 years (s.5 of the Perpetuities and Accumulations Act 2009) and since few commercial leases exceed that period, a perpetuity period should be specified. It is suggested that the beneficiaries should be the persons who will be the tenants of the building (or estate) immediately before the expiry of the perpetuity period, rather than the contributors to the reserve fund or the tenants from time to time. The reason is threefold.

Firstly, if there is no vested interest the trust is closer to a purpose trust, which is the real intention of the parties. Secondly, there is no danger that the tenants at any particular time collectively decide to put an end to the trust and appropriate the trust fund (under the rule in *Saunders v Vautier* (1841) 4 Beav. 115). Thirdly, it avoids the need for each assignment of a lease to contain an assignment of the tenant's interest in the trust fund. The disadvantage is that in a case where a settlement is created with no interest in possession, a periodic charge to inheritance tax may arise (Inheritance Tax Act 1984 Chapter III). However, the practical likelihood of a charge being levied is small because (a) the charge will only arise if the tenant's contributions to the fund exceeds the current exemption limit and (b) application of the principle that any addition to the fund is treated as the creation of a separate settlement means that payments can be arranged so that the funds are applied within the statutory period.

Provision should be made for the payment of any income tax which arises on interest accruing to the trust fund as well as any other tax. At the expiry of the perpetuity period any surplus should be distributed amongst the tenants in defined shares. The most convenient shares are those specified for the payment of the service charge itself.

Finally, it is suggested that the landlord should have the statutory power to appoint a new trustee, so that in the event of a sale of the reversion the new landlord can be quickly and cheaply appointed as the new trustee.

Whilst the creation of a sinking fund is theoretically advantageous for the tenant because the occupier will not be faced with a disproportionately heavy bill at any one time, it does have the disadvantage that the tenant may not see the benefit of its contributions if it assigns its lease or vacates prior to the expiration of the term at a time when the fund has not been called upon. The funds are also expensive to administer.

Where the reserve is intended to defray regular non-annual items of expenditure, a simpler approach is possible. The landlord should be required to pay the fund into a separate bank account and to pass on the moneys standing to the credit of the account in the event of a sale of the reversion. In this way, the tenant will have a contractual right to ensure that the fund is available for use for the intended purpose. It may be that the court would infer that even this approach involved the creation of a trust (cf. *Re Chelsea Cloisters Ltd (In Liquidation)* (1980) 41 P. & C.R. 98).

If the lease permits the landlord to include in the total service cost a reasonable sum for future repairs and renewals but does not provide for the creation of a reserve fund, the money held in reserve and the excess retained in a year of light expenditure, will be treated as sums which will be used to meet the costs incurred in a year of heavy expenditure, and to reduce the demands made upon the tenant in those years. In the absence of any provision as to what is to happen to unspent funds at the end of the lease, they will be returned to the tenant (*Brown's Operating System Services Ltd v Southwark Catholic Diocesan Corp* [2007] L. & T.R. 25).

In summary, reasonable and fair provisions may include that: **8–43**

(1) any monies accumulated in a reserve or sinking fund should be held in interest bearing trust accounts separate from the landlord's own money;
(2) the landlord should act reasonably in estimating the amount of the sinking or reserve fund contributions to be included within the service charge;
(3) the contributions could relate to specifically identified expenditure only, for example the roof or the boiler, rather than unidentified future expenditure;
(4) if the contributions relate to specifically identified expenditure only, the landlord should have regard to a realistic assessment of the anticipated life-cycle of the item in question and the funds accumulated from previous service charge periods;
(5) the landlord should make all payments into the sinking or reserve fund accounts for void premises;
(6) the annual budget and reconciliation accounts should clearly state contributions to and expenditure from the sinking and reserve fund accounts together with the account opening and closing balances and the amount of interest earned and tax paid in the relevant period; and
(7) upon completion of any assignment of the landlord's interest, the landlord should pass all sinking or reserve fund monies held, together with accrued interest, to the assignee.

(k) Certification of charges

8–44 Every service charge should make provision for the certification of the charge and for the recovery of the cost of certification to be recoverable as part of the charge. Usually, the issue of a proper certificate is a condition precedent to the tenant's liability to pay (cf. *CIN Properties Ltd v Barclays Bank Plc* [1986] 1 E.G.L.R. 59; *Northways Flats Management Co (Camden) v Wimpey Pension Trustees* [1992] 2 E.G.L.R. 42, submission of estimates for approval a condition precedent).

The RICS Code states that the purpose of certification of the service charge accounts is, basically, to provide the tenant with the comfort and certainty that the accounts produced:

(a) represent a true and accurate record of the expenditure incurred by the landlord (or upon the landlord's behalf, or in accordance with the terms of the lease (as appropriate)), in supplying the services to the building; and
(b) that the expenditure the landlord is seeking to recover is in accordance with the terms of the lease.

The tenant's adviser should ensure that the lease provides that the annual statement is certified to state that it complies with these statements. The RICS Code states that the certifier needs to be an appropriately qualified competent person, with a duty of care to both landlord and tenant to act with professional care, diligence, integrity and objectivity (para.4.2.2).

The lease should state the credentials of the person required to certify the annual statement, commonly the landlord's surveyor or accountant, or the manager of a shopping centre or building. In circumstances where the identity of the landlord dictates that a very specific individual or office holder is to provide the certificate, an extended class of individuals or office holders should be permitted to provide the certificate in the alternative (see *St Modwen Developments (Edmonton) Ltd v Tesco Stores Ltd* [2007] 1 E.G.L.R. 63, where the original landlord was a local authority and the service charge provisions simply provided for the service charge to be certified annually by the "Council's Borough Treasurer").

Where the lease requires certification by someone other than the manager the costs of certification, together with the fees of an independent accountant, should be stated to be recoverable through the service charge. Where the manager may certify, the costs should be comprised within the management fee.

Where the lease provides that the certifier is to act as an expert he must act impartially and hold the balance between landlord and tenant (*Concorde Graphics Ltd v Andromeda Investments SA* [1983] 1 E.G.L.R 53; *New Pinehurst Residents Association (Cambridge) Ltd v Silow* [1988] 1 E.G.L.R. 227). This means that he cannot be the landlord himself (*Finchbourne Ltd v Rodrigues* [1976] 3 All E.R. 581) nor the landlord's managing agent where in that capacity he has been putting forward the landlord's case (*Concorde Graphics Ltd v Andromeda Investments SA* [1983] 1 E.G.L.R 53) unless the lease expressly provides for this.

The certificate is often expressed to be final. It is now established that where parties to a contract entrust a function to an expert, they usually intend him to perform that function according to the contract as correctly interpreted, and that his interpretation is open to review by the court (*Mercury Communications v Director-General of Telecommunications* [1996] 1 W.L.R. 48). It appears, therefore that a certificate may only be final on matters of fact. This should be expressly stated in the lease. The landlord's position is sufficiently protected if the tenant is precluded from challenging the interim payments (thus maintaining the landlord's cash flow) but is entitled to challenge items on the final annual account.

If the lease does not say that the certificate is final, either party may reopen the certificate if a mistake has been made in calculating the service charge (*Universities Superannuation Scheme v Marks & Spencer* [1999] 1 E.G.L.R. 13).

(i) Auditing of the service charge accounts

References to "auditing" of service charges in older leases may not **8–45** have been intended to reflect modern auditing and accounting standards and practice. It must therefore be recognised that a reference to auditing will now involve a process that is to be carried out to International Auditing Standards ("IAS") (UK and Ireland), and that must be performed by a registered auditor. The RICS Code defines an audit as an independent external review process that adds to the credibility of an entity's disclosures. As such, an audit involves performing procedures to obtain evidence that a specified process is being followed in order to give tenants sufficient comfort that there is no material misstatement within the service charge accounts and information subject to the audit. This is likely to be a time consuming and expensive exercise. As part of the process the auditor may well have to employ an expert to review the relevant leases and to summarise the expenses that may be charged to the tenants.

In the case of a large building or development the tenant's adviser should consider the value of attempting to include a provision that the service charge accounts are to be audited on a routine basis. If the accounts are to be audited the landlord should ensure that the lease includes express provision that the auditor's reasonable and proper costs and fees, are to be recovered through the service charge.

(ii) Independent accountant's report

8–46 In circumstances where an audit may not provide best value for tenants and is likely to be disproportionate, an alternative is to provide that the landlord must engage an independent reporting accountant to examine the service charge accounts. The lease would require the service charge statement be prepared and certified by the landlord or their manager, and then reviewed by an independent accountant. The independent accountant's role is to check whether the figures contained in the information were extracted correctly from the accounting records maintained by the manager; and/or (based on a sample) whether entries in the accounting records were supported by receipts, other documentation or evidence inspected. The procedure should be described, and it should be made clear that this review is not intended to take the form of an audit.

In the case of a small property, and dependent upon the quantum and nature of the expenditure within the service charge, the reporting accountant might be engaged to prepare the statement from the landlord's accounting records, as well as providing an independent accountant's report.

(l) RICS Code Best Practice

8–47 In the case of commercial properties, the RICS Code recommends best practice as the preparation of annual statements of service charge expenditure certified by the landlord's manager to confirm that they represent a true and accurate record of the expenditure incurred by the landlord in supplying the services to the building, and that the expenditure the landlord is seeking to recover is in accordance with the terms of the leases. This should be followed (save in the case of smaller properties, where the requirement is optional) by review by an independent accountant. The lease may also provide for an audit unless (the majority of) the tenants confirm in writing that this is not required.

(m) Renewal leases

The terms of any new tenancy granted under the Landlord and Tenant Act 1954 are determined, in the absence of agreement, by the court. In determining those terms the court must have regard to the terms of the current tenancy and to all relevant circumstances (s.35 of the Landlord and Tenant Act 1954). This means that the burden of persuading the court to impose a change in the terms of the current tenancy against the will of either party rests on the party proposing the change. The change proposed must be fair and reasonable and should take into account the relatively weak bargaining position of the tenant and the general purpose of the Act, which is to protect the business interests of the tenant (*O'May v City of London Real Property Co Ltd* [1983] A.C. 726). **8–48**

Where the current lease contains a service charge, it is likely that the court would order its retention in the terms of a new tenancy. However, where the lease does not contain a service charge, or the charge is not as comprehensive as the landlord wishes, different considerations arise. In relation to those items which can be described as day-to-day housekeeping items, inherent in the use and occupation of property (e.g. cleaning, common parts, lighting, etc.) it is likely that the court would order the inclusion of a service charge. In *Hyams v Titan Properties Ltd* (1972) 24 P. & C.R. 359, Buckley L.J. said:

> "It is a fairer arrangement between landlord and tenant that the tenant should pay a proportion of the costs year by year than that an arbitrary figure should be fixed at the inception of the lease to continue in force throughout the term as the amount payable in respect of services."

However, in respect of risk items, inherent in the ownership of a long-term interest in property (e.g. renewal of plant and repairs to the structure) the court is unlikely to impose a service charge on the tenant (*O'May v City of London Real Property Co Ltd* [1983] 2

A.C. 726). But where the service charge does not require the tenant to contribute to the capital cost of replacement of items, nor to the cost of structural repairs, it is likely that the court will order him to pay it (*Leslie & Godwin Investments v Prudential Assurance Co* [1987] 2 E.G.L.R. 95).

(n) Dispute resolution

8–49 It is in the interests of both landlord and tenant to include dispute resolution machinery within the service charge provisions of a lease. If work is required or proposed, or a new service is introduced, it is often necessary to reach a speedy decision as to whether the relevant costs will be recoverable. The RICS Code recommends that all new leases should provide for alternative dispute resolution of service charge disputes. The Code also recommends that when disputes are resolved basic rate interest should be paid or allowed in respect of the period during which the relevant amount has been underpaid or overpaid.

It is suggested that either a provision for independent expert determination or an arbitration clause should be included. It will always be possible for the parties to agree to proceed by way of mediation as an alternative.

Example 8.8 Tenant's covenant to pay service charge: limited payment in advance, and provision for variation in tenant's percentage

(1) To pay to the Landlord in accordance with the provisions of this clause [ ] per cent of the costs and expenses incurred or deemed to have been incurred by the Landlord in connection with the services specified in the Schedule hereto.

(2) Those costs and expenses and the Tenant's percentage of them shall be certified in respect of each financial year by the Landlord's auditors (acting as experts) as soon as practicable after the end of the financial year in question and each such certificate shall be conclusive as to all matters of fact which it purports to certify.

(3) The Tenant shall pay to the Landlord on account of his liability under sub-clause (1) above in the first year of the term the sum of £[ ] and in each year thereafter such sum as may be specified by the Landlord (but it shall not exceed 80 per cent

of the amount certified as the Tenant's percentage for the preceding financial year) payable by four equal instalments in advance on the usual quarter days.

(4) Within twenty-one days after the issue of a certificate under sub-clause (2) above the Tenant shall pay to the Landlord or as the case may be the Landlord shall pay to the Tenant the difference between the advance payments made under sub-clause (3) above and the amount certified as the Tenant's percentage.

(5) The expression "financial year" means a period of 12 months beginning on [   ] in each year.

(6) The percentage specified in sub-clause (1) above may be varied by the Landlord in the event of any material change of circumstance during the term which affects the Tenant's liability under this clause.

Example 8.9 Service charge provision for reserve and payment in advance, and dispute resolution procedure

(1) In this clause the following expressions have the following meanings:
   (a) "financial year" means a period of twelve months ending on [   ] in each year
   (b) "the specified percentage" means [   ] per cent
   (c) "the service costs" means the total sum computed in accordance with sub-clauses (4) (5) and (6) of this clause
   (d) "the service charge" means the specified percentage of the service costs
   (e) "the expert" means a professionally qualified surveyor or accountant (who may be a person employed by the landlord).

(2) The tenant covenants with the landlord to pay the service charge during the term by equal payments in advance at the times at which and in the manner in which rent is payable under this lease.

(3) The service costs in respect of any financial year shall be calculated not later than the beginning of the financial year in question.

(4) The service costs shall consist of a total sum equal to:

(a) the expenditure estimated by the expert as likely to be incurred by the landlord in the financial year in question in connection with the items specified in sub-clause (5) of this clause together with

(b) an appropriate amount as a reserve for or towards such of the items specified in sub-clause (5) as likely to give rise to expenditure either after the expiry of this lease or only once during its then unexpired term or at intervals of more than one year (for example such matters as the decoration of the exterior and common parts of the building and the replacement of lifts boilers and other equipment) PROVIDED THAT where any expenditure is to be incurred on any such item in the financial year to which the estimate relates the expert shall in computing the total sum give credit for the amount then standing to the credit of the reserve in respect of the item in question.

(5) The items to be included in the service costs are the following:

(a) the costs of and incidental to the performance of the landlord's covenants in clauses [ ] to [ ] (inclusive) of this lease

(b) the costs of and incidental to the carrying out by the landlord of any work in pursuance of any requirement of any Act of Parliament or of any local or public authority

(c) the amount of any rates taxes assessments or outgoings of any nature whatsoever payable in respect of the building and paid by the landlord

(d) the full cost of employing porters cleaners and other staff of a like nature including the cost of uniforms bonuses national insurance contributions pensions and (where the landlord provides accommodation for such persons) an amount equal to the market rental value of such accommodation and any rates or council tax payable for it

(e) the cost of periodical inspection repair and maintenance of the common parts of the building and the periodical inspection repair maintenance and replacement of the lifts boilers and other plant machinery and equipment in the building

(f) the cost of preparing accounts and certificates relating to the calculation of the service costs or the service charge

(g) the cost of employing managing agents (save in relation to the collection of rent or the letting of any property) in respect of the building or if the landlord does not employ managing agents then a fee for the landlord of 10 per cent of the total of the foregoing amounts.

(6) As soon as practicable after the end of each financial year the expert shall determine and certify the amount by which the estimate referred to in paragraph (a) of sub-clause (4) of this clause exceeds or falls short of the actual expenditure incurred by the landlord in respect of the items specified in sub-clause (5) in the financial year in question (giving credit for any amount applied from the reserve in payment of items of expenditure incurred during that year) and shall supply the tenant with a copy of the certificate.

(7) Within 21 days of the receipt by the tenant of the said certificate the tenant shall pay to the landlord the specified percentage of the deficiency or as the case may be the landlord shall repay to the tenant the specified percentage of the excess.

(8) During any period when any part of the building is not let upon terms that the tenant of it is liable to pay a service charge corresponding to the service charge payable under the lease the landlord shall contribute to the reserve an amount equal to the total that would have been payable by way of such contribution if such part of the building had been so let and the reserve shall be calculated accordingly.

(9) If in the opinion of the expert it is equitable to do so he may increase or decrease the specified proportion.

(10) Any dispute arising out of the provisions of this clause shall be referred to the decision of a single arbitrator to be appointed on the application of either party by the President for the time being of the Royal Institution of Chartered Surveyors whose decision shall be final but this sub-clause shall not confer upon the tenant the right to challenge the amount of the total sum computed under sub-clause (4)(a) of this clause.

Example 8.10 Tenant's right to require an audit following issue of a certificate by the landlord's manager

The Tenant may within [3] months of the issue of the certificate for any service charge year request the Landlord to commission an independent audit of the service costs

If no audit is requested within [3] months of the issue of the certificate for any financial year the certificate shall be conclusive as to all matters of fact which it purports to certify.

Example 8.11 Trust of reserve fund

(1) Any reserve paid to the landlord shall be held by the landlord upon trust during the perpetuity period to apply it and any interest accruing upon it for the purposes for which it was collected and subject to that upon trust for the persons who immediately before the expiry of the perpetuity period are contributing to it in shares equal to the proportions in which they contribute to it

(2) The landlord may invest the reserve in such manner as he thinks fit but is under no obligation to do so

(3) The power of appointing a new trustee is vested in the landlord

(4) The perpetuity period is [125] years.

CHAPTER 9

REPAIRS AND IMPROVEMENTS

1. REPAIRS

(a) The norm

The normal way of allocating responsibility for the physical condition of commercial buildings is by reference to the concept of "repair". From time to time suggestions have been made that this is not the appropriate concept. The Law Commission has suggested that responsibility should be defined by reference to keeping the property fit for use, but this suggestion has not been adopted in the market. More recently, it was recommended in the Code for Leasing Business Premises in England and Wales 2007 that, unless expressly stated in the heads of terms, tenants should only be obliged to give the premises back at the end of their lease in the same condition they were in at the date of grant. The Code also recommended that a tenant's repairing obligations should be appropriate to the length of term and the condition of the premises. **9–01**

Nevertheless, the "repairing covenant" is not the only means by which one or other party to a lease may assume responsibility for its physical condition. The covenant to comply with statutes, and the covenant to pay outgoings may also impose liability to carry out work to the property. In terms of both repair and improvement, the parties will also wish to consider green leasing issues as discussed in Chapter 11.

(b) The standard framework

When dealing with a covenant to repair, most practical problems can be addressed by answering the following questions: **9–02**

(1) What is the subject matter of the covenant?

(2) Has the physical subject matter of the covenant deteriorated since some earlier time?
(3) If so, what work is necessary to restore it to its undeteriorated condition?
(4) As a matter of fact and degree can that work fairly be called work of repair?

(c) Interpretation of covenants to repair

9–03 A covenant to repair is construed with reference to the age and nature of the property in question at the beginning of the lease (*Lurcott v Wakely* [1911] 1 K.B. 905; *Smedley v Chumley and Hawke Ltd* (1981) 44 P. & C.R. 50; *Mason v TotalFinaElf UK* [2003] 3 E.G.L.R. 91). This principle applies both to determine the standard of repair required and to restrict the nature of the work that can be required of the covenantor. Thus, where a tenant covenants to keep in repair an old building the landlord cannot require him to keep it in a condition appropriate to a new building or to modernise it (for example, by updating the electrical system or installing a damp-proof course). It follows that where the landlord is himself a tenant a repairing obligation contained in the headlease and repeated word for word in the sublease may impose on the subtenant a lighter obligation than that contained in the headlease if the grant of the headlease and the grant of the sublease are separated by a significant length of time. In such a case, the draftsman can protect the landlord by inserting in the sublease a covenant "to observe and perform the covenants in the headlease so far as they affect the demised property". Such a covenant is more than a covenant of indemnity: it amounts to an express covenant to perform the covenants in the headlease (*Ayling v Wade* [1961] 2 Q.B. 228).

If the demised property is out of repair at the beginning of the tenancy the covenant to repair will be construed as requiring the property to be put into repair (*Proudfoot v Hart* (1890) 25 Q.B.D. 42), although the standard of repair will depend on the age of the property. If the tenant wishes to protect himself against liability to carry out initial repairs the covenant should be amended to read "to keep the demised property in no worse condition than that in which it was at the beginning of this lease". In addition, a full schedule of condition should be agreed between the parties and annexed to the lease. The schedule should take the form of a full structural survey, with photographs, otherwise it will not be of much practical use at the end of the lease. In some cases a video film with commentary may be useful. It is not advisable to prepare the schedule solely by reference to sample rooms or buildings within a large building or complex of buildings unless there is no other practical alternative. If this approach is adopted, there will be ample scope for argument at the end of the term.

A covenant to repair and keep in repair imposes a continuing duty throughout the term. An obligation on a tenant to keep the property in good repair and condition and to carry out all repairs necessary to keep the property in good repair and condition, does not however impose an obligation upon the tenant to indemnify the landlord against whatever liability he may have as a result of service of a statutory dangerous structure notice (*Riaz v Masaku* [2001] L. & T.R. 22). Equally, a duty to maintain or repair or to keep in good condition does not equate to a duty to keep safe or to put in good condition or to a statutory warranty that premises are reasonably safe (see *Alker v Collingwood Housing Association* [2007] 2 E.G.L.R. 43, where a claim against a landlord for damages for breach of statutory duty under s.4 of the Defective Premises Act 1972 failed).

(d) Subject matter of the covenant

Close attention should be paid to the subject matter of the covenant. **9–04**
It is arguable that, if the covenant amounts to a series of separate covenants to repair component parts of the demised property, the obligation will not extend to the replacement of the whole of one of those component parts. Accordingly, it is suggested that the draftsman should not attempt to enumerate all the parts of the demised property that the covenantor is called upon to keep in repair. The covenant should, whenever possible, be expressed simply as a covenant to "keep the demised property in repair". Such a covenant also has the advantage of preventing an argument whether the express inclusion of some parts of the demised property in the covenant is to be taken as impliedly excluding all other parts.

The scope of a repairing covenant is closely linked to the definition of the demised property in the parcels clause of the lease. If, for example, loadbearing walls are excepted from the demise, a tenant who covenants to keep the demised property in repair will not be obliged to repair those walls and would be guilty of a trespass if he attempted to do so. Similarly, the placing of a phrase in the parcels clause such as "hereafter called the demised property" may affect liability to repair. If, for example, a right of way is granted to the tenant, and the grant of the right precedes that phrase, it is at least arguable that the way must be kept in repair under a covenant to keep the demised property in repair. Provision should be made for the repair of means of access and of services.

Particular problem areas in the context of repairing obligations include:

(1) windows, window frames, glass;
(2) floors, screeds, beams, columns;
(3) flat roofs, canopies;
(4) cladding panels.

These problems occur most frequently where a building is multi let. In such cases it is vital to ensure that the dividing line between those parts of the building for which the landlord is responsible and those parts for which the tenant is responsible is clear. A phrase such as "the interior of the demised property" is likely to lead to uncertainty about windows, doors, etc. (*Reston v Hudson* [1990] 2 E.G.L.R. 51; and see Chapter 3, para.3–18).

In addition, it is helpful for the draftsman either to visit the building or at least to have a clear explanation of its method of construction. Too often a lease of a steel framed building will refer to the main walls and timbers, although the court will interpret such phrases as encompassing steel girders, where appropriate (*Manchester Bonded Warehouse v Carr* (1880) 5 C.P.D. 507).

(e) Physical deterioration

9–05 Before it can be said that work is work of repair, it must be shown that the building (or other subject matter of the covenant) is in a condition which is worse than that in which it was at some earlier time (*Quick v Taff-Ely BC* [1985] 3 All E.R. 321 at 328). Thus, if the tenant covenants to keep the structure of the building in repair, it must be shown that the structure has deteriorated before the tenant's covenant begins to bite. So where the basement of a building became flooded, but no damage was done to the building itself, the tenant was held not liable to repair (*Post Office v Aquarius Properties* [1987] 1 All E.R. 1055). The tenant's repairing obligation is not therefore to be construed as a warranty that deficiencies in the original design or construction of the building will be rectified in any event. If, for example, a building is built with designed floor loadings of 50 kg per sq metre but achieves a loadbearing capacity of 30 kg per sq metre, the tenant cannot be compelled to strengthen the building. If, however, a deficiency in the original design or construction of the building causes the condition of the building to deteriorate, then the tenant may be liable if, as a matter of fact and degree, the necessary remedial work can fairly be called work of repair.

By contrast, a covenant to keep in good condition may be broken even if there is no physical deterioration in the subject matter of the covenant (*Welsh v Greenwich LBC* [2003] 3 E.G.L.R 4).

(f) Meaning of repair

Repair is restoration by renewal or replacement of subsidiary parts **9–06**
of a whole. Renewal, as distinguished from repair, is the reconstruction of the entirety, meaning by the entirety not necessarily the whole but substantially the whole of the subject matter under discussion (*Lurcott v Wakely* [1911] 1 K.B. 905). This is the classic definition of repair that will govern the construction of any repairing covenant. So a covenant to keep an industrial unit in repair will oblige the tenant to replace the roof where it can no longer be patched (*Elite Investment Ltd v TI Bainbridge Silencers Ltd* [1986] 2 E.G.L.R. 43; and *Carmel Southend Ltd v Strachan & Henshaw Ltd* [2007] 3 E.G.L.R. 15, where patch repair remained sufficient on the facts and overcladding was held to be unnecessary). It appears to make no difference whether the covenant is a covenant to keep "in repair", "in good repair", "in sufficient repair" or "in tenantable repair" (*Anstruther-Gough-Calthorpe v McOscar* [1924] 1 K.B. 716, per Bankes and Scrutton L.JJ.). Whether the end product of work requiring to be done properly constitutes "repair" is a question of degree in each case. The correct approach is to conclude on a fair interpretation of the precise terms of the lease in relation to the state of the property at the date of the lease whether the work can be called repair or not; and, in coming to that

conclusion one must look at the work as a whole and not at individual parts of it (*Brew Bros Ltd v Snax (Ross) Ltd* [1970] 1 Q.B. 612). The common form covenant "well and substantially to repair", does not require that the premises be kept in perfect repair (*Proudfoot v Hart* (1890) L.R. 25 Q.B.D. 42, *Mason v TotalFinaElf UK Ltd* [2003] 3 E.G.L.R. 91; *Riverside Property Investments v Blackhawk Automotive* [2005] 1 E.G.L.R. 114). The work for which the tenant is liable will include the eradication of the cause of the inherent defect if that is what a sensible practical man would do, provided that the work does not amount to the rebuilding of the whole subject matter of the covenant (*Stent v Monmouth DC* [1987] 1 E.G.L.R. 59).

A variety of tests have been suggested to help in answering this question of fact and degree:

(1) whether the alterations go to the whole or substantially the whole of the structure or only to a subsidiary part;
(2) whether the effect of the alterations is to produce a building of a wholly different character to that which has been let;
(3) what is the cost of the work in relation to the previous value of the building and what is their effect on the value and lifespan of the building (*McDougall v Easington DC* [1989] 1 E.G.L.R. 93).

9–07 The "fact and degree" approach will prevail no matter what the cause of the defect under consideration. Even if the work is necessitated by reason of an inherent defect in the design or construction of the demised property a covenant to repair will oblige the covenantor to eliminate that defect if it is not substantial (*Ravenseft Properties Ltd v Davstone (Holdings) Ltd* [1979] 1 All E.R. 929); but a covenant to repair will not oblige him to eliminate the defect if to do so would amount to the construction of property different in kind to that demised (*Pembery v Lamdin* [1940] 2 All E.R. 434; *Sotheby v Grundy* [1947] 2 All E.R. 761). In determining whether work is such as to amount to the construction of property different in kind to that which was demised, it is clearly necessary to compare one with the other. So in the case of an old building a covenant to repair does not require the replacement of wooden windows with aluminium double glazed windows (*Mullaney v Maybourne Grange (Croydon) Management Co Ltd* [1986] 1

E.G.L.R. 70). But in the case of a new building the relevant comparison is between the property contemplated by the parties at the date of the lease and the property as changed by the necessary works (*Smedley v Chumley and Hawke Ltd* (1981) 44 P. & C.R. 50; *Crédit Suisse v Beegas Nominees* [1994] 4 All E.R. 803). In almost every case the building contemplated by the parties will be one that has been properly designed and constructed in the light of good practice at the date of construction. It follows that work necessary to correct faults in the design or construction of a new building will frequently fall within the scope of a covenant to repair. To avoid any doubt, some landlords specifically provide that the obligation to repair applies notwithstanding that any want of repair may be due to an inherent or latent defect in the premises (see *Gibson Investments Ltd v Chesterton Plc* [2003] 1 E.G.L.R. 142). In the case of a new building, the tenant's adviser should seek to include in the repairing covenant an exclusion of liability for such work. It is not satisfactory simply to exempt the tenant from liability to eradicate "inherent defects". First, this expression has no clear meaning. Secondly, it may extend to defects which only become defects in the light of a change in standards (e.g. the presence of asbestos in workplaces). To exempt the tenant from liability in such a case is to make serious inroads into a full repairing liability. It is suggested, therefore, that the yardstick should be linked to a negligence or breach of contract test. If the landlord could have established liability against someone other than the tenant (e.g. the designer or constructor of the building) the tenant should not be held liable.

In addition to excluding liability for such matters, the tenant's adviser should seek to ensure that parallel wording is included so that the landlord is obliged to remedy any such problems. Although a tenant of a new build who signs a full repairing lease may have the benefit of collateral warranties, and would be expected to have the opportunity to seek redress from the warrantors for disrepair resulting from design or construction defects, difficulties may arise. Unlike the freehold owner, the tenant will often have had no involvement in agreeing the terms of the warranties, and the warranties may not be comprehensive, or the warrantor may not be solvent at the date that it is called upon.

Example 9.1 Exemption of liability

Provided that the tenant shall not be liable to remedy any defect in the design or construction of the demised properly in respect of which the landlord or its predecessor in title is (or but for the operation of the Limitation Acts would be) entitled to claim damages from some person not a party to this lease

9–08 The tenant's adviser may also seek to tackle the problem of defective new buildings in a different way. The original design and construction team will owe a duty of care to the tenant as occupier of the building. But that duty is limited in two ways. Firstly, it is limited to a duty to take reasonable care that the building is not a danger to health or safety. Defects in the building which fall short of causing a danger to health or safety are not covered by the duty of care. Secondly, loss is not recoverable if it is pure economic loss; i.e. the cost of putting right defects. In order to be recoverable the loss must consist of damage to property other than the defective building itself (*D&F Estates Ltd v Church Commissioners* [1988] 2 All E.R. 992). In the light of the restricted scope of the duty of care, the tenant's adviser should beware of accepting merely a "duty of care deed" which acknowledges the duty. It must go further and amount to a contractual warranty that the building has been erected in a good and workmanlike manner in accordance with the specification; and that the building has been designed in accordance with proper professional standards. Following the Contract (Rights of Third Parties) Act 1999, the tenant should now seek to ensure that the contracts between the landlord and the professional team are enforceable by him too.

If the tenant is not in contact with the design and construction team (e.g. because the building has already been built before the tenant appears on the scene) the tenant's adviser may seek to obtain from the landlord an undertaking to pursue such remedies as he has against the design and construction team and to apply any damages recovered in remedying any defect discovered. Such an undertaking will inevitably be personal to the original landlord or developer, and will not bind the landlord's successors in title.

(g) Wider forms of covenant

9–09 It is, of course, possible as a matter of drafting to impose obligations on the tenant which go beyond mere repair. Thus, in *Gooderham and Worts Ltd v Canadian Broadcasting Corp* [1947] A.C. 66, the tenant covenanted to keep a radio broadcasting station "modern and up-to-date"; in *Norwich Union Life Insurance Society* *v British Railways Board* [1987] 2 E.G.L.R. 137 the tenant covenanted to keep a building in repair "and when necessary to rebuild reconstruct or replace the same" and in *Gibson Investments Ltd v Chesterton Plc* [2003] 1 E.G.L.R. 142, the tenant covenanted to keep in good and substantial repair and, where appropriate, to rebuild the whole of the demised premises. Such forms of covenant will take effect according to their terms, and will oblige the tenant to do more than merely keep the existing structure in repair. Because the covenant to rebuild may give rise to onerous obligations, the court will not, however, interpret the covenant so that it is given any greater effect than it naturally bears and will interpret it to have a relatively narrow meaning (*Gibson Investments Ltd v Chesterton Plc* [2003] 1 E.G.L.R. 142). In *Post Office v Aquarius Properties Ltd* [1987] 1 All E.R. 1055, Slade L.J. indicated that it would be possible by clear words to impose upon a tenant a liability to eradicate inherent defects in a building before they had caused any damage to the building, but added that this was not an obligation which tenants under a commercial lease might readily be expected to undertake. In *Crédit Suisse v Beegas Nominees* [1994] 4 All E.R. 803, the landlord covenanted to maintain repair "and otherwise keep in good and tenantable condition" certain parts of a building. It was held that a covenant to keep in good condition did not require proof of any deterioration in the subject matter of the covenant before the obligation came into play. Further, whether the subject matter of the covenant was in good and tenantable condition was to be judged not by reference to the actual state of the building at the date of the demise, but by reference to the requirements of a hypothetical reasonably minded tenant likely to take it. The Court of Appeal reached a similar conclusion in *Welsh v Greenwich LBC* [2000] 3 E.G.L.R. 41, *Fluor Daniel Properties Ltd v Shortlands Investments Ltd* [2001] 2 E.G.L.R. 103 and *Mason v TotalFinaElf UK Ltd* [2002] 3 E.G.L.R. 91. The same interpretation would, it is thought, apply to a tenant's covenant in the same form. Thus a covenant to keep in good condition (as opposed to a covenant to keep in repair) is potentially a far more onerous obligation.

Whilst an obligation to keep in good condition has been interpreted as extending beyond an obligation to repair, it has been held that preventative works cannot be justified simply to prevent the consequences of the equipment failing because a piece of equipment is old and because there must inevitably come a time when the equipment must be replaced if, in the meantime, it continues to perform its function, (*Fluor Daniel Properties Ltd v Shortlands Investments Ltd* [2001] 2 E.G.L.R. 103 and *Mason v TotalFinaElf UK Ltd* [2002] 3 E.G.L.R. 91.)

If the draftsman contemplates extending the tenant's liability in one of these ways, he should carefully consider the impact which this would have upon the rent recoverable on review. In *Norwich Union Life Insurance Society v British Railways Board* [1987] 2 E.G.L.R. 137, a combination of the length of the lease (150 years) and the rebuilding obligation resulted in a reduction in the rent of 27.5 per cent.

(h) Divided responsibility for repairs

9–10 In the case of a lease of part only of a building or of a unit in a shopping centre, it will not usually be practicable for one party to be responsible for all repairs. In such a case, the tenant will usually be responsible for repairs to the internal non-structural parts of the demise, while the landlord undertakes the repair of the structure and common parts, recovering his costs of so doing through a service charge.

For many years it could be confidently asserted that the law would not imply any repairing obligation by a landlord in a lease, even where the tenant undertook some obligations as respects the repair or maintenance of the property (*Sleafer v Lambeth BC* [1960] 1 Q.B. 43; *Tennant Radiant Heat v Warrington Development Corp* [1988] 1 E.G.L.R. 41). However, in *Barrett v Lounova (1982) Ltd* [1989] 1 All E.R. 351, the Court of Appeal held that a landlord was liable for structural repairs where it was necessary that the structure of a building be put in repair in order to enable the tenant to comply with her obligation to keep the interior of the property in repair. But it has been subsequently held that since there are cases in which neither landlord nor tenant has any responsibility for repairs (or for certain categories of repair), the court should not be astute to imply obligations (*Demetriou v Poolaction* [1991] 1 E.G.L.R. 100); and it now seems unlikely that *Barrett v Lounova (1982) Ltd* would be followed (see *Adami v Lincoln Grange Management* [1998] 1 E.G.L.R. 58).

Nevertheless, the draftsman should make sure that the allocation of responsibility for repairs is fully covered by the lease, and that there are no gaps in that responsibility, particularly since it will not be presumed that the landlord will be entitled to recover all expenditure through the service charge.

The draftsman should also make sure that the allocation of responsibility does not overlap. Where the repairing obligations in a lease result in the landlord and tenant having overlapping obligations, the lease will be construed in accordance with the good sense of the agreement to avoid such an impractical result unless it is literally impossible to do so (*Petersson v Pitt Place (Epsom) Ltd* [2001] 82 P. & C.R. 276; *Holding & Barnes v Hill House Hammond* [2000] L. & T.R. 428; *Ibrahim v Dovecorn Reversions* [2001] 2 E.G.L.R. 46).

Where repairs are to be carried out by a management company, there is no implied term to the effect that the landlord will undertake those obligations if the management company defaults (*Hafton Properties v Camp* [1994] 1 E.G.L.R. 67).

When defining the scope of the landlord's repairing obligation the **9–11** expression "structural repairs" should be avoided. It has been observed that "structural repairs" mean "repairs of or to a structure" (*Granada Theatres Ltd v Freehold Investment (Leytonstone) Ltd* [1958] 2 All E.R. 551, per Vaisey J.). That definition divides all repairs between structural repairs and decorative repairs and may enlarge the obligation to carry out structural repairs beyond that intended by the draftsman. It is suggested that the draftsman should attempt to define with more clarity the parts of the property to be repaired by each party. Thus, for example, the landlord's repairing obligation might be "to keep in repair the roof and loadbearing walls and main beams of the Building and the common parts of it". Even this may not be adequate where the external walls of the building are not themselves loadbearing, but rest upon a loadbearing frame. In such a case, the landlord's obligation should extend to external walls. If the obligation is to repair "external walls of the demised property", the obligation will extend to all the walls enclosing the demised property, whether or not they are exposed to the air (*Pembery v Lamdin* [1940] 2 All E.R. 434). Thus, if the repair of external walls is excepted from the repairing obligations of a tenant of an office suite he will not be liable to repair a partition wall separating his suite from the corridor. It is suggested that if "loadbearing walls" or external walls "of the Building of which the demised property forms part" are excepted instead his obligation will extend to partition walls enclosing his suite.

9–12 The expression "main walls" has been said to mean those walls which support the structure or have directly to do with its stability (*The Holiday Fellowship Ltd v Hereford,* unreported per Harman J., approved on appeal in [1959] 1 All E.R. 433).

The landlord's obligation is sometimes expressed as a covenant to keep in repair "the structure and exterior of the Building of which the demised property forms part". This is a less onerous obligation than a covenant to keep in repair "the structure and exterior of the demised property". In the latter case, but not the former, the obligation will extend to the repair of inner party walls (e.g. walls separating one part of the building from another) (cf. *Campden Hill Towers Ltd v Gardner* [1977] 1 All E.R. 739 construing the expression "structure and exterior of the dwelling house"). Indeed, subject to any specific drafting, it has been held in the residential context that internal plaster to walls or ceilings forms part of the "structure" of a building, and that the exact nature of the plaster work is irrelevant (*Grand v Gill* [2011] 1 W.L.R. 2253). As such, "structure" can be taken to include both old-fashioned and substantial lathe and plaster and plaster that is merely "a smooth constructional finish to walls and ceilings".

The "exterior" of a building will include access ways and staircases (*Brown v Liverpool Corp* [1969] 3 All E.R. 1345).

The repair of glass should always be considered, particularly where a substantial part of the demised property is enclosed by glass. Generally, windows will not be part of the "main walls" of a building (*The Holiday Fellowship v Hereford* [1959] 1 All E.R. 433). Whether they are so is a question of fact and degree. Where, for example, property is enclosed by large plate glass windows, the windows will be part of the walls of the property and will not be included in an obligation to keep the interior of the property in repair (*Boswell v Crucible Steel Co* [1925] 1 K.B. 119). Thus, the tenant of an office suite will be liable to repair the windows if the building is constructed of brick with normal size windows, but not if it is constructed of steel and glass. Accordingly, the draftsman should take full instructions as to the construction of the property in question before drafting any repairing obligation. The draftsman should also consider defining precisely the limits of liability, particularly where the responsibility for repair is divided between landlord and tenant. See also Chapter 3 in this regard.

Example 9.2 Definition of structure [N.B. to exclude internal plaster]

"The structure of the building" means:

(1) the roof and foundations of the building
(2) its loadbearing walls and columns (excluding plaster or other decorative finishes)
(3) its floor structures (including beams and joists but excluding floorboards floor screeds and floor finishes)
(4) all surfaces of the building exposed to the elements except surfaces made of glass and window frames.

Example 9.3 Definition of interior of the demised property [N.B. to include internal plaster]

"The interior of the demised property" includes:

(1) all non-loadbearing walls wholly within the demised property
(2) one half (severed vertically) of all non-loadbearing walls separating the demised property from any other part of the building
(3) all plaster or other decorative finish applied to any wall bounding the demised property and not falling within (1) or (2) above or applied to any column or loadbearing wall within the demised property
(4) the whole of all doors door frames windows and window frames bounding the demised property
(5) all ceilings bounding the demised property
(6) all floor finishes floorboards and floor screeds.

(i) Air conditioning

From 1 January 2015, it will be illegal to top up air conditioning systems with the widely used refrigerant, HCFC Gas R22. Its use contravenes European Regulation 1005/2009, commonly referred to as the ODS Regulation (Ozone Depleting Substance). Under the Regulation, it is the "operator", defined as the "person exercising actual power over the technical functioning of the equipment and system", who is responsible for compliance. Compliance includes regularly checking for and repairing leakage, maintaining service records and recovery of gases. Appropriately qualified personnel **9–13** must be employed. As a result, it is clear that plant and machinery designed to use R22 will effectively become un-maintainable and will, eventually, need to be replaced.

In any case where the plant and machinery in a building incorporates an air conditioning system using R22, express provision should be incorporated within any new or renewal lease stating whether:

(1) the landlord or the tenant is to be responsible for the repair, maintenance and replacement of air conditioning that uses R22;
(2) the landlord or the tenant is to be responsible for compliance with the regulations;
(3) the cost of any relevant works is to be borne by the landlord or the tenant or included within, or excluded from, the service charge.

In any case where a tenant assumes responsibility of any kind, the rent review clause should also be considered to ensure that the tenant is not both paying for the works and paying an increased rent as a result of the operation of an assumption or disregard.

(j) Fair wear and tear

9–14 The exception of fair wear and tear is rarely found in commercial leases. It relieves a tenant from liability for repairs that are decorative and from remedying parts that wear out or come adrift in the course of reasonable use, but it does not exempt him from anything else. If further damage is likely to flow from the wear and tear he must do such repairs as necessary to stop that further damage (*Regis Property Co Ltd v Dudley* [1959] A.C. 370). In practice, it is usually very difficult to determine what amounts to disrepair and what is covered by the exception. For that reason, it is suggested that the landlord should resist the exception of fair wear and tear as it almost always leads to a dispute over terminal dilapidations. For the same reason, the parties should beware of a liability to repair qualified by reference to a schedule of condition. Such schedules are almost invariably too vague and generalised to be of any assistance at the end of the lease. If the repairing liability is to be qualified in this way the schedule should be in the nature of a full structural survey and should be accompanied by an agreed photographic record of the building.

(k) Wind and watertight

In some short leases of poor quality property, the tenant is sometimes simply obliged to keep the property merely "wind and watertight". There is, however, no judicial definition of this expression in a modern commercial context. In practice, it is suggested that a preferable course is to limit the tenant's obligations by reference to a schedule as described above. **9–15**

(l) Fire damage

Although a tenant who covenants to repair property is not generally liable to rebuild the whole of the property, he is liable to rebuild if it is destroyed by fire (*Matthey v Curling* [1922] 2 A.C. 180). Accordingly, where the landlord is bound to insure, the tenant's adviser should see that the repairing covenant exempts the tenant from liability to repair damage caused by a peril against which the landlord has insured. The landlord will usually wish to qualify this by restricting it to cases where the insurance has not been avoided or vitiated by the tenant. **9–16**

The standard form of clause may not be entirely satisfactory to the landlord, particularly in the case of a total loss. The insurers may be entitled to limit the extent of the indemnity to the market value of the building if that is less than the reinstatement cost (*Leppard v Excess Insurance Co Ltd* [1979] 2 All E.R. 668). In the case of a partial loss, the claim may be subject to average. Thus, the tenant may have been released from liability exempting him from having to remedy damage caused by an insured risk, yet the sum which the landlord recovers from his insurers may be insufficient to pay for the work. Accordingly, the draftsman should consider casting the clause in the form of an exemption from liability "to the extent that the landlord recovers the cost of the necessary work from its insurers". Such a form of words would deal both with the possibility that the insurance had become vitiated, and with the possibility that the measure of indemnity was insufficient to pay for the work. If the draftsman chooses this form of covenant, the tenant's adviser should be especially careful to see that the landlord is under an obligation to maintain adequate insurance cover. Thus if the landlord fails to insure, or underinsures, the tenant will have a remedy against him.

(m) Repair on notice

9–17 Where a landlord covenants to repair the demised property his obligation does not arise unless and until he had notice of a defect in the property, and he will not be in breach of his obligation thereafter if he carries out the necessary repairs with reasonable expedition (*O'Brien v Robinson* [1973] A.C. 912). This does not have to be expressly provided in the lease, but is implied by law. A landlord's obligation to effect repairs to the demised property carries with it an obligation to make good any consequential damage to decorations (*McGreal v Wake* [1984] E.G.L.R 42). Where the landlord's obligation is to repair property which falls outside the demise, his obligation is not dependent on notice (*British Telecommunications v Sun Life Assurance Society* [1995] 4 All E.R. 44). He is in breach of covenant as soon as the property in question falls into disrepair. The draftsman may wish to consider making the landlord's obligation to repair an obligation which is expressly dependent on notice being given of any defect.

Where a tenant covenants to repair it is common to impose on him an additional, but subsidiary, obligation to repair on notice. The draftsman should reserve to the landlord a power to enter the demised property to inspect the state of repair and a power to serve notice of disrepair. The tenant should covenant to repair on service of such a notice. The usual provision is "to repair within three months" of service of a notice. The usual three month period will often suffice for minor repairs, but major repairs may well take longer. In such a case the tenant may be at risk of forfeiture for breach of the covenant to repair on notice. It is suggested that a fairer obligation for both parties is for the tenant to covenant to begin the repairs within a shorter period (say 42 days) and to proceed expeditiously to carry them out. In that way, the tenant has sufficient time to arrange for contractors but he is not exposed to the risk of forfeiture if the repairs take a long time.

9–18 In all cases where the tenant covenants to repair on notice, the draftsman will usually seek to provide for the landlord to have the right to enter to carry out the necessary repairs if the tenant fails to comply with his obligation. In the absence of an express right to entry the landlord will not be entitled to carry out the work if the tenant defaults (*Regional Properties Ltd v City of London Real Property Co Ltd* [1981] 1 E.G.L.R 33). Accordingly, such a right should be reserved. See further at para.3–31 above. However, the reservation of such a right will impose upon the landlord a duty of care towards third parties (s.4(4) of the Defective Premises Act 1972). The draftsman should therefore require the tenant to indemnify the landlord against such liability if the liability arises as a result of a defect the existence of which is a breach of the tenant's obligations. The cost expended by the landlord in exercising his right of entry should be expressed to be recoverable from the tenant as a debt. There had been a conflict of authority at first instance on the question whether a landlord's right to enter to carry out work which the tenant ought to have done, and then charge the tenant with the cost, fell within the Leasehold Property (Repairs) Act 1938 requiring the leave of the court to be obtained. However the Court of Appeal has decided that the landlord's remedy is a remedy in debt, not damages, with the consequence that it falls outside the scope of the Leasehold Property (Repairs) Act 1938 (*Jervis v Harris* [1996] 2 W.L.R. 220). It would no doubt be helpful if the clause itself described the sum as a debt, but it is not considered essential to do so. Although the Court of Appeal did not say so in terms, it appears to follow that such a clause is also outside the statutory limitation on damages imposed by s.18 of the Landlord and Tenant Act 1927. Thus, provided that he acts while the tenancy is still running, a landlord can ensure that the property is repaired at the expense of the tenant and, subject to the tenant's financial position, will recover his expenditure in full. Thus major pieces of legislative protection for tenants may be readily avoided. In those circumstances, although a clause giving the landlord the right to enter to carry out work at the tenant's expense has been a standard feature of leases for generations, the tenant's adviser should now consider whether to resist the inclusion of such a clause. If such a clause is to be included, the tenant's adviser should consider restricting the landlord's power to a power to remedy only those breaches which cause damage (or substantial damage) to the reversion.

(n) Supervision of works by landlord's surveyor

9–19 Where the landlord wishes to retain control over the execution of repairs the draftsman may provide that the tenant must repair to the satisfaction of the landlord's surveyor or that the repairs are to be carried out under the supervision of the landlord's surveyor. If the works are to be carried out to the satisfaction of the landlord's surveyor it appears that the appointment of a surveyor is a condition precedent to the tenant's liability under the covenant (*Combe v Greene* (1843) 11 M. & W. 480); and, further, that there will be no breach of covenant if the surveyor ought to have been satisfied (*Doe (dec'd) Baker v Jones* (1848) 2 Car. & Kir. 743). The surveyor can prescribe what works should be done, however he will not have carte blanche over what to require. Against the background of a standard full repairing covenant, the works have to be works to make good a want of repair or absence of good condition. However, provided the surveyor comes to a decision that a reasonable surveyor could reach, it will not matter that the tenant's surveyor favours another cheaper but no less reasonable, option (*Mason v TotalFinaElf UK Ltd* [2003] 3 E.G.L.R. 91 (Ch. D.)). On the other hand, if the works are to be carried out under the supervision of the landlord's surveyor the appointment of a surveyor does not appear to be a condition precedent to the tenant's liability (*Cannock v Jones* (1849) 3 Exch. 233). It is suggested that the draftsman should provide for the tenant to repair to "the reasonable satisfaction of the landlord or his surveyor". It is conceived that this formula overcomes the difficulties of a failure to appoint a surveyor while at the same time preventing the landlord from being capriciously dissatisfied.

(o) Planned maintenance

9–20 In the public sector, standard covenants to "repair" are sometimes now modified to enable the tenant to carry out repair and maintenance through a planned maintenance programme. The approach recognises that some public sector tenants may require time to apply for funding under a central funding agreement, and are subject to budgetary constraints. Whilst the public sector tenant takes a full repairing lease, the tenant's covenant to repair on notice, and the forfeiture clause, are modified such that whilst any serious disrepair, and issues of statutory compliance, must be resolved promptly, more minor and routine matters may be the subject of an agreed programme of scheduled maintenance over a set period of time, with the tenant having the opportunity, and the time, to apply for the requisite funding well in advance.

(p) The landlord's obligation

The draftsman should consider the inter-relationship of the landlord's covenant to repair and the covenant for quiet enjoyment, and make express provision to resolve any potential conflict. Where the two provisions come into conflict they will be interpreted and applied so as to give proper effect, if possible, to both of them. The obligation on the landlord to keep the building in repair must co-exist with the tenant's entitlement to quiet enjoyment of the premises. That points to a threshold for disturbance by repairs where the landlord takes all reasonable precautions, rather than all proper precautions (*Goldmile Properties Ltd v Lechouritis* [2003] 1 E.G.L.R. 60 (CA)). **9–21**

(q) Decorative repairs

A tenant who covenants to repair is liable to do such repapering and painting as would be necessary to satisfy a reasonably-minded tenant of the class likely to take the property (*Proudfoot v Hart* (1890) 25 Q.B.D. 42). However, there is doubt as to the scope of this obligation, particularly with regard to decoration during the term rather than at the end of it. Accordingly, the draftsman should make express provision for redecorating the demised property. Note, however, that in some circumstances a tenant may be relieved against liability to decorate (s.147 of the Law of Property Act 1925). **9–22**

The most common fault in decorating covenants is that the nature of the property has not been considered. Thus, one finds covenants "to paint with three coats of good oil paint" property that is constructed of brick, aluminium and plate glass. If the draftsman does not know what decorative process is necessary to keep the property in sound decorative condition he should not attempt to be specific. The tenant's obligation should be an obligation "in a good and workmanlike manner and with appropriate materials of good quality to redecorate the demised property". However, it is convenient to specify the number of coats of paint which should be applied where painting is appropriate, because this is often a point of dispute in dealing with a terminal schedule of dilapidations.

In the case of a large office building, the draftsman should consider whether the tenant should be required to undertake annual inspections of the exterior with a view to monitoring the performance of cladding panels, window frames, mastic joints and the like.

In most cases the tenant is required to redecorate at fixed intervals. The requirement has the advantage for the tenant that he can plan his programme of redecoration well in advance, but it is doubtful how far such an obligation is really in the interest of either party. In so far as the tenant is concerned, an obligation to redecorate at fixed intervals may expose him to the risk of forfeiture for breach of the covenant at a time when the property is not in need of redecoration. Even if he is granted unconditional relief against forfeiture he may still become involved in tiresome litigation.

Conversely, from the landlord's point of view, the right to forfeit for breach of a covenant to redecorate in a specified year is easily waived. Once the year has passed the breach is complete. It is not a continuing breach of covenant and, accordingly, the receipt of rent in the following year will waive the right to forfeit once and for all (cf. *Stephens v Junior Army and Navy Stores* [1914] 2 Ch. 516: breach of covenant to build by a specified date waived by acceptance of rent after that date).

It is usually a matter of practical indifference to the landlord when the tenant redecorates during the term. However, for the purposes of rent review, the building will be hypothetically more easily lettable if it has been recently redecorated. The draftsman should therefore consider linking the years in which the tenant is required to redecorate to the rent review dates. Since the rent review will be conducted on the assumption that the tenant has complied with his covenants, the property will be assumed to have been redecorated whatever the position in reality.

An obligation to decorate "in the last year of the term" will not oblige the tenant to redecorate if his tenancy comes to a premature end by the service of a break notice (*Dickinson v St Aubyn* [1944] K.B. 454) or, it is thought, forfeiture or surrender. It would be otherwise if the obligation was to decorate "in the last year of the tenancy however determined and in the year preceding any surrender of it".

It is suggested that many of the problems of the timing of periodical redecoration can be overcome if the tenant covenants to decorate "as often as is reasonably necessary", or if the landlord wishes to retain greater control, "as often as in the opinion of the landlord is reasonably necessary but not more often than once in every three years".

Where the landlord covenants to redecorate and recovers the cost from the tenant by way of service charge, the draftsman should not impose a fixed timetable on him. If a fixed timetable is imposed and not complied with, the tenant may refuse to pay such part of the cost of the redecoration as is attributable to a rise in cost between the time when the redecoration ought to have been carried out and the time when it was in fact carried out. The landlord will be better protected if he covenants to redecorate "as often as in his opinion is reasonably necessary".

(r) Covenants to comply with statutes

A covenant to comply with statutes or regulations or notices served under statutes is incorporated in most leases. An obligation on a tenant to keep the property in good repair and condition and to carry out all repairs necessary to keep the property in good repair and condition, does not impose an obligation upon the tenant to indemnify the landlord against whatever liability he may have as a result of service of a statutory notice (see *Riaz v Masaku* [2001] L. & T.R. 22, where a dangerous structure notice was served). Whether the amount of that liability may coincide with a damages claim will depend upon what work is actually carried out by the local authority and whether the amount charged for it is reasonable in the circumstances. The landlord's adviser may, therefore, wish to include a covenant that the tenant indemnify the landlord in respect of any such liability. **9–23**

Regulations such as the Control of Asbestos Regulations 2012 (SI 2012/632) impose duties on those who manage or occupy non domestic property. Under the Control of Asbestos Regulations 2012, the "dutyholder" is someone who has an obligation "of any extent" in relation to the maintenance or repair of non-domestic premises, or the means of access to and egress from those premises, whether by contract or tenancy (Reg.4(1)). There may be more than one "dutyholder" at any one time. Where there is more than one dutyholder, the relative contribution to be made by each such person in complying with the requirements of the regulation will be determined by the nature and extent of the maintenance and repair obligation owed by that person. The dutyholder must ensure that a suitable and sufficient risk assessment is carried out as to whether asbestos is or is liable to be present in the premises, and must take such steps as are reasonable and must consider the condition of any asbestos found when carrying out the assessment (Reg.4(4)).

Landlords, tenants and managing agents also need to consider their respective duties in relation to fire safety and health and safety legislation. The Regulatory Reform (Fire Safety) Order 2005 (SI 2005/1541, as amended by SI 2006/484), impose duties on a defined "responsible person". This will be the employer if the workplace is to be under his control, otherwise it will be the person in control of the premises in connection with the carrying on of a trade, business or other undertaking, or, in other cases, the owner of the premises (Art.3). A person will be a person in control if that person has an obligation of any extent in relation to the maintenance or repair of any premises or the safety of any premises (Art.5). The duties are set out in Part 2 and include an assessment of the risks to any person who is or may be lawfully on the premises, to any person in the immediate vicinity of the premises who is at risk from a fire on the premises, and to fire fighters on the premises carrying out fire authority duties. The general fire precautions identified in the risk assessment must be put in place and maintained. The assessment must be kept under review. Failure to comply with a duty under the Order is an offence; the current maximum penalty in the magistrates court is £5,000, and in the crown court an unlimited fine or imprisonment for up to two years, or both (Art.32. See *R v New Look Retailers Ltd* [2011] 1 Cr App. R (S) 57, where the retailer responsible for complying with all fire and safety precautions at the retail premises it leased was fined £400,000). In multi-occupied premises there is likely to be more than one "responsible person": there may be a number of tenant employers on different floors and the landlord may retain the common parts. Where two or more responsible persons have duties in respect of premises, they are required to co-ordinate and co-operate with each other in carrying out their duties (Art.4).

Example 9.4 Tenant's covenants to repair and decorate
(1) To keep the demised property in good repair
(2) To decorate the demised property in a good and workmanlike manner and with appropriate materials of good quality as often as in the opinion of the landlord is reasonably necessary but not more often than once in every three years and to decorate as aforesaid in the last year of the tenancy however determined and in the year preceding any surrender of it
(3) To permit the landlord and his agents at reasonable times and upon reasonable notice to enter the demised property and to inspect its condition and state of repair
(4) Within 42 days after the service of a schedule of dilapidations to begin and to proceed expeditiously to comply with the same
(5) If the tenant shall not within 42 days after the service of such schedule (or immediately in case of need) have begun or be proceeding expeditiously to comply with the same the landlord may (without prejudice to his right of re-entry) enter the demised property and execute such works as may be necessary to comply with the schedule and whose cost (including all professional fees and value added tax) shall he a debt payable by the tenant to the landlord on demand and in default shall be recoverable as rent in arrear.

Example 9.5 Landlord's restricted power to enter to repair
If the tenant does not within 42 days after the service of such schedule (or sooner in case of need) have begun or be proceeding expeditiously to comply with it the landlord may:
(a) enter the demised property and
(b) carry out works to remedy such of the defects specified in the schedule as have caused or are likely to cause substantial damage to or diminution in value of the landlord's reversion and the cost of those works (including all professional fees and value added tax associated with them) shall be a debt payable by the tenant to the landlord on demand.

Example 9.6 Tenant's covenant to maintain plant and machinery
(1) To keep all plant, machinery and equipment properly maintained and in good working order

(2) To employ reputable contractors to inspect and service all plant, machinery and equipment at least once a year
(3) To renew or replace all parts of the plant machinery and equipment when necessary
(4) To keep full service and maintenance records and records of any work carried out to the plant machinery and equipment and to make them available to the Landlord within seven days of any written request to see them.

Example 9.7 Tenant's covenant to repair and rebuild: insured risks excepted
(1) To keep the demised property in repair
(2) If necessary to rebuild the demised property in accordance with plans and specifications approved by the landlord (such approval not to be unreasonably withheld)
(3) To replace any landlord's fixtures or other plant and machinery which during the term become incapable of economic repair
(4) In the last year of the term to ensure that the electrical system in the demised property complies with the then current regulations of the Institute of Electrical Engineers
(5) The above obligations do not extend to damage by any insured risk save to the extent that the landlord is unable to recover the cost of any necessary works from its insurers.

Example 9.8 Tenant's covenant to repair interior
To keep the interior of the demised property (including its windows window frames doors and door frames) in repair.

Example 9.9 Tenant's covenant to decorate
(1) In every fifth year of the term and in its last year to decorate the inside of the demised property in a good and workmanlike manner and with appropriate materials of good quality
(2) In every third year of the term and in its last year to decorate the outside of the demised property in a good and workmanlike manner and with appropriate materials of good quality
(3) In the last year of the term the redecoration must be carried out with colours and materials approved by the landlord (such approval not to be unreasonably withheld)
(4) Where decoration involves the redecoration of previously painted surfaces they must be properly prepared and not less than two coats of paint must be applied.

Example 9.10 Tenant's covenant to decorate linked to rent review dates

(1) In the six months preceding any rent review date under this lease and in its last year to decorate both the inside and the outside of the demised property in a good and workmanlike manner with materials of good quality
(2) In the last year of the term the redecoration must be carried out in colours approved by the landlord (such approval not to be unreasonably withheld)
(3) Where decoration involves the redecoration of previously painted surfaces they must be properly prepared and not less than two coats of paint must be applied.

Example 9.11 Tenant's covenant to inspect

To cause a professional inspection of the demised property (both inside and out) to be carried out at least once a year for the purpose of identifying any defects in it.

Example 9.12 Landlord's covenants to repair exterior and to decorate

(1) To keep in repair the roof and loadbearing walls (excluding the windows and doors therein) and main beams of the Building and the common parts of it.
(2) To decorate in a good and workmanlike manner and with appropriate materials the exterior and common parts of the Building as often as in the opinion of the landlord is reasonably necessary.

Example 9.13 Tenant's covenant to repair (fire damage excepted)

To keep the demised property in good repair (excepting damage caused by fire or any other peril against which the demised property is insured by the landlord under a policy which has not been vitiated by any act or omission of tenant or any person deriving title under him).

Example 9.14 Tenant's covenant to carry out work required by statute, etc.

To execute all works required by or by virtue of any Act of Parliament or regulation or directive of the European Union or any local or public authority to be done in or in respect of the demised property whether by the landlord or the tenant or any other person (however described).

OR

(1) The Tenant shall:
   (a) comply with all existing and future Acts of Parliament and subordinate legislation made thereunder or regulation or directive of the European Union or of any local or public authority applicable to the Premises and/or their occupation and use
   (b) carry out any works to the Premises required by or as may be necessary to prevent any liability or claim against the owner the Landlord the Tenant or any occupier of the Premises under any Acts of Parliament and subordinate legislation made thereunder or regulation or directive of the European Union or of any local or public authority and
   (c) immediately give written notice to the Landlord of any damage to or defect in the Premises which might give rise to any obligation, duty of care or liability on the Landlord under any Acts of Parliament and subordinate legislation made thereunder or regulation or directive of the European Union or of any local or public authority and

(2) If the Tenant receives any notice order proposal or communication made given or issued under any Acts of Parliament and subordinate legislation made thereunder or regulation or directive of the European Union or of any local or public authority it shall immediately forward a copy to the Landlord and if in the Landlord's reasonable opinion such notice order proposal or communication is contrary to the interests of the Landlord the Tenant shall make such objection or representation against it as the Landlord reasonably requires and at the Landlord's cost

(3) Where any such notice order proposal or communication requires works to be carried out to the Premises the Tenant shall so far as compatible with such notice order proposal or communication also comply with the provisions of the Lease in relation to such works.

2. ALTERATIONS AND IMPROVEMENTS

(a) Covenant against alterations

A covenant against "alterations" is wider than a covenant against "improvements". Even minor operations may be caught by a covenant against alterations. On the whole, the purpose of the covenant is to ensure that the tenant does not change the nature of the landlord's property or imperil its stability or safety. For that reason the word "alteration" will usually be construed as meaning something which alters the form or construction of a building (*Bickmore v Dimmer* [1903] 1 Ch. 158). Thus, a tenant will be entitled to erect a neon sign advertising his business (*Joseph v LCC* [1914] 111 L.T. 276). He will also be entitled to replace items of plant (e.g. air-conditioning equipment) by other items designed to fulfil the same function (*Hagee (London) v Co-operative Insurance Society* [1992] 1 E.G.L.R. 57). Where the letting is of a large office, the tenant's adviser should satisfy himself that the covenant permits the erection and removal of internal partitioning. Similarly, the tenant of a shop will require the right to alter the shop front. This may be done by limiting the covenant to alterations to the main structure or by inserting a proviso expressly permitting the work. Alternatively, the form of covenant previously recommended by the Law Commission may be used; namely, "not to carry out any alterations or other works of which the actual or probable result is to destroy or alter the character of the property or any part of the property to the detriment of the interest of the landlord therein" (Law Com. No.67, p.78). **9–24**

If the landlord wishes to retain greater control, the draftsman should prohibit "alterations to the demised property (including alterations to its appearance or lay-out)". This form of covenant will prohibit such activities as letting a wall for bill-posting (*Heard v Stuart* (1907) 24 T.L.R. 104). In the case of an actively managed shopping centre, the landlord may well wish to keep greater control over the appearance of the individual units, including their shop fronts and fascias. Often this is done by requiring any alterations to comply with a tenant's handbook which in turn contains detailed rules about materials, dimensions and other such matters. An alteration by a tenant may also have an impact upon or affect the calculation of service charge liabilities between tenants (see the RICS Information Paper, "Apportionment of Service Charges and Tenant's Alterations").

9–25 In older buildings it may be appropriate for the lease to contain a covenant against cutting or maiming the main walls or timbers of the building. This form of covenant will prevent the tenant from attaching substantial fixtures to the building (*LCC v Hutter* [1925] Ch. 626) or from notching the joists to receive ductwork (*Hagee (London) v Co-operative Insurance Society* [1992] 1 E.G.L.R. 57).

A covenant against alterations may be absolute (i.e. all alterations are prohibited) or qualified (i.e. alterations are prohibited except with the consent of the landlord). A common form of covenant is qualified as regards nonstructural alterations and absolute as regards structural alterations. If a covenant is fully qualified, the court will apply the principles approved by Balcombe L.J. in *International Drilling Fluids Ltd v Louisville Investments (Uxbridge) Ltd* [1986] Ch. 513, in considering whether consent has been unreasonably withheld (*Iqbal v Thakrar* [2004] 3 E.G.L.R. 21 (CA)). Where the covenant is qualified, the consent of the landlord may not be unreasonably withheld if the proposed alteration amounts to an improvement (s.19(2) of the Landlord and Tenant Act 1927). If the statutory scheme, taken as a whole, is more favourable to the tenant than the contractual provisions of the lease, the lease must yield to the statute (*Sargeant v Macepark (Whittlebury) Ltd* [2004] 3 E.G.L.R. 26). If the proposed alteration does not amount to an improvement the landlord may arbitrarily withhold consent unless the lease itself provides that he may not. Whether an alteration amounts to an improvement must be judged from the point of view of the tenant (*Lambert v FW Woolworth & Co Ltd (No.2)* [1938] Ch. 883). Surprisingly, "an alteration may be an improvement although it produces damage or diminution in the value of the premises or does not add to the letting value of the holding so that the mere fact of damage or diminution in the value arising to the premises from their alteration will not of itself prevent the alteration from being an improvement" (ibid., per Slesser L.J.). If the covenant against alterations is absolute the statutory proviso does not operate. It will, therefore, be in the landlord's interest to insist on an absolute covenant. However, an absolute covenant against alterations may have a detrimental effect on the rent recoverable on review.

Where the lease contains an absolute covenant against alterations, or certain classes of alteration, the question arises whether the landlord has an "absolute right" to refuse to allow the tenant to carry out alterations (or alterations of the prohibited class). This question is relevant because where the landlord has an "absolute right" to refuse to allow a variation of the lease, and the lease is in fact varied neither a former tenant nor a guarantor will be liable to pay any amount in respect of the covenant to the extent that the amount is referable to the variation (s.18 of the Landlord and Tenant (Covenants) Act 1995). In deciding whether the landlord has an absolute right to refuse to allow a variation, regard must be had to the effect of any statute. Part I of the Landlord and Tenant Act 1927 will be of particular relevance in this respect. If the tenant could have obtained a certificate under that Act that the alteration was a proper improvement, then it is considered that the landlord would not have an absolute right to refuse to allow the variation.

(b) Statutory modification of covenants

A number of Acts of Parliament have modified the effect of covenants against alterations and improvements. The most important of them, and the widest ranging, is the Landlord and Tenant Act 1927. **9–26**

(i) Section 3 of the Landlord and Tenant Act 1927

Whether a covenant against alterations is absolute or qualified, a tenant of business premises may apply to the court for authority to carry out improvements. The tenant must comply with the procedure laid down in s.3 of the Act, and the landlord is entitled to an opportunity of being heard if he objects. **9–27**

Having heard all interested persons the court may certify that an improvement is a proper improvement if it is satisfied that the improvement:

(1) is of such a nature as to be calculated to add to the letting value of the holding at the termination of the tenancy;
(2) is reasonable and suited to the character thereof (taking into account evidence that the improvement will not injure the amenity or convenience of the neighbourhood); and

(3) will not diminish the value of any other property belonging to the same landlord or to any superior landlord from whom he holds directly or indirectly (s.3(1) of the Landlord and Tenant Act 1927).

If the court issues a certificate, or if the landlord does not object in time, the tenant is entitled to carry out the improvement notwithstanding any covenant in the lease (s.3(4) of the Landlord and Tenant Act 1927). This means that the tenant can carry out the improvement even if there is an absolute covenant against alterations in the lease. Moreover, the tenant's right to carry out alterations despite an absolute covenant is not dependent on the giving of a certificate by the court. If the tenant gives notice to the landlord of his intention to make an improvement and the landlord does not object within three months, the tenant has the right to carry out the improvement. In addition, this right exists not only against the landlord but also against any superior landlord. In most cases the tenant will be entitled to compensation for the improvement on quitting.

(ii) Other Acts

9–28 Many other Acts of Parliament empower the court to modify obligations in leases if the effect of the obligation would be to prevent the tenant from carrying out works required by the Act in question. The most important of these in practice are the Regulatory Reform (Fire Safety) Order 2005 (SI 2005/1541, as amended), the Building Act 1984 (ss.76–83), the Equality Act 2010 (Part 4 and Sch.4, in particular) and the Equality Act 2010 (Disability) Regulations (SI 2010/2128).

Under the Electronic Communications Code, the court has extensive powers to override covenants in leases in order to enable telecommunications equipment to be installed (s.134 of the Communications Act 2003). In addition, where the tenant is granted a waste management licence subject to conditions, and the conditions require him to carry out works or do things which he is not entitled to carry out or do, it is the duty of any person whose consent would be required to enable the conditions to be fulfilled to grant that consent (s.35(4) of the Environmental Protection Act 1990). Similar provisions apply where a remediation notice has been served in respect of contaminated land (s.78G of the

Environmental Protection Act 1990). These provisions also require a person whose consent is required before anything required by a remediation notice can be done to grant or join in granting such rights in relation to any of the relevant land or waters as will enable the appropriate person to comply with the requirements of the remediation notice. Thus they require the landlord to consent to variations in a lease which have the effect of prohibiting compliance with such conditions.

Some works required by statute are required to be carried out by the owner of the property in question, others by the occupier. For this purpose the owner is often defined as the person entitled to receive the rack rent of the property in question. This will usually be the landlord, unless the letting was initially made for a rent less than the rack rent, in which case the owner will be the tenant.

Many such Acts also empower the court to apportion any expenditure on improvements required by the Act in question between persons having an interest in the property in such proportions as is just and equitable. Section 102 of the Building Act 1984 also requires the court to consider the nature of the work and the benefit of the work to the different persons concerned. Thus, the common covenant by the tenant "to execute all works required to be carried out by any Act of Parliament whether by the owner or occupier or any other person and to bear the cost of all such works" may be overridden by the court. Indeed, it appears that the court has no jurisdiction to entertain an action on the covenant itself (*Horner v Franklin* [1905] 1 K.B. 479). Nevertheless, such a covenant is a material consideration in the apportionment of expenditure, and it will often persuade the court that the expenditure in question ought to have been in the contemplation of the tenant when he took the lease (*Monro v Burghclere* [1918] 1 K.B. 291). The draftsman should, therefore, insert such a covenant in the lease for the protection of the landlord. Although the landlord cannot bring an action on the covenant, it may be indirectly enforced through the apportionment mechanism. The tenant can be protected to some degree if the covenant is qualified by the insertion of some financial limit; for example, "to bear the cost of all such works up to an amount equal to three times the rent payable under this lease at the commencement of such works". Although the court can override such a financial limit, again it will be material in the apportionment of the expenditure (*Bedford v University College Medical School* (1974) C.L.Y. 2063, County Court).

9–29 Where the landlord carries out work required by statute, he too is entitled to apply for an apportionment. Where he incurs costs in carrying out such work which he wishes to recover by way of service charge, it would seem that he cannot do so in the absence of an order from the court apportioning the expenditure.

Where the tenant has covenanted to comply with statutes, and carries out an improvement required by statute the effect on rent of the improvement will not be ignored in determining a new rent on a renewal under the Landlord and Tenant Act 1954 (and often on a rent review). Thus, the imposition on the tenant of an obligation to carry out works required by statute confers a double benefit on the landlord. This may, however, be redressed by the court in the exercise of its discretion to apportion expenditure. Thus the fact that the landlord will derive a rental benefit from the improvement, may be a reason for requiring him to contribute towards the capital cost of the improvement; while the fact that the improvement will be disregarded on review may be a reason for leaving the burden on the tenant.

(c) Initial improvements

9–30 At the beginning of the tenancy it is often intended that as part of the bargain between the parties the tenant will carry out improvements to the demised property, often in consideration of a rent free period. Sometimes the tenant enters into a contractual undertaking to carry out the improvements in question. Whether this is in the interest of either party depends on the circumstances of the case, so the draftsman should not automatically impose on the tenant such an obligation.

The problem arises where the lease is less than 50 years for tax purposes. Where a lease of a duration not exceeding 50 years is granted on terms that the tenant is obliged to carry out any works on the demised property, the landlord is treated as having received a premium equal to the amount by which the value of his reversion immediately after the commencement of the lease exceeds the value it would have had at that time, if the obligation to carry out the work had not been imposed on the tenant (s.34 of the Income and Corporation Taxes Act 1988, substituted by the Finance Act 1998 s.38; s.287 of the Income Tax (Trading and Other Income) Act 2005). Tax will be charged on a sliding scale, depending on the length of the lease: a reduction of two per cent of the notional premium is made for each full year of the term after the first year. What is taxed is not the cost of the works but the benefit accruing to the landlord as a result of the works. The benefit may accrue on a rent review or at the expiry of the term.

In addition, where the grant of a rent free period is linked to an obligation by the tenant to carry out work, the rent foregone may be liable to VAT as being a supply by the tenant to the landlord of the rent foregone (*Ridgeons Bulk v Commissioners of Customs & Excise* [1994] S.T.C. 427; [1994] E.G.C.S. 68).

Set against the charge to tax are two advantages to the landlord. First, the tenant is not entitled to claim compensation under Part I of the Landlord and Tenant Act 1927 in respect of improvements that he was obliged to make under a contract made for valuable consideration (s.2(1)(b) of the 1927 Act). Secondly, on a renewal of his lease under the Landlord and Tenant Act 1954 the tenant will have to pay a rent for the demised property as improved since the court will only disregard voluntary improvements in assessing the rent (s.34(2) of the 1954 Act). Further, as many rent review clauses follow the form of s.34 of the Landlord and Tenant Act 1954, the tenant may pay a higher rent on an intermediate review if an obligation to improve is imposed.

It will usually be better for the tenant if he is not under an express covenant to carry out improvements since he will be entitled to claim compensation for them under the Landlord and Tenant Act 1927 and will not have to pay rent for the demised property as improved. Moreover, the absence of a covenant will minimise the risk of a charge to VAT arising. For the landlord, on the other hand, whether a covenant should be imposed will depend upon the weight of the respective financial burdens that he will have to bear. If an obligation to improve is imposed, the Revenue accept that the landlord will be able to avoid paying tax if, in addition to the covenant to improve, he also imposes on the tenant an obligation to reinstate at the expiry of the term if so required by the landlord. The logic of this is hard to see, especially if in consequence of the improvements the landlord is entitled to exact a higher rent from his tenant on a rent review.

(d) Hidden obligations to improve

9–31 The tenant's adviser should be on his guard against hidden obligations to improve. Such an obligation usually arises in one of two ways.

Firstly, a covenant to repair may require the covenantor to carry out improvements that are inherent in the particular repair. If, for example, a wall has to be rebuilt and the building regulations for the time being in force require it to be rebuilt with deeper footings the regulations must be complied with even if compliance involves a certain degree of improvement (*Lurcott v Wakely* [1911] 1 K.B. 905). Equally, if modern building techniques involve a certain degree of improvement such improvement will be included in the obligation to repair (*Ravenseft Properties Ltd v Davstone (Holdings) Ltd* [1979] 1 All E.R. 929). It appears that nothing can be done to avoid these obligations.

Secondly, a covenant to comply with Acts of Parliament may impose on the covenantor an obligation to carry out statutory improvements; for example, the installation of fire-resisting doors. If such a covenant is included in the lease, the tenant's adviser should check that the relevant statutes contain a power for the court to apportion expenditure required thereby between the landlord and the tenant. In some cases no such power exists. In any event the tenant's adviser should press for the effect of such works to be disregarded in assessing the rent on a review.

Alternatively, the tenant's adviser may seek to limit the tenant's liability, either by reference to a financial limit or to a category of work. Examples are given below.

(e) Environmental matters

9–32 The control of pollution has become of great concern in recent years, particularly with respect to industrial processes. Greater enforcement powers have been conferred on the regulatory authorities. Enforcement powers may now require the carrying out of extensive work in order to prevent pollution or to deal with the effect of past pollution (see, for example, *R (On the Application of National Grid Gas Plc) v Environment Agency* [2006] 1 W.L.R. 3041, and *Possfund Custodian Trustee Ltd v Kwik-Fit Properties Ltd* [2009] 1 E.G.L.R 39). These powers are contained in Part IIA of the Environmental Protection Act 1990 (inserted by s.57 of the Environment Act 1995). An environmental permit is not required where the storage of waste is temporary at the premises on which it is produced, pending its collection, and is for twelve months or less, (see Environmental Permitting (England and Wales) Regulations 2010 (SI 2010/675), as amended). Thus no licence is required for waste placed outside a factory or workshop pending its removal.

The enforcement authorities may recover costs incurred in works to prevent or remedy pollution of controlled waters, including groundwater (Environmental Permitting (England and Wales) Regulations 2010 (SI 2010/675).

But even in the absence of such powers, the landlord will wish to be protected against the effect of pollution and contamination of his property. In an extreme case, the contamination of property with the waste products of an industrial process may result in the building having to be pulled down and the subsoil excavated and carted away. The traditional repairing obligation is not wholly adequate to deal with this problem, and in any case what is required may be alteration or even improvement. In cases of industrial property the covenant to comply with statutes should refer expressly to the Environmental Protection Act 1990 (which deals with contamination and pollution) and also to the Environmental Permitting (England and Wales) Regulations (which deal with discharge of effluent). The problem of leakage of potentially contaminative substances is not confined to industrial property. For example, a dry cleaner will use chemicals which could cause problems of pollution if they escape into the aquifer. Similar problems might arise in the case of a warehouse storing chemicals or a DIY retail outlet selling paint and solvents. In addition, the draftsman should seek to impose on the tenant an obligation at the end of the term to yield up the demised property in a state which will enable it to be lawfully and immediately used for industrial purposes without expenditure on works. The tenant may resist such an obligation or at least qualify it so that it only applies where the unfitness arises out of the tenant's activities during the term. In some cases, the conditions attached to a licence may not be capable of being performed at the expiry of the lease (e.g. methane gas may require to be burned off a landfill site for many years, or safety precautions may be required to be kept in place). In such a case the landlord should seek to require the tenant to provide security for the expenditure involved in compliance with such conditions.

9–33 Where the building has previously been used for industrial purposes, the incoming tenant may inherit a liability for pollution or contamination which arose during the time of a previous occupier. Ideally, the tenant's adviser should secure a warranty from the landlord that at the date of the lease the property is fit for use for industrial purposes without expenditure on works. But most landlords will be unwilling to give such a warranty. In such a case, the tenant's adviser should consider excluding the soil and sub-soil from the demised premises so that it takes a "pie-crust" lease, or seek to exclude liability for dealing with such pollution or contamination from the tenant's covenants, including the tenant's covenant to comply with statutes and to carry out such works as may be required under any statutory notice, and the tenant's covenant to pay service charge. He may also consider pressing for a tenant's break-clause exercisable in the event that statutory liability is imposed on the tenant over a stated amount (e.g. three times the annual rent).

Reinstatement

9–34 The landlord may wish to include a covenant enabling it to require the tenant to reinstate any authorised (or unauthorised) alterations that the tenant has made prior to the end of the term of the lease, and to make good. If the service of a notice by the landlord is a condition precedent to the tenant's obligation to reinstate, the landlord can determine prior to the end of the term whether it will or will not be to its benefit (or that of an incoming tenant), at that stage to retain the alterations.

If no specific time limit is stated for service of the landlord's notice, it has been held that the notice simply has to be served prior to the end of the term, requiring the tenant to start the work before the expiry date, and then allowing a reasonable time thereafter for the completion of the work (*Scottish Mutual Assurance Society Ltd v British Telecommunications Plc* [1999] E.G.C.S. 43, where the relevant clause obliged the tenant to "reinstate the property to its original design and layout at the expiry of the lease at its own cost should the lessor reasonably so require", and notice was served only seven days before the lease expiry date). Service of a Schedule of Dilapidations listing works of reinstatement, without service of any separate specific notice requiring reinstatement, has also been held to constitute a valid notice to reinstate (*Westminster City Council v HSBC Bank Plc* [2003] 1 E.G.L.R. 62; [2003] 16 E.G. 103).

The Code for Leasing Business Premises in England and Wales 2007 makes two recommendations. Firstly, that landlords should not require tenants to remove permitted alterations and make good at the end of the lease, unless reasonable to do so. Secondly, that landlords should notify tenants of their requirements at least six months before the termination date.

It is suggested that the tenant's adviser should press for the inclusion of a set period within which notice of reinstatement must be served, and that it should be accepted that such notice can either be served separately or as a component part of a Schedule of Dilapidations. The landlord's adviser will, however, wish to ensure that any such time limit is applicable only in the event that the lease expires by effluxion of time, and that it does not operate to deprive the landlord of the opportunity to seek reinstatement in the event that, say, a break notice is served giving six months' notice to bring the lease to a premature end (whether compliance with the covenant to reinstate is a condition precedent to the effective operation of the break clause, or not). In the event that compliance with a covenant to reinstate was to be a condition precedent to the right to break, the tenant's adviser should seek to include a timetable for service of any notice requiring reinstatement following service of the break notice such that the tenant would have certainty as to the steps that it had to take, and so as to enable the tenant time to comply in good time prior to the break date.

If the lease contains provision that a notice must be served to trigger the obligation to reinstatement, and the lease is protected by the provisions of the Landlord and Tenant Act 1954, a notice should be served before the end of the original contractual term, and a reinstatement clause reflecting the alterations already made should be incorporated into the terms of any new lease granted on a renewal under Part II of the Landlord and Tenant Act 1954.

Example 9.15 Tenant's covenant against alterations

(1) Not without the consent in writing of the landlord to make any alteration or addition to the demised property

(2) Upon each application for such consent to supply the landlord with drawings and specifications of each proposed alteration or addition for approval by him
(3) Not to carry out any works to which the landlord has consented save in accordance with drawings and specifications approved as aforesaid
(4) Before beginning any approved works to enter into such covenant with the landlord relating to the reinstatement of the demised property as the landlord may reasonably require.

Example 9.16 Tenant's covenant against structural alterations; qualified covenant against non-structural alterations
(1) Not to make any structural alteration or addition to the demised property
(2) Not to unite the demised property with any other property
(3) Not without the landlord's written consent (such consent not to be unreasonably withheld) to carry out any non-structural alteration
(4) A non-structural alteration is one which:
  (a) does not affect any loadbearing part of the demised property or consists of alterations to the electrical system or to service pipes or other conducting media or consists of the installation or removal of demountable partitioning and
  (b) is carried out in accordance with plans and specifications previously approved in writing by the landlord
(5) To carry out any approved non-structural alteration:
  (a) in a good and workmanlike manner
  (b) with materials of good quality and
  (c) to the reasonable satisfaction of the landlord
(6) On demand to remove any alteration which:
  (a) has not been approved in writing by the landlord or
  (b) is required to be removed by any legislation or
  (c) is required to be removed by the terms of any consent to the making of that alteration
  and in any such case to make good all damage caused either by the alteration or by its removal or reinstatement.

Example 9.17 Tenant's covenant relating to statutes
To comply with all present and future Acts of Parliament and subordinate legislation made thereunder relating to the demised

property or the use of it and to execute at his own expense any work required to be carried out in the demised property whether such work is required to be carried out by the owner or the occupier or any other person.

Example 9.18 Proviso limiting tenant's liability
Provided that this covenant shall not require the tenant to expend in any period of 12 months an amount greater than 3 times the amount of the annual rent then payable under this lease.

Example 9.19 Alternative proviso limiting tenant's liability
Provided that this covenant shall not impose upon the tenant any liability to carry out work which is not fairly described as work of repair.

Example 9.20 Tenant's covenant to carry out improvements
(1) To carry out in a good and workmanlike manner the works described in the plans and specifications approved by the landlord and attached hereto within [ ] months from the date of this lease or such further period as the landlord may allow in writing
(2) If so required by the landlord to reinstate the demised property to the state in which it now is on the expiry or sooner determination of this lease.

Example 9.21 Tenant's covenant to yield up in a fit state
At the expiry or sooner determination of the term to yield up the demised property:
(1) in repair and
(2) free from contamination by substances potentially harmful to:
    (a) humans or
    (b) the environment or
    (c) the demised property and
(3) in such a physical condition as will enable it to be used for industrial purposes without expenditure on works.

Example 9.22 Covenant by tenant to give security for compliance with conditions
(1) In any case where:

(a) the carrying on of any activity on the demised property is lawful by reason only of the grant of a permission licence or authorisation under environmental or planning legislation and

(b) the permission licence or authorisation imposes conditions in connection with the carrying on of those activities (whether or not those conditions fall to be performed after the end of the term or after those activities have ceased) and

(c) fulfilment of those conditions after the expiry or sooner determination of the term would fall to be undertaken by the landlord or a person (other than the tenant) deriving title under him,

the tenant shall:

(a) indemnify the landlord against any loss damage cost or expenditure incurred or suffered in connection with compliance with those conditions and

(b) on demand (whether made before or after the expiry or sooner determination of the term) provide security in such form as the landlord may reasonably require for the estimated cost of complying with those conditions.

(2)

(a) "Environmental legislation" means the Environmental Protection Act and the Environmental Permitting (England and Wales) Regulations as amended from time to time and any other legislation relating to the control of pollution or the protection of the environment

(b) "Planning legislation" means the Planning Acts 1990 and any other legislation relating to town and country planning or the control of development

(c) "Legislation" includes Acts of Parliament and regulations made under them and also regulations and directives of the European Union.

CHAPTER 10

USE OF THE DEMISED PROPERTY

1. WARRANTIES AS TO FITNESS FOR USE

Generally, there is no implied covenant or warranty by the landlord that the demised property is legally or physically fit for the use that the tenant proposes to make of it, even if the lease itself contains restrictive use covenants (*Hill v Harris* [1965] 2 Q.B. 601). It is, therefore, incumbent on the tenant to ensure that his use of the property will be lawful both in terms of planning control and in terms of any restrictions imposed by a lease under which his landlord or any superior landlord holds, or any restrictive covenants that bind the land. An undertenant should call for his landlord's title to be produced in all but the most straightforward case, even if he is not strictly entitled to it (under s.44 of the Law of Property Act 1925). Many landlords will cooperate with a tenant but a recalcitrant landlord should be asked for a warranty that the tenant's proposed use will be lawful. If all else fails, a tenant may still be able to sue his landlord for negligent misstatement (*Esso Petroleum Co Ltd v Mardon* [1976] Q.B. 801: misstatement as to earning potential of petrol filling station); and it may be that the mere description of property (as, for example, "offices") is of itself a representation that the property may lawfully be used as such during the term of the lease (*Laurence v Lexcourt Holdings Ltd* [1978] 2 All E.R. 810). **10–01**

Express warranties by landlords that the property is fit for use are unknown in the current market. However, the problems of contamination and industrial pollution are likely to become of increasing importance in the future. In cases where the tenant is proposing to take a lease of property which has previously been used for industrial purposes, he should consider requiring the landlord to warrant either that the building is fit for use or that no work is required as at the date of the lease in order to deal with historic contamination or pollution.

2. TOWN AND COUNTRY PLANNING ACT 1990

10–02 The Town and Country Planning Act 1990 and the Orders made under it place statutory limits on the use that may be made of property and the operations that may be carried out on it. It is, nevertheless, common in leases for the tenant to covenant with the landlord to comply with the Town and Country Planning Act and not to apply for planning permission without the landlord's consent. Both of these covenants are important to the landlord and the draftsman should not lightly omit them. If the tenant commits a breach of planning control and the local planning authority decides to take enforcement proceedings, the enforcement notice will be served on the "owner" of the land in question and any other person having an interest in that land (ss.172(2) and 336(1) of the Town and Country Planning Act 1990); that is, it will be served on the landlord. If the landlord falls within the statutory definition of "owner", i.e. the letting was originally at a rack rent (s.336(1) of the Town and Country Planning Act 1990; *Borthwick-Norton v Collier* [1950] 2 K.B. 594) he may be liable to prosecution if the notice is not complied with (s.179(1) of the Town and Country Planning Act 1990). A covenant prohibiting a breach of planning control by the tenant adds the weapon of forfeiture to the landlord's armoury and may protect him against a prosecution.

The covenant prohibiting the tenant from applying for planning permission without the landlord's consent is equally important. If it is not included the tenant may lawfully change the use of the demised property, or carry out operations on it, although the landlord would have the opportunity of making representations to the local planning authority if he objected to the application. Such activity by the tenant may prove very detrimental to the landlord because a change of use by the tenant may result in the abandonment of an existing use, so that planning permission might be necessary to revert to that use.

In addition, the landlord should have control over the entry into any planning obligation under s.106 of the Town and Country Planning Act 1990 and the modification and discharge of planning obligations under s.106A and appeals under s.106B (as substituted by s.12(1) of the Planning and Compensation Act 1991), and should prohibit the giving by the tenant of any unilateral undertaking under those sections or any replacement sections.

If the tenant applies for planning permission with the landlord's consent, he may be granted planning permission for a limited period (s.72(1)(b) of the Town and Country Planning Act 1990). In such a case the permission will often be subject to a condition that the land to which it relates be reinstated at the expiry of the permission. In the absence of any specific provision in the lease, if the lease expired before the planning permission the tenant would be entitled to vacate, leaving the landlord to comply with the planning conditions. Accordingly, the draftsman should impose on the tenant an obligation to carry out any works required by the planning permission before the expiry of the lease. In addition, the draftsman may consider requiring the tenant to give security for performance of this obligation and for such security to be provided before the planning permission is implemented. Security could be provided by the deposit of cash in a joint account or by the provision of a bond. The tenant's adviser should seek to limit an obligation to carry out works required by planning conditions to those required by permissions granted during the term.

Clearly, the tenant's obligations will be very different in the case of a lease under which the tenant is to carry out substantial improvements to the demised property. It would be inappropriate in such a lease for the tenant to covenant not to carry out development on the demised property, or even not to carry out material development thereon. Nevertheless, it is suggested that the draftsman should restrict the tenant's right to carry out development on the demised property as much as is consistent with the intention of the parties. **10–03**

Some leases require the tenant not to make an application for an established use certificate without the landlord's consent. The reason behind the covenant was to prevent previous use rights from being lost and replaced with an established use. An established use was one which was immune from enforcement proceedings but was not lawful. Now, however, once the time for taking enforcement action has passed a use becomes lawful (s.191(2) Town and Country Planning Act 1990, as substituted by the Planning and Compensation Act 1991) and an application for a certificate of lawfulness may be made (s.192). The danger of an anomalous position arising is therefore lessened. Nevertheless, the landlord may have a legitimate interest in ensuring that he keeps control over changes of use under the Planning Acts, since such changes may have repercussions beyond the term of the lease.

Example 10.1 Tenant's covenant relating to planning and development

(1) Not to commit any breach of planning control
(2) Not without the consent in writing of the landlord (such consent not to be unreasonably withheld):
  (a) to apply for planning permission to carry out any development in or upon the demised property and in any event to supply to the landlord a copy of any application for planning permission together with such plans and other documents as the landlord may reasonably require and to supply to the landlord a copy of any planning permission granted to the tenant or
  (b) to enter into any binding agreement with the local planning authority or to give any legally binding unilateral undertaking to such an authority
(3) To pay and satisfy any charge that may be imposed upon any breach by the tenant of planning control or otherwise under the Town and Country Planning Act 1990
(4) Unless the landlord shall otherwise direct to carry out before the expiry or sooner determination of this lease any works required to be carried out to or upon the demised property as a condition of any planning permission which may have been granted during the term of this lease irrespective of the date before which such works were thereby required to be carried out
(5) Expressions used in this clause shall be construed in accordance with the Town and Country Planning Act 1990.

Relationship with covenants to build

10–04 A covenant by the tenant with the landlord to complete the erection on the demised land of a building development for uses within specified use classes of the Town and Country (Use Classes) Order, will not be interpreted to mean that the building may be used only for such specified uses during the term, but only that the building must be suitable for such uses (*Ashworth Frazer Ltd v Gloucester City Council (No.2)* [2002] 1 E.G.L.R. 15).

3. ABSOLUTE AND QUALIFIED RESTRICTIONS ON USE

A restriction on the use of property may be absolute or subject to the proviso that the use may not be changed without the landlord's consent. In either case the landlord may withhold his consent arbitrarily (*Guardian Assurance Co Ltd v Gants Hill Holdings Ltd* [1983] 2 E.G.L.R 36; *Pearl Assurance Plc v Shaw* [1985] 1 E.G.L.R. 92). Accordingly, the tenant's adviser should insert a requirement that consent is not to be unreasonably withheld. If the restriction is not absolute the landlord is prohibited by statute from demanding a fine or premium as a condition of consent to a change of use (s.19(3) of the Landlord and Tenant Act 1927). The fine or premium may not be disguised as increased rent or as the introduction of a landlord's break-clause (*Barclays Bank v Daejan Investments (Grove Hall)* [1995] 1 E.G.L.R. 68). **10–05**

However, the landlord will still be entitled to require the payment of expenses incurred in connection with consent to a change of use and a reasonable sum in respect of any damage to or diminution in the value of the demised property or any neighbouring property that belongs to him. If the change of use would involve structural alterations to the property the statute does not apply, and the landlord is free to demand a fine or premium (or increased rent) as a condition of consent to the change of use. A change of use "involves" a structural alteration if the alteration is included in the proposed change of use even if it is not necessary to enable that change to take place (*Barclays Bank v Daejan Investments (Grove Hall)* [1995] 1 E.G.L.R. 68). In practice there are very few changes of use which do not involve some alterations. It then becomes a matter of debate whether or not they are structural. If the tenant wishes to protect himself against such a demand he must stipulate for an express provision that no fine or premium (or increased rent) will be demanded as a condition of consent to a change of use. It is, however, unlikely that a well-advised landlord would agree to such a provision.

Where the lease contains a covenant against changes of use without the landlord's consent, but does not state expressly that the landlord's consent is not to be unreasonably withheld, the question arises whether the landlord has an "absolute right" to refuse to allow the change. The relevance of this is that if the landlord does have an absolute right to refuse to allow the change, but nevertheless allows it, a former tenant or guarantor will not be liable to pay any amount in respect of the covenant to the extent that the amount is referable to the variation (s.18 of the Landlord and Tenant (Covenants) Act 1995). In deciding whether the landlord has an absolute right to refuse to allow a variation, regard must be had to statutory provisions. Bearing in mind that, unless the change of use involves structural alterations, the landlord cannot charge a fine or premium as the price of consent, it is considered that he does not have an absolute right to refuse. Moreover, it is arguable that where the covenant contemplates that consent might be given, and it is in fact given, there is no variation of the lease at all (cf. *Forte & Co v General Accident Life Assurance Co* [1986] 2 E.G.L.R. 115).

10–06 It will usually be in the interests of the landlord if the use of the demised property is capable of being changed with his consent because a greater rent will be payable on a rent review or under a new tenancy granted by the court (see *Plinth Property Investments Ltd v Mott, Hay & Anderson* (1977) 38 P. & C.R. 361, where the rent would have been 50 per cent higher if the use of the property had been capable of being changed). Nevertheless, the landlord may wish to impose limits on the extent to which the use can be changed in order to avoid the impact of the Town and Country Planning Act 1990 or for reasons of estate management. One problem, however, is that "good estate management" is a phrase of no fixed meaning. In order to meet this difficulty the draftsman should consider framing a hybrid covenant which permits changes of use within absolute limits.

One possible compromise is for the clause to prohibit changes of use without the landlord's consent, but not to go on to provide that the landlord's consent may not be unreasonably withheld. This will preclude the landlord from charging a premium for consent to a change of use, but will not be as damaging on the rent review as an absolute covenant (*Forte & Co Ltd v General Accident Life Assurance Co Ltd* [1986] 2 E.G.L.R. 115). The recommendation in The Code for Leasing Business Premises in England and Wales 2007 is that landlord's control over changes of use and alterations should not be more restrictive than is necessary to protect the value, at the time of the application, of the premises and any adjoining or neighbouring premises of the landlord.

Where the clause contemplates that the landlord may consent to a change of use, it is implicit that he will only do so at the request of the tenant (*C&A Pension Trustees Ltd v British Vita Investments Ltd*

[1984] 2 E.G.L.R 75). Thus the landlord will not be able unilaterally to widen the use covenant in order to increase the rent. However, for the purposes of rent review, the question will not usually be whether the landlord has actually permitted a wider use, but what prospects the hypothetical tenant would perceive of obtaining consent to a change (*Tea Trade Properties v CIN Properties* [1990] 1 E.G.L.R. 155).

Some landlords of shopping centres wish to maintain tight control over the permitted use of the trading units, but nevertheless to avoid any diminution in the rental income. The dual objective may be achieved by including in the rent review clause an assumption that the hypothetical lease contains a wider use clause than the actual lease. But since this requires the tenant to pay for a freedom which he has not got, the tenant should not accept an artificial assumption about the permitted use.

However, even where the covenant is a fully qualified one, a landlord who has a rational tenant mix policy and refuses consent on the ground that the proposed change of use would conflict with that policy, will expect that his refusal will be upheld by the courts (*Crown Estate Commissioners v Signet Group* [1996] 2 E.G.L.R. 200; *Chelsfield MH Investments v British Gas* [1995] N.P.C. 169; *Moss Bros Group v CSC Properties* [1999] E.G.C.S. 47). **10–07**

Example 10.2 Hybrid use covenant

The demised property shall not be used otherwise than as a shop nor without the landlord's consent in writing (such consent not to be unreasonably withheld) otherwise than for the sale of [ ].

Example 10.3 Alternative hybrid use covenant

Not to use the demised property except as a shop for the sale of [ ] or for such other goods (not being goods which in the opinion of the landlord would be detrimental to the proper management of the centre) as the landlord may approve in writing.

4. NEGATIVE AND POSITIVE OBLIGATIONS

A tenant's use covenant is usually negative in form (i.e. "not to use the demised property otherwise than as …"). This form of covenant effectively prevents the tenant from carrying on the prohibited use. However, it does not impose on him a positive obligation to use the **10–08** property for any particular use, or indeed at all. Thus, the landlord will have no remedy against the tenant if he allows the property to remain empty. In normal circumstances, this will not concern the landlord, at all events if the tenant remains able to pay the rent; but there are cases in which the interest of the landlord may be seriously affected if the property is unused for business purposes.

Firstly, a positive obligation to use the property for business purposes may help the landlord to prevent a business letting from turning into an assured tenancy. A tenancy cannot be an assured tenancy if it is one to which Part II of the Landlord and Tenant Act 1954 applies (Sch.1, para.4 of the Housing Act 1988). Where a tenancy has once been a tenancy to which Part II of the 1954 Act applies, it ceases to be such a tenancy if the tenant gives up business occupation (*Esselte v Pearl Assurance* [1997] 1 W.L.R. 891).

Secondly, in the case of a shopping centre, an empty unit may have a significant effect on the rental value of other units in the centre, as the traders are reliant on a high pedestrian flow. Thus the landlord may find himself penalised upon his rent review. Although an injunction to compel the tenant to trade is unobtainable (*Co-operative Insurance Society v Argyll Stores (Holdings)* [1998] A.C. 1), a positive obligation will give the landlord a remedy in damages (*Costain Property Development Ltd v Finlay & Co Ltd* [1989] 1 E.G.L.R. 237; *Transworld Land Co v J Sainsbury* [1990] 2 E.G.L.R. 255). If required to enter into a positive covenant the tenant's adviser should ensure that no breach is caused if the unit is closed for repairs, refitting, stocktaking and the like. Where a positive use covenant is imposed on a retailer, it is often argued that this depresses the rent on rent review. In the case of a shopping centre, however, this should not unduly concern the landlord if the rental comparables will themselves come from the centre and are themselves let on similar terms. Moreover, it may fairly be said that in such a case all tenants benefit from the fact that their fellow traders can be compelled to keep open (see *Boots the Chemist v Pinkland* [1992] 2 E.G.L.R. 98).

Thirdly, if the rent is payable on a turnover basis, the landlord will wish to ensure that the maximum amount of revenue is generated.

Fourthly, the landlord may be entitled to capital allowances on the cost of constructing a building or structure if it is or is to be in use for a "qualifying trade" or is to be a qualifying hotel, a qualifying sports pavilion or, in relation to qualifying Enterprise Zone expenditure, a commercial building or structure (s.271 and see ss.274, 279, 280 and 281 of the Capital Allowances Act 2001). But capital allowances may be lost and a balancing charge may become payable if the building ceases to be used for a purpose qualifying for capital allowances (Capital Allowances Act 2001, Chapter 8). However, temporary disuse will not bring these provisions into play (s.285 of the Capital Allowances Act 2001).

Fifthly, under the (now repealed) provisions relating to rating surcharge on unused commercial property, the person entitled to occupy the property became liable to pay a rating surcharge after the property had been unoccupied for more than six months (s.17A of the General Rate Act 1967; suspended by the Rating Surcharge (Suspension) Order 1980 (SI 1980/2015)). Under those provisions, if the occupier failed to pay the surcharge, the rating authority was entitled to register a local land charge for the amount due. When registered, the charge bound not only the occupier's interest but also the landlord's reversion (*Westminster City Council v Haymarket Publishing Ltd* [1980] 1 All E.R. 289). If a surcharge is ever brought back into force, a positive obligation will enable the landlord to forfeit the lease before any liability to pay the surcharge arises.

Where the parties have agreed on a positive use covenant, the obligation to trade or to use premises in a certain way must be clearly expressed. Each covenant must be interpreted in the context of the particular lease, and cases in which particular but dissimilar covenants have been considered are not usually helpful (*Blumenthal v The Church Commissioners for England* [2005] 1 E.G.L.R. 78). The court sometimes holds that what appears on the face of it to be a positive obligation is in fact no more than an "emphatic negative" (*Tea Trade Properties v CIN Properties* [1990] 1 E.G.L.R. 155; *JT Sydenham v Enichem Elastomers* [1989] 1 E.G.L.R. 257; *Montross Associated Investments v Moussaieff* [1990] 2 E.G.L.R. 61). The draftsman should therefore use an expression such as "to keep the demised property open for trading during normal business hours". **10–09**

The tenant must consider what his position is on Sunday trading. Sunday trading is now permitted (Sunday Trading Act 1994). A covenant made before 26 August 1994 which requires the tenant to keep open during normal business hours will not compel him to open on Sundays unless it refers specifically to Sundays. However, this does not apply to covenants entered into or varied after that date. Accordingly normal business hours may now include Sundays. If this is undesirable from the tenant's point of view, Sunday should be excepted from the positive covenant.

Example 10.4 Positive covenant: business use only

(1) To use and occupy the demised property for the purpose of the tenant's business of the sale of [ ] or such other business as may be approved in writing by the landlord and not to use the demised property for any other purpose

(2) To keep the demised property open for business during normal business hours.

Example 10.5 Tenant's proviso to keep open covenant

Provided that:

(1) this covenant shall not apply to Sundays

(2) the tenant is entitled, notwithstanding this covenant:

  (a) to close the demised premises for reasonable annual holidays

  (b) to cease to trade if and so long as the tenant requires to carry out repairs or alterations to the demised property which would be substantially more expensive or cause substantially more inconvenience if carried out while the demised properly remained open for trading and is carrying out such repairs or alterations with all reasonable speed

  (c) to cease to trade for not more than one month on the occasion of the assignment or subletting of the demised property (in either case to a person approved by the landlord)

  (d) to cease to trade if unconditionally required to do so by any regulation or requirement of any competent authority and for as long as an unconditional prohibition on trading remains in force

  (e) to cease to trade if and so long as physically prevented from trading by damage caused by an insured risk.

Example 10.6 Positive covenant: mixed use

To use and occupy the demised property (as to the ground floor and basement) for the sole purpose of the tenant's business of [ ] or such other business as may be approved in writing by the landlord and not to permit any person to sleep or reside there and (as to the upper floors) solely as the residence of the tenant and his household or of a person employed by the tenant and required by the tenant to reside there for the better performance of his duties.

5. Defining the permitted use

In defining the permitted use a great responsibility rests on the tenant's adviser because in most cases the tenant will know with more precision than the landlord what use is intended to be made of the property. The concern of the tenant's adviser is to ensure that the use covenant is sufficiently wide to enable the tenant to carry on his business (taking into account possible changes in the range of the business or the manner in which it is carried on) and to be able to dispose of the lease if necessary or, if the tenant is an investor rather than an occupying tenant, sufficiently wide to enable him to grant occupation leases to a wide class of potential occupiers. If the use covenant is too narrow the tenant's beneficial enjoyment of the property may be hampered, but on the other hand if it is too wide the tenant may be liable to pay a higher rent when the rent is reviewed. It is, as so often, a question of balance. The concern of the landlord will usually be to maximise the earning potential of the demised property while at the same time protecting himself against possible liability to others; and, if he is also interested in other property, protecting the earning potential of that other property. The use covenant should be drawn with those ends in mind. **10–10**

The permitted use may be defined in various ways. Firstly, it may be described by the name of the business which the tenant is to carry on (e.g. "the business of a butcher" or "solicitors' offices"). It will be a question of fact what is included in the permitted use, but it should be noted that the scope of the permitted use will be fixed by reference to the meaning of the description at the time of the demise (see, for example, *St Marylebone Property Co Ltd v Tesco Stores Ltd* [1988] 2 E.G.L.R. 40, and *Joint London Holdings Ltd v Mount Cook Land Ltd* [2005] 3 E.G.L.R. 119, where the user covenant in a long lease granted in 1950 prohibited the use of the premises for the business of "victualler, vintner, tavern keeper, vendor of malt liquor, restaurant or coffee house keeper", without the consent of the landlord). Thus, if the scope of the permitted business changes during the term of the lease it may be that the change will not be permitted under the lease. It is suggested that this difficulty may be overcome by framing the covenant to include a proviso that the permitted use shall extend to such trade or business as is from time to time usually carried on by persons in the named business. This would not however entitle the tenant to use the property for a business which had superseded the named business. Thus a covenant not to use the property otherwise than for the business of a blacksmith would not entitle the tenant to use the property as a motor repair workshop (*St Marylebone Property Co Ltd v Tesco Stores Ltd* [1988] 2 E.G.L.R. 40).

Secondly, the use may be defined by reference to an existing statutory definition; for example, a definition in the Town and Country Planning (Use Classes) Order 1987 (SI 1987/764) as amended by the Town and Country Planning (Use Classes) (Amendment) (England) Order 2005 (SI 2005/84). The advantage of such definition is that a greater flexibility is given to the tenant while at the same time the landlord is able to prevent the development of the demised property. This form of definition is particularly useful where the landlord is not interested in other property and is not, therefore, concerned to prevent competition between his tenants. The draftsman should, however, make it clear whether the permitted use is to be restricted to the use class as defined by the Use Classes Order in force at the time of the demise (*Brewers Company v Viewplan* [1989] 2 E.G.L.R. 133) or whether it is capable of change if amendments are made to the Order during the term. Modern leases usually have a clause that updates legislative references to include later amendments, modifications and re-enactments. If the permitted use is to be frozen in accordance with its meaning at the date that the lease was granted, the Use Classes Order should be specifically excluded from this clause. When the Town and Country Planning (Use Classes) (Amendment) (England) Order came into force on 21 April 2005, Class A3 of the Town and Country Planning (Use Classes) Order 1987 (use for the sale of food or drink for consumption on the premises or hot food for consumption off the premises) was deleted and replaced by new Classes A3, A4 and A5 (A3: restaurants and cafes - sale of food and drink for consumption on the premises; A4: drinking establishments - a public house, wine-bar or other drinking establishment; A5: hot food takeaway - sale of hot food for consumption off the premises). The Order also added use as an internet café to Class A1 (shops), and excluded use of premises as a retail warehouse club, or as a night club from the Principal Order. Corresponding amendments were made to the General Permitted Development Order.

Thirdly, the permitted use may be defined by enumerating the various activities to be carried on in the demised property. This form of definition is more suitable to lettings of shops than other business lettings, although it can be used for lettings of factories. The characteristic of this form of definition is that it regulates the use of the property with more certainty (e.g. "the sale of raw meat, poultry, rabbits and game" rather than "the business of a butcher"). If the landlord wishes to retain strict control over his tenant (as, for example, in a shopping development) this form of definition has much to recommend it. However, the tenant's adviser will in such a case need to take more detailed instructions as to the nature of the business the tenant proposes to carry on. If this form of definition is chosen it should be coupled with the ability to extend the permitted activities with the landlord's consent in order to accommodate unforeseen changes in the business. The draftsman adopting this form of clause should ensure that the landlord's rent will not be adversely affected on review. Sometimes the permitted use is defined as "the tenant's business of ...". This form of definition will restrict the use of the property to the carrying on of a business by the tenant himself and will not permit it to be used for the carrying on of the same business if it is carried on by someone who is not the tenant (cf. *Cramas Properties Ltd v Connaught Fur Trimmings Ltd* [1965] 2 All E.R. 382), unless the expression "tenant" is itself widely defined. This form of definition may be unobjectionable in a short occupation lease where subletting is absolutely prohibited; but in another case its effect might be to destroy the value of the tenant's right to sublet since, because a subtenant is not a tenant, the consent of the landlord to a change of use would have to be obtained on any subletting. **10–11**

From time to time, the description of the permitted trade is prefaced with the epithet "high class". It has been suggested that this phrase is incapable of definition, but that it is possible to categorise an establishment as one which is not high class (*Rossi v Hestdrive Ltd* [1985] 1 E.G.L.R. 50, provision of takeaway food not inconsistent with high class licensed restaurant). However, it has also been suggested that "high class" means "rather much better than average" or "very much better than average" (*Patoner Ltd v*

Lowe [1985] 2 E.G.L.R. 154 at 156L, per Russell J.); and that a "high class" business is one which is respectable (*Ropemaker Properties v Noonhaven* [1989] 2 E.G.L.R. 50). In view of the uncertainty, such phrases are probably best avoided.

10–12 The case of *C&J Clark International Ltd v Regina Estates Ltd* (2003) EWHC 1622, exemplifies the trap a retail tenant may fall into if it simply considers its own specific requirements and does not consider how circumstances may change in the future. The tenant applied for consent to assign to a company whose primary business was the sale of ladies clothes, with the sale of footwear accounting for 25 per cent of its business. The landlord refused consent on the basis that the assignee would use the premises in breach of the user covenant. The lease contained a covenant that the tenant was "not to use or permit to be used the premises except for the permitted use". The "permitted use" was defined as:

> "A retail shop within Class A1 in the Schedule to the Town and Country Planning (Use Classes) Order 1987 for the sale of footwear and as ancillary thereto other items from the range of goods from time to time sold by C&J Clark International Limited and such other merchandise consistent with the use of the premises as a high-class shop that the landlord shall from time to time approve in writing such approval not to be unreasonably withheld or delayed."

The landlord contended that the sale of footwear was the single permitted use and that there were two classes of ancillary use. Accordingly, it submitted that the clause should read:

> "A retail shop within Class A1 in the Schedule to the Town and Country Planning (Use Classes) Order 1987 for the sale of footwear and as ancillary thereto:
>
>> other items from the range of goods from time to time sold by C&J Clark International Limited; and
>>
>> such other merchandise consistent with the use of the premises as a high-class shop that the landlord shall from time to time approve in writing such approval not to be unreasonably withheld or delayed."

The tenant contended that two distinct categories of use were permitted, with one ancillary class applicable to the first category. It read the clause as:

> "A retail shop within Class A1 in the Schedule to the Town and Country Planning (Use Classes) Order 1987 for the sale of:
>
> > footwear and as ancillary thereto other items from the range of goods from time to time sold by C&J Clark International Limited; and
> > such other merchandise consistent with the use of the premises as a high-class shop that the landlord shall from time to time approve in writing such approval not to be unreasonably withheld or delayed."

Neuberger J. held that as a matter of syntax the definition could be read in either way, but that the landlord's construction resulted in the words flowing more naturally to an ordinary speaker of English. Furthermore, if the tenant's interpretation was correct, the second "and" should really have been an "or" because (a) and (b) would be alternatives and the word "and" normally has a conjunctive rather than a disjunctive meaning. The words "such other" before "merchandise" also connected back to the words "other items" earlier in the definition. Accordingly, the tenant's adviser had agreed terms that catered only for the expansion of C&J Clark's own user, and had failed to incorporate an alternative to the sale of footwear by way of a distinct permitted user, rather than as an ancillary user to the sale of footwear.

6. WIDENING A PROHIBITION

A prohibition on a specified use of property can take one of four forms, which are listed below in ascending order of severity: **10–13**

(1) "not to use the demised property otherwise than as";
(2) "not to use or permit the demised property to be used otherwise than as";
(3) "not to use or permit or suffer the demised property to be used otherwise than as";
(4) "the demised property shall not be used otherwise than as."

Form (1) will effectively prohibit the tenant himself from using the demised property for the specified use, but it will not affect the activities of any subtenant or licensee of his.

Form (2) extends the provision wider. A covenant not to permit the carrying on of a prohibited activity will be broken if the prohibited activity is carried on by the covenantor himself (*Oceanic*

Village v United Attractions [2000] 2 W.L.R. 476). The word "permit" also means one of two things: either to give leave for an act that could not be legally done without that leave; or, to abstain from taking reasonable steps to prevent the act where it is within a man's power to prevent it (*Berton v Alliance Economic Investment Co Ltd* [1922] 1 K.B. 742, per Atkin L.J.).

The distinction between a covenant expressed in the active voice, such as "not to use", and a covenant expressed in the passive voice, such as "shall not be used", is well established. It is clear that a tenant who has covenanted not to use premises in a particular way cannot commit a breach of the covenant except by his own act or that of his agent. The same is true of a covenant not to permit. The use in the one case and the permission in the other must be something which can be predicated of the defendant or the defendant's agent. It is not sufficient to show that the premises have been used in a way which would constitute a breach of the covenant; it must further be shown that the use is by the defendant or his agent, or that it is permitted by the defendant or his agent (*Berton v Alliance Economic Investment Co Ltd* [1922] 1 K.B. 742, per Atkin L.J. at p.759, cited with approval in *Earl of Sefton v Tophams Ltd (No.2)* [1967] 1 A.C. 50, and *Roadside Group v Zara Commercial* [2010] 3 E.G.L.R. 41).

Form (3) goes wider still. The word "suffer" is wider than the word "permit" (*Barton v Reed* [1932] 1 Ch. 362), although it is far from clear how much wider. In a residential context, it has been held that a tenant may "suffer" a nuisance even if they have no legal power to prevent it if they have influence and could probably have influenced an abatement of the nuisance (*Courtney Lodge Management Ltd v Blake* [2005] L. & T.R. 2).

Finally, Form (4) is an absolute prohibition. A covenant that something shall not be done on demised property may be broken by an event over which the tenant has no control (*Prothero v Bell* (1906) 22 T.L.R. 370).

7. RESTRICTIONS ON COMPETITION

10–14 Either the landlord or the tenant may wish to restrict the other's right to carry on, or to permit someone else to carry on, a competitive business. Subject to the impact of the Competition Act 1998 in any given factual circumstances, if a landlord or tenant wishes to restrict competition it must be done expressly. In the absence of express provision, or exceptional factual circumstances regarding the terms and background to the lease (*Oceanic Village Ltd v Shirayama Shokusan Co Ltd* [2001] L. & T.R. 35), the landlord will be entitled to let property next door to the demised property to a trade rival of the tenant even if the profitability of the tenant's business is thereby reduced (*Port v Griffith* [1938] 1 All E.R. 295). If the tenant has sufficient bargaining strength he may insist on the landlord entering into a covenant restricting his ability to deal with other property owned by him (*Oceanic Village Ltd v Shirayama Shokusan Co Ltd*, as cited above). Commonly, such a restriction takes the form of a covenant by the landlord "not to let" adjoining property for the purposes of the tenant's business. Such a covenant will be narrowly construed, and the tenant's advisers should ensure that it encompasses all the landlord's property in the vicinity.

> "A covenant not to let other premises for the purpose of trade A does not prohibit a letting for trade B unless the carrying on of trade B can fairly be said to be, or to include, the carrying on of trade A, or, perhaps, a substantial part of it. In deciding this, what matters is the substance: it is not enough merely to establish that there is a minor degree of identity between the types of articles sold in the two trades." (*Rother v Colchester Corp* [1969] 2 All E.R. 600, per Megarry J.).

Moreover, "a covenant not to let premises for a particular purpose is not broken by the use of the premises for that purpose if the lessor has inserted in the lease a prohibition wide enough to prohibit the use. 'Not to let' and 'not to permit the use' are two different concepts" (as cited above). The tenant will, therefore, be better protected if the restriction imposed on the landlord is in the form that adjoining property "shall not be used" for the purpose of the specified business. Where, for example, the covenant does not make the tenant liable for the acts of its subtenant, the scope of the covenant will not be extended by reading in the words contained in s.79 of the Law of Property Act 1925 (*Roadside Group v Zara Commercial* [2010] 3 E.G.L.R. 41).

In defining a prohibited use it should be noted that a covenant prohibiting the carrying on of a specified business will not prohibit the carrying on of a business that overlaps with the specified business to a minor degree (*Lewis (A) & Co (Westminster) Ltd v*

Bell Property Trust Ltd [1940] Ch. 345). Moreover, it has been held that an obligation not to carry on a particular business is not an obligation not to carry on part of that business (*Stuart v Diplock* (1889) 43 Ch. D. 343).

Sometimes the landlord is willing to enter into a restriction on letting where the restriction only applies while the original tenant remains in occupation. Other variants are for the landlord to restrict initial lettings in a shopping centre, to limit the restriction in time to a certain specified period, or to limit the restriction to particular units or sizes of units. These types of restrictions protect the tenant while a shopping centre gets up and running, but leaves the landlord with flexibility in the longer term. The landlord should ensure that ancillary uses in other premises are not prohibited. The draftsman should expressly exclude any units let at the date of the restriction from its ambit. Whilst the existing use of such a unit might not breach the restriction, it may do so in future if the lease of that unit permits a change of use.

(a) The Competition Act 1998

10–15 A restriction on competition must comply with the Competition Act 1998. On 6 April 2011, the Competition Act 1998 (Land Agreements Exclusion Revocation) Order 2011 (SI 2010/1709) ("the 2010 Order"), came into force. As a consequence, all land agreements between undertakings (as defined below) are now subject to Chapter I of the Competition Act 1998 ("the Chapter I prohibition"), whether entered into before or after the commencement of the Act or the 2010 Order.

The Chapter I prohibition is that, subject to certain exemptions (see Schs 1 to 4 of the Act), agreements between undertakings, decisions by associations of undertakings or concerted practices which:

(1) may affect trade within the UK; and
(2) have as their object or effect the prevention, restrictions or distortion of competition within the UK,

are prohibited unless exempt under the Act (s.2(1)). This applies in particular, to agreements, decisions or practices which:

(1) directly or indirectly fix purchase or selling prices or other trading conditions;
(2) limit or control production, markets, technical development or investment;
(3) share markets or sources of supply;
(4) apply dissimilar conditions to equivalent transactions with other trading parties, thereby placing them at a competitive disadvantage;
(5) make the conclusion of contracts subject to acceptance by the other parties of supplementary obligations which, by their nature or according to commercial usage, have no connection with the subject of such contracts (s.2(2)).

It is for the party wishing to rely on exemption to prove that the criteria are satisfied. Parties therefore need to assess whether the criteria apply on a case by case basis. The four cumulative criteria which must be satisfied to qualify for exemption are:

(a) the agreement must contribute to improving production or distribution, or to promoting technical or economic progress;
(b) it must allow consumers a fair share of the resulting benefits;
(c) it must not impose restrictions beyond those indispensable to achieving those objectives;
(d) it must not afford the parties the possibility of eliminating competition in respect of a substantial part of the products in question.

The Chapter I prohibition does not apply to an agreement to the extent it is a planning obligation (Sch.3 para.1 of the Act). This includes planning obligations made under s.106 of the Town and Country Planning Act 1990.

Guidance has been issued by the Office of Fair Trading on the application of the Competition Act to land agreements: "Land Agreements: the application of Competition Law following the revocation of the Land Agreements Exclusion Order" (24 March 2011), OFT 1280a. A land agreement is an agreement between undertakings which creates, alters, transfers or terminates an interest in land, or an agreement to enter into such an agreement, together with any obligation and restriction to which Article 5 applies" (Competition Act 1998 (Land Agreements Exclusion and

Revocation) Order 2004 (SI 2004/1260), Art.3). That includes leases, assignments of leasehold interests and agreements to enter into land transactions. An undertaking is any natural or legal person carrying out commercial or economic activities relating to goods or services, irrespective of that person's legal status (OFT Guidance, paras 2.6–2.9).

The OFT Guidance states that there is no presumption that a restriction in a land agreement is anti-competitive. The Chapter I prohibition is only against agreements that prevent, restrict or distort competition to an "appreciable" extent. The OFT Guidance states that agreements between firms do not appreciably restrict competition if:

- the aggregate market share of the parties to the agreement does not exceed 10 per cent of any of the relevant markets affected by the agreement where the agreement is between competing undertakings (often called "horizontal agreements"), or
- the market share of each of the parties to the agreement does not exceed 15 per cent of any of the relevant markets affected by the agreement where the agreement is made between non-competing undertakings (that is, firms which are neither actual nor potential competitors on any of the markets concerned, which usually means firms operating at different levels of the supply chain) (para.2.13).

In both cases, the thresholds are reduced to five per cent where competition on the relevant market is restricted by the cumulative foreclosure effect of parallel networks of agreements having similar effects on the markets. The OFT Guidance indicates that it is generally unlikely to take action in respect of a land agreement where none of the parties to the agreement has a market share exceeding 30 per cent of the relevant market (para.1.22, and Part 8). In assessing whether a restriction infringes competition law key factors will include the definition of the relevant markets, the parties' position in the markets and the nature of the restriction.

An "exclusivity arrangement" is an example of a potentially relevant restriction. That is where a landowner agrees with a particular type of tenant not to allow another similar type of retailer to operate from one or more sites owned by a landowner. The OFT Guidance includes a number of worked examples, and these presently provide the best guide to practical application (paras 9.37–9.43). If a landlord of a parade of shops enters into an exclusivity agreement with a tenant planning to operate a coffee shop so that other similar coffee shop businesses will not be able to operate from the parade, it will be important to consider whether the relevant market extends beyond the parade so that the tenant may face competition from existing and future coffee shops in the area. The market will comprise all the land or premises which are suitable for use by a coffee shop, café or sandwich bar within the area to which the customer in search of a cup of coffee would be prepared to travel. This type of restriction is thought to be less likely to appreciably restrict competition in the context of a parade of shops than in a large out of town destination shopping centre where the market affected by the exclusivity agreement is likely to be only the market within the shopping centre itself. Any market belonging to a single undertaking and enjoying a captive consumer base is likely to merit careful consideration, for example retail areas at airports or stations and markets requiring specialist premises or land with special characteristics. In analogous cases in a retail context, the OFT has used a catchment area as a pragmatic approximation to geographic market definition. From the customer's perspective, the Guidance states that most retail markets are inherently local if they require a visit to a physical store or outlet. Drive times have been used by the OFT and the Competition Commission to define catchment areas in the following sectors:

(a) cinemas, a 20 minute drive-time catchment area has been used (*Terra Firma Investments (GP) 2 Ltd/United Cinemas International (UK) Ltd and Cinema International Corp (UK) Ltd* (OFT ME/1322/04, January 2005) and *Vue Entertainment Holdings (UK) Ltd/A3 Cinema Ltd* (Competition Commission, February 2006));
(b) supermarkets, a 10 or 15 minute drive-time catchment area has been used for supermarkets of 1400sq m and over, and a 5 or 10 minute drive-time catchment area for supermarkets of under 1400sq m (*Safeway Plc and Asda Group Ltd (owned by Wal-Mart Stores Inc)*; *Wm Morrison Supermarkets Plc; J Sainsbury Plc; and Tesco Plc*: A report on the mergers in contemplation (Competition Commission, August 2003));

(c) sports equipment stores, a 15 minute drive-time catchment areas has been used (*Sports Direct/JJB Sports* (Competition Commission, March 2010)).

In relation to other businesses, such as licensed betting offices, a distance measure has been used to define the catchment area (for example, 400m and 880m distances from the betting office were used in *William Hill Plc/Stanley Plc* (OFT ME/1716/05, August 2005)).

A provision which relates to use is generally unlikely to raise competition issues unless an exclusivity agreement has been entered (OFT Guidance, para.4.30). The commonplace provisions in leases permitting certain uses and prohibiting others are unlikely to infringe Chapter I as they are likely to contribute to the attractiveness of the retail venue to consumers by encouraging a good variety of traders. Accordingly, a landlord is likely to be able to continue to rely upon a tenant mix policy or estate management objectives in considering an application for permission to a change of use. Other provisions which are unlikely to give rise to competition concerns include:

(1) covenants relating to service charges and meeting certain financial criteria; and
(2) restrictions imposed on a tenant regarding alterations, repairs, obstructions to the premises, applications for planning permission, advertisements or hours of use (OFT Guidance, para.4.29).

However, where a land-owner is also active in a related market and seeks to limit the availability of its land to its downstream competitors by restricting the use of its land for a particular purpose, this has the potential to restrict competition. For example, a land owner who operates a number of convenience stores in a particular area may restrict how a tenant of a particular unit may use the premises, by prohibiting the tenant from using the unit as a convenience store, or conversely by providing that it must be used for a particular purpose other than as a convenience store. This has the potential to restrict competition in the related market for convenience stores (OFT Guidance, para.4.12).

An agreement or decision which is prohibited by the Chapter I prohibition is void (s.2(4) of the Competition Act). The compatibility of a land agreement with the prohibition needs to be assessed taking into account present and also possible future circumstances. An agreement which does not infringe the Chapter I prohibition at the time when it is entered into may, subsequently and as a result of change in its economic context, infringe the prohibition and become void and unenforceable. Assessing the possibility of an agreement infringing competition law in the future is important when an agreement can make it more difficult for other businesses to compete effectively in a market. For example, the assessment may be affected by the entry and exit of competitors on that market or the availability of suitable sites for use in that market (OFT Guidance, para.2.18). **10–16**

The court may sever the provisions of an agreement which infringes the Chapter I prohibition. If it does sever the provisions, the other terms of the agreement will remain valid and enforceable (see *Crehan v Courage Ltd; Byrne v Inntrepreneur Beer Supply Co Ltd* [1999] Eul.R 834 at 896E et seq.).

Such covenants are intended to protect the tenant, often an anchor tenant, from competition, and have the potential to foreclose the related market. Whilst potentially anti-competitive if those involved have sufficient market power, it is possible that the arrangement may benefit from an exemption from the Chapter I prohibition if of limited duration, or if the benefits outweigh, or at least match, the negative impact on competition, and if consumers are allowed a fair share of those benefits. The OFT Guidance contains the example of the developer of a new shopping centre who wishes to grant a lease to a major department store [A] as anchor tenant (para.9.20). The developer intends to grant a 25 year lease, with an exclusivity covenant that it will not grant a lease of other premises to a department store competitor. The centre will contain many other small and medium size retailers selling similar products, but no other department store. The great majority of A's customers will come from within 25 minutes drive time of the centre. Within 10 minutes drive there is a town centre. Within 15 minutes drive, an established shopping centre anchored by a department store let to B, a rival of A. The proposed exclusivity covenant in the lease to be granted to A may not be objectionable:

(1) if the shopping centre would not have been built at all if an anchor tenant could not be guaranteed exclusivity, the covenant may be interpreted as pro competitive. That would require consideration of the fact specific barriers to market entry and the possibility of a department store retailer gaining access to the relevant market without the benefit of the restriction;

(2) because there are other established retail centres, including a department store, within the catchment of the new development, and because there are to be many other outlets in the shopping centre, it may be found that the exclusivity covenant does not have an appreciable effect on competition. That would require consideration of the relevant market;

(3) if the covenant did appreciably restrict competition it would be necessary to consider whether it could benefit from exemption. The OFT view is that a covenant for the whole of the 25 year lease is unlikely to be necessary in order to protect A's investment or to ensure the profitability of the shopping centre. The duration of the minimum restriction necessary to provide the required protection would require consideration of the time necessary for the store to achieve a stable revenue and customer base.

A tenant with the benefit of an anti-competition covenant must register that covenant against the landlord's title at the Land Registry. The covenant will then bind the landlord's successors in title and future tenants of other units.

The Groceries Market Investigation (Controlled Land) Order 2010 came into force on 30 April 2010. The Order also prohibits large grocery retailers from entering into restrictive covenants which restrict grocery retailing. The Order applies only to major grocery retailers, and not to independent retailers.

(b) Enforcement

10–17 Where the landlord gives a covenant restrictive of the use of land, it is enforceable not only against an assignee, but also against any other person who is the owner or occupier of the premises to which the covenant relates even though there is no express provision in the tenancy to that effect (s.3(5) of the Landlord and Tenant

(Covenants) Act 1995). If, for example, part or parts of the demised premises were assigned to a different person or persons and one of those persons surrendered their part of the demised premises back to the landlord, the landlord would only be free to use that part of the premises subject to the restriction (*Oceanic Village Ltd v United Attractions Ltd* [2000] 1 E.G.L.R. 148). The effect of s.3(5) has been confined to the premises demised by the lease in question, and has been held not to extend to premises other than those demised by the lease (*Oceanic Village Ltd*, as cited above). It is not possible to contract out of this section (s.25).

In *Williams v Kiley(t/a CK Supermarkets Ltd)* [2003] 1 E.G.L.R. 46, a letting scheme was held to exist where two tenants held adjoining shops under separate leases from the Council, each containing covenants restrictive of user. The covenants were identical in form and carefully constructed to dovetail with the other leases in the group of five shops. They were not directed simply at protecting the interests of the landlord and contained clear evidence of an intention to create reciprocity of obligation. The tenants were, therefore, entitled to enforce the covenants directly between themselves. No arguments were heard on the competition aspects. **10–18**

Example 10.7 Covenant by tenant
That the demised property shall not be used for the purpose of the business of [ ] or for the sale by way of trade or business of any of the following articles namely [ ].

Example 10.8 Covenant by landlord which may infringe the Chapter I prohibition
That no part of the Shopping Centre shall be used for the purposes of the business of a [ ] or for any other business which is likely substantially to compete with the business lawfully carried on in the demised property.

8. COVENANTS ANCILLARY TO USE

In addition to the principal use covenant, it is likely that a number of ancillary covenants will be necessary. **10–19**

(a) Illegal and immoral use

10–20 It seems that there is no implied obligation on the tenant not to use the demised property for an illegal purpose, and it has been held that there is no implied obligation against immoral use (*Burfort Financial Investments Ltd v Chotard* [1976] 2 E.G.L.R. 53, property in Soho used for prostitution). Accordingly, the draftsman should always include such a covenant in the lease. A covenant against immoral use will be construed as prohibiting the kind of conduct that the great majority of people in this country would condemn as being immoral (*London Scottish Properties Ltd v Mehmet* (1970) 214 E.G. 837). It should be noted that, if the tenant is convicted of keeping a brothel, the landlord may require him to assign the lease to a person approved by him, and in default thereof, within three months the court that convicted the tenant may make a summary order for possession (s.35(2) and Sch.1 of the Sexual Offences Act 1956).

(b) Licensing requirements

10–21 In many cases, the carrying on of a business in property may not be lawfully done without a licence. The loss of such a licence may be very serious. Accordingly, the tenant should be required to covenant to do all things necessary to maintain, and from time to time to renew, the licence and to comply with all requirements of the licensing authority. In addition, the draftsman should also consider whether the loss of the licence is a risk against which the tenant ought to be obliged to insure. Special considerations affect property licensed for the sale of intoxicating liquor. The tenant should be required to conduct the business in an orderly manner and to transfer the licence to any assignee and, on termination of the lease, to the landlord's nominee. He should also be required to comply with any undertakings given to the licensing justices, and with any conditions attached to the licence. Example 10.12 and Form 12 contain covenants appropriate to licensed property.

(c) Regulation of competition: exclusivity and dominant position

Article 101 of the Treaty on the Functioning of the European Union (the Lisbon Treaty or "TFEU") (formerly Article 81 of the EC Treaty) and the Chapter I prohibition in the Competition Act 1998 apply to both informal and formal agreements between businesses, whether or not they are in writing, that have as their object or effect the prevention, restriction or distortion of competition. Chapter I and Article 101 provide an identical illustrative list of examples of agreements to which they apply (see para.10–23). The most frequent circumstances in which Article 101 and Chapter I have previously proved relevant in a landlord and tenant context were those of an exclusive purchasing arrangement, such as a "tie" in a lease of a public house or a "solus agreement" in a lease of a petrol station. **10–22**

Chapter I applies where the agreements at issue have an effect on trade within the UK. Article 101 applies where the agreements at issue have an effect on trade between Member States of the EU. Where an agreement affects trade within the UK and trade between the Member States, both Chapter I and Article 101 apply.

The fact that an agreement requires a trader to obtain its supplies from one supplier or contains a minimum purchase obligation does not automatically mean that the agreement infringes Article 101. The question is whether there is significant foreclosure of the market, either to new entrants or by preventing existing competitors from increasing their market shares (*Delimitis v Henninger Bräu AG* (C-234/89) [1991] E.C.R. I-935, 995, [1992] 5 C.M.L.R. 210). Because the court is concerned with the economic effect of an agreement, the agreement may be invalid whilst its benefit is enjoyed by a supplier with a large market share, but may become valid if the benefit of the agreement is assigned to a supplier with a small market share (*Passmore v Morland Plc* [1999] 1 E.G.L.R. 51). If a term of an agreement is void on the ground that it infringes Article 101, the automatic nullity only applies to those elements of the agreement which infringe the Article, unless they are not severable from the remainder of the Agreement, when the whole agreement will fall. Where a beer tie in a lease arguably infringed Article 81, the tie was severed from the remainder of the lease and the tenant was held to remain liable to pay rent and perform the other covenants (*Inntrepreneur Estates v Mason* (1993) 68 P. &

C.R. 53). Where an option to renew a lease was conditional on the purchase by a tenant of a specified quantity of beer, and the condition was invalid, the option without the condition was so different in character to the option with the condition that the whole option was invalid (*Byrne v Tibisco* [1999] 2 E.G.L.R. 145).

Article 101 may be declared inapplicable to certain agreements and concerted practices (Council Regulation 1/2003, which replaced Council Regulation 17/62). Different regulations empower the Commission in the areas defined by them to grant regulations which declare Article 101(1) inapplicable to certain categories of agreements, decisions by associations of undertakings and concerted practices (block exemption regulation). The motor vehicle sector has its own block exemption, for example (Reg.461/2010). The current block exemption is found in Reg.330/210, (which replaced Reg.2790/99/EC). It exempts from Article 101 agreements and concerted practices entered into by two or more undertakings each of which operates, for the purposes of the agreement, at a different level of the production or distribution chain, and relating to the conditions under which the parties may purchase, sell or resell certain goods or services ("vertical agreements"). The exemption applies on condition that the market share held by the supplier does not exceed thirty percent of the relevant market on which it sells the contract goods or services. The exemption does not apply to vertical agreements which contain restrictions which are likely to restrict competition and harm consumers or which are not indispensable to the attainment of "the efficiency-enhancing effects". In particular, vertical agreements containing certain types of severe restrictions of competition such as minimum and fixed resale-prices, as well as certain types of territorial protection, will be excluded from the benefit of the block exemption established by the regulation irrespective of the market share of the under-takings concerned. (Article 10) The Commission may also grant individual exemptions in particular cases. The category of agreements which can be regarded as normally satisfying the conditions laid down in Article 101(3) for exemption include vertical agreements for the purchase or sale of goods or services where those agreements are concluded between non-competing undertakings, between certain competitors or by certain associations of retailers of goods.

10–23 Article 102 of the Treaty on the Functioning of the European Union (formerly Article 82 of the EC Treaty) and the Competition Act

1998 Chapter II prohibit any abuse by one or more businesses of a dominant position within the common market or a substantial part of it in so far as it may affect trade between Member States. Article 82 and Chapter II give examples of specific types of conduct that are particularly likely to be considered as an abuse where the business is in a dominant position. These include:

- imposing unfair purchase or selling prices;
- limiting production, markets or technical development to the prejudice of consumers;
- applying different trading conditions to equivalent transactions, thereby placing certain parties at a competitive disadvantage; and
- attaching unrelated supplementary conditions to contracts.

A dominant position essentially means that the business is able to behave independently of competitive pressures, such as other competitors, on that market (*Hoffman-La Roche v Commission* [1979] E.C.R. 461). A range of factors will be relevant in determining dominance. Previously these have included::

- market share - generally, a business is unlikely to be considered dominant if it has less than 40 per cent;
- the number and size of competitors and the potential for new competitors to enter the market.

Chapter II applies to the abuse of a dominant position which may affect trade within the UK, whereas Article 102 applies to the abuse of a dominant position which may affect trade between Member States. It is possible for both Chapter II and Article 102 to apply where the abuse affects trade within the UK and trade between Member States. The terms of a lease are capable of amounting to an abuse of a dominant position (see *Heathrow Airport v Forte (UK)* [1998] E.G.C.S. 13, where an airport authority granted a lease of buildings within the airport perimeter for use for the provision of in-flight catering at a rent of six percent of turnover, and subsequently removed a similar charge imposed on other in-flight caterers). Whilst circumstances in which one undertaking will enjoy a dominant position in the context of land will be relatively rare, airports and ports are, perhaps, prime examples of situations where the operator will have control over access to facilities (see also, *Purple Parking v Heathrow Airport* [2011] U.K.C.L.R. 492 and *Humber Oils Terminal Trustees v Associated British Ports* [2012] U.K.C.L.R. 71).

(d) Nuisance and annoyance

10–24 It is common to find in leases a covenant against nuisance and annoyance. Such a covenant is of particular importance where the use of the property is otherwise relatively unrestricted. The word "nuisance" is likely to be construed in its technical sense; that is, "an inconvenience materially interfering with the ordinary comfort physically of human existence, not merely according to elegant or dainty modes and habits of living, but according to plain and sober and simple notions among the English people" (*Walter v Selfe* (1851) 4 De G. & Sm. 315), with the proviso that a nuisance in one area may not be a nuisance in another. However, "annoyance" is a wider term than nuisance, and "if you find a thing which reasonably troubles the mind and pleasure, not of a fanciful person or of a skilled person but of the ordinary sensible English inhabitant of a house … that is an annoyance although it may not appear to amount to physical detriment to comfort" (*Tod-Heatly v Benham* (1888) 40 Ch. D. 80). Although couched in the language of the nineteenth century, these definitions are still good law.

If the draftsman wishes to give the landlord a greater control over the activities carried out on the demised property the covenant may be a covenant against anything "which in the opinion of the landlord" amounts to a nuisance or annoyance. Provided that the landlord directs his mind to the particular activity in question and forms his opinion honestly, he need not give the tenant an opportunity to be heard; nor, it seems, need his opinion be reasonable (*Zetland (Marquess) v Driver* [1939] Ch. 1). It is suggested that a covenant of this kind, coupled with a wide permitted use, is less likely to have a detrimental effect on a rent review than a more restricted use and a covenant against nuisance and annoyance of the conventional kind. A covenant against nuisance and annoyance will usually prohibit acts that would be a nuisance or annoyance to owners and occupiers of "adjoining" or "adjacent" or "neighbouring" property. It is a question of construction of the individual lease whether those words are limited to property in physical contact with the demised property. The modern tendency is to construe such words as not being limited to property in physical contact with the demised property (see *Norton v Deane (Charles) Productions Ltd* (1969) 214 E.G. 559, following *Cave v Horsell* [1912] 3 K.B. 533). However, the draftsman should take care to be consistent in his choice of expression because if one expression is found in one part of the lease and another expression in another part the two expressions will be taken to have different meanings (*White v Harrow* [1902] 86 L.T. 4, "adjoining" restricted to property in physical contact because of the use elsewhere of the expression "adjoining or neighbouring").

In addition to a covenant against nuisance and annoyance, a tenant often covenants not to carry on any "offensive" or "dangerous" trade or business on the demised property. It is suggested that in most cases the carrying on of such a trade or business would in any event be a breach of a covenant against nuisance or annoyance. If it would not be a breach of that covenant it is questionable whether it is reasonable to impose on the tenant an additional restriction, breach of which is unlikely to cause the landlord any damage.

The landlord does, however, have a legitimate interest in protecting both the property and himself from liability to deal with pollution or contamination engendered by the tenant's activities. The draftsman should therefore impose on the tenant an obligation to indemnify the landlord against any liability arising as a result of pollution or contamination caused or permitted by the tenant. In addition, the tenant should have a contractual obligation to use the best practicable means to eliminate or minimise environmental pollution or the contamination of the building.

The draftsman should however be aware that if the landlord has **10–25** extensive powers to prevent environmental pollution and fails to exercise them, he may himself be exposed to liability as a person who "permitted" the pollution to take place. If the landlord has powers, it is important that he exercises them.

Example 10.9 Covenant ancillary to use: short form

That the demised property shall not be used:

(1) for any illegal or immoral purpose

(2) in such a way as in the opinion of the landlord causes or might cause nuisance or annoyance to the landlord or to the owners or occupiers of adjoining property.

Example 10.10 Covenant ancillary to use: long form

Not:

(1) to use the demised property for any illegal or immoral purpose

(2) to store in or bring on to the demised property anything which is:

- (a) dangerous
- (b) offensive
- (c) explosive
- (d) radio-active or
- (e) easily inflammable (apart from petrol in the tanks of motor vehicles)

(3) to do anything in the demised property which would invalidate any policy of insurance taken out by the landlord or increase the rate of premium payable for it

(4) to do anything which causes nuisance or annoyance to neighbours or to the landlord

(5) to reside or sleep on the demised property

(6) to hold any political meeting or sale by auction on the demised property

(7) to use any machine on the demised property other than:

- (a) a normal office machine (including computers)
- (b) a machine necessary for carrying out repairs or authorised alterations

(8) to discharge into any pipe or drain any greasy oily or corrosive materials or anything likely to damage or block them or any substance likely to cause harm to humans living organisms or the environment if it escapes into any aquifer

(9) to discharge into the soil or into the air any contaminative harmful noxious or polluting substance

(10) to permit or suffer anything prohibited by the preceding paragraphs of this sub-clause.

Example 10.11 Covenant not to pollute

(1) To use the best practicable means to avoid or minimise pollution or contamination of the environment as a result of anything done or omitted to be done in the demised property during the term

(2) To indemnify the landlord against all costs and liabilities incurred by him in connection with carrying out work to prevent minimise or deal with the effects of pollution or contamination of the environment as a result of anything done or omitted to be done in the demised property during the term
(3) In this clause
  (a) the "environment" means land, water and air
  (b) "pollution" means the release into the environment of substances or articles capable of causing harm to humans or to any living organism supported by the environment or to any building or other structure
  (c) in interpreting "best practicable means"
    (i) "practicable" means reasonably practicable having regard among other things to local conditions and circumstances, to the current state of technical knowledge and to the financial implications
    (ii) the means to be employed include the design installation maintenance of plant and machinery and the design construction and maintenance of buildings
    (iii) the fact that the tenant has a limited interest in the demised property shall be disregarded.

Example 10.12 Covenant relating to licence
To do all things necessary to maintain and from time to time renew the licence for [ ] and not to do or permit or suffer to be done anything which might prejudice the future grant or renewal of such licence (whether to the tenant or any future occupier of the demised property) and to comply with all requirements and recommendations of the licensing authority.

Example 10.13 Landlord's covenant in relation to use of multi-occupied building
The landlord covenants with the tenant:
At the request and cost of the tenant (and subject to the tenant providing adequate security for costs if reasonably required) to enforce those of the covenants or other provisions in the tenancy documents in respect of the residential flats forming part of the Building which if breached would adversely affect the tenant's ability to trade.

9. MODIFICATION OF USE COVENANTS

10–26 Usually a use covenant may only be modified or varied with the consent of the parties to the lease. However, where the lease was granted for a term of more than 40 years and 25 years of the term have expired, the Lands Tribunal has power to discharge any restriction on use (s.84 of the Law of Property Act 1925).

10. RENEWAL LEASES

10–27 On the grant of a new tenancy under Part II of the Landlord and Tenant Act 1954, the restrictions on use will be such as are agreed by the landlord and the tenant or, in default of agreement, such as are determined by the court having regard to the terms of the old tenancy and to all relevant circumstances (s.35 of the Landlord and Tenant Act 1954). The terms of the new tenancy should be such as to enable the tenant to carry on his business as it is at the date of the renewal. They should not be cut down so as to prevent the tenant from carrying on an important part of it (*Gold v Brighton Corp* [1956] 3 All E.R. 442). But the tenant's reluctance to accept a "keep open" covenant was no justification for removing it from the lease (*Boots the Chemist v Pinkland* [1992] 2 E.G.L.R 98). However, the court will not alter the restrictions on use merely to give a rental advantage to one or other party. Thus, where a tenant sought to introduce a restriction on use for the sole purpose of reducing the rent, the court refused to allow the change (*Aldwych Club Ltd v Copthall Property Co Ltd* (1962) 185 E.G. 219). Similarly, where the landlord sought to relax restrictions upon use for the purpose of increasing the rent, the court refused to allow the relaxation (*Clements (Charles) (London) Ltd v Rank City Wall Ltd* [1978] 1 E.G.L.R 47).

CHAPTER 11

GREEN LEASES AND UNDERSTANDINGS

A "green" lease is a standard commercial lease that includes additional clauses intended to encourage collaborative sustainable practices by landlord and tenant. Whether green provisions are contained in the lease itself or in a tenants' handbook or memorandum of understanding, green issues are increasingly likely to impact on the operation of many standard lease clauses, including those governing the levying of service charges and payment for utilities, the carrying out of landlord's and tenant's repairs and decoration, tenant's alterations, user, and waste and re-cycling. **11–01**

Increases in energy costs and the introduction of new legislation and regulations mean that both landlords and tenants will need to consider issues associated with sustainability in the construction and operation of leasehold premises when negotiating a new lease. These issues have been brought to the fore by the Climate Change Act 2008; the Planning and Energy Act 2008; the Energy Act 2011; the Waste Electrical and Electronic Equipment Regulations 2006; the Energy Performance of Buildings (Certificates and Inspections) (England and Wales) Regulations 2007 ("the 2007 Regulations") and the Site Waste Management Plans Regulations 2008. They are likely to become even more important with initiatives such as the European Commission's *Green Public Procurement Handbook* which is designed to help public authorities implement green strategies, including buildings and electricity usage ("Buying Green!", indicative 2nd edn, November 2011). Since 6 April 2012, the 2007 Regulations have been in force for all buildings, and apply whenever a lease is granted.

1. THE PARTIES' INCENTIVES

11–02 For a developer landlord of high quality grade A space, an energy efficient state of the art building will be attractive in a competitive market. There will be savings in operational and maintenance costs and an increased likelihood of tenant retention. For an institutional landlord with space to develop or let, a commitment to carbon reduction and energy efficiency is often a facet of corporate social responsibility as well as a desire to maximise marketability, reduce void space, and to obtain the highest rents. The inclusion of appropriate provisions is likely to be reflected in valuation and on rent review.

A landlord of an existing building seeking to make improvements in order to encourage new lettings will generally have to fund energy improvements itself unless its tenants are willing to contribute to the costs. From the point of view of many landlords the incentive will also be marketability, the potential for a letting at a higher rent and increased energy efficiency.

The impact of environmental regulation is likely to be much more difficult for smaller landlords with existing ageing premises and/or premises in tertiary locations. However, if and when regulations come into force barring the letting or continued letting of premises with poor energy efficiency, the landlord's incentive may become the ability to let its premises at all, or to halt a decline in their value. Regulations under the Energy Act 2011 (s.49) are to be brought into force no later than April 2018, but may be implemented earlier. These may make all F and G rated commercial premises unlettable. The British Property Federation estimate is that this will impact 18 per cent of all commercial properties in the UK (BPF Newsroom, 6 March 2012). In the meantime, it is probable that obsolescence will be accelerated without the implementation of some sustainability measures.

From a tenant's point of view, relevant considerations will include corporate social responsibility, the allocation of costs associated with capital improvements to the landlord's building, the potential for the reduction of its energy bills, and concerns as to whether compliance with green clauses is to be voluntary, or, if mandatory, the consequences of non-compliance. A tenant will also wish to ensure its operational requirements and freedom to assign are not adversely affected.

2. SHADES OF GREEN

There is no standard green lease. Rather there are many shades of green depending upon individual circumstances. The inclusion of green provisions must be based upon the specific design and operational characteristics of the building in question. The landlord's and tenant's agenda for the negotiation and agreement of any green clauses will always be shaped by: **11–03**

- the age of the building;
- the use of the building;
- the size of the building;
- the location of the building;
- the consequential impact on the valuation of the reversion and the level of rent payable;
- the financial constraints of the parties;
- the degree of commitment of landlord and tenant to green issues; and
- existing sustainability commitments.

The resolution of these issues will be more complex in the case of a multi-occupied building or development.

The three common benchmarks are light, mid and dark green leasing provisions. The parties may adopt a combination of these provisions. **11–04**

Light green leasing represents a light touch commitment to the green agenda. The provisions rely on co-operation and voluntary adoption and are not legally binding. The provisions are often contained in a memorandum of understanding entered simultaneously with the lease rather than in the lease itself. The memorandum should cover the practical ways in which the landlord and tenant can work together. Points may include a new building management system, the reduction of emissions, and recycling. The tenant may undertake to do nothing that would prejudice the existing energy performance rating of the building at the date of letting. This may include avoiding or minimising any detrimental effect of tenant's alterations. As a memorandum of understanding will not bind an assignee or subtenant, the parties will need to enter a new memorandum on an assignment or sub-letting.

Mid green leasing provisions are often contained in building or estate regulations or tenants' handbooks, although may also be contained in a memorandum of understanding. The provisions will be legally binding if they are incorporated in the lease by reference: "The Tenant covenants to comply with all reasonable regulations notified by the Landlord from time to time and contained in the Tenants' Handbook". The focus is normally on on-going energy use and commits the parties to aspire to achieve some compliance with environmental targets, and to protect the existing asset rating. A mid green lease may adopt a standalone dispute resolution procedure in the event of non-compliance.

A "dark green" lease is a lease that contains covenants by the landlord and the tenant. The provisions often require a significant level of commitment to environmental issues and relate to actual energy use, including operational obligations, waste, recycling and water efficiency to ensure that such costs are kept low. The lease may include tenant's covenants to act sustainably in terms of repairs, alterations, fit out and, possibly, alienation. These covenants are likely to be reflected in the landlord's covenants in respect of repair and service charge. A dark green lease will require specific consideration in terms of the impact of the parties' obligations on rent review, particularly if the premises are contained in an existing building and the landlord is, effectively, seeking to improve its building at the tenant's cost. A dark green lease may treat the sustainability clauses in the same way as any other obligation and attach the same remedies, but breaches may also be dealt with through alternative dispute resolution rather than forfeiture.

Light green leasing has proved most popular in the market at the date of writing, and provides a useful starting point for collaboration. Subject to the length of the lease, and its protection under the Landlord and Tenant Act 1954 Part II, the rapid and unpredictable nature of change in this area also suggests that the most practical solution may be to include sustainability objectives in a memorandum of understanding or tenants' handbook rather than in the body of the lease. This solution should allow the parties flexibility to adjust their objectives throughout the term of the lease as practices and technology develop and standardise, and external requirements for compliance evolve. A memorandum will often be time limited and can be updated, say every three years, to set new targets and update actions to cut energy use.

In terms of rising energy costs and efficiency ratings, many landlords may seek to remove utility costs from the service charge in future. Tenants will therefore pay for the utilities they use themselves within their premises, sharing the costs for the common parts. If this course is adopted the tenant will not be prevented from using their premises, or illuminating them, 24 hours a day 7 days a week if it so requires or desires, but the tenant will be directly responsible for the relevant costs. In so far as a multi-occupied building or centre was not constructed or developed with the installation of separate metering, a new lease should include provisions for the landlord to obtain access to install separate metering, and, in any case, for the landlord to have the right to periodic access in order to read the meters. It will be necessary to ensure that these costs are passed onto any subtenant. **11–05**

Given the on-going consultations and legislative change in this area, the landlord's draftsman is advised to ensure that any definitions of "energy levels" and "utilities charges" or "utilities costs" are as widely drawn as possible to ensure that all charges, costs and potential climate change levies are included. It is not advisable to refer to current regulations as at the date of grant of the lease. It has also yet to be tested whether any such levy would be held to be recoverable under a clause that the tenant pays "all rates and taxes".

In so far as the landlord may be required to guarantee the performance of equipment or plant, a landlord's adviser may wish to include provision that the standard of performance is only guaranteed during the warranty period or an initial specified time period. This will be unacceptable to a tenant with its own sustainability standards to meet. A compromise may be to permit the landlord to include the amortised cost of replacing equipment that no longer meets standards in its annual operating expenses if reasonable maintenance cannot return the equipment or plant to the required performance level.

The parties' advisers will also wish to have regard to the fact that energy rating standards are evolving. It appears probable that the equivalent standard of building will receive a lower rating in future than that which it would be awarded at present.

Both parties should consider the impact of relevant environmental ratings on rent review. At the date of writing, these are Energy Performance Certificates (EPC's) and the Building Research

Establishment Environmental Assessment Method (BREEAM) performance ratings. Again, it is recommended that the draftsman does not make reference to these specific provisions, but instead refers to "any relevant statutory or regulatory environmental obligations".

A landlord may wish to include an assumption that the premises enjoy a valid EPC (or equivalent replacement) with a specified asset rating, or to include a disregard of a poor EPC rating, or an assumption that the premises enjoy an "excellent" BREEAM (or equivalent replacement) rating. Unless the lease contains "dark green" clauses and such an assumption reflects the parties' agreed targets to improve energy efficiencies, the tenant's adviser should reject such drafting. Even in the case of a dark green lease the tenant's adviser should ensure that the tenant is not penalised for its own efficiencies, and may instead wish to seek the inclusion of an appropriately drafted disregard. A fair compromise is always likely to be that it is assumed that the premises have a rating that is at least as high as at the date the lease was granted.

Example 11.1 Some sample provisions that may be included in a Memorandum of Understanding

1. The tenant is prohibited from doing or omitting to do anything which adversely affects the EPC rating of the Property.
2. The landlord and tenant agree to co-operate to:
    a. reduce carbon emission;
    b. reduce energy consumption and to implement energy saving initiatives;
    c. reduce water consumption and to implement water saving initiatives;
    d. re-use/recycle waste.
3. The landlord and tenant agree to share information with regard to environmental performance and energy consumption.
4. The specified industry accepted methodology [….] should be used to ensure consistency of data.
5. At a minimum annual consumption data should be shared on an annual basis.
6. The landlord and tenant agree to share maintenance records for major services equipment.
7. Named contacts between landlord, tenants and managing agents on environmental performance should be provided and updated as necessary.

8. This Memorandum of Understanding is personal to the parties and will apply only for so long as the landlord owns the Building and the tenant occupies the Premises. If either the landlord or the tenant disposes of its respective interest in the Building or the Premises the landlord or tenant will encourage the new owner or new occupier or subtenant to enter into a similar Memorandum of Understanding.
9. At the end of the period of [3] years the parties will review the progress which has been made in improving the environmental performance of the Premises and Building and will renew this Memorandum for a further period of three years or review and redraft the Memorandum as appropriate.
10. This Memorandum of Agreement is not supplemental or collateral to the Lease.
11. The parties agree that information provided to the other shall be used only for the purposes of implementing this Memorandum of Understanding and for no other purpose whatsoever and that they shall keep all such information confidential and will not disclose it other than if required to do so by law or with the written consent of the other party.

The parties agree that paragraph 11 is legally binding.

Example 11.2 Some sample provisions that may be included in a Tenant's Handbook

1. The landlord is obliged to put in place an environmental management plan.
2. The landlord and tenant are obliged to comply with the environmental management plan.
3. A Building Management Committee shall meet periodically to review the environmental management plan and the date and other information shared by the parties and any changes in law and practice relevant to the performance of the Premises and the Building.
4. The landlord and tenant are obliged to share information with regard to:
    a. environmental performance;
    b. energy consumption;
    c. amounts of waste sent to landfill and recycled;
    d. water consumption;
    e. use of grey water.

5. The purpose of data collection and use of date shall be agreed in advance.
6. Separate metering facilities are to be installed for individual utilities, individual occupiers and special usages (such as data centres).
7. Joint targets shall be set for energy and carbon reductions.
8. Energy consumption shall be reviewed by the landlord annually to identify and address changes in operational performance and to set future objectives.
9. Joint targets shall be set for recycling and the implementation of building waste strategies.
10. Waste date shall be reviewed by the landlord annually to identify and address changes in the amount of waste generated and recycled and to set future objectives.
11. Water consumption date shall be reviewed by the landlord annually to identify and address changes in the amount of water consumed and to identify water loss through leaks and overflows.
12. Cleaning contractors shall be obliged to comply with waste management, energy and water conservation policies.
13. Simple replacement of equipment and plant shall be avoided. Improvements in performance shall be sought in energy rating.
14. Suitability for purpose when altering or replacing equipment and plant shall include consideration of energy consumption, sustainable sourcing and climate change adaptation.
15. Equipment and plant shall be well-maintained and serviced in accordance with manufacturer's recommendations in order to ensure optimum performance.
16. The landlord and tenant shall not, without appropriate consultation, carry out any alterations without prior consideration of the effect of those alterations on the environmental performance of the Premises and the Building.
17. The landlord and tenant shall agree to consider alterations that reduce the need for air conditioning.
18. Where the landlord controls the hours of operation of any heating lighting or air conditioning services to the Premises and Building the tenant shall provide the landlord details of its standard hours of occupancy and its requirements for heating lighting and air conditioning and will notify the landlord in writing of any changes in its requirements.

19. The landlord shall give reasonable consideration to not including reinstatement requirements on the grant of any Licence for Alterations where such alterations improve the environmental performance of the Premises and / or the Building and the landlord considers that it will not need to remove or reinstate the alterations at the end of the term of the Lease.

Example 11.3 Some sample clauses that may be included in a lease

1. The landlord and tenant agree to cooperate in good faith (but without legal obligation) to ensure that the Building and the Premises are run in a manner which is as sustainable and efficient as reasonably possible from time to time in accordance with a Memorandum of Understanding and with the aim of reducing energy and water consumption and waste generation.
2. The landlord shall set up a building management committee comprising a representative of the landlord, the tenant and such other third parties as the parties deem necessary and are involved from time to time in the operation and management of the Building to agree targets and strategy to:
   a. reduce energy use
   b. water consumption
   c. waste management
   d. implement matters recorded in the Memorandum of Understanding.
3. The tenant shall cooperate in the setting up and meeting of the building management committee on the provision of prior reasonable written notice by the landlord.
4. The landlord shall provide to the tenant the data it holds in respect of energy and water use and waste recycling.
5. The tenant shall submit to the landlord sufficient information to enable the landlord to assess the impact of any proposed alteration on the energy efficiency or operational asset or energy rating of the Premises or the Building.
6. The tenant shall provide to the landlord access to date reasonably required for the preparation of an Energy Performance Certificate or equivalent.
7. The tenant shall permit the landlord to enter the premises on reasonable prior written notice for the purposes of compliance

with the Energy Performance Certificate Regulations as shall be in force from time to time or any similar or replacement Regulations and shall cooperate with the landlord's compliance with any such Regulations.

8. The tenant shall permit the landlord to enter the premises on reasonable prior written notice to install metering equipment (including smart metering equipment) on the electricity, water and gas utilities connected to the premises.
9. The tenant shall pay all charges relating to the supply and consumption of Utilities to or at the Premises and also that part of the Landlord's Energy Management Costs which the Landlord's Surveyor reasonably attributes to the Premises.
10. The landlord and tenant will keep the data each discloses confidential and will only use such data for the purposes of ensuring that the Building is run in a sustainable way that minimises its environmental impact.
11. The tenant may with the landlord's prior written consent (not to be unreasonably withheld) carry out non-structural alterations to the Premises intended to reduce energy use water consumption or waste management efficiencies provided such works do not adversely affect the performance of any other plant or equipment or services in the Building or adversely affect the environmental rating of the Building.
12. At the determination of the term the tenant shall not be required to reinstate any lawful tenant's alterations which improve the energy use water consumption or waste management of the Premises.

11–06 The Better Buildings Partnership ("BPP") a group of leading commercial property owners and allied organisations including the British Council for Offices, British Property Federation, Office of Government Commerce and Royal Institution of Chartered Surveyors, was launched in 2007. The BPP first issued Guidance on "Green Leases" in November 2008. The Guidance stated that, as a minimum, provisions regarding sharing of data, establishment of a building management committee and co-operation on reduction strategies should be achievable in all cases. The recommendation was that new leases should include some green clauses.

The BBP has also issued subsequent "Guidance on Green Leases" and the "Green Lease Toolkit" (re-issued 2011). The

Toolkit sets out the provisions which the BBP consider necessary to achieve a minimum level of sustainability for multi-let office buildings, but which will also be appropriate for single occupiers and shopping centres. It includes a model memorandum of understanding to address data sharing, building management committee and system, reinstatement of alterations and co-operation. The Toolkit includes model green lease clauses to address co-operation, an environmental management plan, building management committee, data sharing/metering, flexibility, restrictions on tenant's alterations and landlord's works, dilapidations and rent review. The BPP has also produced "Managing Agents'" and "Transactional Agents'" Toolkits.

CHAPTER 12

ASSIGNMENT AND SUBLETTING

In the absence of an express covenant to the contrary, a tenant is entitled to assign or underlet the demised property without the consent of his landlord. His right to do so may only be cut down by clear words, and a covenant against alienation will usually be construed strictly against the landlord. See *Sweet & Maxwell Ltd v Universal News Service Ltd* [1964] 2 Q.B. 699, where Buckley J. said: **12–01**

> "to underlet is an important incident of the normal property right which belongs to the tenant: it is one of the ways in which he can turn his property to good account and make it profitable to himself; and as a matter of construction I think a tenant should not be treated as deprived of that right except by clear words or circumstances which make it clear that the parties so intended."

The form of covenant now commonly found in a lease of commercial property is a covenant "not to assign underlet or part with or share the possession of the demised property or any part thereof without the consent of the landlord (such consent not to be unreasonably withheld)". Such a covenant is in reality four separate covenants that are not mutually exclusive (*Marks v Warren* [1979] 1 All E.R. 29). Each part of the covenant will be examined in turn, before turning to the interpretation of virtual assignments.

1. NOT TO ASSIGN

A covenant against assignment is not broken by anything short of a legal assignment (*Gentle v Faulkner* [1900] 2 Q.B. 267; *Clarence House Ltd v National Westminster Bank Plc* [2010] 1 W.L.R. 1216 (CA). Thus, a tenant may, without breaking the covenant: underlet the demised property (*Sweet & Maxwell Ltd v Universal News Services Ltd* [1964] 2 Q.B. 699); mortgage it (*Doe d. Pitt v Hogg* (1824) 4 Dowl. & Ry. K.B. 226); allow a potential assignee into **12–02** possession pending completion of the assignment (*Horsey Estate Ltd v Steiger* [1899] 2 Q.B. 79); declare a trust of the lease (*Gentle v Faulkner* [1900] 2 Q.B. 267); or form a partnership that is to use the demised property for the purposes of the partnership business (*Gian Singh & Co v Nahar* [1965] 1 All E.R. 768), provided that no legal assignment takes place (*Langton v Henson* (1905) 92 L.T. 805). In the case of a lease which is registered at Land Registry, the legal estate will not be transferred until the transfer is itself registered. Thus the mere execution of a transfer is not itself an assignment (*Brown & Root Technology v Sun Alliance & London Assurance* [1997] 1 E.G.L.R. 39). Most of these activities will be effectively prohibited by the other parts of the covenant. It is, however, unusual to find in a lease a prohibition on declaring a trust of the lease except in the limited case of a declaration of trust for the tenant's creditors. This is sometimes made a condition of the lease, breach of which entitles the landlord to forfeit. More consideration should be given by draftsmen to specifically prohibiting all declarations of trust (and see the discussion of "virtual assignments" at para.12–07 below). The reason for this suggestion is that if the tenant declares a trust of the lease and the demised property is occupied by a beneficiary under the trust the tenant will continue to be entitled to the protection of Part II of the Landlord and Tenant Act 1954 (s.41), whereas if the occupier is a licensee of the tenant the protection will be lost. If the covenant prohibits holding the tenancy on trust, the tenant's adviser should ensure that an exception is made in the case of joint tenants each of whom has a beneficial interest in the tenancy, because they will automatically hold the tenancy on trust. In addition, where the business to be carried on is operated under franchise, the franchisor may take the lease in its own name and declare a trust of it in favour of itself and the franchisee, thereby preserving security of tenure under the Landlord and Tenant Act 1954. For the tenant, therefore, the ability to hold the lease on trust may be a valuable right.

A rent factoring arrangement may amount to a transfer of an interest in land, and hence a breach of the covenant, because it amounts to an assignment either short term or by way of security only (*John Lewis Properties Ltd v Commissioners of Inland Revenue* [2002] 1 W.L.R. 35 (Ch)).

Finally, where the original tenant has personal rights which determine on assignment, the draftsman may wish to enlarge the definition of an "assignment" so as to include the unconditional execution of a transfer.

2. NOT TO UNDERLET

A covenant against underletting will not prevent the tenant from granting licences of the demised property; nor, it is submitted, will it prevent him from granting equitable leases of it. This may be of great importance to the landlord since a tenant under an equitable underlease will be entitled to the protection of Part II of the Landlord and Tenant Act 1954 (s.69(1); *Brimex Ltd v Begum* [2009] L. & T.R. 21). However, the grant of equitable leases will effectively be prohibited by a covenant against parting with possession of the demised property. Since the decision of the House of Lords in *Street v Mountford* [1985] 2 All E.R. 289, it is now clear that, save in exceptional circumstances, a person having exclusive possession of property for a term at a rent, will be held to be a tenant. The status of possessory licensee has all but disappeared. Accordingly, many more transactions will now fall within the scope of a covenant against underletting. **12–03**

A covenant against underletting the demised property will probably effectively prevent the tenant from mortgaging his lease (*Sergeant v Nash Field & Co* [1903] 2 K.B. 304) because any mortgage of a leasehold interest must be effected either by way of sublease (s.86(1) of the Law of Property Act 1925) or by way of legal charge, which takes effect as if a sublease had been created (s.87(1) of the Law of Property Act 1925), although it was assumed but not decided in *Re Good's Lease* [1954] 1 All E.R. 275 that the grant of a mortgage by way of legal charge was not a breach. Accordingly, where there is likely to be any equity value in the lease (as where the tenant has paid a premium for it or where there is a long interval between rent reviews) the tenant's adviser should ensure that the tenant is entitled to charge the lease. This may be effected either by a proviso to the effect that the grant of a charge over the lease shall not be deemed to be a breach of covenant or by including in the lease a separate covenant dealing with the charging of the lease. Under the Land Registration Act 2002, a mortgage of registered land cannot now be created by demise or sub-demise (s.23(1)). A legal charge must either be created as a charge expressed to be by way of legal mortgage or by charging the estate with the payment of money.

A covenant against underletting "the demised property" will not prevent the tenant from underletting part only of the property (*Cook v Shoesmith* [1951] 1 K.B. 752), unless the underlettings in aggregate amount to an underletting of the whole (*Chatterton v Terrell* [1923] A.C. 578). If the draftsman intends to prevent underlettings of part of the demised property this must be clearly dealt with in the lease. Conversely, where the intention of the parties is that the tenant should be entitled to grant occupation leases of parts of the demised property, which in aggregate will amount to an underletting of the whole, the tenant's adviser should ensure that the tenant is not exposed to forfeiture when the last part of the demised property is underlet. However, a covenant against underletting "any part of the demised property" will prohibit an underletting of the whole (*Field v Barkworth* [1986] 1 E.G.L.R. 46; *Troop v Gibson* [1986] 1 E.G.L.R. 1).

A covenant against underletting will not prevent an undertenant from sub-underletting the demised property since the covenant will bind only the tenant and not an undertenant of his (*Mackusick v Carmichael* [1917] 2 K.B. 581). If the draftsman wishes to prevent sub-underletting it appears that he may do so only by providing that any underlease shall contain a covenant by the undertenant not to underlet without the consent of the superior landlord. If the covenant is expressed to be made with the landlord, he will be able to take the benefit of the covenant even though he is not a party to the underlease (*Amsprop Trading v Harris Distribution* [1997] 2 E.G.L.R. 78), and the tenant will be under an implied obligation not to release the subtenant from the covenant (*Drive Yourself Hire Co (London) Ltd v Strutt* [1954] 1 Q.B. 250 at 270, per Denning L.J.). Some draftsmen prefer to make the implied obligation an express one.

3. NOT TO PART WITH POSSESSION

12–04 A covenant not to part with possession of the demised property is wider than a covenant not to assign or underlet it. It may be broken by allowing a potential assignee into possession of the property pending completion (*Abrahams v MacFisheries Ltd* [1925] 2 K.B.

18) or by letting a wall for advertising (*Heard v Stuart* (1907) 24 T.L.R. 104). However, the word "possession" should be construed strictly and given its natural and technical meaning, and will not be extended to prohibit occupation falling short of possession (*Akici v LR Butlin Ltd* [2006] 1 W.L.R. 201). Where the tenant entitled to possession is alleged to have parted with possession to an entity which is in occupation, the ultimate question is whether the tenant has effectively ceded possession: to that other entity (as cited above, per Neuberger L.J. at 211). A covenant which forbids a parting with possession,

> "is not broken by a lessee who in law retains the possession even though he allows another to use and occupy the premises. It may be that the covenant, on this construction, will be of little value to a lessor in many cases and will admit of easy evasion by a lessee who is competently advised but the words of the covenant must be strictly construed, since if the covenant is broken a forfeiture may result."

(*Lam Kee Ying Sdn Bhd v Lam Shes Tong* [1975] A.C. 247).

Thus the tenant will be entitled to grant licences of the property under which exclusive possession does not pass.

4. NOT TO SHARE POSSESSION

A covenant not to share possession of the demised property should be given its normal, and technically legally correct meaning, and should not be construed to extend to sharing occupation (*Akici v LR Butlin Ltd* [2006] 1 W.L.R. 201). If a tenant is alleged to have breached the covenant against sharing possession, the question will be whether the tenant retained possession in itself alone and merely permitted another to occupy, or whether the company shared possession? (as cited above, per Neuberger L.J. at 210). **12–05**

In an attempt to prevent the "easy evasion" of a covenant against parting with possession of the demised property, draftsmen have included in leases a prohibition against "sharing possession or occupation or use" of the demised property. Such a covenant will effectively prohibit anyone except the tenant from using the property. To part with possession is one thing; it is very much another to permit premises to be occupied by some other company without yielding up possession. In the case of associated companies carrying out industrial work in adjoining premises, it might be **12–06** necessary to conduct a precise analysis of which employees working in which premises were employed by which company before any answer could be made to the question whether there has been a parting with possession (*VT Engineering v Richard Borland & Co Ltd* (1968) 19 P. & C.R. 890, per Megarry J.).

A covenant against sharing possession or occupation or use of the demised property should only reluctantly be accepted by the tenant. In most cases, such a covenant goes beyond what is required for the protection of the landlord, while it imposes unwarranted restrictions on the tenant's ability to use the property. The problem is particularly acute in the case of a letting of a large shop, for in such a case it is becoming usual for the tenant to permit other traders to occupy portions of the shop on a licensed basis. Such occupiers seldom have exclusive possession of the portion of the property that they occupy. There is no precise test of the meaning of sharing occupation: the question is a mixed question of fact and law in any given case (*Mean Fiddler Holdings Ltd v Islington LBC* [2003] 2 E.G.L.R. 7). The fact that the tenant remains exclusively responsible for everything concerned with the premises may be indicative of the fact that it has not shared occupation (as cited above, per Carnwarth L.J. at p.10). The test is whether the third party is operating a separate business on the premises from that carried on by the tenant (as cited above, per Sir Christopher Staughton at p.10). If, the tenant is carrying on a business and the third party participates in that business under the tenant's supervision and control, the third party would not be sharing occupation of the demise premises (as cited above).

Where the tenant is a member of a group of companies, the tenant's adviser should press for the right to share occupation with companies in the same group. However, if such a right is granted, the draftsman should ensure that the share capital of a company in occupation cannot be transferred without the landlord's consent, otherwise the right would be capable of being used to circumvent restrictions on alienation. The landlord may only have been willing to grant the lease initially because the tenant was a member of a certain group.

5. "VIRTUAL ASSIGNMENTS"

Virtual assignments are a relatively new type of commercial arrangement, and the draftsman now needs to consider whether such an arrangement is or is not to be prohibited by adding additional drafting to the standard alienation covenant. A "virtual assignment" is an arrangement under which all the economic benefits and burdens of the relevant lease (including any management responsibilities) are transferred to a third party, but without any actual assignment of the leasehold interest or any change of the actual occupancy of the premises in question. The device has typically been employed by tenants where a lease contains covenants against assigning or parting with the possession of the premises without the consent of the landlord, and there are concerns either that the landlord may be unwilling to consent to a legal assignment because of perceived concerns about the financial standing of an assignee, or the landlord's consent may not be available in advance of the scheduled date for completion of the transaction (per H.H.J. Hodge QC, approved by the Court of Appeal in *Clarence House Ltd v National Westminster Bank Plc* [2010] 1 W.L.R. 1216). A virtual assignment can also be employed as a means of removing lease liabilities from the balance sheet: capital can be released to be better invested elsewhere in the assignor's business; property risks can be transferred to a third party; and the assignor's business liabilities can be more closely aligned with its business needs because surplus property can be vacated before the term ends. **12–07**

In circumstances where premises have already been underlet by a tenant to an undertenant, a "virtual assignment" by the tenant to a third party has been held not to infringe the provisions of a standard alienation covenant (*Clarence House Ltd v National Westminster Bank Plc* [2010] 1 W.L.R. 1216 (CA)). In *Clarence House* the third party was appointed by the tenant as its agent to collect the rent from the undertenant. The tenant also executed a power of attorney appointing the third party as its attorney in respect of dealings with the premises. As a result, the virtual assignment was held not to transfer any proprietary right or interest in the premises. Prior to the assignment, the occupier and person in possession was the undertenant, and not the tenant, and that state of affairs was unaltered following the assignment. The virtual assignment between tenant and third party was intended to pass to the third party, as buyer, all, but *only*, the economic benefits and burdens of the lease. It mimicked the economic effect of a legal assignment without altering the underlying relationship between landlord and tenant or changing the legal position of third parties. The third party was obliged to pay the rent and to manage all the dealings with the landlord and any undertenants as if the premises had been assigned to it. The money received by the third party from the undertenant belonged to it under the virtual assignment, but it collected the rent and received it as agent of the tenant and in the tenant's name, not in its own name. The arrangement was purely contractual and did not amount to a transfer to the third party of the right to receive the rent and profits as envisaged by the definition in s.205 of the Law of Property Act. In any event, an assignment of the rent would not by itself amount to a sharing or parting with possession (*Kataria v Safeland Plc* [1998] 1 E.G.L.R. 39.)

On the basis that the arrangement is founded in contract rather than equity, the virtual assignment has been held not to amount to a declaration of trust of the lease. The cornerstone of the relationship is agency, and not a bare trust (*Clarence House*, as cited above). The third party is obliged to obey the covenants in the lease, including the covenant not to assign without the consent of the landlord. Accordingly, the third party does not have the right to put an end to any "trust" by calling for a transfer of the tenant's legal title. The landlord's cooperation is required, and the tenant cannot compel the landlord to agree to the assignment. The arrangement was also held not to breach the covenant against underletting because no privity of estate was created.

If the landlord wishes to prohibit a virtual assignment or similar arrangement, either absolutely or without landlord's prior consent, the alienation provision in the lease must be drafted in comprehensive terms, and should, for example, specifically prohibit equitable assignments and virtual assignments (being the assignment of any of the benefits or burdens of the lease).

A tenant's adviser may argue that such an arrangement should be of no concern to the landlord because the identity of the tenant remains unchanged. In the event of any breach of covenant, the landlord's rights are against the tenant as before. The landlord's adviser may however argue that it has no interest in dealing with a third party company, and would not have chosen to do so; that the tenant's covenant strength is diminished by the fact that it will not be in receipt of any sub-rents; and that its interest in the premises, and in ensuring compliance with its own covenants and the undertenant's covenants, may also be reduced. It is common, for example, to find that such a provision not only permits the third party to retain the surplus income from the sublease rents, but also to determine the identity of any future subtenants and the terms of any new subletting.

If the alienation covenant does seek to prohibit virtual alienation or any similar arrangements, the tenant's adviser should ensure that, if necessary, the tenant is not prohibited from charging the lease or rent factoring, or, at minimum, that the prohibition is qualified such that it is subject to the landlord's consent not to be unreasonably withheld. However, such drafting remains to be tested by the courts and may, perhaps, be self-defeating. An alternative is to enter a genuine management agreement that does not breach the alienation provisions.

6. ABSOLUTE PROHIBITIONS ON ALIENATION

There is nothing to prevent a landlord from imposing on the tenant **12–08**
an absolute prohibition on alienation of the demised property. Such a prohibition is, however, unusual and should not be accepted by the tenant except in special circumstances. Nevertheless, it is not uncommon for the landlord to impose an absolute prohibition on alienation of part of the demised property. Such a prohibition enables him to prevent the fragmentation of his estate and may be amply justified on management grounds. In the case of a letting of a large building, the draftsman should always consider the desirability of preventing the tenant from underletting small portions of the demised property. This is usually done by imposing an absolute prohibition on underletting or parting with possession of a part of demised property whose area is less than, say, one whole floor or a given number of square metres.

However, where the demised property consists of both business and residential property (e.g. a shop with residential accommodation over) an absolute prohibition on underletting part is highly desirable. If there is no such prohibition, and the tenant underlets the residential part, the residential subtenant may be entitled to the protection of the Housing Act 1988.

Even where the demised property consists entirely of business property (e.g. a large suite of offices) an absolute prohibition on underletting part may be of great advantage to the landlord. For example, if the tenant underlets a small part of the demised property to a business occupier and then vacates the remainder at the expiry date of his lease the occupying subtenant will be entitled under Part II of the Landlord and Tenant Act 1954 to hold over on the terms of his underlease. Thus, the landlord may find that the property is virtually unlettable, and in any event the terms on which the subtenant holds over may be wholly different from the terms of the original lease.

If the landlord imposes an absolute prohibition on alienation it will always be open to him to permit the tenant to deal with the demised property in a particular case. However, he will be entitled to refuse his consent to a proposed transaction without having to be reasonable in his refusal. The reason for this is that no statutory proviso to the effect that consent to an assignment or underletting may not be unreasonably withheld is read into an absolute prohibition on alienation (see, however, the contrary observations in *Property & Bloodstock Ltd v Emerton* [1968] Ch. 94, per Dankwerts L.J.). In addition, an absolute covenant against alienation is not caught by the Landlord and Tenant Act 1988 which applies only to covenants against alienation without consent, where that consent cannot be unreasonably withheld (s.1(1) of the Landlord and Tenant Act 1988). The advantages to the landlord of an absolute covenant are that he is able to regulate precisely who is to occupy the property and on what terms; and if the tenant wishes to leave the property he has the ability, if he chooses, to compel a surrender as the only practical way for the tenant to be rid of his obligations. The disadvantages are that the property is likely to be far less marketable with an absolute covenant against alienation; and even if a tenant is found, the effect of the restrictions on the rent achievable at rent review is likely to be significant.

12–09 However, some of the advantages of an absolute covenant may be preserved if the absolute covenant is confined to certain aspects of alienation. This technique is used more often in relation to prohibitions upon subletting rather than prohibitions on assignment. For example, it will be desirable to prevent the tenant from granting a sublease of property which extends beyond the boundaries of the property comprised in the lease. If the tenant grants such a sublease, the landlord may be unable to determine it under Part II of the Landlord and Tenant Act 1954 (*Nevill Long & Co (Boards) Ltd v Firmenich & Co* (1983) 268 E.G. 572). Equally, an absolute prohibition may be combined with specified exceptions to the general prohibition. Many landlords for example insist upon an absolute covenant preventing the tenant from sub-letting except at a rack rent. If the tenant is prepared to accept such a clause, the tenant's adviser should try to provide for some machinery to determine disputes over value. If, however, the covenant is drafted as a covenant not to underlet at less than the passing rent without the landlord's consent, the provisions of the Landlord and Tenant Act 1988 will apply to the covenant (*Clinton Cards (Essex) Ltd v Sun Alliance & London Assurance Co Ltd* [2002] 3 E.G.L.R. 19).

In many cases landlords have sought to impose a covenant which prohibits subletting at less than the rent payable under the lease, or in the case of a subletting of part, an apportioned part of it. The justification for this is that the landlord wishes his tenant to be in a position to pay the rent, and if the tenant has sublet the whole, and is therefore no longer trading in the property, his ability to pay the rent may be compromised. In addition, in the eyes of many landlords a subletting at less than the passing rent establishes a bad precedent as to value and may have a detrimental effect on the capital investment of the investment. However, from the tenant's point of view such a clause is dangerous. At best, its freedom to sublet is curtailed. In a falling market, it may effectively mean that the property cannot be sublet. Alternatively, the tenant may have to consider the payment of a large reverse premium in order to maintain the rent.

Two contrasting cases demonstrate the lengths to which tenants have gone to attempt to circumvent such a covenant. In *NCR Ltd v Riverland Portfolio No.1 Ltd* [2005] 2 P. & C.R. 27, the lease provided that any underletting had to be at the best rent obtainable in the open market (achieved without payment of a premium or other capital consideration to the grantor), or, if greater, at the then passing rent. The prospective tenant agreed to take an underlease at the passing rent, but required payment of a reverse premium of £3 million in return. It was held that the proposed underletting was within the terms of the headlease and that payment of a genuine reverse premium did not breach those terms. However, in *Allied Dunbar Assurance Plc v Homebase Ltd* [2002] 2 E.G.L.R. 23 the tenant's subterfuge was held to be ineffective. In that case, the lease provided that the rent of any underlease should not be "less than the full market rent reasonably obtainable", and that the underlease should contain covenants in the same terms as the lease. Whilst the draft underlease complied with the terms of the underletting provisions in the lease, a collateral deed was also prepared, personal to the parties, that contained terms by which the tenant would indemnify the subtenant for the difference between the rents under the lease, and also in respect of the more onerous repairing obligations. The Court of Appeal held that the combined effect of the proposed underlease and collateral deed was as if the relevant provisions had been included in the underlease, and that the requirements set out in the lease were not, therefore, fulfilled. It was irrelevant that those undertakings were enforceable only as between the original parties and not as between whoever might be the landlord and the tenant for the time being.

The signs are, however, that landlords' insistence upon a covenant in these terms may be coming to an end. On 20 April 2005, the British Property Federation issued a declaration calling on its members not to use occupational leases that contain a provision requiring sublettings, whether of the whole or part, to be at the higher of the passing or reserved rent and the market rent. The BPF expressed the view that it wished this to become standard industry practice. The declaration was endorsed by a number of leading companies. The Code for Leasing Business Premises in England and Wales 2007 states that if subletting is allowed, the sublease rent should be the market rent at the time of subletting. The Code also recommends that subleases that are to be excluded from the protection of the Landlord and Tenant Act 1954 Part II should not have to be on the same terms as the tenant's lease.

In any case where the landlord and tenant agree that the lease is not to contain provisions requiring sublettings to be at the higher of the passing rent and the market rent and/or on the same terms as the lease, the landlord's advisers should establish that the landlord is not prevented by an existing contractual arrangement, such as with a provider of finance or superior landlord, from agreeing such terms and should, if necessary, seek to vary that existing contract.

The parties should also now consider the potential for the application of the Competition Act 1998 to such "restrictions", and whether they will be classed as "hardcore restrictions". That is restrictions presumed by their very nature to restrict competition to an appreciable extent. The list contained in Article 11 of the European Commission Notice on Agreements of Minor Importance (2001/C 368/07), states that in the case of agreements between non-competitors any restriction which, directly or indirectly, has as its object the restriction of the buyer's ability to determine its sale price is a hard core restriction. Clauses such as covenants restricting the tenant's right to underlet at a rent lower than market rent or to take a premium on the grant of an underlease (or on an assignment on the same basis) may be argued to infringe the provisions of the Act because the price at which the tenant wishes to resell the right to use the premises is the rent for the underletting or the premium that would be payable. In the event that the premises are over rented, for example, the tenant will be prevented from offering the premises at the current market rent, and this will probably prove a substantial impediment to the tenant's ability to dispose of the premises.

Leases may also contain a prohibition on subletting except in units of a given size; or without including provision for rent review at dates which coincide with the review dates under the head-lease; or without including provision that the underlease contains covenants in the "same" terms as the lease (*Allied Dunbar Assurance Plc v Homebase Ltd* [2002] 2 E.G.L.R. 23), or covenants in the "like" terms (*Crestfort Ltd v Tesco Stores Ltd* [2005] 3 E.G.L.R. 25). Covenants will be in "like terms" if they are the same in substance, if not in form, as those in the lease (*Crestfort*, as cited above). In addition, a lease may place a limit on the number of permitted sublettings (e.g. in an office building not more than two per floor). If the landlord wishes to retain tight control over sub-lettings of the demised property, a hybrid covenant of this kind may be the most acceptable compromise between the parties. **12–10**

However, the tenant should be much less willing to accept fetters on his right to assign. An assignment is the primary means by which the tenant is able (in practical terms) to shed his liabilities under the lease and the tenant's adviser should ensure that this will be as easy as possible. It is probably acceptable for the tenant to agree to an absolute prohibition upon assignment except to a respectable and responsible assignee who has entered or is willing to enter into a direct covenant with the landlord to perform the tenant's obligations for the residue of the term. Further restrictions are likely to be required by landlords using the rights introduced by the Landlord and Tenant (Covenants) Act 1995. These are considered below.

Even if an absolute covenant is imposed on the tenant, the landlord is not entitled to withhold permission if to do so would amount to discrimination (s.34 of the Equality Act 2010). The protected characteristics include disability, race and sex (s.4 of the Act).

7. SPECIFIED CIRCUMSTANCES IN WHICH THE LANDLORD MAY WITHHOLD CONSENT OR IMPOSE CONDITIONS

12–11 Where a covenant against assignment, underletting, charging or parting with possession is a qualified covenant, there is a statutory proviso to the effect that consent cannot be unreasonably withheld (s.19(1) of the Landlord and Tenant Act 1927). The parties cannot contract out of this proviso, nor may they themselves determine what is reasonable (see, for example, *Royal Bank of Scotland Plc v Victoria Street (No.3) Ltd* [2009] L. & T.R. 17). The question is objective: is it reasonable to withhold consent? That question will be decided without regard to the interpretation the parties have put on that expression (*Re Smith's Lease* [1951] 1 T.L.R. 254).

However, in the case of a lease which is a new tenancy for the purpose of the Landlord and Tenant (Covenants) Act 1995 (other than a residential lease) there is a major exception to this rule. The parties may enter into an agreement specifying circumstances in which the landlord may withhold consent to an assignment or specify conditions which the landlord may impose on an assignment (s.19(1A) of the Landlord and Tenant Act 1927). The following points should be noted:

(1) The agreement must be one which specifies the circumstances or conditions "for the purposes of this subsection". It is not clear whether the subsection must be expressly mentioned in the agreement, but it is clearly safer if it is.
(2) The agreement will only apply to assignments; it will not apply to underlettings, charges or parting with possession which will continue to be governed by s.19(1) in its unamended form.
(3) The agreement applies only to the giving or withholding of consent by the landlord. It will not apply to the consent of anyone else (e.g. a superior landlord or mortgagee).

Where the parties have entered into such an agreement then the landlord will not be regarded as unreasonably withholding consent to an assignment if he withholds it on the ground that any of the specified circumstances exist and they do in fact exist. It follows therefore that in most cases the specified circumstances must be ones which can be objectively verified. Equally, the landlord will not be regarded as giving consent subject to unreasonable conditions if he gives it subject to the specified conditions. **12–12**

If the specified circumstances or conditions are framed by reference to any matter falling to be determined by the landlord or by any other person for the purposes of the agreement, s.19(1A) will not apply unless:

(a) that person's power to determine the matter is required to be exercised reasonably; or
(b) the tenant is given an unrestricted right to have any such determination referred by a person independent of both landlord and tenant whose identity is ascertainable by reference to the agreement, in which case the agreement must provide for the determination to be conclusive (s.19(1C) of the Landlord and Tenant Act 1927).

It is generally accepted that the person referred to in para.(a) includes the landlord, and is not restricted to the other person previously referred to. The tenant's right to a review must be "unrestricted". This appears to mean that no time limit may be imposed within which the tenant must apply for a review. In practice, most landlords prefer to impose conditions under which the landlord must act reasonably, rather than conditions which give the tenant an unrestricted right of review. If there is a challenge to the landlord's decision, it will be for the court to decide whether he was reasonable.

These important amendments were designed to give landlords more certainty of control over assignments of new tenancies, where the tenant is released from liability on assignment. **12–13**

The tenant may, however, be required to enter into an Authorised Guarantee Agreement under which he guarantees the obligations of the immediate assignee (s.16 of the Landlord and Tenant (Covenants) Act 1995). The detailed requirements of an Authorised Guarantee Agreement are considered in Chapter 14, below.

However, it is important to note that a Guarantee Agreement will only be Authorised if the tenant cannot assign without consent, and consent is given subject to a condition (lawfully imposed) that he is to enter into the Guarantee Agreement. It is considered that such a condition will be lawfully imposed in two cases only:

(1) where it is reasonable to impose the condition; or
(2) where the lease specifies for the purpose of s.19(1A) that on any assignment the tenant is to enter into a Guarantee Agreement.

In order to achieve certainty, the draftsman should make it an express term of any alienation clause that on assignment consent may be given subject to the condition that the tenant enters into a Guarantee Agreement.

The amendments to the law now give landlords the opportunity to specify in advance their requirements for an assignee. In framing those requirements, the draftsman should take account of the changes to the contractual liability of the outgoing tenant. Since the outgoing tenant will be released from liability on assignment, the landlord should be able to withhold consent if rent or service charge is unpaid at the date of the assignment. The draftsman should also consider whether the landlord should be able to withhold consent if there are significant breaches of the tenant's obligations as respects repair and maintenance of the property. Since the tenant is released from liability on assignment, any guarantor for the tenant will also be released (s.24(2) of the Landlord and Tenant (Covenants) Act 1995; and see *Good Harvest Partnership LLP v Centaur Services Ltd* [2010] Ch. 426 and *K/S Victoria Street (a Danish Partnership) v House of Fraser (Stores Management) Ltd* [2012] 2 W.L.R. 470). The draftsman should therefore consider whether the landlord should be able to require a fresh guarantor for the assignee.

It has been confirmed, albeit obiter, that a guarantor of the tenant can be required to guarantee the obligations of the tenant under an Authorised Guarantee Agreement (*K/S Victoria*, as cited above). A condition requiring the guarantor to guarantee the tenant's obligations under an Authorised Guarantee Agreement (sometimes referred to as a "GAGA", a Guarantor's Authorised Guarantee Agreement, or a sub-guarantee) should, therefore, be included. A severability clause could also be included so that the remainder of the alienation clause will stand unaffected if such a condition is subsequently held to be invalid.

It has been suggested that a guarantor could be required to act as a co-guarantor with the tenant under an Authorised Guarantee Agreement (*K/S Victoria*, as cited above, per Lord Neuberger M.R.). However, the validity of such a provision was expressly said to be an issue for future determination, and is therefore not assured.

The potential for intra group assignments causes particular problems for the draftsman if it is the potential guarantor, rather than the would-be tenant, that is actually the company with good covenant strength. A landlord may well wish the parent covenant to enter into the lease as either tenant or joint tenant instead. A further alternative in the event of an intra group assignment is to include provision that such an assignment is only permitted if a valid guarantee is provided from amongst a defined group of guarantors. The risk being that a company's covenant strength might alter between the date of grant of the lease and the date of any assignment.

In evaluating the covenant strength of the assignee some landlords apply rules of thumb in looking at the assignee's pre-tax profits. The landlord now has the opportunity to make explicit in the lease the policy which he adopts. A requirement that the assignee must be of at least the same covenant strength as the tenant will be inappropriate in most situations. However, it may be important for a landlord to make such provision where the return on the letting is specifically linked to the covenant strength of the original tenant.

8. LIMITED LIABILITY PARTNERSHIP ASSIGNEES

Since the coming into force of the Limited Liability Partnerships Act 2000, and given the growing popularity of the Limited Liability Partnership ("LLP"") as a legal entity (e.g. amongst solicitors' and accountants' practices), the draftsman may also wish to consider the possibility of a proposed assignment to a LLP and to impose specific conditions in that regard so as to prevent any argument that what the landlord is requiring is unreasonable. If the LLP is a newly formed LLP such conditions might include personal guarantees from an appropriate number of members of the LLP, say for three **12–14** years until an institutional profits test was satisfied. Alternatives to guarantors include rent deposits, letters of credit and other alternative security arrangements.

In the case of LLPs which have existed for more than seven years, with their annual return and accounts filed at Companies House, an appropriate condition may be that all the assets of the business are required to be held within the LLP. The landlord should also require disclosure of the extent to which members of the proposed LLP assignee are obliged to contribute if the LLP is wound up. Some LLP agreements do not oblige members to contribute in the event of a winding up.

A landlord should also consider the drafting of the forfeiture clause in the lease to ensure that it is drafted in terms which include the entry of the LLP into administration or liquidation.

Example 12.1 Absolute prohibition

Not to assign charge underlet hold upon trust for another share or part with possession or share or part with occupation of the demised property or any part of the demised property.

Example 12.2 Absolute prohibition on alienation of part; qualified as to whole

(1) Not to assign underlet or part with or share possession or occupation of part only of the demised property

(2) Not without the landlord's consent in writing (such consent not to be unreasonably withheld) to assign underlet or part with or share possession or occupation of the demised property as a whole

(3) At his own expense to procure that any assignee of the demised property enters into a direct covenant with the landlord in such form as the landlord may reasonably require to pay the rent and perform the tenant's covenants herein

(4) Within one month after any transfer or devolution of the tenant's interest in the demised property or any part thereof to produce to the landlord's solicitors a copy of the instrument or other document under which it was made or which evidences the same and to pay a reasonable fee for its registration.

Example 12.3 Absolute prohibition subject to exceptions

Not to assign underlet or part with the possession of part only of the demised property except where the proposed transaction consists of an underletting

(1) for a term of less than one year and
(2) at a rent equal to the rack rental value of the part in question at the date of the proposed transaction and
(3) to a person first approved by the landlord (such approval not to be unreasonably withheld).

Example 12.4 Absolute conditions for alienation

Not to assign underlet or part with possession or share occupation of the demised property or any part of it unless each of the following conditions is fulfilled:

(1) in the case of a proposed assignment the proposed assignee has before taking possession entered into a covenant with the landlord to perform and observe the tenant's covenants contained in this lease during the residue of the term
(2) in the case of a proposed underletting:
    (a) the proposed undertenant has before taking possession entered into a covenant with the landlord to perform and observe the tenant's covenants contained in this lease (except the covenant to pay rent) during the term created by the underlease so far as they affect the property to be underlet
    (b) the property to be underlet does not include any property or any right over any property which is not demised by this lease
    (c) the rent to be reserved by the underlease is the best rent reasonably obtainable for such underletting and the underlease provides for the upward revision of the rent payable thereunder at dates coincident with the dates upon which the rent is revised under this lease
    (d) the underlease is otherwise in a form approved by the landlord
(3) if the proposed assignee or undertenant is a limited company (other than a public limited company) two of its directors of satisfactory standing or a public limited company stand surety for the performance of its obligations to the landlord and enter into the standard form of surety covenant from time to time of the landlord

(4) the landlord has consented to the proposed transaction (such consent not to be unreasonably withheld)
(5) the transaction is completed by way of legal assignment or underlease within three months after the giving of consent.

Example 12.5 Circumstances in which the landlord may withhold consent to an assignment: objective criteria
The landlord may withhold consent to an assignment in any of the following circumstances which are specified for the purpose of section 19(1A) of the Landlord and Tenant Act 1927:
(a) at the date of the application for consent to assign the rent is in arrear or any other sums payable by the tenant have not been paid
(b) at the date of the application for consent to assign there are [substantial] breaches of the tenant's obligations as respect the repair and maintenance of the demised property
(c) the proposed assignee has traded for less than three years immediately preceding the date of the application for consent to assign
(d) the proposed assignee has not demonstrated by production of audited accounts that in each of the three years immediately preceding the application for consent to assign it has made annual profits equal to at least three times the rent payable under this lease at that date
(e) the proposed assignee has no assets in England and Wales or no address for service in England and Wales.

Example 12.6 Circumstances in which the landlord may withhold consent to an assignment: subjective criteria
(1) The landlord may withhold consent to an assignment in any of the following circumstances which are specified for the purpose of section 19(1A) of the Landlord and Tenant Act 1927:
    (a) in the landlord's opinion the proposed assignee will be less able than the tenant to pay the rent and perform the tenant's obligations under this lease for the residue of the term
    (b) in the landlord's opinion the use of the demised property proposed by the proposed assignee will reduce the capital value of the landlord's reversion

(c) in the landlord's opinion the substitution of the assignee for the tenant will reduce the capital value of the landlord's reversion

(d) in the landlord's opinion the use of the demised property proposed by the proposed assignee will be detrimental to the mix of uses current in the Centre at the date of the application to assign

(2) If the tenant is aggrieved by any opinion formed by the landlord for the purposes of subclause (1) above he may require it to be reviewed by an independent surveyor appointed (in default of agreement) by the President of the Royal Institution of Chartered Surveyors and the independent surveyor's determination on the review shall be conclusive.

Example 12.7 Conditions which the landlord may impose on assignment

On any assignment the landlord may impose all or any of the following conditions which are specified for the purpose of section 19(1A) of the Landlord and Tenant Act 1927:

(a) a condition that the tenant enters into an Authorised Guarantee Agreement in the form set out in the [ ] Schedule

(b) a condition that any person who guarantees the obligations of the tenant under this lease enters into a guarantee of the tenant's obligations under the Authorised Guarantee Agreement

(c) a condition that the assignee will procure two persons of suitable standing to stand surety for the performance of his obligations under this lease

(d) a condition that the assignee procures a bank guarantee from an English clearing bank for the performance of his obligations under this lease

(e) a condition that the assignee deposits with the landlord an amount equal to one year's rent as security for the performance of his obligations

(f) a condition that the assignee deposits with the landlord an amount equal to the service charge payable during the last finalised service charge year as security for the performance of his obligations

(g) a condition that before completion of the assignment the tenant makes good to the reasonable satisfaction of the landlord any breach of obligation of which the landlord has previously notified the tenant in writing

PROVIDED THAT any provision in this sub-clause which is void pursuant to section 25 of the Landlord and Tenant (Covenants) Act 1995 shall be severed from the remaining provisions and such remaining provisions shall be unaffected.

Example 12.8 Proviso permitting group company sharing
Provided that nothing in the preceding provisions of this subclause shall prevent the tenant from sharing occupation with another member of the same group of companies (as defined in section 42 of the Landlord and Tenant Act 1954 (as amended)) if and so long as that other member remains a member of that group and no relation of landlord and tenant subsists between the tenant and that other member.

Example 12.9 Provisions regulating group company sharing
(1) For the purposes of this sub-clause:
  (a) two bodies corporate are members of the same group if and only if one is for the time being a subsidiary of the other or both are for the time being subsidiaries of a third body corporate
  (b) "subsidiary" has the same meaning as in section 1159 of the Companies Act 2006 (as amended)
(2) Where this lease is vested in [*name of original tenant*] or a body corporate to whom this lease has been lawfully assigned the tenant may by written notice to the landlord bring this subclause into operation until the next lawful assignment of this lease
(3) While this sub-clause is in operation:
  (a) the tenant shall be entitled to share occupation of the demised property with another member of the same group and
  (b) the tenant shall procure that that member does not cease to be a member of that group
(4) This subclause may be brought into operation once only during the tenure of any particular tenant.

Example 12.10 Franchisees
The tenant may share occupation of the demised property with third party franchisees on the basis that the tenant does not grant the franchisee exclusive possession or otherwise transfer or create a legal estate or create the relationship of landlord and tenant.
The tenant acknowledges that if the landlord accepts payment of the rent or any sum due under this Lease from any such franchisee the landlord shall be entitled to assume without further enquiry that the payment has been tendered by the franchisee as agent for the tenant.

9. QUALIFIED COVENANTS AGAINST ALIENATION

Where a lease contains a covenant against assigning, underletting, **12–15**
charging or parting with the possession of the demised property or any part thereof without licence or consent, it is deemed to be subject to a proviso that licence or consent cannot be unreasonably withheld (s.19(1) of the Landlord and Tenant Act 1927). The proviso does not, however, prevent the landlord from requiring payment of a reasonable sum in respect of legal or other expenses incurred in connection with the grant of licence or consent.

In relation to new tenancies for the purposes of the Landlord and Tenant (Covenants) Act 1995, the parties may now specify circumstances in which the landlord may withhold consent to an assignment and conditions which he may impose on assignment. This does not apply to consents to underletting or other forms of disposition, to which s.19(1) will continue to apply with full rigour. In such cases, the parties cannot restrict its operation by stipulating that this or that shall not be deemed to be unreasonable. The question is objective: is it reasonable to withhold consent? That question will be decided without regard to the interpretation the parties have put on that expression (*Re Smith's Lease* [1951] 1 T.L.R. 254).

Many draftsmen seek to widen the ambit of the covenant by providing, for example, that on any assignment or underletting the tenant shall procure that the assignee or undertenant enters into a direct covenant with the landlord to pay the rent and observe the covenants in the lease. Since this is a freestanding obligation which is not dependent on consent, it is an effective obligation (*Vaux Group v Lilley* [1991] 1 E.G.L.R. 60), although if the lease were silent, the landlord probably could not impose such a liability as a condition of consent. Moreover, since the assignee or undertenant will be released from liability on assignment, such a covenant will cease to have effect at that time. In a case where the landlord sought to require a proposed undertenant to enter into a direct covenant with him to observe the terms of the headlease it was held that the landlord was acting unreasonably, although if the proposed transaction had been an assignment he might not have been (*Balfour v Kensington Gardens Mansions Ltd* (1932) 49 T.L.R. 29). The landlord might have been protected if the lease had contained an absolute covenant against underletting except on the terms of the lease. On the other hand, it has been held reasonable for a landlord, who occupies part of a building and lets off another part to a tenant who seeks to underlet, to require the undertenant to enter into a direct covenant with him not to underlet further (*Re Spark's Lease* [1905] 1 Ch. 456). If the draftsman wishes to impose terms on the tenant in relation to alienation of the demised property more extensive than the simple requirement that the landlord's consent be obtained the safer method of doing so is to frame the covenant as an absolute one. See Example 12.4 above. Even so, its effectiveness may yet be open to challenge.

12–16 Although the parties cannot restrict the operation of the proviso they may by agreement restrict the landlord's freedom to withhold his consent. Therefore, where the parties (probably by mistake) provided that the landlord's consent was "not to be withheld in the case of a respectable and responsible person" it was held that once a respectable and responsible person had been produced the landlord could not withhold consent even on reasonable grounds (*Moat v Martin* [1950] 1 K.B. 175). The word "respectable" points to the behaviour of the person, primarily in carrying on his business but probably also in the whole of his external relations (*Willmott v London Road Car Co Ltd* [1910] 2 Ch. 525); while the word "responsible" means able to pay the rent and perform the covenants and other obligations in the lease (*Re Greater London Properties Ltd's Leases* [1959] 1 All E.R. 728). Where the tenant is a company the tenant's adviser should seek to ensure that the lease permits the tenant to share occupation of the property with other members of the same group of companies without the need to obtain the landlord's consent.

Sometimes the statutory proviso is spelt out in the lease. The form of the proviso varies. It may be provided that the landlord may not withhold consent "unreasonably" or "wholly unreasonably" or "without reasonable cause" or "arbitrarily". Whichever of these forms is chosen the effect is the same (*Mills v Cannon Brewery Co Ltd* [1920] 2 Ch. 38).

It is well established that if the tenant's covenant not to assign, etc. without consent is merely qualified by a proviso that the consent of the landlord is not to be unreasonably withheld, there is no implied covenant by the landlord that he will not unreasonably withhold his consent. In the absence of an express covenant to that effect the tenant cannot maintain an action for damages against him for withholding it (*Ideal Film Renting Co Ltd v Neilson* [1921] 1 Ch. 575). The position at common law was altered by the Landlord and Tenant Act 1988. Where a lease contains a qualified covenant against alienation, any person whose consent is necessary to a proposed transaction owes the tenant a duty within a reasonable time:

(1) to give consent except in a case where it is reasonable not to give consent;
(2) to notify the tenant in writing of his decision; and
    (a) if the consent is conditional, of the conditions;
    (b) if the consent is withheld, of the reasons for withholding it (s.1(3) of the Landlord and Tenant Act 1988).

In order to satisfy the duty, any condition imposed must be reasonable (s.1(4)). Section 1(5) of the Act provides:

> "For the purpose of this Act it is reasonable for a person not to give consent to a proposed transaction only in a case where, if he withheld consent and the tenant completed the transaction, the tenant would be in breach of a covenant."

Although the drafting of this subsection is obscure, it is thought that it is not intended to change the law. Accordingly, if the completion of the proposed transaction without the landlord's consent would be a breach of the covenant against alienation, then the landlord will be justified in withholding consent under the Act. In order to appreciate the significance of this it is necessary to appreciate that at common law the effect of an unreasonable withholding of consent is to release the tenant from the covenant to obtain the landlord's consent (*Treloar v Bigge* (1874) L.R. 9 Exch. 151), and consequently alienation in such circumstances would not be a breach of the covenant. Although the Act imposes the burden of proof on the landlord, so that it is for the landlord to show that his consent was reasonably withheld, it has not altered the rule that the landlord need not justify as matters of fact the matters on which he relies, if a reasonable person in his position could have reached the same conclusion as the landlord actually did (*Air India v Balabel* [1993] 2 E.G.L.R. 66; *NCR Ltd v Riverland Portfolio No.1 Ltd (No.2)* [2005] 2 E.G.L.R. 42).

The Act also imposes a duty upon the landlord to notify the tenant of its decision and the reasons for the decision within a reasonable time (s.1(3)). The reasonableness of the landlord's refusal will be judged at the expiry of the reasonable time. When this period expires will depend upon all the circumstances of the case, but, unless the situation is very unusual and complex, the period for response will be relatively short once all the necessary information is available (see, for example, *Go West v Spigarolo* [2003] 2 W.L.R. 986).

If the lease contains a covenant compelling the tenant, in the event of a proposed subletting, to provide the landlord with a certificate setting out the rent and service charges under the proposed sublease, the statutory duty will apply from the date that consent to sublet is requested even if the request does not contain the certificate (*Blockbuster Entertainment v Barnsdale* [2003] EWHC 2912 (Ch). This is also the case if it is stated that the landlord's prior written consent to the form of the draft sublease is required in principle prior to any subletting (*Lombard North Central Plc v Remax Herbarne Ltd* [2009] L. & T.R. 14). Equally, if a fully qualified covenant against underletting is made subject to a proviso that the landlord will be entitled to refuse consent if it is not reasonably satisfied that any proposed underletting is to be at a full rack rent, it will be for the landlord to request details of the rent and to do so clearly and promptly. No requirement will be implied that any request for consent must be accompanied by details of the proposed rent as it is a matter for the landlord as to whether it is concerned with the proposed level of rent and whether it exercises the right granted by the proviso (*Norwich Union Linked Life Assurance Ltd v Mercantile Credit Co Ltd* [2004] 4 E.G. 109).

The Act imposes a statutory duty rather than introducing an implied term into the lease. It follows, therefore, that the original landlord will not be liable for breach of the duty once he has parted with his interest in the property.

A claim that a person has broken the statutory duty is actionable in tort (s.4). In *Mount Eden v Folia* [2003] N.P.C. 95, the judge granted a declaration and awarded indemnity costs against the landlord. In *Design Progression Ltd v Thurloe Properties Ltd* [2005] 1 W.L.R. 1, the Judge ordered compensatory and exemplary damages against the landlord.

The Act does not expressly say whether parties may contract out of the duty, but it is most improbable that they can (cf. *Johnson v Moreton* [1980] A.C. 37). However, it is possible that the landlord could require an indemnity from a third party (e.g. the surety) against his potential liability under the Act.

10. THE FORM OF LANDLORD'S CONSENT

It is commonly stated that the landlord's and superior landlord's consent must be obtained in writing. This is sensible as it avoids the scope for misunderstanding. A requirement that any consent must be embodied in a deed prevents argument that a consent given "in principle" is sufficient (see, for example, *Alchemy Estates Ltd v Astor* [2009] 1 W.L.R. 940 and *British Telecommunications Ltd v Rail Safety & Standards Board Ltd* [2012] L. & T.R. 35). **12–17**

Example 12.11 Tenant's qualified covenants against alienation

(1) The tenant must not assign underlet charge part with possession of or share possession or occupation of the demised property or part of it or hold this lease on trust except to the extent expressly permitted by this clause (save that floating charges granted to a financial institution to secure the financial obligations of the tenant do not require consent)

(2) The tenant may assign the demised property as a whole if (and only if) each of the following conditions is fulfilled:
   (a) the intended assignee:
      (i) is respectable and responsible and
      (ii) enters into a covenant with the landlord to pay the rent and perform the tenant's covenants while he remains tenant

(b) if the landlord reasonably requires two persons of satisfactory standing to stand surety for the performance by the intended assignee of his obligations
(c) the tenant obtains the landlord's written consent (such consent not to be unreasonably withheld)
(d) the assignment is completed and registered within one month after the giving of consent

(3) The tenant may underlet the demised property as a whole if (and only if) each of the following conditions is fulfilled:
(a) the intended undertenant:
(i) is respectable and responsible
(ii) enters into a deed covenanting with the landlord to perform the tenant's obligations contained in the underlease
(iii) enters into a deed covenanting with the landlord to perform the tenant's covenants under this lease (except the covenant to pay rent) while he remains undertenant
(b) the intended underlease:
(i) is granted without a premium and at a rent approved by the landlord (such approval not to be unreasonably withheld)
(ii) contains provisions approved by the landlord (such approval not to be unreasonably withheld) for rent review at the same times and on the same basis as in this lease
(iii) is so far as possible in the same form as this lease (except that all further sub-letting must be prohibited)
(c) the tenant obtains the landlord's written consent (such consent not to be unreasonably withheld)
(d) the underletting is completed and registered within one month after the giving of consent

(4) The tenant may underlet part only of the demised property if (but only if) each of the following conditions is fulfilled:
(a) the intended undertenant:
(i) is respectable and responsible
(ii) enters into a deed covenanting with the landlord to perform the tenant's obligations contained in the underlease

(b) the intended underlease:
  (i) is granted without a premium and at a rent approved by the landlord (such approval not to be unreasonably withheld)
  (ii) contains provisions approved by the landlord (such approval not to be unreasonably withheld) for rent review at the same times and on the same basis as in this lease
  (iii) is so far as possible in the same form as this lease (except that all further subletting must be prohibited)

(c) the grant of the intended underlease will not result in the demised property being occupied in more than three different parts

(d) the property comprised in the intended underlease is either one whole floor of the demised property or a multiple of whole floors (but it may include rights to use car parking spaces and ancillary easements)

(e) the provisions of sections 24 to 28 of the Landlord and Tenant Act 1954 as amended are excluded in relation to the intended underlease

(f) the tenant obtains the landlord's written consent (such consent not to be unreasonably withheld)

(g) the underletting is completed and registered within one month after the giving of consent.

The drafting of the above form could be simplified if "consent" and "approved" were defined terms.

11. THE CODE FOR LEASING BUSINESS PREMISES IN ENGLAND AND WALES 2007

The Code for Leasing Business Premises in England and Wales 2007 contains a number of recommendations. Firstly, that leases should allow tenants to assign the whole of the premises with the landlord's consent not to be unreasonably withheld or delayed. Secondly, that leases should not make reference to any specific circumstances for refusal, although (it is stated) a lease will still be "Code compliant" if it requires that any group company taking an assignment, when assessed together with any potential guarantor, must be of at least equivalent financial standing to the assignor **12–18** (together with any guarantor of the assignor). Thirdly, that Authorised Guarantee Agreements should not be required as a condition of the assignment, unless at the date of the assignment the proposed assignee, when assessed together with any proposed guarantor: (a) is of lower financial standing than the assignor (and its guarantor) or (b) is resident or registered overseas. It is recommended that for smaller tenants a rent deposit should be acceptable.

12. BUILDING LEASES

12–19 If the lease is for more than 40 years and is a building lease (i.e. it is wholly or partially in consideration of the erection or the substantial improvement, addition or alteration of buildings) a further proviso is implied. If such a lease contains a qualified covenant against alienation no consent or licence is required if the transaction in question is effected more than 7 years before the end of the term and written notice of the transaction is given to the landlord within 6 months (s.19(2) of the Landlord and Tenant Act 1927). The proviso does not apply if the landlord is a government department, a local or public authority, or a statutory or public utility company; nor does it apply to mining leases. In addition, if the lease is a new tenancy for the purposes of the Landlord and Tenant (Covenants) Act 1995, and is not a residential lease, the proviso does not apply to assignments. This means that the landlord's consent to an assignment must be obtained, and that the landlord cannot withhold consent except:

(1) on reasonable grounds; or
(2) in circumstances which have been specified in the lease.

But even in relation to a new tenancy the proviso will apply to underlettings.

Where a lease is both a building lease and a rent sharing lease, the draftsman may be faced with a difficulty in ensuring that the tenant is required to keep the property underlet at full market rents. However, s.19(2) of the 1927 Act does not apply to an absolute covenant even if it takes effect only on assignment (*Vaux Group v Lilley* [1991] 1 E.G.L.R. 60). Since s.19(2) does not apply to absolute covenants against alienation, the solution is to create a series of absolute conditions which must be satisfied before a sub-letting takes place, and for which no question of consent arises. Plainly, however, a tenant who carries out substantial building works is unlikely to accept highly onerous restrictions on his right to alienate the property; nor indeed should he.

Example 12.12 Restrictions on alienation in building lease

(1) not to underlet the whole or any part of the demised property:
  (a) at a rent or rents less than the best rent reasonably obtainable for such underletting without a premium but taking into account any rent-free period granted to the undertenant
  (b) without providing for the rent or rents thereby reserved to be increased at intervals of not more that the prescribed number of years to the rack rental value of the property comprised in the underlease at the date of the increase without fine

(2) "the prescribed number of years" means;
  (a) five years or
  (b) such other number of years as the landlord may from time to time prescribe in writing; or
  (c) if the tenant objects in writing within 28 days (time being of the essence) such numbers of years as may be determined by an expert to be appointed by the President for the time being of the Royal Institution of Chartered Surveyors (acting as an expert) having regard to:
    (i) the terms of any existing tenancy of the property to be underlet and the rights (if any) of the undertenant thereof under the Landlord and Tenant Act 1954 as amended from time to time and any other Act of Parliament in respect of that property and
    (ii) market practice current at the time when any such underletting is to take place in relation to property of the same nature as the property to be underlet.

13. REQUIREMENT TO SURRENDER BEFORE ASSIGNING OR SUBLETTING

12–20 Draftsmen have attempted to avoid the effect of the implied proviso that consent to alienation is not to be unreasonably withheld by imposing on the tenant an obligation to offer to surrender his lease before asking for consent. Such an obligation is usually called an "offer back clause". It enables the landlord to control the identity, use and character of the business more tightly than on an application for consent to an assignment or underletting, but without the adverse rental consequences of an absolute prohibition. It is not a usual term "either in the technical or the colloquial sense, and it is a harsh term when applied to a business letting in which considerations of the sale of goodwill may arise" (*Cardshops Ltd v Davies* [1971] 2 All E.R. 721, per Widgery L.J.). The tenant should, therefore, resist the inclusion of such a term.

After some doubt as to the effectiveness of such clauses (*Greene v Church Commissioners for England* [1974] Ch. 467), it has now been established that if the tenant is obliged to offer to surrender before asking for consent to a proposed transaction, the landlord has an absolute discretion to accept or refuse the offer, and the statutory proviso that consent may not be unreasonably withheld never comes into play (*Bocardo SA v S&M Hotels Ltd* [1980] 1 W.L.R. 17). The reason for this is that the offer to surrender is a condition precedent to the right to apply for consent to alienation. This is to be distinguished from the case in which the parties purport to provide for what is or is not a reasonable ground for refusing consent to a transaction once an application for consent has been made. In the latter case, the clause is invalid (*Re Smith's Lease* [1951] 1 All E.R. 346). This is, therefore, a case in which the form of the drafting is crucial.

An offer back clause will be upheld by the court, even in a lease which is protected by Part II of the Landlord and Tenant Act 1954 (*Allnatt London Properties Ltd v Newton* [1981] 2 All E.R. 290). Thus the tenant is required to make the offer to surrender as stipulated in the lease. However, if the landlord accepts the offer, an agreement to surrender will come into existence. If the tenancy is one to which Part II of the Landlord and Tenant Act 1954 applies at the date of the acceptance of the offer, the agreement to surrender will be void and hence unenforceable by either party (*Allnatt London Properties Ltd v Newton* [1984] 1 All E.R. 423; *Ultimate*

Leisure Ltd v Tindle [2008] 1 P. & C.R. DG11). The operation of such a clause may therefore produce a deadlock, in which the tenant is unable to assign, but the landlord is unable to compel a surrender.

If at the date of the landlord's acceptance of the tenant's offer to surrender, the tenancy is not one to which Part II of the Act applies (e.g. the tenant has already moved out) the resulting agreement to surrender will be mutually enforceable.

If the tenancy is "contracted out" of the 1954 Act, the clause will be fully enforceable. This is because an agreement to surrender a tenancy protected by the 1954 Act is only void because it has the effect of precluding the tenant from applying to the court for the grant of a new tenancy (s.38(1) of the Landlord and Tenant Act 1954: *Joseph v Joseph* [1967] Ch. 78). If the tenant cannot make such an application anyway, the agreement to surrender cannot have that effect.

It seems that the operation of an offer back clause will not be affected by s.2 of the Law of Property (Miscellaneous Provisions) Act 1989 (*Spiro v Glencrown* [1991] 2 W.L.R. 931). Thus no special drafting precautions need to be taken in this respect.

The clause may provide that the surrender is or is not to be for consideration. If the clause requires the surrender to be on the same terms as to payment as the proposed assignment or underletting, the tenant will normally suffer no commercial disadvantage in surrendering rather than assigning, and is likely to make the surrender. However, if the surrender is to be for consideration, the landlord should include provision that the tenant is to provide written evidence reasonably satisfactory to the landlord that the terms of the proposed assignment or underletting have been negotiated in good faith and at arms length with the proposed assignee or underlessee, and that such evidence is provided within a prescribed time frame. The tenant will be disadvantaged if the proposed assignment or underletting is part of a group reorganisation, or business assets sale. The tenant's adviser may wish to amend the landlord's clause so that it does not apply to intra-group dealings, although landlords are likely to be concerned that such a concession could be abused if the assignee or underlessee then leaves the group and is sold.

Example 12.13 Requirement to offer to surrender

Not to assign underlet or part with possession of the demised property or any part thereof unless each of the following conditions is fulfilled:

(1) the tenant has offered in writing to surrender this lease to the landlord without consideration at the expiry date of four weeks from such offer

(2) the landlord has not within two weeks of such offer accepted the same

(3) not more than six months have elapsed since the last such offer and then not to assign underlet or part with possession of the demised property or any part thereof without the consent of the landlord (such consent not to be unreasonably withheld).

14. FINES AND PREMIUMS

12–21 Where the lease contains a covenant against alienation without licence or consent, the covenant is deemed to be subject to a proviso that no fine or sum of money in the nature of a fine shall be payable for or in respect of such licence or consent (s.144 of the Law of Property Act 1925). The proviso does not preclude the right to require payment of a reasonable sum in respect of legal or other expense incurred in relation to such licence or consent. More important, the proviso can be excluded by agreement. It may be desirable to exclude the proviso where the lease is a lease of property expected to be sublet on terms that require the subtenants to pay premiums to the tenant. In such a case, if the proviso is not excluded the landlord may find that if the headlease is determined his rental income declines sharply without any capital benefit having being received.

The proviso will prevent the landlord from asking for an increase in the rent as the price of his consent (*Jenkins v Price* [1907] 2 Ch. 229) but it will not prevent him from requiring an assignee to enter into a direct covenant to pay the rent reserved by the lease (*Waite v Jennings* [1906] 2 K.B. 11). If the landlord does demand a fine and the tenant pays it, although not obliged to do so, he may not afterwards recover it from the landlord (*Comber v Fleet Electrics Ltd* [1955] 2 All E.R. 161).

Example 12.14 Simple exclusion of section 144
Section 144 of the Law of Property Act 1925 shall not apply to this lease.

Example 12.15 Exclusion of section 144 where amount of permitted premium is defined
Notwithstanding anything in section 144 of the Law of Property Act 1925 the landlord shall be entitled to require as a condition of the grant of licence to assign or underlet the whole or any part of the demised property the payment by the tenant of an amount equal to one third of any fine or premium payable to the tenant by any proposed assignee or undertenant under the terms of the transaction for which the landlord's licence is sought.

15. COSTS

The draftsman should always impose on the tenant an express obligation to pay the landlord's costs incurred in connection with an application for licence to assign or underlet even if the licence is not in the event granted. This obligation should extend to costs that the landlord reimburses to any superior landlord. Where the court assesses costs which are payable under the terms of a contract, the costs payable under those terms are, unless the contract expressly provides otherwise, to be presumed to be costs which: **12–22**

(a) have been reasonably incurred; and
(b) are reasonable in amount,

and the court will assess them accordingly (CPR Ord.48 r.3). Thus the draftsman should provide that the costs should be paid on an indemnity basis.

Example 12.16 Costs
To pay to the landlord on demand on an indemnity basis the amount of any costs or professional fees incurred by him in connection with any application for any licence required under the terms of this lease (including any costs or fees which are payable by the landlord to any superior landlord) whether or not such licence is in fact granted.

Example 12.17 Costs: fuller version
To pay on an indemnity basis all costs and expenses incurred by the landlord including professional fees (or their equivalent in the case of solicitors or surveyors employed by the landlord) in connection with:

(1) the preparation or service of a schedule of dilapidations or a notice under section 146 of the Law of Property Act 1925
(2) any application made by the tenant for any licence or consent under this lease (even if such licence or consent is not granted or the application is withdrawn)
(3) the preparation and engrossment of this lease and its counterpart.

16. RENEWAL LEASES

12–23 In determining the terms of a renewal lease the court is required to have regard to the changes in the law brought about by the Landlord and Tenant (Covenants) Act 1995 (s.35(2) of the Landlord and Tenant Act 1954). Even so, the court has refused to allow a landlord to impose on a tenant an unqualified obligation to enter into an Authorised Guarantee Agreement on assignment, but instead ordered the tenant to covenant to enter into such an agreement only if it was reasonable to do so (*Wallis Fashion Group v CGU Life Assurance* [2000] 2 E.G.L.R. 49).

Chapter 13

STATUTORY PROTECTION

1. Part II of the Landlord and Tenant Act 1954

If Part II of the 1954 Act applies to a tenancy, four main consequences will follow: **13–01**

(1) the tenancy may not be determined except in accordance with the Act;
(2) even if the tenancy is determined, the tenant will be entitled to apply to the court for the grant of a new tenancy;
(3) the tenant's advisers should consider the impact of the Stamp Duty Land Tax regime where the tenant holds over (see the Guidance provided by the Revenue in SDLTM14060);
(4) if the court is unable to renew his tenancy, or if he makes no such application, he may in some circumstances be entitled to compensation on quitting. Part II of the Landlord and Tenant Act 1954 applies "to any tenancy where the property comprised in the tenancy is or includes premises which are occupied by the tenant and are so occupied for the purposes of a business carried on by him or for those and other purposes" (s.23(1)).

2. Tenancy

The Act applies only to tenancies. Thus if the occupier of business premises is a licensee, the Act will not apply. If the licence is a genuine licence it will be upheld by the court. **13–02**

> "One has first to find out what is the true nature of the transaction and then see how the Act operates on that state of affairs. One should not approach the problem with a tendency to attempt to find a tenancy because unless there is a tenancy the case will escape the effects of the statute."

(*Shell-Mex and BP Ltd v Manchester Garages Ltd* [1971] 1 All E.R. 841, per Buckley L.J.).

In the absence of exceptional circumstances, a contractual arrangement giving exclusive possession to an occupier at a rent will be held to be a tenancy (*Street v Mountford* [1985] 2 All E.R. 289). Accordingly, if the parties wish to create a licence, the draftsman must take care that the licensee does not acquire exclusive possession. This may be achieved by including in the licence terms which are inconsistent with the grant of exclusive possession (provided that the terms are genuine). For example, a term requiring the occupier not to impede the exercise by the owner of the owner's rights of possession and control of the property was held to be fatal to a claim by the occupier to be a tenant (*Shell-Mex and BP Ltd v Manchester Garages Ltd* [1971] 1 All E.R. 841). Similarly, exclusive possession may be negatived where the occupier does not have unlimited use of the property (*Manchester City Council v National Car Parks Ltd* [1982] 1 E.G.L.R 94; *National Car Parks Ltd v Trinity Development Co (Banbury) Ltd* [2002] 2 P. & C.R. 18) or where the owner is entitled to require the occupier to move to different premises (*Dresden Estates Ltd v Collinson* [1987] 1 E.G.L.R. 45). Thus the grant of front of house rights in a theatre was held to amount to a licence (*Clore v Theatrical Properties Ltd* [1936] 3 All E.R. 483). However, where two persons shared the use of a shop, each having a separate counter and using the area between the counters together, it was held that a tenancy had been created (*Piper v Muggleton* [1956] 2 Q.B. 569). Had services been provided by the owner, it is suggested that the result would have been otherwise (cf. *Ross Auto Wash Ltd v Herbert* [1979] E.G.L.R 95). Terms which point towards the grant of exclusive possession include:

(1) the reservation of limited rights of entry (*Facchini v Bryson* [1952] 1 T.L.R. 1386);
(2) an express prohibition against subletting (as cited above);
(3) a covenant for quiet enjoyment (*Addiscombe Garden Estates Ltd v Crabbe* [1957] 1 Q.B. 513);
(4) a proviso for re-entry on breach of obligation (as cited above).

Some of the cases contain detailed analyses of whether terms are more consistent with the grant of a tenancy than a licence. Such analyses should be treated with the greatest caution in the light of the decision of the House of Lords in *Street v Mountford* [1985] 2 All E.R. 289.

In addition, the Act does not apply to the following kinds of tenancy:

A tenancy at will

A tenancy at will may be created by implication (e.g. where the tenant holds over or is let into possession pending negotiations for the grant of a lease or the renewal of a lease) or by express agreement. In neither case will the Act apply (*Wheeler v Mercer* [1957] A.C. 416; *Hagee (London) Ltd v Ericson (AB) and Larson* [1976] Q.B. 209; *Essex Plan Ltd v Broadminster Ltd* [1988] 2 E.G.L.R. 73; *Cameron Ltd v Rolls Royce Plc* [2007] EWHC 546 (Ch). **13–03**

A tenancy granted for a term of years certain not exceeding six months (s.43(3))

This exception will only apply in the case of new businesses. The exception will not apply if the tenant (together with any predecessor of his carrying on the same business) has been in occupation for a period exceeding 12 months (s.43(3)(b)). Note that occupation need not be as tenant. Thus, if the tenant is let into occupation as licensee pending completion of the lease that period of occupation will count towards the 12 months. Equally, if the landlord sells his own business to the tenant, the landlord's occupation may be aggregated with that of the tenant. Where a tenancy is granted for a term of 6 months to a person who begins a new business in the demised property it may be renewed once for a similar term before the Act applies; but the first tenancy must not contain any provision for renewing the term or for extending it beyond 6 months from its beginning, otherwise the Act will apply to it (s.43(3)(a)). Thus, even if the parties contemplate that the tenancy will in fact be renewed the lease itself should be silent on the point. **13–04**

A tenancy granted for a term of years certain (of any length) excluded from the protection of ss.24 to 28 (inclusive) of the Act before the parties become contractually bound (s.38(4))

13–05 A tenancy made for a term certain can be contracted out of the security of tenure of the Act. The term may be for less than one year (*Re Land and Premises at Liss* [1971] Ch. 986) and the terms of the tenancy may include a break clause (*Receiver of Metropolitan Police v Palacegate Properties* [2000] 3 W.L.R. 519). The parties cannot authorise the exclusion of the Act in relation to a periodic tenancy (*Nicholas v Kinsey* [1994] 2 W.L.R. 622). The purported grant of a contracted out lease "for a term from and including 1 January 2003 to 28 September 2004 (hereinafter called "the term" which expression shall include any period of holding over or extension of it whether by statute or at common law or by agreement)" has been held not to be for a term certain, and not therefore capable of contracting out of the protection of the Act, with the consequence that the contracting out order obtained was invalid and the tenant enjoyed the protection of the Act (*Newham LBC v Thomas Van-Staden* [2009] L. & T.R. 5 (C.A.)). As leases normally include an extended definition of "the term" to ensure that all relevant parties remain bound by the provisions of the lease if the tenant remains in occupation after the contractual term has expired, care should be taken to ensure the extended definition refers to "any statutory continuation" rather than to "any period of holding over" if the lease is to be excluded for the protection of the Act, such that there is no doubt that the term remains a term certain.

The procedure for excluding protection

13–06 The procedure for excluding leases and agreements for lease from the security of tenure of the Act is set out in the Regulatory Reform (Business Tenancies) (England and Wales) Order 2003 (SI 2003/3096), and must be complied with before the tenant becomes contractually bound to enter into a new lease. The landlord will serve a prescribed form of notice upon the tenant confirming the new lease is to be excluded from the Act's security of tenure provisions, and the tenant will then sign a declaration confirming it has received the notice and understood its contents. Both the warning notice and declaration are required to be "substantially" in the form prescribed by the Order. Unless the requirements of the Order are met, the agreement to contract out will be void.

The landlord's notice must be served at least 14 days before the date on which the tenant enters the new lease or, if earlier, becomes contractually bound to do so. It is likely that a landlord's notice can be served at any stage once heads of terms have been agreed. The best advice is, however, for a landlord to wait to serve its warning notice until the form of the lease has been fully agreed so that there is no scope for the tenant to challenge the validity of the exclusion once the lease has been granted. Under the old court order procedure, the exclusion order made by the court would remain valid if the parties made minor amendments to the lease between the date of the court order and the eventual grant of the tenancy (*Receiver of Metropolitan Police v Palacegate Properties* [2000] 3 W.L.R. 519), however any material changes to the form of the lease after the order was obtained would invalidate the exclusion. A fresh notice should be served if the lease terms change materially after any notice is served and before the tenant is contractually bound. It is sensible to attach the agreed form of the lease to the landlord's notice, although there is no formal requirement for this to be done.

The landlord's notice must be addressed to the tenant, not the tenant's solicitor. There is no formal requirement for the notice to be dated or signed, but it appears wise to date and sign it to avoid the potential for dispute as to the date the notice was given.

The tenant's declaration must be in the form of a statutory declaration unless the landlord's notice has been served on the tenant 14 days or more before the tenant becomes contractually bound when a non-statutory declaration will suffice (see *The Chiltern Railway Co Ltd v Patel* [2008] 2 E.G.L.R. 33. In practice, it is sensible that all declarations are statutory so that there can be no risk as a result of inadvertent short service, and the parties do not have to delay executing the lease for a further 14 days once the terms have been agreed and the landlord's notice has been served.

There does not appear to be any reason why the tenant's solicitor cannot swear the declaration on the tenant's behalf. The declaration should, however, state that the tenant has personally received and read the landlord's notice. The form of landlord's notice set out in the tenant's declaration must remain uncompleted to comply with the Order.

The exclusion agreement must be contained in the tenancy agreement and the tenancy agreement must also contain a reference to the notice and the declaration. If the tenant's declaration is not made by the tenant personally, additional wording may be included whereby the tenant confirms that the person making the declaration on the tenant's behalf was duly authorised to do so. Additional wording may also be included to confirm whether or not there was an agreement for lease and, if there was, the date.

Agreements for lease should prohibit assignment unless the assignee complies with the contracting out procedure before becoming contractually bound. A fresh warning notice can then be served on the assignee, and the declaration in response obtained, before the assignee becomes contractually bound. Consideration should be given to the service of landlord's warning notices on any guarantors if the lease is to contain a guarantor's put option under which the guarantor will take a new lease in the event of the tenant's default. If no notice is served, the guarantor may later refuse to cooperate with the procedure, or subsequently claim that the procedure was invalid.

Example 13.1 Exclusion of 1954 Act

The Landlord and the Tenant agree that the provisions of sections 24 to 28 (inclusive) of the Landlord and Tenant Act 1954 shall not apply to this tenancy.

The Tenant confirms that before the date of this Lease OR before the Tenant became contractually bound to enter into the tenancy created by this Lease:

The Landlord served on the Tenant a notice in a form complying with Schedule 1 to the Regulatory Reform (Business Tenancies) (England and Wales) Order 2003 dated [ ] in relation to the tenancy created by this Lease; and

The Tenant, or a person duly authorized by the Tenant, made a statutory declaration in reply notice in a form complying with Schedule 2 to the Regulatory Reform (Business Tenancies) (England and Wales) Order 2003 dated [ ] in relation to the tenancy created by this Lease.

The Landlord and the Tenant confirm that there is no agreement to which this Lease gives effect OR The Landlord and the Tenant confirm that the agreement to which this Lease gives effect was made on [ ].

3. IDENTITY OF THE TENANT

(a) Service tenancy

The Act does not apply where the tenancy is granted because the tenant is the holder of an "office appointment or employment" from the landlord, provided that the tenancy determines automatically (or may be determined by the landlord) on the tenant ceasing to hold the office, appointment or employment in question or comes to an end at a time fixed by reference to the tenant ceasing to hold it (s.43(2)). Thus, the Act may be avoided if before the tenancy begins the tenant is given an "appointment" by the landlord. It is thought that the appointment must not only be genuine (see *Teasdale v Walker* [1958] 3 All E.R. 307; *Wang v Wei* (1975) 119 S.J. 492 and *Brumell v Powys CC* [2012] 1 P. & C.R. DG18, where "management agreements" were held to be tenancies) but must also be related to the use the tenant is to make of the property. Thus, it is suggested that a mere agency to sell the landlord's products in the course of the tenant's business does not qualify (Woodfall, *Landlord and Tenant* (looseleaf), para.22.035). The position may be different if the tenant is not permitted to sell anything except the landlord's products (i.e. the property is "tied"). **13–07**

A service tenancy will only escape the Act if it is granted in writing and the written agreement states the purpose for which the tenancy is granted (s.43(2)).

Example 13.2 Statement of purpose of tenancy
It is hereby declared that this tenancy is granted in consequence of the appointment of the tenant by the landlord as [ ] and in order to facilitate the duties of that appointment.

(b) Non-occupying tenant

The Act only applies where the demised property is occupied by the tenant and is so occupied for the purposes of a business carried on by him (s.23(1)). Thus, the Act will not apply where the tenancy is granted to a person who does not occupy the demised property. Where, for example, a business is to be carried on by a limited company, a tenancy granted to a director of the company will not attract the protection of the Act (*Pegler v Craven* [1952] 2 Q.B. 693; *Tunstall v Steigmann* [1962] 2 Q.B. 593), unless the tenancy is **13–08** held on trust for the company (contrast *Palmer v Weaver* (1952) 159 E.G. 141 and *Beech v Bloomfield* (1953) C.L.Y. 1988, both County Court cases). A similar situation arises where a tenancy is granted to a company engaged in franchising. The franchisor tenant will not be in occupation, while the franchisee occupier will not have security of tenure. If the tenancy is held on trust and the demised property is occupied by a beneficiary under the trust who has a right to occupy it by virtue of his beneficial interest (rather than by virtue of a commercial arrangement made between him and his trustee (*Frish v Barclays Bank Ltd* [1955] 2 Q.B. 541)) the beneficiary's occupation will be sufficient to attract the protection of the Act (s.41). It may be that for all practical purposes the Act may be avoided if the tenancy contains an absolute covenant against holding the lease on trust. In those circumstances, if the tenant sets up a claim to hold the tenancy on trust for a business occupier he will simultaneously expose himself to the risk of forfeiture. The tenant would of course have the right to apply for relief against forfeiture.

If the tenancy is granted to a limited company and the demised property is occupied for business purposes by another company that is a member of the same group of companies the Act will apply to the tenancy (s.42).

(c) Joint tenants

13–09 Where a tenancy is granted to joint tenants, all the joint tenants must be parties to any application to the court for the grant of a new tenancy (*Jacobs v Chaudhuri* [1968] 2 Q.B. 470). Thus, it may be that the Act may be avoided if the tenancy is granted to two persons, one of whom will not occupy and who will not join in an application for renewal. Where joint tenants are the sole beneficial owners of the tenancy the court will not compel an unwilling tenant to join with the other in applying to the court (*Harris v Black* (1983) 266 E.G. 628). The position may be different where other beneficiaries are involved or where the unwilling joint tenant is a mere nominee (*Sykes v Land* [1984] 2 E.G.L.R. 8; *Featherstone v Staples* [1985] 1 E.G.L.R. 1. However, the decision in *Jacobs v Chaudhuri* [1968] 2 Q.B. 470 has been reversed in so far as it relates to partnership property (s.41A).

4. NATURE OF THE PROPERTY

The Act applies only where the demised property includes "premises which are occupied by the tenant". Premises are not confined to buildings and may include open land (*Bracey v Read* [1963] Ch. 88). However, a letting of fixtures and fittings is not within the Act (*Mirabeau v Scheckman* (1959) 174 E.G. 39. It has been held that an incorporeal hereditament, such as the right to use a parking space, can constitute premises for the purposes of the Landlord and Tenant Act 1954 s.23, on the ground that a tenant does not have to be physically present in the premises if he is using them in some other way as an incident in the ordinary course or conduct of business life, and provided that the premises are not occupied by another business occupier and are not used for any non-business purpose (see *Pointon York Group Plc v Poulton* [2007] 1 P. & C.R. 6 (CA) where the lease of office premises included the right to use three parking spaces, cf. *Land Reclamation Co Ltd v Basildon DC* [1979] 1 All E.R. 993 and *Jones v Christy* (1963) 107 S.J. 374). The landlord may therefore wish to consider excluding the right to park in any defined spaces from the lease of any other premises to be demised to the tenant, and entering a separate arrangement so that its hands are not tied if it wishes to use the car park in some other way in future (see, for example *Picture Warehouse Ltd v Cornhill Investments Ltd* [2008] 1 E.G.L.R. 29). **13–10**

5. USE OF THE DEMISED PROPERTY

The Act does not apply where the demised property is used for certain specified purposes. **13–11**

(a) Use in breach of covenant

The Act does not apply where the tenant is carrying on a business in breach of a prohibition (however expressed) of use for business purposes (s.23(4)). The prohibition must be a general prohibition, and not a prohibition of use for a specified business or of use for any but the purposes of a specified business. Thus, if the lease contains a covenant "not to use the demised property except for the purpose of a bakery" the Act will continue to apply if the use is changed to use as a butcher's shop. However, the prohibition may **13–12** be a prohibition of use for trade in general or professional use in general. Thus, if the lease contains a covenant "not to use the demised property otherwise than for professional purposes" or "otherwise than as a dentist's surgery", it seems that the Act will not apply if the use is changed to use as the offices of a building society. If the use of the property has been changed in breach of covenant the Act will apply if the immediate landlord or his predecessor in title has consented to the breach, or the immediate landlord has acquiesced in it. Acquiescence is a passive failure to do anything in the face of knowledge of the breach, while consent involves something of a positive nature which amounts to an express affirmation of what is being done (*Bell v Franks (Alfred) and Bartlett Co Ltd* [1980] 1 All E.R. 356). Note that the prohibition must be one that is binding on the tenant. Thus, where a subtenant is let into possession in breach of a covenant against subletting, the subtenant will be entitled to the protection of the Act (*D'Silva v Lister House Development Ltd* [1971] Ch. 17).

(b) Agricultural use

13–13 The Act does not apply to a tenancy of an agricultural holding or to a farm business tenancy (s.43(1)(a)); nor does it apply to a grazing and mowing licence for less than one year; nor to a tenancy approved by the Minister before it was entered into.

(c) Use for mining

13–14 The Act does not apply to a tenancy created by a mining lease (s.43(1)(b)). A mining lease means a lease for mining purposes (defined in s.25 of the Landlord and Tenant Act 1927) and extends to a lease for the extraction of sand and gravel (*O'Callaghan v Elliot* [1966] 1 Q.B. 601).

(d) Licensed premises

13–15 The former exclusion from the protection of the Act in relation to licensed premises was removed in stages by the Landlord and Tenant (Licensed Premises) Act 1990. All tenancies of licensed premises in existence on July 11, 1992 (whenever granted) and all tenancies of such premises granted since July 11, 1989, are capable of qualifying for protection if the ordinary criteria of occupation by the tenant for business purposes are satisfied.

6. EXCLUDING THE RIGHT TO COMPENSATION

If the landlord opposes the renewal of a tenancy on any of the grounds set out in s.30(1)(e), (f) or (g) of the 1954 Act, and no other ground is made out, the tenant will be entitled to compensation on quitting. If the business has been carried on in the property for 14 years the amount of the compensation will be the product of the appropriate multiplier and twice the rateable value of the holding; in all other cases it will equal the product of the appropriate multiplier and the rateable value of the holdings (s.37). The right to compensation may be excluded by agreement where the business has been carried on in the property for less than 5 years preceding the date on which the tenant quits. Occupation by the tenant's predecessors may be aggregated for this purpose provided that the same business has been carried on throughout (s.38(2)). Once the business has been carried on for more than 5 years, the agreement becomes void. **13–16**

At the beginning of a tenancy granted to a tenant who is to begin a new business in the property it will not be known whether an agreement excluding the right to compensation will be effective by the time that the tenant quits. Nevertheless, the draftsman should wherever possible seek to exclude that right. It may be worth doing so in a lease granted for a term exceeding five years just in case the tenant quits before the expiry of the term or there is a change both in the occupier and the business carried on.

Example 13.3 Exclusion of right to compensation
The landlord and tenant hereby agree in so far as they are permitted to do so by section 38(3) of the Landlord and Tenant Act 1954 that the tenant shall not be entitled to compensation under section 37 of that Act on quitting the demised property or any part thereof.

7. PROPERTY WHERE SUBLETTING IS ENVISAGED

Special problems arise where the tenant is expected to sublet the demised property (either in whole or in part). The first question is whether he is protected by the 1954 Act at all. If he sublets on a **13–17** regular basis there is nothing to prevent the sub-letting itself from being a business for the purposes of the 1954 Act (*Bagettes Ltd v GP Estates Co Ltd* [1956] Ch. 290). In most cases the problem will be to determine whether the tenant "occupies" the demised property. Where the subtenant is residential, joint occupation by both tenant and subtenant is possible, although the normal inference will be that the subtenant has exclusive occupation (*Smith v Titanate* [2005] 2 E.G.L.R. 63 (County Court)). Even if the tenant retains possession of the common parts of the property, storage space and temporary voids, that will not be "occupation" for the purposes of the 1954 Act. Equally, the mere fact that the tenant provides furniture for his subtenants will not entitle him to claim to occupy (*Narcissi v Wolfe* [1960] Ch. 10). Where the tenant sublets parts of the property as part of his business, the subtenants will be entitled to the protection of the Act (if they are in occupation) and the tenant will not. The tenant cannot be said to occupy property in respect of which he has granted the right to exclusive possession to another (*Graysim Holdings v P&O Properties* [1994] 4 All E.R. 831).

If the 1954 Act does apply to the letting, the second problem is to anticipate its effect both on the letting itself and on subtenancies. Even if the tenant does not occupy the whole of the demised property for the purposes of the 1954 Act, his tenancy of the whole will nevertheless continue until it is determined in accordance with the provision of the Act (s.24(1)). Once it has been determined, usually by notice served under s.25 of the Act, the tenant will only be entitled to renew his tenancy of the part that he actually occupies (s.32) unless the landlord requires him to take a new tenancy of the whole (s.32(2)).

If the tenant is not entitled to renew his tenancy of the whole of the demised property, the subtenants may nevertheless be entitled to do so. Moreover, if the tenant does not occupy the demised property for the purposes of the Act the subtenancies will nevertheless continue provided that the subtenants are in occupation. Prima facie, the terms on which the subtenancies continue are those agreed between the subtenants and the tenant, not the terms of the agreement between the tenant and the landlord. This may involve a radical change in the terms (*Poster v Slough Estates Ltd* [1969] 1

Ch. 495). It therefore becomes all the more important that the landlord be given the right to approve the terms of any proposed subletting.

8. RESIDENTIAL ACCOMMODATION

In some circumstances, a tenancy of residential accommodation may be protected by the Act. Activities which are merely incidental to residential occupation do not amount to occupation for the purposes of a business although they may properly be described as used for business. The businessman who takes work home in the evening which he does in a study set aside for that purpose may very well be said to be using the premises partly for carrying on business; but he is not occupying the premises for the purposes of a business. It is only if the business activity is part of the reason for and part of his aim and object in occupying the premises that the Act will apply (*Cheryl Investments Ltd v Saldanha* [1979] 1 All E.R. 5). Where the tenant takes a tenancy of residential accommodation for the purpose of providing housing accommodation for his employees, the tenancy will not be protected by the Act unless the occupation of the employees is in furtherance of the business activities (*Chapman v Freeman* [1978] 3 All E.R. 878, as explained in *Linden v DHS* [1986] 1 W.L.R. 164). Thus where a flat let to a medical school was used to house students with a view to fostering a corporate spirit and thereby advance the educational process, the tenancy was protected by the Act (*Groveside Properties Ltd v Westminster Medical School* [1983] 2 E.G.L.R 68), as was a house used by a health authority for housing employees of the National Health Service at a nearby hospital (*Linden v DHS* [1986] 1 W.L.R. 164). **13–18**

Property let for mixed use (i.e. partly for business purposes and partly for residential purposes) will not usually qualify for protection under the Rent Act 1977 (*Henry Smith's Charity Trustees v Wagle* [1989] 1 E.G.L.R. 124). The same approach would probably be adopted under the Housing Act 1988 in relation to assured tenancies.

CHAPTER 14

THE LIABILITY OF SURETIES AND GUARANTORS

The surety's obligation is to make good any default by the tenant. The draftsman's duty is, therefore, to ensure that the liability of the surety is co-extensive with that of the tenant so that the landlord does not find that the surety is unexpectedly released or discharged during the term, or for any period when the guarantee would otherwise remain in place. **14–01**

1. CO-EXTENSIVENESS

In principle, the surety's liability is co-extensive with the tenant's. Under a covenant of guarantee it is the duty of the surety to ensure that the tenant performs his covenants. If the tenant breaks any of his covenants, the breach automatically and instantly places the surety in breach of his own obligations (*Cerium Investments v Evans* (1990) 62 P. & C.R. 203). In addition, the surety usually agrees to indemnify the landlord against losses suffered as a result of the tenant's breach of obligation. This is not a guarantee but an indemnity, and is usually dependent on both a breach and a demand by the landlord for compensation. An obligation to indemnify is not capable of being discharged following an accommodation reached between the landlord and a subsequent holder of the term (*Scottish & Newcastle Plc v Raguz* [2008] 1 W.L.R. 2494 (HL)). **14–02**

If the landlord and tenant agree that the liability of the tenant under the lease and under any Authorised Guarantee Agreement is limited to a partnership's assets (and does not extend to the personal assets of individual partners, present, past or future), the guarantor can take advantage of such a limitation on recoverability against it if the true interpretation of the agreement permits this conclusion, or it is able to rely upon the provisions of the Contracts (Rights of Third Parties) Act 1999 (see, for example, *The Prudential Assurance Co Ltd v Ayres* [2007] 2 E.G.L.R. 31 (Ch)).

Where the tenant is released from liability by the Landlord and Tenant (Covenants) Act 1995, the surety will also be released from liability to the same extent (s.24(2) of the Landlord and Tenant (Covenants) Act 1995). In certain circumstances, the tenant may be required to enter into an Authorised Guarantee Agreement guaranteeing his immediate assignee's liabilities under the lease. The surety's obligation should require the surety to guarantee the tenant's liabilities under an Authorised Guarantee Agreement as well as his liabilities under the lease (see *K/S Victoria Street v House of Fraser (Stores Management) Ltd* [2012] 2 W.L.R. 470, where this sub-guarantee arrangement was considered, albeit obiter). This is of real importance where the tenant itself has no covenant strength with the result that any Authorised Guarantee Agreement is equally worthless. However, the court has made it clear that in no circumstances can a tenant's existing guarantor directly guarantee the immediate incoming assignee. Any requirement to that effect, whether contained in the lease, a separate guarantee, the subsequent assignment or a licence to assign, is of no effect (*K/S Victoria*, as cited above).

2. TERMINATION OF THE TENANCY

14–03 Prima facie, the surety's obligations will come to an end on the date on which the contractual term is expressed to expire. Thus, if the tenant holds over as a continuation tenant under s.24 of the Landlord and Tenant Act 1954, the surety will not be liable during the continuation period unless the lease provides to the contrary (*Junction Estates Ltd v Cope* (1974) 27 P. & C.R. 482; *Plesser (A) & Co Ltd v Davis* [1983] 2 E.G.L.R 70). Curiously, although a surety is not liable during a period in which the tenant holds over lawfully, he will be liable to pay damages if the tenant holds over unlawfully as a trespasser (*Associated Dairies Ltd v Pierce* [1983] 1 E.G.L.R 45). But the surety will not be obliged to enter into a guarantee of the tenant's obligations under a renewed lease, and the absence of a surety is not a ground for objecting to a renewal (*Barclays Bank Ltd v Ascott* [1961] 1 All E.R. 782). However, the provision of a surety is a term of the new tenancy that the court could order under s.35 of the Landlord and Tenant Act 1954 (*Cairnplace Ltd v CBL (Property Investment) Co Ltd* [1984] 1 All E.R. 315). Further, there appears to be nothing to prevent the landlord from taking a covenant from the surety to guarantee a renewed lease (cf. *Hollies Stores Ltd v Timmis* [1921] 2 Ch. 202, where an option to renew a lease failed because one of the guarantors of the original lease had died).

Example 14:1 Basic covenant by surety

In consideration of the grant of this lease to the tenant having been made at his request the surety hereby covenants with the landlord that:

(a) the tenant will punctually pay the rent and will observe and perform all the tenant's covenants in this lease both during the term hereby expressed to be granted and during any continuation or renewal thereof and

(b) the tenant will comply with any obligations imposed on him under an Authorised Guarantee Agreement and

(c) that in case of any default by the tenant in the payment of the rent or the observance or performance of his covenants or obligations as aforesaid the surety will make good to the landlord all loss damage costs and expenses arising out of such default and suffered or incurred by the landlord.

Example 14:2 Obligation to provide a new surety

The Tenant covenants that it shall:

(a) within 21 working days of any of the events listed below give written notice of that event to the landlord and

(b) if within 21 working days thereafter the landlord so requires provide some other person reasonably acceptable to the landlord to covenant with the landlord within 21 working days thereafter in the terms set out in the surety's covenant at clause [ ] of this lease.

The events are:

if any surety,

(1) being an individual (or where the surety comprises more than one individual then any one of those individuals) dies or has a bankruptcy order made against him or

(2) being a company has an administration order made against it or is wound up either voluntarily (except by merger consolidation or other similar corporate transaction previously approved

in writing by the landlord such approval not to be unreasonably withheld or delayed) or by the court or if the surety shall for any reason cease to maintain its corporate existence or if a receiver (of any kind) liquidator (of any kind) or manager of its business or any part of its business shall be appointed or

(3) being either an individual or a company if any interim official or other receiver is appointed or if the surety shall propose or make any composition or propose to enter into any voluntary or other arrangement with the creditors of the surety or if the surety shall otherwise cease for any reason to be or remain liable under its covenants.

3. DISCHARGE OF THE SURETY

14–04 The surety will be discharged from liability under his guarantee if the landlord acts to his prejudice since the landlord must act with the utmost good faith towards him. This rule may be modified or excluded by the express terms of the guarantee. Thus, it has become usual for the basic obligation to be qualified by a proviso that any time given to the tenant or any neglect or forbearance on the part of the landlord to enforce the covenants shall not discharge the surety. From the landlord's point of view it may be that the usual form of proviso does not go far enough. For example, if the tenant is in breach of covenant but tenders the rent the landlord will almost invariably refuse to accept it in order not to waive the breach. It is doubtful whether a refusal by the landlord to accept rent tendered falls within the expression "neglect or forbearance". Accordingly, it may be that the surety would be discharged once rent has been tendered by the tenant and refused. It has, however, been suggested that the landlord is not obliged to accept a tender of rent from a third party where the acceptance would prejudice him (*Richards v De Freitas* (1974) 29 P. & C.R. 1); but the tenant is not a third party, so this rule may not extend to the refusal of a tender by the tenant. It is suggested that the draftsman should make express provision for this eventuality.

The surety will be similarly discharged if the tenant surrenders part of the demised property, even if the rent is reduced (*Holme v Brunskill* (1877) 3 Q.B.D. 495), because his rights of subrogation are thereby prejudiced. There seems to be nothing in principle to prevent the draftsman from providing that in the event of a surrender of part of the demised property the surety's liability should continue in respect of the remainder. In all cases the draftsman should consider doing so.

Where the lease provides that the surety is not to be discharged if the landlord "gives time" to the tenant, the surety will not be discharged even if the landlord contractually binds himself not to sue for the rent or agrees to authorise an alteration made in breach of covenant (*Selous Street Properties Ltd v Oronel Fabrics Ltd* [1984] 1 E.G.L.R 50).

Another method of dealing with the possibility of inadvertently discharging the surety is to provide that as between the landlord and the surety he is to be treated as a principal debtor. In addition the surety may be asked to confer irrevocable authority upon the tenant for the time being to bind him with reference to the subject matter of the lease. A provision to this effect is likely to defeat most defences based upon alleged variations to the lease. The words of the provision must be clear, as the court construes contracts of suretyship strictly in favour of the surety. Thus where the contract provided that the surety should not be released in certain circumstances, it was held that the clause did not cover new terms introduced by a licence to assign (*West Horndon Industrial Park v Phoenix Timber Group* [1995] 1 E.G.L.R. 77; *Howard de Walden Estates v Pasta Place* [1995] 1 E.G.L.R. 79). **14–05**

Whilst it is now commonplace for leases to include an anti-release clause to the effect that the surety's liability will not be released by any variation, waiver or modification of any of the terms of the lease, the question will always be whether the contract as varied or modified remains a contract within the general purview of the original guarantee (*Triodos Bank NV v Dobbs* [2005] EWCA 630, per Longmore L.J.). As such, the fact that a guarantor has agreed to the inclusion of an anti-release clause is not the end of the matter. The issue will remain whether the proper interpretation of the original agreement, including the anti-release clause, permits the actual variations which have taken place without the guarantor's further express consent. The true variation of an existing obligation will be caught. The entering of what is, in fact, a different obligation, even though it may purport to be no more than a variation, will not.

However, where the principal debtor has ceased to be tenant as a result of an assignment, and the surety remains liable on his guarantee, he is not liable to pay any amount in respect of a tenant covenant of the tenancy to the extent that the amount is referable to any relevant variation of the tenant covenants of the tenancy effected after the assignment (s.18(2) of the Landlord and Tenant (Covenants) Act 1995). A relevant variation is one which the landlord has an absolute right to refuse, or would have had such a right but for a previous variation which was effected after the assignment (s.18(4)). The effect of this provision is that although the draftsman may provide for the surety to be bound by variations effected while the principal debtor remains tenant, he cannot provide for the surety to be bound by variations made after an assignment by the principal debtor. Indeed, it appears to be the case that a surety will not be bound by a variation effected after an assignment by a principal debtor even if he expressly consents to the variation. The practical answer for landlords is to refuse to agree to variations of the tenancy unless the surety enters into a fresh guarantee. However, the section does not say that the surety is discharged by a relevant variation, and it seems probable that although the surety's liability cannot be increased by such a variation, the draftsman can provide that his original liability will continue despite such a variation.

Example 14:3 Proviso limiting discharge of surety
Provided that:

(1) no neglect or forbearance of the landlord in enforcing the payment of the rent or the observance or performance of the tenant's covenants nor any refusal by the landlord to accept rent tendered by or on behalf of the tenant during a period in which the landlord is entitled or would after service of a notice under section 146 of the Law of Property Act 1925 be entitled to re-enter the demised property nor any time given by the landlord to the tenant shall discharge the surety either in whole or in part or in any way affect his liability under this covenant

(2) in the event that the tenant surrenders part of the demised property the liability of the surety shall continue in respect of the part of the demised property not so surrendered after making any necessary apportionments under section 140 of the Law of Property Act 1925.

Example 14:4 Surety deemed to be principal debtor
Provided that as between the landlord and the surety the surety shall be deemed to be a principal debtor and accordingly the landlord shall be at liberty to forbear or refuse to accept payment of the rent hereby reserved or enforce performance or observance of the tenant's covenants or to give time to the tenant or to vary the terms of this lease without discharging the surety wholly or partly or in any way diminishing his liability under this covenant.

Example 14:5 Surety to be bound by variations
The surety agrees:
(a) to be bound by any variation of this lease made in good faith by the landlord and the tenant at any time before an assignment of this lease by the tenant
(b) that any variation of this lease after such an assignment will not discharge his liability under this guarantee.

Example 14:6 Comprehensive anti-release clause
The surety agrees:
(a) to be bound by any variation waiver release or modification of any of the terms of this lease made in good faith by the landlord and the tenant at any time before an assignment of this lease by the tenant
(b) that any variation waiver release or modification of this lease after such an assignment will not discharge his liability under this guarantee.

4. DISCLAIMER

If the tenant for the time being becomes insolvent his trustee in bankruptcy (or in the case of a company the liquidator) may disclaim the lease (ss.178–182 (companies) and ss.315–321 (individuals) of the Insolvency Act 1986). **14–06**

Disclaimer of a lease will not discharge a surety (*Hindcastle v Barbara Attenborough Associates* [1996] 1 All E.R. 737) or a guarantor under an Authorised Guarantee Agreement (*Doleman v Shaw* [2009] 2 E.G.L.R. 35 (CA)). However, the surety's obligations will come to an end if the landlord retakes possession (*Active Estates Ltd v Parness* [2002] 3 E.G.L.R. 13). It follows that in order to retain his rights against a surety the landlord must leave the property empty. If he wishes to avoid this undesirable result, the draftsman should include a covenant on the part of the surety to take a lease of the demised property if the existing lease is disclaimed. Some clauses place a time limit on a request by the landlord to the surety. If a time-limit is imposed, it should run not from the date of the disclaimer, but from the date on which the landlord receives notice of it.

If the lease was excluded from the protection of the Landlord and Tenant Act 1954 Part II, the landlord will want the new lease to be contracted out too. This will require compliance with the necessary health warning/declaration procedure at the time that the guarantor becomes legally obliged to take the new lease. The landlord and guarantor must also consider the standard of repair under the new lease. If the standard of the area has changed since the date of grant of the lease, the repairing obligation under the new lease granted to the guarantor may be different (applying the *Proudfoot v Hart* [1890] 25 Q.B.D. 42 approach). The landlord may wish to include an express provision that the standard of repair should be fixed as at the date of grant of the original lease. Both landlord and guarantor will also wish to consider the terms of the new lease if the tenant has made permitted alterations during the term of the lease, subject to an obligation to reinstate at the end of the term. The landlord should seek to ensure that the new lease includes an express obligation on the guarantor to reinstate the alterations made under the lease. The guarantor will seek to ensure that the standard rent review disregard of tenant's permitted alterations "carried out during the term" or, sometimes, "during any earlier period of occupation arising out of an agreement to grant the term" is extended to ensure that alterations made during the term of the disclaimed lease are disregarded for the purposes of rent review under the new lease (see, Emma Slessenger, "Requiring a Guarantor to Take Up a Fresh Lease Following Disclaimer" (2012) 16 *Landlord & Tenant Review* 43–46).

Although the surety enters into a covenant to take a new lease on disclaimer as a principal (since *ex hypothesi* his liability as surety will have come to an end before the time for performance arrives), nevertheless he remains collaterally liable. Thus, if the surety is discharged from liability under the covenant imposing his primary liability upon him, he will also be discharged from his obligation to take a lease on disclaimer (*Selous Street Properties Ltd v Oronel Fabrics Ltd* [1984] 1 E.G.L.R 50). However, the disclaimer itself does not discharge the surety from his obligation to take a new lease (*Re Yarmarine* [1992] B.C.L.C. 276). The covenant runs with the land, and consequently a successor in title to the original landlord may enforce it (*Coronation Street Industrial Properties v Ingall* [1989] 1 W.L.R. 304). So long as the surety's obligation to take a new lease subsists, the benefit of that obligation will pass to a new reversioner even after the lease has been disclaimed (*Scottish Widows v Tripipatkul* [2004] 1 P. & C.R. 29).

Example 14:7 Covenant by surety to take a lease on disclaimer
If:
(a) a liquidator or trustee in bankruptcy disclaims this lease so that it comes to an end or
(b) the tenant (being a company) is dissolved or struck off the Register of Companies or
(c) this lease vests in the Crown as bona vacantia and is disclaimed by the Crown

then at the written request of the landlord (made not more than three months after notice of the event in question has been given to him or the event has otherwise come to his knowledge) the surety will take from the landlord a new lease of the demised property:
(i) for a term equal to the residue of the term unexpired at the date of the event in question
(ii) at the rent then payable under the terms of this lease
(iii) otherwise on the terms of this lease and will pay the landlord's costs of the grant of the new lease.

Example 14:8 Covenant by a guarantor under an Authorised Guarantee Agreement to take a new lease on disclaimer
If:
(a) a liquidator or trustee in bankruptcy disclaims this lease so that it comes to an end or
(b) the tenant (being a company) is dissolved or struck off the Register of Companies or
(c) this lease vests in the Crown as bona vacantia and is disclaimed by the Crown

then at the written request of the landlord (made not more than three months after notice of the event in question has been given to him or the event has otherwise come to his knowledge) the guarantor will take from the landlord a new lease of the demised property:

(i) for a term equal to the residue of the term unexpired at the date of the event in question

(ii) at the rent then payable under the terms of this lease

(iii) otherwise on the terms of this lease and will pay the landlord's costs of the grant of the new lease.

5. PROTECTING THE SURETY

14–07 In recent years more thought has been given to the position of the surety and to ways of protecting him against unlimited liability. Where a surety is required upon the grant of a lease the selected person is usually closely connected with the tenant (e.g. a director or parent company of a limited company, or a relative of an individual tenant). For as long as the original tenant holds the lease the surety is likely to be aware of the tenant's financial strength; indeed he may directly control it. However, once an assignment takes place the surety will lose direct contact and is likely to become aware of his liability only when he is faced with meeting a demand from the landlord. Accordingly, in the first instance the surety should seek to limit his liability to the tenure of the original tenant.

If the landlord will not agree, the surety should seek to limit his retrospective liability. For this purpose Example 14:1, above, may be suitably adapted. If such a limitation is introduced into the lease, the landlord will be under pressure to enforce his remedies in good time, and the surety will be to a large extent protected against the width of a proviso enabling the landlord to refrain from enforcing obligations.

Since the surety will be liable to pay not only the rent initially agreed, but also any increased rent which becomes payable on review, he should seek to secure a right to participate in the determination of the reviewed rent. It seems that this may be done by requiring rent review notices to be served on "the parties" rather than on "the tenant" (*Cressey v Jacobs* (1977), unreported. Digested in Reynolds and Fetherstonhaugh, *Handbook of Rent Review* (looseleaf). A surer way would be to require the surety to be a party to any rent review memorandum. From the landlord's point of view this would have the added advantage of preventing any later argument that the review had been irregularly conducted.

To some extent, the surety will be protected by the provisions in s.17 of the Landlord and Tenant (Covenants) Act 1995. The Act requires that, in order for a landlord to recover fixed charges from either a former tenant or the surety of a former tenant, a default notice must be served upon that party within six months of the sums becoming due (s.17). The provision for service of a notice has been held to extend to service of a notice under s.17(2) of the Landlord and Tenant (Covenants) Act 1995 in order to preserve an original tenant's or guarantor's liability in respect of such sums as may become due and owing once an outstanding rent review has been determined (*Scottish & Newcastle Plc v Raguz* [2008] 1 W.L.R. 2494 (HL)).

Notice

It is sensible for a surety to seek protection through the inclusion of a notice provision so they receive warning of a problem with payments by the tenant and can take whatever informal steps are open to them to minimise their exposure. In *Greene King Plc v Quisine Restaurants Ltd* [2012] 2 E.G.L.R. 64, a provision in the following terms was held to impose an effective contractual obligation to use all reasonable endeavours to notify the surety of any occasion when the rent was more than two months in arrear, but not to operate as a condition precedent to the surety's liability to pay. **14–08**

> "The Tenant hereby undertakes with the Undertenant's Guarantor to use all reasonable endeavours to give written notice to the Undertenant's Guarantor each and every time the rents reserved by the Underlease are more than two months in arrear."

Finally, since the role of the surety is essentially passive, he may find it advantageous to convert his role into an active one. Thus, consideration should be given to enabling the surety to require the tenant to assign the lease to him if he is called upon under the guarantee. Although the surety will not escape liability, he will at least have the opportunity of finding a solvent assignee. Such an option would amount to an estate contract and must be protected by registration. The surety should stipulate, where possible, for a **14–09** provision exempting the transaction from the requirement of obtaining the landlord's consent. The need to obtain consent may be time consuming, and the tenant, who is being compelled to assign, may be reluctant to expend energy in obtaining it. It is not unreasonable to expect the landlord to waive the requirement of consent, since he will have initially approved the surety as a person of financial responsibility. These questions are more fully discussed in Reynolds and Fogel, "Commercial Lettings: Liability of Original Tenant and of Successive Sureties After Assignments", Blundell Memorial Lecture of May 22, 1984.

Since the Landlord and Tenant (Covenants) Act 1995 a surety who pays in full an amount which he has been required to pay is entitled to the grant of an overriding lease. The overriding lease will be on the same terms as the lease itself (subject to any agreed modifications) and will be for the residue of the term of the lease plus three days (s.19 of the Landlord and Tenant (Covenants) Act 1995). This may be sufficient for a surety to dispense with a contractual right to call for an assignment, although the grant of an overriding lease will still leave the defaulting tenant in possession of the property.

Example 14:9 Surety's right to require assignment

(1) At any time after the surety has been lawfully required by the landlord to discharge any liability of the tenant and has discharged that liability either wholly or partly he shall be entitled to serve notice on the tenant under this clause

(2) Within 14 days after service of such notice on the tenant he shall deliver up vacant possession of the demised property and shall execute and deliver to the surety an assignment of this lease and the surety shall accept it

(3) The landlord's consent to any such assignment is not required.

Other concurrent leases

14–10 Some guarantee provisions are drafted to allow the landlord to call on the guarantor to take a concurrent lease if the tenant defaults. This sits above the lease making the guarantor the immediate landlord of the tenant. The guarantor receives the tenant's rent and can enforce the tenant's covenants, having the ability to exercise more control over the tenant and having the ability to forfeit the tenant's lease. For some landlords this is preferable to the s.17 Landlord and Tenant (Covenants) Act 1995 process because the decision whether to call for the concurrent lease is that of the landlord rather than the guarantor. This may be a valuable comfort for a landlord if it is concerned about its proposed tenant's covenant strength.

6. AUTHORISED GUARANTEE AGREEMENTS

Under the Landlord and Tenant (Covenants) Act 1995, a tenant is released from liability on an assignment of his lease (unless the assignment is an excluded assignment). However, the landlord may require him to guarantee the obligations of his immediate assignee. This can only be done by an Authorised Guarantee Agreement. An agreement is an Authorised Guarantee Agreement if: **14–11**

(1) under it the tenant guarantees performance of the tenant covenants of the tenancy to any extent by the assignee;
(2) it is entered into in the following circumstances:
  (a) by virtue of a covenant against assignment (whether absolute or qualified) the assignment cannot be effected without the consent of the landlord or some other person;
  (b) consent is given subject to a condition (lawfully imposed) that the tenant is to enter into an agreement guaranteeing the performance of covenants by the assignee; and
  (c) the agreement is entered into by the tenant in pursuance of that condition;
(3) its provisions conform with s.16(4) and (5) of the Act (s.16 of the Landlord and Tenant (Covenants) Act 1995).

The formal conditions are that the agreement must not:

(1) impose on the tenant any requirement to guarantee in any way the performance of the relevant covenant by any person other than the assignee; and
(2) impose on the tenant any liability, restriction or other requirement (of whatever nature) in relation to any time after the assignee is released from liability by virtue of the 1995 Act.

14–12 However, an Authorised Guarantee Agreement may:

(1) impose on the tenant any liability as sole or principal debtor in respect of any obligation owed by the assignee under the relevant covenant;
(2) impose on the tenant liabilities as guarantor in respect of the assignee's performance of that covenant which are no more onerous that those to which he would be subject in the event of his being liable as sole or principal debtor in respect of any obligation owed by the assignee under that covenant;
(3) require the tenant, in the event of the tenancy assigned by him being disclaimed, to enter into a new tenancy of the premises comprised in the assignment:
    (a) whose term expires not later than the term of the tenancy assigned by the tenant; and
    (b) whose tenant covenants are no more onerous than those of the tenancy;
(4) make provision incidental or supplementary to any provision made by virtue of (1) to (3), above (s.16(5) of the Landlord and Tenant (Covenants) Act 1995).

Example 14.10 Authorised Guarantee Agreement

AN AGREEMENT made the [ ] of [ ] between [ ] ("the Tenant") (1) and [ ] ("the Landlord") (2)

RECITES THAT

(1) the Tenant is the tenant of [ ] under a lease dated [ ]
(2) the Tenant has applied to the Landlord for consent to assign the lease to [ ] ("the Assignee")
(3) the Landlord has granted consent subject to the condition that the Tenant enters into this agreement
(4) the condition was lawfully imposed
(5) the Tenant enters into this agreement in pursuance of that condition

AND NOW WITNESSES

1. In consideration of the grant of consent by the Landlord to the assignment of the lease to the Assignee the Tenant covenants with the Landlord that:
    (a) from completion of the assignment until he is released from liability by the Landlord and Tenant (Covenants)

Act 1995 the Assignee will punctually pay the rent reserved by the Lease and will perform all the tenant covenants contained in it

(b) in case of any default by the Assignee the Tenant will indemnify the Landlord against all loss damage costs and expenses suffered or incurred by the Landlord

2. As between the Landlord and the Tenant the Tenant shall be treated as a principal debtor and accordingly:
   (a) the Tenant's liability under clause 1 is not dependent on any demand being made by the Landlord
   (b) the Tenant's liability will not be discharged by any forbearance or indulgence by the landlord or by the giving of time to the Assignee or by any refusal on the part of the Landlord to accept rent from the Assignee
   (c) the Tenant's liability will not be discharged by any variation of the terms of the Lease made after the Lease has been assigned to the Assignee

3.
   (a) In the event of the Lease being disclaimed the Landlord shall be entitled to require the Tenant to enter into a new tenancy of the property comprised in the assignment:
      (i) for a term equivalent to the term of the Lease unexpired at the date of the disclaimer
      (ii) on the same terms as the terms of the Lease at that date
   (b) The Landlord requires the Tenant to enter into a new tenancy by giving written notice to that effect not later than three months after the disclaimer has come to his notice
   (c) The Tenant shall complete the new lease within ten working days after receipt of written notice under sub-clause (b).

7. CHANGE OF LANDLORD

It has now been authoritatively determined that a covenant by a surety that the tenant will perform his obligations runs with the land, and subsequently may be enforced by a successor in title to the original landlord (*P&A Swift Investments v Combined English Stores Group Plc* [1988] 2 All E.R. 885). Accordingly, the problems **14–13** which had previously been thought to exist no longer apply. All that is necessary is for the lease to state clearly that "the landlord" includes successors in title.

8. RENEWAL LEASES

14–14 On a renewal, the court has no power to order the grant of a new tenancy to be conditional on the provision of a surety, since this could be to introduce a new non-statutory ground of opposition into the Landlord and Tenant Act 1954 (*Barclays Bank Ltd v Ascott* [1961] 1 All E.R. 782). However, the court may order the new tenancy to contain a term which requires the tenant to procure a person to stand surety for him within a fixed period (*Cairnplace Ltd v CBL (Property Investment) Ltd* [1984] 1 All E.R. 315).

Where the liability of the tenant is guaranteed under the current tenancy, it will usually be fair and reasonable to order the provision of sureties in the new tenancy. Breach of the obligation would entitle the landlord to forfeit the new tenancy, and it is unlikely that the tenant would obtain relief against forfeiture unless the sureties were provided. However, failure to provide sureties within a fixed period would amount to a once and for all breach, and consequently would be capable of inadvertent waiver. The draftsman should therefore provide for the period to be capable of extension by the landlord.

Example 14:11 Requirement to provide sureties

(1) Within 28 days of the grant of this lease (or such longer period as the landlord may from time to time prescribe by notice given to the tenant) the tenant shall procure that two persons approved by the landlord shall stand surety for the performance of the tenant's obligations under this lease
(2) The landlord's approval shall not be unreasonably withheld
(3) The obligations to be assumed by the sureties shall be contained in a deed and shall take such form as the landlord shall reasonably require.

Example 14:12 Alternative form of surety covenant including obligation to take lease on disclaimer

(1) The surety covenants with the landlord:
    (a) that the tenant will pay the rents promptly and perform all his other obligations under this lease

(b) to make good to the landlord all losses occasioned by any breach of paragraph (a) above
(c) if this lease is disclaimed in circumstances in which the disclaimer brings it to an end to take a new lease of the demised property for the residue of the term as at the day preceding the disclaimer on the same terms as this lease

(2) The surety's liability will not be discharged or diminished by:
(a) any neglect or forbearance by the landlord in enforcing payment of rent or performance of the tenant's obligations
(b) any refusal by the landlord to accept rent following a breach of covenant by the tenant
(c) any time given to the tenant
(d) any variation of this lease or any consent given under it (and the surety's liabilities will extend to the lease as varied so far as permitted by the Landlord and Tenant (Covenants) Act 1995)
(e) any surrender of part of the demised property (except that the surety's liability will be limited to the part not surrendered).

9. ALTERNATIVE FORMS OF SECURITY

Rent deposits

As maintaining the rental stream is generally the landlord's most basic requirement, rent deposits can provide a less complicated form of security for a landlord. The security offered by a rent deposit is readily accessible to remedy the default of a tenant, and can have considerable benefits where the lease is short or is not of high value. The deposit may prove less attractive however if the tenant's inability to pay the rent means that it also does not have the finance to replenish the deposit in the event of a draw down by the landlord. From a tenant's point of view however a rent deposit locks up a large amount of cash for a relatively long period. **14–15**

Bank guarantees

14–16 If a bank guarantee is available it may prove preferable to a landlord. The bank contracts with the landlord to meet the tenant's obligations under its covenants in the lease up to a set level. Again, this may be attractive to a landlord if the lease is granted for a relatively short term.

Release

14–17 The Code for Leasing Business Premises England and Wales 2007 recommends that the lease terms should clearly state the conditions for releasing rent deposits and guarantees. It also recommends that the tenant should be protected against the default or insolvency of the landlord.

Form 1

Standard Form of Lease for Letting of Shop in Parade

[**General note**: In this form the Prescribed Clauses are set out and all the variable parts of the lease are collected, so far as possible, at the front, thereby reducing the possibility of mistakes. Care must be taken to avoid any conflict between the completion of the Prescribed Clauses and the content of the clauses forming the body of the lease. The lease contains a "keep open covenant" subject to exceptions.] **F1-01**

THE PRESCRIBED CLAUSES

LR1. Date of lease	[ ]
LR2. Title number(s)	**LR2.1 Landlord's title number(s)** *Title number(s) out of which this lease is granted. Leave blank if not registered.* [ ] **LR2.2 Other title numbers** *Existing title number(s) against which entries of matters referred to in LR9, LR10, LR11 and LR13 are to be made.*

LR3. Parties to this lease *Give full names and addresses of each of the parties. For UK incorporated companies and limited liability partnerships, also give the registered number including any prefix. For overseas companies, also give the territory of incorporation and, if appropriate, the registered number in the UK including any prefix.*	**Landlord** [ ] **Tenant** [ ] ***Other parties*** *Specify capacity of each party, for example "management company", "guarantor", etc.* [ ] Surety
LR4. Property *Insert a full description of the land being leased* *or* *Refer to the clause, schedule or paragraph of a schedule in this lease in which the land being leased is more fully described.* *Where there is a letting of part of a registered title, a plan must be attached to this lease and any floor levels must be specified.*	**In the case of a conflict between this clause and the remainder of this lease then, for the purposes of registration, this clause shall prevail.**

LR5. Prescribed statements etc. *If this lease includes a statement falling within LR5.1, insert under that sub-clause the relevant statement or refer to the clause, schedule or paragraph of a schedule in this lease which contains the statement.* *In LR5.2, omit or delete those Acts which do not apply to this lease.*	***LR5.1 Statements prescribed under rules 179 (dispositions in favour of a charity), 180 (dispositions by a charity) or 196 (leases under the Leasehold Reform, Housing and Urban Development Act 1993) of the Land Registration Rules 2003.*** ***LR5.2 This lease is made under, or by reference to, provisions of:*** *Leasehold Reform Act 1967* *Housing Act 1985* *Housing Act 1996* *Housing Act 1996*

LR6. Term for which the Property is leased *Include only the appropriate statement (duly completed) from the three options.* *NOTE: The information you provide, or refer to, here will be used as part of the particulars to identify the lease under rule 6 of the Land Registration Rules 2003.*	From and including To and including *OR* The term as specified in this lease at clause/schedule/paragraph *OR* The term is as follows: [ ]
LR7. Premium *Specify the total premium, inclusive of any VAT where payable.*	
LR8. Prohibitions or restrictions on disposing of this lease *Include whichever of the two statements is appropriate.* *Do not set out here the wording of the provision.*	This lease does not contain a provision that prohibits or restricts dispositions. *OR* This lease contains a provision that prohibits or restricts dispositions.

LR9. Rights of acquisition etc. *Insert the relevant provisions in the sub-clauses or refer to the clause, schedule or paragraph of a schedule in this lease which contains the provisions.*	**LR9.1 Tenant's contractual rights to renew this lease, to acquire the reversion or another lease of the Property, or to acquire an interest in other land** **LR9.2 Tenant's covenant to (or offer to) surrender this lease** **LR9.3 Landlord's contractual rights to acquire this lease**
LR10. Restrictive covenants given in this lease by the Landlord in respect of land other than the Property *Insert the relevant provisions or refer to the clause, schedule or paragraph of a schedule in this lease which contains the provisions.*	
LR11. Easements	**LR11.1 Easements granted by this lease for the benefit of the Property** **LR11.2 Easements granted or reserved by this lease over the Property for the benefit of other property**

LR12. Estate rentcharge burdening the Property *Refer here only to the clause, schedule or paragraph of a schedule in this lease which sets out the rentcharge.*	
LR13. Application for standard form of restriction *Set out the full text of the standard form of restriction and the title against which it is to be entered. If you wish to apply for more than one standard form of restriction use this clause to apply for each of them, tell us who is applying against which title and set out the full text of the restriction you are applying for.* *Standard forms of restriction are set out in Schedule 4 to the Land Registration Rules 2003.*	The Parties to this lease apply to enter the following standard form of restriction [against the title of the Property] or [against title number]

LR14. Declaration of trust where there is more than one person comprising the Tenant *If the Tenant is one person, omit or delete all the alternative statements.* *If the Tenant is more than one person, complete this clause by omitting or deleting all inapplicable alternative statements.*	
	The Tenant is more than one person. They are to hold the Property on trust for themselves as joint tenants. *OR* The Tenant is more than one person. They are to hold the Property on trust for themselves as tenants in common in equal shares. *OR* The Tenant is more than one person. They are to hold the Property on trust [*Complete as necessary*]

PARTICULARS

Column 1	*Column 2*
Landlord	
Tenant	
Surety	
Property	
Commencement Date	
Term	
Initial Rent	
Review Date	
Permitted Use	

THIS LEASE which is made on the [ ] of 20[ ] between the Landlord (1) and the Tenant (2) and the Surety (3) WITNESSES as follows:

F1–02 1. (1) In this Lease the following expressions have the following meanings:

(a) expressions in Column 1 of the preceding table have the meanings assigned to them by Column 2 thereof

(b) the Landlord and Tenant include the persons deriving title under them respectively

(c) the Parade means [ ]

(d) [*Definition of rate of interest*, "*the Prescribed Rate*" - *see Example 6.36*].

(2) Where the Tenant or the Surety is more than one person their covenants shall be joint and several.

(3) Any reference to an Act of Parliament includes a reference to that Act as amended or replaced from time to time and to subordinate legislation or byelaws or regulations made thereunder.

F1–03 2. In consideration of the rents and covenants on the part of the Tenant contained below the Landlord DEMISES the Property to the Tenant TOGETHER with the rights set out in Part I of the First Schedule but EXCEPTING AND RESERVING the rights set out in Part II of that Schedule TO HOLD the Property to the Tenant from the Commencement Date for the Term YIELDING AND

PAYING therefor the Initial Rent (exclusive of value added tax) (subject to review as set out in the Second Schedule) by equal quarterly payments in advance on the usual quarter days the first payment (or a duly apportioned part of it) to be made on the date hereof.

3. The Tenant hereby covenants with the Landlord as follows: **F1–04**

(1) (a) to pay the rent promptly without any legal or equitable set-off or deduction whatsoever

(b) to pay interest on all arrears of rent and other moneys due under the Lease at the Prescribed Rate.

(2) to pay on demand such sums as the Landlord may expend from time to time in insuring the Property or as the case may be a proportion calculated by reference to the proportion which the net internal area of the Property measured in accordance with the Royal Institution of Chartered Surveyors Code of Practice (as issued from time to time) bears to the net internal area of all the buildings comprised in the Parade of the sums expended by the Landlord in insuring the Parade.

(3) to pay all rates and outgoings payable in respect of the Property or its ownership or occupation (except such as are payable on a disposal of the Landlord's interest in the Property and income tax charged on the Landlord).

(4) to execute all works required in pursuance of any Act of Parliament or required by any local or public authority to be done in respect of the Property whether by the Tenant the Landlord or any other person (however described).

(5) [*To repair and decorate - see Example 9.4, substituting "the Property" for "the demised property"*].

(6) [*Not to alter without consent - see Example 9.15 substituting "the Property" for "the demised property"*].

(7) (a) not to use or permit or suffer to be used the Property for any purpose other than the Permitted Use and to keep the Property open for business during normal business hours PROVIDED THAT it shall not be a breach of this clause if during a period of twenty-four months the Property is not open for business for a period not exceeding three months by reason of:

(i) the carrying out of works (whether of repair or not) to the Property

or

(ii) the tenant having ceased to trade in the Property with a view to disposing of it either by way of assignment or sublease.

(b) not to carry on any offensive or noisy trade or business nor to hold any sale by auction in the Property nor to permit any person to sleep or reside therein nor to do anything therein which in the opinion of the Landlord causes or might cause nuisance or annoyance to the Landlord or any tenant of his.

(8) [*Planning covenant - see Example 10.1, substituting "the Property" for "the demised property"*].

(9) [*Not to cause increase in premium, etc. - see Example 7.13, substituting "the Property" for "the demised property"*].

(10) not to exhibit any signboard advertisement placard or name-plate on or in the Property except:

(a) as part of a normal window display

or

(b) with the previous approval in writing of the Landlord.

(11) [*Covenant against assignment etc. - see Examples 12.1 and 12.6, substituting "the property" for "demised property"*].

(12) not to permit any easement to be acquired or encroachment made against or upon the Property and promptly to give notice to the Landlord of any attempt to make or acquire the same and to take such steps (whether by legal proceedings or otherwise) to prevent the same from being acquired or made as the Landlord may reasonably require.

(13) not to stop up darken or obstruct any window or other aperture in the Property.

(14) to pay all costs charges and expenses (including any professional fees) incurred by the Landlord in and about the preparation or service of a schedule of dilapidations or a notice under section 146 or 147 of the Law of Property Act 1925 (even if forfeiture is avoided otherwise than by relief granted by the court).

(15) to pay the Landlord's solicitors costs and disbursements and surveyor's fees in connection with:

(a) the preparation and grant of this lease

(b) any application by the Tenant for any licence or consent under this lease (whether or not such licence or consent is actually granted).

F1–05 4. The Landlord hereby covenants with the Tenant as follows:

(1) that the Tenant paying the rent and performing and observing his covenants shall peaceably and quietly hold and enjoy the

Property for the Term without any interruption by the Landlord or any person claiming under or in trust for him

(2) [*Covenant to insure and reinstate - see Example 7.6 substituting "the Property" for "the demised property", and adding the following subparagraph: "(5) for the avoidance of doubt it is hereby declared that the landlord need not maintain a separate policy of insurance in respect of the Property only but may insure the Parade as a whole"*].

5. PROVIDED ALWAYS and it is hereby agreed as follows: **F1–06**

(1) if the rent or any part thereof shall be unpaid for twenty one days after becoming payable (whether formally demanded or not) or if there shall be a breach of any of the Tenant's covenants or the conditions to be performed or observed by the Tenant or if the Tenant allows and distress or execution to be levied on its goods which is not discharged within fourteen days or the Tenant or the Surety (being a company) shall enter into compulsory or voluntary liquidation (otherwise than for the purpose of amalgamation or reconstruction) or if a resolution is passed for its winding up or a proposal is made to the body corporate and its creditors for a composition in satisfaction of its debts or a scheme of arrangement of its affairs or an application is made to the court for an administration order or notice is given of appointment or the intention to appoint an administrator or liquidator or if the Tenant (not being a company) shall become bankrupt or have a receiving order made against him or call a meeting of or enter into any composition with his creditors then and in each such case the Landlord shall be entitled (in addition to any other right) to re-enter upon the Property and thereupon this lease shall absolutely determine.

(2) Re-entry in exercise of the rights set out at clause 5 (1) above does not affect any other right or remedy of the Landlord for breach of covenant or condition by the Tenant occurring before the termination of the Lease.

[*Proviso for abatement of rent - see Example 7.10, substituting "the Property" for "the demised property"*].

(3) [*Tenant's break clause on total loss - see Example 7.11*]

(4) section 196 of the Law of Property Act 1925 shall apply to all notices or schedules required or permitted to be served hereunder.

6. In consideration of the demise contained above and made at the Surety's request (as he hereby acknowledges) the Surety hereby covenants with the Landlord as follows: **F1–07**

(1) [*Basic covenant - see Example 14.1*]

(2) [*To take a lease on disclaimer - see Example 14.7, substituting "the property" for "the demised property"*].

THE FIRST SCHEDULE

Part I: Rights included in the demise

F1–08 1. The right in common with the Landlord and all others having the like right to pass and repass (but not to park) with or without vehicles at all times and for all purposes connected with the Permitted Use but not otherwise over the service road at the rear of the Property but this right is conditional on the Tenant paying a fair proportion (to be conclusively determined by the Landlord's surveyor) of the cost of repairing and maintaining the same.

2. The right in common with the Landlord and all others having the like right to the free passage of water soil gas and electricity through the pipes conduits sewers and wires serving the Parade but this right is conditional on the Tenant paying a fair proportion (to be conclusively determined by the Landlord's surveyor) of the cost of repairing and maintaining the same.

3. The right for the Tenant and the Tenant's customers to pass and repass on foot only at all times and for all purposes connected with the Permitted Use but not otherwise over the common parts of the Parade

4. The right to the support and shelter of any part of the Parade in physical contact with the Property.

Part II: Exceptions and reservations

F1–09 1. Rights corresponding to those granted to the Tenant in Part 1 of this Schedule.

2. The right to enter the Property in case of emergency to carry out any works thereon making good all physical damage caused by such entry.

3. Such other rights of entry upon the Property as are necessary for the proper performance of his covenants by the Landlord making good all physical damage caused by such entry.

4. Section 62 of the Law of Property Act 1925 shall not apply to this lease.

THE SECOND SCHEDULE

F1–10 [*Rent review - see Example 6.39, substituting "the property" for "the demised property", and deleting the definition of "Review Date"*]

Form 2

Lease of Shop in Shopping Centre

[**General note**: This form is suitable where the landlord is to provide services to the shopping centre. Since the landlord may wish to exercise his option to charge VAT on the rent, the VAT has itself been reserved as rent. The landlord recovers a service charge. The service charge deals with major expenditure by allowing the landlord to build up a reserve fund.] **F2–01**

THE PRESCRIBED CLAUSES

[See Form 1 above]

PARTICULARS

Column 1	*Column 2*
Landlord	
Tenant	
Demised Property	the property known as Unit [ ] in the Centre which is described further in Part I of the First Schedule and identified by red edging on the Plan
Term	[ ] years beginning on [ ] and ending on

Basic Rent	£[ ] per annum
Review Date	the [ ] of [ ] and every fifth anniversary of that date
Permitted Use	use as a retail shop for the sale of [ ] or such other goods as the Landlord shall from time to time approve (such approval not to be unreasonably withheld)
Service Charge Proportion	[ ] per cent

THIS LEASE which is made the [ ] of 20[ ] between the Landlord (1) and the Tenant (2) WITNESSES as follows:

INTERPRETATION

F2–02 1. In this Lease

1.1 the following definitions apply:

1.1.1. expressions in Column 1 of the Particulars have the meanings opposite them in Column 2

1.1.2. the "Plan" means the attached plan

1.1.3. the "Landlord's Surveyor" means the surveyor from time to time appointed by the Landlord for the purposes of this lease (who may be employed by the Landlord or an associated company of the Landlord)

1.1.4. the "President" means the President for the time being of the Royal Institution of Chartered Surveyors or a person acting on his behalf

1.1.5. [*Definition of interest rate "the Prescribed Rate" - see Example 6.36*]

1.1.6. the "Centre" means the shopping centre known as [ ] and edged blue on the Plan

1.1.7. [*Definition of the interior of the Demised Property - see Example 9.3 substituting "the Centre" for "the building" and adding "(7) the shop front and fascia"*]

1.1.8. the "Common Parts" means the service roads and loading bays coloured brown on the Plan

1.1.9. the "Public Parts" means the malls stairs escalators lift car parks and other parts of the Centre not comprised in a demise to which the public has access during business hours

1.1.10. the "Retained Parts" means those parts of the Centre whose possession is retained by the Landlord including storerooms restrooms and offices for managerial staff within the Centre

1.1.11. the "Structure" means:

1.1.11.1. the roof and foundations of the Centre

1.1.11.2. its loadbearing walls and columns (excluding plaster or other decorative finishes)

1.1.11.3. its floor structures including structures supporting malls and walkways (but excluding floor screeds and floor finishes outside the Public Parts or the Retained Parts)

1.1.11.4. stairs escalators and lifts within the Public Parts

1.1.11.5. all surfaces of the Centre exposed to the elements

1.1.12. the "Plant" means all mechanical electrical heating air-conditioning and ventilating apparatus and all sprinkler systems within the Centre which have been provided by the Landlord and all wires pipes conduits sewers and flues which serve more than one unit

1.2 the Landlord and the Tenant include their respective successors in title.

1.3 covenants given by or implied on more than one person are joint and several.

1.4 any reference to an Act of Parliament includes a reference to that Act as amended or replaced from time to time and to any subordinate legislation or byelaws made under it.

1.5 the paragraph headings shall not affect the interpretation of this lease.

DEMISE

2. In consideration of the rent and the tenant's covenants the Landlord demises the Demised Property to the Tenant for the Term together with the rights specified in Part II of the First Schedule and Reserving the rights specified in Part III of that Schedule yielding and paying: **F2–03**

2.1 the Basic Rent (exclusive of value added tax) (subject to review in accordance with the Second Schedule) payable (if so required by direct debit) by equal quarterly instalments in advance on the usual quarter days.

2.2 an amount equal to the gross premium (before deduction of discount or commission) paid by the Landlord from time to time in insuring the Demised Property (or if the Landlord chooses the Service Charge Proportion of the amount equal to the gross premium paid by the Landlord from time to time in insuring the Centre) in either case payable on demand.

2.3 the Service Charge calculated in accordance with the Third Schedule and payable as there set out.

2.4 where value added tax is payable on the rent (whether as a result of an election by the Landlord or otherwise) the amount of that value added tax together with interest at the Prescribed Rate from the due date for payment until payment in full.

TENANT'S COVENANTS

F2–04 3. The Tenant covenants with the Landlord:

To pay rent

3.1 to pay the rent promptly and without deduction or set-off.

To pay outgoings

3.2 to pay all rates taxes charges and outgoings of any kind which are now or may during the term become payable in respect of the Demised Property or its ownership or occupation (except such as are payable on a disposal of any interest in reversion to this lease and income or corporation tax charged on the Landlord).

Services

3.3 to pay all charges (including statutory charges and equipment rental) for gas electricity oil and telecommunication used in the Demised Property during the term and to comply with all requirements and recommendations of the appropriate statutory undertaker or public corporation.

Statutory works

3.4.1. to execute all works required by or by virtue of any Act of Parliament or by any local or public authority to be done in or in respect of the Demised Property whether by the Landlord or the Tenant or any other person (however described).

3.4.2. without prejudice to paragraph 3.4.1 above to comply in all respects with the Offices Shops and Railway Premises Act 1963, the Fire Precautions Act 1971 and the Health and Safety at Work etc Act 1974.

Repair and decoration

3.5 [*Covenants to repair and decorate - see Example 9.4 substituting "the interior of the Demised Property" for "the demised property"*].

Alterations

3.6 [*Covenant restricting alterations - see Example 9.15*]

The Tenant shall not be required to reinstate any Tenant's alterations which have been made lawfully during the term and which improve the energy or water efficiency of the Demised Property unless such reinstatement is reasonably required by the Landlord having regard to its intentions in respect of the use or re-letting of the Demised Property after the expiry or sooner determination of the Term.

Planning and Development

3.7 [*Covenant relating to planning and development - see Example 10.1*].

Notices

3.8.1. upon receipt by the Tenant of any notice proposal or order likely to affect the Demised Property forthwith to supply a copy of it to the Landlord

3.8.2. if any such notice proposal or order comes to the attention of the Tenant (without having been received by him) forthwith to supply the Landlord the best particulars of it which the Tenant is able to give.

Use

3.9.1. not to use the Demised Property otherwise than for the Permitted Use.

3.9.2. not to use the Demised Property:
3.9.2.1. for any illegal or immoral purpose
3.9.2.2. for any offensive or dangerous trade or business
3.9.2.3. in such a way as in the opinion of the Landlord's Surveyor is likely to cause nuisance or annoyance to neighbours.
3.9.3. [*Covenant not to avoid insurance - see Example 7.13*].
3.9.4. not to accumulate any refuse or trade empties in or outside the Demised Property.
3.9.5. not to display or offer for sale any goods outside the Demised Property.
3.9.6. not to permit or suffer any obstruction of the Public Parts and not to load or unload goods in or convey goods through the Public Parts.

Roads and parking

3.10.1. not to obstruct any service road.
3.10.2. not to park on any service road.
3.10.3. to comply with any scheme of traffic management from time to time promulgated by the Landlord.

Advertisements

3.11 not to exhibit any advertisement signboard name-plate or inscription upon any part of the Demised Property except:
3.11.1. as part of a normal window display or
3.11.2. on the fascia to the shop front or
3.11.3. with the previous written consent of the Landlord (such consent not to be unreasonably withheld).

Plate glass insurance

3.12 to insure all plate glass in the Demised Property to its full reinstatement value in a reputable insurance office and to produce to the Landlord on demand the receipt for the last premium payable.

Alienation

3.13 [*Covenant restricting alienation - see Examples 12.1, 12.4 and 12.6*].

Registration

3.14 to give notice to the Landlord within one month after the creation transfer or devolution of any interest in the Demised

Property and to produce to the Landlord a copy of any instrument effecting or evidencing it and to pay a reasonable registration fee.

Costs of notices and consents

3.15 to pay all costs and expenses incurred by the Landlord (including professional fees) in connection with

3.15.1. the preparation or service of a notice under section 146 of the Law of Property Act 1925 or a schedule of dilapidations

3.15.2. any application made by the Tenant for any licence or consent under this Lease (even if such licence or consent is not granted or the application is withdrawn).

To yield up

3.16 at the expiry or sooner determination of the term to give vacant possession of the Demised Property in conformity with the covenants contained in this clause (especially those relating to repair and decoration).

Tenant's fixtures

3.17 on quitting to remove such tenant's fixtures as the Landlord may require.

Not to permit breaches

3.18 not to permit or suffer the doing of anything expressly prohibited by this clause.

LANDLORD'S COVENANTS

4. The Landlord covenants with the Tenant: **F2–05**

Quiet enjoyment

4.1 that on condition that the Tenant pays the rent and performs and observes his covenants he shall have quiet enjoyment of the Demised Property as against the Landlord and persons lawfully claiming in trust for it.

To insure

4.2 [*Covenant to insure - see Example 7.9 substituting "the Centre" for "the building"*]

To provide services

4.3 to try his best to provide the services and to carry out the works listed in the Third Schedule.

ADDITIONAL PROVISIONS

Forfeiture

F2–06 5.1 the Landlord shall be entitled to re-enter the Demised Property or any part of it in the name of the whole in any of the following cases:

5.1.1. the rent or any part of it is in arrear for fourteen days after becoming due (whether formally demanded or not)
5.1.2. the Tenant fails to comply with any of his covenants
5.1.3. the Tenant or a surety for the Tenant has a receiving order made against him or is adjudged bankrupt
5.1.4. a receiver is appointed of all or any of the Tenant's assets
5.1.5. the Tenant or a surety for the Tenant (being a company) goes into liquidation (otherwise than for amalgamation or reconstruction) or ceases to exist

and upon such re-entry this lease shall absolutely determine but without prejudice to any accrued cause of action.

Rent suspension

5.2 [*Proviso for rent suspension - see Example 7.10 omitting the concluding words after "President"*]

Interest

5.3.1. if any sum payable by the Tenant is not paid in full on the due date for payment it shall bear interest at the Prescribed Rate from that date until payment in full.
5.3.2. an instalment of rent is due on the date fixed for payment under Clause 1 above even if the amount of the instalment is not then ascertained.

Standard of work

5.4 any work carried out by the Tenant (whether of repair or not) shall be carried out to the reasonable satisfaction of the Landlord's Surveyor.

Service of notices

5.5 any notice or other document required or permitted to be served under the terms of this lease may be served in accordance with section 196 of the Law of Property Act 1925.

Memorandum of Understanding

6. The Landlord and Tenant agree in good faith but without legal obligation to agree and implement a Memorandum of Understanding with the aim of reducing energy and water use within the Centre and the Demised Property and reducing and recycling waste.

EXECUTED AS A DEED, etc.

THE FIRST SCHEDULE

Part I

DESCRIPTION OF THE DEMISED PROPERTY

1. The Demised Property includes **F2–07**
    1.1. all landlord's fixtures and fittings in or upon the Demised Property
    1.2. all additions to the Demised Property.
2. The Demised Property excludes the Structure and the Plant.

Part II

THE TENANT'S RIGHTS

1. A right for the Tenant and all persons authorised by the Tenant (in common with the Landlord and all others entitled to the like right): **F2–08**

1.1 of way with or without vehicles over the Common Parts

1.2 of way on foot only over the Public Parts

1.3 to use the loading bay hatched brown on the Plan for the sole purpose of loading and unloading vehicles

1.4 to use the Plant serving the Demised Property

1.5 to the free passage and running of water soil gas electricity and other services through and along the pipes drains wires cables and other conductors which are now or may within the Term be within the Centre and serve the Demised Property.

2. The right of shelter protection and support from all parts of the Centre in physical contact with the Demised Property.

Part III

The Landlord's Rights

F2–09 1. Rights over the Demised Property corresponding to those set out in paragraph 1 of Part I of this Schedule.

2. The right for the Landlord and all persons authorised by it at reasonable times and on reasonable written notice (but in emergency at any time and without notice) to enter the Demised Property for any or all of the following purposes:

2.1 carrying out work (whether of repair or not) to the Structure or the Plant

2.2 inspecting the Demised Property

2.3 showing the Demised Property to any person with a view to that person acquiring an interest in it

2.4 measuring the Demised Property

2.5 carrying out work (whether of repair or not) for which the Landlord or the Tenant is liable under the terms of this lease.

3. The right to build on alter or deal with the Centre and every part of it (including the right to erect scaffolding or hoardings) even though the amenity of the Demised Property or access to it or the flow of light or air to it may be diminished or obstructed.

THE SECOND SCHEDULE

Rent review

F2–10 1. The Basic Rent payable from any Review Date shall be the higher of:

1.1 the Basic Rent contractually payable immediately before that Review Date (disregarding the operation of clause 5.2) and

1.2 the Market Rent of the Demised Property on the Review Date in question.

2. [*Disputes procedure - see Example 6.15*]

3. [*Definition of Market Rent - see Example 6.26*]

THE THIRD SCHEDULE

Service charge

1. In this Schedule the following definitions apply: F2–11

1.1 Financial Year means a period of twelve months ending on [ ] in each year or such other period as the Landlord may specify

1.2 the Service Costs means the total sum computed in accordance with paragraph 3 below

1.3 the Service Charge means the Service Charge Proportion of the Service Costs

1.4 the Expert means the Landlord's Surveyor or professionally qualified accountant (who may also be employed by the Landlord or an associated company of the Landlord).

2. The Service Costs in respect of any Financial Year shall be calculated not later than the beginning of the Financial Year in question.

3.1 The Service Costs are:

3.1.1. the expenditure estimated by the Expert as likely to be incurred by the Landlord in the Financial Year in question in connection with the Services and

3.1.2. the Major Expenditure Contribution less any amount standing in the Reserve referred to in paragraph 7 below to be applied towards Major Expenditure to be incurred by the Landlord in that Financial Year.

3.2 Major Expenditure is expenditure on one or more of the Services which in the opinion of the Expert:

3.2.1. is likely to be substantial and

3.2.2. is likely to be incurred once only during the term or at intervals of more than one year or is likely to be incurred after the expiry of the term.

3.3 the Major Expenditure Contribution is the sum determined by the Expert as being an appropriate annual contribution towards that Major Expenditure to be held by the Landlord as a Reserve.

4. The Service Charge shall be paid by the Tenant in equal quarterly instalments in advance on the usual quarter days.

5.1 As soon as practicable after the end of the Financial Year in question the Expert shall determine and certify the amount by which the estimate referred to in paragraph 3.1.1 above exceeds or falls short of the actual expenditure incurred by the Landlord in connection with the Services in that Financial Year.

5.2 The Expert shall also certify those items of expenditure which are Major Expenditure and the amount (if any) applied from the Reserve in or towards payment of them.

5.3 The Tenant shall be supplied with a copy of the certificates.

6. Within fourteen days after the receipt by the Tenant of the certificates the Tenant shall pay to the Landlord the Service Charge Proportion of the deficiency or as the case may be the Landlord shall give credit to the Tenant for the Service Charge Proportion of the excess.

7. [*Trust of major expenditure contribution - see Example 8.11*]

8. Nothing in this lease shall confer upon the Tenant the right to challenge the Service Costs.

9. The Services are:

9.1 the repair maintenance and renewal of the Common Parts

9.2 the repair maintenance cleaning lighting heating ventilation cooling and decoration of the Public Parts and the Retained Parts

9.3 the inspection servicing repair maintenance and renewal of the Plant

9.4 the repair maintenance and renewal of the Structure

9.5 the provision of security to the Centre and the management of traffic in it

9.6 the maintenance of public liability insurance to such sum as the Landlord considers adequate and the insurance of the Plant

9.7 the provision of ornamental features displays and decorations in the Public Parts

9.8 the employment of such staff (including managerial staff surveyors and accountants) as the Landlord considers desirable to facilitate the provision of the services (including uniforms national insurance contributions pensions bonuses gratuities and perquisites)

9.9 the supply of materials and equipment necessary for the provision of the services

9.10 if the Landlord thinks fit expenditure on advertising the Centre including promotion displays and exhibitions

9.11 any outgoings payable by the Landlord in respect of the Retained Parts (including a sum equal to the fair letting value of any office accommodation in the Centre used by the Landlord's employees in managing the Centre)

9.12 compliance with all statutory obligations affecting the Centre

9.13 any other service or expenditure relating to the Centre requested by a majority in number of the tenants

10. [*Provision entitling landlord to replace plant - see Example 8.2*]

Form 3

Underlease of Whole: Retail Unit/Car Showroom

[**General Note**: Shops selling and displaying motor vehicles, petrol filling stations, hostels providing no significant element of care, scrap yards, retail warehouse clubs, nightclubs, launderettes, taxi businesses, amusements and casinos are all sui generic uses under the Town and Country Planning (Use Classes) Order 1987 (as amended) so planning permission will be required for any change of use for such purposes. **F3–01**

Note also the restrictions imposed on the storage and use of petrol in workplaces by the Petroleum (Consolidation) Act 1928 as amended by the Dangerous Substances and Explosive Atmospheres Regulations 2002 (DSEAR). which are reflected in the user covenants in this form.]

THE PRESCRIBED CLAUSES

[See Form 1]

BY THIS UNDERLEASE which is made on the [ ] of 20[ ] between [ ] of [ ] ("the Landlord") (1) [ ] of [ ] incorporated and registered in England and Wales with company number [ ] whose registered office is at [ ] ("the Tenant") (2) and [ ] incorporated and registered in England and Wales with company number [ ] whose registered office is at [ ] of [ ] ("the Surety") (3)

BACKGROUND

(A) The Landlord is entitled to possession of the Demised Property under the terms of a Superior Lease of [ ] dated [ ] and made between [ ] as landlord and [ ] as tenant (a copy of which has been given to the Tenant and receipt of which is acknowledged).

(B) The Landlord has agreed to grant an underlease of the Demised Property to the Tenant on the terms set out in this Lease.

The Landlord in consideration of the rents and covenants on the part of the Tenant contained below DEMISES ALL THAT [ ] ("the Demised Property") TOGETHER WITH the following rights set out in Schedule 1 (to the exclusion of all others) but EXCEPTING AND RESERVING the rights set out in Schedule 2 TO HOLD the Demised Property to the Tenant for a term of [ ] years beginning on [ ] YIELDING ANY PAYING THEREFOR the annual rent of £[ ] payable by equal quarterly instalments in advance on the usual quarter days and subject to review in accordance with Schedule 3.

F3–02 1. The Tenant hereby covenants with the Landlord as follows:

(1) to pay the rent promptly without any deduction counterclaim or legal or equitable set-off whatsoever. The payments shall be made by banker's standing order.

(2) to pay all present and future rates taxes and other impositions and outgoings payable in respect of the Demised Property and its use and any works carried out there or the ownership or occupation of it (subject to any statutory provision expressly to the contrary) other than:

(a) any taxes payable by the Landlord in connection with any dealing with or disposition of the Landlord's reversion or the Landlord's interest under the Superior Lease
(b) any taxes payable by the Superior Landlord in connection with any dealing with or disposition of the Superior Landlord's reversion in the Superior Lease
(c) any taxes, other than VAT, payable by the Landlord or the Superior Landlord or by reason of the receipt of the receipt of the rent due under this Lease or the Superior Lease.

(3) to pay interest at the rate of [ ]% per annum above the base rate from time to time of such UK clearing bank as the

Landlord may choose on any rent which remains unpaid after the due date and on any other amount payable to the Landlord under this Lease which remains unpaid 7 days following of the due date.

(4) to pay all costs in connection with the supply of electricity gas water sewage telecommunications data and other services and utilities to or from the Demised Property.

(5) to comply with all laws and regulations of the relevant suppliers not to make any application to alter the rateable value of the Demised Property without the prior written approval of the Landlord and the Superior Landlord.

(6) [*To insure and reinstate - see Example 7.5*].

(a) to comply with all requirements of the insurers in relation to the Demised Property
(b) not to do anything which may adversely affect any insurance policy covering the Demised Property.

(7) [*To repair and decorate - see Example 9.4*].

(8) [*Not to alter without consent - see Example 9.16*] Save that the Tenant may instal internal counters shelves display cases and partitions and other shopfittings in the Demised Property subject to such items being removed by the Tenant at the end of the term with any damage being made good and any consequential redecoration being carried out prior to the end of the term

(9) [*Planning covenant - see Example 10.1*]

(10) (a) the Demised Property shall not be used otherwise than as a shop nor without the Landlord's consent in writing (such consent not to be reasonably withheld) otherwise than for the sale of motor cars and motor vehicles
(b) not to have or store on the Demised Property any petrol or other inflammable substance of a like nature save for such quantity of petrol (not exceeding ten litres per vehicle or two hundred and sixty five litres in total whichever is the less) as may be from time to time in the petrol tanks of vehicles awaiting sale or collection
(c) not to carry out any repairs to or work on any motor vehicle
(d) not to display or store more than [ ] vehicles on the forecourt of the Demised Property at any one time
(e) [Covenant ancillary to use - see Example 10.10]

(f) that the demised property shall not be used for any sale by auction.

(11) not without the Landlord's consent in writing (such consent not to be unreasonably withheld) to exhibit any signboard advertisement placard or name-plate on the Demised Property.

(12) (a) not to obstruct any window light or other aperture of the Demised Property
(b) not to permit any encroachment into the Demised Property nor to permit any easement to be acquired over it
(c) forthwith to notify any activity known to the Tenant which might be or result in encroachment or the acquisition of a right or easement.

(13) [*Not to stop up windows - see Form 1, clause 3(13)*]
(14) [*To pay costs of notices - see Example 12.16*]
(15) to observe and comply with the covenants which the Landlord is liable to observe and comply with under the headlease of the Demised Property (except the covenant to pay rent) in so far as they relate to the Demised Property
(15) [Covenant against alienation - see Examples 12.1, 12.5 and 12.6]

F3–03 2. The Landlord hereby covenants with the Tenant as follows:
(1) punctually to pay the rent reserved by and to indemnify the Tenant against breach by the Landlord of covenants in the headlease under which the Landlord holds the Demised Property.
(2) on condition that the Tenant performs his obligations he shall have quite enjoyment of the Demised Property as against the landlord and those lawfully claiming under him.

F3–04 3. PROVIDED ALWAYS and it is hereby agreed as follows:
(1) [*Proviso for re-entry - see Form 1, clause 5(1)*].
(2) [*Proviso for abatement of rent - see Example 7.10*].
(3) any notice or schedule required or permitted to be served under the provisions of this underlease shall be validly served if served in accordance with the provisions of section 23 of the Landlord and Tenant Act 1927.
(4) the expressions "the Landlord" and "the Tenant" include their respective successors in title.

4. In consideration of the demise contained above and made at the Surety's request (as he hereby acknowledges) the Surety hereby covenants with the Landlord as follows: **F3–05**

(1) [*Basic covenant - see Example 14.1*].

(2) [*To take a lease on disclaimer - see Example 14.7*].

(3) [*Proviso limiting discharge of surety - see Example 14.3*].

EXECUTED AS A DEED, etc.

Form 4

Lease of Secondary Shop with Upper Part

[**General note**: This form is designed to be as simple as possible. It is a non-institutional form written in plain English, suitable for secondary property.] F4–01

THE PRESCRIBED CLAUSES

[See Form 1]

THIS LEASE is made the [ ] of [ ] 20[ ] Between [ ] of [ ] ("the Landlord") and [ ] of [ ] ("the Tenant") (2)
And WITNESSES that:

1. In consideration of the rent and the Tenant's covenants the Landlord LEASES to the Tenant the property known as [ ] (the Property) identified by red edging on the attached plan for a term of [ ] years beginning on [ ] at an annual rent of £[ ] (exclusive of value added tax) (subject to increase but not decrease every five years) payable by equal quarterly instalments in advance on the usual quarter days. **F4–02**

2. The Tenant covenants with the Landlord: **F4–03**
   (1) to pay the rent promptly without any deduction or set off
   (2) to pay all rates taxes and other outgoings payable in respect of the Property.
   (3) to reimburse the Landlord on demand the amount of the insurance premium payable by the Landlord for insuring the Property.

(4) to keep the Property clean tidy and in repair.

(5) to decorate the Property (both inside and outside) every five years in a good and workmanlike manner with appropriate materials.

(6) promptly to comply with any schedule of dilapidations served by the landlord.

(7) if the Tenant does not comply with sub-clause (6) above then the Landlord may do so and may enter the Property and carry out works for that purpose and the cost of those works will be a debt payable by the Tenant to the Landlord on demand.

(8) not without the Landlord's written consent to alter or add to the Property or its external appearance.

(9) (a) not to commit any breach of planning control
(b) not to carry out any development in the Property
(c) expressions used in this subclause have the same meaning as in the Town and Country Planning Act 1990 (as amended).

(10) (a) not to part with possession of the Property or any part of it except by an assignment of this lease
(b) not without the Landlord's written consent to assign this lease
(c) to notify the Landlord within fourteen days of any assignment.

(11) (a) not to use the Property except as a shop on the ground floor and as a residence on the upper floors
(b) not to use the Property for any illegal or immoral purpose or in such a way as to cause nuisance to neighbours.

(12) to pay the Landlord's costs in connection with any application for consent under this lease (whether or not the consent is granted) and of any notice of breach of obligation served on the Tenant.

(13) at the expiry or sooner termination of the tenancy to deliver up all keys to the Property and give up vacant possession of the Property and to remove all tenant's fixtures and to reinstate the Property and make good.

F4–04 3. The Landlord covenants with the Tenant:

(1) that the Tenant shall have quiet enjoyment of the Property as against the Landlord and anyone lawfully claiming under him.

(2) to keep the Property insured in a sum equal to its full reinstatement value against damage by fire and other risks selected by him and to expend moneys payable under the policy in reinstating the damage which gave rise to the payment.

4. It is also agreed that: **F4–05**

(1) the Landlord may repossess the Property and forfeit this lease if:

(a) the rent is in arrear for fourteen days (whether formally demanded or not)
or
(b) the Tenant fails to comply with his obligations
or
(c) the Tenant becomes insolvent.

(2) arrears of rent and other moneys carry interest at the rate of two per cent over [ ] Bank plc base rate from the due date for payment until payment in full.

(3) notices may be served in accordance with section 196 of the Law of Property Act 1925.

5. (1) With effect from every fifth anniversary of the beginning of the tenancy the rent shall be increased to the Market Rent as at that anniversary. **F4–06**

(2) if the parties have not agreed the Market Rent three months after the relevant anniversary it shall be fixed by an independent expert appointed (in default of agreement) by the President of the Royal Institution of Chartered Surveyors.

(3) the Market Rent is the rent which the Property would fetch if let in the open market by a willing landlord to a willing tenant on the terms of this lease for the unexpired residue of the term disregarding the Tenant's occupation and goodwill and improvements carried out by him.

EXECUTED AS A DEED, etc.

Form 5

Quarterly Tenancy of Lockable Stall in a Market or Store

[**General note**: A periodic tenancy cannot be contracted out of the Landlord and Tenant Act 1954.] **F5–01**

AN AGREEMENT MADE the [ ] of [ ] 20[ ] between [ ] of [ ] ("the Landlord") (1) and [ ] of [ ] ("the Tenant") (2)
WHEREBY IT IS AGREED as follows:

1. The Landlord lets and the Tenant takes the property ("the Demised Property") known as Stall No [ ] at [ ] for a term from the date hereof until [insert the next quarter day] and thereafter from quarter to quarter until determined as provided below. **F5–02**

2. The rent shall be £[ ] *per* quarter (exclusive of value added tax) payable in advance on the usual quarter days the first payment or an apportioned part of it to be made on the signing hereof. **F5–03**

3. The Tenant agrees with the Landlord as follows: **F5–04**
   (1) to pay the rent as aforesaid without any deduction or set-off whatsoever.
   (2) to keep the Demised Property in good repair.
   (3) not to alter the Demised Property or change its external appearance.
   (4) not to use the Demised Property for any illegal or immoral purpose nor for any purpose other than the sale of [ ].
   (5) not to cause or permit any nuisance or annoyance to the Landlord or to any stallholder.
   (6) not to permit the accumulation of any rubbish in or about the Demised Property.

(7) not to bring or do on the Demised Property anything which may invalidate or increase the premium payable for any policy of insurance of the Demised Property maintained by the Landlord.

(8) not to hold any sale by auction in or about the demised property.

(9) not to assign underlet or part with or share possession of the demised property or any part thereof.

(10) to pay £[ ] as a contribution towards the cost of preparing this agreement.

F5–05 4. The Landlord agrees with the Tenant as follows:

(1) to pay the general and water rates payable in respect of the Demised Property.

(2) to permit the Tenant and his staff to use the sanitary facilities provided for stallholders and to keep the same clean and in good order and properly equipped.

(3) to permit the Tenant and his staff to have access to the Demised Property at all reasonable times.

(4) to try his best to keep the market open for trading on at least six days per week (excluding public holidays).

(5) that the Tenant paying the rent and complying with the terms of this agreement shall have quiet enjoyment of the Demised Property for the duration of this tenancy without any interruption by the Landlord or any person lawfully claiming under or in trust for him.

F5–06 5. This tenancy may be determined by either party giving to the other not less than one quarter's notice in writing expiring on one of the usual quarter days (and in the case of a notice given to the Tenant it may be left for him on the Demised Property).

F5–07 6. The Landlord reserves to himself:

(1) the right to enter the Demised Property for the purpose of inspecting it and of carrying out any works therein which the Tenant ought to have carried out but has failed to carry out.

(2) the right to deal with any adjoining property belonging to him in such way as he thinks fit without making any compensation to the Tenant.

F5–08 7. It is hereby agreed that the Landlord may re-enter the Demised Property (in which case this tenancy shall immediately determine) in any of the following cases:

(1) the rent is in arrear for more than fourteen days after becoming due (whether formally demanded or not)
(2) the Tenant is in breach of any of his obligations under this agreement
(3) the Tenant ceases to occupy the Demised Property
(4) the Tenant has a receiving order made against him or is adjudicated bankrupt or execution is levied against him on the Demised Property or any goods in it.

Signed, etc.

Form 6

Underlease of Office Accommodation above a Shop

[**General note**: This form is intended for use where the property is not a large office building, and where no services are provided, but the tenant contributes towards repair and maintenance.] F6–01

THE PRESCRIBED CLAUSES

[See Form 1]

THIS UNDERLEASE which is made the [ ] of [ ] 20[ ] between [ ] of [ ] ("the Landlord") and [ ] of [ ] ("the Tenant")
WITNESSES that

1. Interpretation F6–02

1.1 In this Underlease the following definitions apply:

1.1.1. the Property means the Property described in Part I of the Schedule.

1.1.2. the Building means the building of which the Property forms part and known as [ ].

1.1.3. the Headlease means a lease of the Building made the [ ] of [ ] between [ ] (1) and [ ] the Landlord (2).

1.1.4. the Head Landlord means the person from time to time entitled to the reversion immediately expectant upon the determination of the Headlease.

1.1.5. Interest means interest both before and after any judgment calculated daily from the due date to the date of payment at the rate of [ ]% a year above the base rate from time to time of [ ] Bank.

1.1.6. Consent means the written consent of the Landlord and the Head Landlord.

1.2 the Landlord and the Tenant include their respective successors in title.

1.3 where two joint or more persons are the Tenant their obligations are joint and several.

1.4 expressions used in this Underlease which are used in the Town and Country Planning Act 1990 (as amended) have the same meaning as in that Act.

F6–03 **2. Demise**

The Landlord demises the Property to the Tenant together with the rights set out in Part II of the Schedule but reserving the rights set out in Part III of that Schedule and subject to all rights vested in the Head Landlord by virtue of the Headlease to hold to the Tenant for a term beginning on [ ] and ending on [ ] yielding and paying the following rents:

2.1 until the [ ] of [ ] the annual rent of £[ ] (exclusive of value added tax).

2.2 from the [ ] of [ ] the higher of the rent specified in clause 2.1 above and the Market Rent on that date ("a Review Date").

2.3 from the [ ] of [ ] the higher of the rent payable under clause 2.2 above and the Market Rent on that date ("a Review Date") in each case payable by equal quarterly instalments in advance on the usual quarter days.

2.4 if value added tax is payable on the rent (whether because of an election by the landlord or not) the amount of the value added tax.

F6–04 **3. Tenant's covenants**

The Tenant covenants with the Landlord:

3.1 to pay the rent (if so required by banker's standing order) promptly and without deduction or set-off.

3.2.1. to pay the general and water rates payable for the Property or (if the Property is not separately assessed for rating) a fair proportion of the general and water rates payable for the Building.

3.2.2. to pay all taxes assessments and outgoings payable for or in respect of the Property.

3.3 to pay Interest on any rent (including VAT) which remains unpaid after the due date.

3.4 [*To keep the interior in repair - see Example 9.7*].

3.4.1. to decorate the interior of the Property with appropriate materials of good quality and in a good workmanlike manner every five years and in the last year of the tenancy (however terminated).

3.4.2. where any part of the Property is to be painted at least two coats of paint shall be applied and in the last year of the tenancy the colours shall be approved by the Head Landlord.

3.5

3.5.1. within twenty eight days after the service of a schedule of dilapidations to begin and to proceed quickly to comply with it.

3.5.2. if the Tenant does not comply with clause 3.5.1 above then the Landlord or Head Landlord may do so and may enter the Property and carry out works for that purpose and their cost will be recoverable from the Tenant as a debt payable on demand together with interest at the Prescribed Rate from the date of demand.

3.6

3.6.1. to pay the Landlord on demand [ ] percent of the expenditure incurred from time to time by the Landlord in keeping the structure and exterior of the Building in repair.

3.6.2. the amount of the Landlord's expenditure shall be certified from time to time by the Landlord's surveyor (acting as an expert) whose certificate shall be conclusive of all matters of fact which it purports to certify.

3.6.3. to reimburse the Landlord a fair proportion of any sums payable by the Landlord to the Head Landlord pursuant to the terms of the Headlease.

3.7 not without consent to alter or add to the Property.

3.8

3.8.1. not to commit any breach of planning control

3.8.2. not without consent to apply for planning permission

3.9

3.9.1. not to use the Property except as offices.

3.9.2. not to use the Property in such a way as in the opinion of the Landlord:

3.9.2.1. would be in contravention of the terms of the Headlease.

3.9.2.2. is likely to cause nuisance or annoyance to neighbours.

3.9.2.3. might avoid or make more expensive any policy of insurance maintained by the Landlord or the Head Landlord in respect of the Building.

3.10

3.10.1. not to display or erect any sign or advertisement without (a) consent and (b) obtaining any necessary approval from the local planning authority.

3.10.2. to remove any such sign or advertisement at the end of the tenancy.

3.11 not to assign underlet hold on trust charge part with or share the possession or occupation of the whole or any part of the Property save that the Tenant may assign the Property as a whole with the prior written consent of the Landlord.

3.12

3.12.1. to supply the Landlord within one month of its date a copy of any instrument effecting or evidencing the disposition or creation of any interest in the Property and to pay a reasonable registration fee.

3.12.2. promptly to notify the Landlord of any change in the Tenant's address or registered office.

3.13 [*Costs of consent - see Example 12.17*].

3.14 to permit the Landlord and the Head Landlord and all persons authorised by either of them to enter the Property at all reasonable times and (except in emergency) on reasonable notice for any of the following purposes:

3.14.1. inspecting the Property.

3.14.2. carrying out any works (whether of repair or not) to the Building.

3.15 during the last six months of the tenancy to permit the Landlord to maintain a letting board on the Property.
3.16 at the end of the tenancy to give vacant possession of the Property and to remove all tenant's fixtures.
3.17 not to permit or suffer anything which would be a breach of the Headlease or which is expressly prohibited by this clause.

4. Landlord's covenants

The Landlord covenants with the Tenant: **F6–05**
4.1 that if the Tenant pays the rent and complies with his obligations he shall have quiet enjoyment of the Property during the tenancy as against the Landlord and all persons claiming under or in trust for it.
4.2 to keep the structure and exterior of the Building in repair.
4.3 to indemnify the Tenant against any breach by the Landlord of its obligations under the Headlease.

5. Provisos

Provided always and it is agreed: **F6–06**
5.1 the landlord shall be entitled to re-enter the Property (or any part of it in the name of the whole) in any of the following cases:
5.1.1. the rent or any part of it is in arrear for more than twenty-one days (whether formally demanded or not).
5.1.2. the tenant breaks any of his obligations.
5.1.3. the tenant becomes insolvent or goes into administration or liquidation otherwise than for the purpose of amalgamation or reconstruction and upon such re-entry the lease shall terminate but without prejudice to accrued causes of action
5.2 [*Proviso for abatement of rent - see Example 7.10*]
5.3 [*Service of notices - see Form 2, clause 5.5*]

6. Rent Reviews

6.1 [*Definition of Market Rent - see Example 6.26*] **F6–07**
6.2 [*Disputes procedure - see Example 6.16*]

EXECUTED AS A DEED, etc.

THE SCHEDULE

Part I

ALL THAT property on the first and second floors of the Building excluding: **F6–08**

1. the roof and roof timbers of the Building
2. the external surfaces of exterior walls.

Part II

F6–09 1. The right to use the staircase from the ground floor to the first floor on foot only for obtaining access to and egress from the Property.

2. The right to the free passage of water gas electricity and soil through any wire pipe or conduit in the Building and serving the Property.

Part III

F6–10 3. All rights reserved to the Head Landlord by the Headlease.

4. The right to use the Building in any manner in which the Landlord thinks fit without making any compensation to the Tenant.

Form 7

Lease of Office Block: Rent Geared to Sublettings

[**General note**: This form is designed for a lease taken primarily for investment purposes. If the tenant erected the building, and the lease is for more than forty years, s.19(1)(b) of the Landlord and Tenant Act 1927 will apply to any qualified covenant against alienation (other than assignment). In the case of assignment, parties can specify circumstances in which the landlord may withhold consent, and conditions which he may impose in a licence to assign. The tenant should delete clauses 2(10)(c) and (d) which may make the lease unmortgageable.] **F7–01**
The Landlord and Tenant should consider the inclusion of Green Lease clauses - see Chapter 11, Example 11.3.

THIS LEASE which is made the [ ] of [ ] 20[ ] between [ ] of [ ] ("the Landlord") (1) and [ ] of [ ] ("the Tenant") (2)
WITNESSES as follows:

1. In consideration of the sum of £[ ] (receipt of which the Landlord acknowledges) and of the rents and covenants contained below the Landlord DEMISES to the Tenant ALL THAT [ ] ("Demised Property") BUT RESERVING to the Landlord the right to build on develop deal with and use any adjoining property owned by the Landlord (whether at the date hereof or in the future) in such manner as he thinks fit even though the amenity of the Demised Property or the access of light or air thereto may be lessened thereby and without making any compensation to the Tenant TO HOLD to the Tenant for a term of [ ] years beginning on [ ] YIELDING AND PAYING (exclusive of value added tax) [see Example 6.7]. **F7–02**

F7–03 2. The Tenant covenants with the Landlord as follows:

(1) to pay the rent as aforesaid without any deduction or set-off whatsoever.

(2) to pay all existing and future rates taxes assessments and outgoings payable in respect of the Demised Property or the ownership or occupation thereof (except such as are charged on a disposition of any interest in reversion to this lease).

(3) [*To insure and reinstate - see Example 7.5*].

(4) [*To repair and decorate - see Example 9.4*].

(5) [*To comply with statutes - see Example 9.14*].

(6) (a) not to make any external additions to the Demised Property.

(b) not without the Landlord's consent in writing to make any alteration to the structure of the Demised Property and not to make any such alteration save in accordance with drawings and specifications first approved by the Landlord.

(7) [*Planning and development covenant - see Example 10.1*].

(8) that the Demised Property shall not be used for any purpose other than as offices.

(9) [*Not to cause nuisance, etc. - see Example 10.10*].

(10) (a) not to assign part only of the Demised Property

(b) not to assign underlet or part with possession of the Demised Property as a whole without the Landlord's consent in writing (such consent not to be unreasonably withheld in the case of a respectable and responsible person).

(c) not to underlet or otherwise part with or share the possession of part only of the Demised Property:

(i) being less than one whole floor of the demised property (excluding lift shafts staircases and common parts)

(ii) for a term exceeding five years without the Landlord's consent in writing (such consent not to be unreasonably withheld in the case of a respectable and responsible person)

(d) not to mortgage or charge this lease without the Landlord's consent in writing (such consent not to be unreasonably withheld).

(e) within one month after any assignment underletting mortgage or charge of the whole or any part of the

Demised Property or any transfer or devolution of the Tenant's title thereto to produce and register with the Landlord any document by which the same was effected or which evidences the same and to pay the Landlord a reasonable fee for such registration.

(f) subject to the preceding provisions of this subclause to try his best to keep the Demised Property fully let at rack rents and to maximise the income derived from it.

(11) to supply the Landlord with a copy of any order notice direction permission or consent issued by any local or public authority in relation to the Demised Property within seven days of the receipt thereof by the Tenant.

(12) to take all reasonable steps to prevent encroachment on the Demised Property and to notify the Landlord forthwith of any such encroachment or any adverse claim to the Demised Property or any notice or proceeding known to him (whether addressed to or taken against him or not) which may affect the Landlord's interest in the Demised Property.

(13) not to stop up darken or obstruct any window or other aperture in the Demised Property.

(14) [*To pay costs - see Example 12.17*].

3. The Landlord covenants with the Tenant that if the Tenant pays the rent and observes and performs his covenants he shall peaceably hold and enjoy the Demised Property for the term of this lease without any interruption by the Landlord or any person lawfully claiming under or in trust for him. **F7–04**

4. PROVIDED ALWAYS and it is agreed as follows: **F7–05**

(1) the Landlord shall be entitled to re-enter the Demised Property or any part thereof in the name of the whole upon the happening of any one or more of the following events:

(a) the rent or any part of it is in arrear for twenty one days or more (whether formally demanded or not).

(b) the Tenant fails to comply with any of his covenants.

(c) the Tenant makes any composition with his creditors or execution against the Tenant is levied on the Demised Property.

(d) the Tenant enters into liquidation whether compulsory or voluntary (otherwise than for the purposes of amalgamation or reconstruction) or a resolution is passed for a creditors' winding up or a proposal is made to the body corporate and its creditors for a composition in satisfaction of its debts or a scheme of arrangement for its affairs or an application is made to the court for an administration order or notice is given of the appointment or intention to appoint an administrator or liquidator or the Tenant is adjudicated bankrupt or a receiving order or interim receiving order is made against him and upon such re-entry this lease shall absolutely determine but without prejudice to any accrued cause of action.

(2) any notice or schedule required or permitted to be served under this lease may be served in accordance with section 196 of the Law of Property Act 1925.

(3) the expressions "the Landlord" and "the Tenant" include their respective successors in title and any reference to any Act of Parliament includes a reference to that Act as amended or replaced from time to time and to any subordinate legislation made thereunder.

EXECUTED AS A DEED, etc.

SCHEDULE

F7–06 [*Detailed provisions for calculation of rent - see Example 6.7*].

Form 8

Lease of Suite of Offices

[**General note**: This form is suitable where the Landlord is to provide services. **F8–01**
Green lease provisions could include a Building Management Committee, data sharing and monitoring and restrictions on Tenant's alterations, see Chapter 11.
The Landlord may wish to reserve its rights to grant a Feed In Tariff Lease on a separate demise of the roof, see Chapter 3.]

THIS LEASE which is made the [ ] of [ ] 20[ ] between [ ] of [ ] ("the Landlord") (1) [ ] of [ ] ("the Tenant") (2) and [ ] of [ ] ("the Surety") (3) WITNESSES as follows:

1. (1) In this lease the following expressions have the following meanings: **F8–02**
   (a) "the Landlord" and "the Tenant" include their respective successors in title.
   (b) "the Building" means [ ].
   (c) [*"the structure of the building" - see Example 9.2*].
   (d) "the exterior of the Building" means all surfaces of the Building exposed to the elements except surfaces made of glass.
   (e) ["the interior of the demised property" - see *Example 9.3*].
   (f) [*"the prescribed rate" - see Example 6:36*].

(2) any reference to any Act of Parliament includes a reference to that Act as amended or replaced from time to time and to any subordinate legislation made thereunder.

2. In consideration of the rents and covenants on the part of the Tenant contained below the Landlord DEMISES to the Tenant ALL THAT suite of rooms on the [ ] floor of the Building ("the **F8–03**

Demised Property") TOGETHER WITH the following rights (to the exclusion of all others):

(1) [*Right of way - see Example 3.13*]

(2) [*Right to use lifts - see Example 3.14*]

(3) [*Right to display advertisement - see Example 3.18*]

(4) [*Right to use sanitary facilities - see Example 3.19*]

(5) the right to use the existing and future drains sewers and gas electricity and telephone and other wires and pipes serving the Demised Property and which pass through the Building.

(6) all rights of shelter protection and support now enjoyed by the Demised Property.

(7) such rights of entry upon the Building as are necessary for the proper performance of the Tenant's covenants and for the purpose of escape in case of fire or other emergency.

BUT EXCEPTING AND RESERVING to the Landlord [*see Example 3:20*]

TO HOLD to the Tenant for a term of [ ] years from [ ] YIELDING AND PAYING therefor (exclusive of value added tax) first the annual rent of £[ ] (subject to review as provided in the First Schedule) payable by equal quarterly payments in advance on the usual quarter days the first payment (or a duly apportioned part of it) to be paid on the date hereof and secondly by way of service charge the annual sum calculated in accordance with the Second Schedule and payable as therein provided.

F8–04 3. The Tenant covenants with the Landlord as follows:

(1) to pay the rent and service charge as aforesaid without any deduction or set-off whatsoever together with interest at the prescribed rate on all arrears from the due date for payment until payment in full.

(2) to pay the general and water rates payable in respect of the Demised Property and all charges for gas electricity and telecommunications (including any standing charges) used or consumed in the Demised Property.

(3) to clean the windows at least once a month.

(4) [*To repair and decorate - see Example 9.4 and 9.7 substituting "the interior of the demised property" for "the Demised Property"*].

(5) [*Not to alter - see Example 9.16*].

(6) [*Planning covenant - see Example 10.1*].

(7) [*Not to vitiate insurance - see Example 7.13*].

(8) not to use the Demised Property for any purpose other than as offices.

(9) [*Not to assign, etc. without consent - see Examples 12.1, 12.5 and 12.6*].

(10) [*Not to cause nuisance, etc. - see Example 10.10*].

(11) not to overload the floors ceilings or walls of the Demised Property (the permitted loadings being [ ]).

(12) not to display any sign or advertisement in the Demised Property except as expressly provided above.

(13) not to stop up darken or obstruct any window or other aperture in the Demised Property.

(14) not to deposit any refuse save in such place as may be designated by the Landlord.

(15) to comply with any written regulations about the use of the Building which may be made by the Landlord from time to time.

(16) to pay all costs charges and expenses (including any professional fees) incurred by the Landlord in and about the preparation or service of a notice under section 146 or 147 of the Law of Property Act 1925 (even if forfeiture is avoided otherwise than by relief granted by the court).

(17) to pay the Landlord's solicitors' costs and disbursements and surveyors' fees and any stamp duty in connection with:

(a) the preparation and grant of this lease

(b) any application by the Tenant for any licence or consent under this lease (whether or not such licence or consent is actually granted).

4. The Landlord covenants with the Tenant as follows: **F8–05**

(1) [*To insure and reinstate - see Example 7.9*].

(2) to keep in repair the structure of the Building and the exterior of the Building and to decorate the exterior of the Building in a good and workmanlike manner at regular intervals.

(3) to keep the lifts in the Building in good working order and to replace them as and when necessary.

(4) to keep the common parts of the Building in repair properly lit and cleaned and to decorate them in a good and workmanlike manner at regular intervals.

(5) to provide and maintain in adequate supply of hot water to the washbasins and sinks in the Building and to the heating system in the Demised Property.

(6) that the Tenant paying the rent and service charge and performing and observing his covenants the Tenant shall peaceably and quietly hold and enjoy the Demised Property for the term hereby granted without any interruption by the Landlord or any person claiming under or in trust for him.

F8–06 5. PROVIDED ALWAYS that:

(1) if the rent or service charge is in arrear for more than fourteen days after becoming due (whether formally demanded or not) or if the Tenant is in breach of any of his covenants or if the Tenant or the Surety (being a company) shall enter into compulsory or voluntary liquidation (other than for the purpose of amalgamation or reconstruction) or a resolution is passed for its winding up or a proposal is made to the body corporate and its creditors for a composition in satisfaction of its debts or a scheme of arrangement of its affairs or an application is made to the court for an administration order or notice is given of the appointment or intention to appoint an administrator or liquidator or (not being a company) shall have a receiving order made against him or call a meeting of or enter into any composition with his creditors or be adjudicated bankrupt or suffer any distress or execution to be levied on the Demised Property then and in each such case the Landlord shall be entitled (in addition to any other right) to re-enter upon the Demised Property or any part thereof in the name of the whole and thereupon this lease shall absolutely determine.

(2) [*Proviso for abatement of rent - see Example 7.10*].

(3) any notice or other document required or permitted to be served under this lease may be served in accordance with section 196 of the Law of Property Act 1925.

F8–07 6. (1) [*Basic covenant by Surety - see Example 14.1*].

(2) [*Covenant by Surety to take a lease on disclaimer - see Example 14.7*].

(3) [Proviso limiting discharge of Surety - see Example 14.3].

EXECUTED AS A DEED, etc.

THE FIRST SCHEDULE

F8–08 [*Provision for rent review - see Example 6.39*]

THE SECOND SCHEDULE

[*Provision for Service Charge - see Example 8.9, adapting as necessary*] **F8–09**

Form 9

Lease of Industrial Property on Industrial Estate

[**General note**: This form includes a limited form of service charge for the upkeep of common parts of the estate and the cost of insurance.] **F9–01**

THIS LEASE which is made the [ ] of [ ] 20[ ] between [ ] of [ ] ("the Landlord") (which expression includes his successors in title) (1) and [ ] of [ ] ("the Tenant") which expression includes his successors in title) (2) WITNESSES as follows:

1. In consideration of the rents and covenants contained below the Landlord DEMISES to the Tenant ALL THAT [ ] ("the Demised Property") TOGETHER WITH the following rights (to the exclusion of all others): **F9–02**

(1) [*Right of way over estate roads - see Example 3.12*].

(2) the right in common with the Landlord and all others having the like right to park not more than [ ] private motor cars and motor cycles in the area designated "Car Park" on the attached plan.

(3) the right to the free passage of water soil gas and electricity through the pipes drains and wires now serving the Demised Property.

(4) the right to maintain a signboard of a size and form approved by the Landlord in a position along the perimeter of the estate of which the Demised Property forms part ("the Estate") such position to be designated by the Landlord.

BUT EXCEPTING AND RESERVING to the Landlord:

(1) the right to the free passage of water soil gas and electricity through the pipes drains and wires passing through the Demised Property (whether at the date hereof or in the future).

(2) the right at reasonable times and (except in emergency) on reasonable notice to enter the Demised Property for the purposes of inspecting the condition and state or repair thereof carrying out any works (whether of repair or otherwise) for which the Landlord or the Tenant is liable under this lease or carrying out any works (whether of repair or otherwise) to any property adjoining the Demised Property or to any party structure pipe drain or wire or other thing used by the Tenant in common with others but making good any physical damage caused by such entry.

TO HOLD to the Tenant for a term of [ ] years beginning on [ ] YIELDING AND PAYING therefor (exclusive of value added tax) the annual rent of £[ ] (subject to revision in accordance with the Schedule) payable by equal quarterly instalments in advance on the usual quarter days the first payment to be made on [ ] and also by way of additional rent payable on demand a service charge calculated in accordance with clause 2(3) of this Lease.

F9–03 2. The Tenant covenants with the Landlord as follows:

(1) to pay the rent as aforesaid without any deduction or set-off whatsoever.

(2) to pay all rates taxes and outgoings payable in respect of the Demised Property or the occupation thereof.

(3) to pay on demand an amount equal to [ ] per cent of the costs incurred by the Landlord in and about:

(a) the repair maintenance and replacement from time to time of all roads parking areas and loading bays on the Estate and any pipe drain wire or other thing not used exclusively by a single tenant on the Estate.

(b) the repair maintenance and replacement from time to time of the fence enclosing the Estate.

(c) the insurance of the Estate.

(d) the lighting of any common part of the Estate.

(e) the cultivation of any planted or grassed part of the Estate the said amount to be certified in writing by the Landlord's surveyor for the time being.

(4) [*To repair and decorate - see Example 9.4*].

(5) [*Not to alter - see Example 9.16*].

(6) To comply in all respects with the provisions of statutes from time to time, and the requirements of any competent authority, relating to the Demised Property or the Estate, or anything sone in or on them by the Tenant and to keep the Landlord indemnified against the Tenant's failure to comply.

(7) at least once in every six months to cause the sprinkler system and other fire-fighting equipment to be inspected by a competent person and to keep the same in efficient working order at all times and not to permit any fire door to be locked.

(8) [Not to cause increase in insurance premiums - *see Example 7:13*].

(9) not to use or permit or suffer to be used the Demised Property for any purpose other than one falling within class B1 or B2 or B8 of the Town and Country Planning (Use Classes) Order 1987 (as amended).

(10) to perform and observe the requirements of the Town and Country Planning Acts and all other statutes and regulations relating to town and country planning and environmental protection applying to the Demised Property and to obtain any development or other consent permit or licence by reason of the development or manner of use of the Demised Property by the Tenant.

(11) to keep the Landlord indemnified against liability by reason of the Tenant's failure to obtain any consent or permit or licence or in complying with the requirements of statutes and regulations.

(12) to give full particulars to the Landlord of any notice or proposal for a notice or order or proposal for an order made or given to the Tenant under the Town and Country Planning Acts or environmental protection acts or otherwise within 7 days of receipt by the Tenant.

(13) immediately to take all reasonable and necessary steps to comply with any such notice or order.

(14) not to permit or suffer any person to park any vehicle on any road in the Estate.

(15) not to permit or suffer any accumulation of refuse or trade empties in or about the Demised Property.

(16) not to affix any machinery to the roof or walls of the Demised Property without the Landlord's consent in writing.

(17) that the Demised Property shall not be used for any illegal or immoral purpose or in such a way as in the opinion of the Landlord causes or might cause nuisance or annoyance to the owners or occupiers or any neighbouring property.

(18) [*Covenant against alienation - see Examples 12.1, 12.5 and 12.6*].

(19) [*To pay costs - see Example 12.16*].

(20) during the last six months of the term to permit the Landlord to affix to a conspicuous part of the Demised Property a notice advertising the same for reletting and to permit all persons authorised by the Landlord to inspect the same.

(21) to comply with any written regulations made by the Landlord from time to time in connection with the use of the common parts of the Estate.

(22) [*Covenant to yield up in a fit state - see Example 9.21*].

F9–04 3. The Landlord covenants with the Tenant as follows:

(1) that the Tenant paying the rent and performing and observing his covenants the Tenant shall peaceably hold and enjoy the Demised Property during the term without any interruption by the Landlord or any person lawfully claiming under or in trust for him.

(2) [*To insure and reinstate - see Example 7.6*].

(3) to take reasonable care to keep in repair all roads parking areas and loading bays on the Estate and the fence enclosing the Estate.

(4) to take reasonable care to ensure that the common parts of the Estate are adequately lit during the hours of darkness.

(5) to keep any planted or grassed part of the Estate properly cultivated.

F9–05 4. PROVIDED ALWAYS and it is hereby agreed as follows:

(1) if the rent or service charge is in arrear for more than fourteen days after becoming due (whether formally demanded or not) or if the Tenant is in breach of any of his covenants or if the Tenant enters into administration or liquidation (otherwise than for the purposes of amalagamation or reconstruction) or a receiving order is made against him or he is adjudicated bankrupt then the Landlord shall be entitled to re-enter the Demised Property or any part thereof in the name of the whole and thereupon this lease shall

absolutely determine but without prejudice to any accrued cause of action.

(2) [*Proviso for abatement of rent - see Example 7.10*].

(3) any notice or other document required or permitted to be served hereunder may be served in accordance with section 196 of the Law of Property Act 1925 (as amended by the Recorded Delivery Service Act 1962).

(4) arrears of rent and other moneys due under this lease shall bear interest at the rate of two percent above the base lending rate from time to time of [ ] Bank plc ("the Prescribed Rate").

EXECUTED AS A DEED, etc.

THE SCHEDULE

1. In this Schedule: **F9–06**

(1) "the Review Date" means the [ ] of [ ] and every fifth anniversary of that date.

(2) "the President" means the President for the time being of the Incorporated Society of Valuers and Auctioneers.

2. With effect from each Review Date the rent payable by the Tenant shall be the higher of: **F9–07**

(1) the rent contractually payable immediately before that date and

(2) the Market Rent on that date.

3. [*Definition of Market Rent - see Example 6.24*]. **F9–08**

4. [*Disputes procedure - see Example 6.16*]. **F9–09**

5. [*Payment on account - see Example 6.38*]. **F9–10**

Form 10

Underlease of Part of Building Let as Clothing Factory

THE PRESCRIBED CLAUSES

See Form 1

THIS UNDERLEASE which is made the [ ] of [ ] 20[ ] between [ ] of [ ] ("the Landlord") (which expression includes his successors in title) (1) and [ ] of [ ] ("the Tenant") (which expression includes his successors in title) (2) and [ ] of [ ] ("the Surety") (3) WITNESSES as follows: **F10–01**

1. In consideration of the rent and the covenants contained below the Landlord DEMISES to the Tenant ALL THAT property comprising [ ] ("the Demised Property") and being part of the building at [ ] ("the Building") TOGETHER WITH the following rights (to the exclusion of all others): **F10–02**

(1) [*Right of access - see Example 3.13*].

(2) [*Right to display advertisement - see Example 3.17*].

(3) [*Right to use sanitary facilities - see Example 3.19*].

(4) the right to use the existing and future drains sewers and gas electricity telephone and other wires and pipes serving the Demised Property and which pass through the Building.

(5) such rights of entry upon the Building as are necessary for the proper performance of the Tenant's covenants and for the purpose of escape in case of fire or other emergency.

BUT EXCEPTING AND RESERVING to the Landlord and the Superior Landlord [*see Example 3.20*]

TO HOLD to the Tenant for a term of [ ] years beginning on [ ] YIELDING AND PAYING THEREFOR the annual sum of £[ ] (exclusive of valued added tax) payable by equal quarterly payments in advance on the usual quarter days.

F10–03 2. The Tenant covenants with the Landlord as follows:

(1) to pay the rent promptly without any deduction or set-off whatsoever.

(2) to pay all rates taxes assessments and outgoings of any nature payable in respect of the Demised Property or the ownership or occupation thereof and to pay a fair proportion of such of them as are payable in respect of the Building as a whole.

(3) to pay a fair proportion of the cost of repairing and maintaining all party structures sewers drains means of access or escape in case of fire wires and pipes the use of which is common to the Demised Property and other property.

(4) to pay a fair proportion (having regard to the area of the Demised Property and the use of the Demised Property and other parts of the Building) of the cost to the Landlord of insuring the Building in accordance with his covenant in that behalf.

(5) to comply with any conditions relating to the insurance of the Demised Property and the Building.

(6) to repair and keep in repair the interior of the Demised Property and all windows and doors enclosing the same (except damage caused by fire or any other peril against which the Demised Property is insured by the Landlord under a policy which has not been vitiated by any act or omission of the Tenant or any person deriving title under him).

(7) [*To comply with statutes - see Example 9.17*].

(8) not to make any alteration or addition to the Demised Property save such as are required in order to comply with the last preceding sub-clause.

(9) that the Demised Property shall not be used:

(a) for any illegal or immoral purpose.
(b) in such a way as to cause nuisance or annoyance to any other occupier of the Building or to the Landlord or the Superior Landlord.

(c) with the Landlord's consent in writing (such consent not to be unreasonably withheld) for any purpose other than the manufacture of clothing and as ancillary offices.

(10) [*Planning covenant - see Example 10.1*].

(11) at any time when any person is working in the Building to keep closed but not locked all fire doors in the demised property and not to permit or suffer any obstruction of any means of escape in case of fire.

(12) [*Not to vitiate insurance - see Example 7.13*].

(13) [*Covenant against alienation - see Examples 12.1, 12.5 and 12.6*].

(14) at least once each day to sweep up all waste material and to place the same in such place as may be designated from time to time by the Landlord.

(15) not to overload the floors walls or ceilings of the Demised Property.

(16) not to stop or obstruct any window or other aperture in the Demised Property.

(17) to pay all costs charges and expenses incurred by the Landlord (including any professional fees stamp duty and any sum payable by him to the Superior Landlord) in connection with:

(a) the preparation and grant of this underlease.

(b) any application by the Tenant for any licence or consent hereunder (whether or not such licence or consent is actually granted).

(c) the preparation or service of a schedule of dilapidations or a notice under section 146 of the Law of Property Act 1925 (even if forfeiture is avoided otherwise than relief granted by the court).

(18) during the last six months of the term (unless the Tenant shall have made an application to the court for a new tenancy of the Demised Property) to permit the Landlord to affix and maintain on the Demised Property a notice for the reletting of the same.

3. The Landlord covenants with the Tenant as follows: **F10–04**

(1) [*To insure and reinstate - see Example 7.6 substituting "the building" for "the demised property"*].

(2) [*To repair exterior and to decorate - see Example 9.12*].

(3) to keep clean and in good order the sanitary facilities in the Building.

(4) that the Tenant paying the rent and performing and observing his covenants he shall peaceably and quietly hold and enjoy the Demised Property for the term hereby granted without any interruption by the Landlord or any person claiming under or in trust for him.

F10–05 4. PROVIDED ALWAYS and it is hereby agreed as follows:

(1) if the rent is in arrear for twenty one days after becoming due (whether formally demanded or not) or if the Tenant is in breach of any of his covenants or if the Tenant or the Surety calls a meeting of his creditors or has a receiving order made against him or is adjudicated bankrupt or (being a company) goes into liquidation otherwise than for the purpose of amalgamation or reconstruction or a resolution is passed for a creditors' winding up or a proposal is made for a composition in satisfaction of its debts or scheme of arrangement of its affairs or an application is made to the court for an administration order or a notice is given of the appointment of or intention to appoint an administrator or liquidator or if any execution or distress is levied on the Demised Property then and in each such case the Landlord shall be entitled (in addition to any other right) to re-enter the Demised Property or any part of it in the name of the whole and thereupon this demise shall absolutely determine.

(2) [*Proviso for abatement of rent - see Example 7.10*].

(3) where the consent of the Landlord is required for anything under this underlease the consent of the Superior Landlord is also required.

(4) any dispute as to any proportion payable by the Tenant under clauses 2(2) 2(3) or 2(4) hereof shall be determined by the Landlord's surveyor for the time being acting as an expert.

(5) any notice or schedule required or permitted to be served hereunder may be served in accordance with section 196 of the Law of Property Act 1925.

(6) any reference to any Act of Parliament includes a reference to that Act as amended or replaced from time to time and to any subordinate legislation made thereunder.

F10–06 5. In consideration of the demise contained above and made at the Surety's request (as he hereby acknowledges) the Surety covenants with the Landlord as follows:

(1) [*Basic covenant by a Surety - see Example 14.1*].

(2) [*Covenant by a Surety to take a lease on disclaimer - see Example 14.7*].

(3) [*Proviso limiting discharge of Surety - see Example 14.3*].

EXECUTED AS A DEED, etc.

Form 11

Tenancy Agreement of Start Up Premises

[**General note**: This form is designed for property to be used by small businesses; and it is therefore drawn in plain English]. F11–01

BY THIS TENANCY AGREEMENT [ ] THE LANDLORD [ ] of [ ] LETS TO [ ] THE TENANT THE PROPERTY known as [ ] from [ ] to [ ] on the following terms:

1. Rent

(1) Your rent is £[ ] per month (exclusive of value added tax). F11–02

(2) Your rent is due monthly in advance on the first day of each month.

(3) You may pay your rent in cash or by cheque.

(4) If you pay your rent in cash you must bring it to the office of the landlord's managing agents at [ ] during normal office hours. If you pay your rent by cheque you may sent it by post to that address.

(5) Rent arrears are not allowed and may lead to the landlord terminating your tenancy.

(6) Your rent is exclusive of general and water rates and does not include charges for electricity or gas or value added tax.

(7) The landlord may increase the rent by giving you two months' written notice.

2. Repairs and maintenance

(1) The landlord is responsible for repairs to the structure (including the roof walls and floor) of the property. F11–03

(2) You are responsible for the general cleanliness of the property and for doing ordinary running repairs which would normally be done by a householder.

(3) The landlord may ask to enter the property in order to inspect it; to read or empty meters; to do repairs or other work or for other reasonable purposes. You must not refuse if it is a reasonable time of day, but you can insist on twenty-four hours' written notice.

(4) If a repair is needed to the property you must report it to the landlord as soon as possible. You should not instruct a builder yourself unless you have the landlord's permission to do so.

(5) At the end of the tenancy you will have to pay for the redecoration of the property to a reasonable standard.

(6) If any damage is caused to the property by you or your visitors you will be responsible for the cost of putting it right.

(7) You must not make any alteration to the property even if you think the alteration would be an improvement.

3. Your general responsibilities

F11–04 (1) You must pay the rent on time.

(2) You must pay the general and water rates and any other outgoings and utility charges (including gas and electricity).

(3) You must occupy the property personally.

(4) You must use the property only for the business of [ ].

(5) You must not assign this tenancy without the landlord's permission (not to be unreasonably refused).

(6) You must not sublet the property or any part of it or share the use of it with anyone else.

(7) You must not do anything which causes a nuisance or annoyance to neighbours.

(8) You must comply with planning control.

(9) At the end of the tenancy you must vacate the property and take with you all your belongings including machinery and equipment installed by you.

4. The landlord's general responsibilities

F11–05 If you comply with your obligations the landlord will make sure that you are allowed to occupy the property until the tenancy ends (but the landlord cannot be responsible for persons over whom he has no control).

5. Termination of the tenancy

(1) Either you or the landlord may terminate the tenancy by four weeks' written notice if the property burns down or is otherwise unfit for use. **F11–06**

(2) The landlord may also terminate the tenancy without notice if the rent is two weeks in arrear (even if he has not formally demanded it) or if you do not comply with your obligations. If the landlord does terminate the tenancy this may lead to a court order making you vacate the property.

6. Deposit

On signing this agreement you must pay the landlord a deposit equal to one month's rent. The landlord will keep the deposit until the end of the tenancy. At the end of the tenancy the landlord will take out of the deposit any compensation to which he may be entitled on account of any breach by you of your obligations as tenant. Any balance of the deposit remaining will then be returned to you. You may not use the deposit to pay the last month's rent. **F11–07**

Signed, etc.

Form 12

Lease of Hotel: Rent Based on Turnover

[**General note**: Capital expenditure incurred on the construction of certain hotels may qualify for capital allowances under the Capital Allowances Act 2001. The hotels that qualify are those defined in s.279 of the Capital Allowances Act 2001. Since the definition depends in part on the use of the hotel in question and the nature of the service provided for guests, this Form has been drawn so as to ensure that the hotel does not cease to be a qualifying hotel. In some areas a hotel proprietor may need to be registered with the local authority (see, for example, the Greater London Council (General Powers) Act 1984, s.17). A general power to compel registration of hotels exists under the Development of Tourism Act 1969, but to date the power has not been exercised.] **F12–01**

PRESCRIBED CLAUSES

[See Form 1]

THIS LEASE which is made the [ ] of [ ] 20[ ] between [ ] of [ ] ("the Landlord") (1) and [ ] of [ ] ("the Tenant") (2) WITNESSES as follows:

1. In this Lease: **F12–02**

(1) the expressions "the Landlord" and "the Tenant" include their respective successors in title.

(2) any reference to any Act of Parliament includes a reference to that Act as amended or replaced from time to time and to any subordinate legislation made thereunder.

F12–03 2. In consideration of the rents and covenants on the part of the Tenant contained below the Landlord DEMISES to the Tenant ALL THAT building known as the [ ] Hotel together with the gardens and grounds belonging to it ("the Demised Property") more precisely delineated and edged in red on the attached plan TOGETHER WITH the exclusive right to take fish from so much of the River [ ] as flows through the Demised Property BUT RESERVING to the Landlord the right to build on develop deal with and use any adjoining property owned by him (whether at the date hereof or in the future) in such manner as he thinks fit even though the amenity of the Demised Property or the access of light or air thereto may be lessened thereby and without making compensation to the Tenant TO HOLD to the Tenant for a term of [ ] years beginning on [ ] YIELDING AND PAYING therefor (exclusive of value added tax) by equal quarterly payments in advance on the usual quarter days:

(1) the annual sum of £[ ] ("the Basic Rent") and

(2) such sum as is calculated in accordance with the Schedule hereto ("the Turnover Rent").

F12–04 3. The Tenant covenants with the Landlord as follows:

(1) to pay the rents as aforesaid without any deduction or set-off whatsoever.

(2) to pay all rates taxes and outgoings payable in respect of the Demised Property or the ownership or occupation of it (subject to any statutory direction to the contrary).

(3) [*To insure and reinstate - see Example 7.5*]

(4) to execute all works required in pursuance of any Act of Parliament or required by any competent local or public authority to be done in the respect of the Demised Property whether by the Tenant or the Landlord or any other person (however described)

(5) that at all times there shall be a valid and subsisting fire certificate in respect of the Demised Property.

(6) [*To repair and decorate - see Example 9.4*].

(7) (a) not without the consent in writing of the Landlord nor (where such consent is required by any Act of Parliament) without the consent of the licensing justices to make any alteration or addition to the Demised Property.

(b) upon each application to the Landlord or such consent to supply him with drawings and specifications of each proposed alteration or addition.

(c) not to carry out any work save in accordance with drawings and specifications approved as aforesaid and in accordance with any directions which may be given by the licensing justices.

(d) before beginning any approved works to enter into such covenant with the Landlords relating to the reinstatement of the Demised Property as the Landlord may reasonably require.

(8) (a) not to use the Demised Property for any purpose other than as a high class hotel.

(b) to keep the Demised Property open for business for at least four months during the months of April May June July August September and October in each year.

(c) during the time when the Demised Property is open for business to offer sleeping accommodation consisting wholly or mainly of bedrooms available to the public generally.

(d) not to permit any person to occupy a bedroom for more than one month save for staff employed in the Demised Property.

(e) to provide for guests services including the provision of breakfast and an evening meal the making of beds and the cleaning of rooms.

(9) (a) that nothing shall be done or omitted to be done on the Demised Property whereby any justices' licence may be forfeit suspended or otherwise imperilled.

(b) to do all things necessary to maintain and from time to time renew any such licence and not to do or permit or suffer to be done anything which might prejudice the future grant or renewal of such licence (whether to the Tenant or any future occupier of the Demised Property) and to comply with all requirements and recommendations of the licensing justices.

(10) to cultivate and maintain the gardens and grounds forming part of the Demised Property and to keep them properly planted with healthy plants.

(11) that no person shall fish in such part of the River [ ] as flows through the Demised Property during any close season.

(12) [*Planning consent - see Example 10.1*].

(13) [*Covenants ancillary to use - see Example 10.9*].

(14) (a) not to assign part only of the Demised Property nor to underlet the whole or any part thereof.

(b) not to assign the Demised Property as a whole without the Landlord's previous consent in writing (such consent not to be unreasonably withheld).

(c) not to part with or share possession of the Demised Property or any part thereof save that the Tenant shall be entitled with the Landlord's previous consent in writing (such consent not to be unreasonably withheld) to grant a licence to a respectable and responsible person for the occupation of a part of the hotel building not exceeding [ ] square metres in area for the sale of newspapers periodicals tobacco confectionery and other like goods.

(d) at his own expense to procure that any assignee of the Demised Property enters into a direct covenant with the Landlord in such form as the Landlord may reasonably require to pay the rent and perform the tenant's covenants herein.

(e) within one month after any assignment or devolution of the Tenant's interest in the Demised Property or any part thereof to produce to the Landlord's solicitors a copy of the instrument or other document whereunder the same was made or which evidences the same and to pay a reasonable fee for the registration thereof.

(15) not to permit any easement to be acquired or encroachment made against or upon the Demised Property and promptly to give notice to the Landlord of any attempt to acquire or make the same and to take such steps (whether by way of legal proceedings or otherwise) to prevent the same from being acquired or made as the Landlord may reasonably require.

(16) to pay all costs charges and expenses (including any professional fees) incurred by the Landlord in and about the preparation or service of a notice under section 146 or 147 of the Law of Property Act 1925 (even if forfeiture is avoided otherwise than by relief granted by the court).

(17) to pay the costs incurred by the Landlord (including any professional fees) in connection with:

(a) the preparation and grant of the Lease

(b) any application by the Tenant for any licence or consent under this Lease (whether or not such licence or consent is actually granted).

4. The Landlord covenants with the Tenant that the Tenant paying the rents and performing and observing his covenants shall peaceably and quietly hold and enjoy the Demised Property for the term hereby granted without any interruption by the Landlord or any person lawfully claiming under or in trust for him. **F12–05**

5. PROVIDED ALWAYS and it is hereby agreed as follows: **F12–06**

(1) if the rents or any part thereof shall be unpaid for twenty one days after becoming payable (whether formally demanded or not) or if there shall be a breach of any of the Tenant's covenants or if the Tenant (being a company) shall enter into compulsory or voluntary liquidation otherwise than for the purposes of reconstruction or amalgamation or if a resolution is passed for its winding up or a proposal is made to the body corporate and its creditors for a composition in satisfaction of its debts or a scheme of arrangement of its affairs or an application is made to the court for an administration order or notice is given of the appointment or intention to appoint an administrator or liquidator or if the Tenant (not being a company) shall have a receiving order made against him or call a meeting of his creditors or be adjudicated bankrupt or if any distress or execution shall be levied on the Demised Property then and in each such case the Landlord shall be entitled (in addition to any other right) to re-enter upon the Demised Property or any part thereof in the name of the whole and thereupon this lease shall absolutely determine.

(2) [*Proviso for abatement of rent - see Example 7.10, substituting "the Basic Rent" for "the rent"*].

(3) section 196 of the Law of Property Act 1925 shall apply to all notices or schedules required or permitted to be served hereunder.

EXECUTED AS A DEED, etc.

THE SCHEDULE

1. In this Schedule the following expressions have the following meanings: **F12–07**

(1) "gross turnover" means the aggregate of all sums:

(a) received by the Tenant in return for the provision of accommodation services goods facilities food and drink at the Demised Property or received by the Tenant in the course of carrying on any trade or business in or from the Demised Property and

(b) payable to the Tenant by any person (other than an overnight guest) in consideration of the use or occupation of any part of the Demised Property.

(2) "a rental year" means a period of twelve months beginning on [ ] in each year.

(3) "net turnover" means the gross turnover less:

(a) any sum actually paid by the Tenant to HM Revenue and Customs by way of value added tax or other tax payable on the supply of goods and services

(b) any sum received by the Tenant which is exclusively attributable to any revenue or excise duty imposed on intoxicating liquor or tobacco and

(c) any sum refunded by the Tenant to his guests or customers in respect of defective or unsatisfactory goods or services.

(4) "qualified accountant" means a member of the Institute of Chartered Accountants in England and Wales.

F12–08 2. The Turnover Rent for a rental year shall be:

(1) [ ] per cent of the net turnover for the year immediately preceding that rental year exceeding £[ ] but less than £[ ] and

(2) [ ] per cent of the net turnover for the year immediately preceding that rental year exceeding £[ ] but less than £[ ].

F12–09 3. Within one month after beginning of each rental year (time being of the essence) the Tenant shall deliver to the Landlord a certificate signed by a qualified accountant giving particulars of the Tenant's gross turnover and net turnover for the year immediately preceding that rental year.

F12–10 4. The Tenant shall upon reasonable notice permit the Landlord or his agent to inspect and take copies of the Tenant's books of account or any other document or record which in the opinion of the Landlord or such agent is relevant to the determination of the

Turnover Rent and shall bear the costs of such inspection if there shall be any material discrepancy between the information supplied by the Tenant under paragraph 3 above and the results of such inspection.

5. The Turnover Rent shall be determined by an expert to be appointed by the President for the time being of the Institute of Chartered Accountants in England and Wales **F12–11**

(1) if the Tenant fails to supply a certificate in accordance with paragraph 3 above (in which case the Landlord's costs of the determination and the expert's fee shall be borne by the Tenant) or

(2) if there shall be any dispute between the parties as to the calculation of the Turnover Rent (in which case the costs of the determination and the expert's fee shall be borne as the expert directs).

6. Until the determination of the Turnover Rent of any rental year the Tenant shall continue to pay rent at the rate payable immediately before the beginning of the rental year in question and upon such determination there shall be due as arrears of rent or as the case may be refunded to the Tenant the difference (if any) between the rent paid by the Tenant for that year and the rent which ought to have been paid by him for that year plus (if the Turnover Rent is determined by an expert) such amount of interest as maybe directed by the expert. **F12–12**

7. If the Turnover Rent for any rental falls below £[ ] the Landlord may by notice in writing served on the Tenant not more than one month after the determination of the Turnover Rent for that rental year (time not being of the essence) require that there be substituted for the Basic Rent and the Turnover Rent for that rental year the amount for which the Demised Property might reasonably be expected to be let in the open market at the beginning of the rental year in question for a term equal to the then unexpired residue of this Lease and on the same terms as this Lease (save as to rent but on the assumption that the rent may be revised upwards only every five years) there being disregarded the matters set out in section 34 of the Landlord and Tenant Act 1954 (as amended) and the effect on rent of works carried out by the Tenant in pursuance of any requirement of the fire authority or the licensing justices and in default of agreement the said amount shall be determined by an independent surveyor (acting as expert not as arbitrator) to be **F12–13**

appointed by the President for the time being of the Royal Institution of Chartered Surveyors and whose fee shall be borne as he directs.

Form 13

Lease of Licensed Squash Club

[**General note**: Because of the difficulty of finding comparable properties for the purposes of rent review, a rent based on turnover has been adopted. An alternative method of rent fixing would have been to tie the rent to a notional building - *see Example 6.19*]. **F13–01**

Prescribed Clauses

[See Form 1]

THIS LEASE which is made the [ ] day of [ ] 20[ ] BETWEEN [ ] of [ ] ("the Landlord") (1) and [ ] of [ ] ("the Tenant") (2)
WITNESSES that

1. (1) In this Lease the following definitions apply: **F13–02**

 (a) "the Demised Property" means the property described in the First Schedule.
 (b) "the Landlord" and "the Tenant" include their respective successors in title.
 (c) "the Licensing Authority" means the licensing authority for the licensing district in which the Demised Property is situated.
 (d) "Liquor" means ale beer porter and other malt liquors and all cider perry wines spirits liqueurs and alcoholic cordials and British wines.
 (e) [*Definition of rate of interest, "the Prescribed Rate" - see Example 6.36*].

(2) where the Tenant is more than one person the Tenant's covenants are joint and several.

(3) any references to any Act of Parliament includes a reference to that Act as amended or replaced from time to time and to any subordinate legislation made under it.

F13–03 2. In consideration of the rent and the Tenant's covenants the Landlord DEMISES the Demised Property to the Tenant for a term of [ ] years beginning on [ ] and ending on [ ] YIELDING AND PAYING (exclusive of value added tax) for the first year of the term of rent of one peppercorn and thereafter a rent determined in accordance with the Second Schedule to be paid by equal quarterly instalments in advance on the usual quarter days.

F13–04 3. The Tenant covenants with the Landlord:

(1) to pay the rent punctually and without deduction or set-off.

(2) to pay interest at the Prescribed Rate on all arrears of rent and other moneys due under this lease from the due date for payment until payment in full.

(3) to pay all rates taxes charges duties assessments and outgoings of whatsoever nature which are now or may during the term become payable in respect of the Demised Property or its ownership or occupation (except such as are payable on a disposal of the landlord's reversion).

(4) [*To insure and reinstate - see Example 7.5*].

(5) [*To comply with statutes - see Example 9.17*].

(6) that there shall at all times during the term be a valid and subsisting fire certificate for the Demised Property.

(7) [*To repair and decorate - see Example 9.4*].

(8) (a) not without the previous written consent of the Landlord (such consent not to be unreasonably withheld) and of the Licensing Authority (where such consent is required by virtue of any Act or Parliament) to make any addition or alteration to the Demised Property.

(b) upon each application to the Landlord for such consent to supply it with drawings and specifications of each proposed addition or alteration.

(c) not to carry out any works save in accordance with drawings and specifications approved as aforesaid and in accordance with any directions or conditions which may have been given or imposed by the Licensing Authority.

(9) not without the previous written consent of the Landlord (such consent not to be unreasonably withheld) to display any sign or advertisement on the exterior of the Demised Property.

(10) [*Planning covenant - see Example 10.1*].

(11) (a) as soon as may be to apply for the grant to an individual approved by the Landlord (such approval not to be unreasonably withheld) of the Licensing Authority's licence for the sale of Liquor in the Demised Property and for such purpose to give all necessary notices.

(b) not without the previous written consent of the Landlord to apply for the insertion of any conditions in the Licensing Authority's licence.

(c) to apply for and try his best to obtain the renewal of the Licensing Authority's licence as and when it becomes renewable.

(d) not without the previous written consent of the Landlord to surrender or try to surrender the Licensing Authority's licence or allow it to lapse or become forfeit or to take any steps to procure its transfer to any other premises.

(e) that nothing shall be done or omitted to be done on the Demised Property whereby any Licensing Authority's licence may be forfeit suspended or otherwise imperilled.

(12) (a) not without the previous written consent of the Landlord to have any gaming machine or machine for amusement with prizes in the Demised Property.

(b) in the case of any such machine permitted by the Landlord to be in the Demised Property:

(i) not to install it until all necessary licences and permits have been obtained and the appropriate duty (if any) paid.

(ii) to display all licences and permits as required by law and to produce them to HM Revenue and Customs as and when required.

(13) (a) [*Covenants ancillary to use - see Example 10.10*].

(b) that no more than one hundred persons shall simultaneously be in the Demised Property.

(c) not without the previous written consent of the Landlord (such consent not to be unreasonably withheld) to use the Demised Property or permit it to be used otherwise than as a private members' club for playing of squash rackets and the provision of ancillary facilities including light meals and refreshments and a bar for the sale of Liquor.

(d) notwithstanding paragraph (c) above the Tenant shall be entitled to hold not more than twice a month exhibition matches of squash rackets attended by members of the public.

(14) [*Covenant restrictive of alienation - see Examples 12.1, 12.5 and 12.6*].

(15) to supply the Landlord with a copy of any order notice direction permission or consent issued by any local or public authority or by the Licensing Authority in relation to the Demised Property within seven days of its receipt by the Tenant.

(16) [*To pay costs - see Example 12.16*].

(17) to keep full and accurate books of account recording all the Tenant's receipts and expenses in connection with the business carried on in the Demised Property.

(18) at the expiry or sooner termination of the term to give vacant possession of the Demised Property and to remove such tenant's fixtures as the Landlord directs in writing.

F13–05 4. The Landlord covenants with the Tenant that on condition that the Tenant pays the rent and complies with his covenants he shall have quiet enjoyment of the Demised Property as against the Landlord and those claiming under or in trust for it.

F13–06 5. It is agreed and declared that:

(1) the Landlord may forfeit this lease in any of the following cases:

(a) the rent or any part of it is more than fourteen days in arrear (whether formally demanded or not).

(b) the Tenant is in breach of any of his obligations under this lease.

(c) the Tenant is adjudicated bankrupt or (if a company) is wound up by order of the court.

(2) [*Proviso for abatement of rent - see Example 7.10*].

(3) section 196 of the Law of Property Act 1925 applies to any notice or schedule required or permitted to be served under this lease.

EXECUTED AS A DEED, etc.

THE FIRST SCHEDULE

[Description of the Demised Property]. **F13–07**

THE SECOND SCHEDULE

1. In this Schedule: **F13–08**

(1) "Accountable Receipts" means the aggregate of all sums received by the Tenant (or any associated company of the Tenant) by way of:

(a) membership subscriptions
(b) court fees (including any separate charge made for the provision of electricity changing facilities hot water and hire of equipment)
(c) payment for sales of meals refreshments and Liquor
(d) entrance fees for attendance at exhibition matches
(e) sale of sports equipment
(f) any other income received by the Tenant in the ordinary course of carrying on business in the Demised Property less any sum actually paid by the Tenant by way of value added tax excise duty or tobacco duty.

(2) "the Rent Fraction" means the fraction of which the numerator is £[ ] and the denominator is the Accountable Receipts during the first year of the term.

(3) "Qualified Accountant" means a member of the Institute of Chartered Accountants in England and Wales.

(4) "Review Date" means the sixth anniversary of the beginning of the term and every fifth anniversary thereafter.

(5) "Review Period" means the period between one Review Date and the next and between the last Review Date and the expiry date of the term.

2. The rent for the second to fifth years (inclusive) of the term shall be £[ ] per annum.

3. The rent for each Review Period shall be an annual sum equal to the product of the Accountable Receipts for the year immediately preceding the beginning of the Review Period in question and the Rent Fraction.

4. Within one month after the beginning of each Review Period (time being of the essence) the Tenant shall deliver to the Landlord a certificate signed by a Qualified Accountant giving full particulars of the Accountable Receipts for the year immediately preceding the beginning of the Review Period in question.

5. The Tenant shall upon reasonable notice permit the Landlord or his agent to inspect and take copies of the Tenant's books of account or any other document or record which in the opinion of the Landlord or such agent is relevant to the determination of the Accountable Receipts and shall bear the costs of such inspection if it reveals any material inaccuracy in the information supplied by the Tenant under paragraph 4 above.

6. The Accountable Receipts shall be determined by an independent Qualified Accountant (acting as an expert) to be appointed in default of agreement by the President for the time being of the Institute of Chartered Accountants in England and Wales:

(1) if the Tenant fails to deliver a certificate in accordance with paragraph 4 above (in which case the costs of the determination shall be borne by the Tenant) or

(2) if there is any dispute about the calculation of the Accountable Receipts (in which case the costs of the determination shall be borne as the independent accountant may direct).

7. If the membership subscription or the court fees are materially less than the average membership subscription or court fees charges by other similar members' clubs in the counties of [ ] then in the calculation of the Accountable Receipts the Tenant shall be deemed to have received such amounts as would have been received if the membership subscription and/or the court fees had been equal to such average (but on the assumption that there would have been no fewer members or court bookings).

8. Until the determination of the annual rent for any Review Period the Tenant shall continue to pay rent at the rate payable immediately before the beginning of the Review Period in question and upon such determination there shall be due as arrears of rent (or as the case may be refunded to the Tenant) the difference (if any) between the rent paid by the Tenant for the period and the rent

which ought to have been paid together with interest at the Prescribed Rate calculated from the date when each instalment of rent fell due.

Form 14

Agreement for Lease of Land to be Used as Car Park Pending Redevelopment

[**General note**: It would be advisable for the provisions of the Landlord and Tenant Act 1954, ss. 24-28, to be excluded from the Agreement. It includes a redevelopment break clause.] **F14–01**

PRESCRIBED CLAUSES

[See Form 1]

AN AGREEMENT made the [ ] day of [ ] 20[ ] between [ ] of [ ] ("the Landlord") of the one part and [ ] of [ ] ("the Tenant") of the other part WHEREBY IT IS AGREED as follows:

1. The Landlord agrees to let and the Tenant agrees to take ALL THAT [ ] ("the Demised Property") for a term of [ ] years beginning on [ ] determinable as provided below YIELDING AND PAYING therefor (exclusive of value added tax) the annual sum of £[ ] payable by equal quarterly payments in advance on the usual quarter days. **F14–02**

2. The Tenant agrees with the Landlord as follows: **F14–03**

(1) to pay the said rent as aforesaid without any set-off or deduction whatsoever.

(2) to pay all rates taxes and other outgoings (except such as are charged on a disposal of the Landlord's reversion) payable in respect of the Demised Property or the ownership or occupation thereof.

(3) to erect as soon as may be and thereafter keep in repair a close boarded fence along the boundaries of the Demised Property.

(4) to keep the Demised Property properly drained and in good order and condition and free from rubbish.

(5) not to use the Demised Property for any purpose other than as a car park for motor cars and motor cycles only.

(6) to provide attendants to supervise parking in the Demised Property at all times.

(7) not to assign underlet hold on trust charge part with or share the possession of the Demised Property or any part thereof without the prior written consent of the Landlord (such consent not to be unreasonably withheld) provided that it shall not be a breach of this covenant if the Tenant grants to another the right to park not more than ten vehicles in a specified part of the Demised Property for a period of not exceeding one year at a time.

(8) to keep the Landlord indemnified against any claim loss or damage whatsoever in respect of any loss or damage to any person using the Demised Property.

(9) not to carry out any development on the Demised Property other than the use thereof as a car park as aforesaid nor to apply for planning permission to carry out any such development.

(10) not to use the Demised Property for any illegal or immoral purpose nor for any purpose which causes or might cause a nuisance or annoyance to the Landlord or to neighbouring occupiers.

(11) to permit the Landlord at any time during the term to erect and maintain a notice or advertisement for letting or selling any interest in the Demised Property.

(12) to permit the Landlord and all persons authorised by him at reasonable times and on reasonable notice to enter the Demised Property for the purposes of inspecting surveying or repairing the same or for storing any plant machinery or materials in connection with the development of any adjoining property belonging to the Landlord.

(13) to supply to the Landlord a copy of any notice order direction consent or permission relating to the Demised Property within four days of the receipt thereof by the Tenant.

(14) not to bring or do anything upon the Demised Property which may invalidate or increase the premium payable for any policy of insurance of the Demised Property maintained by the Landlord.

(15) to take all reasonable steps to prevent any encroachment on the Demised Property or the acquisition of any easement thereover

and promptly to notify the Landlord of any attempt or claim to make or acquire the same.

3. The Landlord agrees with the Tenant that the Tenant paying the said rent and performing and observing his agreements the Tenant shall peaceably hold and enjoy the Demised Property for the term hereby granted without any interruption by the Landlord or any person claiming under or in trust for him. **F14–04**

4. Provided always that if the rent or any part thereof shall be in arrear for 14 days after becoming payable (whether formally demanded or not) or if the Tenant shall commit any breach of agreement or shall be adjudicated bankrupt or (being a company) enter into liquidation or administration or any creditors' or members' voluntary arrangement then and in each case the Landlord shall be entitled to re-enter the Demised Property or any part thereof in the name of the whole and thereupon this agreement shall forthwith determine but without prejudice to any accrued right of action vested in the Landlord. **F14–05**

5. [*Landlord's break clause - see Example 5.4*]. **F14–06**

Signed, etc.

Form 15

Renewal of Lease by Reference to Expired Lease

[**General note**: The covenants in a lease are construed by the reference to the date of the demise. Accordingly, when granting a lease by way of renewal it will be in the interest of the landlord if some obligations (particularly those relating to repair) are construed by reference to the date of the original demise, rather than to the date of the renewal. This form provides for all obligations to be construed as if entered into at the date of the original demise. The operation of section 62 of the Law of Property Act 1925 is excluded, in order to avoid informal licences being upgraded into legal easements.] **F15–01**

PRESCRIBED CLAUSES

[See Form 1]

THIS LEASE which is made the [ ] of [ ] 20[ ] between [ ] of [ ] ("the Landlord") (1) [ ] of [ ] ("the Tenant") (2) and [ ] of [ ] ("the Surety") (3)
SUPPLEMENTAL TO a Lease made the [ ] of [ ] between the Landlord (1) the Tenant (2) and the Surety (3) ("the Original Lease") WITNESSES as follows:

1. In consideration of the rent and the covenants contained below the Landlord DEMISES to the Tenant ALL THAT property ("the Demised Property") which was demised to the Tenant by the **F15–02**

Original Lease TOGETHER WITH the rights granted to the Tenant by the Original Lease and subject to the exceptions and reservations therein containing TO HOLD to the Tenant for a term of [ ] years beginning on [ ] YIELDING AND PAYING (exclusive of value added tax) by equal quarterly payments in advance on the usual quarter days the annual rent of £[ ].

F15–03 2. The Tenant covenants with the Landlord to observe and perform all the covenants and conditions on his part contained in the Original Lease.

F15–04 3. The Landlord covenants with the Tenant to observe and perform all the covenants and conditions on his part contained in the Original Lease.

F15–05 4. PROVIDED ALWAYS and it is agreed as follows:

(1) if the rent or any part of it is in arrear for twenty one days after becoming payable or there is any breach of any of the Tenant's covenants or if the Tenant is adjudicated bankrupt or (being a company) goes into liquidation otherwise than for the purpose of amalgamation or reconstruction or a resolution is passed for a creditors' winding up or a proposal is made for a composition in satisfaction of its debts or a scheme of arrangement of its affairs or an application is made to the court for an administration order or notice is given of the appointment or intention to appoint an administrator or liquidator then in any such event the Landlord may re-enter the Demised Property or any part of it in the name of the whole and thereupon this Lease shall absolutely determine.

(2) the covenants given by the Landlord and the Tenant shall be construed as if they had been given at the date of the Original Lease.

F15–06 5. In consideration of the demise contained above which was made at the request of the Surety (as he acknowledges) the Surety covenants with the Landlord as follows:

(1) [*Basic Covenant by Surety - see Example 14.1*].

(2) [*Covenant by Surety to take a lease on disclaimer - see Example 14.7*].

(3) [*Proviso limiting discharge of surety - see Example 14.3*].

6. Section 62 of the Law of Property Act 1925 shall not apply to this Lease. **F15–07**

EXECUTED AS A DEED, etc.

Form 16

Licence to Share Professional Offices

[**General note**: This form is reproduced from *Lease or Licence* (Longman, 1991) by the Consultant Editor.] **F16–01**

BY THIS LICENCE which is made the [ ] day of [ ] 20[ ] of [ ] ("the Licensor") grants to [ ] of [ ] ("the Licensee") licence to share with the Licensor the use of the Licensor's offices at [ ] ("the Offices") from until determined in accordance with the provisions of this Licence.

1. The Licensee shall pay the Licensor £[ ] a month on the first day of each month (the first payment to be made on signing). **F16–02**

2. The Licensee shall be entitled: **F16–03**

(1) to carry on business as in such part of the Offices (consisting of not less than one private office and [ ] square feet of other space) as the Licensor shall from time to time direct.

(2) to use (in common with the Licensor) the sanitary facilities in the Offices.

(3) to install a telecommunication line and equipment for his own exclusive use.

(4) to install his own office furniture and equipment in the Offices.

3. The Licensee shall not: **F16–04**

(1) impede or interfere with the Licensor's rights of possession and control of the Offices.

(2) use the Offices for any purpose other than for the business mentioned in clause 2(1) above.

(3) be entitled to a key to the Offices.

(4) do anything which may avoid or increase the premium payable for any policy of insurance maintained by the Licensor or to which he is liable to contribute.

(5) alter the Offices or their internal layout.

(6) interfere with the conduct of the Licensor's business as a [ ].

(7) solicit or attempt to solicit any client of the Licensor.

(8) read or make copies of any books (other than published works of reference) papers or documents addressed to or in the possession or custody of the Licensor.

(9) permit or suffer the doing of anything prohibited by this clause.

F16–05 4. The Licensor shall:

(1) try his best to give the Licensee and his staff and clients access to the Offices during normal office hours.

(2) pay the general and water rates payable for the Offices and the rent payable to the Licensor's landlord.

(3) keep the sanitary facilities in working order and properly cleaned and equipped.

(4) keep the Offices adequately heated and lit during normal office hours.

(5) indemnify the Licensee against any breach by the Licensor of any of the terms upon which the Licensor holds the Offices.

F16–06 5. The Licensor shall not:

(1) interfere with the conduct of the Licensees' business.

(2) solicit or attempt to solicit any client of the Licensee.

(3) read or make copies of any books (other than published works of reference) papers or documents addressed to or in the possession or custody of the Licensee.

(4) permit or suffer the doing of anything prohibited by this clause.

F16–07 6. Either party may terminate this agreement by three months' written notice and the Licensor may also terminate it by two weeks' written notice if the Licensee commits a serious breach of his obligations.

Signed, etc.

Index

All references are to paragraph number